Franz Joseph was the last of the Habsburg emperors, the oldest dynasty in Europe. Succeeding to the imperial throne in the wake of the 1848 revolution, he ruled over Europe's largest empire for the next sixty-eight years until the First World War brought about the dissolution of Austro-Hungary. Professor Bled begins with an account of Franz Joseph's privileged childhood as a member of the imperial family. He then examines the state of the Austro-Hungarian empire on the eve of the 1848 revolution, and of Franz Joseph's succession at the age of eighteen. Professor Bled's account examines not only the key political events of the period but also social conditions and life at court. This story is set against the turmoil of late nineteenth-century Europe and the conflict between two ideals and two cultures: that of the multinational state and that of the nation state.

This is a highly readable and well-informed account of Franz Joseph's life and reign, set in the context of the momentous changes in European society over which he presided and wielded great influence.

Franz Joseph

FRANZ JOSEPH

Jean-Paul Bled

Translated by Teresa Bridgeman

BLACKWELL
Oxford UK & Cambridge USA

English translation first published 1992

Blackwell Publishers
108 Cowley Road
Oxford OX4 1JF
UK

238 Main Street, Suite 501
Cambridge, Massachusetts 02142
USA

British Library Cataloguing in Publication Data

A CIP catalogue record for this book is available from
the British Library.

Library of Congress Cataloging-in-Publication Data

Bled, Jean-Paul.
[François-Joseph. English]
Franz Joseph/Jean-Paul Bled; translated by Teresa Bridgeman.
p.   cm.
Includes bibliographical references and index.
Translation of: François-Joseph.
ISBN 0–631–16778–1
1. Franz Joseph I, Emperor of Austria, 1830–1916. 2.   Austria –
Kings and rulers – Biography.   3. Austria – History – Francis Joseph,
1830–1918.   I. Title.
DB87.B5713   1992
943.6'04 – dc20   91–44881
                                                              CIP

Typeset in 9½ on 11 pt Ehrhardt
by Graphicraft Typesetters Ltd, Hong Kong
Printed in Great Britain by TJ Press (Padstow) Ltd, Padstow, Cornwall

Contents

1
Childhood (1830–1848)

From the day of his birth on 18 August 1830 the young Archduke Franz Joseph seemed destined for great things. His mother, the Archduchess Sophie could allow herself the hope that he would one day rule the Austrian Empire. According to the order of succession he was not the direct heir of the Emperor Franz who had ruled for thirty-eight years over the states of the House of Habsburg. Traditionally on the death of the sovereign, his oldest son, in this case the Archduke Ferdinand, should succeed. But should the latter have any shortcomings, the crown would pass to his younger brother, the Archduke Franz Karl, Franz Joseph's father. The likelihood of the newborn boy's succession to the throne would, however, be seriously reduced if Ferdinand, hitherto without descendants, were to have a son.

The Ambitions of the Archduchess Sophie

The Archduchess Sophie's dream was not an unrealistic one. Though the Archduke Ferdinand was the direct heir, the members of the court recognized his deficiencies. He suffered from frequent epileptic attacks (it was known for him to have up to twenty in one day), and this might affect his ability to rule. The chance that he would father an heir appeared very slight. His marriage with Marie Anne, princess of Savoy, in the year following Franz Joseph's birth probably gave Sophie cause for uncertainty for a brief moment, but the doctors were quick to reassure her. She soon announced triumphantly to her mother that it was unlikely that Ferdinand could have children. Marie Anne was to be more of a nurse than a wife. In light of all this, it was permissible for Sophie to cherish the hope of being the future empress of Austria. Two of her sisters, Elisabeth in Prussia and Amelia in Saxony, had made royal marriages. How could Sophie not dream of a distinguished future for herself as well?

As was to all intents the rule in force in the courts of Europe at the beginning of the nineteenth century, the nineteen-year-old Sophie had not made a love match. The Archduke Franz Karl was the child of the Emperor Franz's second marriage, and was a dull young man, who had little to recommend him, mentally or physically. In the tradition of such unions between the Habsburgs and the Wittelsbachs, the marriage was a response to calculations which extended far beyond the individual figure of the young princess. Her father, King Maximilian Joseph of Bavaria, sought after his error of judgement of the Napoleonic period to increase the prestige of Bavaria once again through a series of alliances with many of the main German dynasties, while at the emperor's court in Vienna, there were hopes that the marriage would reinforce Austrian influence in southern Germany.

Sophie was thus obliged to submit to the fate that had been decided for her. Her resignation does not seem to have made Franz Karl any the more attractive to her. Her inclination for romanticism, the result of adolescent years in Munich, must have made it hard for her to adapt to the prosaic tastes of an unreceptive husband. Nor was it surprising that in the course of the years which followed her establishment in Vienna she amused herself in the company of the duke of Reichstadt who, although he was six years younger than her, was possessed of a charm and elegance which contrasted with the boring insipidness of her husband. Furthermore there was a certain similarity in their situations which was likely to draw them together. Transplanted into surroundings which were at first strange to her, Sophie took to this young man who, separated from his mother, and placed under Metternich's supervision, lived at the Viennese court in a kind of exile.

Although Sophie was not impervious to the attractions of this friendship, she was too aware of the duties of her position to allow it to develop further, for her husband seemed destined by then to become the next emperor of Austria. Indeed, all the evidence suggests that she was the dominant partner in the marriage. Franz Karl had received no preparation for the exercise of power. Moreover, his nature was not imperious enough to be able to draw on its own resources to compensate for this omission and his tastes inclined him in the opposite direction, preferring as he did a simple and peaceful life. On the other hand, Sophie was possessed of strong convictions. An ardent Catholic, she was a vociferous defender of the divine right of kings and avowed an unwavering hatred for liberalism, which she saw as an absolute evil. Established very early, this mode of thought would constantly guide her behaviour and choices. Secure in her clearly defined principles, Sophie revealed herself to be a forceful character who directed her energy towards the implementation of her beliefs and, when put to the test, remained level-headed and determined. All of these factors indicated that, should Franz Karl come to the throne, she would be capable of exercising considerably greater influence on affairs of state than might normally have been possible for the empress.

Because of the obstacle placed in her way by Metternich's plans, Sophie did not have the chance to realize this ambition. With the emperor's advancing years, the succession was becoming a matter of some urgency. Although he was not blind to the problems which a sovereign who was not capable of the full assumption of his responsibilities would create for the monarchy, Metternich was also of the view that if the order of succession was not respected, this would be a blow to the principle of legitimacy which would cause even more damage. In advising this choice, was he placing his own interests before all others? With a monarch who was incapable of concerning himself with affairs of state, he would obviously have no reason to fear for his own power. Whatever the ulterior motives of his chancellor may have been, the emperor lent his support to the argument in favour of legitimate succession and was in any case predisposed to take this view by his affection for the poor invalid.

Sophie must certainly have been frustrated by this decision which threatened to destroy for ever her dream of becoming empress of Austria. Should we therefore conclude that she nurtured a long-term resentment against Metternich for this? Nothing is less likely. In this matter, it is not unimportant that Metternich's way of thinking corresponded very closely to Sophie's own. In fact, the chancellor initiated a policy which followed the wishes of the archduchess. During Ferdinand's reign, she and her husband were among his most solid supporters in the imperial family. On the other hand, Count Kolowrat, his great rival, never figured as one of Sophie's intimate circle. And how can her choice of the old chancellor as Franz Joseph's tutor in the art of politics fail to be seen as proof of her confidence in him?

Despite this, Franz's decision led Sophie to consider the future in a new light. Now that her prospects of one day becoming empress of Austria were rapidly diminishing, she transferred her hopes to her eldest son who, in due course, might succeed Ferdinand. This change of viewpoint fitted in better with her own estimation of the situation. Following the reign of a sickly and retiring sovereign, there would be a need for a young, robust, and brilliant emperor who would lend lustre to the institution of the monarchy. With the new turn of events in the succession Sophie soon assumed the more prominent role of mother of the emperor-to-be.

Infancy

Following her marriage, Sophie had been obliged to wait six years before becoming a mother. In 1826 and 1827 she had two miscarriages, which led some courtiers to begin to question whether she would be able to fulfil her role as a parent. At last, in 1830, her third pregnancy went to its full term. This time the doctors left nothing to chance, and did not hesitate to confine Sophie to her quarters for several months. The birth took on the appearance of a court ceremony. No sooner had the midwife announced, in the afternoon of 16 August, that the longed-for birth would take place before the day was out, than Sophie's bedchamber was invaded by a crowd of relatives and courtiers. It was nevertheless the beginning of a long wait. Sophie's labour pains began only on the following morning and lasted for an entire day. Finally, on 18 August, at a quarter to ten, Sophie brought a son into the world. Even then, the birth was a difficult one, with forceps being used to deliver the child.

The newborn infant, who was at once treated as a future sovereign, was given the name Franz Joseph. The choice had not been left to personal preference. New to the traditions of the family, this combination was the announcement of a political programme. The choice of the first name was primarily in response to the need to honour the child's paternal grandfather. But Franz was also the name of Maria Theresa's husband, the founder of the Habsburg–Lorraine dynasty. Through this association it represented a continuation of the baroque age, one of the high periods of Austrian greatness and one of the major features of the Habsburg tradition. His second name embodied another side of the Habsburg heritage in its reference to Joseph II, whose entire reign symbolized devotion to the imperial office, the Habsburg attachment to progress and the primacy of the state over personal interests.

Little Franzi, as she called him, was Sophie's pride. A lively baby, he had a fine rosy complexion which led the duke of Reichstadt to observe that he looked like 'a strawberry ice cream topped with whipped cream'.[1] Very soon the young archduke was provided with a royal household appointed by Sophie. Through all its years she was to supervise everything that concerned Franz Joseph's education with jealous care. Baroness Maria von Sturmfeder was selected as his governess, a happy choice which would be repeated for his younger brothers. After the long wait of the early years, child after child appeared. Sophie gave Franzi three brothers; Ferdinand Maximilian who would be called Maxi by all the family was born in 1832, Karl Ludwig in 1833, and Ludwig Victor in 1842. Baroness Sturmfeder created an atmosphere of warm affection around the children, who were placed in her charge until their sixth year, and they would cherish fond memories of her after leaving her care.

Apart from summer sojourns at Ischl in the Upper Austrian Alps, Franz Joseph's early childhood was spent in the imperial residences of Vienna. Although he was not allowed into certain parts, his personal universe included his parents' apartments, the corridors and terraces of the Hofburg and Schönbrunn palaces and his own room. The emperor's study was often open to his grandson, whose company diverted him. Also, the little archduke was admitted to the blue drawing-room where he would find the imperial family. There, he was the joy of his grandparents when he came to snuggle up to them on the couch where they sat, a scene which confirms that, in private, the imperial family led a simple, almost bourgeois life, which was a far cry from the pomp they displayed at official ceremonies.

If Franz enjoyed the company of his grandson, he also considered him to be the hope of the monarchy. Many facts bear this out. On the emperor's orders, Franzi was provided with a six-horse carriage when he went out. As another notable mark of respect, when he appeared the guards on duty had to present arms to him – which led to the comical sight of elderly veterans paying honour to a brat squalling in his pram. Franz was interested in the education of his grandson even before he was provided with tutors. While Sophie taught the boy to read, Franz taught him the first rudiments of Italian. The ties which bound him to his grandfather explain the young boy's distress when he died at the beginning of March 1835. This disappearance was Franz Joseph's first experience of death. It was true that the duke of Reichstadt had already been carried off in 1832 by the consumption which had worn him down for many years. But Franz Joseph had been too young at the time to remember the event. On this occasion things were different; he now had to collect himself when confronted by his grandfather's remains, and this sight combined with all the ceremony which surrounded the emperor's funeral service was to mark him for a long time.

These years also revealed a precocious taste for military life in Franz Joseph. Ferdinand Waldmüller, the great painter of the Austrian *Biedermeier* has left us a portrait of him as a gentle fair-haired child in a charming suit of white lace, wearing a grenadier's cap. Surrounded by warlike trappings, he holds a rifle in one hand and caresses a wooden soldier with the other, while a sword is belted at his waist. As a tiny child of two, Franzi followed the manoeuvres of the Hofburg guard with passion, and he then practised these movements with his playmates in the Schönbrunn gardens. His parents knew how to give him pleasure by presenting him when he was five with a Christmas gift of a cavalryman's uniform. Although such incidents are trifling, they nevertheless shed light on a tendency in Franz Joseph's character which was showing even before he was placed in the care of his tutors.

The Formative Years

When he was six, a new stage in Franz Joseph's life began. Baroness Sturmfeder was now eclipsed by a grand master of the court (*Obersthofmeister*) who would, in particular, have charge of the boy's education. Metternich and the Archduchess Sophie once again showed themselves to be in agreement by their appointment of Count Heinrich Bombelles to this position. To these two conservatives, united in their rejection of the revolution, this son of a French emigré offered the best guarantee of total orthodoxy. In addition, Count Heinrich had loyally served Metternich's political schemes as ambassador in Lisbon and Turin. Such was Metternich's confidence in his protégé that he would number him, in his *Memoirs*, among the privileged few whom he considered to have had a perfect understanding of his system of thought. The similarity of their opinions qualified Bombelles, in the eyes of the chancellor, to bring up the young prince according to conservative principles and to prepare him for the counter-revolutionary fight. To assist him in his task, Count Bombelles received the help of Count Johann Coronini, an officer of the Engineers, who, whilst reporting to Bombelles, would be closely involved with the young archduke's education. Coronini's status as an officer brought him the natural sympathy of his pupil, and it was with Coronini that Franz Joseph had the closest relationship during these years.

In its excesses, the regimen of studies perfected by Bombelles and Coronini confounded good sense. Probably, knowing that the child in their care had every chance of becoming emperor, they were concerned to provide him with a broad and varied knowledge. This aim failed to recognize the old adage that a well-trained mind is worth more than a well-filled mind. Although at first the timetable only scheduled thirteen hours of teaching a week, this rose dramatically. Increased to thirty-two hours from the following year, it went up to fifty hours on Franz Joseph's thirteenth birthday.

This programme of studies subjected Franz Joseph to a severe regimen. He would be up by six in the morning and would rarely end the day's work before nine in the evening. This sytem imposed a severe physical test on him, all the more so because his daily environment was, in itself, trying to the health. This was not just a question of the comfort of the imperial palaces, which in certain aspects was rudimentary by modern standards. Hard to heat because of its high ceilings and long corridors, Schönbrunn was a veritable icebox in winter. Franz Joseph himself lived in the room where the duke of Reichstadt had fought against the advance of his tuberculosis. In these adverse surroundings in which, moreover, he developed a tendency to angina, the robustness of his constitution which was to be the key to his longevity asserted itself. He also acquired here a lifestyle which, with time, would become spartan in its austerity.

The timetable of Franz Joseph's studies contained a certain number of subjects which were the traditional basis of the education of a young gentleman: fencing, dancing, music, and drawing. Franz Joseph, however, showed little interest and even less aptitude for music. In this he was a clear exception to the family tradition. As his surviving pictures (book illustrations, patriotic scenes, and evocations of battle) confirm, the young archduke showed a greater talent for drawing, which he would, however, have little chance to make use of in later life.

In addition to these traditional disciplines the study of languages had an important place in Franz Joseph's curriculum. At first, naturally, he studied German, his native tongue, but almost equal importance was placed on French which was then the *lingua franca* of European aristocratic society and the language of international relations. This portion of his timetable did not, however, really distinguish Franz Joseph from the other young princes of his time. The originality of his education lay in the fact that he had also to learn Czech, Hungarian, Polish, and Italian all of which were spoken in the Austrian Empire. As future sovereign, it was his duty to learn the principal languages of his subjects. It says something for his ability that he managed to do so.

In this part of his study programme, Franz Joseph showed a worthy degree of application but where his military training was concerned, he displayed outright enthusiasm. At first he had only to perform a series of simple exercises every two days, but from the age of twelve, his training became more intensive. Franz Joseph was now handed over to the authority of an officer, Commander Franz von Hauslab, the victor in the battle of Aspern, who had been recommended to Sophie by Archduke Karl. Hauslab decided that he would first make his pupil serve as a simple trooper, laying down the principle that 'He who is called to command should first have known how to obey'. For his apprenticeship to be complete, the young archduke served successively as a foot soldier, a dragoon, and an artilleryman. But it is the privilege of princes not to be subjected to the ordinary rules of promotion. This period of his military training was deemed to have been completed after a few months. Franz Joseph received, for his thirteenth birthday, the brevet of regimental colonel in the Dragoons. He clearly took this promotion to the grade of colonel very seriously. During the years that followed, the visits which he paid to his regiment, then stationed in Moravia, were proof of this. These visits gave him the opportunmity to be part of a world which had long attracted him and in which he felt naturally at ease. He also found in the army the model of a society in which relationships were founded on the principles of hierarchy and obedience. The lesson would not be lost on him.

His thirteenth birthday brought more to Franz Joseph than his officer's papers. It was of special importance for another reason, for on the following day Franz Joseph was allowed to take part in his first hunt. This was the beginning of a true passion for the sport which he pursued into old age. He shared this passion with his father, and they would hunt together for many years.

During this time, Franz Joseph continued his studies, which developed according to the dictates of those responsible for his education. His timetable was enriched with new subjects: astronomy, law, and philosophy. His philosophical training was placed in the hands of the priest Joseph Othmar von Rauscher. A well-known theologian and director of the Eastern Academy in Vienna, he was already recognized as one of the stronger personalities among the Austrian clergy, amongst whom he represented the movement for Catholic restoration which had developed since the beginning of the century in reaction to Josephism. As one of the leaders of this tendency, he supported the abolition of the legislation originally passed by Joseph II which placed the Church in a subordinate role to the State, and offered, in return for power, the support of the Church, which would be recognized as independent, in the fight against liberalism. These attitudes, which earned him the support of the zealot party at court, naturally recommended him to Sophie and Metternich in their choice, for they were both strong supporters of the redefining of the relationship between Church and State. In the post to which he was appointed, Rauscher did not omit to educate his pupil in these beliefs.

As the crowning glory of this educational programme, it remained for the young archduke to be taught the art of governing men and of conducting affairs of state. Metternich reserved this task for himself, under Sophie's benevolent eye. For almost an entire year he instructed Franz Joseph in the guiding principles of his conservative politics. Franz Joseph would always keep in mind Metternich's assertion that a Constitution founded on the principle of representation would be incompatible with the pluralist nature of the Austrian monarchy. Even though events would not always allow him to follow this political line, the gradual seizing-up of the Austrian constitutional machinery in the final years of his reign would confirm him in this belief.

However we judge Franz Joseph's education, it had the merit of coherence. Although it was broadly based, his tutors' concern was always to inculcate an aversion to liberalism in the prince, and to prepare him for authoritarian methods of government. This aspect of his education left an indelible mark on him. The demanding nature of his training left him with little free time. Although he did enjoy playing with his brothers when he had the opportunity, such moments were rare. The regimen prescribed left him no time to read for pleasure and because he did not develop the habit in his youth, he did not feel the need for it later in life. This workload was partly the result of the particular characteristics of the Habsburg monarchy which obliged Franz Joseph's tutors to include the main languages spoken in the empire in his studies. This wealth of subjects studied by the young Franz Joseph did not allow him sufficient objectivity to be able to distinguish essential from peripheral matters, or to understand the underlying structure of power within the empire. The example of his military training is representative of these defects. Here, his tutors were above all concerned with the external forms of command, while showing themselves to be far less forthcoming on matters concerning tactics, and even less so concerning strategy. The seriousness of this omission became obvious when, in June 1859, Franz Joseph decided to take command of the army in Italy: he then perceived his inability to assume this supreme responsibility for lack of the appropriate military training.

As the hope of the monarchy, Franz Joseph began to take on a diplomatic role before he had even finished his studies. His youth was a trump card for the monarchy, for which he was a more appealing representative than the sickly emperor. The general opinion at court was that his appearances would confirm his subjects in their loyalty and would rekindle allegiances which had been inclined to waver. His journeys first took him in 1847 to Hungary. Franz Joseph appeared to advantage on these missions which were not without difficulty as a result of the atmosphere of tension which hung over relations between Vienna and Hungary at that time. The elegance of his bearing, his fluency in Hungarian, and the care which he took to wear the uniform of the Hungarian hussars brought him a favourable reception, although it is true that all, or almost all of this goodwill would have disappeared in less than two years.

In the course of the following years, Franz Joseph would certainly have further assumed the role of representative for the monarchy while awaiting the time when he would succeed Ferdinand, but events decided otherwise. The revolution of 1848 precipitated the day of reckoning. Because a change of sovereign appeared to the ruling party to be the prerequisite for the rejuvenation of the power of the monarchy, Franz Joseph was brought to the throne when he was only just eighteen.

2
Austria on the Eve of the 1848 Revolution

Eighteen forty-eight was known as the 'springtime of the people' or the 'year of madness'. Although revolution did not break over completely untroubled waters, the Habsburg monarchy was still strong enough to resist the shock wave which shook its foundations and threatened to topple it. But the clouds were gathering and behind the still-brilliant façade of the monarchy, the forces of change which were eventually to destabilize the empire were at work. Strengthened by the revolutionary upheavals in the rest of Europe, their conjunction was to lead in 1848 to a violent explosion within the Habsburg Empire.

Austria, the 'European House of Lords'

At the end of the wars of the French Revolution and the Empire, Austria embodied the politics of the restoration, forming a barrier against which it was hoped that the forces of liberalism would be shattered. Already, the choice of Vienna as host to the peace conference which was to reshape the face of Europe was a tribute to the part played by the Habsburg monarchy in the allied victory over Napoleonic France. Austria not only emerged from the conference confirmed in its role as a great power, but having been a major contributor to the birth of the new international order, it also appointed itself its guardian. This political stance assured Austria a long-term dominant role in European affairs, but to be successful the monarchy had itself to be a model of conservative society. It thus fell to Austria, in the words of Prince Metternich, to act as 'the European House of Lords'.

The Absolutist State

Founded on the divine right of kings, the Austrian Empire was run according to absolutist principles. The emperor, as sovereign, was the source of all power. He initiated policy, closely followed its implementation and would intervene at a later stage if the need arose. Such a system obviously did not prevent a group of influential ministers from ranging themselves around the sovereign. Chancellor Kaunitz had the ear of two great monarchs, first Maria Theresa and then Joseph II, and Metternich was in undisputed control of the monarchy's foreign policy.

In practice, events often do not follow their predicted pattern. Attentive to detail as well as larger matters, Franz I had carried out his duties as sovereign with a scrupulous conscientiousness. Jealous of his authority, he would never have allowed one of his ministers, even Metternich, to take a decision without first consulting him. Following Joseph II's example, he set aside much of his time for paperwork, showing himself to be the empire's chief bureaucrat. But under Ferdinand, the situation changed completely. Although by his father's wish he wore the imperial mantle, both his physical and mental condition prevented him from exercising his prerogatives. It thus fell to the empire's officials and administration to compensate for this weakness so as to keep the fiction of a strong central power alive.

The Austrian state remained loyal to the policy of centralization which had been developed by Maria Theresa after the Austrian War of Succession and was continued by Joseph II. The Habsburg lands, still a patchwork of disparate provinces when Maria Theresa came to the throne, were transformed under these two great rulers into a political whole, and solid structures of state were set up according to contemporary standards. The autonomy of the constituent parts of the monarchy was gradually reduced, and they were replaced by the central institutions which multipled as the sphere of their activities grew. One victim of this policy was the Chancellorship of Bohemia, in which the sovereignty of the Kingdom of Saint Wenceslas lay, and which became merged with the Chancellorship of Austria.

During this process, the monarchy's lands came under the control of a network of state officials who were directly answerable to the authority o the central administration in Vienna. The Diets, whose opinions had still had influence at the beginning of the century, were generally reduced to a mere honourary role. Although the central government judged it to be wiser to preserve them for appearance's sake, it now felt strong enough to ignore their rights. Although they had a constitutional right to self-rule in matters of taxation, the government neglected to convene certain Diets for several years running without suffering any inconvenience. Beyond the individual concessions agreed by Leopold II, whose main aim had been to provide the Diets with a sop to their self-esteem, no modification was made to this policy of centralization during subsequent reigns. The Diets thus continued to stagnate in the obscurity to which they had been relegated by the absolutist system, and when the central power agreed to convene them it made sure that they did not exceed their role as simple recording offices.

It is true that this process had not reached the same stage throughout the empire. It was already well-advanced in the Austro-Bohemian group, which had expanded at the end of the eighteenth century to include Galicia, the part of Poland given to Austria, but it had developed only slowly in Hungary. The main reason for this difference, which was acknowledged in Habsburg society well before the Compromise of 1867, was that historically Hungary had evolved separately from the other areas of the monarchy, and the greater part of the Hungarian territory had indeed been under Ottoman rule for over a century and a half. It was only after the collapse of the second siege of Vienna, in 1683, that the Habsburgs were able to regain the whole of the Kingdom of Saint Stephen. During this period of Ottoman domination the first steps had been taken in the other Habsburg countries towards a policy of centralization, and these had prepared the ground for Maria Theresa and Joseph II. No such process had been possible in Hungary where, in order to be able to assert their authority following the reconquest, the Habsburgs were obliged to recognize the authority of the kingdom's traditional institutions.

Of course the Habsburgs attempted to reduce Hungary to the status of their other possessions, but each time that they resorted to force in this aim they encountered a stubborn resistance which was eventually victorious. While Maria Theresa had been careful to mount no direct attacks and had managed to gain ground on several points, Joseph was obliged to admit defeat in his dealings with Hungary. Ignoring the Hungarian Constitution, he tried to place Hungary under direct Viennese authority with the intention of integrating it into a rationalized Austrian state. Faced with a country on the point of secession, he was obliged to withdraw these measures shortly before his death.

Franz I experienced failure in his turn, although he managed to avoid such drama in his relations with Hungary. He did not convene the two Houses of the Hungarian Diet from 1812 onwards, thus allowing the constitutional rights of the kingdom to be neglected. When in 1825 he decided to recall them, he was obliged, however, to acknowledge that they would not be content just to record Vienna's wishes. This recalcitrance continued to grow until 1848. Although the Austrian authorities were not very concerned over the spirit of revolt which was stirring up certain other Diets at that time, Hungarian resistance to their rule gave them cause for real disquiet, for the Hungarian Constitution was still in operation and, despite the efforts of the Habsburgs to dismantle it, it continued to dictate the form of Austrian relations with the Hungarian nation, headed by its nobility. On the eve of 1848, the Austrian Empire as standard-bearer of absolutism in Europe, was thus obliged, paradoxically, to tolerate a constitutional regime on part of its territory. Although its other possessions submitted to absolute rule, Hungary would not, and Vienna was obliged to come to terms with this.

The Austrian state of the restoration and of the *Vormärz* (the period which led up to March 1848) saw itself as the inheritor of the Theresian and Josephist eras. As such, it officially assumed the ideology of enlightened despotism working for the good of its subjects, giving them the benefits of progress, but without allowing them any part in the management of affairs. Nevertheless the great fear brought about by the French Revolution had profoundly modified the government's perspective. From that time on, priority was no longer given to social change, or even a more modest development; instead, the emphasis was placed on civil peace and order, *Ruhe und Ordnung*, which to some extent became the administration's motto.

Under Franz I and Ferdinand I, the state was careful not to relinquish the system it had inherited. We already know that the administration pursued the policy of centralization begun under previous reigns, and censorship and the political police, the future pillars of the regime, were not new inventions. The difference lay not in the structures of government but in the attitude towards absolutism. Where Josephism perceived it as an instrument of policy, the Austrian rulers now saw it as an essential method of government to combat the revolution.

After 1815 the powers of the censors and the police were increased. At their head was Count Sedlnitzky who, secure in Metternich's confidence, was to occupy this post until the revolution. The task of the services under his command was to prevent Austrian subjects from coming into contact with liberal ideas. Their activities were first concentrated within the empire. Their primary target was the press, which they watched closely. Newspapers and journals could only be produced if they had been given prior authorization. Literature, too, was placed under close observation. Among the ruling classes the role of writers and philosophers in the gestation of the French Revolution had not been forgotten. Many works critical of society thus fell under the censor's axe. One such was *Promenades of a Viennese Poet*, the collection of poems banned in 1831 in which, under the pseudonym of Anastasius Grün, Count Anton Auersperg mocked the vices of the Austrian absolutist political system. The theatre did not escape either. Passages hostile to the Habsburgs had to be cut from Schiller's *William Tell* before it could be performed. Franz Grillparzer, the great Austrian dramatist of the period was also obliged to submit to the censor's knife.

In order to be effective, censorship had to go further and place Austria in a sort of quarantine, by ensuring that works considered to be dangerous did not enter the monarchy, and this task intensified when writers banned in Austria began to publish their writings in other countries. The situation was aggravated by some German and Swiss publishers who specialized in works which were banned in Austria, and the censored *Promenades of a Viennese Poet* was thus published in Germany. But it was also necessary to guard against the pernicious ideas to be found in foreign works of subversion, especially those published in the various languages spoken within the empire. Metternich was particularly concerned by the writings of Polish emigrés and by Italian publications, for he saw the revolutionary nature of the Polish movement, and he also feared for Austria's Italian possessions. But it was in the case of the German language that the chancellor's vigilance was at its most active. Because of the strong position of the Germans in the monarchy, he feared that the main danger lay in this quarter. In the face of the growth of liberal ideas, which in Germany were rapidly becoming both democratic and nationalistic, he allowed no relaxation in his attitude towards the literature which propagated them. These defences against illegal imports were not, however, without weaknesses and despite the vigilance of the authorities, many forbidden works managed to enter Austria and were covertly circulated.

It would be wrong, however, to look on Metternich's Austria as a totalitarian state. Such a label would in any case be an anachronism, for no European state of the nineteenth century, even Tsarist Russia, had such powers. Furthermore, the restoration and *Vormärz* rulers of Austria had no wish to force the whole population to assume an official ideology. They were content to maintain order and to protect society against the threats of a revolutionary upheaval.

Nor should the Austria of this period be seen as a cultural desert. Naturally, the restrictions enforced by the government inhibited freedom of thought and artistic creation, but their efforts were already restricted by the limited practical power of the state in a society which had not yet fully entered the technological age. There was also a certain nonchalance prevalent among the Austrian people which lessened the severity of the restrictions. Moreover, the vigilance of the censors gave priority to political works and, although it was not always easy to establish the dividing line between political and literary works, non-political writers were generally left alone. Metternich himself, the mastermind of this great witchhunt for liberal ideas, was also a man of culture, whose *salon* was open to men of letters, scholars, and scientists. It was certainly not his intention to prevent all artistic expression within the monarchy. On the whole, although censorship stood in the way of artistic creation, it did not render it sterile.

The truth of this is demonstrated by the flourishing of creativity in a wide variety of genres during these years. Grillparzer, for example, certainly had to suffer the harassments of censorship, but these did not prevent him from producing most of the plays which made him the spokesman of his Austrian homeland during this period. At this time, too, the Viennese stage was dominated by two great writers, Raimund and Nestroy, whose works, rich in popular language, still number today among the Austrian literary classics.

This phenomenon was not confined to the German-speaking countries. In some areas this was the time of the revival of a national consciousness, in others it was newly awakened, especially among the Slavs. These movements could not have developed had they been based on the oral tradition alone. Although they were widespread they needed to be communicated through a whole range of printed works, dictionaries, and grammatical and orthographical treatises, which provided these peoples with a basis for national identity which combined their language and their past. Those men who aroused the Czech nation, Dobrovsky, Jungmann, Palacký, and Safarik, were thus able to publish the results of their philological, literary, and historical research without having to suffer the thunderbolts of the censor.

Nor did the constraints of a police state smother musical creativity. As the inheritors of the baroque tradition, the lands of the Danube provided an excellent environment for music, having both aristocratic taste and the vitality of popular tradition, and great works were created during this period. Vienna remained one of the great centres of European music, and it was there that Beethoven finally settled, remaining there until his death in 1827, although he had to face living conditions which were often difficult. It was also in the Vienna of the restoration that Franz Schubert's genius flourished, his discreet melancholy blending with the muted colours of the Austria of the *Biedermeier* school. The masters of the waltz, Joseph Lanner and Johann Strauss caused the censors no problems. Their music might have been created for the purpose of distracting the Viennese from unhealthy political preoccupations as they danced gaily to its strains.

Scientific life presented the same varied picture. The Austrian universities did not bear comparison with their German rival, whose fame at that time was spreading throughout Europe. Locked into a rigid system of constraints, their organization did not lend itself to high standards of scientific development. The professors were not free to select the content of their own lectures and this had inevitable consequences. The authorities feared that the Austrian universities might become the home of liberalism, following the example of their German counterparts, and considered this control to be a guarantee against the risk of dangerous deviations. They were not so concerned about the possible damage to the quality of the teaching, because the primary aim of the universities was to train good and loyal subjects, fit for the emperor's service.

There were nevertheless some areas of Austrian science which escaped this fate. In the steps of their eighteenth-century predecessors, the medical schools could declare themselves to be of the same standard as those of the rest of Europe. Great professors such as Rokitansky and Skoda maintained the reputation of the Vienna School of Medicine. The Austria of the *Vormärz* period also included experts in Eastern studies from outside the university world, such as Hammer-Purgstall and Prokesch von Osten. It was Metternich's administration which finally founded the Academy of Science in 1846, filling the gap left by preceding reigns, and this institution attracted leading contemporary scholars in many fields to Vienna.

The Vestiges of Feudalism

Despite the beginning of the decline of the nobility, Austrian society still retained a strong feudal flavour. The Diets' loss of influence affected the nobility most of all, and the nobles could also see the evidence of their decline on their own lands.

Until the major reforms which took place under Maria Theresa and Joseph II, there was no direct relationship between the sovereign and most of his or her subjects. Outside the limits of the towns, the authority of the crown was exercised through the nobles, although there were a few exceptions. Little by little, however, a local administration responsible directly to Vienna grew up, and by taking the enforcement of state legislation into the nobles' holdings, it curbed their powers. On the eve of 1848, this transfer of authority from the nobility to the state was widely advanced. The only significant rights still left to the feudal lord on his own lands were those of local policing and local justice.

Despite the crisis in the feudal system, the nobility still retained a large degree of economic power. The monarchy's economy continued to be strongly dominated by agriculture and in most areas the noble's estate remained by the basic unit of rural organization with its classic division between the lord's demesne, farmed by the landowner with the help of his peasants' labour, and the lands of the village, farmed by the peasants themselves, although there were considerable variations within the system. The first was the difference in the size of each demesne. There was a strong contrast between the many small estates in the alpine areas, and the vast possessions of the Hungarian magnates and the Bohemian and Polish aristocracy. This contrast was accentuated because the great families almost always owned more than one estate. The branch of the Schwarzenbergs alone held 640,000 hectares in Bohemia and the Liechtensteins owned as many as 145,000 hectares. The more modest holdings of the Thun-Hohenstein von Tetschen family in northern Bohemia still covered 57,000 hectares.

Differences also existed in farming methods. The small estates of the Alps often used old-fashioned methods of farming, and among the larger estates, too, there were some, mainly in Hungary and Galicia, in which the vast lands were partly left to lie fallow, or were over-cultivated, giving a poor yield. In contrast, there were the large estates, especially in Bohemia and Moravia, which set an example of a dynamic agriculture. These estates rationalized their farming methods, gradually eradicating the old practice of leaving land fallow by increasing fodder crops, improving their livestock, introducing new root crops such as sugar beet, and reclaiming farmland under a programme of major improvements.

The aristocracy's share in economic expansion was not limited to agriculture. They were also involved in the industrial development of the monarchy. This involvement should not be exaggerated, as only a minority of the richer aristocracy owned industrial interests. Indeed, in the course of these years a gap opened up between the industrial production of the Habsburg monarchy and western European states. Nevertheless, although development was slower, Austria was affected by the industrial revolution which had begun in England. The nobility's interest was chiefly concerned with the sectors of the food industries in which they were traditionally strong. One such was the beer industry, particularly in Bohemia where many large landowners had breweries on their estates. Introduced under the influence of the continental system, the cultivation of sugar beet naturally led to the development of a sugar industry, which again was usually established on the estates where the raw material was grown.

The nobility did not neglect to invest in areas directly linked to the industrial revolution such as the textile industries and although the rise of these industries was certainly not due to the nobility alone, for bourgeois families such as the Schoellers and the Skenes built up major manufacturing complexes during this period, the aristocracy did play an important part in this development: Prince Salm-Reifferscheid, for instance, added interests in textile mills to his fortune in land. Even more important was their role in the iron and steel, and metallurgic industries. As owners of the mineral rights of their estates, they controlled many of the Bohemian and Moravian coal deposits and naturally invested in the mining industries.

The diversification of their interests also led the members of the nobility to explore the possibilities which had opened up with the development of steam travel. The potential profits to be made from the expansion of the railway system did not escape those nobles who were most involved in the process of economic development. The advantages of the growth in river transport, which the development of steam also made possible, drew their attention as well. The most spectacular project was certainly that of Count Istvan Széchényi, who, in founding the Vienna–Pest *Donauschiffahrtsgesellschaft* (Danube Shipping Company) in 1830, improved Hungary's link with the main centres of development in Europe and contributed to that country's modernization.

Of course not all members of the nobility were in the same position, and this extension of the field of their economic interests required a level of funding not possible for the minor nobles. It does, however, reveal a capacity to adapt in one group of the aristocracy, allowing the business magnate of the capitalist age to surface from beneath the feudal lord.

Austria and Europe

As it had on the home front, the Austria of the restoration and the *Vormärz* was occupied in matching its foreign policy to its conservative principles. Indeed, the administration was convinced that any separation of these two spheres of action would be artificial. In both the common enemy was the spirit of revolution. To this end, relations between states were organized in such a way that no foothold was provided for revolutionary activity.

During this period, Metternich was the uncontested master craftsman of the monarchy's foreign policy. He had defined its rules, and supervised its conformation to these principles. In the international system of which he had been the main architect when the collapse of the Napoleonic Empire had necessitated the rebuilding of Europe, Metternich assigned a pivotal role to Austria. He had wanted to found this new European order on the principle of balance, as it was defined in the spirit of the eighteenth century by Friedrich von Gentz (who was later to become his adviser) in 1805: 'Equilibrium, or the balance of power, is made up of parallel or closely linked systems under which no one party can threaten the independence or essential rights of another without encountering effective resistance, thus placing itself in danger.'[1] After a decade of Napoleonic domination, Metternich had wanted to establish a relationship of strength between the five great European powers under which none of them could secure a dominant position. The survival of this sytem required a lasting accord between these states and Metternich had also arranged that all of them should be involved in preserving this balance. To this end, the directing body would have regular meetings to decide on a joint policy in any crisis which threatened to disturb it.

In this pentarchy, Metternich placed the whole of central Europe under the aegis of Austria. In Metternich's mind this included Germany and Italy, with the Habsburg Empire at the natural centre of such a system, allowing it to contain the pressures which threatened it. To the west, the danger came from a France still suffering from the revolutionary itch. If no barrier was erected against it, it was to be feared that the evil would gradually contaminate the rest of Europe. To the east, Metternich suspected that Russia might abandon itself to the temptation of an expansionist policy. He also foresaw that Russian ascendancy would expose Europe to the threat of an Eastern despotism. Because of its position at the heart of Europe, only Austria could stand in the way of these two pressures. Metternich therefore appointed it the guardian of European balance.

Austria would only be in a position to fulfil this role if it could subdue Germany and Italy. For many centuries, the Habsburgs had retained the elected crown of the Holy Roman Empire. But, whatever the prestige which still surrounded it, the holder of this position had been gradually stripped of the powers which he had originally held over the other German princes. While this was happening the Habsburgs owed their power far more to their hereditary possessions than to a title which, although glorious, had retained little substance. After Napoleon decided to abolish the Holy Roman Empire and chased Austria out of Germany in 1806, the monarchy lost interest in the title, and in 1815, it opposed a plan to restore the imperial office in Germany. Franz I had in any case created the Austrian Empire in 1804, thereby setting the seal of the law on Austrian domination and making it unnecessary to assume a second crown which would have been devalued in certain respects in relation to the first. Metternich preferred to organize Germany as a confederation, with the Austrian emperor as president. It was thus that the German Confederation (*Deutscher Bund*) was born, whose thirty-nine states were joined through the Habsburg monarchy to the Austro-Bohemian group, which extended as far as Trieste.

Metternich required this Confederation to provide the Germanic world with the necessary unity to face up to its European responsibilities. He also insisted that its structure should remain flexible so as not to harm the sovereignty of the member states and not to hinder the monarchy's freedom of manoeuvre. In addition to its legal pre-eminence as president, Austria made use of the special relationship which it had with the courts of southern Germany and certain other states, such as Hanover and Saxony, to exert its influence in the heart of the Confederation.

Austrian supremacy was also dependent on the quality of relations with Prussia. Metternich was aware that the Austro-Prussian dualism of the time of the Holy Roman Empire had contributed to the undermining of the Habsburg position in Germany. To dissuade the Hohenzollerns from being tempted to form a united Germany with Prussia at the centre, he realized the necessity to restrict Prussia through a close alliance. For many years, this union of the two monarchies was one of the axes of Metternich's diplomacy, for he perceived their solidarity to be not only a condition of the strengthening of Germanic unity, but also a means to control Prussia, thus assuring Austrian pre-eminence in Germany.

Italy, as a traditional field of intervention for Habsburg power, was the other major area of Austrian activity in Europe. Following the collapse of Napoleonic dominance, Austria regained a degree of influence there which exceeded that which it had held before the French Revolution. There were clear signs of its ascendancy. First, there was direct control in Lombardy-Venetia over which Austria held sovereignty. Then, other side branches of the Habsburg family became established in Florence and Modena, and Maria Louisa had been given the Duchy of Parma in return for the loss of her imperial crown. Further south, the Papal States and the Kingdom of Naples were firmly attached to the Austrian system through their counter-revolutionary zeal. There remained Piedmont-Sardinia, which was less susceptible to Austrian influence but was unlikely to conduct too independent a policy in view of its king's aversion to liberalism. Furthermore, there were hopes that Princess Marie Anne's marriage to the heir to the throne would help to consolidate the relationship between the two monarchies.

Metternich's Europe was an intricate mechanism and was therefore fragile. Its different parts were closely linked and the modification of any one element threatened repercussions throughout the whole. It was here that the second ruling principle of Metternich's diplomacy, that of legitimacy, came into play. He advocated total respect for existing international treaties and after 1815 he devoted himself to the European system formulatd at the Vienna Congress, thereby supporting the integrity of those states designated by the Congress. This could be achieved by holding regular meetings between the powers. But these meetings needed to be not only a forum for the opinions of the participants but also a place where decisions were made and carried out. As the guardian of European order, Metternich's Austria delighted in its role as the practical arm of the great powers. Metternich was nevertheless careful to limit these interventions to areas of direct interest to the monarchy. A clear example of this was Austria's action in sending an expeditionary force to crush the revolution which had broken out in Naples following the Troppau Congress of December 1820.

Metternich nowhere pushed the principle of legitimacy as far as he did in the Balkans. He based his ideas on the conviction that any incursion into the territory of the Ottoman Empire would serve as a justification for other frontier modifications and political upheavals in the rest of Europe, and would certainly bring the system born of the Vienna Congress into question. Metternich's policy was still based on the belief that the gradual expulsion of the Ottoman Empire from Europe would sooner or later lead to a direct confrontation between Austria and Russia in the Balkans.

Only by preserving Ottoman rule in Constantinople could such a confrontation, with its attendant dramatic results, be avoided. Metternich also realized that the creation of a number of nation-states among the ruins of the Ottoman Empire would represent a serious danger to the monarchy because they would encourage the development of separatist tendencies among the Austrian peoples.

In this we can see that two different, but not contradictory, interpretations can be placed on Metternich's diplomacy. First there is his own declaration that his decisions were made in the greater interests of Europe. There is no question that he did indeed care for this. He was too influenced by eighteenth-century tradition not to have a universal vision of Europe's destiny which influenced his policies. It would, however, be short-sighted to accept this as his only motivation, for Metternich's policies were equally dictated by Habsburg interests. His defence of the status quo in the Balkans provides an illustration of this. But how should we view Austria's interventions in the name of the counter-revolution? It is impossible to ignore the fact that they all took place in Italy and Germany, in those areas where the power of the Habsburgs was directly in question.

The Faults of the System

As an intellectual construct, the system with which Metternich's name is associated certainly had the merit of coherence, balanced as it was by its internal logic. Moreover, Metternich was always prepared to indulge in an explanation of the principles which directed his politics. However, to say that his contemporaries were not in complete agreement with him would be to understate the case. Liberal and nationalist writers did not weary in their denunciations of the Austrian 'prison of the peoples'. Charles Sealsfield, an Austrian subject who emigrated to the United States, uttered in 1828 a merciless condemnation of the Austrian regime: 'an absolutism which is as perfect and refined as Austrian absolutism has perhaps never existed in any other civilized country.'[2]

It goes without saying that neither Metternich's complacent description of his system, nor the diatribes of his opponents can be considered as disinterested evidence for the historian. He must simply ask himself whether this fine system was actually fragile despite its appearance of cohesion, and whether it stood up to the test of events. In this he is obliged to acknowledge that, despite its brilliant façade, the edifice was not without flaws.

The Paralysis of Governmental Power

The truth was that the regime was sinking into increasing lethargy as the years passed. A major cause of this was the change of direction effected during the traumatic years which followed the French Revolution. There was still sufficient momentum in policy for certain reforms to be effected, but these soon fell off and the guiding principle of the reign soon developed into a hostility towards change, as the administration feared that the slightest alteration in the balance of power would lead to the collapse of the whole structure. Metternich himself suffered from this attitude.

Avoiding the finality of an outright refusal, Franz I simply refrained from following up various suggestions for reform. To confirm this as the golden rule for the heads of the monarchy, in his will made in February 1835 he called on Ferdinand to 'make no changes to the foundations of the state'.[3]

Personal quarrels further contributed to the increase in this paralysis. The most serious was that between Metternich and Count Franz Kolowrat. As the head of the political section of the Council of State since 1826, Kolowrat occupied himself with the task of preventing Metternich from extending his control of foreign policy to embrace home affairs. This conflict was partly the result of political differences. As well as being the spokesman for the aristocracy, Kolowrat represented Josephist ideals at the heart of the governmental machine, while Metternich believed that religious politics should favour Catholic interests more. However, this disagreement soon outgrew the strictly political context and developed into a confrontation between two strong personalities. Despite this, it suited the emperor to allow them to clash, for the rivalry protected him from the influence of too powerful a minister, allowing him to retain mastery of the game.

On the death of the old emperor the chancellor appeared to gain the advantage, for Franz, in his will, ordered his son to take no decisions without first consulting Metternich. In his last wishes he called for the establishment of a diarchy shared by his youngest brother, Achduke Ludwig, and Metternich who would share the task of making up for the inadequacies of the new emperor. This formula was suggested by Metternich, and would have placed the real power of the empire in his hands, as he was clearly the stronger of the two men. His victory was shortlived, however, in the face of strong opposition from Kolowrat and the Josephist party. Eventually a compromise was reached and a Council of Regency, the *Staatskonferenz*, was formed which included both rivals and the Archduke Ludwig.

Now that the sovereign was not capable of the full exercise of his powers, this confrontation only increased administrative paralysis. The government machine was subjected to contradictory directives which were successful only in cancelling each other out. Lacking the intervention of a higher authority, the administration was left to resolve the problem, and this naturally enhanced its power. The complexity of the empire's government structure added to the confusion. Austria was still without modern organization on the lines of the French or British systems of government. There were high-level ministerial appointments, but there was no collective authority in the form of a cabinet of ministers. Real decision-making took place in sort of privy council, Franz I's *Konferenzrat* or Ferdinand I's *Staatskonferenz*, which in turn was assisted by a State Council, divided into many sections. There was no cohesive unit of administration. The monarchy's administrative activities were divided among many chancelleries, (the Austro-Bohemian chancellery, the Hungarian and Transylvanian chancellery, those of Galicia and Lombardy-Venetia). In the case of Hungary, and of Lombardy-Venetia, these units were relatively autonomous, whereas the Galician chancellery was primarily a concession to the self-esteem of the Polish and barely screened the direct intervention of Vienna. The drawbacks of this decentralization of the power bases would not attract much attention while the emperor co-ordinated the whole, but with a monarch who was just a figurehead they would come to the fore. Without a central guiding hand, this heavy and archaic machinery revealed itself to be an unsuitable tool for coherent governmental action.

The Awakening of the Opposition Parties

The result of this stagnation was that the state became progressively less able to supply the needs of a changing society. Such a situation was favourable to the formation of an opposition movement and from 1830 onwards, affected by the general climate in Europe, Austria became open to such a movement, which eventually developed during the final years of the *Vormärz*. As was appropriate to the slow development of Habsburg society which was only just beginning to be affected by the industrial revolution, most of the opposition's demands were moderate. With the exception of a few marginal groups, it was based among the new middle classes and, although its members called for a transformation in government, they made it clear that they did not dispute the authority of the monarchy. The proposed reforms themselves went no further than the establishment of a constitutional monarchy which would retain most of its prerogatives while guaranteeing the landowning upper classes a part in government.

The local Diets occupied a central position in this opposition movement. Although most of them had no real power they were still a forum for the expression of opinions in countries subject to censorship. Furthermore, in spite of their diminished powers they had still managed to survive and they provided support for the reforms proposed by the opposition, as they had been the focus for local patriotism in the face of centralization for over a century and a half. As in Bohemia, opposition to the *Vormärz* regime could take the form of an aristocratic reaction. The ancient feudal lords were eager to recover the political privileges which they had lost to the Vienna bureaucrats, and to reverse the policies which had made Bohemia a mere Austrian province. The nobles were aware that the rebellion of 1620 had not deprived the states of their legal freedoms and privileges, and, although they were now ignored, these rights had never been abolished. On the basis of this, the Bohemian nobles proposed a political system for the empire, claiming historical rights in the place of arbitrary decisions by the sovereign, and proposing a government based on a contract between the prince and his subjects as an alternative to absolute rule. The Diet soon acted on these principles by refusing in 1847 to pay a portion of the taxes demanded of it, and it made a solemn protest over Vienna's decision to crush this resistance.

It seems likely that if the role of the Diets were to grow, there would be a corresponding growth in the numbers of their members. Unchanged for centuries, their organization was the reflection of a feudal and fundamentally agricultural society which, although it had certainly not disappeared, was now encountering a new force in the rise of the middle classes who had begun to expand during the Enlightenment and who became established in Austria during the period of economic change which the country had entered. Although this new power was only just emerging, it was sufficiently developed in several provinces for a rich middle class to have formed and this class, allied with bourgeois intellectuals, aspired to a political influence in proportion to its increasing economic power. This was also true of the class of wealthy farmers which had grown up in areas where the feudal system had already disappeared.

The nobles, who had until this time enjoyed a comfortable majority in the Diets, were obliged to face up to the issue raised by this social transformation. They had to decide how far they were prepared to support a process which was likely to turn the hierarchical system of government into a representative system under which they would inevitably become a minority group.

The decision of the Bohemian nobles was a restrictive one. Their alliance with the Czech middle-class nationalists against Viennese centralization disposed them to accept an increase in the towns' representation in the Diet but they were not prepared to include the farmers. This was because, althouh it was no longer all-powerful, the feudal system was still strong in Bohemia, and most of the farmers were still dependent on the nobility for their lands.

In *Austria and its future*, however, Baron Andrian-Werburg declared himself to be in favour of a broader composition of the Diets while expressing the hope that the nobility would be able to regain some political influence through their renewed activity. In proposing to extend membership of the Diets to new sections of the population and even to those to whom the Diets had been hostile, he hoped for a growth in the representation of the urban middle classes, and for the possibility of representation for the farming classes who until then had been excluded except in the Tyrol.

One of the main centres of opposition to the *Vormärz* regime, the Diet of Lower Austria which met in Vienna, was of the same opinion. The nobility here was not so powerful as that of Bohemia, and was less entrenched in feudal traditions. The social groups from which the members of the Diet were drawn had also been more affected by liberal ideas. Liberalism found active promoters in Vienna, among societies whose continued existence, barely troubled by police surveillance, in fact demonstrated the limits of the oppressive character of the regime. This was true of the *Juridisch-Politischer Leseverein* (legal and political reading society) in which deputies from the Diet mixed with senior civil servants, professors from Vienna University, lawyers and doctors, all of whom were critical of the political system of the *Vormärz*. Compared with the whole of Viennese society these groups remained very much in the minority, but recruited as they were from among the elite and the able, the members of the *Juridisch-Politischer Leseverein* were all men of note whose influence extended beyond the personal sphere. Their visits to this centre for political exchange and comment made them familiar with liberal theory, although the cutting edge of ideas was blunted because Austria dragged so far behind western Europe in liberal thought. These men had already been anaesthetized against the risk of democratic temptation.

We can find an echo of this mild liberalism in the motion formulated by the Lower Austrian Diet, which called for the convocation of a central parliament in Vienna, which would be drawn from the Diets, would meet once a year to set the rates of taxation and would advise the crown. The most daring proposal of the period, this project aimed to bring to Austria a form of constitutional government that was not as advanced as those already in operation in England and Belgium, or even in France.

National Pluralism

The Austria of the *Vormärz* also saw the rise of nationalist movements which gave a new flavour to liberalism. The multinational nature of the Habsburg Empire was one of its main characteristics. Of course other states were not totally unified, but although Prussia, for instance, had Polish subjects, it was nevertheless undeniably a German state. The Russian Empire, too, contained many ethnic minorities, but the Russian people were broadly in the majority. In the Habsburg Empire, however, there was no one dominant people, at least in terms of numbers. The largest individual population, the Germans, did not even represent a quarter of the total (24.8 per cent in 1851*) and the distribution of nationalities was such that the term minority did not really apply to most of the nationalities under Habsburg rule.

This national pluralism was complex. This is hardly surprising, given that the 35 million inhabitants of the Austrian Empire were split into eleven national groups. These nationalities were divided among several great ethnic groups (the Germans, the Latin peoples, Magyars, and Slavs). But these classifications could cover so many differences that it is hard to leave it at that. For instance, the Slavs were divided into northern Slavs (Czechs, Slovaks, Poles, and Ruthenians) and southern Slavs (Slovenians, Croats, and Serbs). Being a member of the same group did not necessarily imply any similarity of development. The two branches of the Latin line, the Romanians and the Italians, were too far apart to have any close ties. There could also be a lack of fellow-feeling, for instance in Galicia the Poles and the Ruthenians were in perpetual opposition. The variety of languages also created subdivisions in these classifications. Although the Germans and the Magyars were homogenous linguistic units, the Slavs and the Latin peoples comprised as many languages as nationalities.

Religious variations added to this diversity. As a result of the Counter-Reformation, most of the empire's subjects were Catholic, like their rulers. But the empire also contained both Lutheran and Calvinist minorities. These were often to be found within a national group, for instance there was Magyar Calvinism and Slovak Lutheranism. Finally, on the eastern borders of the empire, Romanians and Serbs beloned to the Orthodox Church.

There were also historical differences within the empire, and even the traditional distinction between 'historical' and 'non-historical' peoples often appears artificial. For various reasons, the Czechs, Magyars, and Croats could claim a continuous national heritage, which, although it had sometimes wavered, had nevertheless continued through the centuries. There were still kingdoms of Bohemia, Hungary, and Croatia of which the emperor was sovereign. The case of Poland was different. Although by the agreement of the great powers, the Kingdom of Poland had been eradicated from the map of Europe, its disappearance had not wiped out the living memory in the hearts of the Poles. All peoples shared a national culture which had developed over a period of time, and which provided them with a sense of identity, even through periods of suppression, such as the Czechs had suffered after the battle of the White Mountain.

There was a second category of peoples, such as the Slovaks, the Slovenes, and the Ruthenes, who had never existed historically as constitutional nations. Here there were no traditions of the state or culture developed through the ages. Having long remained only potential historical entities, these peoples were just beginning to enter a process of national awakening.

* This figure does not include the population of Lombardy and Venetia. With it, it falls to 21.6 per cent.

Also for historical reasons, some of these peoples were not all contained within the boundaries of the empire. The Czechs, Slovenes, Magyars, and Slovaks certainly escaped this fate, but the Germans, Poles, Romanians, Serbs, Italians, and Ruthenians all had fellow nationals in one or more neighbouring states. For the present, with the exception of the Italians, this situation did not cause any serious problems for the monarchy. It could quickly become a danger, however, should these peoples seek national unity. To add to the complexity, the administrative divisions of the empire did not follow the territorial boundaries of the different peoples. They had been drawn up piecemeal as each area was acquired by the empire with no consideration for the nationalities of its inhabitants. Often intermingled, the peoples themselves did not occupy single areas, making a mosaic of any map of the different nationalities of the empire.

While it is clear that each of these peoples had its own individual characteristics, the simultaneous growth of nationalist movements also suggests that they were responding to a common cause. There were many factors in the development of nationalism. One influential element was the Josephism of the Habsburg monarchy. The reactions provoked by the moves towards centralization under Maria Theresa and Joseph II created a favourable climate for the declaration of a national consciousness. But the influence of Josephism was also a positive one. Joseph II's education system, which increased the spread of knowledge and helped to popularize the ideas of the Enlightenment, together with his policies of social reform, allowed a class of intellectual professionals to grow up among the subject peoples of the empire who could inspire movements of reform and of national awakening and promote them among the population.

Unlike Josephism, Romanticism was an external influence, which came from Germany. It spread easily because all the founders of nationalist movements could speak German and some had even been to German universities. The Czech nationalist leader, Kollar, had attended the University of Iena, which was one of the major centres of German Romanticism. Romanticism provided this generation with the opportunity to encounter an intellectual movement which numbered nationalism among its preoccupations. It supplied them with various theories, such as that of *Volksgeist* which saw the people as a living organism, and which valued language for its consolidation of national identity. They read Herder whose work pleaded in favour of the Slav people whom he described as a peaceful race living in harmony with nature, and this work anticipated Palacký's portrait of the Czech people in his *History of Bohemia*.

Despite the attempts of the authorities to suppress them, ideas awakened by the French Revolution also left their mark on nationalist movements deep within the empire. They taught that all peoples had the right to develop a national character. French thought had directly influenced the southern Slavs during the brief period of French sovereignty over Croatia, Carniol, Carinthia, and Istria, which were transferred to the Illyrian Provinces along with Dalmatia following the Peace of Vienna in 1809. This French presence did not last, but it triggered the rise of a desire for unity, and the memory of this influence inspired the Illyrian movement which aimed at the unification of all southern Slavs.

The Austrian Germans occupied a different part of the picture. There was certainly the feeling among them that they formed a single cultural community with the Germans of the *Bund*, but very few of them shared the hope for a united Germany. They felt the need for it even less because, generally unaware of the growth of feeling among the other nationalities, they could not imagine Austria as a non-German power and they were confirmed in this belief by the predominance of Germans in the key posts of the empire. Although Hungary and Lombardy-Venetia were separate states, they were still well-integrated ino the body of the monarchy, so the Germans saw little reason to participate in a movement which might break up the empire.

For the Czechs (12.8 per cent of the empire's population) the problems were quite different. Here feelings of nationalism were reawakening following the long period of eclipse after the battle of the White Mountain. This Czech renaissance had benefited from a combination of circumstances which, although they were not exclusive to Bohemia, were at their strongest there: the influence of the Enlightenment was strong in Bohemia and had created a climate favourable to the growth of an elite prepared to head any nationalist movement; the proximity of Germany increased the influence of Romanticism; and widespread political resistance to centralization led to an agreement between the nationalists and a sector of the nobility. As the creation of scholars, writers, and historians, this nationalist revival was at first purely cultural but it soon took on political overtones. This was not yet really true of Kollar's glorification of the Slav peoples who stretched as far as Russia. Despite appearances, he did not promote a Pan-Slavic movement centred on Russia. He was the fervent apostle of a spiritual unity which had no application in the political field, but sympathy towards Russia would remain part of Czech nationalism for a long time. Nevertheless, at that time, Palacký and the journalist Havliček were revealing the true face of the Romanov Empire to their fellow countrymen and attacked the illusion of Russian-backed emancipation. On a different front, the desire to combine the nationalist movement with the Hussite tradition soon took on political implications because it turned its back on Catholicism and pushed its supporters down a natural path to liberalism. Palacký's interpretation of Bohemia's past in the light of antagonism between Germans and Czechs did much the same thing.

Their subsequent common destiny makes it logical to examine the Slovaks after the Czechs. From this period onwards, there was a current of opinion among the Slovaks which favoured the union of the two peoples. Although they were of Slovak origin, Kollar and Safarik chose to express themselves in Czech. The state of the languages also seemed to favour union. At the beginning of the nineteenth century, the Slovak language had not yet stabilized and the Slovak dialects were related to Czech. The Czecho-Slovak option found supporters among the Slovak Protestants who used bibles printed in Czech. However, the Catholic Slovaks who were in the majority feared Protestant dominance and as a reaction they worked to establish a Slovak national identity. The historical situation also contributed to the separation of Czechs and Slovaks, for the Czechs were part of Austro-Bohemia, whereas the Slovak territories were part of the Kingdom of Hungary. The unification of the two peoples could only take place if the integrity of the Kingdom of Hungary were threatened.

The Slovaks did not yet consider this to be an option. The victims of the politics of Magyar integration employed against them by the Hungarian authorities in the final years of the *Vormärz*, their response was a programme of national autonomy which united Catholics and Protestants. Those who supported the use of the Czech language soon admitted to the lack of realism shown by their proposal and the choice for a new national language fell on the dialect of the area of Turciansky Sväty Martin. But there was no desire for secession from the Kingdom of Hungary and the Protestants among them recognized that they benefited from greater religious tolerance as part of Hungary than they would elsewhere in the Austrian Empire. The Magyars would have been wrong, however, to ignore the growth of the Slovak nationalist movement which, although it was still ruled by loyalty to Hungary, could cause them problems in the future.

To the Austrian government, it seemed that the greatest problems always originated in Hungary. The repercussions of Joseph II's attempt to bring Hungary into line could still be felt. Hungary also stood out from the rest of the monarchy. A new element was developing in the hardening of the opposition. Until this time it had confined itself to the framework of the historial Constitution of the Kingdom of Saint Stephen, but from now on, it would be influenced by liberal ideas entering Hungary, especially after the revolutionary shake-up of 1830, and it supported a policy which no longer included the integrity of the Constitution as an article of faith. In the belief that the traditional oligarchy was outmoded, the opposition demanded popular suffrage and called for the formation of a Hungarian government answerable to the Diet. Its members also asked for the abolition of tax concessions for the nobility. Under the impulsion of new men, among them Lajos Kossuth, the opposition gained a majority in the Lower Chamber of the Diet. The pressure was so strong that the government felt constrained to take some action. It gave up its attempt to suppress the rise of the opposition through a policy of repression and allowed the political debate to unfold. At the risk of losing all credibility, the government's partisans were obliged to promote a programme of reforms. At this cost, the government avoided the worst, managing to hold onto its majority in the Upper Chamber and retaining a strong minority in the Lower Chamber.

But the Austrian government must have seen its future threatened on all sides. Unable to live up to the counter-revolutionary role assigned to it by Metternich, the Austrian state had shown itself unable to prevent the gradual growth of liberal political practices in one of its subject nations. The political groups of the empire were beginning a reorgnization process which turned them into real parties, at least according to the standards of the times. Their confrontation dominated public life at election-time, in the debates in the Diet, and in the newspapers.

Equally serious were the demands for the creation of a Hungarian government. The most lucid members of the opposition such as Ferenc Deák or Baron Eötvös did not expect the future of Hungary to be separated from that of Austria, but the most ardent among them, such as Kossuth, would not be daunted by such an extreme solution if Vienna attempted to interfere with their programme of reform. Even if a compromise were reached, the ties between Hungary and the rest of the empire would have been fatally loosened.

Resistance to the centralization policies of Joseph II had stimulated the development of a Magyar nationalism which rapidly became extreme. The tradition of strife with Vienna fed this nationalism, but it was given a new impetus by the introduction of the language question. Before that time, the political classes, that is the nobility, were in theory made up of many nationalities, and the use of Latin in the Diet and in the administration reinforced this image of supranationality. But actually, by the time the nineteenth century approached, this national plurality was almost nothing but a memory. With the exception of the Croats, the nobility of other nationalities had allowed themselves to make increasing use of the Magyar tongue. The turning-point was reached when Joseph II decided to replace Latin with German. When this had failed, the adoption of the Hungarian by the Diet and the administration became one of the major demands of Hungarian political classes, and this demand was gradually satisfied. Simultaneously, the idea that the Hungarian language belonged to the citizens of Hungary began to take hold. As long as membership of the political body remained restricted to the nobility, the damage was slight. This could no longer be so when liberalism set out to include new social classes in political life. These might include representatives of other nationalities, and the logic of this interpretation of the principle of citizenship led to the promotion of Magyar in politi- cal life. Although nobody would be prevented from speaking his or her mother tongue in everyday life, political competence was associated with the mastery of Hungarian.

It was true that the nationalists did not yet have the means to impose this programme, although the gradual conversion of secondary education to Hungarian served this aim. But weight of numbers favoured the Magyars. Compared with other nationalities, they made up 36.5 per cent of the population in Hungary, while in the empire as a whole they represented as much as 15.5 per cent.

A Croat nationalist movement developed in reaction to that of the Magyars. Ljudevit Gaj, its founder, did not, however, separate the destiny of his people from that of other southern Slavs. Influenced by his memory of the French occupation, and by Kollar's teachings, he called for the unification of all southern Slavs under the Habsburgs. These demands were in direct opposition to the wishes of the Magyars, since most of the Croats and the Serbs in the empire lived in Hungary and success would have resulted in secession from the Kingdom of Saint Stephen.

In creating a language common to both Croats and Serbs, Gaj paved the way for future developments. But there were dissenters. In the Styrian, Carinthian, and Carniol mountains the Slovenes, who were directly under Viennese authority, re- mained aloof from this movement. As an archivist in Vienna under Metternich's protection, Bartholomäus Kopitar fixed the Slovene language in a form which preserved its differences with Serbo-Croat. In addition, the linguistic union between the Serbs and the Croats was not complete, each people retaining its own alphabet. This partial integration demonstrates that the two peoples could not overcome entirely the traditional antagonism which reflected the historical frontier which separated them, and split southern Europe into two worlds: Latin and Greco-Byzantine, and two churches: Catholic and Orthodox.

The temporary restriction of Illyrianism pushed Croatian nationalist feeling towards the field of Hungarian politics where, in declaring Croatian rights, it was strongly opposed to Magyar nationalism. Already the will to subjugate Croatia to Hungarian authority was in evidence, foreshadowing future conflicts.

The Romanians were not such a serious cause of concern for the Magyars. Although alone they represented more than half the population of Transylvania, they were deprived of all political rights, and therefore had no voice in the Diet. Most were farmers who generally lived in poor conditions under the authority of the great

Magyar landowners. Lacking a national aristocracy, the only positions of authority open to them were in the still embryonic middle classes and among the Orthodox clergy. The driving force was provided by the principalities of the Danube, Moldavia and Wallachia, which, although still legally part of the Ottoman Empire, became autonomous in 1829 and henceforth became the centre of Romanian nationalism. At first, however, the Transylvanian Romanians did not seek more than an improvement in their living conditions under the monarchy, with political recognition as a priority, but this alone was enough to render them suspicious to the Magyars.

The Poles and the Ruthenians formed another conflicting pair. Although the Poles were still in the minority (40.9 per cent against 50 per cent), this statistic, which would soon be reversed (51.5 per cent and 42.9 per cent in 1880), concealed major differences in their demographic distribution. Whereas western Galicia was populated almost entirely by Poles, the Ruthenians were in the majority in the eastern part of the province. Furthermore, there were social and economic differences which aggravated the nationalist dispute. In each province, the farmers made up the body of the population, but in eastern Galicia the Ruthenian farmers were ruled by Polish landowners. The Ruthenians lacked a national aristocracy. The Catholic clergy, headed by the Chapter of Saint George's cathedral in Lvov (Lemberg), was not strong enough to compensate for this on its own. On the opposing side, although dominated by the nobility, Polish society had already diversified enough to benefit from a broader framework.

Unlike the Poles, who had an ancient national culture, the Ruthenians were still searching for a national identity and the difference between the two peoples was accentuated by their different stages in national development. This was exacerbated by the hold which the Polish had over the school system. Although they did not control the administration in Galicia, the cultural and social domination of the Poles led to resentment among the Ruthenians which, although it was generally contained, could lead to outbursts of frustrated violence. This was demonstrated by the great uprising of 1846 which ravaged the countryside, especially in the eastern part of the province, during the course of which over 1,500 Polish nobles were killed or wounded.

The Italians, for their part, were scattered among many provinces of the empire. They lived in the Trient district, many were to be found in Istria and Trieste, and they formed the middle classes of the towns along the Dalmatian coast. But it was in Lombardy-Venetia that they caused the most trouble for the Austrian government although it is with the latter that the credit lies for the improvement of this region. Of all the regions of Italy it was the most economically advanced but the number of Italians in the administration was diminishing. Although the administration was honest and efficient, it committed the sin of being increasingly run by foreigners who were indiscriminately and mistrustfully labelled as *tedeschi* by the locals. This was a situation which could not fail to inhibit the relations between the Italians and the Habsburgs. Many of the Italians forgot the material advantages gained by Lombardy-Venetia from the Austrian presence and were aware only of being forced to live under the domination of a foreign power. In fact, this discontent had little effect on the farmers, who were content with the relative prosperity brought about by Austrian rule. On the other hand, the feeling of frustration was acute among the nobility and the middle classes and made the social elite receptive towards the desire for national unity. This growth of opinion was still easily contained by the Austrian police who were joined by the best regiments of the imperial army under the command of Marshal Radetzky. Lombardy-Venetia was nevertheless one of the Habsburg possessions likely to be roused by nationalist feeling if a major crisis were to shake the monarchy's defences on other fronts.

In all, the nationalist problems of the Habsburg monarchy were very varied. Austria cannot be blamed for failing to espouse the principle of the nation-state which some European liberals defended, for to do so would have been to pronounce her own death sentence. This refusal did not mean, however, that she exercised a policy of systematic repression when faced with the growth of national awareness among her subject states.

It would be wrong to ascribe a desire for Germanization to Austria, although the Germans remained pre-eminent and some of the key texts of other nationalist movements were written in German. The first volume of Palacký's *History of Bohemia*, for instance, was first published in German. But at the same time, national languages were making advances in the educational system. In areas under the direct authority of Vienna they were used in primary schools and were often taught as full disciplines in secondary schools and even in universities. Of course German remained the standard language of teaching once primary school was finished, but these changes nevertheless demonstrate that, faced with the growth of nationalism, the Austrian government was prepared to adopt positive measures.

The official line of conduct was to refrain from any expression of hostility towards these movements as long as they were confined to cultural matters. It is true that it was easy for such matters to become political, but even then the Austrian authorities considered each case individually. A clear example of this can be seen in their authorization of an Illyrian nationalist review which was published by Gaj in 1835, which they hoped would weaken the Magyars. Nevertheless, when their actions did spill over into the political domain, very few nationalists, with the exception of some Italians in Lombardy-Venetia and a few Hungarians and Poles, imagined a future for their peoples outside the framework of the Habsburg monarchy. In short, most of them hoped for a monarchy adapted to the multicultural needs of its peoples, not for its removal.

As has been seen, it would also be a mistake to suppose that the nationalist problems in Austria could be reduced to the system of direct relations between Vienna and its subject states. In Hungary the Magyars, far from displaying the same flexibility as the central government, were already instituting policies within the limits of the kingdom's autonomy which aimed to subjugate other nationalities, and this explains the strong anti-Magyar feeling among these peoples.

The Austrian government was certainly not a disinterested spectator to these antagonisms. Hungarian opposition had always stood in the way of the unification of the empire, and the government was certainly tempted to support the resistance movements of the smaller nationalities. Such support remained discreet, however, and was periodically withdrawn. The efforts of Metternich to consolidate the conservative camp in Hungary in the final years of the *Vormärz* led him to drop this policy. Vienna could still threaten an alliance with the minorities in order to prevent the Magyars from pushing their demands too far. Whatever happened, if relations with Hungary deteriorated to the level of a major crisis, it would be easy to form a common front with the minorities, who still saw the emperor as their natural protector.

In some countries the tensions caused by two peoples living side by side added to the complexities of nationalist problems. The empire contained several conflicting pairs, Germans and Czechs in Bohemia, Poles and Ruthenians in Galicia, and Croats and Italians in Dalmatia. These conflicts gave the government a freedom of movement which left it largely in control of events. Although it had not created them, the monarchy could at least make use of these divisions to consolidate its power.

For the time, Vienna controlled these movements throughout the empire. They nevertheless had an explosive power capable of releasing a formidable force which would be beyond the control of the empire's officials. This was because the principles on which they were based would ultimately contradict the very nature of the Habsburg monarchy. For as long as some sort of compromise succeeded in reconciling the demands of the multinational state and national aspirations the danger could be contained but should this balance be upset, it would soon become clear that the threat could destroy the monarchy.

Economic Weaknesses

The weaknesses which afflicted the economy increased the vulnerability of the Austrian *Vormärz* government. In the agricultural sector which alone employed three-quarters of the active population of the monarchy, the great problem was the *Robot*, which, for as long as it was preserved, would stand in the way of development in the countryside. Its obligations did not affect all the empire's peasants for in areas such as Lower and Upper Austria, Styria, Carinthia, and the Tyrol it only existed as a residual practice, or had completely disappeared. Elsewhere, however, it remained the rule. The mediocre standard of the work supplied under the *Robot* condemned it. Count Széchényi placed its value at a third of that of free labour. Many of the major landowners were beginning to understand, notably in Bohemia, that it acted as a brake to the modernization of their estates, and admitted the need for its abolition, hoping to replace it with a system of agricultural salaries. Several Diets echoed this desire in the final years of the *Vormärz*.

The responsibility for the preservation of the old system lay less with the nobility than with the central power which feared that such a decision would lead to the collapse of the whole social system. And yet these fears were counterbalanced by anxiety over the atmosphere of tension in the countryside, fed by the continuation of the *Robot*. In the areas where it was still imposed, it was universally hated by the peasantry. Although there are many other possible reasons for the 1846 uprising which shook Galicia, it acted as a warning to the authorities, revealing the depth of discontent in the country, and emphasizing the urgency of finding a solution.

Besides the *Robot* there was a need to question the whole patrimonial system left over from feudal times which still held the greater part of rural Austria in its grip. This was all the more essential because the effects of the *Robot* extended to the rest of the economy. This is not surprising because such a high proportion of Austrian society was agricultural, and development in other areas was necessarily connected to the prosperity of the countryside.

Statistics and travelogues describe a well-to-do farming class. Though this class was mostly based in the western part of the empire, it was present in all areas. This group was not the only one to work the land, though. Most areas were seriously underdeveloped and as a result of demographic pressure, most holdings had been divided up in the course of time. Thus, in Lower Austria, although it was one of the more prosperous regions, only 20,443 holdings survived untouched at their full original size, 27,119 comprised about half the original holding, 23,556 only a quarter, while 62,131, making up nearly half the total, were even smaller than this. The rural areas belonging to the monarchy were even lower on the social scale, inhabited by a mass of peasants who, besides their cottages, owned only a tiny garden which they could cultivate. There was a final category of peasants without land, sometimes even without a roof over their heads, who hired out their labour to a lord or a rich farmer for a meagre payment in kind.

This situation created great inequality in the Austrian countryside. The only real unifying factor for the peasantry lay in the wish of its various members to free themselves from the system of duties and constraints to which the nobility subjected them. But it was likely that, once this had been achieved, these differences which were partly concealed by the feudal system would become dominant and would create a class system within the countryside.

In the meantime, except for the well-off minority, the poor yield of most farming concerns provided the farmers with only small revenues, and this was made worse by the imposition of state taxes and duties to the local landlords. As for the landless farmworkers, theirs was a miserable lot, below even a minimum standard of living. In consequence, the home market could not be sustained by a strong demand for goods from the rural areas. This contraction of the domestic market penalized Austrian industry which also suffered from a lack of labour caused by the estates' huge requirement for labour, and this slowed its development. But despite these problems, this period was not one of economic stagnation.

The driving force was only rarely supplied by the administration which was split between many economic philosophies and had difficulty in defining a coherent industrial policy. The funds which were necessary for the development of industry came in part from the nobility who, careful to diversify their sources of income, also elected to invest in this area of the economy. This was not only true of the older nobility. Some banks already had close connections with the empire's industrial development. Thus Baron Salomon Rothschild was behind the initiative for Austrian railway construction. These years also saw the foundation of middle-class dynasties with fortunes based in industry. The empire still welcomed foreigners, especially Germans and English, and these set up businesses. As well as the traditional Austrian products (glass and leather), new industries developed. The big landowners began to build sugar refineries on their lands. Another sign of the influence of the industrial revolution was the rapid growth of the textile industries. Although still in its early stages, railway construction was a positive influence, stimulating coal extraction in Bohemia and Silesia and the development of the iron and steel industries.

This expansion should not, however, conceal the limits of the industrialization process which exposed serious regional disparities. Industrial development was actually confined to a few areas such as Bohemia and Moravia, Lombardy-Venetia, Vienna and its surroundings, while other regions such as Galicia and Transylvania were hardly affected. The limits of progress became even clearer in the European context. The portion of the active population of Austria working in industry and manufacturing in 1846 was only 16.73 per cent. This shows that, although individual areas belonged completely to one category or the other, Austria as a whole occupied a middle ground between the advanced industrialization of western Europe and under-developed eastern Europe.

The relative fragility of Austrian industry led the authorities to protect the monarchy with high customs duties. This fear of foreign competition prevailed when Austria was obliged to state its position on possible membership of the *Zollverein*, the customs union which, created in 1834 at the instigation of Prussia, included most of the German states among its members. Against the advice of Metternich who feared the political consequences of a refusal, the government gave in to pressure from industry which feared that if Austria joined the *Zollverein* it would lead to a collapse of the economy, by leaving the domestic market wide open to foreign goods.

Diplomatic Failures

The insistence with which Metternich supported Austrian entry to the *Zollverein* suggests that this was not merely an economic issue. His failure is also an indication that the system of international relations which he had built up was being demolished.

This was not the first reverse suffered by the chancellor. Metternich's system, which as we know only recognized historical states, ran directly counter to the prin-ciple of the nation-state in period of growing nationalism. In 1829, Greece obtained its independence from France and Russia with the help of Britain. One year later the revolution broke out which resulted in the establishment of Belgium as an independ-ent state. Each of these upheavals ran counter to the aims of Austrian foreign policy.

Even more seriously, other areas besides those traditionally under Austrian influ-ence were being shaken by the nationalist movement. In Germany, the status quo was threatened by more than constitutional demands. Moving beyond the student demonstrations which had led to harsh measures from Metternich at the Carlsbad conference of 1819, nationalist ideas were widely supported amongst the liberal middle classes, and also among the democrats, who dreamed of a German republic. More and more Germans were becoming dissatisfied with the confederate structure proposed by Metternich in 1815, and many, especially Protestants, looked to Prussia to achieve the unification of Germany.

In Italy, the unification movement was gaining ground, although the danger was certainly diminished by disagreements among the Italian patriots over their pro-posals. One possible focus was the Kingdom of Piedmont in a similar role to that which Prussia was widely expected to play in Germany. There were also proposals by Gioberti for a united nation centred on the Vatican and by Mazzini for a republic. These differences must certainly have sustained Metternich in his conviction that Italy was no more than a 'geographical term', but it is hard to believe that they managed to mislead him over the real nature of the threat. Above their disagree-ments, the various currents of the *Risorgimento* shared a common hostility towards Austria, and the accomplishment of their national objectives would entail the dis-mantling of the hegemony which the empire had established in the Italian peninsula.

Metternich could no longer rely on the pentarchic system to combat this rising tide of nationalism. Although the series of conferences held between 1817 and 1822 had at first seemed to give it some substance, Britain was the first to leave the alliance after Castlereagh's death. France soon did likewise. The advent of the Greek question followed by that of Belgium confirmed the demise of this council of the great powers. Realizing that the five nation system was dead, Metternich set out to replace it with an alliance of the three great conservative monarchies of central and northern Europe. Prussia still had close links with Austria and raised no difficulties, but Russia was another matter. Metternich had never been confident in his dealings with Alexander I, whose appetite for power and liberalism worried him. Relations with Nicolas I held more promise, for his commitment to autocracy precluded any dangerous quirks of behaviour. It is true that the Tsar's support for Greek independence had at first affected this relationship, but Russia's position on the revolutionary crisis of 1830 and the Polish insurrection had improved relations between the two empires and the meeting between Franz I and Nicolas I at Münchengraetz in September 1833 set the official seal on this.

From this time on, confronted with the rise of liberalism, the common cause of conservative interests prevailed. The efficiency of this new line of defence had still to be tested. How could three nations uphold what five could not? This worry was heightened by remaining doubts over the solidarity of the common front. Austria's two partners themselves threatened to become contaminated with the nationalist fever. Already, with the founding of the *Zollverein*, Prussia revealed its desire to build up a united Germany around itself, and although Russia's agreement with Austria led to the restriction of its expansionist policies in the Balkans there was no guarantee that this was anything more than a lull in hostilities. Metternich could not therefore afford to ignore the existence of parties in Berlin and Saint Petersburg which were working to persuade their sovereigns to adopt a policy of aggression which must automatically affect Austrian interests.

All this could be seen as the prelude to a serious crisis. Austria found itself forced into a defensive position on all fronts and at first it suffered from a lack of real government, the ultimate paradox for an absolutist regime. Because of Ferdinand's weakness, the empire appeared to be a 'monarchy without a monarch'. This problem was one reason for Nicolas I's expressed scepticism over Austria's future. On the other hand it was an advantageous situation for Franz Joseph, whose youth made him a good substitute if the monarchy should enter a period of crisis. But in the meantime the problem was rendered more acute as the governmental machinery, lacking the necessary direction of the head of state, tended to go in circles. The administration's detachment from reality which resulted from this paralysis meant that no solution to the problems of Austrian society was available. This state of immobility prevented all hope of a compromise with the opposition. Even when its demands were modest they were still too much for a regime whose creed was hostility to liberalism. Government inactivity also increased dissatisfaction in rural areas where the constraints of the feudal system were gradually becoming less acceptable. The problems caused by administrative methods and the organization of society spread throughout every state of the empire.

The unique multinational structure of Austria was to play an important part in its future relationship with nationalism. Each people had its individual characteristics and the central power could certainly exploit this diversity in the exercise of its own authority but it could also bring hostile peoples together. The separatists had in any case only limited support. Nevertheless there was a clear possibility of losing authority since the uncontrolled development of a national movement would automatically undermine the foundations on which multinational Austria was built. In foreign affairs, Austria was also having to face the same nationalism. Over the years, the empire was obliged to back down over a series of issues and its own spheres of influence were infected by nationalism. If the concept of the nation-state were to take hold, Austria would not long be able to resist.

At the end of this period, Austria had not completely lost its lustre of 1815, but its position had weakened. Metternich had long since lost his hold on the reins of European politics, and his policies had been reduced to defensive measures. In internal affairs, under the veneer, the edifice was crumbling. But the empire had not lost all its assets. Although weakened, conservative forces were still strong, but the faults of the system reduced their capacity to resist or act. In all, on the eve of the revolution, Austria seemed ill equipped to fight the defiance of the new age. Franz Joseph's heritage threatened to be a heavy one, should he come to the throne.

3

Franz Joseph Succeeds to the Throne: the Farewell to Childhood

As 1848 dawned there were a number of presages of the serious events to come, for the previous two years had seen a rapid deterioration in the political climate. After the uprising which shook Galicia in February 1846, the government, fearing that the unrest would spread, was obliged to put an end to the policy of inactivity which it had pursued until that time. The Declaration of 18 December 1846 proposed the abolition of all existing financial demands on farmers in exchange for the payment of a cash annuity or purchase instalment, but the implementation of this measure was dependent on the agreement of both parties and therefore provided no real solution to the peasant problem. The growth of a movement to reject the *Robot* in the course of the following years underlined this. At the beginning of 1848 the government therefore had to face an escalation of the agricultural crisis. Rural discontent was increased by the series of poor harvests from 1845 onwards and by flooding in Galicia, Hungary, and Lombardy. The consequences of these disasters were felt by the whole of Austrian society. The price of staple foods rose to a level which was beyond the means of the urban lower classes.

The situation was all the more serious because the decline of the domestic market, which was linked to the fall in demand for manufactured goods from rural areas, led to a sharp rise in unemployment in industrial regions. The areas most affected were Bohemia and Silesia where the textile industries were particularly hard hit. Vienna also suffered, for on top of its permanent working population the city attracted unemployed labourers from elsewhere. Already many workers, often Bohemian or Moravian, had succumbed to the dream of the capital. The relative security of the working population of Vienna in the first years of the *Vormärz* had disappeared and a growing number of citizens were poverty-stricken.

The crisis also encouraged radical trends in public opinion. In Bohemia, liberals such as Palacký were not the only ones to speak for the Czech people. Democratic ideas gained ground among the victims of the economic slump and spread to the ranks of the lower middle classes. In Hungary, the opposition had managed to gain a majority in the Lower Chamber of the Diet. Croatia was seeking independence from Hungary, and the *Sabor*, the Agram (Zagreb) Diet, passed a resolution demanding the unification of Croatia with Dalmatia, the occupied zones, and Fiume.

In Italy, unrest grew following the election of Monsignor Mastai as Pope Pius IX, whose first acts earned him the reputation of a liberal patriot, much to Metternich's consternation. Piedmont no longer concealed its intention to head a crusade for the unification of Italy. The lands directly under the administration of the central government were also affected, and at the end of December 1847, there were demonstrations in the streets of Milan. To withstand the growing Italian threat, Vienna could only call on an army which had suffered repeated economic cuts. The ageing Marshal Radetzky – who was eighty-two in 1848 – had been in command since 1831, and had managed to turn it into a fine military machine, but with a total of only 34,000 men at his disposal he had little hope of holding Austria's possessions in Italy without reinforcements.

Franz Joseph was not unaware of these problems in 1848, but he still had no authority to act on them. Once back from his stay in Hungary, he returned to his studies. The type of teaching he received in philosophy, constitutional law, and history must have confirmed him in his hostility to liberalism, but his only real contact with contemporary politics was his Sunday lesson with Metternich.

Revolutionary Outbursts

The great upheaval which was to shake Europe to its roots, and which would culminate in the overthrow of the *Vormärz* regime, began in Italy. The shock wave caused by the January revolt in Sicily gradually affected the whole peninsula. The danger grew when in February the Second Republic was declared in Paris, for France was traditionally the flagship of European revolution.

The effects of events in Paris were soon felt within the empire. The first blow was struck by Kossuth, who on 3 March demanded the formation of a Hungarian government. Then Bohemia began to stir. In Prague, an assembly was called by the radical groups and it decided on 11 March to present an address to the government which contained the same demands as had been made in Bohemia.

Local reception of these demands depended on Vienna's response. When the Bohemian delegation arrived in the capital it encountered a new ruling body. Once Vienna in its turn had been overtaken by the revolutionary fever, it took only three days for events to run their course. On 13 March a confrontation took place between a disoriented and divided government and a crowd of middle and working class men and students, united in their hostility to absolute rule. For a time it seemed that the strength of the government would triumph and the crowd was dispersed by troops, but not without the use of force. Taking fright at this turn of events, the court decided to withdraw its troops and by evening the demonstrators controlled the streets. Fearing that the protests would turn to revolt, the imperial family now decided to cut its losses. Metternich would be sacrificed as the symbol of the despised regime. It was hoped that once this had been done, matters would return to normal. Abandoned by all, the old chancellor had no choice but to tender his resignation. The time had come when the statesman who had directed the empire's foreign policy for so long was finally alone. The imperial family did not concern themselves with his fate, and he was obliged to take the road to exile, aided only by his old ally Baron Salomon Rothschild who gave him financial support.

The announcement of Metternich's resignation caused an explosion of joy in the city but the demonstrators did not reduce their demands. Only a solemn promise from the sovereign to allow a Constitution could now restore order. This became clear when the crowd remained unsatisfied by the announcement on 14 March that a civilian guard was to be created and censorship abolished.

The decisive step was taken during the afternoon of 15 March with the announcement by the palace that the emperor had taken the necessary measures to convene a representative assembly of the countries of the monarchy as soon as possible in order to draw up a Constitution. The news of these concessions had the desired effect. In the following weeks, the situation appeared to stabilize. A new government based on a constitutional model had indeed been called, but it was mostly made up of the chief figures of the old regime. While awaiting the meeting of a constituent Assembly, the imperial court could congratulate itself on having come through this test without too much damage, assuming of course that the March days had not released forces over which the central government would never really regain its former authority.

Even when they called for constitutional freedom, the middle classes remained highly mistrustful of disorder, but democratic ideas dominated among the students who had played such an important role during the March events. The academic 'legion' which they formed was almost completely beyond the control of the government. They found allies in the capital's craftsmen and labourers who, during the March days had also demonstrated their strength by occupying the suburbs, and pillaging the factories and even setting some on fire. Although the fever had died down there were nevertheless many supporters for the radical wing of the Viennese revolution. These democratic forces acted as a sort of counterbalance which restricted the goverment's freedom of action. The students, especially, set out to maintain a climate of ferment.

For the men who directed affairs of state, the situation became daily harder to grasp. With the loss of the Viennese government's authority the unity and integrity of the empire were also threatened. First there was Hungary, which was moving towards a simple direct relationship with Austria. On 17 March, suffering from the blow of events in Vienna, the emperor authorized the formation of a Hungarian government with Count Batthyány at its head. The inclusion of such wise minds as Deák and Széchenyi among his ministers can be seen as a commitment to moderation. But their influence was to carry little weight against that of Kossuth who was also a member of the government and who, with the people behind him, was likely to push the government to more extreme policies. In any case, accompanied by Franz Karl and Franz Joseph, Ferdinand travelled to Presburg on 11 April to sanction the laws passed by the Diet which not only established a constitutional government on liberal lines in Hungary but also recognized the Kingdom of Saint Stephen as a semi-sovereign state within the Habsburg lands.

The case of Hungary threatened to influence others. Although it left decisions over the unification of Bohemia with Moravia and Silesia to the future imperial assembly, the Bohemian charter nevertheless ordained that in Bohemia itself the deputies elected in the towns and the countryside would combine with the States General to control all the internal affairs of the kingdom. To this was added the proclamation of the total equality of Germans and Czechs both in the administration and in education. Nevertheless, matters did not appear as threatening as they did in

Hungary. The conviction remained among the Bohemian Czechs that independence would leave them at the mercy either of the Germans or of Russia. Their own interests therefore led them to continue to support the monarchy in the hope that an empire reconstructed along principles of equality would allow the Slavs political influence in proportion to their numbers. This theory led to Palacký's famous comment: 'Indeed, had Austria not already been in existence for some time, we would have felt ourselves obliged to create it in the interest both of Europe and of humanity itself.'[1] Even uttered as it was under the colours of Austro-Slavism this pro-Austrian profession of faith seemed to protect the monarchy from the risk of Bohemian self-rule getting out of control.

Another process filled with perils of a different kind was the unification of Germany, where, towards the end of April and the beginning of May, a constitutional parliament was elected. If it was going to include the Austrian lands which had belonged to the German Confederation, this movement threatened to destroy the whole empire. The inclusion of part of the empire in a unified German state would have the inevitable consequence of cutting it off from the rest of Habsburg possessions. Revolutionary fever quickly took hold in the Germanic countries of Austria, and it was fired by the possibility of the inclusion of these lands in the new Germany, which would force Austria to move closer to democracy. Students began to wear the black, red and gold cockade, and the fashion quickly spread among the members of the Viennese left. Soon Ferdinand was obliged to suffer the ultimate humiliation in allowing the German revolutionary flag to fly over the Hofburg, the symbol of an ideology which was incompatible with the very existence of the Habsburg monarchy. The unification movement in Germany soon created tensions at the heart of the empire. The elections for the Frankfurt Parliament strengthened the opposition between Germans and Czechs in Bohemia, the former participating in them and the latter boycotting them. To express his disapproval Palacký even took the initiative of calling a Slav congress in Prague.

The situation was equally critical in Italy where the Milanese were quick to revolt. Rather than wear out his troops in hand-to-hand combat on the streets which might cut him off from reinforcements, Radetzky made the decision at the end of March to withdraw to the Quadrilateral, a natural stronghold commanding Peschiera, Verona, Mantua, and Legnano with what remained of his army. With the exception of this last bastion, the rest of the Italian peninsula was lost to Austria. On 21 March, Venice rejected Habsburg sovereignty. On 23 March the Piedmont army entered Lombardy, while contingents from the other Italian states supported this war of national liberation. Faced with general mobilization, Radetzky could only regroup his forces and wait for better days, ensconced in the Quadrilateral.

The Baptism of Fire

It was there that Franz Joseph joined him on 29 April. The government had decided to make him *Statthalter* (governor) of Bohemia, but instead of going to Prague Franz Joseph set out for Italy. This move was decided by the Archduchess Sophie. She considered that Franz Joseph would have nothing to gain in the current situation if he took on political responsibilities which would compromise him in the eyes of the revolutionaries. It was important for him not to be tied down in preparation for the day he would succeed to the throne. But for the same reasons it was imperative for him to leave Vienna where the danger was just as great. What better means to him keep away from the trouble spots than to send him to join the army in Italy? At a time of flux, the army would protect the monarchy to the last.

When Franz Joseph left for Italy he had already made up his mind about the revolution. His opinions mirrored those of his mother. Although she had been obliged to accept Metternich's departure, Sophie immediately showed a total hostility to the revolutionary movement. Her diary betrays the anguish she felt over the course of events. She used the harshest of terms to describe the events of March: 'Terrible and disastrous days, which have left me with a pain in my heart, a shattering memory which will never fade.'[2] On 19 March, she lamented to see the 'spirit of disorder and sedition'[3] at work everywhere. Shortly after she wrote: 'The coming of Spring which has always brought me joy leaves me unmoved now that I am so disturbed, so distressed, with no place to rest my heavy heart.'[4] The strength of her convictions made Sophie the representative of the essence of the court faction, the famous 'camarilla' which was scandalized by the weakness displayed concerning the revolution and whose members had already set out to nullify the concessions which had been torn from Ferdinand. Aided by the Empress Marie Anne and by Franz I's widow, Caroline Augusta, she constantly urged those in positions of responsibility to resist.

Franz Joseph reacted in the same way. Sophie's son and Metternich's pupil, it was inevitable that he should suffer at the spectacle of the victorious revolution. Although it had not yet taken on the characteristics of extremism, it offended his sense of order and of monarchical authority. As he passed through the Tyrol, Franz Joseph was already breathing a different atmosphere. In it, he found a province which had never wavered in its loyalty to the crown. This first contact with Austrian reality outside Vienna gave him the chance to discover that, at least in the German countries of the empire, the revolution remained an isolated phenomenon. Indeed, outside the walls of Graz, any resonance of the turmoil of the capital was practically unknown.

Franz Joseph's stay at Innsbruck was only a brief halt on his journey to Verona where he was to present himself to Radetzky. He was delighted at the prospect of rejoining the army, for he had always been attracted by military life. He was also exultant that he would probably have the chance to experience his first real battle. Even before he had arrived at his destination, he declared himself convinced that the situation in Italy was not as critical as was generally thought in Vienna. Now that the old marshal had consolidated his forces within the walls of the Quadrilateral, he would be able to take up the offensive again and open up the road to Milan. Franz Joseph even imagined the imperial army pursuing its advantage as far as Turin. He also believed that it was important that the force of the military thrust should not be interrupted by political decisions. He was well aware that many of the new administrators of the monarchy considered Lombardy to be a lost cause and were prepared to hand it over to Piedmont. A diplomatic mission was even projected to seek agreement on the basis of this. It was natural that the young prince should revolt against such an attitude which would end centuries of Austrian presence in Italy:

In the name of God, there must be no diplomatic negotiations! It would be an infamy. We owe it to our honour, to our country and to our position in Europe as a whole not to rest before we have driven the Piedmont army from our lands, and raised the standard of the two-headed eagle in Turin.[5]

Once in Verona, Franz Joseph was nevertheless obliged to admit that the situation was less favourable than he had hoped. While waiting for reinforcements, Radetzky remained on the defensive. A first victory was won, however, on 6 May at Santa Lucia at the gates of Verona. Although it was only a small skirmish it was nevertheless of considerable importance because at last the advantage had begun to swing to the Austrian side. It also had a wider significance beyond the conflict between Austria and Piedmont. This first success after a long series of withdrawals served to shore up the confidence of the supporters of the old Austria who had kept quiet since mid-March, awaiting a suitable moment to raise their heads once more. It was also important that the army had caused this change of fortune, thus reconfirming its position as the defender of the monarchy. If it was concerned today with the defence of the integrity of the empire, it could serve tomorrow as the sword which could win back the rights of the sovereign.

Santa Lucia was also the scene of Franz Joseph's first battle. He was naturally eager to announce the event with pride to his mother: 'For the first time I have heard cannon balls whistle around me and I am perfectly happy.'[6] Three days later he described the events of the battle to her in great detail, although he was careful not to alarm her, neglecting to inform her of the risks he had taken or of the shell that had exploded close enough to have frightened his horse which had almost unseated him.

His departure for Italy did not prevent Franz Joseph from continuing to observe the course of events in Vienna. The publication on 25 April of a proposal for a Constitution drawn up by the minister of the interior, Baron Pillersdorf, had re-awoken the unrest. Although it was inspired by the Belgian and Badois constitutions which were the yardsticks of European liberalism, and although it affirmed fundamental freedoms, it was considered to be too conservative by all the radicals. In it, Pillersdorf had proposed the implementation of a bicameral system in which the Upper Chamber would be made up partly of life members nominated by the emperor and partly of great landowners nominated by their peers. In addition, the sovereign would still retain the right of veto, and it is not hard to deduce that it thus included enough material to antagonize anybody who had hoped for a democratic government.

This recurrence of the unrest came to a head on 15 May, after the government announced the electoral procedures for the nomination of the members of the Lower Chamber. By excluding workers paid by the day or week, domestic servants, and those receiving charity, from whom the democrats expected to draw considerable support, the government precipitated a new crisis. The authorities could not withstand another day of revolution. Under pressure from the people, they decided to withdraw their proposal for a Constitution and to reconsider the restrictions on the right to vote.

These events aroused the indignation of Franz Joseph. His anger was concentrated on the 'faithless Viennese' who were jeopardizing the security of the imperial family and who threatened to destroy the authority of the state by their actions. Nor did he spare the ministers whose weakness was at the root of the worsening situation. Franz Joseph's letters are filled with criticisms of them. As for the attitude to be adopted in the face of this new crisis, it is easy to guess the inclinations of the young prince. Such excesses should no longer be tolerated. Only a policy of strength which allowed for the use of force could succeed: 'It is time at last', he wrote to his mother, 'to put an end to these excesses which are the weaknesses of a constitutional state.'[7] This remark says much for his feelings about the prospect of Austria's entry into constitutional government. But how could he hope for strength from a regime which in the course of the previous two months had displayed nothing but weakness? Franz Joseph naturally compared it with the army which displayed energy and efficiency in intervening against the troublemakers.

These impressions would affect him permanently. They convinced him that military strength provided a model of coherence at the centre of a hierarchical structure. They also awoke in him a mistrust of civilians which would influence his decisions during the first decade of his reign. Aware of the inability of the government to make the Viennese citizens return to the confines of duty, he could see no other hope for the imperial family than to regain its freedom of action by leaving Vienna. He felt confident that the citizens of Tyrol would receive them with enthusiasm and would offer their honour to serve them as a shield.

He was greatly relieved when he learned that the imperial family had chosen to flee Vienna after the events of 15 May and had arrived safely in Innsbruck. He immediately wrote to his mother: 'I cannot describe my joy on being awoken at six o'clock this morning to receive an officer of the *Kaiserjäger* who brought me the happy news that the emperor and all of you have arrived in Innsbruck, having abandoned the heathen Viennese to their fate.'[8] Now that this decisive step had been taken, he urged his family not to give in to the pressure of those who advised them to return to Vienna as though nothing had happened. This was aimed in particular at the ministers who had not been party to the imperial family's plans and had not accompanied them to Innsbruck. These ministers were now insisting on their return to Vienna while expressing concern for their security. If the imperial family were to do this, he believed that it would suffer the same fate as the French monarchy after Varennes, and make itself a prisoner of the revolution. The blunt refusal of the invitations of the Viennese government delivered Franz Joseph from his fears. But now that the imperial family had found refuge in Innsbruck there was little justification for his continued presence with the army in Italy, and Sophie, who was now aware of the dangers which her son had risked at Santa Lucia, obtained Radetzky's agreement that it would be wise to avoid any further exposure of the future emperor of Austria to danger. Franz Joseph was recalled to Innsbruck on 5 June. Although he made no protest, he nevertheless obeyed with a heavy heart. He found it hard to return to civilian life which appeared dull to him after the excitement of the weeks spent in the company of the officers and soldiers of the Italian army. As events in Prague prevented him from taking up his post as governor of Bohemia, Franz Joseph returned to his place at the heart of the imperial family and remained in Innsbruck until the question of a return to Vienna was raised at the beginning of August.

The Beginning of the Recovery

When it arose, this return no longer appeared to be a display of weakness. From the court's point of view, the situation had changed for the better on many fronts. The flight of the imperial family had accelerated the split in the revolutionary camp into extremists and moderates who wanted an agreement with the crown. The elections to the constitutional assembly confirmed the isolated position of the radicals, and the moderates (whose members were drawn from all the less extreme political groups) won a clear victory.

Although they were still strained, relations with Hungary had not reached a point of no return. In Frankfurt, the nomination of a Habsburg, the Archduke Johann, as vicar-general for the interim period before a future sovereign could be chosen, demonstrated that the majority of the parliament did not intend to drive Austria out of Germany. But, and this was even more important, the forces of the counter-revolution were on the march. In Italy, after having convinced the government to put an end to its tentative proposals for a diplomatic conclusion of the conflict, Radetzky crushed the Piedmont army at Custozza on 25 July. A few days later the campaign came to an end when Charles Albert was obliged to request an armistice. This victory had a considerable affect on public opinion, mainly because it showed that Austria did not have to submit to events. It also acted as a sign to conservative groups that the wheel of fortune had begun to turn. These included not only those who had never accepted the revolution, but also those people who had been disappointed in the revolution, who had at first sympathized with the uprising but who were later alienated by its excesses, and who now wished for a return to order, while still hoping that it would not take the form of absolutism.

For these conservative and patriotic Austrians, the army, basking in the glory of its success, appeared to be the supreme hope of the empire. This is what Grillparzer, who was one of those who had been disappointed in the revolution, wanted to express in his famous lines addressed to Radetzky: 'Austria is in your camp, / We are only its ruins.'[9] It appears that the victory of Custozza changed the balance of power. Although Venice had not yet fallen, the victory released troops who could then be deployed elsewhere within the empire.

In Bohemia too, fortunes were changing. A return to order had begun there even before events in Italy brightened the horizon to the south. Whereas in Lombardy the army was fighting an outside enemy, in Bohemia it was engaged for the first time in the fight against revolution within the borders of the monarchy itself. The counter-revolution found its champion in the person of Prince Alfred Windischgraetz who commanded the troops stationed in Bohemia. From 13 March onwards this prince from one of Bohemia's greatest aristocratic families was one of the few to side with Metternich and he considered it to be his mission to wipe out the revolution. After a long period of restraint he considered that his hour had come when the control of the Slav Congress escaped from the hands of the moderate members of the Czech nationalist party. Its organizers had hoped that this congress would provide an unequivocal support for the cause of Austro-Slavism. Instead it was very soon overrun by extremists, some of whom, such as Bakounine and a number of the Poles, were not even subjects of the monarchy. Although at first the concern had been to declare the solidarity of the empire's Slavs, this objective had gradually faded into the background and was replaced by support for a broader fraternity which included all Slavs. As the expression of this radical change, the congress had adopted a manifesto which contained many clauses, such as the solemn protest against the division of Poland, which were not acceptable to the monarchy.

The convening of the congress also coincided with an economic crisis caused by a recession in the textile industries. The effects of this struck the workers of Prague hard and the conjunction of these factors created an atmosphere which was favourable to revolutionary activity. This development provided Windischgraetz with the excuse he needed to restore order in Prague, which he envisaged as a first step in the return to order of the whole empire. On 12 June, when the demonstrations had degenerated into a riot and the old town was filled with barricades, he bombarded Prague after isolating it from outside help, a tactic which was to be just as effective twenty-three years later when it was used by Thiers in the Paris Commune.

Strong in his victory, Windischgraetz would have liked to march straight to Vienna to put down the revolution, but the emperor's refusal restrained him. Under the pressure of the empress and the Archduchess Sophie, who urged him to set up emergency measures, Ferdinand eventually gave way in mid-August, only a few days after the return of the imperial family to Vienna. A secret order, unknown to the minister for war and therefore unknown to the government, placed Windischgraetz at the head of the imperial armed forces with the exception of the Italian army, and gave him full powers in the event of an exceptional situation, that is, in the event of another revolutionary explosion. One of his close friends, Prince Lobkowitz, was to look after the imperial family and, as soon as the need arose, was to take them to Olmütz according to a prearranged plan, where they would be placed under the protection of the army.

During Windischgraetz's stay in Vienna, there also began to be serious discussion, in private circles, of the possibility of the abdication of Ferdinand in favour of his nephew Franz Joseph. At one point, it was even suggested that the ceremony should take place on 18 August, Franz Joseph's birthday. The conviction nevertheless prevailed that to intervene too early would be to compromise his position with the revolutionaries, which would have the opposite effect to that intended. Indeed, it was important that the new sovereign should be freed from these obligations so as to be given a free hand in the reorganization of the empire on the principle of monarchical authority. Windischgraetz could deem himself satisfied. The revolution had been placed under close surveillance. Further, a change of monarch was an integral part of the plan which had been drawn up. At Olmütz, under the protection of the army, Ferdinand would be able to abdicate and Franz Joseph would be brought to the throne under the banner of the counter-revolution. For the rest, Windischgraetz did not conceal his intentions. On revealing to Lobkowitz the stages of his plan which would follow the arrival of the imperial family in Olmütz, he confided in him that 'I will take over in Vienna, and his Majesty will abdicate in favour of his nephew, the Archduke Franz Joseph, then I shall take Buda.'[10]

sketchy knowledge of internal affairs. His knowledge of European matters, on the other hand, could turn out to be valuable if the restoration of the external affairs of the monarchy demanded a firm diplomatic hand. Schwarzenberg's decision to retain the post of foreign minister for himself confirmed the importance which he placed on this field of government activity.

Although there was an element of the risk-taker in this aristocratic thoroughbred, he was also a man with a political mind of his own. In spite of the fact that he had served under Metternich for more than twenty years, his ideas were somewhat different from those of the old chancellor. The need for European balance, for an understanding between the conservative states, and the defence of legitimate rule were less important to him than the power of the Habsburg monarchy. Filled with the glory of Austria, Schwarzenberg set the restoration of its power in Europe as his primary objective, and this must first be achieved at the heart of the continent.

The tone of his first official declaration as first minister marked him as a defender of Austrian rights. In his reply to the Frankfurt Parliament whose draft Constitution had appeared to involve the break-up of the monarchy into one area which would be part of united Germany and another which would be separate, he declared: 'Keeping Austria as one state is both a German and a European necessity.'[11] In his view, this aim would best be accomplished through a policy of centralization within the empire. Austria must be transformed into a united state in order to carry her full weight in relations between the powers.

It remained to be seen whether this creation of a single state could be accomplished within the framework of a constitutional regime or whether it would be necessary to return to absolute rule. When he presented his government on 27 November to the deputies at Kremsier, Schwarzenberg declared to them 'We sincerely wish for a constitutional monarchy.'[12] Was this a proposal dictated by circumstance? Perhaps it was. Schwarzenberg might have considered that tactical necessities demanded that he should allay suspicion. If this were the case then he would wait until the time was ripe to remove his mask. It is nevertheless possible that the truth was more complex than this. Schwarzenberg surrounded himself with ministers who were all sincere supporters of a constitutional government, although they were in agreement that the rights of the crown should be preserved. One of them, Alexander Bach, had even been one of the figureheads of Viennese democracy, before rallying to the side of the authorities. Also, most of the ministers such as the home secretary, Count Stadion, and the minister of commerce, Baron Bruck, were of the opinion that a dialogue should be maintained with the *Reichstag*. Whatever the truth of the matter, although doubts may remain over his eventual intentions, it would be wrong to describe the new head of government as a reactionary. Schwarzenberg in no way proposed the reinstatement of the *Vormärz* regime. He was too aware that the lack of decision of the heads of government of the time had not been the only reason for the speed with which the revolution had taken hold. This collapse could only be understood in the context of the outmoded practices of the regime itself. The trials which it had undergone required new men who would direct all their energies to the prevention of the revival of the revolutionary threat. But, wise from the lessons of these events, Schwarzenberg also wanted to give a new face to Austria, by introducing a programme of modernization.

Now that the authority of the emperor was no longer opposed in Vienna and

Schwarzenberg's government had taken up its responsibilities, the final phase of the plan which had been conceived in the summer could take place. In the speech outlining his programme of reforms, Schwarzenberg had underlined the need for an injection of youth. Such a suggestion indicated the imminence of Franz Joseph's accession. What better way to illustrate this intention than to give an example of it in the head of the state?

The final decision was made in the first days of November. As it is described in the Archduchess Sophie's diary, it was preceded by many conferences at the heart of the imperial family to which Schwarzenberg was a party. It was first necessary to persuade Ferdinand to abdicate. This task fell to the Empress Marie Anne who had long been convinced that the burden was too great for her husband. In addition, Franz Karl must also be pursuaded to renounce his rights to the succession, and it was Sophie who managed this. It remained for a name to be chosen for the new emperor. At first it was proposed that only his first name should be retained in honour of the memory of his paternal grandfather, but Schwarzenberg managed to throw out this solution which might have given the impression that the new regime intended to restore the *Vormärz* style of government. In the end, under Schwarzenberg's influence, it was decided to keep both his names. In this combination 'Franz' suggested the continuation of and respect for tradition and 'Joseph' echoed the great reforming Emperor Joseph II. This choice also anticipated the plan to construct a unified empire as Joseph II had proposed.

The ceremony of the handing over of power took place on the morning of 2 December in the State Chamber of the archbishop's palace at Olmütz. The secret was well guarded. The circle of those who knew was very small although it would not have been hard to guess that a great event was about to take place. What other reason could there have been for the convocation of the members of the imperial family, the court, Marshal Windischgraetz, General Jellačić, the government ministers and high officials to the archbishop's palace? Furthermore, the garrison at Olmütz received orders during the night for a parade at nine in the morning.

The ceremony began at eight with the entrance of the imperial family to the chamber where those invited were already in their places. For his final official appearance, Ferdinand wore civilian dress as was his habit, unlike his nephew who wore the white tunic and red trousers of a general officer of the imperial army. The Archduchess Sophie was beautiful with happiness at the sight of the achievement of her dream. She described her own dress in her diary: 'A white dress of moire silk, and a coiffure in gold, rose and white; the turquoise and diamond necklace and earrings which my husband gave me on my dear Franzi's birth; the turquoise and diamond corsage and the red and gold indian wrap.'[13] The mystery which surrounded this meeting soon lifted when, in a nervous voice, Ferdinand read out the document which announced his abdication in favour of his nephew Franz Joseph. Once various official acts had been read out by Schwarzenberg, the new emperor of Austria went up to his uncle and knelt before him. Giving the ceremony a touch of good humour, Ferdinand stroked his hair and, lifting him to his feet said to him: 'God bless you! Be good and God will protect you. I have done this willingly.'

Franz Joseph's first act as emperor was to honour the army, represented by Windischgraetz and Jellačić. He wished by this to demonstrate his gratitude for the past and to demonstrate that he considered the army to be the mainstay of the throne. He declared to Windischgraetz, 'We owe you all that is and still remains', and he shook Jellačić's hand warmly in witness to the friendship which he would reserve for only a handful of his servants in the sixty-eight years of his reign. Although Radetzky could not attend the ceremony because he was detained in Milan, he was not forgotten. A letter was immediately written to him expressing his sovereign's gratitude. Franz Joseph wasted no time in selecting his senior aide-de-camp. To this post he appointed Count Karl Grünne, one of Sophie's protégés who had already replaced Count Bombelles during the previous summer. Grünne was to be one of the central figures of the next decade and would be placed at the head of the emperor's military chancellery.

Franz Joseph also received his ministers and to them he revealed the motto which he had selected for his reign. This was *Viribus Unitis* (united in our powers). With this formula, in which the influence of Schwarzenberg can be seen, he intended to express his aim to transform Austria into a united state. Finally, a review of the troops of the Olmütz garrison once again involved the army in the display which closed the official part of this first day of the reign.

It is not hard to guess at the feelings of Franz Joseph at this time. Rather than being filled only with the heady pleasure of power, he must have experienced some pain. At the age of eighteen he was suddenly pushed to the head of the most august dynasty in Europe and placed in control of a vast empire. It was natural that he should have been filled with disquiet in the face of the responsibilities he now held. It is true that his entire education was intended to prepare him for this day but the possibility of his accession had always remained theoretical to a certain extent. Now he could no longer escape the fact that his life had changed, and that he was now embarking on a new life, filled with responsibilities, pomp, and loneliness. It was this painful awareness which drew from him the sigh, 'Farewell to youth'.

4

The Power of the Monarchy Restored (1849–1851)

It was a very young emperor who, through circumstance and through the efforts of a small group, found himself in power. Kriehuber, one of the finest portrait painters of the period, depicts him buttoned into the impeccable uniform of a general officer. In spite of the care taken by the painter to give his subject a military air, it is Franz Joseph's youth and grace which hold our attention. His figure and his waist are slender and he has a long face, still beardless, with regular features. His full lips are nevertheless well moulded and his rather large and slightly hooked nose does not detract from the grace of his face. Under straight brows his gaze is clear and a high forehead is surrounded by carefully combed hair. Above all, the portrait gives the impression of aristocratic elegance and evokes a small girl's Prince Charming rather than a soldier.

Influences

From the time of his accession, Franz Joseph displayed a personality which would remain unchanged throughout his reign. He immediately applied himself to his job as sovereign with a rigour and a sense of duty which would have been surprising for an eighteen-year-old youth, had he not already demonstrated the same serious attitude in his approach to his studies. His capacity for work was most impressive. In a letter to Metternich, Schwarzenberg noted that he worked for at least ten hours a day.[1] From the first, too, Franz Joseph showed a marked taste for the execution of his office. To him, the paperwork which already took up a large part of his time was not just a formality, as can be seen by the many marginal notes in his hand to be found in reports. He would often go so far as to return them, Schwarzenberg wrote, asking for further information.

However, it was natural that such a young man who had never previously had control of his affairs should be subject to the influence of others when he became emperor. The first figure to spring to mind in this context is the Archduchess Sophie, who remained politically active after her son came to the throne. Even had her guidance ceased at this time, such had been the degree of her control over Franz Joseph's education that she would still be an important formative influence, for the attitudes and values which she had instilled in the young archduke had a permanent effect on his character. Although her dearest wish had been fulfilled, Sophie did not lose interest in affairs of state. She believed that it was her duty as a mother to help her son, 'the pure young soul, devoted to his duty',[2] to bear the burden of power which he had assumed. Her role appears to have been discreet. Officially she had no part in decision-making. She did not attend ministerial councils or audiences, and had no knowledge of the contents of state documents. Her influence was non the less real, founded on the mother–son relationship which continued even after Franz Joseph had become the most powerful figure in the empire. As a child, he had always been obedient, as emperor he did not lose this trait and continued to rely on his mother. The filial devotion with which he surrounded her, the deference which he showed towards her and the confidence which he had in her powers of judgement led him to hold her opinions and advice in the highest esteem.

Sophie's opinions had not changed since the time when she had supervised her eldest son's education. Convinced that the monarch held a divine right to power, she instilled in Franz Joseph a great respect for the role of emperor, which became second nature to him. Any attempts to limit his sovereign powers thus appeared to him to be an undesirable infringement of his authority. Had there been any need for it, the 1848 revolution would only have confirmed in him his hatred of liberalism. Sophie naturally defended authoritarian measures. It went without saying that she displayed no sympathy for the *Reichstag*, even when it had been purged of its extremist elements. The Frankfurt Parliament was described by her as 'the infamous Diet of Frankfurt'.[3] She also disliked the Magyars, whom she simply saw as rebels and encouraged Franz Joseph to make a firm example of these symbols of the revolution.

Although the troubles were over, it was still important to guard against their re-emergence. The archduchess had long hoped for a close alliance between Church and State, hoping that the influence of the Church would protect men's souls from the troublemakers who distracted them from their duties. Because of this, Sophie was prepared to support the current of opinion which looked for a new relationship between Church and State, calling for the abolition of Josephist legislation and for an agreement with Rome. The policies to bring about such a development from 1849 onwards certainly owed much to her.

Another major influence was that of Schwarzenberg, the only one of Franz Joseph's senior ministers for whom he felt a mixture of affection and admiration. Here there was no family tie, but instead the influence of a strong personality. From their first meeting, the young archduke had been impressed by the prince's calm and cold determination. Although Schwarzenberg's appointment as first minister was made without Franz Joseph's collaboration, he must have been pleased with the choice. Once Franz Joseph had completed his general political education, it fell to Schwarzenberg to initiate him in his role as sovereign. Franz Joseph found him a most energetic teacher who, when others might allow themselves to be controlled by events, would himself direct them, leaving his personal mark on them. In addition to the attraction of his strength of character, Franz Joseph was also attracted to the belief in the greatness of Austria which inspired Schwarzenberg's policies both at home and abroad. His wary attitude towards the revolution was also clearly in accordance with Franz Joseph's feelings. He was as influential as Sophie in reinforcing the young emperor's taste for authority, for although he did not immediately outline his policies for the future organization of Austria, it was accepted from the first that he would build up the system in such a way as to assure the dominant role of the monarch. Schwarzenberg was also a greater believer in the use of force to support policy and as a foundation for power than Metternich had been, the latter's diplomacy having been based on principles which were not always practicable. Although he had little interest in the concept of a balance of power, as both soldier and diplomat, Schwarzenberg believed firmly that the relationships between states were determined by their relative strength. This vision encouraged Franz Joseph's inclination to believe that an empire could be governed along the same lines as an army. He therefore found nothing to cavil at in his first minister's readiness to use the threat of force, and to carry out that threat should the need arise in order to ensure that his ideas prevailed.

A soldier like Schwarzenberg, but lacking his brilliance, Count Grünne held a key position beside Franz Joseph. Appointed his senior aide-de-camp from the day of the emperor's accession, he saw him daily and rapidly gained his confidence. His influence was confirmed when he was placed at the head of the empire's armies although he had never held a position of command in battle. This allowed him to gain gradual control over the army, especially as from 1853 there was no longer a minister for war to stand in his way, as the position was abolished at this time. From the strong position of this powerful military role, Grünne would later attempt to extend his influence into the political sphere. Grünne's devotion to his young master was unquestionable but his political influence was more problematic. His political philosophy boiled down to a belief in the application of military discipline to civil society in order to rid it of any subversive impulses. Corresponding to this narrow exaltation of the military spirit reduced to a devotion to hierarchy and obedience, was his rejection of the values sacred to the civil world. He was particularly wary of the concept of culture, which he suspected all the more for being a possible vehicle of liberal thought.

During the first years of his reign, Franz Joseph expressed his mistrust of cultural matters to the point of caricature. Thus, when he was required to attend a performance of *Torquato Tasso* given to celebrate the centenary of Goethe's birth, his reaction was: 'We could have saved ourselves this pointless celebration; there are better causes and better figures to celebrate.'[4] The responsibility for this narrowmindedness did not lie only in Grünne's hands. He was nevertheless guilty of encouraging Franz Joseph's predilection for a military system which he saw as an alternative to civil society. The creation of such a cocoon, cutting him off from contemporary thought and developments, jeopardized his ability to exercise his role as sovereign.

Although they displayed themselves in different ways, these influences all presented an authoritarian image of monarchical power, and Franz Joseph would soon demonstrate that he had learned this particular lesson by his re-establishment of absolute rule. Although he would later be obliged by circumstances to make concessions to liberalism, even then he would contrive to preserve the monarchy's supremacy, by retaining those prerogatives which he considered to be fundamental. In this new context, he would once again show himself to be the worthy pupil of his childhood advisers.

The Kremsier Parliament's Constitutional Project

For the time being, the most pressing problem was the organizational structure of the monarchy. In the manifesto with which he began his reign, Franz Joseph did not go back on Ferdinand's promise to allow his subjects a Constitution. Far from dismissing it, he announced that he was awaiting a constitutional proposal from the *Reichstag* which should be submitted to him as soon as possible. But in a cleverly calculated move, he also fixed the limits for such a Constitution. Although he declared himself ready to 'share Our rights with the representatives of Our peoples', he also announced his intention of preventing any attempt to reduce the brilliance of the crown. Taking the initiative, he again announced his intention to turn the empire into a single state. By doing so he closed the door on the possibility of a federal system and expressed his opposition to any separatist movement.

Confirmed in its task, the *Reichstag* set to work. The outline worked out in committee was submitted for full discussion on 4 January 1849. Although they had dissociated themselves from the more radical elements of the revolution, most of the members of the *Reichstag* remained true to their convictions. They proclaimed their support for the principle of popular rule, declaring that the source of all power was the people. Nevertheless, the monarch would be far more than a figurehead in the scheme devised by the Kremsier Parliament. The emperor would retain control of foreign policy, have the power to appoint and dismiss ministers, and would have the power to dissolve parliament. He would also have a right of veto over the bills passed by parliament.

The exercise of these powers was, however, subject to strict rules. The principle of ministerial responsibility was introduced and there would be guarantees to protect the parliament against a return to absolute rule. If the new parliament were to be dissolved, it must meet again within three months, and the emperor could not dissolve it again for a year. The *Reichstag* could not adjourn for more than a month and should a conflict arise between the two bodies, the parliament, not the sovereign, had the final decision. Lastly, the sovereign could not take up his position without having sworn to abide by the Constitution.

The deputies continued to follow liberal ideas in establishing the equality of all men before the law. The legal system was expected to protect individual liberties against the arbitrary judgements of the state. Their proposal listed a long catalogue of liberties which, if they were respected, would place Austria on a par with the great liberal states of western Europe: freedom of the press, of expression, of conscience, of association, of movement, and of education. The principle of equality was again in operation in questions of nationality. Article 21 of the proposed Constitution declared the right of the peoples of the empire to affirm their national identity, specifically according them the right to use their own language at school and in the administration.

This article illustrated the concern of those who supported the Constitution to address the problems caused by Austria's multinational structure. The final form of the organizational model for the empire confirmed this, expressing the desire to discover a formula which would allow these peoples to live in harmony within the same political unit. The solution which was reached bore the marks of a compromise between the supporters of centralization and the federalists. The lands of the monarchy would participate in the bicameral system proposed by the Kremsier Parliament in their historical territorial form. While the first Chamber would be directly elected by the people, the second, on the model of the American Senate, would be made up of representatives from the Diets, who acted as the political voice of these lands. The designers of the Constitution chose to deal with the national problem on the level of the political unit which came immediately below the Diet, the *Kreis*, or circle. Because of its size, this constituency had the advantage of presenting a greater national homogeneity which recommended it to the members of the Kremsier Parliament who supported national autonomy. This solution also satisfied the supporters of centralization because the extension of the powers of the *Kreis* would result in a reduction of the influence of provincial institutions. It was thus decided to hand over some of the responsibilities which would otherwise have devolved on the Diets to the *Kreis*, and their administration would be run by a local executive which would itself be appointed by an elected assembly.

The project elaborated at Kremsier was not a simple copy of the liberal Constitutions already in operation in Europe or the United States. Its great originality lay in the account it took of the national plurality of the Habsburg monarchy and its proposal of solutions which allowed for this. For the representatives of the peoples of the empire, this text was significant as an act of loyalty to Austria as a multinational state. This desire to live together helped them to agree finally on a compromise acceptable to all parties in spite of the differences in their original positions.

Such an effort was no doubt easier at a time in which national antagonisms had not yet reached the aggravation point they would reach by the end of the century. Could the implementation of this compromise have prevented relations between different nationalities from deteriorating, or would it eventually have been subsumed under the pressure of nationalist passions? The only certainty is that such a course of action was never attempted.

The Dissolution of the Reichstag and the Constitution of 4 March

It is certainly regrettable that the new rulers of the empire chose to bury this proposal, but it was not in their nature to satisfy its demands. By temperament and belief Franz Joseph was firmly convinced from the time he came to the throne that there should be a return to absolute rule. Schwarzenberg's position was probably less clear, but he was not inclined to tolerate a document which praised the principle of rule by the people. As for the ultras of the counter-revolution, they could not understand why the government did not dissolve the *Reichstag*.

The government soon came round to this view themselves. The break came at the beginning of January when the contents of the constitutional proposal agreed in committee became known. The reference to popular rule was felt to be a scandal by all the government ministers, even those who were most open to liberal ideas, such as

Count Stadion. On 20 January they agreed on the principle that the *Reichstag* should be dissolved. However, the move to dissolve the parliament came only on 7 March, as the government needed time to draw up an alternative Constitution to that of the *Reichstag*. Also, Schwarzenberg still had to obtain Windischgraetz's agreement, as he had undertaken to refer all major decisions to him. This was not a simple matter because it turned out that the two men had very different attitudes.

Windischgraetz expected the Constitution to restore its old influence to the aristocracy: 'A monarchy cannot exist without its nobility', he wrote to Schwarzenberg, 'To look to other factions to support the monarchy is, in my opinion, no more than a dream.'[5] In his view, the middle classes could not fill this role because their loyalty was suspect and, entrenched as he was in the traditions of a feudal order, Windischgraetz could not conceive of any other role for the farmers than that they should be represented by their former lords. He thus envisaged the establishment of an aristocratic monarchy in which the Diets would have roughly the same composition as they had before 1848. Formed of deputies elected by the Diets, the senate, the only chamber planned by Windischgraetz, would also be under the control of the nobles. He further assumed that the economic power of the nobles in the countryside would not come under attack and, from the eve of Franz Joseph's accession, Windischgraetz had warned him against the danger of depriving the aristocracy of any of their lands.

Schwarzenberg's analysis of the situation was completely different. Although he bore one of the greatest aristocratic names in Austria he was sceptical about the political abilities of his peers: 'Our aristocracy is unfit for power', he would later confide to Metternich.[6] It would also be a serious mistake to make the nobility the mainstay of a monarchical system. Schwarzenberg envisaged instead an alliance of the wealthy classes. The revolution had sobered the middle classes and led them to support the authorities once again, and in the rural areas the emancipation of the farmers led them to establish themselves in a conservative position, forming a common front with the nobility.

Because of the brilliance of his services to the crown, Windischgraetz could not be treated lightly, even when his didactic manner began to annoy the emperor and his first minister. It took Schwarzenberg a long time to wear down his brother-in-law's resistance and to induce him to approve the Constitution which had been prepared by Stadion under his own guidance. Even then, his consent was only given grudgingly. Windischgraetz was no doubt pleased that the document drawn up by the government gave the monarch a central position, but although he finally gave in, it was only because he believed that, being a simple tactical expedient, this Constitution would probably never come into force.

Once this obstacle had been removed it became possible to move on to the final phase of the plan outlined in January. This was urgent because the *Reichstag* had chosen 15 March as the date to make their document public. The government therefore took the initiative and staged a double coup on 7 March. As their own Constitution which the emperor had approved three days earlier was promulgated, a proclamation announced the dissolution of the *Reichstag*.

In comparison with the document devised by the now defunct *Reichstag* the Constitution announced by Franz Joseph displayed quite a different perspective. It was nevertheless not in complete contrast with the first document, for it did confirm some basic freedoms, even if it fenced them about with restrictions. Although formulated along more general lines, the right of the peoples of the empire to the development of their own identities was reiterated.

The project for the decentralization of power was not abandoned by Stadion. Although he did not go so far as suppress the *Land*, he did at least undertake to retain the provincial institutions in a subordinate role. The benefits of decentralization were spread among the three lowest division (the *Kreis*, the district and the commune) in the pyramid structure which he retained. Convinced, like Tocqueville, that local autonomy was the lifeblood of liberty – the Constitution postulated that 'the free commune is the foundation of the free state' – he left the direction of local affairs to these divisions, through their elected assemblies.

The most important feature of this Constitution, though, was that the monarch once more became the central figure in the Austrian political system. As was to be expected, all reference to popular rule had disappeared. The sovereign was still required to swear allegiance to the Constitution, but it gave him such rights that this oath was turned into a formality. From now on the emperor would truly have total executive power and if he chose to exercise his power through his ministers they would be responsible to him alone. His right of veto over proposed legislation passed by the assemblies was no longer limited to that of suspension, and the right of dissolution which the Kremsier Parliament had allowed him was no longer subject to any limitations. Lastly, outside the parliamentary sessions the emperor had the right to legislate by decree if exceptional circumstances should demand it.

In the normal state of affairs the emperor would share his powers of legislation with the assemblies, but the prerogatives accorded him were so great that there could be no balance between the two sides. As the practical embodiment of Schwarzenberg's ideas, the voting system for the two Chambers which made up the *Reichstag* was intended to favour a coalition of conservative forces which would support the monarchy. There was no longer any question of universal suffrage. A system based on property ownership was established for the Lower Chamber which excluded the popular classes from the right to vote, while the composition of the Upper Chamber reflected Schwarzenberg's poor opinion of the nobility. He again chose wealth as a basis for selection but the threshold was raised much higher, making the Upper Chamber of the *Reichstag* the preserve of a wealthy elite made up of both aristocrats and members of the bourgeoisie.

Finally, the Constitution outlined the creation of the single state which Schwarzenberg hoped for. The decentralization measures outlined by Stadion were not intended to change this. They only concerned the lower echelons of provincial organization. At the upper levels of government, centralization became the rule. Unlike Kremsier's proposal, the Constitution of 4 March included Hungary in its proposals. This desire to treat Hungary simply as a part of the single Austrian state also explained the government's delay in announcing the Constitution, for Schwarzenberg was waiting for the military situation to stabilize, which it appeared to have done by the beginning of March.

Although the Hungarian Constitution was not revoked, little of it remained, following the declaration that there was only a single crown, that of the Austrian Empire, and the request to the Hungarians to send representatives to the Austrian *Reichstag*. In addition, the unity of the Kingdom of Saint Stephen was shattered.

Transylvania which had attached itself to Hungary in 1848 became separate once more and, in return for its services to the cause of greater Austria, Croatia-Slavonia gained the status of a crown province, and the government of Voivodia could expect the same privilege in the near future. Deprived of its rights and divided within itself, Hungary was reduced to the same level as the other provinces of the monarchy with no regard for its historical and constitutional individual identity.

Now that the Emperor's authority had been restored on a solid basis and the army held the Austro-Bohemian lands firmly under control, it would soon be possible for the government to return to Vienna. The proximity of the border with Hungary was another reason for this return as Franz Joseph was eager to visit it. He moved back to Vienna on 5 May, while the rest of the family lingered a little longer at Olmütz.

The Hungarian Front

Despite its political success of 7 March, the government's difficulties were not over. In some respects, by setting out the field of conflict in such exact terms, the government's measures became the cause of an increase in hostilities in the areas where Austria was still fighting.

The Italian front flared up again when, on 13 March, Charles Albert rejected the terms of the armistice of the previous August and resumed hostilities. This turned out, however, to be a fruitless move. It took Radetzky only a few days to inflict a new and humiliating defeat on the Piedmont army at Novare. In his disappointment Charles Albert decided to abdicate that same evening in favour of his son Victor Emmanuel. After this final eruption in Piedmont, Austria re-established a hegemony over most of the Italian peninsula which resembled that which had existed before 1848. In northern Italy only Venice still eluded its authority, but for a short time only. The city's fall on 22 August came as no surprise to anybody.

More serious was the threat which Austria faced in Hungary. The promulgation of the Constitution seemed to make the assumption that Hungary's fate was decided, but the government had not yet resumed control in the kingdom, and the Hungarian question would continue to trouble Schwarzenberg's government into the summer.

Windischgraetz at first imagined that this campaign would be a simple military expedition. The army had set out in mid-December and Buda fell on 5 January. But the commander-in-chief lingered there to negotiate the terms of an agreement with the representatives of the Magyar aristocracy, now called the Old Conservatives, which was intended to confirm the suppression of the revolution while recognizing the national identity of the Hungarians. These discussions were pointless, for Schwarzenberg refused to countenance any alternative to the integration of Hungary into the rest of the monarchy. Pressed by the government to continue his military offensive, Windischgraetz had a further success, albeit on a small scale, at Kapolna at the end of February, and this put Schwarzenberg in a position to promulgate the Constitution.

Forced back onto Debrecen, Kossuth's government had taken advantage of this delay to regroup its forces. General Görgey, the new Hungarian commander-in-chief had managed to transform the army, the *honved*, into a fine military machine. Also, once it had returned to the offensive, the Hungarian army soon gained an advantage on the various fighting fronts. While Bem, a Pole who had offered his services to the Hungarian revolution, reconquered Transylvania, Görgey drove the Austrians back from Buda. In mid-April, Hungary was almost entirely lost to the empire. Now that military superiority had been established, the Hungarian revolutionaries could take up the challenge of Schwarzenberg's Constitution. They had already responded to Franz Joseph's accession by continuing to recognize Ferdinand, the crowned monarch, as their legitimate sovereign. Following the promulgation of the Constitution, they took a further revolutionary step and announced on 14 April that the Habsburg-Lorraine dynasty had failed.

This sudden deterioration in the situation called for emergency measures from the Austrian government and the series of military defeats raised the question of the command of the armies. No doubt Schwarzenberg wished to avoid the dismissal of a man who, despite his faults, was still the saviour of the empire. His first move was therefore to dispatch Baron Kübeck as an adviser to assist Windischgraetz. But this half-measure had little effect on the military situation and it also led to indignation on Windischgraetz's part at the implication that he no longer had the full confidence of the government.

When the advance of the *honved* drew near to the Austro-Hungarian border Schwarzenberg's scruples disappeared. The government took the decision on 12 April to ask Franz Joseph to relieve Windischgraetz of his command. Two days later he was informed of his fall from favour. It must have been painful for Franz Joseph to have to take this decision, for he was aware of the debt of gratitude which the empire owed to Windischgraetz, as his words to him on the day of his coronation bear witness. Despite this, the young emperor already had mixed feelings over this matter. As time went on he suffered Windischgraetz's behaviour with a diminishing degree of equanimity, for the older man implied that his services to the empire had earned him the right to act as Franz Joseph's adviser. Although there were sufficient reasons of state to explain Franz Joseph's agreement to the government's request, it seems likely that he was also influenced in this by the state of his personal relations with Windischgraetz.

Windischgraetz considered his removal from office to be an affront and he would never forgive his brother-in-law for asking it of the emperor. His subsequent dealings with Franz Joseph also showed that the wound never healed. He reacted to his dismissal with pride, but also with the style of a great feudal lord. His reply to Franz Joseph is couched in a tone which few subjects would have been able to use without exciting their monarch's wrath:

> The sacrifices which I have agreed to for sake of the imperial House, the absolute devotion with which I have served your Majesty, your dynasty, the monarchy and the army, and what I can describe without false modesty as my achievements, are apparently not great enough for me to wear the badge of office which you have taken away from me. In addition, your Majesty must excuse me and the world must not judge me harshly, when I find myself constrained to leave the titles and decorations which have been bestowed on me by the imperial House at your feet.[7]

The choice for a new head of the army in Hungary fell on General Welden, who was a devoted soldier but who was lacking in genius and soon showed himself incapable of the task of setting the military situation to rights. The inferior numbers of the imperial forces in Hungary precluded any hope of victory on their part and they were in need of immediate reinforcements, but the situation in the rest of the empire made it impossible to spare any troops. Radetzky did not consider it feasible to withdraw any forces from Italy and a further section of the army was tied up with the task of maintaining order in Austro-Bohemia and in Galicia.

The only remaining hope lay in Russian support. Nicolas I could not refuse to send help to Austria when he had so loudly declared his support for the counterrevolution. He must also have been conscious of the risk of unrest spreading to Poland if the revolution succeeded in Hungary. For the Austrian leaders, it was a difficult decision to call for Russian aid and Schwarzenberg had dismissed Windischgraetz's earlier suggestion of a request for Russian help in the middle of March. He must still have hoped that the situation was only a temporary one and that in time his own forces would be strong enough to allow Austria to regain control of Hungary. A month later, the progress of the war crushed this hope. It gradually became accepted that the only path left open to the Austrian government was to call on Russia for help. Franz Joseph and Schwarzenberg made the bitter decision to turn to Nicolas I and the latter was quick to respond to their call, made on 1 May, notifying them of his agreement practically by return of post.

Shortly after this, Franz Joseph journeyed to Warsaw in the company of his first minister to find out the details of Nicolas I's plans to provide aid. From this meeting he brought away an agreement which sealed the fate of the Hungarian revolution. Although it did not begin until the middle of June, when it came, the effect of the intervention of more than 100,000 Russian troops was enormous. Under the command of the duke of Warsaw, General Paskiewicz, the Russian offensive began on the left bank of the Danube. In itself, the choice of Paskiewicz, the man who had put down the Polish uprising of 1831, was enough to indicate Russia's intentions to Kossuth and his followers. Paskiewicz could be expected to use to advantage the knowledge which he had acquired against the Polish in his campaign against the Hungarians. Finally, and this provides a fair indication of the relative power of the partners of this alliance of conservative powers, the Russian army would have the right to a complete freedom of action within its field of operations.

In the division of tasks between the two allies, the Austrian army would be deployed on the right bank of the Danube. Before the counter-offensive was launched a further change took place in the army's command and Welden, who was certainly not competent, was replaced by one of the generals of the Italian army, Baron von Haynau. This appointment of one of Radetzky's finest lieutenants gave the army new life. However, it was not only his military zeal which distinguished Haynau; he was also reputed to be possessed of a cold cruelty which had been especially in evidence during the taking of Brescia, earning him the nickname of 'hyena of Brescia'. As the final element of the plan, in the south, Jellačić was marching at the head of his Croats to make his own contribution to victory. The plan of campaign of the Austro-Russian allies involved a pincer movement which would leave the enemy surrounded and force them to capitulate. Their superior numbers in both men and supplies gave the allies the greater chance of victory, for the Hungarians had only 150,000 men and 450 cannons to pit against the allies' 280,000 men and 12,000 cannons.

Once the counter-offensive had been launched, Franz Joseph could not resist joining the fight. He first took part in the taking of Raab (Györ) on 28 June, and a little later he again participated in the fight for Komorn (Komarom), and here he was involved in an incident similar to that at Santa Lucia when a shell exploded a few metres away from him. After this Schwarzenberg quickly put an end to his military career. Convinced that his position as emperor was too important for him to be allowed to continue to risk his life in such a careless way, the statesman managed to persuade him to withdraw from the vicinity of the fighting.

Franz Joseph was thus obliged to follow the final phase of the war from Vienna. For the Hungarians, who were suffering from their inferior numbers, the situation was rapidly becoming desperate. The *honved* withdrew at the beginning of August to the south-eastern part of Hungary and appeals for public support brought no response from a country exhausted by war. Perceiving no point in the continuation of a fruitless struggle, Görgey decided to surrender. By choosing to give himself up to Paskiewicz rather than Haynau, Görgey inflicted a final insult on the Austrians. Franz Joseph must have been deeply affected by this act which deprived him of the satisfaction of receiving the capitulation of his faithless subjects. But its main effect was to remind him that he owed his victory to the help of a foreign power. Far from soothing this affront, the terms in which Paskiewicz notified the Tsar of Görgey's surrender on 13 August at Vilagos were likely to twist the knife in the wound: 'You are the sole victor, Sire; Hungary is at your feet and the war is over.' For Kossuth, the other great figure of the revolution, this was the beginning of the time of exile. After burying the crown of Saint Stephen on Hungarian soil, he fled to Turkey and thence to England.

Now that peace had been restored, Franz Joseph found himself at a crossroads. He could choose a policy of appeasement which would heal the wounds caused by the revolution and the war, and which would look for a way in which Hungary could be integrated into the Austrian state without violence. He could alternatively choose repression. The second course was more in keeping with his inclinations and his advisers did nothing to direct him towards an attitude of clemency. Schwarzenberg considered that all Magyars were 'rebels to be destroyed, to be put out of action once and for all'.[8] Archduchess Sophie cursed them, and Count Grünne felt no less hostility towards them. A policy of repression was therefore adopted. It was decided to make an example of those Hungarians who had held positions of responsibility in the uprising and the war. In particular, the senior officers who had broken their vows to the emperor and had served with the *honved* could expect no mercy. Haynau was even given a free hand to dispense capital punishment to the offending officers. Although Görgey was fortunate enough to be under the protection of the Tsar because he had surrendered to the Russian army, thirteen generals were executed on 6 October in Arad. On the same day, many civilians suffered the same fate, among them Count Batthyány, the former head of the Hungarian government, although he had resigned in the summer of 1848, withdrawing his support from Kossuth. In all, 114 men were executed and nearly 2,000 were imprisoned.

The harshness of these measures augured ill for any chance of an improvement in relations between Hungary and the empire. There was one group which, although its members remained silent during the rule of the extremists, was in favour of a compromise with the Habsburgs. This was the group of Old Conservatives, the only Hungarians to be in a position, as a result of their connections with the Austrian aristocracy, to approach the Viennese ruling party in the hope that the March Constitution had not provided a definitive form for Austro-Hungarian relations. They no doubt agreed that the leaders of the revolution should be treated with severity but they disputed the legitimacy and the wisdom of forcing the whole Hungarian nation to suffer the consequences of the crimes of the revolution. Despite their antagonism towards the Hungarian constitutional laws of April 1848 they were not supporters of absolutism. In the name of the principle of legitimacy they asked Austria to restore historical rights and to revive the Hungarian Constitution which had been in force before the revolution.

The Magyar magnates found allies among some of the conservatives of Austro-Bohemia. Such prestigious advocates as Windischgraetz and the old Prince Metternich pleaded their cause before Schwarzenberg. Metternich recommended that rather than adopting a policy of force which he believed to be destined to fail, as it had done under Joseph II, an attempt should be made, however difficult it might seem, to come to an agreement with the conservatives, on whom he had relied in the last years of the *Vormärz*.

These arguments had little effect on either Franz Joseph or Schwarzenberg. Franz Joseph believed at that time that all Hungarians were rebels. Even the Magyar nobles had no virtue in his eyes: 'the conservatives are the cause of many problems in Hungary. They are just troublemakers like the others and should be treated as such.'[9] Nor was Schwarzenberg to be swayed by these pleas when he decided to make use of the situation to incorporate Hungary into a single state.

The treatment of Hungary, following the defeat of the revolution, ran counter to the more liberal arrangements written into the March Constitution which still made reference to the Hungarian Constitution. This problem was solved by Bach, the new minister of the interior, replacing Stadion, whose nervous disposition had not been strong enough to resist the pressures he was under. Bach managed to persuade the government to use the Diet of Debrecen's declaration of the collapse of the Habsburg dynasty as an excuse to relieve Austria of its obligations.

Placed under the authority of a military governor, Hungary was treated like an occupied country. It was divided into five areas which were controlled by army officers. In addition, all trace of local autonomy was eradicated. Previously under the control of the nobility, the local assemblies were reduced to the status of simple administrative bodies. The plan to absorb Hungary into the rest of the monarchy was extended to other areas. Two such measures were spectacular in character: the introduction of the Austrian system of taxation, and the abolition of the customs barriers between Hungary and the other countries of the empire. This final reform, which had been pushed through by Karl von Bruck, the dynamic minister for commerce who hoped to make Austria the heart of a vast customs union from the North Sea to the Adriatic and from the Rhine to the Carpathians, used the political unity of the empire as a basis for economic unification.

These policies were all aimed at the absorption of Hungary into the empire. It no longer existed in the letter of the law except as part of the greater Austrian state, for the Kingdom of Saint Stephen had disappeared as an autonomous political body.

The Duel with Prussia

Austria was also active on the German front. There too, it was Schwarzenberg who controlled events. Armed with Franz Joseph's support, his ultimate aim was the entry of the entire empire into a renewed German Confederation. Austria would gain primacy in Germany, not through its ancient rights, but through force of numbers. This 'greater-Austrian' design also explained the single structure which Schwarzenberg intended for the empire, and the customs unification of the Habsburg lands could equally be seen as the preliminary step towards Austria's entry into the German customs union, the *Zollverein*. This project demonstrates that Schwarzenberg's policies were directed towards increasing Austrian power, and were not dictated by nationalist preoccupations, for such a move would run counter to hopes for a unified Germany, and would bring together not only Germans, but Slavs, Magyars, and Italians. Schwarzenberg had a fall-back scheme, however, should opposition to his plan prove too strong. In such a case, he would content himself with the revival of the ancient Confederation, with Austria as its president but with only part of the empire participating.

There were, on the other hand, two possible situations which Schwarzenberg was determined to prevent: the establishment of a national parliament at home and the creation of a German Federation of states dominated by Prussia. Of these two threats, the first was the one immediately confronting Austria, but it soon became apparent that Prussia was opposed to the consolidation of the Austrian empire. By specifying that the limits of the German Empire should correspond to those of the German Confederation and that a member state could only be allied with non-German countries through a private union (the first articles of the constitutional proposal adopted by the Frankfurt Parliament at the end of October 1848), Austria was left with no choice, if it agreed with this scheme, but to sacrifice its own unity. If Austria were to reject the scheme it could no longer be a part of the Germanic group.

Schwarzenberg was not prepared to be trapped into this dilemma. On 9 March he informed the Frankfurt Parliament of his proposals for the reform of Germany which would allow the Habsburg monarchy to retain all its possessions on its entry on an empire of 70 million inhabitants. Instead of a national parliament there would be a States General comprising seventy members of which thirty-eight would come from Austria alone. In this move, Vienna was laying its cards on the table and making a clear announcement of its intention to re-establish rule in Germany.

It is unlikely that Schwarzenberg cherished any illusions over the possible reactions of the Frankfurt Parliament. It would have been unthinkable for it to approve a project which was so opposed to the principle of the nation-state. Realizing that the recovery of Austria would make it difficult for its own proposal to be put into operation, the Assembly had already begun to reconsider its position. Its president, Heinrich von Gagern had prevailed on its members in mid-January to reach an agreement on the proposal for a smaller Union centred around Prussia which could enter into alliance with Austria. The official approval given to Schwarzenberg's plan precipitated events. On 27 and 28 March the Assembly reacted to this challenge by offering the German imperial crown to the King of Prussia, Friedrich Wilhelm IV.

For Austria, should the king accept, the matter would become critical. The army was occupied on other fronts and was not in a position to intervene. It was true that

Schwarzenberg felt that he could count on the Prussian king's refusal. Brought up under the influence of Romanticism, filled with nostalgia for medieval Christendom, Friedrich Wilhelm IV had shown great attachment to the feudal ethic. He therefore considered himself to be the inheritor of the Holy Roman Empire's bans. Nor did he wish to receive an honour which would place him at the head of the whole of Germany from any other authority than his peers. He was thus following his own views when he declared himself unable to accept a crown 'made of mud and clay', tarnished by its popular origin.

This reply sealed the fate of the Assembly. On 6 April, Schwarzenberg recalled the Austrian representatives from Frankfurt. As a logical result of Friedrich Wilhelm's decision, the Prussian government did likewise at the end of May. Dismantled, and soon to be expelled from Frankfurt, the Assembly fell back on Stuttgart, and continued a pale existence for a while before falling under the blows of the Wurtemberg troops.

In spite of the removal of this obstacle, Schwarzenberg still had to cope with Prussian ambitions, for Friedrich Wilhelm's refusal did not mean that he was not tempted by power. His own ambitions, ironically, mirrored von Gagern's plan, for he pictured himself at the head of a small Union, but appointed, not by popular vote but by the other German princes. The smaller German Union would form a larger but separate union with Austria. Although it appeared to allow Austria the right to enter a new confederate pact as a single body, it would nevertheless exclude the monarchy from a Germany dominated by Prussia. As such it was unacceptable to Schwarzenberg.

Before the two powers had even come into open conflict Austria had begun to take counter-measures. These were at first concentrated on the states of southern Germany which traditionally had a special relationship with the monarchy. Although these relations had not always been ideal, both Bavaria and Wurtemberg wanted an ally in facing Prussia's attempt at domination, and their refusal to join the smaller Union was the first setback experienced by Prussia. At least the latter could be pleased with the consent of Saxony and Hanover with whom agreement was reached on 26 May 1849. Although it could not control the whole of Germany immediately it could still hope to extend its power to the Main area, which already represented a considerable increase in its sphere of political influence.

At first events seemed to confirm this expectation. A conference of sovereigns held in Berlin gave the presidency of the Union's ruling body to Prussia and also the supreme command of the army. It appeared quite possible that this success would finally overcome the reluctance of Bavaria and Wurtemberg, especially as Prussia already had a bridgehead into southern Germany in the form of the Grand Duchy of Baden. However, this hope soon faded, for Saxony and Hanover had been prudent enough to make their support for the Union dependent on the agreement of Bavaria and Wurtenberg, and with the refusal of Munich and Stuttgart to join they were released from their undertakings.

With this double defection, the power relationships shifted in October in Austria's favour. Prussia had by no means abandoned its plans, but their future did not appear hopeful without the agreement of the other four Germanic kingdoms. In addition, since the summer, Austria had resolved its problems in Hungary and Italy and this enabled the government to increase the number of troops in Bohemia as a continued means of pressure on that state. Lastly, Russia had come to a decision over German matters. As in the Hungarian question, it backed Austria, whose rights to dominance in Germany had a historical basis. In Russian eyes, the claims of Prussia for a united nation with itself at the centre was an application of liberal ideas.

Prussia's position continued to weaken. The two rivals agreed on a temporary solution with the creation of a provisional confederate commission which would sit until 1 May 1850. This scheme allowed room for a compromise but its main function was to gain time for both sides, as neither had renounced its ambitions in joining this commission. Prussia continued to hope for the smaller Union, and Austria saw the commission as the first step in a move to restore the Germanic Confederation.

These opposing viewpoints meant that there was no respite in the Austro-Prussian conflict, but the initiative had now passed to Austria. Already, Prussia's aspiration to share the presidency of the commission with Austria and thus place itself on an equal footing with the monarchy had met with Schwarzenberg's refusal. When the time of the commission ran out on 1 May 1850, tensions rose to a new level. Acting in its capacity as president of the Germanic Confederation, Austria decided to call the Confederate Assembly in Frankfurt according to the procedures of the old *Bund* Constitution.

For Prussia, this move was filled with menace, because it set up an alternative to the Union which, as it derived its authority from the principle of legitimacy and had the strength of the support of Austria and its allies, seemed likely to smother it. Its immediate effect was to harden antagonisms and Germany thus found itself divided into two hostile camps: on one side, the states still loyal to the Union, and on the other, those who agreed to send representatives to the Frankfurt Diet.

This split was bound to cause problems sooner or later. The crisis came when the Prince of Hesse-Cassel called on the help of the *Bund* in a dispute with his local Diet. This would have been a relatively simple matter had he not also been a member of the Union. Prussia reacted immediately, contesting the right of the *Bund* to involve itself in the affairs of a state belonging to the Union. This reaction was all the stronger because Hesse-Cassel separated old Prussia from its possessions on the Rhine. Perceiving its own interests to be under threat, Prussia decided that an intervention by the Confederation would threaten the security of its communications with its western possessions.

Schwarzenberg hailed the opportunity created by this crisis to settle the conflict with Prussia once and for all, by forcing Berlin to renounce its ambitions, either through diplomatic channels or if necessary by force. He did not confine himself, therefore, to informing the Prussian cabinet on 27 September that Austria would support any government which appealed to the Germanic Confederation. He also perfected military plans which would restore order in Hesse-Cassel. These were announced on 12 October in Bregenz where Franz Joseph was in conference with the kings of Bavaria and Wurtemberg.

The military agreement signed by the three partners gave Bavaria responsibility for the operation. If Prussia should resist, then Austria and Wurtemberg would also join in. The main role would then fall to the five units of the Austrian army assembled in Bohemia under Radetzky's command, which would strike at the heart of Prussia with the help of the army of Saxony. Hesse-Cassel's decision to ask the Confederation's help was made official on 15 October and this plan was put into operation. When ten days later, Prussia took the initiative by occupying the principality, war loomed.

Despite the decisiveness of this move, Prussia had reason for concern as its isolation became apparent in the wake of Schwarzenberg's anticipatory diplomatic activity. Nicolas I, who had met Franz Joseph for a second time in Warsaw on 25 October, pronounced himself in favour of Austria. The Prussian side could not match this with the support of any other European power, so it was obliged to face the final stage of the dispute alone. This diplomatic isolation and the superior military strength of Austria and its allies, who at the end of November could command 130,000 men against only 50,000 Prussians, finally forced Prussia to make concessionary moves. This retreat took place only in stages, for the Prussian leaders were divided over policy. Although some sought an honourable compromise, others were prepared to go the extent of an armed confrontation over supremacy in Germany. Those in favour of resistance suffered a setback when, on 2 November, Friedrich Wilhelm IV decided in favour of a peaceful solution and declared himself ready to dissolve the Union. This moment of relief from the conflict did not last for long, however, as Prussia was also unwilling to withdraw from Hesse-Cassel, and in order to protect its rights there, called for a general mobilization on 6 November. Nor was there any reduction in tension in the field, where Prussian and Bavarian soldiers soon clashed, and the first shots were fired on 8 November.

This alarm was nevertheless followed by a new conciliatory gesture from Prussia, which officially dissolved the Union on 15 November. This concession which had still been unthinkable a few weeks earlier was naturally considered by Schwarzenberg to be a great victory. Peace was not yet assured, though, as the Prussian army remained in Hesse-Cassel. Schwarzenberg's recent success did not make him any more accommodating. He chose instead to press the Prussians even harder: Austria presented Prussia with an ultimatum on 25 November which demanded its submission to the decisions of the Confederation within 48 hours.

Events then took an unexpected turn, for in reply Friedrich Wilhelm IV announced that he was sending his first minister, Baron von Manteuffel, to Olmütz. Austria could have considered this to be a delaying tactic and have acted, but instead Schwarzenberg agreed to receive Manteuffel.

Knowing itself to be in a strong position, Austria could afford a gesture of goodwill, but it soon transpired that the decision to receive the Prussian minister was due to the intervention of Franz Joseph who was not content to follow his first minister's advice, and wished to have a personal say in events. He was prepared to go to war if there were no other option open but, brought up in the traditions of Austro-Prussian accord, he hoped that every other possible means to preserve the peace would first be explored. He also feared that an armed conflict between two great conservative powers would help the cause of liberalism, exciting a spirit of revolution which, although it had been suppressed for the time being, might still raise its head given the right circumstances. The Austrian authorities also had to take Russia's views into account. Although Nicolas I was ready to support Austria in any conflict, he considered it to be a last resort and placed his own hopes on the rebuilding of a common front of the three great conservative powers in northern and central Europe.

The interviews between Schwarzenberg and Manteuffel which took place, significantly, in the presence of Baron Meyendorff, the Russian ambassador to

Vienna, ended in agreement. The conclusion to this crisis has commonly been called the 'retreat' or 'humiliation of Olmütz' giving a categorical judgement of its nature, but Heinrich von Srbik, the great historian of German unification, has nevertheless suggested that this agreement left 'neither victor nor vanquished'.[10]

The report of the encounter can actually be interpreted in many ways. In the Hesse-Cassel affair Austria was undoubtedly successful, as Prussia finally agreed to allow the Bavarian troops to occupy the grand duchy. However, the agreement did not achieve any overall settlement of the German question. In order to reshape the political organization of Germany, it was decided to hold a conference at Dresden in the near future, in which all the states would participate.

It remains to provide an explanation for Schwarzenberg's comparative moderation, for the results with which he satisfied himself at Olmütz were less far reaching than his original aims. It was true that he could expect to see his ideas prevail at Dresden, but this would not be enough. The factors which led Austria to accept the Olmütz meeting were also in play in the decision to temper the demands of the monarchy. The state of the empire's finances were a further disincentive for war, if it were possible to obtain the same results through negotiation. Schwarzenberg was also aware that the prospect of a war with Prussia was not viewed favourably in military circles. This situation was a different one from that which the army officers had known in both Hungary and Italy, where they had been fighting against the forces of the revolution. Furthermore, they still remembered the comradeship in arms which had existed in the fight against Napoleonic France, and Radetzky did not forget that he had been Schwarzenberg's commanding officer at the battle of Leipzig.

There were nevertheless those who deplored Austria's decision to stay its hand at the moment when it held Prussia at its mercy. They feared that a historic chance had been allowed to slip by which could have provided a long-term settlement of the German question to Austria's advantage by reducing Prussia to a position from which it could offer no threat to the monarchy.

Schwarzenberg appears to have been of this opinion: 'You would have liked us to take them apart, so would I', he confided to Beust.[11] For his part, von der Pfordten, the Bavarian first minister, predicted that: 'The fight for control of Germany has been settled and Austria has lost.'[12] Whether or not it should be seen as a lost opportunity, Olmütz was the high-water mark of Austria's relations with Germany. Once over, a decline began which, although it was not continuous, and was even occasionally reversed, would continue until the break of 1866.

On the Prussian side, however, the Olmütz agreement was felt to be a humiliation. This wound created a deep resentment of Austria and fed a desire for revenge which would inevitable act as an obstacle to good relations between the two kingdoms. At first glance, this might seem surprising, given that Franz Joseph in his desire for agreement had made sure that Schwarzenberg showed moderation. After all, Austria did not treat Prussia at Olmütz as Napoleon had following his victory at Iena. The reason for this feeling of humiliation is to be found elsewhere. It was impossible for many Prussians to come to terms with the fact that Austria had prevented Prussia from gaining supremacy in Germany. All hope of the speedy fulfilment of the project for a united Germany had disappeared in Berlin. The Olmütz episode had therefore not succeeded in getting rid of the clash of Austrian and Prussian interests; all it had done was to postpone the reckoning. But it had also struck a blow to Prussian expansionism and it was for this that many Prussian patriots could not forgive Austria.

In accordance with the plan formulated by the two countries, negotiations began again in Dresden in April 1851, but the atmosphere was less troubled now that the threat of war had receded. This relaxation nevertheless barely concealed the continuation of the duel between the two rivals. Each brought its own secret agenda to Dresden.

Schwarzenberg intended to strengthen the direction already taken at Olmütz with the help of his allies and in this his aim was twofold. He still wished to obtain entry for Austria with all of her empire into the new Germany. This would be complemented by the inclusion of Austria and all her dependent states in the *Zollverein*. Prussia, on the other hand, intended to prevent the success of a plan which, should it succeed, would be a long-term threat to Prussia's own advance. At best, it was prepared to allow the entry of Austria as a whole into the German political unit on condition that the Austrians embraced its own plan for a Union.

Schwarzenberg, however, was no more inclined to agree to this than he had ever been. Nor was Prussia prepared to help Austria's entry to the *Zollverein*. Prussia planned that if it could not manage to gain support for the Union, it would work towards its recognition by the confederate institutions as Austria's equal. But this was another demand to which Schwarzenberg was not prepared to accede.

Schwarzenberg failed at Dresden to overcome Prussian resistance, especially as Prussia had succeeded in ending its isolation. Certain of the German states which had supported Austria against Prussian attempts at dominance rebelled when it seemed that Austria in its turn wished to extend its influence in Germany. Perhaps Schwarzenberg might still have succeeded if he had not also come up against strong opposition from elsewhere. Neither Palmerston's Britain, nor Louis Napoleon's France looked favourably on a plan which would result in the upsetting of the continent's balance of power. Palmerston notified Schwarzenberg that such a change could only take place with the agreement of the signatories of the Treaty of Vienna. Louis Napoleon realized for his part that if such a political entity were to come into being, it would probably upset French hopes of obtaining the changes to the treaties of 1815 which were his main objective.

But it was mostly Russia's attitude which convinced Schwarzenberg to follow a prudent course. Although Russia was opposed to the Prussian plan to lead a united Germany, it did not mean to allow Austria to head a similar empire which would be both vast and powerful, and which could interfere with Russian influence on German affairs and could damage Russian expansion in the Balkans.

Without the imposition of Schwarzenberg's programme, the solution agreed by the German states could, in principle, satisfy both parties, for its advantage lay in that it did not compromise any future plans. It was decided simply to restore the Constitution and territorial boundaries of the German Confederate states to their 1848 status. Could this be described as a limited success or a limited failure for Austria?

This arrangement conformed to Schwarzenberg's minimum requirements when he assumed responsibility for the Austrian diplomatic negotiations. Although there was no longer any question of Austria bringing all its possessions into the Confederacy, Schwarzenberg could at least congratulate himself that the plans for Union had been dismissed. But Austria had not succeeded in breaking into the *Zollverein*, despite the provision that the application was to be reconsidered in February 1858, providing Austria with the chance, in the intervening seven years, to put its economy in order. But it was impossible to ignore the fact that Prussia placed quite a different interpretation on the delay. Berlin's first concern was to delay events in the hope that in seven years the balance of power would have evolved sufficiently to enable it to prevent Austria's entry to the *Zollverein*.

Franz Joseph was certainly confirmed as the senior German prince, and this gave both him and his first minister cause for satisfaction. But, after three years of confrontation, this ending did not really settle the Austro-Prussian question, and it would eventually cause Franz Joseph considerable difficulties.

The Restoration of Absolutism

Now that Hungary had returned to Viennese rule and that the status quo had been restored in Germany, it remained for the monarchy to regain its full power. This called the fate of the March 1849 Constitution, which had never been enforced, into question. The state of siege under which not only Vienna and Prague, but also Galicia and Transylvania found themselves, and the period of military dictatorship in Hungary and Lombardy-Venetia provided a plausible justification for this delay.

Should it then be assumed that the Austrian leadership had intended from the first to treat the Constitution as valueless? Such was not the intention of Count Stadion, its main deviser, but, weakened by illness, he had left the government. Following his departure there were still several ministers who continued to support a constitutional government. This is borne out by the resignations of Schmerling, the minister of justice, in January 1851 and of Bruck in May of the same year, both of whom chose to leave the government when they realized that they were powerless to prevent the return to absolute rule. The other ministers who opposed this move managed to continue their resistance for a further six months before giving way to the inevitable.

There remains the case of Schwarzenberg himself. Although he was not a man to be constrained by scruples, there is no evidence that he had already decided in March 1849 on a return to absolutism. It is likely that he did not intend to take Stadion's Constitution as gospel and envisaged some revisions to it. In his conviction that the monarchical system should henceforth be founded on an alliance of the landed classes which would primarily act to bring the aristocracy and the middle classes together, it is feasible that he should have considered it desirable that Austria should remain a constitutional state. This position was in fact very close to that of his ministers, whom he had been careful to choose from the ranks of 'liberal conservatives' and not from the fiercer reactionaries. But although the process of the restoration of absolute rule was not initiated by him, he did not resist it as strongly as some of his ministers and in fact came quite quickly to support it. Perhaps, being less sensitive to matters of principle and more concerned with matters of power, he considered that it was not possible for him to change the course of events in this matter and so felt it best to join those in favour of absolute rule, thus at least leaving himself in a position to influence it.

The driving force in this decision to rid Austria of the Constitution came from

Franz Joseph and this was no doubt another reason for Schwarzenberg's behaviour. There is some credibility in Helmut Rumpler's thesis that of all those who were in power at the time, it is only in Franz Joseph that we can be certain of a resolve to restore absolute rule in Austria from the outset of his reign in 1848. Franz Joseph never showed anything other than aversion for modern constitutionalism. His education predisposed him to this view and, in offending his sense of sovereign dignity, the vision of a triumphant revolution confirmed him in this opinion. Nor did he consider the declaration of the March Constitution as anything other than a concession dictated by circumstance which in no way bound him for the future.

Until the end of 1850, Franz Joseph was prevented from any precipitate action by the German war. Many of the Austrian allies had a constitutional form of government, so to go back too quickly on the promises of the March Constitution would have been to compromise Austria's position in Germany. But by the beginning of 1851, when the crisis appeared to be coming to an end, Franz Joseph could feel that his hands were no longer tied.

His advisers also supported this policy. Archduchess Sophie and Grünne certainly did not dissuade him from following such a course, but the major role in this stage of the development of the return to an absolute monarchy was played by Baron von Kübeck. When Franz Joseph called him to office, this old member of the *Vormärz* administration already had a long career behind him. The son of a working-class family, Kübeck had overcome this disadvantage of birth through his personal qualities of intelligence and efficiency. An effective administrator, with a thorough knowledge of financial and economic affairs, he had gradually risen in the state hierarchy. In 1840, he was placed at the head of the *Hofkammer*, giving him control over the finances of all the monarchy except Hungary. He was a conservative Josephist and, in his view, it was the government's responsibility to raise the standard of living throughout its lands, although there was no need to call on the populace to participate in such matters. As a result of his humble origins, Kübeck retained an antagonism towards the old aristocracy which led him to mistrust any mediators between him and the throne, and it was these views which led him to champion the cause of absolute monarchy.

It was as president of the *Reichsrat* (Council of the empire) that Kübeck encouraged his young sovereign in his plans to re-establish absolute rule. On 19 October 1850 Franz Joseph made him responsible for the drawing up of the statutes of the Council, which had been provided for in the March Constitution. His report, presented on 1 November, received the emperor's approval and Kübeck was appointed the first president of the *Reichsrat*.

The interest in Kübeck's report lies in the fact that it attacked the government. Kübeck denounced the ministerial Council as a western import which stood in the way of the supremacy of the sovereign and he cleverly connected it to the Constitution. The vow taken by the ministers to obey the Constitution prevented the government from acting as the executive body of imperial policy which Kübeck wished to represent as its primary function. The restoration of the monarch's personal authority was thus implemented through the reduction of the role of the Council of ministers who were to disappear as an autonomous group. To enable this to happen, Kübeck proposed that the *Reichsrat* should act as adviser to the emperor. To this end, any policy prepared by the administration would be submitted to the

Reichsrat for approval. With the benefit of this advice, the emperor would then be in a position to take decisions through a full act of sovereignty.

It is significant that, being aware of these ideas, Franz Joseph should have chosen to appoint Kübeck to the presidency of the *Reichsrat*. This decision suggested that, despite his admiration for Schwarzenberg he was becoming increasingly dissatisfied with the role of guardian which he felt that the government was still assuming towards him. The possibilities of this scheme appealed to him because of the freedom of action which they would allow him. The final version of the statutes reflected Kübeck's views by placing the *Reichsrat* in opposition to the government designed to limit its powers. Once Kübeck had made a careful choice of its members from the ranks of high-level administrators of the *Vormärz* regime who were, like him, radically hostile to the revolution, but who also had their reservations concerning the government, the *Reichsrat* took office on 13 April 1851.

The turning-point in relations between the emperor and the government came on 10 June 1851, when Franz Joseph first presided over his Council of ministers in person. This move put an end to the appointment of president of the Council. Although this title could clearly not be taken from Schwarzenberg, it became unlikely that he would have a successor. On a more general level, Franz Joseph's intentions were clear. By choosing to run the Council himself, he wished to make it clear that, far from being an independent body, it was subordinate to him. Matters were thus made explicit even before a further step towards absolutism was taken on 17 August 1851 when it was decided that ministers would hold their authority directly from the emperor. This was not yet a complete revocation of the Constitution but it was clear that its days were numbered.

In his intervention in the affairs of the Council, Franz Joseph did not conceal his ultimate aim, reminding them that such a liberal constitutional system as was in operation in France or Britain could never be applied in Austria. He was in any case aware that most of the groundwork had been achieved, and in writing of the news to his mother he did not conceal his satisfaction: 'We have thrown the principle of a Constitution overboard and Austria will only have one master from now on. Now I must work even harder. Thank God that in three years we have almost reached the position we wish for.'[13]

Franz Joseph's emergence in the front line of politics was received with enthusiasm in counter-revolutionary circles. Usually sparing in his compliments, Windischgraetz wrote: 'I am happy to be able to salute Your Majesty as my true emperor.'[14] Metternich, who was about to return to Austria (another sign of the changes taking place), celebrated the declaration of 20 August which made public the decisions of 17 August as 'the most important act of the new era'.[15]

It still remained for the death blow to be delivered. Franz Joseph was only awaiting the right moment to complete his work, and this presented itself when Louis Napoleon established a dictatorship in France following the *coup d'état* of 2 December. Taking advantage of this situation, Franz Joseph abolished the Constitution with the patent of 31 December 1851 which removed the final legal obstacle to absolute rule.

Just three years after coming to the throne, Franz Joseph had good reason to congratulate himself on his progress. Order was restored to the empire as a whole, the separatist movements had been destroyed and the liberal and democratic opposition parties muzzled; all obstacles to an absolute monarchy, such as the parliamentary Assembly, the Constitution, and the regency of a too-influential Council of ministers had been overcome and in Franz Joseph's words to his mother, Austria had a single master. Abroad, the Austrian position was re-established; in Germany, Prussia's rise had been checked and the Austrian emperor had regained his primacy which, although the plan approved by Schwarzenberg had only a theoretical basis, still left him as the first prince of Germany.

Of course there were gray areas in this situation. Austria had needed the help of a foreign power to reconquer Hungary, and Franz Joseph's pride had been wounded by having to request it under conditions which might be considered somewhat inglorious for a state which aspired to play a major role in Europe. The order which had returned to the whole monarchy was also fragile in character, and it was likely that the military solutions chosen by Franz Joseph might contain the seed of future crises. Although the mobilization of the army and the vigilance of the police prevented the expression of any organized opposition by subversive elements within the empire, the desire for freedom was unlikely to be contained for long. Hungary was restored to the body of the monarchy, but the conditions under which the revolution there had been suppressed threatened to push the whole Hungarian nation into revolt against Austria. In the Italian peninsula the balance of power was in a very similar situation to that which had existed before 1848, but the nationalist spirit had not been ousted, and indeed it had gained ground. In Germany the status quo had returned, but because of the humiliation of the Olmütz agreement, many Prussians dreamed of revenge.

In short, the achievements of the monarchy on various fronts were likely to prove to be Pyrrhic victories, but for the time being, untroubled by doubts, Franz Joseph allowed himself to be seduced by the pleasures of power. All he chose to see in the events of these three years was the attainment of his chosen objectives. The way was thus open for a period of neo-absolutism during which Franz Joseph would command the total power which his political philosophy demanded.

5
Neo-absolutism (1852–1859)

It would be wrong to think of the regime during these years as a simple return to pre-1848 absolutism. The powers held by Franz Joseph exceeded any which had been held by his predecessors. Although this period was to be the swan-song of absolutism, it also represented the culmination of the process of secularization.

The taming of the Diets had begun in the seventeenth century and was not yet over, for the government had been confronted by an uprising of many provincial assemblies just before the events of 1848. The Diets could still act as a counterweight, however slight, to the great imperial power, but with the disappearance of the last vestiges of provincial autonomy, this potential restraint vanished. The lords who formed part of the feudal system had also acted as a barrier between the emperor and his subjects until 1848. Maria Theresa had begun to demolish this barrier and with time the breaches had widened, but this process also remained incomplete. The local lords still held certain rights of police and justice over which the state had no control. The eventual destruction of the feudal system put an end to this anomaly and the state stepped into the gap. The neo-absolutist state's field of influence was thus enlarged and it relied on an even larger body of civil servants, with greater resources for the exercise of power than any preceding administration.

It would not only be a simplification, but also misleading to describe neo-absolutism as a reactionary exercise. Although there were reactionary features in its programme, there was no intention of re-imposing the *Vormärz* system. It was already significant that no attempt had been made to revoke the abolition of the feudal system. Instead, the patent of 31 December 1851 took care to confirm this measure, thereby gaining for the government the support of the peasants. On a more general level, a further difference with the old regime can be found in the spirit of modernization which characterized neo-absolutist thought, contrasting with the stagnation of the *Vormärz* administration. This can be demonstrated by many of its internal policies (economic growth, development of communications, transformation of the urban landscape, and school and university reform).

In these respects, Austrian neo-absolutism was not dissimilar to the authoritarian phase of the Second Empire in France. Restored to a position which fitted into the historical continuity of Austrian government, it partly resumed the tradition of Josephism, the Habsburg version of enlightened despotism, providing a model for government reform conducted by the state without reference to the people. This inheritance can be seen in the neo-absolutist desire to turn Austria into a single empire.

The Ministers

Franz Joseph at first relied on his ministers to carry out his policies. Although the intention of the Declaration of 20 August 1851 was to reduce their importance by making them simply the executors of the imperial will, in reality this system did not prevent strong personalities from carrying out policies of their own devising. Not all the ministers had this degree of freedom, however. Franz Joseph considered the diplomatic field to be his own preserve and the minister for foreign affairs, once Schwarzenberg was no longer in office, was primarily the loyal executor of his wishes. His colleagues, however, did have a greater degree of freedom of manoeuvre although no decision of any importance could be made before the emperor had studied the relevant papers and given his consent. Some of his ministers had strong personalities and were capable of influencing government policy. Schwarzenberg did not remain long at their head, though. Struck down by a heart attack, he died on 5 April 1852. Franz Joseph felt this loss badly, as can be seen in a letter written while still under the shock of events:

> A terrible thing has happened to me, to us all. It would be impossible to imagine a greater loss, a figure harder to replace, than the one taken from us so brutally yesterday. The man who has remained at my side since the beginning of my reign, dealing loyally with every difficulty, showing me absolute devotion, a man with iron determination and an inextinguishable energy has died, and there will never be anyone like him again. I still cannot really believe that this has happened and I have to exercise great control to preserve my countenance, I have to look courageously on a difficult future, and have to uphold 'the principles which must not go to the grave with the great man' with fortitude.[1]

At the beginning of the spring of 1852 Schwarzenberg and Franz Joseph had certainly outgrown the roles of master and pupil. The young emperor had gradually gained in confidence. On certain occasions he had even had the strength to impose his own views. Franz Joseph nevertheless continued to feel a mixture of admiration and affection for Schwarzenberg, and it was therefore natural that he should have wept sincerely for his loss. But there was more than gratitude for guiding his first steps in Franz Joseph's attitude towards Schwarzenberg. Time had made no difference to the confidence which he had in him, and although their relationship had gradually changed, he knew that he could always rely on him. Now that Schwarzenberg had died, Franz Joseph found himself alone, and this solitude frightened him. However, Franz Joseph soon recovered from this first reaction. As much as his first letter to Sophie had betrayed his distress, so did his letter to her of 14

April, nine days later, express his determination to control the empire single-handed: 'I must do more myself. From now on I cannot refer to somebody else as I did with Schwarzenberg, but this is not without its advantages.'[2]

In effect, nobody succeeded the dead man. He was of course replaced at the head of the empire's diplomatic service, by Count Karl Buol-Schauenstein who, after being posted to London, had been Austria's representative to Nicolas I from 1848 to 1851. The links which Buol had forged during his stay in Saint Petersburg certainly spoke in his favour. The new foreign minister also had the advantage of being well acquainted with Germany, another area of priority in Austrian foreign policy, for he had held many postings there before 1848 and had also been chosen to attend the Dresden conference. Although Schwarzenberg had intended him to succeed him, Buol had neither his predecessor's authority nor his charisma. In the role which he was destined to play, the main feature of his performance would be the loyal (and sometimes clumsy) execution of his sovereign's own policy, and he would have no say whatsoever in the processes of government.

Alexander Bach, the minister of the interior, had a stronger personality. Since he had succeeded Stadion he had become one of the central figures of the government. A brilliant Viennese barrister, he had been one of the pillars of the *Juridisch-Politischer Leseverein* during the final years of the *Vormärz* regime. The outbreak of revolution saw him in the front line and, with his liberal reputation to support him, he was included in Baron Wessenberg's government of July 1848. This appointment began the conversion which would gradually turn him into a servant of neo-absolutism. The break with democratic circles was confirmed when he rallied the *Reichstag* to the cause of the great landowners who were seeking compensation for the loss of part of their lands. After Schwarzenberg had asked him to remain in government, Bach supported the measures which one by one led to the re-establishment of absolutism in Austria. It seems very likely that Bach, like many members of the middle classes, had gradually been moved by the course of events to support authoritarian measures. Perhaps his behaviour can also be explained by his hope of achieving the unification of the administrative system, to which aim he had devoted himself since his arrival at the ministry of the interior. He actively supported Schwarzenberg's proposal to turn Austria into a single empire, believing that its multiple nature demanded a strongly centralized administration. He went so far as to suggest that 'the emperor would destroy his throne should he ever abandon this principle.'[3]

It was in the light of these opinions that he initiated a reorganization of the Austrian administrative system which had been made both possible and necessary by the abolition of the feudal system. This was a massive task and it made him, in certain respects, the father of the modern Austrian state. Equal to the task of reinforcing the political weight of the administration he had controlled since Vienna, Bach became the strongest minister in the government after Schwarzenberg's death, and such was his influence that the regime often bears his name.

On the other hand, the minister of the interior aroused strong opposition, and even enduring hatred. For the democrats, and those liberals who had not gone over to neo-absolutism, he was a complete renegade. At the other end of the spectrum, many members of the old aristocracy shunned him because they could not forgive him his past. These circles greatly resented his policies which were hostile to the traditional elite. By refusing to consider the great landowners as a special case which would have left them beyond the authority of the new administration, his policies demonstrated the desire of those in power to rid the aristocracy of its influence in local matters. Their interests were affected by the taming of the Diets. Bach's position as minister of the interior also made him responsible for agricultural reform and this fuelled the nobles' antipathy towards him. Finally, in the Magyar lands, Bach was certainly one of the least popular figures of neo-absolutist Austria. Its officials, who formed a tight network across Hungary, were called 'Bach's Hussars' by the Hungarians, which emphasized their role as the agents of the armed force which controlled the country.

Baron Karl von Bruck was another minister who was regarded with suspicion by the more conservative members of Austrian society. The son of a lower middle class Rhenish family, he became the founding president of the Austrian Lloyd in 1832 in Trieste, which concerned itself, as did the London office, with insurance, trade, and shipping, and he had already expressed his belief that the future would be dominated by large economic enterprises. With this in mind, he set out to turn Trieste into one of the major international trading centres, in its position of meeting point between northern and central Europe and the Mediterranean. Underlying this scheme was the idea of turning the *Zollverein* and the Austrian Empire into a vast integrated commercial unit. Although, as minister of commerce in Schwarzenberg's cabinet, he failed in his attempt to force Austria's entry into the *Zollverein*, at least the empire benefited from being turned into a single customs area.

After leaving the government in May 1851 Bruck did not remain absent from state matters for long. He was soon given the task of negotiating the 1853 commercial treaty with the *Zollverein* which, although all it achieved was the agreement of a slightly lower rate of duty between the two parties, had the merit, from Austria's point of view, of leaving open options for the future. The following year he was sent to Constantinople to represent his country, where he had the opportunity to consider the possibilities for an alliance between the Ottoman and Danubian empires. During the Crimean War he was recalled to serve as minister of finance with the task of reducing the budget deficit which in the course of the years had taken on alarming proportions, and had further grown under the weight of military spending in reaction to the international crisis. This task did not prevent him from initiating fresh reforms. Convinced that the monarchy's economic development would be stimulated by such enterprises, Bruck supported initiatives to strengthen the banking system and continued to express innovative views. An example of this can be found in his support for the proposed Suez canal which fitted in with his vision of a central European organization whose commercial influence would extend to the Near East and beyond.

The presence of Bruck in the government demonstrates the rise of the business classes. In this respect, neo-absolutism differed from the old administration. Certainly, Bruck's rise brought him enemies as well as friends, for the financier continued to be regarded with suspicion among the ranks of the old aristocracy, even when they admitted that he was a necessary evil. Like Bach, Bruck was also suspected of preserving liberal sympathies and, furthermore, the army would not forgive him the swingeing cuts he imposed in military spending in order to reduce the budget deficit.

Count Leo Thun, the minister for religion and education, came from an old Bohemian aristocratic family. He soon demonstrated concerns and assumed stances which marked him as a reforming conservative. During his early years, influenced by the two branches of Josephist tradition and the teachings of Bolzano the philosopher, he developed a conviction that the aristocracy had a social function to fulfil, and he expressed a Catholic confidence in the powers of human reason which made him receptive to concepts of progress. This confidence in man's capacity to improve himself explains his dominant interest in the improvement of the education system.

The revolution of 1848 pushed him to the forefront of the political stage. In April, the government sent him to Prague where he was to assist the young Archduke Franz Joseph in his duties as governor of Bohemia. Franz Joseph having finally gone to Italy instead, Leo Thun replaced his absent monarch. Espousing the Austro-Slav cause, he worked for an alliance between the nobility and the moderate wing of the Czech nationalists under Palacký and his son-in-law Rieger. He even went to the lengths of creating a Bohemian ministry at the end of May without consulting the Viennese government, in which representatives of the nobility and of the Czech middle classes sat side by side. However, the June revolution put an end to these efforts.

Relieved of his duties in July, Leo Thun spent a brief period in retirement which ended on 28 July 1849 when he entered Schwarzenberg's cabinet as minister for religion and education. He was to keep this portfolio for eleven years, during which time his name would became associated with the elaboration of the concordat and the remoulding of the school and university systems.

His participation in the government of this neo-absolutist period may appear surprising. Had he not made himself the champion of historical federalism, a role which fitted ill with the centralization policies of the regime? Although this was certainly the case, it seems likely that his reflections on the revolution during the year which he spent away from political affairs had led him to modify his position. Thun was also one of the generation of young noblemen who, realizing the state of stagnation to which the *Vormärz* regime had condemned the monarchy, had adopted a critical attitude towards it. He thus agreed to participate in an undertaking which took this same realization as its starting-point, and which intended to modernize Austria.

After the 1848 revolution, Leo Thun's outlook also moved closer to the views of the Catholic restoration which rejected Josephism and the traditon of the Enlightenment. The enthusiasm with which he negotiated the concordat and the understanding which he showed in this process for the Roman point of view are indications of the genuine nature of this change in his views. Because of this, certain liberals perceived him as a zealot.

Leo Thun did not, however, go so far as to break completely with Josephism. The reforms which he introduced in schools and universities demonstrate the enduring quality of their influence. The ideal which inspired his reform of the universities was the product of an enlightened conservatism. His aim was to make the Austrian universities the mainstay of a Catholicism which took account of scientific matters, and which could meet the challenge to liberalism.

The Bureaucracy

Beyond its striking individual features, the neo-absolutist state was founded on a number of bodies and institutions which were the traditional pillars of the European authoritarian regimes of the period. Supported by the bureaucracy, the army, and the Church, the neo-absolutist government considered itself to be in a position to oppose any renewed revolutionary attack.

With the measures taken by Maria Theresa and Joseph II towards centralization, an administrative apparatus had been set up in each member province of Austro-Bohemia which had even succeeded in penetrating the structure of individual domains. With the abolition of the feudal system a new state began. By replacing the feudal administration with a state apparatus, Bach's reforms obliged the already dwindling aristocratic estates to give way to the wealthy landowners, thereby ending a process which had begun a century earlier. Furthermore, Hungarian resistance had finally given way and the kingdom, which despite Joseph II's battering had managed to retain control of its administration, had been absorbed into the general system. As its influence grew at the edges of the monarchy, this expansion in the administration's role brought about an increase in the number of imperial officials, many of whom were recruited among the old employees of the local lords.

Strongly hierarchical in structure – there were no fewer than twelve grades – the bureaucracy was not a homogeneous unit. There was little common ground between the governor of a province or the chief of a ministerial department and a humble office scribe. This diversity did not, however, prevent certain shared characteristics.

The use of German was already a help in the unification of the Austrian administration. It was not uncommon to address those concerned in their own language, but German was the most suitable internal language of the administration, although its recruits were by no means all of German origin. For example, although the population assumed them to be Germans, Bach's Hungarian Hussars numbered many Czechs among their ranks. In this multinational empire, the common language acted as both a means of identification and of integration.

Loyalty to the crown and an awareness of the state were the prime virtues of this administration. This was all the more so because, following Joseph II's example, Franz Joseph set himself up as a model. It was soon a commonplace to describe him as the 'first administrator of the empire'. This rule of service to the state as represented by the emperor's person emphasized the effect of Josephist values on the administrative body, and they continued, clearly, to fulfil a dual purpose under neo-absolutist rule. On the one hand, their duty was to act as the agents of Franz Joseph's absolute will. This area of their service could sometimes involve acts of repression. But they also served the neo-absolutist principles of modernization and habitually saw themselves as the executors of policies for the improvement of society. Above all, the bureaucracy – and in this it was still a bastion of Josephism – was bound by both conviction and self-interest to the plan for a unified Austria to which it would remain loyal into the final days of the monarchy despite the changing course of events.

The Army

From the time of the *Vormärz* regime, the imperial army had been fighting the revolution on a number of fronts but only in locations beyond the empire's frontiers where the existence of the monarchy itself was not in question. In 1848 and 1849, on the other hand, the army was called upon to fight within the empire for the survival of the Habsburg lands. At a time when the other traditional supporters of the monarchy were absent or paralysed, the monarchy owed its success in overcoming these troubles to the loyalty of the army alone. Speaking to his men, Radetzky said: 'While everything was in flux around our august throne, you did not waver. As the waves of a tempestuous sea break on the rocks, so treason, perjury, and rebellion were broken on your noble breasts.'[4] These two years of fighting against the enemy within were to leave indelible marks on the military institution. Even more than before 1848 the Austrian officers considered themselves to be the soldiers of legitimate rule and of the counter-revolution. Their experience led them to believe that theirs was the only body which truly represented the unity of the monarchy. They concluded from the events of 1848 and 1849 that the army was the dynasty's final defence against forces working for Austria's downfall both within the empire and outside it.

This internal mission did not end with the suppression of the revolution. It now became the army's responsibility to protect the civil peace. The state of siege continued in Vienna, Graz, and Prague until September 1853; in Hungary and Lombardy-Venetia it did not end until May 1854, and it continued for several more months in Transylvania. This gradual relaxation of the state of siege did not bring the army's job within the empire to an end, as can be seen by the military detachment kept in Vienna to ensure that the city remained in a state of submission, for it was still suspected of harbouring dangerous temptations. Near the *Südbahnhof* (south station) a massive arsenal was built on a hill overlooking the town which was crisscrossed with a network of strategically placed barracks. As an additional measure, there were frequent military parades of the troops stationed in Vienna to remind everyone of the government's intention to suppress any tendency to disorder.

The privileged position of the army under the neo-absolutist state cannot be explained without alluding to the ties between it and Franz Joseph. The course of events after 1848 only confirmed in him the attachment which he had shown for the army from an early age. In particular, events had convinced him that it was the only institution not contaminated by the ferment of disintegration which attacked the monarchy as a whole. Because it had been the last defence of the House of Austria, he was inclined to look on the army as an essentially dynastic body. In other terms, his view of the relationship between army and sovereign remained a feudal one for the most part.

These ties were again in evidence during the years of neo-absolutism in which Franz Joseph elected personally to act as the commander-in-chief of the army. He exercised this authority through his military chancellery headed by Count Grünne, who was increasingly in his confidence. This department had continued to gain influence through the years until it had become the true decision-making centre.

This imperial guardianship of the army did not only have positive aspects.

Naturally, Franz Joseph wished to create an army which shared his own views. In this, his often quoted remark should be remembered: 'The value of my army lies not in its cultured officers, but in those possessed of courage and chivalry.'[5] It is too easy to mock at such a declaration, to see it as the proof that Franz Joseph encouraged obscurantism in his army. But this statement was really a manifestation of Franz Joseph's feudal attitudes which led him to consider the greatest value of the army to lie in loyalty to its sovereign. The Austrian officers were thus simply the modern successors of the knights of old who had fought for their lord. This view of the army acquired an unassailable moral virtue among its officers and future conflicts were to confirm that most of them subscribed to it. It was nevertheless questionable whether this ethic was enough to prepare the Austrian army for modern warfare in which the military art increasingly demanded the assimilation of the techniques of the industrial revolution.

Although he had proved his physical courage under fire, Franz Joseph had neither the experience nor the theoretical knowledge necessary to a commander-in-chief. His knowledge of war was confined to a few battles in which he had held no position of authority. His military education had led him to value good discipline on the parade ground, the neat execution of manoeuvres, and well-kept uniforms, but had provided him with no training for an overall military strategy.

Such ideas resulted in the Austrian army falling behind many of its European equivalents during these years, especially the Prussian army. There was little evolution in weaponry, and strategic studies were almost completely neglected. Certainly a few officers had been trained by Radetzky in the conduct of a campaign, but they were seldom to be found at court with Grünne. Radetzky, succumbing to old age, died in 1858, having been relieved of his Italian command a short time previously. His replacement was one of Grünne's protégés, Count Gyulai, who, although he had the advantage of youth, was not competent to command, as events would show. These deficiencies would turn out to be disastrous when the army came up against a foreign enemy, although they did not prevent the army from carrying out its duties within the empire.

The Church

The neo-absolutist regime also relied on the support of the Catholic Church. This was the culmination of a long process set in motion at the end of the eighteenth century by Joseph II who established the supremacy of the State over the Church and set out to liberate Austrian Catholicism from the yoke of baroque devotion.

Although still based on the principle of revelation, Josephism offered believers a religion which was very different from the forms which the expression of faith had taken in the Habsburg lands since the triumph of the Counter-Reformation. Josephism had been rejected in some Catholic circles whose members had taken advantage of the doubt shed on the teachings of the Enlightenment by the French Revolution, and had found a powerful instrument for communication in Father Hofbauer, the founder of the Austrian Order of Redemption, and in the Viennese Romantic movement. This movement put forward a programme of Catholic restoration as an alternative to Josephism, calling for the end of the subjugation of the Church and advocating a religion which combined the tradition of the counter-Reformation with Romantic soul-searching.

With the exception of the group headed by Anton Günther which had chosen to limit its thought to the theological field, but which would gradually slide towards a form of Catholic liberalism, the Catholic restoration rapidly assumed a counter-revolutionary character and proposed an alliance with the *Vormärz* regime in return for the abolition of Josephist legislation. Despite a small number of limited successes, it had not succeeded by 1848 in reversing the government's religious policies. Franz I was too respectful of the advantages of the existing system to have any wish to dismantle it, and the administrative bureaucracy remained broadly attached to Josephist principles.

The triumph of the counter-revolution at the end of 1848 strengthened the position of those Catholics who, like Monsignor Rauscher, hated liberalism and favoured an alliance with the absolutist government. It is likely that there could never have been a more favourable situation for the practical accomplishment of their theories. Their continued influence in Austrian society, especially in the country areas, recommended them to the government as a precious ally in its planned reconstruction of the monarchical order. The ecclesiastical hierarchy did not hesitate to exploit this argument in its attempts to obtain concessions from state officials, as Rauscher insisted: 'If the fight for grace and renewal is to succeed, the power of the spirit must unite with the power of the sword.'[6]

The programme outlined by the Austrian bishops in June 1849 presented a catalogue of extensive demands which called for nothing less than the total dismantling of the Josephist system. The bishops hoped that the Church would regain the freedom to organize itself according to its own rules and to direct its own affairs with no interference from the state. In the hope of establishing a direct link with Rome, they called for the abolition of the *placet* which, since Joseph II's reign had acted as an obstacle to their relations with the Holy See.

This proposal also involved the opening up of civil society to the Church's influence. In order to achieve this objective, it would be necessary to bring the marriage service into line with canon law. The organization of the education system was also a matter of concern for the bishops who wished the Church to gain control of primary education. Making it a rule that children should only be entrusted to teachers of irreproachable religious and moral beliefs, they asked for a right of veto over the selection of teachers.

The Church's demands were satisfied in two stages, first by the imperial commands of 18 and 23 April 1850, and then by the concordat of 18 August 1855. Franz Joseph was directly involved in these decisions. Not content with closely following the progress of events, he took a decisive role in the decision-making procedure. One example of this was his imposition on a reluctant government of Count Thun's proposals, which involved in particular the restoration of ecclesiastical courts of law and the abandoning of the *placet*. This proposal, and especially the arrangements for the re-establishment of direct links between the Austrian bishops and the Pope, had met with an unenthusiastic and sometimes frankly hostile reception from the ministers, who, with a typically Josephist reaction, feared that the loss of these prerogatives would harm the authority of the state. Finding himself alone against his colleagues – even Schwarzenberg expressed reservations – Thun at one point considered offering his resignation. In the face of this opposition, nothing less than the intervention of Franz Joseph could push through the legislation. But it was enough for him to pronounce himself to be in favour of Thun at the Council of 14 March 1850 for the matter to be decided. The orders of 18 and 23 April included the measures suggested by Thun, and it was also announced that the remaining questions would be decided in a concordat with the Pope.

Signed on 18 August 1855, the emperor's birthday, the concordat largely satisfied the demands of the episcopate. It handed over authority on matrimonial matters to the ecclesiastic courts and agreed to a reorganization of the education system according to the wishes of the bishops. The concordat made the Church responsible for primary education and ordered that only Catholic teachers would be allowed to teach in schools with Catholic pupils, and this proviso applied to most schools, given the distribution of religious groups across the empire.

The bishops were therefore justified their self-congratulation over the privileges which the concordat had bestowed on the Church, and Cardinal Schwarzenberg, archbishop of Prague, became their representative to Franz Joseph in the expression of their gratitude. Satisfaction was also the uppermost sentiment in the lay community: Metternich spoke for them when he hailed the concordat as 'the most important of contemporary events'.[7] Neo-absolutism thus conferred a freedom of action on the Church which had been denied it since the end of the eighteenth century. There was no question, however, of a separation between Church and State, for this was not desired by either partner. The state chose to stand down in favour of the Church in a certain number of areas, but it saw it as an ally which would unfailingly support its policies. For its own part, the Church recognized the state as the guarantor of its social influence. Their relationship was to be one of distinct powers with common interests.

The break with Josephism was nevertheless not complete. The choice of Rauscher as a negotiator for Austria in the concordat demonstrates this. It was certainly true that he was one of Franz Joseph's intimates who had been known and appreciated by the emperor since his student years, but it is still significant that Franz Joseph should have chosen a churchman to serve the interests of the Austrian state in the course of these negotiations. This choice showed that Josephism was still alive in the formulation of a treaty which was intended to announce its death sentence. The limits of the emancipation of the Church were set out in this decision.

Although the concordat was designed to free the Church from its restraints, Franz Joseph still saw the Church as his predecessors had done, as the servant of the state. For the rest, Rauscher honoured the confidence placed in him, and did not hesitate to oppose many of the Pope's suggestions which appeared to him to be exorbitant. In assuming this stance he demonstrated that Josephism had too profound an influence on the Austrian Church to be forgotten. It affected the bishops' conduct, for their desire for independence was tempered by loyalty to the crown which had developed in the traditions of the Counter-Reformation, and a century of Josephism.

The concordat was not, however, received with universal approval. Although the Catholics were generally satisfied, the liberal reaction was quite different. The liberals considered the concordat to be the unpardonable fault of a government influenced by aggressive clericalism. They were also indignant that such a transfer of power from the neo-absolutist government should be allowed to take place. Later, in describing his first reaction to the concordat, one of the liberals, Count Anton Auersperg, would declare to the *Reichsrat*: 'My patriotism revolted at this treaty which seemed to me to be another Canossa... by which nineteenth-century Austria threw out the Josephism of the eighteenth century.'[8] The constraints at that time imposed on free speech prevented the liberals from making any great show of their opposition. But, as soon as neo-absolutism gave way to a constitutional order, they would single out the concordat as one of the particular targets of their aggression, and would only drop it when it had been abolished.

The example of the concordat nevertheless demonstrated that although the neo-absolutist state could count on the loyalty of the forces which maintained it, it did not exist as a monolithic whole. Thus, Josephism remained a strong influence among the bureaucracy, and also among the members of the army. As a result, although the Church was delighted with a treaty which gave it a special position at the heart of society, there were many who deplored it. These Josephist conservatives feared above all that the state in giving way to the pressures of the ecclesiastical hierarchy had allowed a serious blow to be inflicted on its authority. Summing up their feelings, Count Hartig suggested that 'it would have been difficult to conclude a more fatal treaty.'[9]

These differences were not without their consequences. Once Austria had entered the constitutional era, they would lead to a division among the forces on which neo-absolutism had depended. For the time being, though, they did not have any serious results and though the concordat was ill-received among some sectors of the administration and the army, this reaction did not go an further than a few displays of bad humour, most of which took place in private. These divergent views of religious policy nevertheless give us a different perspective of the relations between the various pillars of the regime.

These relations had their tensions. The civil administration and the army shared a feeling of annoyance at the growing power of the Church. The members of the army were also harshly critical of the bureaucracy, party as a result of the mistrust in which they held the whole of civil society, but also because of the interventions of the administration in areas which they considered to come under their sole authority. For example, many army officers deplored the gradual lifting of the state of siege which resulted in, among other things, a reduction in the influence of the military. In the field, relations between Bach's Hussars and the army were often far from cordial.

These frictions were nevertheless insufficient to threaten the neo-absolutist regime. On the contrary, this combination of different powers, each with its own sphere of influence, supported and helped the structuring of Austrian society, and it remained effective for as long as it could avoid the test of an economic crisis or any major challenge from another nation.

Policies of Centralization and Nationalities

During these years, the neo-absolutist state extended its hold over society and systematized the centralized regime. The patent of 17 March 1849 which gave autonomy to local groups, from the *Kreis* or circle to the commune, had only begun to be applied in a timid fashion with the election of the municipal councils. After the return to absolute rule, these councils were held under close surveillance and the political authorities began to limit their power.

There was less hope than ever that there could be elected local assemblies. Although the statutes for certain areas were enlarged by the minister of the interior, they remained effective on paper only. Provinces, *Kreise*, and districts certainly still existed, but only as administrative divisions. These years were instead marked by the reinforcement of government control. The patent which had established the independence of legal procedures and introduced the jury system was revoked. Once this had been achieved, the government held the entire judicial hierarchy under its control.

At the same time, the process of centralization continued and Hungary became increasingly integrated into the single empire. There, as in the other lands of the monarchy, German was the language of the administration. Hungary was also subjected to the common rule and was divided up into *Kreise* and districts with no regard for its old administrative structure. The territories which had become independent from Hungary received no better treatment. The rigour of the policy of centralization did not spare the Croats whose regiments under Jellačić had helped to save the empire. In its turn, Croatia was divided into districts which were directly responsible to the Viennese ministerial departments. In view of this state of affairs, it seems that the Hungarians had reason to say to the Croats: 'What we have been given as punishment you have been given as a reward.'

The educational policies of the neo-absolutist state were also inclined towards centralization. There too, a uniform system was applied to the whole empire. The growing role of the German language favoured this phenomenon, although there was no question of a deliberate policy of Germanization. In the Josephist tradition, the neo-absolutist state wished to be supranational. The preference given to German was not intended to serve the interests of a particular Austrian people, but was a matter of reason and expediency. The unity of the empire required that each subject should have at least the rudiments of one of the empire's common languages in addition to his or her own tongue. Although primary schooling was usually given in the mother tongue, there were changes even at this level. The number of 'mixed schools' in which the vernacular and German were both used was growing. Furthermore, the influence of German was growing in the secondary schools where it was becoming an obligatory subject, and where it was often the language of teaching even in the non-German countries of the monarchy. Finally, the process of Germanization extended to higher education. Only the universities of Lombardy-Venetia escaped this process.

Although the government had no intention of favouring any one of the empire's nationalities it was hard for the non-German ones not to suspect it of harbouring such a secret aim. The discontent remained underground, as the military and police forces which patrolled the monarchy not only prevented any unrest but also suppressed any organized expression of opinion. In addition, the repressive measures which had followed the victory of the counter-revolution had either dispersed or put out of action the groups which could have led such an opposition. To cap this, the revolutionary upheaval was still too close for people's minds to have recovered from its trauma. It should also be mentioned that among the middle classes, and not only in the Germanic countries, there were many who were grateful to the regime for the restoration of peace and the period of prosperity which it seemed to herald.

Hungary avoided this temptation. Here, the few government supporters were isolated in the midst of a hostile population. The Hungarians did not forgive the neo-absolutist government for having dismantled the Kingdom of Saint Stephen in the face of all their historical rights, and for having imposed laws and an administrative system which were alien to what remained of their country. Certainly, as was the case elsewhere, the revolutionary opposition was disorganized, and the resistance therefore took a passive form, but it extended throughout the country, and during the whole of this period the central government had no success in establishing itself. The government's choice of a policy of force, which was supported by Franz Joseph, only brought about the appearance of a solution. The chances of a reconciliation had not, however, disappeared. Although Kossuth's name had taken on mythical proportions, many Hungarians rejected his extremism and, like Baron Eötvös who was one of Tocqueville's disciples, or Ferenc Deák, the nation's sage, they remained receptive to a compromise which would guarantee Hungarian rights while respecting the necessities of Austrian power. The time was not yet ripe, though, and Franz Joseph would have to face many crises before he came round to supporting this viewpoint.

The Libenyi Assassination Attempt

The feelings of rancour directed at Austria which had build up in Hungary could have led to a brutal end to Franz Joseph's reign. He was the victim of an assassination attempt on 18 February 1853, while walking along the ramparts of the old town of Vienna in the sole company of one of his aides, Count O'Donell. It was only through luck that Franz Joseph survived, for a woman, on seeing a man armed with a knife advancing towards a senior officer, cried out. This led Franz Joseph to turn round in the act of leaning over to watch some soldiers exercise on the ground at the foot of the ramparts. It was this movement which saved him and the blow intended for his back struck his neck which was protected by the collar of his coat and the edge of his cap. Prevented from striking again by Count O'Donell, his assailant was finally overcome with the help of passers-by who had been alerted by the cries.

The assassin turned out to be a young Hungarian, a member of the guild of tailors called Janos Libenyi. As one of Kossuth's supporters he wished to strike down the man he held responsible for his country's misfortunes. In the moments which immediately followed the assassination attempt it appeared possible that he had succeeded in his aim for the wound was bleeding freely and suggested the worst. However, on examination, the wound turned out to be more impressive than it was deep. Although the incident turned out in the end to be less serious than it had at first appeared, Franz Joseph was nevertheless confined to his bed for several weeks.

The initial emotional effect which this attempt on Franz Joseph's life had on the population was to bring him a popularity which he had not enjoyed since coming to the throne, for his subjects blamed him for the constraints imposed on them, especially in the areas which were under military control. In addition, Franz Joseph had often given the appearance of a stiffness which was disliked, especially among the Viennese who had been accustomed by his grandfather and even poor Ferdinand I, to greater friendliness in their emperor. Under the emotion of the moment, these grievances tended to disappear, if only temporarily.

One of the monuments of imperial Vienna preserves the memory of the Libenyi assassination attempt. This is the *Votivkirche* which today stands near the university. The originator of the idea to construct a church in thanksgiving for the divine protection of the emperor's life was his brother Ferdinand Max. After Franz Joseph had agreed, the foundation stone, which was brought from the cave on the Mount of Olives, was laid on 26 April 1856. In the history of Austrian architecture this building marked the beginning of a new era. The work of Heinrich Ferstel, it was the first official building to be constructed in the neo-gothic style. Furthermore, it served to consecrate the rise of the 'historic style' which would soon inspire the architects of the *Ring*.

Franz Joseph's Sentimental Education

Although it almost began with tragedy, 1853 ended with the jubilation of Franz Joseph's engagement. As was common among the royal families of the time, his education in gallantry was not neglected. Count Grünne, it was whispered, was given the responsibility of supplying him with 'clean mistresses'. But for Franz Joseph these years were also those of his emotional education.

Very soon after the emperor's return from Olmütz the great aristocrats returned to their palaces in Vienna and, with this return, life at court was resumed. Indeed, it took on a vigour which had been lacking during the previous reign. Although this was due in part to the relief felt at the return of order after the revolutionary upheaval, it was also due to the youth of the new sovereign. Franz Joseph regularly attended the balls and entertainments which animated the life of the court. Buttoned into his fine officer's uniform, he drew all eyes and more than one young lady's heart secretly beat faster for this emperor who had the features and figure of a Prince Charming.

Matters were likely to become more serious when Franz Joseph apparently fell in love with one of his cousins, Archduchess Elisabeth, who was the daughter of Archduke Joseph, the previous Palatine of Hungary. His feelings were not in doubt. What other conclusion should be drawn from the morning walks of the two young people in the Prater? The loving looks which Franz Joseph bestowed on his cousin seemed to be a declaration.

This love was not, however, favoured by Sophie and a marriage between the cousins was hard to imagine. The emperor should traditionally marry a foreign princess, and matters were made worse because Elisabeth belonged to a branch of the family which was in semi-disgrace. Her father had already displayed a sympathy for Hungary in the exercise of his functions as Palatine which he would continue to hold to the day of his death. Then, in 1848, his brother the Archduke Stephen had espoused the Hungarian cause. Certainly, in attempting to act as mediator between Austria and Hungary, he had not believed himself to be failing in his duty of loyalty towards the emperor, but his actions resulted in his banishment. Had there been any need, this sympathy for the Magyar cause would have been enough to discredit Elisabeth in Sophie's eyes, and the emperor's mother intervened with her usual spirit of firmness. Taking advantage of the absence of Franz Joseph from Vienna, Sophie paid a visit to Elisabeth during which she commanded her to marry at the earliest possible moment, and the young girl believed this to be on the emperor's own orders. On his return, Franz Joseph discovered that his cousin had left Vienna. Shortly afterwards in his role as head of the family he was called upon to give his consent to the marriage of Elisabeth and the Archduke Ferdinand Karl. The culminating irony of the situation was the letter of congratulations which it was his duty to send the couple!

The Meeting with Elisabeth

That Franz Joseph should have given way without protest demonstrated the hold which his mother still had over him. He may have reigned as emperor of Austria by the grace of God and been one of the most powerful of rulers, but he still remained an obedient son.

The preparatory phase of plans for his engagement confirmed this. It was Sophie who directed the search for a German princess. This choice corresponded with one of the basic principles of Austrian diplomatic policy. After the Olmütz and Dresden conferences, the Austrian desire to become the first power in Germany not only continued but increased in strength. The restoration of the German Confederacy provided it with a legal basis for this aspiration. A marriage with a German princess would have the advantage of reinforcing this position of dominance.

To this end, the archduchess set her personal network of contacts into motion, and this extended into the German courts, thanks mainly to the positions of several of her sisters. She would have preferred an alliance with Prussia which would have provided the official confirmation of the reconciliation between Vienna and Berlin while also confirming that Austria held the upper hand. Despite the assistance of her sister Elise, who was Friedrich Wilhelm IV's wife, the project soon failed. Such a union did not enter into the plans of the Prussian government who, scenting the trap, had no intention of binding their country to Austria. Sophie also undertook some discreet enquiries at the Dresden court where she could count on the support of the queen, her sister Maria. The links between Austria and Saxony, one of the traditional German allies of the Habsburg monarchy, favoured such an event. But Princess Sidonia was considered by Franz Joseph to be too unattractive.

Thanks to her sister Ludovica who had married Duke Max in Bavaria, Sophie had no difficulty in proposing an alternative. The bride destined for Franz Joseph was his cousin Helena, the eldest daughter of the duke and duchess. It would certainly be a less prestigious marriage than the others which had been considered. The duke's family was only a secondary branch of the Wittelsbach dynasty, and Helena's parents lived as retired a life as possible, away from the Munich court. Sophie nevertheless hoped that this marriage, although it was a modest one for an emperor of Austria, would create closer ties between Bavaria and the empire, and would thus strengthen Vienna's position in southern Germany.

Sophie could rely on the active support of Ludovica in the achievement of this aim, as she was delighted at the prospect of marrying her eldest daughter to the emperor of Austria. She was fully aware that Helena had the necessary qualities for an empress. The eldest of five girls, she was naturally expected to make the best marriage. Because of this her mother had been careful to provide her with an excellent education, at least in terms of what aristocratic society expected of a young girl. Her natural seriousness and her firm Catholic faith spoke in her favour. They made it likely that she would have both the moral and intellectual capabilities to carry out the duties which would befall her if she were to share Franz Joseph's future. Helena would nevertheless have to accustom herself to a very different way of life from that which she had led with her family. Her parents both hated the constraints of protocol and etiquette. It was for this reason that they were often far from court on their Possenhofen estate on the shores of the Starnberger See, where they could live in freedom and simplicity according to their tastes.

Sophie and Ludovica together devised a scheme which would lead to the engagement. Franz Joseph's birthday on 18 August was an ideal excuse to have a family reunion at Ischl. At the end of this stay, the official announcement of the two young people's engagement would be made. But a small matter, to which nobody paid any attention at the time, was to upset the plans made by the two sisters. In order to distract her from her first love affair, Ludovica decided to bring Elisabeth, Helena's younger sister with her, whom the whole family called by her nickname, Sissi. Once in the company of his cousins, Franz Joseph only had eyes for Sissi. Although he was perfectly aware of the reason for this meeting, Helena's half-stiff, half-awkward air made no impression on him. Elisabeth was probably no more comfortable than her sister, but her entire future did not hang on a few hours, and above all, she had a freshness which fascinated Franz Joseph. Barely grown to maturity, Elisabeth at fifteen was at that uncertain age which had not yet shaken off the final ties of childhood. With her long plaits, she was graceful in a childlike fashion, but it was precisely this guileless charm which bewitched Franz Joseph.

Franz Joseph made no attempt to conceal his feelings. Sophie's diary reports the words with which he immediately expressed his enthusiasm to his mother: 'How delicious Sissi is...She is as fresh as an almond which springs from its shell, and her face is framed by such a splendid crown of hair! She has such beautiful gentle eyes! And her lips are like strawberries!'[10] If any doubts remained as to his intentions, the events at the ball attended by the young people removed them. It was with Sissi that he chose to dance, leaving poor Helena with no other choice than to accept matters with good grace. It was to Sissi that he gave a bouquet. On the next day, which was his birthday, he hastened to order his mother to discover what Sissi's feelings were. He probably took care that she should not feel pressured, adding: 'My responsibilities are so great that God knows that it could not be a pleasure to share them with me.'[11]

These scruples were to Franz Joseph's credit but what choice did Sissi have but to agree to the Austrian emperor's proposal? Her reaction did show, however, to what extent she was overcome by the course of events: 'How could he consider me?' she asked, 'I am so insignificant!'[12] But her main feeling was one of anxiety: 'I like the emperor so much, but if only he were not emperor!'[13]

The tears which were abundantly shed by Sissi during her stay at Ischl were not only tears of happiness; they must also have contained distress when confronted by a future for which she was vaguely aware that she had received no preparation. How could she have done so? Her education had not been conducted in the expectation of so elevated a future. Until that time her life had been free of the constraints of court life, protected by her youth and her parents' choice. Her tastes and dreams were those of a romantic adolescent, with a love of nature and solitude, and inclined to melancholy.

It is therefore hardly surprising that Elisabeth was distraught. Many young ladies of her rank would have felt as lost as she did had they found themselves in her position, but it was part of the nature of their position that they might be called to such a future. Most did manage, however, to overcome this moment of crisis and to adapt to their new identities. Elisabeth's tragedy was not that she experienced this moment of disarray, but that she never subsequently managed to assume the role which this change in her circumstances demanded of her.

The Wedding

Eight months passed between the engagement and the wedding, during which time Franz Joseph visited Sissi in Munich three times. Although Elisabeth's feelings continued to be divided between pleasure and doubt, Franz Joseph was unequivocally happy. The test of these early separations only strengthened his love, as he confided to his mother: 'I could never thank you enough for having given me such happiness. Each day I love Sissi more and become more convinced that nobody could suit me better than she.'[14]

This delay also served to make up for lost time and to prepare Elisabeth for her future duties as empress. In the course of a few months, she was taught French and the history of her new country. To teach her this, a knowledgeable Magyar, Count Johann Mailath, was called on, and despite his absolute loyalty to the Habsburgs, he tended to favour the Hungarian point of view in his teaching, and this was to influence his pupil. Sissi was also familiarized with the rules of conduct and the subtleties of Viennese court protocol.

Also during this time certain official arrangements were made. Among them was the marriage contract under which Elisabeth would receive the sum of 150,000 florins, of which a third would be given by her father and two-thirds by Franz Joseph. The latter would also provide her with an annual income of 100,000 florins, and in addition it was understood that he would cover her everyday expenses. The young bride's trousseau also had to be prepared, filling twenty-five trunks, and which, although it may appear to have been large, was in fact quite modest by Austrian aristocratic standards, especially when we remember that most of her jewels were gifts from Franz Joseph or Sophie. During this period, the archduchess concerned herself with the preparation of the apartment in the Hofburg allocated to the young couple.

The date of the wedding was fixed for 24 April. It was decided that Elisabeth would travel to Vienna along the Danube. She would thus have the opportunity to see some of the beautiful scenery of her new country, but, more importantly, she would be seen by all the new subjects who would hasten to acclaim her. It was at Linz, where her fiancé welcomed Elisabeth, that she had her first contact with Austria and also a foretaste of the duties which would be a part of any future journey across the empire. That evening in a town lit up in her honour, she would have to divide her time between a theatre visit, a torchlight procession, and a choral concert. On the following day the triumphal procession to Vienna was resumed, but without

Franz Joseph who had returned to the capital to welcome his fiancée. For the whole length of the journey she was obliged to be on display to the crowd which had collected along the river banks, without ever betraying her weariness.

But she finally arrived at Nussdorf from where she was to continue her journey to Schönbrunn by carriage. Hübner described the scene in his *Memoirs*:

> No sooner had the steamboat reached the quay than the young emperor ran towards his young wife-to-be, meeting her on the gangway where he embraced her *coram populo*. The princess, who was tall and slender and had a majestic carriage and classical features, and yet who was still a young girl, immediately won all hearts. There were groups of peasants on the banks but few members of the court or society. A sweet and joyful emotion was to be seen on every face. Each spectator seemed to feel himself the brother or cousin of the imperial couple.[15]

Elisabeth's official duties did not end with her arrival in Vienna. At Schönbrunn she was presented to the various members of the imperial family and then to the high dignitaries of the court. After this, she was then obliged to attend a gala dinner. On the following day, Sunday 23 April, she made her solemn entry into Vienna, accompanied by the ringing of all the capital's church bells and drawn by eight Lippizaner horses.

The eve of Sissi's wedding thus arrived, after four tiring days which had been a sore test to her nerves. From her first moment in Austria she realized that she no longer had a private identity. Knowing herself the object of all eyes, she had to assume expressions, smile at will, meet new people, learn to follow a timetable, change her toilette many times a day, and she had to do all this while assailed with moments of worry and self-doubt at the approach of an event which would mark a complete break in her personal lifestyle.

After all these preliminaries, the wedding was finally celebrated by Cardinal Rauscher in the late afternoon of 24 April in the Augustinian church. Once the religious ceremony was over, the husband and wife had not finished their official duties. On their return to the Hofburg it was the turn of the diplomatic corps to be presented to the empress, and the young couple were then congratulated by the court dignitaries and ladies.

For Elisabeth the torture was not yet over, she was now expected to direct the conversation of the circle of ladies who had collected around her. As she had no experience of this sort of situation, she appeared gauche, and this increased her embarrassment. At last the official part of the day ended, but the couple were still unable to be alone. Archduchess Sophie accompanied her son into the nuptial chamber where Elisabeth had been put to bed in her mother's presence:

> Louise and I accompanied the young bride to her chamber. I left her with her mother and settled myself in the small room next to the bedroom until she had been put to bed, upon which I went in search of my son and brought him to his young wife's side, whom I found, on saying goodnight to her, with her pretty face surrounded by a profusion of fine hair buried in a pillow, as a frightened bird hides in its nest.[16]

This scene should not be judged by modern standards. Sophie in no way sought to subject her daughter-in-law to a further ordeal. Nor did she have any intention of humiliating her. Furthermore, this ceremony was far more simple that the ritual still followed in several European courts. Now that the emperor and empress were no longer in their official roles, events became a matter for the family. Far from intending to persecute her, it is likely that Sophie thought that Elisabeth would feel secure with her mother and mother-in-law nearby as the consummation of the marriage drew near. But, whatever her intentions, the ceremony must certainly have wounded Elisabeth's sensibilities.

The Modernization of Austria

The town which Elisabeth had just discovered still had its traditional appearance, which was described by Gérard de Nerval on his stay in Vienna in 1840: 'One travels through extensive suburbs with identical houses; then, in the middle of a ring of walks, surrounded by ditches and walls, one finally comes to the city, barely the size of a Paris *quartier*.'[17] There was much talk at the time of demolishing the ramparts which surrounded the old town. These fortifications had long since lost all military value. If this were done, the neo-absolutist government could hope to construct major roads through them along which it would be simple to bring cannon should there be a riot. Construction on part of the surrounding land would also help to ease the housing crisis, which was already acute in a town which had been the destination of a large proportion of the empire's internal migratory movement.

These arguments were not altogether sufficient to explain Franz Joseph's decision to demolish the ramparts which was announced in the Declaration of 20 December 1857. This plan met with strong opposition in some military circles in which it was feared that this measure would be of greater benefit to the revolutionaries than to the authorities. As for the settlement of the housing crisis, the allocation of this land could only be a sop. Reserved for wealthy clients, the luxury apartments which were to be built in these new areas would not be accessible to the population of the suburbs. Franz Joseph's decision was mainly a result of his desire to turn Vienna into the metropolis of the unified empire of neo-absolutist dreams. The realization of this ambition required the razing of the ramparts which held the city in a grip which prevented its physical development. Once this obstacle had been removed it would be possible to initiate a programme of urban rebuilding and embellishment in Vienna which would raise it to the level of the other great metropolises, London and Paris.

The Declaration of 20 December 1857 announced the construction of a series of edifices intended to house the cultural institutions necessary to a great metropolis: an opera house, archives, libraries, galleries, and museums. The great circular boulevard which was to become the *Ringstrasse* which surrounded the old city was part of the same plan. It was intended to represent the prestige of Austria's renewed grandeur. The demolition work began immediately. This area was turned into an immense building-site for nearly twenty years. Vienna's new face took shape only very gradually. But the impetus had been given and this choice became a symbol, for it illustrated the policies of modernization which were one of the features of neo-absolutism.

The Austrian economy entered a period of growth during these years, and was a further manifestation of this policy of modernization. Economic development figured among the priorities of the neo-absolutist government, and although this was in any case in line with one of the main tendencies of the age, the government also hoped that material progress would distract the middle classes from the old political temptations and would consolidate the coalition of the wealthy on which it wished to form the sociological base of the regime. Nor did it escape its notice that economic power was one of the means to political power. Finally, the government hoped that by favouring material interests, this new era could lead Franz Joseph's subjects away from nationalist influences.

Economic speculation benefited from a period of expansion from 1849 to 1857 serving neo-absolutist aims. But although it was part of a favourable international situation, this growth was also the result of a deliberate policy. The regime here chose a course of economic liberalism which contrasted with its political inclinations. The government first opted in favour of free trade, a move consecrated by the abolition of interior customs duties and the creation of a common commercial market, and it then began the reduction of international tariffs for Germany. It also opened up agriculture to the influence of market forces and gradually introduced economic freedom. Another aspect of this policy was the Declaration of 14 September 1854 which gave private firms the task of constructing and running the railway system.

This decision to support economic liberalism did not mean that the state deprived itself of all powers of intervention and control. It introduced, for example, agricultural reforms which served to liberate the forces of production, and although the reforms first affected the countryside they had an effect on all areas of the economy. Their first result was to transform the legal relationships between the landowning nobility and the peasants and farmers, although attitudes did not change so quickly. With the transfer of lands from the old lords to the peasants, yesterday's tenants became today's landowners in their own right.

This change did not benefit all peasants to the same extent, and it would often accentuate the social differences which already existed in the Austrian agricultural world before 1848. It certainly contributed to the growth of a class of wealthy farmers which became a centre for development in the heart of the rural areas. The abolition of the *Robot* also acted as a factor in the evolution of agricultural practices. Whereas the lords had previously had the use of very cheap labour which was nevertheless not an effective labour force, the great landowners now employed salaried agricultural workers. Although the financial outlay was greater, the return for money was greatly increased by this change.

The great landowners were the other beneficiaries of the reform, despite appearances and the alarmist predictions of some of those concerned. It is true that the lesser nobles who drew most of their income from their lands were seriously affected by this change. Some minor nobles were even plunged into a situation of pecuniary distress. But the aristocracy only really suffered from the loss of its power which it had preserved until 1848, and which allowed it to assert itself in the countryside. This was a matter of rank and not of fortune, for in economic terms the agricultural reforms tended to consolidate the power of the aristocracy and speeded up the process of the transformation of the great estates into profit-making organizations.

The substitution of salaried labour for the *Robot* partly explains this. But it was also due to the sums of money paid to the great landowners in exchange for the loss of part of their lands. These compensatory sums were considerable. In Bohemia, Moravia, and Silesia alone they totalled 72,250,000 florins divided among 1,912 people. Far from going out of circulation, this capital often went towards the modernization of the estates and increased their orientation towards a speculative form of agricultural production. This tendency led many large developments to create production units which included both agricultural and industrial elements. The development of sugar beet production and of the distilling industry in Bohemia and Moravia illustrates this.

The growth of these industries was only one aspect of Austrian industrial development in the 1850s. This development first occurred in areas directly associated with the industrial revolution and the growth of an effective system of transport, such as the textile and iron and steel industries. The state invested in the construction of the railway system: it was concerned, for instance, with the great programme of engineering works which overcame the technical challenge of the Semmering Pass and thus made the link between Vienna and Trieste possible. Its involvement was increased following the Declaration of 14 September 1854. Nevertheless, as much as a fifth of private investment was absorbed by railway construction.

The nobility was also involved in the development of transport and industry, investing in them a portion of the money it had gained through the agricultural reforms. But it did not have a monopoly in any branch of industry. Middle-class families also invested money, and some, such as the Hornbostels and the Schoellers, themselves developed into real dynasties. By contrast, the financial power of the aristocracy gradually declined, though they did retain control over some food industries.

This economic development occurred at the same time as an increasing diversification of the Austrian banking system. The traditional savings banks were joined by lending banks which aimed to participate in the financing of the economic development. Created in 1855, the largest of these was the *Österreichische Credit-Anstalt für Handel und Gewerbe* (the Austrian Institute of Credit for Trade and Industry). The composition of the governing board illustrated the practical alliance which had been formed between the more dynamic members of the aristocracy and the upper echelons of the bourgeoisie. The *Credit-Anstalt* elected Prince Johann Adolf Schwarzenberg, head of the senior branch of the illustrious Bohemian aristocratic family, as its president. He was assisted in his task by other great scions of the nobility, Prince Vinzenz Auersperg, Prince Max Egon zu Fürstenberg, and Count Otto Chotek. These sat on the board with representatives of international finance such as Anselm Rothschild and Louis von Haber and prominent industrialists such as Theodor Hornbostel and Alexander Schoeller.

This economic development was not, it is true, beneficial to all producers or to all areas. There was already a tendency towards specialization in the agricultural sector where for many small farmers the pleasure of becoming landholders did not last. Their lands lay below the threshold of profitability and many of them soon entered the spiral of mounting debt. At the end of this process they would have no other choice than to sell their lands, swelling the ranks of paid farm labourers, unless they succumbed to the dreams of the city or chose to emigrate.

This phenomenon of concentration also hit the industrial sector hard. Particularly vulnerable were the textile industries in which a part of production had until now been supplied by small artisans. These now often found themselves powerless to resist the competition of the larger enterprises which could afford to buy machines and thus benefit from mass production. A similar disparity could be observed on a regional basis. The centres for industrial development were only to be found in certain areas: the north of Bohemia, Moravia, in urban areas such as Vienna and Prague, and in the alpine valley of Styria. The rest of the empire presented a strong contrast, often verging on underdevelopment.

These disparities explain why, despite the indisputable economic expansion of this period, Austria did not manage to catch up with the countries of western Europe, after having fallen behind during the first half of the century. It continued to occupy the middle position between the industrial west and the underdeveloped east. While areas such as the north of Bohemia were comparable with western Europe, the stagnating economies of Galicia, Bukovina, Transylvania, and even certain parts of Hungary, already made them part of eastern Europe.

The rejuvenation of the university system, carried out by Leo Thun, was another manifestation of the government's programme of modernization. This reform had been made necessary by the failure of the *Vormärz* policies for higher education. The delay in development which had occurred during these years, especially in comparison with the German universities, was the result of a desire to isolate the Austrian intelligentsia from foreign influence. It was also the consequence of the decision that the main aim of the universities should be to produce docile servants of the state. As a result, the universities found themselves muzzled in both their internal organization and in the choice of the subjects to be taught.

Rather than closing in on itself, it was important for the new university to have openness and freedom as its guiding principles. If the elite was kept in an intellectual ghetto, it would be unable to face up to new ideas, especially those of liberalism. It was necessary to open up the universities to the outside world, to bring them into contact with the great currents of thought of the times. Freedom seemed to be the indispensable corollary of this opening up: based on the German model, the Austrian universities were set up as autonomous bodies with their own systems of administration, and the course of studies also recognized the right of the teachers to make their own decisions as to what they would teach their classes.

Although the German university system served as a model for Thun, he did not wish to reproduce it in every detail. The university which he hoped to create in Austria must be Catholic and conservative. It would be the vehicle for a conservative way of thinking which took its inspiration from Catholicism and which would free the Austrian state from the hold of Josephism while leaving it in a position to resist liberalism.

In order to carry out this programme Thun required Franz Joseph's support because there was substantial opposition to it. Many of the universities looked with mistrust on reforms which obliged them to change their habits. In government circles further criticisms were raised, especially at the heart of the *Reichsrat* where the old *Vormärz* officials had difficulty in accepting a system which introduced the principle of freedom into the institution of the university. Certain Catholics went so far as to suspect Thun of seeking to deliver Austrian higher education into the hands of liberalism, under the pretext that he was following the example of Prussia.

Although Thun succeeded in overcoming this opposition, his child was not wholly obedient to his will. Despite his efforts, he did not succeed in turning the Austrian universities into a bastion of Catholicism. The liberalism against which he sought to erect a barrier would firmly establish itself within them. However, Thun's work can be appreciated on other grounds, for it was to survive him and would make of him the founder of the modern Austrian university system. In particular, the credit for raising Austrian universities to an international standard falls to him. After him, the great universities of the empire, Vienna, Prague, and Budapest, would either become or resume their position as centres of European culture.

The Eastern Crisis

Although by the middle of the decade Franz Joseph could observe that Austria had begun the task of rebuilding internal affairs, the international situation was to cause him serious difficulties. The monarchy was naturally concerned by the Eastern crisis which exploded in 1853 and dominated the international scene until the Paris Congress of 1856.

As international tension grew, Franz Joseph became more preoccupied with the Eastern question. The main lines of a policy to deal with this situation could be found in his inheritance from Metternich. The old chancellor had taught him that Austria's interest, as well as the balance of power in Europe, demanded respect for the integrity of the Ottoman Empire. To permit a challenge to it would open up the Balkans to Russian interference and would sooner or later end in a confrontation between Russia and Austria. Following the liberation of Greece, Metternich had contrived to dissuade Russia from expanding in this area. To support this new direction in Russian politics a close alliance had been agreed between the two empires which had been confirmed by Nicolas I's response to Franz Joseph's call for help in Hungary.

But this Russian Intervention in Hungary created a new situation. Now that Austria was tied to Russia through a debt of gratitude, how could the Austrian government oppose the reopening of the Eastern question? Such was Nicolas I's reasoning when he suggested to Franz Joseph that they share the spoils of the Ottoman Empire.

This caused Franz Joseph a bad crisis of conscience. He knew what the monarchy owed to Russia and he himself continued to favour an alliance between the two empires in the sake of conservative interests. But on the other hand, Austria was not prepared to be associated with a policy which went against its own principal interests. The division of the Balkans into areas of foreign influence would end, it seemed, in the creation of satellite nation-states in the Russian zone which would owe allegiance to Saint Petersburg. Franz Joseph feared that the Slavs living in the southern part of the monarchy would follow this lead and that a separatist movement would grow up.

Franz Joseph was also obliged to bear in mind the relationships of the great powers. A Russian offensive towards the Straits would encounter opposition from Britain, and probably from France as well, for the latter's interests in the Mediterranean would be directly threatened by such a move. By siding with Russia, the monarchy would therefore lay itself open to conflict with these two powers. In such a situation Austria would have to look to its Italian possessions, for it was likely that Napoleon III would not hesitate to use the weapon of Italian nationalism to weaken Austria. Hungary might also be in danger, for in the person of Kossuth, Britain and France held a card which they might be tempted to play in order to destabilize the Habsburg monarchy.

Guessing that the two empires would sooner or later come into confrontation in the Balkans, Schwarzenberg had already made the nature of any future decision known when he confided that 'We shall surprise the world with our ingratitude.' Caught between the duty of gratitude and the essential interests of the monarchy, Franz Joseph did not hesitate for long.

Having shied away from Nicolas I's offer, Franz Joseph at first sought to dissuade him from a policy of expansion in the Balkans, but as events progressed he quickly realized that the Tsar paid no attention to his arguments. In July 1853, Russian troops occupied the Danubian principalities of Moldavia and Valachia. But the Ottoman throne, supported by Britain and France, refused to recognize the *fait accompli* and declared war on Russia. When in reply to the destruction of the Ottoman fleet at Sinopoli, a Franco-British squadron passed through the Dardanelles and entered the Black Sea, the conflict appeared certain to escalate to international proportions.

At this time, the tone of the exchanges between Franz Joseph and Nicolas I gradually became less friendly. Both of the two partners clung to his position while still hoping to bring the other round to his own view. The risk that Britain and France might enter the war increased Russia's desire to make Austria declare its position. Franz Joseph, however, saw the threat of international involvement in the fight as an additional reason not to take sides. Not satisfied with giving advice, on 7 January 1854 he intimated to the Tsar that he would encounter Austrian opposition should be continue in his policies, writing to him: 'As for the political relations of Turkey's European provinces, you will remember, dear friend, that I have frequently explained to you both in writing and orally that the emancipation of these countries would affect both our interests. I repeat to you therefore that I could never consent to it, for the reasons which I have already given you.'[18]

In the face of this broadening of the conflict, Austria could have chosen to remain strictly neutral. The government seemed to take this course when on 20 April 1854 it concluded a treaty of alliance with Prussia, thereby forming, with their partners in the German Confederation, a bloc of states at the heart of Europe which, by remaining aloof from both sides, retained the possibility of acting diplomatically to resolve the crisis. It became rapidly clear, though, that Vienna saw this alliance simply as a hostile gesture towards Russia.

This development in Austrian policy was supported by a group which, although it also rejected the idea that the Ottoman Empire should be left alone, supported a confrontation with Saint Petersburg. Its members believed that the monarchy should take advantage of Russia's difficulties to gain a dominant position in the Balkans. This group included many of the major figures of the regime: Count Buol, the foreign minister, Bach, the minister of the interior, Baron Hübner who served Austria at Napoleon III's court, and Baron Prokesch von Osten, Schwarzenberg's ambassador in Berlin who was now in Frankfurt.

As head of the Austrian diplomatic service, Buol was best placed to attempt to guide Franz Joseph's decisions, for each foreign minister had set his own mark on the diplomatic service he directed. Buol hoped that he could persuade his sovereign to declare war on Russia, a measure which Franz Joseph was only prepared to take in the last resort. Despite Buol's influence, Franz Joseph was the true instigator of the monarchy's policies in the Eastern crisis, and Buol merely executed his orders. Diplomacy was one of the chief areas to be controlled directly by the emperor and it would be unthinkable for Buol to authorize any significant action which had not previously received Franz Joseph's agreement.

Franz Joseph's decisions were the result of his conviction that in Eastern affairs 'Russia has always been our natural enemy.'[19] As a result, he made it his objective 'to reduce Russia's power and influence to the limits which they have been allowed to exceed only because of past weakness and differences'.[20] This analysis and this aim dictated the policies of the monarchy. On 3 July 1854 Vienna called on the Russian government to withdraw its troops from the principalities. When, to avoid fighting on two fronts, Russia decided to comply, the Austrian army which had assembled on its eastern frontiers occupied Moldavia and Wallachia, while French and British troops besieged Sebastopol in the Crimea.

This intervention provides an intimation of Austria's inner motivations. For the monarchy, this was not merely question of containing Russia. Although the occupation of the principalities took place with Istanbul's agreement, it became clear that the empire's former policy of non-intervention in Ottoman affairs no longer applied. Austria would not be unhappy to keep these territories for itself. From an objective point of view, in the short term, Vienna's occupation of the principalities served the interests of the two naval powers by tying up a portion of the Russian armed force. The next state in the growth of hostilities was the eventual decision by Austria to join forces with France and Britain. In response to Russia's rejection of the plans to resolve the crisis submitted by the three powers, which were intended to bring a halt to Russian expansion in the Balkans and which proposed a number of guarantees which would prevent its resumption, the monarchy signed a treaty with France and Britain on 2 December 1854 of which the logical result would be Austria's own entry into the hostilities. The empire was not obliged to act on the full implications of its about-face, for the fall of Sebastopol and the death of Nicolas I brought an end to the conflict before Austria was obliged to honour its side of the treaty.

There are many ways of judging Franz Joseph's policies. We can give Austria the credit for having saved Europe from a general conflagration, for had Austria sided with Russia, Napoleon III might have attempted to strike in Italy or on the Rhine. On the other hand, had the monarchy joined in the fighting on Britain and France's side, new fronts would have opened up in the principalities and possibly in Galicia. The complex nature of European interests would have brought about a chain of events leading to general conflict. This questions which had been raised in 1815 and 1848 would inevitably have risen to the surface once more, for each country perceived this war as a means of changing the balance of power to its own advantage and to settle old scores.

Austria did not end its neutrality but it underwent a change in character in the course of these months. This change gives rise to a different evaluation of Austrian policy. It must be admitted that the situation was less favourable at the end of this war than Franz Joseph had hoped. The Paris Congress of 1856 which was the political conclusion of this conflict did not recognize Austria's right to the principalities on the Danube. Indeed, although these provinces continued to belong in theory to the Ottoman Empire, the process leading to Romanian independence had begun.

But the most important result of this crisis was Austria's serious diplomatic isolation. By drawing closer to France, the Austrian government had hoped to protect its Italian possession, but Franz Joseph's delaying had annoyed Napoleon III and Austria soon became aware of the error in its calculations. Far from being grateful for the indirect help it had provided, the French emperor decided to concern himself with Piedmont and Sardinia, which had sent a token expeditionary force to the Crimea, and drew up a plan with Cavour for the reorganization of Italy in which Austria would have no part.

Austria therefore did not win in the west what it had lost in the east, for the decisions which its government had made during this crisis had a serious effect on its relations with Russia which considered its attitude to be an act of betrayal. Nicolas I had felt this behaviour to be a personal insult. He had arranged for the removal of Franz Joseph's portrait from his office and had freely described himself as another idiot who like Jean Sobieski, having saved Vienna, was rewarded only with ingratitude. Later attempts to restore the agreement between the two powers did not succeed in dissipating the mistrust which had now entered their relationship. Russia would never forgive Austria for its behaviour in the Crimean War which had struck a fatal blow to the relationship between Vienna and Saint Petersburg. Austria and Russia now entered an era of rivalry which, despite a few periods of respite, would continue to grow until the explosion of 1914. Austria could no longer expect either understanding or support from Russia in the execution of its affairs.

In Germany the Crimean War reawakened the differences between Austria and Prussia. The Prussian government did not appreciate Vienna's attempt to turn the alliance of 1854 into a weapon against Russia. Prussia would only have followed Austria's lead in this in return for substantial concessions giving Prussia equal status in Germany. As Franz Joseph was not prepared to pay for advances in the south-east with a retreat in Germany, Prussia refused to provide the expected support, reinforced in this by most of the German states, many of whose princes had family ties to the Romanovs.

The Crimean War thus changed the balance of power within the German Confederation. Austria's prestige was weakened and Prussia's moral credit grew. For its part, Russia was grateful to Prussia for the position of loyal neutrality which it maintained throughout the conflict, despite the various approaches which were made to its government. It was further grateful because Prussia had held Austria back from interventionist policies. Prussia could now rely on the prospective help of a Russia ready to use Germany to avenge Austria's betrayal. Thus the Crimean War led to the creation of a Berlin–Saint Petersburg axis which Bismarck would later reinforce and exploit to further his policies. In short, at the end of the Eastern crisis, the diplomatic situation was not very favourable to Franz Joseph's Austria.

Married Life

While the international horizon was filling with clouds, it might be possible for Franz Joseph's happiness in his married life to provide him with the necessary serenity to preserve his emotional state of mind in the face of these difficulties. For Franz Joseph, these years were certainly the happiest period of his marriage. He was clearly deeply in love, and Sissi displayed the same feelings. There is much evidence for this. There were of course the three children which she gave him, two girls, Sophie in 1855 and Gisela in 1856, and a son, Rudolf, in 1858. It could, of course, be the case that she was merely fulfilling her role as empress in producing heirs, with no question of love. But during this period, the young emperor received other irrefutable proofs of Sissi's love. It was for love of him that she forced herself to overcome her timidity and dislike of the court at the beginning of their marriage, and assumed the position assigned to her in the Austrian court hierarchy. That she did not succeed in this does not necessarily mean that she did not try. Elisabeth gave Franz Joseph further proof of her love for him in accompanying him to Lombardy-Venetia in 1857. This journey was not only of considerable importance for the emperor, it would also involve constant dangers because of the tense atmosphere which still reigned in this region. Despite an impressive military and police escort, the possibility of an assassination attempt or of hostile demonstrations could not be ruled out. In spite of these dangers, Elisabeth remained publicly at Franz Joseph's side for the entire journey and, moreover, she brought her presence and charm to bear during the imperial couple's subsequent visit to Hungary, another sensitive Habsburg possession.

There were certainly other journeys undertaken by the pair which were more untroubled and traditional, such as that which took Franz Joseph and Elisabeth to Styria and Carinthia in September 1856, on which they made no attempt to conceal their pleasure in each other's company. This was increased by the marked predilection which they shared for the mountain countries through which they travelled. Far from court, and thus partly excused from the regulations of protocol, surrounded by unsophisticated people and magnificent scenery, Elisabeth was able to imagine that she breathed the same air as that of Possenhofen.

Nevertheless the seeds of the crisis which broke at the beginning of the 1860s were already present, although Franz Joseph did not detect them. Despite her attempts to overcome her lack of ease with the court system, and to adapt herself to her restricted role, Elisabeth never managed to fit into a world which remained foreign to her. She could not suppress her belief that she was an exile in Vienna. Her poems, as the representation of her innermost feelings, are very clear in this respect. The poems which she wrote during the first weeks of her marriage reveal a surprising melancholy in a bride who should have been at the height of her happiness. She constantly returns in them to her memories of Bavaria and of Possenhofen, and more seriously, this nostalgia is associated with a loss of freedom:

> Would that I had never left the path
> which would have led me to freedom.
>
> I awakened in a cage
> with my hands bound.
> And my nostalgia increased all the time.
> And Liberty! You have turned your back on me.[21]

Along with the love which she felt for her husband, Elisabeth experienced a feeling of unease. This raised a question mark over what would happen when their love no longer burned with its first passion and when habit came to dominate their married life. Far from disappearing, this tension was to harden, verging on obsession, to the point of a total and irreversible rejection of the court system.

This problem was exacerbated by the state of isolation in which Elisabeth found herself. Without necessarily blaming Franz Joseph for it, she did not find in him the necessary support to enable her to overcome this difficult situation. From the first day of their marriage, Franz Joseph re-immersed himself in affairs of state. Unfortunately, the first two years of their marriage coincided with the Eastern crisis which took up much of the time which the emperor would, in other circumstances, have devoted to Elisabeth. This applied even during their honeymoon, which was spent at Laxenburg castle, a short distance from Vienna. Early each morning, Franz Joseph would go into Vienna to deal with matters in the East, and Elisabeth, left on her own, fell prey to boredom.

But the worst problem for Elisabeth in the absence of her husband was that she was subject to the surveillance and domination of the Archduchess Sophie who had accompanied the couple to Laxenburg. The conflict which was to divide the two women developed from this time. Whether it was caused by her shyness, her modesty, or her deepest convictions, the main source of suffering for Elisabeth was the loss of her liberty. She wished to make only the most necessary concessions to court life and to maintain a personal freedom over which she had total control. Sophie's priorities were quite different, for she believed that it was an essential part of monarchical power for the sovereigns to be enveloped in a prestige which separated them from the rest of society. Furthermore, in her opinion, this position could only be achieved by a scrupulous respect for protocol and etiquette which would add to the majesty of the imperial couple. Because of this it did not even occur to her that Elisabeth might shrink from her duties. However, aware of her daughter-in-law's upbringing, she knew that Elisabeth was not familiar with the subtleties of the Austrian monarchical system and wished to guide her until such obligations became second nature to her. Far from accepting this supervision, Elisabeth resented it painfully, and she suffered from being constantly corrected when her behaviour failed to conform to the rules of protocol. As a result, she developed an obsessive dislike of Sophie.

The conflict had its source in the conviction of each of the protagonists that she was in the right. Elisabeth clung to her impossible dream and in effect refused to assume her responsibilities as an adult. Because her private life had to take second place to the requirements of her position, an Austrian empress did not have the right to her own identity. The monarchy needed a dutiful sovereign, not a dreamy young girl. Because this was such an important matter, Sophie felt that she had the right to take on Elisabeth's education in order to turn her into an empress who would be aware of her responsibilities.

Elisabeth resented her mother-in-law's interventions, considering them to be unfair and unbearable harassments. Some of Sophie's actions were assaults on those things which Elisabeth held most dear. For instance, when Sophie decided to remove the parrots which had followed Elisabeth from Possenhofen from her room, considering them to be inappropriate to the dignity of the Austrian empress, Elisabeth must have been deeply wounded. This represented a further example of the extent to which Sophie chose to assume an authority over the smallest of details in her daughter-in-law's life, but, above all, the birds had been a reminder of Elisabeth's native Bavaria and had provided a link with her childhood. Her opposition had not yet reached the stage of open revolt, but the constant ill health from which she suffered, even when she was not pregnant, can also be seen as symptoms of an inner unhappiness.

The situation between mother-in-law and daughter-in-law deteriorated a little further with Sophie's decision, when her first granddaughter was born, that she would be brought up under her guidance. The following year, Gisela joined her elder sister in the rooms which Sophie had furnished for them above the imperial apartments. It is possible that Sophie might have taken this step because she thought that Elisabeth would not have time to give her children sufficient attention. Alternatively, she might have felt that her daughter-in-law did not have the maturity necessary for their upbringing.

Whatever the reasons for this decision, it provoked Elisabeth into fighting for the right to look after her children, and pushed Franz Joseph to decide in her favour. On this occasion, for the first time, he took his wife's part. Until now, although he had not displayed the same severity as his mother towards Elisabeth, inclining more towards indulgence under the influence of his love for her, his own training made him unlikely to share her point of view. The product of Sophie's school of thought, he believed the principle that sovereigns should suppress their own personalities in favour of their position, and the constraints imposed on him by protocol had long since become second nature.

But this new conflict arose on different ground. There was no article of protocol which dictated that the emperor's mother should assume the right to bring up the children of the imperial couple. Realizing how much this choice wounded Elisabeth's maternal sentiments, Franz Joseph could decide this time in favour of natural feelings. But he did not do so without hesitation as he had no wish to offend his mother. In order to bring himself to take sides in this dispute he needed the spur of the journey to Styria and Carinthia which took him away from the court, and during which the understanding between husband and wife was obvious to all.

This victory was short-lived, however, as a tragic event occurred which threw it into question. Elisabeth had decided to take her little daughter Sophie with her on the imperial couple's trip to Italy where they were to stay throughout the winter of 1857. Because this absence would last many months Elisabeth refused to be separated from her daughter for so long. Of course her mother-in-law had warned her against the exhausting effects which the travelling would have on the little girl, but these objections were only another reason for Elisabeth to uphold her decision.

The Italian journey took place without any harm to the child's health, but soon after their arrival in Hungary she was taken ill, and despite the reassuring diagnosis of the doctors, her health became rapidly worse. The letters and telegrams from Hungary became increasingly alarming, and finally on 29 May 1857 Franz Joseph telegraphed the fatal news to his family: 'Our daughter is with the angels. After a long struggle she finally gave up her soul in peace. We are overcome with grief.'[22] This sudden death had a lasting effect on the couple. Many months later, Franz

Joseph wrote to his mother: 'Poor Sissi is shaken up by all the memories which assault her everywhere here [Vienna] and she cries a lot. Yesterday, when Gisela sat down on the poor little girl's chair in my study, we wept together.'[23] It was probably Elisabeth who was most deeply affected by the death of the young Sophie. After this loss she gave up the fight against her mother-in-law. Her behaviour suggests that she was overwhelmed with doubts. Turning in on herself, she gave herself up to sadness and appeared to take no interest in the fate of Gisela. For as long as she had fought for the right to look after her children she had not limited herself to a mother's role and showed herself willing to enter into that required of her by her position as empress. Her sudden capitulation suggests that she now renounced even this. The trauma which the younger Sophie's death provoked thus acted as a break-off point for Elisabeth, and which itself anticipated the crisis which would break in the early 1860s. The following year brought confirmation of this, when she made no attempt to claim her newborn son, the Archduke Rudolf.

This birth was nevertheless an important event. Franz Joseph obviously loved his two daughters, but in giving birth to Rudolf, Elisabeth provided him with an heir. The birth of the young archduke was followed by some significant decisions. The choice of his name was meaningful, referring back to his illustrious ancestor who during the great interregnum was the first of the Habsburgs to wear the crown of the Holy Roman Empire. Through this choice, Franz Joseph asserted Austria's intentions to remain true to its undertakings in German matters.

Franz Joseph bestowed gifts of great political significance on his infant son. While still a puling infant Rudolf became a knight of the Order of the Golden Fleece. Even more important, on the day following his birth he received an infantry regiment, along with the rank of colonel. Through this unusual gesture – he himself had not received a regiment until he was thirteen – Franz Joseph intended to strengthen the bond between the army and his dynasty. It was also a recognition of the privileged position of the military in the neo-absolutist state. The dispatch in which Franz Joseph made his decision known left no doubts on this score: 'I wish for the son who has been given to me through the grace of God to belong from his entry into the world to my gallant army. Accordingly, I name him Colonel of my 19th Infantry Regiment of the line which, from this day on, will bear the name of "Crown Prince".'[24]

From Plombières to Villafranca

The birth took place, however, at a time when the finest days of the neo-absolutist era were over. Due to the Eastern crisis, a portion of the army remained mobilized for several long months, in readiness for action, and this aggravated the budget deficit which had now reached enormous proportions. Hoping to reduce the public debt, the government had set up a loan scheme in 1854 which raised 500 million florins. This operation ended in success, but most of the money was diverted from its intended destination and absorbed into military spending. The crowning misfortune was that this crisis in the public accounts coincided with the period of general economic depression which hit Europe from 1857 onwards. These difficulties provoked a current of discontent among the ranks of the middle classes who had been prepared to adapt themselves to the regime for as long as it was benefiting them materially, but who now found themselves strongly inclined to criticized it. In addition, the international horizon was continuing to darken.

The Italian front threatened to flare up again in the near future. The problem for Austria lay not only in conspiracies, which were quickly suppressed, but in the lack of any popular power base in Lombardy-Venetia. Although the peasantry generally remained untouched by nationalistic fervour, an overwhelming majority of the rest of society was hostile to Austria and looked instead to Piedmont for their salvation.

Through a series of political gestures, Franz Joseph had tried hard to rectify the situation. In 1854, the state of siege was raised. Three years later, the imperial couple visited the monarchy's Italian possessions. Franz Joseph hoped that his presence would revive the loyalty of the inhabitants and this journey was further accompanied by conciliatory measures. An amnesty for political prisoners and exiles was announced, and in the cases where the offenders' goods had been forfeit, these were returned to them. Finally, when Marshal Radetzky succumbed to his advanced years and was relieved of his command, civil and military affairs, which until that time had come under a single administration, were made separate and Franz Joseph appointed his brother Ferdinand Max to be the head of the administration of Lombardy-Venetia. He hoped that this choice would be read by the Italians as a sign of his desire to improve relations between Vienna and his Italian subjects.

Franz Joseph did not, however, gain the results he had hoped for from his journey. The reception of the imperial couple remained cold and the upper ranks of society kept away from the ceremonies which they were invited to attend. Nor did the people respond to Franz Joseph's overtures. In short, after this visit, as before, Austria continued to feel itself to be an enemy camped on the soil of Lombardy-Venetia. Ferdinand Max was not slow to realize this and differences of opinion soon appeared between the two brothers. When Ferdinand Max suggested that Lombardy-Venetia should be given a statute of autonomy, Franz Joseph was quick to reprimand him.

Franz Joseph might perhaps have been able to look on the future without disquiet had the Kingdom of Piedmont-Sardinia not been reinforcing its power and increasing its international standing under the direction of Cavour, who had been first minister since 1852. Strengthened by its successes, Piedmont gradually replaced other possible rallying points for the unification of the peninsula in the minds of the Italians, and became the hope of the inhabitants of Lombardy-Venetia who dreamed of driving Austria out of their country. Yet, in spite of the gains made through Cavour's policies, what could he do against the power of Austria if he was obliged to face the empire alone?

But what Cavour had learned from the events of 1848–9 was that a policy based on the slogan of *Italia fara da se* would inevitably end in failure for the Italian movement. To be able to withstand the trials of a conflict with Austria, Piedmont would have to rely on the support of another of the great European powers. Cavour was not long in realizing that such an alliance could only exist with France. In addition to the geographical advantages, he was well aware of Napoleon III's sympathies for the Italian cause, and above all, of the French emperor's desire to dismantle the treaties of 1815 which, sooner or later, would bring him into conflict with Austria as the traditional champion of legitimate rule in Europe. Cavour paved the way by sending an expeditionary force to the Crimea which, although its role in the fighting was only a minor one, was enough to give Piedmont the right to take part in the Paris Congress. Napoleon III was not ungrateful, and he showed this in his support for Cavour when the latter wished to raise the Italian question in front of this great assembly of the European powers.

This diplomatic support had not yet gained the status of a military alliance. The decisive step was taken when Napoleon III and Cavour met on 20 and 21 July 1858 in the little Vosgian resort of Plombières. In the course of their excursions, the two men came reached agreement on a plan for French military intervention in Piedmont's favour should the latter be the victim of Austrian aggression. Should they be victorious, the two states were agreed on the reorganization of Italy as a whole. In the north, Piedmont would extend its borders to include Lombardy and Venetia; central Italy would form a kingdom under Prince Napoleon Jerome; and in the south the Kingdom of Naples would be taken away from the Bourbons and given over to Prince Murat. The Italian states would then be united at the heart of a federation with the Pope as its president.

This plan was intended to end in the expulsion of Austria from Italy. Vienna would not only lose its possessions there, but also all its other bases of influence. While the Kingdom of Naples would escape Austrian influence, the lesser branches of the Habsburg family would be driven out of the central Italian duchies. Of course Cavour was obliged to agree to a number of conditions to obtain Napoleon III's promise of military support. Not only did he have to concede Nice and Savoy, he also had to accept the principle of the establishment of a dominant French influence in Italy, in particular through the two Napoleonic supporters in central Italy and Naples. These conditions meant that such a plan would not further the cause of Italian unification to Piedmont's advantage, should it ever be implemented. Cavour hoped that events would take quite a different turn, and in any case was prepared to manipulate them to deviate from the course set at Plombières.

Following the conclusion of this agreement, relations between Austria and France began to deteriorate. On 1 January 1859, at the formal reception for the diplomatic corps, Napoleon confirmed this deterioration officially through his remarks to Hübner: 'I am sorry that our relations are not as good as I would like them to be, but I beg you to write to Vienna that my feelings for the emperor are the same as they have always been.'[25]

In Vienna, there was much indignation against Napoleon III. The members of the Viennese administration saw him as the leader of the revolution in Europe, or thought him to be its pawn. Although Hübner advised them not to push the French emperor into a permanent alliance with Cavour, Franz Joseph and Buol chose a policy of intransigence which they were convinced would suffice to discourage him from persisting in his plans. They were, furthermore, certain that they could rely on the support of Prussia and the German Confederation should there be an armed conflict, despite the fact that the Prussian officials had been careful to remind Vienna that Berlin was not obliged to give military help if an attack took place outside Confederation territory, as was the case in Lombardy-Venetia. But Franz Joseph was not willing to believe that Prussia would leave Austria to face French aggression alone.

Taking into account the terms of the Plombières agreement, it remained for

Cavour to provoke Austria to the point where the empire would act as the aggressor. Such a 'fine little act of aggression' as Napoleon Jerome hoped for, would serve to remove Napoleon III's hesitations. Following his spectacular trip at the beginning of the year the French ruler now seemed to prefer a diplomatic resolution to the problem. To this end, he proposed a European congress which would meet to discuss a reorganization of Italy. This move annoyed Cavour, as Piedmont could not hope to gain as much as it would through a military victory. As for Austria, it displayed no enthusiasm for the proposal, surmising that it would have to defend itself before such an assembly. Even if the empire managed to restrict the effects of any concessions it was obliged to make, it would still come out of such a meeting in a weakened position.

Austria's aim was instead to make use of the crisis to inflict a searing lesson on Piedmont which would leave the smaller country in no state to be a threat for some time. In the face of the aggravation of tension, both states had begun to mass troops along their borders. Vienna opened by announcing that it would not participate in any congress until Piedmont had withdrawn its troops. This warning shot turned out to be insufficient, and Buol persuaded Franz Joseph to take more extreme measures. On 19 April, he made the decision to send Piedmont an ultimatum declaring that if Piedmont did not disarm, Austria would consider itself to be at war.

The military, with Grünne at their head, objected in vain that it was imperative that a general mobilization order must precede the issuing of the ultimatum. If they were going to be effective in forcing Turin to bend the knee and submit, Austria would have to make a true demonstration of its strength and declare that it was prepared to make use of it if necessary.

Confident in the assurances of his foreign minister, Franz Joseph paid no need to these arguments. Buol contrived to convince him that Piedmont would have no choice but to give in. Although Prussia was only bound to help Austria on Confederation soil, Franz Joseph was sure of its support in a conflict and expected that Napoleon III would advise Cavour to give in rather than face war with all of Germany, and would abandon Piedmont, which would then be obliged to concede.

The illusions on which this policy was founded were soon dispelled. In the space of a few days, Franz Joseph was forced to realize the consequences of his errors. Far from giving way to panic, Cavour was delighted by the announcement of the ultimatum. The condition for French support was fulfilled, as the ultimatum placed Piedmont in the position of the threatened party. Cavour could therefore reject Vienna's demands without fear that he would lose Napoleon III's support. Austria was now harvesting the fruits of its lack of foresight and was obliged to endure the opprobrium of being the agressor both in the eyes of the European governments and in public opinion.

For Vienna, the price of this was an increase in isolation. The British government, which until now had been inclined to favour Austria in opposition to French ambitions in Italy, expressed its disapproval. There was certainly a degree of hypocrisy in some reactions. The Prussian rulers must certainly have been incensed at having been presented once again with a *fait accompli* by Austria, but neither Wilhelm, the Prince Regent who acted for his ailing brother Friedrich Wilhelm IV, nor his government were inclined to take Prussia to war alongside Austria, and this move provided them with the excuse they required to withdraw their support.

This war was interpreted by Franz Joseph as a new episode in the fight between good and evil. The states which he was challenging were for him the perpetrators of a threat to European order. As it had done constantly since 1789, France represented the hearth of the fires of the revolution. As for the French emperor, Franz Joseph judged him harshly. Without mincing his words, he baldly described him 'a scoundrel'.[26] In Franz Joseph's eyes, Napoleon III did not limit his activities to helping Piedmont but curried favour with the heads of European subversion. In order to strike at Austria with greater effect, he did not hesitate to play Kossuth as a card, promising him his help if he could induce Hungary to rise. At the heels of the Italian army Garibaldi played a similar role to that of Kossuth, and Franz Joseph certainly did not see him as an Italian patriot, but rather as a dark adventurer committed to the cause of anarchy.

In the manifesto in which he set out his motivations and his version of events for his subjects, Franz Joseph was careful to emphasize that he also acted on Germany's behalf. Despite the rebuffs to which he had already been subjected, he did not despair of forcing Prussia to take up arms by arousing German nationalist feelings in support of Austria.

Because of its belief that Piedmont would bow to its will, the monarchy had not made proper military preparations. Owing to the nature of its opponents, it seemed imperative to adopt a plan of campaign which exploited the delay between the official opening of hostilities and the arrival of the French army on the battlefield. After crushing the Piedmont army, the Austrians would then bring down the French. If, instead, they were to allow the enemy to join forces, then they would be in difficulties. Because Franz Joseph had failed to order a general mobilization before issuing his ultimatum, he had partly lost this advantage.

A further problem for Austria lay in the mediocrity of the high command. The generalissimo, Count Gyulai, owed his position more to influence than merit and he was not long in demonstrating his incompetence. When reinforcements arrived he made no attempt to derive any benefit from his numerical advantage and once the enemy had joined forces he made the decision to fall back across the Ticino river. On 4 June he was defeated at Magenta, and four days later, Napoleon III and Victor Emmanuel II made their triumphant entry to Milan.

By the defeat at Magenta, Austria had not only lost Lombardy. The whole system of control on which its domination of Italy depended seemed to be crumbling. One after the other, the ruling families of central Italy were thrown out by the revolution, but despite this series of setbacks, Franz Joseph was still not prepared to give up the fight, as can be seen by the measures which he took in the immediate aftermath of Magenta. Having relieved Gyulai of his command he decided to take over the supreme command of the armies himself. It is easy to imagine that he had long dreamed of command, given the fascination which military life had always held for him, and the special attention which he had always given to the army. But this spectacular move was above all intended to make it clear that he was determined not to give up in the face of adversity. He also wished to inspire confidence in his men who could easily have been demoralized by defeat. Knowing themselves to be commanded by the emperor in person, the men would be heartened and regain their taste for victory.

Franz Joseph was not blind to the winning hand held by the enemy, as can be seen in a letter to his mother: 'Our situation is assuredly a difficult one. We are up against a gallant enemy of superior numbers, which is prepared to resort to any means, and is allied to the revolution which provides it with new strength.'[27] This final allusion was a direct reference to the Hungarian legion which Kossuth had been allowed to put together and which Napoleon III was now preparing to launch against Austria from the rear, with the intention of bringing about an uprising in Hungary. Franz Joseph nevertheless believed that it was possible to reverse the tide of events. Although the Austrian army had been beaten at Magenta, it had not been crushed. It had retreated in good order and, once rested, would be in a condition to resume the fight. Nor did he dismiss the possibility that Prussia with the rest of Germany in its wake, might finally decide to emerge from its state of uncertainty and follow its duty: 'I hope', he added, 'that Germany and its bastard Prussians will perhaps support us at the last moment.'[28] His violence of expression nevertheless indicates that even though he might still wish to believe that Berlin would change its mind, he was already gripped by doubts. It also demonstrates the extent of his bitterness at Prussia's behaviour which for him almost amounted to a betrayal.

During these weeks in which the fate of Austria's presence in Italy was at stake, Franz Joseph was not relieved of domestic worries. He was plagued by letters from Elisabeth begging him to allow her to join him. Since he had left for Italy she had in fact been left on her own, without support among the court, in surroundings which she had come to loathe. In order to escape this suffocating atmosphere she hoped to join her husband in Italy. Franz Joseph set himself to explain to her that however painful their separation might be, he could not grant this request. The empress had no place with the army. Furthermore, she could be of more help to him if she remained in Vienna where, rather than cut herself off from society, she should appear in public to encourage the people's spirit which might have been shaken by the news of the defeat at Magenta. Franz Joseph also exhorted her in a letter from Verona to pull herself together and fill the role which fell to her:

> You must stay at your post, where, in these difficult times, you can be of so much help through your presence and that of the children. I beg you, in the name of the love which you have vowed to me, pull yourself together, appear in the town sometimes, visit institutions. You cannot know how helpful you can be to me by doing this. It will revive morale among the Viennese and will keep up the good feeling which I need so badly.[29]

A few days later, Franz Joseph wrote to her of his satisfaction with her behaviour: 'I have already heard from Vienna of the excellent impression which you more frequent appearances have made, and of the way in which you revive everybody's spirits and strengthen every one of them.'[30] Elisabeth was far less accommodating when it came to the question of her health. The slimming diet which she forced herself to follow and her habit of cutting down on her sleep caused Franz Joseph further worries at a time when he should have been giving all his concentration to the outcome of the war: 'Sort yourself out for love of me,' he wrote on 15 June, 'get enough sleep and eat enough so you don't get too thin.'[31] That he returned to this topic, three weeks later, seems to indicate that his pleas had not been heard: 'The hateful habits', he wrote, 'which you have grown accustomed to and which can only destroy your beloved health, leave me in complete despair. I beseech you, give up this way of life immediately and sleep at night, for nature intended the night to be devoted to sleep, not to reading and writing.'[32]

When Franz Joseph wrote this letter, the war was close to its end. On the evening of 26 June, following a scene of great carnage, the Austrian army suffered a second defeat at Solferino. It was certainly not destroyed. In two great masses, the enemy armies had faced each other, without any planned strategy on either side. But the retreat of the Austrian army following the battle allowed the French and Piedmont forces, despite the heavy losses they had suffered, to claim a victory which Franz Joseph had in any case no thought of disputing. He immediately notified Elisabeth of this defeat: 'It is the sad tale of a terrible day in which much was achieved, but during the course of which fortune did not smile on us. I am richer by many experiences and I have discovered how a defeated general feels.'[33] This new failure shook Franz Joseph's morale. Not only did it make him question his own abilities, it also darkened the immediate future even further. Richard Metternich, son of the old chancellor whose recent death had saved him from the pain of knowing of this defeat, summed up the feelings of many when he wrote: 'Only a miracle can save us now.'[34]

Nevertheless, even after Solferino, Franz Joseph did not give up the hope of turning the tide of war. The Austrian army had fallen back to the Quadrilateral, and to force them out would be a perilous task for their opponents, themselves weakened by war. Also, the picture of the conflict could still change if Prussia decided to answer Austria's call. The calculated delay on the part of the Prussian rulers must have angered Franz Joseph, but he was not prepared to declare himself defeated without having tried, one last time, to persuade them to give up their neutrality. To this end, Franz Joseph sent the ageing Marshal Windischgraetz to Berlin. It may have cost him something to have to fall back on his services for this last ditch mission. But, because of his past, Windischgraetz's name also had symbolic value. More than any other, it could illustrate Franz Joseph's reading of this war. Who better than this hero of the counter-revolution to bring the Prussian government to a realization of the true import of this conflict which once more brought the forces of legitimate rule face to face with those of the revolution? If Windischgraetz managed to persuade them of the importance of what was at stake, Franz Joseph believed that Prussia would no longer be able to refuse to support the Austrian army, especially as there was now a risk that it would succumb to the blows which France and Piedmont inflicted on it. Furthermore, in the tradition of Metternich's policies, Windischgraetz had always declared himself to be a strong defender of a close alliance between Austria and Prussia.

These arguments, which were both ideological and emotional, were not enough to gain the support of the Prussian leaders. The Prince Regent was not immune to the appeal for conservative solidarity against the revolution, but his first concern was to protect Prussian interests. For him, there was no question of accepting a solution in which Prussia would help Austria to restore its influence in Italy without any gains in return. He looked for such compensation in Germany. As a security measure he had already assembled two army divisions on the bank of the Rhine, but he had no intention of going any further unless Austria first offered him concessions.

Whether Prussia demanded control of the body of the Confederation's non-Austrian forces, or whether it was prepared to content itself with a system in which it shared command with Austria, its conditions were stiff. Such conditions would in fact be irreconcilable with the preservation of Austrian supremacy in Germany. Franz Joseph now knew that he could only hope to save Lombardy and Venetia at the price of the sacrifice of Austrian rule in Germany. In the face of this dilemma, he did not hesitate long. As he had once rejected Friedrich Wilhelm IV's plans, he now refused the Prince Regent's proposals, and chose to negotiate with Napoleon III.

Matters progressed very quickly now. Windischgraetz had not yet left Berlin when news came of an armistice agreed between France and Austria on 11 July at Villafranca. It must certainly have cost Franz Joseph a great deal to take this step: 'Such a course would not please me, but if it can help the monarchy then I must swallow this pill,' he explained to Elisabeth.[35] Once the decision had been taken not to allow Austria's influence in Germany to be threatened, Franz Joseph was left with no choice but to enter into discussions with Napoleon III if he did not wish to continue the fight alone. This would have been possible from the military viewpoint, but the monarchy's finances could not have sustained it for long, and it might have provoked an internal crisis. Franz Joseph was also aware that, following these successive defeats, his popularity had fallen very low in public opinion. His cousin, Archduke Rainer, who had recently arrived from Vienna, went so far as to recommend him to delay his return to the capital. In addition, he feared that there would be trouble in Hungary if the conflict were to continue.

Franz Joseph was lucky that his main adversary was in a similar situation. Napoleon III knew that to continue the war would be a lengthy process which would cost many lives. He was also in constant fear of the concentration of Prussian troops along the Rhine. This was sufficient reason for him to hope to come to some agreement with Franz Joseph before he found himself up against the whole of Germany.

In Italy itself, events took a different course from that decided on at Plombières. The revolutionary committees which replaced the previous authorities in the duchies were in favour of a solution involving Piedmont, while the Vatican also threatened to succumb to the disease of nationalism. It was therefore possible that Napoleon III felt that he was no longer master of the situation, but above all, he was obliged to take into account the feelings of French Catholics, who formed one of the mainstays of the regime, over the events in Italy. The need to retain their support demanded that he find a rapid solution to the conflict which, while satisfying Italian nationalist feelings, had not reached a level of revolutionary excess. This need to end the war as quickly as possible on Napoleon III's part was a card in Franz Joseph's favour.

When, on 8 July, Napoleon III suggested a meeting, Franz Joseph immediately acquiesced. The interview between the two emperors took place at Villafranca three days later and ended in the signing of a protocol of which the individual clauses were to be discussed and confirmed in a treaty according to the correct form.

Franz Joseph had every right to consider himself satisfied by this agreement. He was only obliged to hand over Lombardy to Piedmont, and Austria manged to keep Mantua and Peschiera, which meant that it kept the Quadrilateral. Austria thus managed to hold Venetia. By keeping this foothold in Italy, Austria could take part in the Confederation of Italian states over which the Pope would be called on to preside. This was not all: Napoleon III had even agreed to the return of the former Austrian rulers to their duchies. Franz Joseph could finally congratulate himself on being freed of the threat of an intervention by Kossuth in Hungary. For the rest,

Cavour's anger at the terms of a treaty which he had not had the power to prevent was reassuring, and the best yardstick of these preliminary peace talks.

In all, although Austria had suffered an undisputable defeat, it had also contrived to limit the ramifications. It remained a power in Italy and, thanks to the cards which it still held there, could hope to regain a considerable influence in the Italian peninsula.

Worrying Prospects

The worst was thus avoided. However, Franz Joseph could not conceal from himself that this war threatened to strike a severe blow to Austrian power, and that the future contained many questions.

In Italy, the agreement between the two emperors remained largely theoretical. The use of force was not an option in restoring the central Italian rulers to their thrones. It was impossible to imagine how the new powers which had emerged could be induced to withdraw. Furthermore, Cavour swore to prevent the implementation of this agreement. To demonstrate his disapproval he resigned as first minister, but he continued to direct the affairs of Piedmont from behind the scenes.

This war had also confirmed Austria's isolation and its ending provided little hope for a quick recovery. Britain was concerned that Italy should not be left under French control, but, especially since the Whigs had returned to power under Palmerston, the British had no intention of helping Austria to regain its old influence. Russia, for its part, observed the Austrian defeats with secret delight. Nor could Austria expect support from France. It was circumstance which had led Napoleon III to cut the war short, and he had no intention of creating a Paris–Vienna axis, even if a few tentative overtures might put people off the scent in the years which followed. Finally, this war served to heighten differences between Austria and Prussia. Although the pact of the Confederation had not obliged Prussia to take up arms in support of Austria, Franz Joseph nevertheless considered himself betrayed. In addition, the conditions suggested by the Prussian rulers in return for their joining the war confirmed that they still hoped for a change in the organization of Germany. Since Franz Joseph chose to negotiate with Napoleon III to prevent such a reorganization, it is not hard to guess that the German question was to occupy the centre stage in years to come. Now that Austria was isolated within Europe, it began this new era under conditions which were not so favourable as those ten years previously when the monarchy had last opposed Prussian pretensions.

The shock wave did not stop there. This series of defeats struck at the heart of the neo-absolutist regime in Austria. Following the crushing of the revolution, neo-absolutism had set itself the task of restoring the power of the monarchy. But this policy was thrown into question after Austria had failed to survive the test of war. For many, these defeats were not only the result of military errors. They were an indictment of the system as a whole.

In fact, a change had taken place in public opinion before the war. The economic recession which hit Austria from 1857 onwards, as it had the rest of Europe, had had the effect of alienating a section of the middle classes, who had previously regarded the government with favour. This reversal of circumstances broke the terms of the tacit compromise which had existed between the two parties. In the ranks of the bourgeoisie, thoughts turned again to the benefits of constitutional rule, and the military reversals served to aggravate the ill-feeling. This ferment of opinion also reached certain subject peoples and the Magyars, who had opposed neo-absolutist rule from the outset, were naturally the first to be affected.

Franz Joseph was not inactive in the face of this deterioration of the internal situation. His first move was to sacrifice the most prominent personalities of the regime. Already, shortly after the beginning of the war which confirmed the failure of his policies, Buol was replaced as first minister by Count Rechberg, an old colleague of Metternich. Following the defeat, many of the top officials of the neo-absolutist regime were removed in turn: Bach, the symbol of the regime, Grünne, who was blamed for the unreadiness of the army, Kempen, the head of police. These dismissals can be interpreted as the announcement of a future change of course. Indeed, on 15 July, Franz Joseph had published a manifesto in which he promised reforms to the people, although he certainly did not propose any great upheaval. The government established under neo-absolutism continued to follow his principles closely. His intention was to make concessions only in small matters in order to protect the main structure of his government. Nevertheless, nothing could ever be the same. Into the breach there flowed an evolutionary tide which would end in the establishment of a constitutional government, however moderate. The death knell of neo-absolutism had rung out over the battlefields of Lombardy and a new era was beginning in the reign of Franz Joseph.

6

From One Defeat to the Next

For Franz Joseph, the years between Solferina and Sadowa were made up of a long series of disappointments. In home affairs, caught between the conflicting proposals of the central and federalist parties and subjected to the pressures of the Magyars, he was trying to achieve a balance which, in the wake of neo-absolutist rule, could generate a new structure for the organization of his government. Suffering from one failure after another, Franz Joseph was repeatedly obliged to return to the drawing board. These internal problems did not fail to have an effect on the monarchy's international position, which had already been weakened by the defeats of 1859, and in external affairs Franz Joseph was in no happier a position. In Italy, the compromise agreed on at Villafranca soon became outdated. Encouraged by its successes, Piedmont was more than ever determined to drive Austria out of Venetia. In Germany the duel between Vienna and Berlin was entering its decisive phase, and although Franz Joseph loudly reaffirmed his rights as first German prince, the balance of strength gradually tipped in Prussia's favour.

Franz Joseph and Elisabeth: the First Crisis

Franz Joseph did not have the consolation of a private life which could compensate for these uncertainties and for his disappointments. During these years his marriage was shaken by a first crisis. Was it possible that this was brought about by new developments? There were certainly persistent rumours which suggested that Franz Joseph was no longer an irreproachable husband.

Whatever the truth of these rumours, they did not fail to get back to Elisabeth and this left her more completely isolated. Until this time, Franz Joseph had given Elisabeth the strength to endure a lifestyle and society which had never had any attraction for her. Although Franz Joseph had never sacrificed his duty as sovereign for her, she knew that she could find refuge beside him. Now she must have imagined that she was going to lose this refuge. This fear contributed to her discomposure and served to convince her that she was a stranger in Vienna. Nevertheless, even if the rumour had been true, Franz Joseph had not changed in his feelings towards her. However, over the years the differences between the husband and wife had grown, and with them a lack of understanding. Franz Joseph had increasing difficulties in understanding his wife, whose complex personality was beyond him. Their gradual estrangement contributed to the precipitation of a crisis which had been developing for many years.

Some aspects of Elizabeth's way of life could be interpreted as indicating that she was undergoing a personal crisis. She forced herself to follow a strict diet in the face of all reason, for, despite three pregnancies in rapid succession, far from getting fatter, she had preserved an exceptionally slender figure: compared with a height of 1.72 metres her weight never went over 50 kilos. It was in vain that Franz Joseph exhorted her to show more moderation; nothing could sway her. These deficiencies in her diet put a severe strain on her nervous system.

To calm her nerves, Elisabeth devoted herself to physical exercises which she followed to the point of exhaustion: long horse rides; walks on which her ladies in waiting had great difficulty in keeping up with her; and fatiguing gymnastic sessions. She even had a gymnasium installed in the Hofburg palace for her personal use. This new excess saddened Franz Joseph, but once again, his cries of alarm had no effect. It is not surprising that Elisabeth's health should have been affected by such a programme. Since her arrival in Vienna she had been the victim of coughing fits and these now began again.

Elisabeth wished for nothing more fervently than to leave Vienna. She grasped at the opportunity to travel with her daughter Gisela to Possenhofen in July 1860. This journey, far from the surroundings which made her feel caged in, became a sort of general rehearsal for the great leave-takings of later years. It took Franz Joseph's birthday on 18 August, which was traditionally celebrated by a family gathering at Ischl, to persuade her back to Austria, for she could not have been absent from such a gathering without creating a scandal.

She had hardly returned to Vienna before the beneficial effects of her stay beside the Starnberger See wore off. In Possenhofen she had soon stopped coughing. On her return to Vienna, she was seized by violent bouts and her health seemed to grow worse. On being called in for a consultation, Škoda, one of the great names of Austrian medicine, gave a categorical opinion: the life of the empress was in danger if she didn't leave Vienna as soon as possible to spend the winter in a more gentle climate. For this sojourn of nearly six months, her choice did not fall on the French or Italian Riviera, where she would have encountered the most elaborate arrangements to receive her, but on the distant island of Madeira. There, Elisabeth was guaranteed sunshine, and no doubt she also sought to put the greatest possible distance between herself and Vienna.

Reported by the Austrian and foreign newspapers, the news of the imminent departure of the empress shocked the public, who had not suspected the gravity of the illness. Queen Victoria even went so far as to offer her personal yacht for the transport of the sick empress. Not everyone at court was convinced, however, that Elisabeth was as ill as official statements made out. In the eyes of some of her visitors, who expected to find her exhausted, she appeared to be in excellent health, completely absorbed by her coming journey. The most widespread opinion in court circles was that they should not be trembling for Elisabeth's life, but rather pitying the deserted Franz Joseph, left alone with his children by a wife who seemed forgetful of her duties.

Having left in November, Elisabeth spent the winter on Madeira and waited for the fine weather to reach Vienna before returning. As she had done the previous year at Possenhofen, she seemed to regain her health. At the same time, one of the characteristics of her personality became clear. She was soon overcome by boredom on an island whose resources were after all limited. She was soon dreaming of new departures: 'More than anything, I would like to go further and further,' she connfided to Grünne. 'Each boat which I see go by gives me a longing to be on board. It doesn't matter whether it is going to Brazil, to Africa or to the Cape! The main thing is not to remain in the same place for so long!'[1] This declaration sheds light on one of the innermost driving forces of Elisabeth's character. For her, it was not only a matter of escaping Vienna, to respond to her wanderlust doubtless also provided her with the chance to escape herself. As her return to Vienna drew near, her feelings were mixed. During this long separation, she had not escaped a longing for her own family, above all, it seems, for her children. On the other hand, the prospect of returning to the company of the Archduchess Sophie left her frozen: 'I can only think of the A— with horror,' she wrote Grünne, 'and the distance only makes me hate her more.'[2]

Elisabeth's return held fresh disappointment for Franz Joseph. The joy of reunion did not last and very soon the symptoms of the illness which, strangely, struck the empress whenever she breathed the Viennese atmosphere, reappeared. Skoda, on being called in again, gave a firm diagnosis: Elisabeth was suffering from consumption and her condition demanded that she should depart immediately for a hot dry climate. The announcement of this new departure caused a shock to opinion which, only a few days earlier, had found the empress to be in apparent good health. The court was devastated and all those who on the first occasion had remained puzzled and even sceptical, were beginning to feel alarm now, the more so because, during the periods of depression which afflicted her, Elisabeth herself thought she was going to die.

For this new stay beyond the empire's borders Elisabeth chose another island, this time Corfu, a place which lay open to the horizon and where, more than anywhere else, she could dream of the absolute and the infinite. The first news was hardly reassuring: still eating as little as ever, Elisabeth became gradually more anaemic. Her coughing fits continued and she remained depressed. On visiting her, her eldest sister, Helena, was horrified to see her gaunt features and pallid complexion. This visit, however, provided the boost to her system which Elisabeth needed to overcome this attack, at least for the present. Soon the news from Corfu improved. Although Elisabeth was still coughing, she was now willing to eat normally. Franz Joseph could detect in this Helena's good influence. The meals reduced to a few pieces of fruit were over. Elisabeth was now eating meat three times a day and drinking beer four times. As a result of these good measures she regained her complexion and became cheerful again. Franz Joseph could therefore consider it a propitious moment to go to Corfu himself.

On his arrival, he found Elisabeth in the condition which Helena had described to him. The report which he sent to Sophie was optimistic. Elisabeth had regained some strength and her face no longer bore the marks of her suffering. Although she was still coughing a little, her chest pains had disappeared. Reassured over his wife's health, Franz Joseph allowed himself to enjoy the beauty of the 'paradise on earth' of Corfu. As a result of his stay, Franz Joseph concluded that the improvement in Elisabeth's condition was great enough for her to be able to leave Corfu. As a return to Vienna would no doubt be premature, it was decided to go to Venice to spend the winter. Sheltered from the hardships of the cold season, the empress would conclude her convalescence on Austrian territory, making it possible for Franz Joseph to visit her more easily. It was also arranged for the children to spend the winter months with their mother, from whom they had been separated for almost a year.

In Venice, Elisabeth was effectively less cut off from the outside world. Franz Joseph visited her on two occasions. Although he was happy to find her in generally good health, he nevertheless noticed that she continued to cough. Archduke Albert, who commanded the troops stationed in Venetia, and his wife, Archduchess Hildegard, also came to see her. But most important, Elisabeth received a visit from her mother, Duchess Ludovica. The latter had until now refrained from interfering in the decisions of the Viennese court. But the persistence of the illness persuaded her to visit her daughter in order to form her own opinion. With her, she brought the family doctor, Dr Fischer.

Dr Fischer's examination resulted in different conclusions from those of his Viennese colleagues. The chest infection, in his opinion was in the course of healing itself, but he diagnosed an advanced state of anaemia in the empress, confirmed by the dropsy from which she was suffering. Her feet were swollen to the point where she could no longer walk without help. He might as well have said that the treatment which she had hitherto been given was no longer appropriate, had it ever been so. No more long voyages, no more long rambles! To cure the illness, Dr Fischer advised Elisabeth to take the waters at Bad Kissingen. This new treatment had the effect of delaying her return to Vienna once again. In May 1862, she set out for Bad Kissingen. The suggested treatment turned out to do her good. Whereas on her arrival she could barely walk, Elisabeth quickly regained an almost perfect use of her legs. All the same, this improvement could also be explained by psychological factors. In Bad Kissingen, Sissi found herself once again in Bavaria, surrounded by her family. Her parents, brothers and sisters created a loving circle around her which helped her to recover her emotional balance as well as her physical health.

Elisabeth finally returned to Vienna shortly before 18 August. Her relations with the court entered a phase of consolidation. The empress's health did not suffer a relapse and there was no longer a need for hurried departures for distant destinations. It is nevertheless hard to describe it as a return to normal. Although for the most part she fulfilled the official obligations of her position, Elisabeth still retained a strong taste for solitude. Above all, Dr Fischer gave her a course of treatment which imposed a regime of sexual abstinence. In addition, during these years, Elisabeth acquired an assurance which meant that she no longer submitted to the course of events without protest. She demonstrated this when she revolted against the type of education given to the young Rudolf.

At the age of five, according to custom, the young archduke had been given over to the care of a tutor. For this task, Franz Joseph chose Count Gondrecourt, a traditionally minded officer, who was instructed to concentrate on the military training of his pupil, to prepare him to be a soldier, and to this end, to harden his body and his character. Gondrecourt therefore did not consider that he was going beyond his authority when, not limiting himself to imposing a spartan lifestyle on the boy, he subjected him to physical exercises which were systematically intended to push him to the limits of exhaustion. This programme had the opposite effect of that intended, however. Far from toughening his body and character, it ruined the young boy's health, shook his nerves, and made him suffer from anxiety attacks. As Rudolf endured this treatment without protest, Elisabeth only became aware of the seriousness of the problem when she was informed of it by one of Gondrecourt's subordinates, Colonel Latour, who was indignant at these methods. Elisabeth reacted immediately by approaching her husband. The following text has been preserved in the archives, revealing a new imperious, almost dominating tone:

> I hope that full powers will be given me in all matters concerning the children, the choice of their entourage, of where they should live, and complete control of their education, in a word, I should have sole powers of decision over them until their majority. Furthermore, I wish for the right to make all decisions concerning my personal affairs, among others, the choice of my own suite, of where I should reside, and control of all decisions concerning the household.
>
> Elisabeth, Ischl, 27 August 1865[3]

This letter, in which the dry tone wipes out all trace of affection, represents an act of emancipation. In the relationship between husband and wife, it even foreshadows, to a certain extent, an inversion in the relative positions; for Elisabeth, who was then at the height of her beauty, was fully aware of the power which this gave her over Franz Joseph. She was also aware that he would be prepared to make concessions in order to avoid the scandal of a new departure on her part, for which no serious medical reasons could be given. Her calculation proved correct. Although he did not like the decision, Franz Joseph bowed to her will, and agreed to dismiss Gondrecourt who was replaced by Latour.

Beyond its immediate implications, this episode marked a turning-point in the relationship between the emperor and empress. The repeated separations and the psychological distance between husband and wife which they accentuated helped Elisabeth to gain some degree of autonomy, and, with this, an assurance which she had previously lacked.

In any case, the lesson was learned. Because a combination of love and a fear of scandal induced Franz Joseph to give in, Elisabeth would no longer refrain from making use of this weapon when she wished to impose her will on the emperor. After many setbacks she had finally reached the point where she could secure for herself the personal freedom for which she had constantly striven. The question remains whether this outcome was in the best interests of the empire. In the specific case of Rudolf's education, her intervention had a good effect. But her demands went well beyond this and, moreover, the means which she used to gain her ends did not reinforce her training as empress. Won in such a way, this success only encouraged her inclination towards capriciousness with no concern for the obligations of her position.

The other lesson to be drawn from this episode was the decline in Archduchess Sophie's influence. In earlier times she would not have allowed Elisabeth to impose her will without a fight. But this time, she did not react. This may have been due to her advancing years which may have weakened her determination. But it was also true that Austrian politics was undergoing a transformation at that time which distressed the archduchess and also demonstrated the waning of her influence in the political sphere.

The October Diploma

The first problem to confront Franz Joseph on his return from Italy was that of the reorganization of his power structure. The general opinion was that, following the defeat, the days of neo-absolutist rule were numbered. The middle classes had completed their break with the system and conservative circles proposed instead a programme of historical federalism which would favour the nobility. But the most important factor lay in the Hungarian situation, where, far from dying down with the return of peace, unrest was growing. Franz Joseph himself recognized the impossibility of maintaining the status quo. Through the Laxenburg manifesto he found the way to announce 'improvements in legislation and administration' but the details of this remained imprecise. This was deliberate, for, after Villafranca, Franz Joseph had no intention of countenancing a global re-evaluation of neo-absolutism. In his opinion there was less chance than ever of introducing a constitutional regime in Austria along the lines of those of western Europe.

It was over a year before Franz Joseph took action. He decided to come to an agreement with the aristocratic party, which was formed of an alliance between the Magyar conservatives and a small part of the old aristocracy of the Austro-Bohemian lands. This party was lucky in that, after ten years in which all political activity had been systematically repressed, it found itself the only organized political group. Also, because of the position of the nobles at court, they were able to approach the emperor and had access to influential contacts among the ruling circles of the monarchy. The urgency of finding a solution to the Hungarian problem represented an additional card in this party's favour. Once the atmosphere of ferment in Hungary appeared to preclude the preservation of the status quo, the Magyar conservatives, who were aware of Franz Joseph's categorical rejection of modern constitutionalism, set out to convince him that the restoration of the historical Constitution of the crown of Saint Stephen would be enough to restore order. He would thus be spared the necessity of making concessions to liberalism.

As the successor to the conservative party which had been formed under the *Vormärz* regime, the Hungarian faction of the aristocratic party was the first to organize itself. The Magyar leaders, among them Count Emil Dessewffy, Baron Jozsef Eötvös and Count Antal Szécsen, considered that their loyalty to her Habsburgs gave them the right to speak out against the fate of their country following the suppression of the revolution, and to urge those in power to change course. As we know, these pleas were in vain. The years of neo-absolutist rule provided a period of withdrawal and reflection, of which this group took advantage to clarify its beliefs and draw up a policy.

The idea that eventually became known, rather cumbrously, as 'historico-political individualism' was the fruit of this ideological maturing process. It began from a premise which proposed the respect of historical rights as a fundamental element of the monarchical state. This was well suited to the Austrian system, for the political elements which made up the monarchy had indeed existed before coming under Habsburg rule. It was as kings of Bohemia that the Habsburgs ruled in Bohemia, as kings of Hungary that they exercised their power in the Kingdom of Saint Stephen. The relationship which was thus built up between these various territories had at first taken the form of a simple personal union. The next stage was officially reached when the Pragmatic Sanction of 1713 transformed these lands into a single organic whole, bound together under the authority of one dynasty. But even before this official act, a central body of power had begun to be sketched out, and the Habsburgs made use of this in their plans to draw together their various possessions.

There was no question that the process by which a central superior authority had assumed power over the constitutive parts of the monarchy should be reinstated. Nor was there any question of refusing the central authority the necessary powers to ensure the continued unity of the Habsburg lands. But this unity was not synonymous with centralization, nor with uniformity. To be able to rest on a solid base, such a power must conform with the principle from which Austria was born. In other words, consubstantial pluralism needed to be part of the very fabric of the monarchy, and, to this end, the central power would have to rely on the countries which formed the substratum of the empire. To wish to reduce them to the status of mere provinces, and even to split them up into geographical sectors along the lines of the French *départements*, would, for Austria, be a denial of the principles of the monarchy's make-up, a betrayal of its vocation, and carried to its conclusion, would place its reason for existence in jeopardy.

At this point in their thought, the proponents of 'historico-political individualism' were faced with the multiple nationalities of the monarchy. These threatened the realization of their proposals because the divisions between national groups rarely matched those between historical countries. This problem was resolved by the separation of the concepts of nationality and of ethnicity. Whereas nationality corresponded to the living human group within a historico-political group, ethnicity was defined by racial and linguistic considerations.

In the case of Austria, the recognition of the principle of ethnicity as the foundation for the organization of states would inevitably lead to the collapse of the monarchy. Ethno-linguistic demands should certainly not be ignored, in so far as they did not compromise the existence of the monarchy. But the only solution compatible with the multiple nature of Austria, in their view, required the satisfaction of 'historico-political' rights, and Eötvös perceived, as had Stadion, the commune and the *Kreis* or circle as the level of government at which these hopes could be best be fulfilled without threatening the cohesion of the Habsburg lands. Following their assessment of the situation, these nobles felt they could safely conclude that, since the pillars of local allegiances transcended linguistic ties, it was appropriate that 'historico-political bodies' should serve as the basis for any constitutional reform which wished to deal with Austria's problems in a realistic way.

In their defence of these theories, the Magyar conservatives were first thinking of Hungary, although logically their application did not stop at Hungary's borders. This project was taken up on their own count by the sector of the ancient Austro-Bohemian nobility which was beginning to organize itself into a separate party by the end of the neo-absolutist decade. Foreshadowed by the uprising which, in the final years of the *Vormärz*, had led several Diets to protest against the central power, the emergence of this political power was a reaction to neo-absolutism. Although neo-absolutist rule was at first well received by the nobility because it had triumphed over the revolution, its true intentions had soon surfaced. The aristocracy did not take long to realize that the central power intended to complete the process of the reduction in status of the nobility begun a century earlier.

This plan was not only the fruit of a defensive stance. Its application would end in no less an achievement than the undoing of Maria Theresa and Joseph II's work, and, in transferring a large number of the powers hitherto monopolized by the state to the Diets, it would restore its lost power to the main body of the nobility. Thus, when the political debate was reopened, the aristocratic party emerged armed with both an ideology and a plan. For more than a generation it was to form one of the dominant elements of Austrian political life. Through it, the option of historical federalism was expressed, and the confrontation between this party and that in favour of centralization was to occupy the limelight for a long time.

Franz Joseph was not at first amenable to the arguments of the aristocratic party. He was as yet unprepared to support a policy which, by restoring the old Hungarian Constitution, would in effect renounce the line taken since 1849. The first steps towards a way out were taken at the beginning of March 1860 when he invited the *Reichsrat* to discuss the budget and proposed legislation set out by the government. This decision was accompanied by a measure which indicated the beginning of a move towards the aristocratic party. The *Reichsrat* which was called was no longer only that which had been devised by Kübeck ten years earliers. It included additional members chosen by the emperor: archdukes, princes of the Church, and most importantly, thirty-eight representatives of the provinces, mainly drawn from the ranks of the upper nobility. These nominations appeared to herald a reversal of the balance of power: while Kübeck's choice had fallen on conservative high-ranking civil servants, brought up in the Josephist tradition, and supporters of centralization, most of the new members were supporters of historical federalism.

Franz Joseph was nevertheless still committed to an utter refusal to make any con-stitutional changes. He was neither ready to permit the newly enlarged *Reichsrat* to assume any legislative powers, nor was he prepared to allow any process of decentral-ization in favour of the Diets to begin. Faced with the motion passed by the *Reichsrat* which called for a total reorganization of the monarchy along federalist lines, his first reaction was one of indignation: 'It is none of their business,' he protested to Leo Thun, 'They may only give an opinion, no more. We do not have a Constitution.'[4]

This display of irritation did not, however, harm the aristocratic party. In the end, it was on the side of the historical federalists that Franz Joseph's choice fell. He already allowed this to be understood when, at the end of September, he called on Court Szécsen, who had recently pleaded the cause of 'historico-political units' in the *Reichsrat*, to join the government. This appointment left the Magyars in a strong position within the aristocratic party. In other words, it was the Hungarian question which had the most influence on Franz Joseph's choice. At the beginning of the autumn of 1860, this worry was uppermost in the sovereign's mind, for he was fully aware of the inability of the authorities to retain control in Hungary. Szécsen, whose influence was dominant during these decisive weeks, did not omit to exploit this concern with an account of the necessity of the restoration of the historical Constitution of the Kingdom of Hungary in a return to historical law, before calm could be re-established. Such a solution would also have the advantage of avoiding the humiliation of a compromise with liberalism.

Having dragged throughout the period since July 1859, events then progressed very quickly. Since he was due to visit Warsaw for a conference with Tsar Alexander II, Franz Joseph wanted the charter for the regulation of the new system to be promulgated before his departure, which was planned for 21 October. Court Szécsen only had the space of a few hours in which to deliver his material, but he was certainly the master of his subject and knew what he wished to achieve. The result of this solitary exercise was the imperial Diploma of 20 October which aspired to rebuild Austria following historical federalist principles.

Franz Joseph was primarily concerned that this basic law should not diminish his power: 'No doubt', he admitted, 'there will be some parliamentarianism. But', he hastened to add, 'power will remain in my hands and the whole system will be adapted to the realities of Austria.'[5] In its solemn declaration that the emperor would continue to hold legislative power, the first article of the Diploma confirmed that it did not have its origins in modern constitutionalism. Of course, there was the small measure of parliamentarianism mentioned by Franz Joseph, for the Diploma contained a provision for the convocation of Diets in the different provinces of the monarchy, which would then designate deputies to represent them in the *Reichsrat*.

The powers given to these assemblies were, however, too limited to threaten the emperor's authority. The Diets and the *Reichsrat* would certainly be involved in the devising of legislation, but they were given no powers of decision in this matter and their role remained purely consultative. The same was true of the financial powers of the *Reichsrat*. Although the Diploma stipulated that any introduction of new taxes or increase of existing ones, any taking out of loans and any conversion of the public debt required the agreement of the *Reichsrat*, this agreement was not a condition for the budget's acceptance. Lastly, the Diploma omitted to introduce a rule of ministerial responsibility, which would have been a way of recognizing the principle of popular rule. Ministers remained responsible only to the emperor.

The other major element was the disparity which the Diploma established between Hungary and the rest of the monarchy. The organization of the *Reichsrat* bore this out. Szécsen proposed that the Hungarian representatives would sit only when matters which were of common concern to all of the monarchy were discussed. As a result, the Diploma also created a more limited *Reichsrat* in which questions concerning other provinces would be discussed without the participation of the Hungarian representatives. The federalist option received positive confirmation through the transfer of authority to the Diets in all matters which were not specifically defined as the concern of the *Reichsrat*. This restriction appeared to presage the return to equilibrium in the relationship between Vienna and the provinces which the conservatives longed for. The powers thus granted to the provinces would include fundamental areas such as religion, education, justice, and agricultural questions. But there was a degree of disparity even in this. In order to satisfy Szécsen's friends, the Diploma granted Hungary the reinstatement of the old Hungarian Constitution, whereas it only offered the other areas of the empire an indication that they would be provided with new statutes which would define their internal structures and their relationships with the central powers.

This disparity had initially been introduced by Szécsen, whose main concern was the fate of his own country. But the fact that Franz Joseph made no criticism confirms that he considered the Hungarian question to have priority. This inconsistency in the treatment of various areas also bore witness to the fact of the duality which had become established between the Austro-Bohemian group and Hungary as a result of their separate evolution.

Schmerling and the Return to Centralization

In the event, the October Diploma was not given the chance to prove itself. Its promulgation did not have the expected effect. Far from restoring calm, it provoked a vast movement of opposition. The German bourgeoisie was incensed that the traditional elites were favoured by it. Elsewhere, the hopes of the Magyar conservatives were disappointed. Besides these limited groups, the Diploma antagonized the whole of the Hungarian political classes. Instead of being the result of a contract between the king and the nation, it was granted by a unilateral act of the Austrian emperor, in defiance of the sovereignty of the Kingdom of Hungary.

The unity of the aristocratic party did not withstand this test. To save the results of their work, the Magyar conservatives broke away from their Austro-Bohemian partners. Performing a complete U-turn, Szécsen and his friends set out to convince Franz Joseph that the hostility of their fellow-countrymen could be nipped in the bud if the Diploma were altered to include a greater degree of centralization in the Austro-Bohemian provinces. Whereas a federalist system threatened to weaken Hungary's position within the Habsburg lands, any move to centralize the administration of the rest of the monarchy would provide additional assurance of Hungary's separate identity and freedoms.

Switching their alliances, the Magyar conservatives now decided to come to an agreement with the Austrian liberals who had the advantage of a larger controlling voice. If the nobles were not strong enough, the German middle classes could replace them as the controlling group in Austro-Bohemia, while the Magyar conservatives would establish a dominant influence in Hungary.

Once again, Franz Joseph followed the advice of his Hungarian counsellors, building up a new team of government around the figure of Anton von Schmerling. The halo of liberalism which surrounded Schmerling from the time of the *Vormärz*, under which he had been one of the opposition spokesmen in the Lower Austrian House, certainly drew him to Franz Joseph's attention. His participation in Schwarzenberg's cabinet did not affect his credit with the German middle classes, and having resigned in 1850, he had not been compromise by either the excesses or the failure of neo-absolutist rule. Lastly, his attachment of the Greater German cause, which was combined with an Austrian patriotism of a quality above suspicion, spoke in his favour at this moment in which the monarchy hoped to reaffirm its primacy at the heart of the German Federation.

Despite appearances, this choice did not represent a break in policy for Franz Joseph. Although he brought men renowned for their liberalism into the government, he retained a profound conviction that he still controlled matters. The liberalism of Schmerling and those who took on ministerial responsibilities beside him was tempered by a solid element of conservatism in the government which prevented policy from taking a democratic turn. Although they considered that absolutism had outlived its usefulness, its members' first loyalty was to a strong government and the supremacy of imperial authority.

For the rest, the concessions made by Franz Joseph remained strictly limited. There was still no question of introducing a parliamentary regime. There was less possibility than ever of the recognition of the principle of ministerial responsibility to the *Reichsrat*. Furthermore, the emperor reserved for himself total control of foreign policy and defence. As these were, in Franz Joseph's opinion, the two most important areas, he could feel satisfied that the real power of the monarchy still lay in his own hands.

Schmerling only needed two months to give a fresh look to the institutions of the monarchy. This was achieved by the patent of 26 February 1861 and by the *Grundgesetz über die Reichsvertretung* (fundamental law on the representation of the empire). Although the October Diploma was never to be implemented, the regime established by Schmerling was to last for some time. Indeed, it set up a constitutional framework which, in its broad lines, would resist the assaults of time and political parties, in Austria at least, until 1907, and, in some of its clauses, would survive until the fall of the monarchy.

There was no basic change to the powers of the *Reichsrat* in the monarchy as a whole. There was, however, a complete reversal in the division of authority between the limited *Reichsrat* and the Diets. Although its powers had been limited by the October Diploma, the smaller *Reichsrat* became the centrepiece of the constitutional edifice. The February patent granted the limited *Reichsrat* all the powers which were not specifically stipulated as having passed either from the greater *Reichsrat* to Hungary, or to the Diets. Running counter to the spirit of the system set out by the October Diploma, this arrangement marked the triumph of centralization.

The other characteristic of Schmerling's regime was the organization of the Diets according to a curial system which would be preserved until 1918. The Diets were split into four *curiae* or colleges (great landowners, rural districts, urban districts, and chambers of commerce and industry), and this division was extended to the *Reichsrat*.

This system did not claim to be founded on egalitarian principles. In the *curiae* of the rural and urban districts, the right to vote was connected to taxes paid and the rate was fixed at a high enough level to limit political power to a small minority. Also, among the *curiae* themselves there were flagrant discrepancies. Fewer voters were required to elect a deputy in the landowners' *curiae* and in that of the chambers of commerce and industry, than in the other two colleges. Finally, Schmerling perfected a clever vote-counting system which ensured that the German bourgeoisie would have a majority in a certain number of Diets. In several provinces with mixed nationalities such as Bohemia, Moravia, Silesia, and Carniol, the right to vote in the urban and rural *curiae* had already been limited to those who paid ten gulden or more indirect taxes, but Schmerling also focused special attention on these areas, taking care to introduce an electoral pattern which would favour the German inhabitants.

Although they expected to benefit the most from this redistribution of power, Franz Joseph's Hungarian advisers became its first victims. Franz Joseph still had no intention of allowing the system of government to move towards dualism, and Schmerling, for his part, had not entered the government in order to remove Hungary from Vienna's jurisdiction.

In Hungary, as was to be expected, the opposition of the political classes was not weakened by the arrival of a new group in the seat of government. Nothing had changed at a fundamental level in relations between Vienna and Hungary. The constitutional documents had been promulgated without consultation. Beyond its authoritarian style, this procedure confirmed Hungary's inferior status in relation to the Austrian Empire, arousing the patriotic spirit of a crushing majority of the Magyar elite. The contents of the February patent also threatened Hungarian sovereignty because they subjected it to the authority of an imperial government and required Hungary to participate in a parliamentary assembly which represented the entire monarchy.

With a majority in the Diet, the opposition party, under the inspiration of Ferenc Deák, agreed on an address to Franz Joseph in April 1861 which, while preserving a respectful tone, proclaimed its categorical refusal to accept the system instituted by the patent. Deák was careful not to burn all his bridges. The Diet declared itself ready to come to an agreement with Austria once its requirement that Hungarian sovereignty should be recognized had been met. The time was not ripe for this, though. Deák's proposal was too much of a contravention of the principle of a unified Austria for Franz Joseph to be prepared to adopt it, and his answer to the address was to dissolve the Diet in August.

Hungary found itself in a position similar to that which it had held during the neo-absolutist period. Once again, it was governed and administered directly from Vienna. Schmerling was not moved by this, for in his view, time was against the Hungarian opposition. Now, it was turn of the Magyar conservatives to experience the results of their failure. Pushed into a minority position within the cabinet and deprived of Franz Joseph's support and that of the general populace, they handed in their resignations.

Schmerling might have thought that he now had a clear field to build up a unified Austria within a system devised to involve both financial and intellectual elites in political matters while respecting the rights of the sovereign, but events soon required that he should rethink his position. Schmerling could repeat in vain that it was enough to play a waiting game, his fine confidence soon came to resemble stubbornness. The determination of the Hungarian political class showed no sign of running out of steam. Furthermore, the opposition party was growing in the Austro-Bohemian lands where the federalist-inspired groups were rejecting Schmerling's system. This was the case for the Czechs who ranged themselves behind their historical leaders, Palacký and Rieger, in defence of the interests of their national group, and formed an alliance with the sector of the nobility who fought Viennese centralization for the cause of the historical rights of the Kingdom of Bohemia. Following the example of the Magyars, the two parties expressed their opposition in material form by deciding to boycott the *Reichsrat*, withdrawing from it in June 1863.

Schmerling's plan as a whole was developing problems. Boycotted by the

Hungarians and the Croats to demonstrate their dissatisfaction that their requirements had not been met, the full *Reichsrat* remained a fictional entity despite Schmerling's protestations to the contrary – he cited the example of the participation of the Romanians and the Transylvanian Saxons. As for the limited *Reichsrat*, following the desertion of the Czechs it gradually became increasingly deserted by the other groups of federalists. Concerned about the waverings of the government over the revision of the concordat, the Austrian Catholics, especially those from Tyrol, followed the same course, so that, after all these departures, the only groups to sit in the *Reichsrat* with the German liberals were a handful of Ruthenian and Italian representatives.

These repeated failures finally shook Franz Joseph who here demonstrated his ability to adapt to a changing situation. The aggravation of the internal crisis led him to draw away gradually from an experiment which did not achieve its objectives, and convinced him that a different way must be found to return the monarchy to the stability which it had lost since the war in Italy.

The Beginnings of Hungarian *Détente*

With the failure of Schmerling's policies, Franz Joseph chose to re-establish links with Hungary. A visit to Pest gave him the opportunity to achieve this in June 1865. This journey was the expression of Franz Joseph's concern to improve relations between Vienna and Hungary. But he went even further than this by taking advantage of his stay to express his desire to come to an agreement with the Hungarian representatives in a declaration which announced the imminent convening of the Diet and the opening of negotiations.

These discussions took place only two months after Deák had outlined a basis for a compromise acceptable to both parties in the *Pesti Naplo* (Pest Gazette). Setting himself apart from those who supported extremist solutions, he put forward in this article the terms of an agreement which, in the spirit of the Pragmatic Sanction, would reconcile respect for Hungarian sovereignty with the security requirements of the monarchy:

> Hungary has no desire to threaten the strength of the Monarchy...There is no conflict between Hungary and the hereditary Austrian lands, they can exist side by side. We are not prepared to sacrifice our liberty merely because there are differences concerning certain rights between the new Constitution of the Cisleithan peoples and ourselves, but we will always be ready to use constitutional means to bring our laws into harmony with the requirements of the security and unity of the Monarchy.[6]

The remarks made by Franz Joseph during his stay in the Hungarian capital could thus be read as a reply to these overtures. They also indicated that Schmerling had lost control of the situation. His dismissal two months later confirmed the change. To replace him, Franz Joseph called on Count Richard Belcredi, a Moravian aristocrat whose qualities he had appreciated while the latter was exercising his function as *Statthalter* of Bohemia. This choice fitted in with his new policies because, if

Belcredi's previous responsibilities in the upper echelons of government were a guarantee of his loyalty, as was his respect for the state, his Moravian connections and his federalist sympathies combined to give his appointment the appearance of a gesture made by Franz Joseph towards the opposition.

The nature of Belcredi's government soon confirmed Franz Joseph's intentions. The patent of 20 September 1865 suspended the February Constitution until a new system of organization for the monarchy could be put in place. On the same day, an imperial manifesto announced the opening of negotiations with the Hungarian Diet, and that the representatives of the other provinces would be consulted over the results of these talks at the appropriate time. Although Belcredi inclined towards a federalist system, these decisions were already moving towards a dualist system as they differentiated between Hungary and the rest of the empire. Despite the rights of consultation for the other provinces set out in the manifesto of 20 September, only Hungary was invited to negotiate with the crown.

This did not mean that Franz Joseph was prepared to agree to all the demands of the Hungarian representatives. He continued to refuse to consider the creation of a Hungarian executive. The road to compromise was still a long one, but the actions of Deák and Franz Joseph combined to undo the impasse which had developed in Austro-Hungarian relations, and the move towards dualism had made a promising start.

Further Retreats in Italy

Franz Joseph's decision to take this course was also influenced by international speculation. The rise of threats to Austria's external frontiers in Italy, and even more in Germany, dictated that Franz Joseph could not allow the internal situation to deteriorate any further.

Following Villafranca, Franz Joseph was doubtless of the opinion that nothing irrevocable had taken place. Despite the military reversals, the worst had been avoided and Austria remained an Italian power. In addition to its most ancient possessions (Trentino and Trieste) the empire had retained Venetia which could, should the occasion arise, serve as a base for the reconquest of Lombardy. In addition, the minor branches of the imperial family in Tuscany and Modena had their rights restored to them. As in the past, the Papal States and the Kingdom of Naples would continue to be a part of the Austrian network.

Of course, Napoleon III had to be taken into consideration, for he would certainly continue to keep an eye on Italian matters. Franz Joseph therefore concluded that the best solution would be to form an alliance between the two empires. He gave serious consideration to this option during the weeks which followed Villafranca. it appealed to him all the more because he was still angry at the defection of Prussia. Baron Hübner's successor in Paris, Prince Richard Von Metternich, received the order to work to draw the two powers closer together.

This fine edifice soon turned out to have been constructed in Franz Joseph's mind and not to have any foundation in fact. Franz Joseph was obliged to cope with successive disappointments. His plan did not take into account the strength of nationalist feeling, which the victories of Magenta and Solferino had served to increase. Already Tuscany and Modena considered the failure of the Habsburgs to be an incontrovertible fact. At the Zurich negotiations which were meant to decide the details of the decisions made at Villafranca, France showed no intention of restoring the deposed Austrian rulers to their thrones. Indeed, the French went as far as to propose a congress to establish the new political shape of Italy. Faced with behaviour which in his view was filled with duplicity, Franz Joseph's anger did not abate: 'The French emperor is, and remains, a scoundrel,' he wrote to his mother.[7]

Signed two months later, the peace treaty certainly preserved appearances but it nonetheless represented a retreat on Austria's part in comparison with the Villafranca agreement. In addition to the confirmation of the annexation of Lombardy by Piedmont, it also provided for an Italian League in which Austria would participate on behalf of its Venetian possessions. But although the rights of the dukes of Tuscany and Modena were reconfirmed, no practical measures were taken to implement this clause of the agreement. In addition, according to Napoleon III's wishes, the principle of a congress to determine the new organizational structure of Italy was retained.

Beyond the surrender of Lombardy, this treaty would soon be no more than an empty shell. Between them, Napoleon III's afterthoughts, Piedmont's ambitions, and the pressure of the Italian populace swept it away. For Franz Joseph, the defeats were accumulating. In January 1860, convinced that this treaty was not going to be put into operation, Cavour returned as head of government in Piedmont. Whether or not Napoleon III was glad of this, or merely resigned to it, in February he gave his agreement to the inclusion of Modena, Parma, and then Tuscany in the Kingdom of Piedmont-Sardinia. For the ruling families who had taken refuge in Austria, it seemed that this time their exile would be a permanent one. The sign that no illusions were cherished in Vienna on this score was given by the reintegration of these branches of the family into the imperial household.

Having struck this first blow against the lands of the Papal States, Piedmont continued to extend its control, still with the consent of the French emperor, this time into Romagna which had revolted against the Pope's authority. The dismantling of what remained of theAustrian system of government in Italy continued with the fall of the Kingdom of Naples. At the head of his redshirts, Garibaldi took over Sicily in under two months. Although there was a close game being played out between Cavour and Garibaldi, when the latter landed on the Italian mainland the young king of Naples, Francis II, had become too weak to change the course of events.

A decisive stage was reached in the unification process when Victor Emmanuel, king of Piedmont-Sardinia, accepted Garibaldi's homage in Naples in November. In the meantime, Piedmont had taken advantage of this crisis to dispossess Pius IX of the Marches and of Umbria. Now, even if Rome and the Latium were still beyond his grasp, Victor Emmanuel's authority extended from the Alps down to Sicily. He could thus proclaim on 14 March 1861 the birth of the Kingdom of Italy, a decision which automatically buried the plan to create an Italian Confederation.

Franz Joseph could only be a scandalized but helpless spectator to this series of events. In his correspondence, he fulminated against 'Garibaldi's banditry, Victor Emmanuel's thievery, and the fraudulent practices of the Parisian scoundrel'.[8] But, in practice, he refrained from military intervention, despite calls for aid from the king of Naples who, having married one of Elisabeth's sisters, had become his brother-in-law. But, with death in his soul, he had to admit that he did not have the resources to take action.

Franz Joseph naturally did not give up the idea of diplomatic action. But the only line he could take was that of the defence of legitimate rule, a diplomatic concept which had already become dated by the end of Metternich's era and had now become quite anachronistic in the context of the new nationalism. Without the support of armed intervention, mere words were powerless to alter the course of events. Franz Joseph was obliged to drink the cup of bitterness to the dregs when he saw Prussia and Russia recognize the new Kingdom of Italy which, in his view, was allied with the powers of evil.

Franz Joseph could certainly console himself with the thought that the Kingdom of Italy was an artificial creation which would not last for long. This was an opinion widely held in Austrian government circles. Despite the fact that Lombardy, central Italy, and the Kingdom of Naples were now united under the House of Savoy, they persisted in perceiving the movement towards unification in Italy as an artificial phenomenon. These successes did not alter the Austrians' belief that the Italians had insufficient life force to create a state for themselves. They were convinced that the entire structure would collapse like a house of cards at the first hurdle. Accordingly, Count Rechberg, head of the Austrian diplomatic service, had no qualms in denouncing the new kingdom as a monster which could only live a few years.

Nevertheless, the balance of power in Italy had been completely altered in two years. Yesterday's dominant power, Austria, was now walled up in its Venetian hide-out, and forced into a defensive position. There were several attempts to persuade Franz Joseph to give up Venetia. Austria was given to understand, by various parties, that it should accept an evolutionary process which sooner or later was going to end in Venetia being united with the rest of Italy. The latter had long been prepared to buy Venetia from Austria, thereby providing a solution which had the advantage of saving the two states from an useless conflict. But this solution was too far removed from Franz Joseph's feudal ethic for him to pay any serious attention to it.

For his part, Napoleon III made many attempts to draw Austria into his plans, making proposals of territorial compensations. Already, following the 1859 war, he had thought of handing over Herzegovina and northern Albania as it stood then, thus removing them from the influence of the Ottoman Empire. The matter took on more flesh when Napoleon III sought to exploit the crisis of 1863 created by the uprising in the Russian area of what had previously been Poland, by attempting a re-organization of the territorial shape of Europe. In particular, Napoleon sought to create a link between the Polish and Italian questions. Austria would return Galicia to an independent Poland and Venetia to Italy. In return, it would receive Silesia, which had been lost to the monarchy since Frederic II had won it from Maria Theresa, and would thereby gain the Danubian principalities which Austria had dreamed of taking over since 1855. Once their relations were re-established along these new lines, the two empires could strengthen the ties between them. Their agreement would form an axis on which the power relationships of Europe would hinge.

Franz Joseph remained deaf to the French siren's song. He suspected Napoleon III of seeking to push Austria and Prussia into conflict. The French emperor did indeed show himself generous with the possessions of others. The Silesian lands which he dangled in front of Franz Joseph's eyes still belonged to the Hohenzollerns, and it is hard to imagine that Prussia would have been prepared to give them up without a fight. There was a final reason behind Franz Joseph's refusal. To accept a deal over Venetia would be to recognize implicitly the principle of nationality, and this might set off a chain reaction which could sound the death knell for Austria.

In the Face of Prussian Ambitions

In Germany, on the other hand, Austria's other traditional area of influence, the Habsburg monarchy still appeared to retain a solid position. Historically, it was still the first of the German powers, a position confirmed by its presidency of the German Confederation. In 1859, Austria demonstrated its wish to defend its supremacy, and it could also count on a network of friendship between the smaller states who were disturbed by the Prussian appetite for power.

Despite this, the situation had not remained static in the years during which Schwarzenberg had directed Austrian foreign policy. In the space of a decade, the balance of power had moved progressively in favour of Prussia. The reaction which followed the revolution of 1848 did not go so far as to re-establish an absolutist regime there. The contrast between the internal development of the two great German states left Prussia with the sympathy of liberal public opinion, which continued to reproach Austria for its religious policy which was considered to be backward-looking. In such circles, those opposed to Austrian neo-absolutism also nourished the conviction that the Habsburg monarchy was not a true German power because of the heterogeneous nature of its subjects.

Thanks to its possessions on the Rhine which assured it, in particular, control of the Ruhr, Prussia underwent a spectacular industrial development which turned it into the economic centre of Germany. The state of the Hohenzollerns had also had the opportunity to make Austria aware that Olmütz had not succeeded in shattering its power. In 1854, Prussia upset Franz Joseph and Buol's plans in the course of the Eastern crisis. Even more importantly, it had managed to close the doors of the *Zollverein* to Austria. Even though the game was not over, this success provided Prussia with a powerful trump card, for it helped it to develop a material bond with the other German states which was not available to Austria. In other words, although the political debate had still to be settled, a nucleus for the development of an independent Germany centred around Prussia was gradually being set in place. When the final act of this drama opened, Franz Joseph was armed with his own beliefs: 'I am a German prince,' he would repeat. It would be wrong, however, to see this as a nationalistic declaration. To understand it correctly, it should be considered in conjunction with another declaration: 'I am Austrian first and foremost.' On this basis, he could describe himself as a German prince, as he was also a Hungarian king, an Italian monarch and a Polish sovereign. This shows that there was no question of a nationalist ideology behind his German policies.

These policies were chiefly dictated by concern for the interests of the Austrian state. The traditions of the House of Habsburg designated Germany as a particular sphere of influence for the family, in their role as first princes of Germany, and

Franz Joseph proposed to maintain this supremacy in the form in which it had been bequeathed to him by his ancestors. But this policy led to inevitable problems in Austro-Prussian relations.

Franz Joseph could choose between two courses of action, both of which had supporters among the political and diplomatic community. These two groups were in agreement that a conflict with Berlin was inevitable, but they differed over the conclusions to be drawn from this. The first group, whose spokesman was Rechberg, believed that Austria should refrain from any aggressive behaviour until its military forces had been built up again. In the tradition of Metternich, this party considered that an understanding between the two powers was the only possible response to the German question which would serve conservative interests. Furthermore, by obliging Prussia to conform to the stipulations of an alliance, Austria would be in a better position to aim at greater power, because of the control it would gain. The final advantage of this solution would be that Austria could hope to obtain a guarantee of the integrity of its possessions from Prussia which, should there be a new conflict with France, would protect Austria from a repeat of the situation in 1859. It remained to be seen whether such a policy had solid foundations for, although Austria might wish to re-establish its ties with Prussia, it would not do so at the expense of its own primacy in Germany. It was hard to believe that Prussia would agree to a form of alliance which would keep it in the role of brilliant second power. Such forbearance could surely not be expected of Bismarck who had been called on to head the government in September 1862. In the event that such an alliance were to be made, it must be assumed that both participants would enter into it with veiled hostility. Should Austria draw closer to Prussia, it would also have to be prepared to suffer a deterioration in its relations with the German states on whose support it had traditionally relied. These states had often supported Austria, but they had considered the hostility between the two largest German powers to act as a safeguard for their own autonomy. The creation of a Vienna–Berlin axis would inevitably entail a reduction in their own freedom of action with the result that Austria's credit would be reduced in their eyes. Thus isolated, the monarchy would be condemned to a close relationship with Prussia which would be heavy with threats.

The other line of thought was that Austria should accept the risk of a confrontation with Prussia. If it were to cut itself off from its traditional partners, Austria would in effect be giving itself over to the machinations of an ally whose sole aim was to exploit this union in order to paralyse the empire, and to move closer to the achievement of its own goals. This camp believed that Austria should instead continue to challenge Prussia and should rely on its own network of alliances among the German states to deter Prussia's empire-building ambitions. As first power in Germany it still fell to Austria to lead a move towards reinforcing the structures of the Confederation, and through this means it could thwart Prussia's ambitions. Those who supported this policy were also high up in the administration. Schmerling was among them. Since 1848, he defended the theory of a Greater Germany centred around Austria. Although his ministerial position meant that his main concern was the internal affairs of the empire, he considered the defence of a Greater Germany to be among his government's priorities. In addition, in initiating a constitutional regime inspired by centralist principles, he was also considering the effects which such a reform would have on Germany. He believed that it would allow the monarchy to regain the ground which it had lost during the neo-absolutist decade, and would help provide a counterweight for Prussian prestige.

Obliged to choose between such contrasting proposal, Franz Joseph inclined towards a closer link with Prussia, although he had initially been furious at Berlin's traitorous action and had dreamed of vengeance. In the grip of his anger he had considered turning instead to Paris, but Napoleon III's refusal to honour his undertakings at Villafranca soon dissuaded Franz Joseph from this temptation. Schwarzenberg's example had certainly prepared him for a view which envisaged political and even military confrontation with Prussia. But he had also been brought up under Metternich's school of thought and he remained loyal to a system which would combine respect for Austrian primacy in Germany with the preservation of a close alliance with Prussia. This choice was in accordance with his desire for a common front among the conservative powers against the dangers of the revolution, embodied by liberalism and nationalism, and it was these two forces which he suspected Napoleon III of manipulating. He had nevertheless learned that Prussia's will to power was a factor to be reckoned with. He was therefore not deaf to those of his counsellors who warned him against Prussia.

It was perfectly natural that Franz Joseph should keep the option of a change of policy open. There was nothing exceptional in the fact that his entourage was made up of supporters of opposing factions. It was, however, a serious matter when these two policies were effectively in operation at the same time. Although he was the head of the Austrian diplomatic corps, Rechberg did not have complete mastery of German affairs and Schmerling, who escaped his jurisdiction, developed his own independent initiatives. The difference of opinion between these decision-makers lent an air of uncertainty to Austrian policy in contrast with the continuity in Prussian diplomatic behaviour. Indeed, these disagreements shed light on an important truth of the period: throughout these years, with the exception of a few rare occasions, of which in any case it was unable to take advantage, Austria was constantly on the defensive towards a Prussia which was both confident and in a position of strength.

Matters promised to become really difficult when, having been recalled from his post as ambassador in Paris, Otto von Bismarck became head of the Prussian government in September 1862. His first task was to resolve the crisis provoked by the Diet's refusal to pass a reform which the king considered necessary to turn the Prussian army into an efficient fighting machine. From then on, Austria was confronted by a figure who was determined to bring about a complete revision of the relationship between the two powers, who was possessed of few scruples as to his choice of means, and who was prepared to cut through Austro-Prussian dualism with steel and blood.

Austria, however, did not have to wait for Bismarck's arrival to suffer from Prussian policy. The attack began in the sphere of commerce, where the Habsburg monarchy found itself in weak position. Friedrich Wilhelm IV had pointed the way: 'I believe', he insisted to his ministers, 'that it is a political necessity to proceed without delay in a reduction of the customs tariffs of the *Zollverein* to an extent that Austria should not be able cope with them.'[9] Having set out his goals, what better way to score against Austria than to conclude a commercial treaty with one of the other great European powers? Prussia would allow the other power tax concessions which would outplay Austria. His objective was achieved on 29 March 1862 when

Prussia signed a commercial treaty with France which, beyond the economic advantages which each of the partners supllied to the other, was intended to hasten the completion of the *Zollverein*. Prussia in fact undertook to extend the application of the treaty to the whole of the *Zollverein*, involving a reform of its internal tariffs.

Without any doubt, this treaty was intended to be a direct attack on Austria. By making necessary a reduction in the internal tariffs of the customs union, its main result was to consolidate the economic ties between Prussia and the other German states and, in so doing, to accentuate a tendency which had already been emerging for some years. At the same time it would serve to turn away a little more German trade from the Austrian marketplace.

Whatever the case, this treaty would weaken Austria's position, if only because it placed the monarchy in a delicate position in relation to its allies among the German states. Above all, it created a favourable climate for the creation of the limited Union which had, until Olmütz, been the objective of Friedrich Wilhelm's policies. Certainly, such a consequence would at first be limited to the economic sphere. But it is not hard to guess that, in the minds of the Prussian rulers, this initial act was intended to lead to a second move, at the close of which Austria would also be excluded from the political body of Germany: 'In the commercial treaty with France', wrote the Swabian economist Albert Schäffle, 'politics play a fundamental role. This is a question of cutting off Austria economically for political reasons.'[10]

The Prussian initiative at first provoked a real hail of protest among all the powers hostile to Berlin's ambition. Among these were the supporters of a Greater Germany who could see clearly that this treaty was a preparation of the way for a political solution which would leave Austria isolated. There were also a number of groups, in particular in southern Germany, who feared a free-trade system, and defended their right to remain separate. Austria could exploit these reactions to cement relations with the lesser German states, and to form a common front with them. Indeed, the monarchy was not slow to act, sending a note to the various German governments on 10 July 1862 which proposed the creation of a commercial zone which would include both the *Zollverein* as it stood at present, and the Habsburg monarchy. Once this agreement had come into force, it was proposed that Austria and Prussia would negotiate with France in the name of the extended *Zollverein* for a number of modifications to the Franco-Prussian treaty. The execution of this plan was dependent on a gesture of goodwill from Prussia, but the latter had no intention of deserting the path it had chosen for itself. Faced with this point of no return, some people went so far as to envisage a denunciation of the *Zollverein* which would then be rebuilt to include Austria but not Prussia. Of course it would be necessary for Austria to agree with this solution and it was already clear that in its very principles this course was repugnant to Franz Joseph who wished to avoid a break with Prussia. To cap this, wavering between two opposing courses of action, Austria failed to choose a coherent and firm policy, especially as protectionist tendencies remained strong.

Profiting from the confusion in the enemy camp, Bismarck pushed the assault to a greater pitch by declaring Prussia to be against the *Zollverein* on 15 December 1863, and demanding the ratification of the Franco-Prussian treaty by the German states as a condition for rejoining it. For the latter, the hour of truth had arrived. Deprived of Austrian support, since the monarchy favoured an understanding with Prussia in order to provide concerted action over the Danish duchies, they had no choice but to agree.

For the monarchy of the Danube, this outcome represented a major defeat. It put a final end to Schwarzenberg and Bruck's plan for the creation of an economic Mitteleuropa centred on Austria. As Schwarzenberg had once attempted to force the doors of the *Zollverein* to ensure a financial foundation for the Habsburg Empire's political hegemony in central Europe, so Prussia exploited the weapon of commerce to strike at its rival. Although the game was not over, Austria had already been forced into a losing position.

The Congress of Princes

Before the die had been irrevocably cast, Franz Joseph attempted to neutralize Prussia's power and to regain the political advantage. From the outset of 1863 the most anti-Prussian among his advisers begged him to take action along lines which would exploit German national feeling. For this undertaking Austria had several points in its favour in addition to the probable support of a large number of the smaller German states. Still steeped in imperial tradition, many Catholics continued to see Austria as the power historically destined to control the fate of Germany. The monarchy could also rely on the support of those who defended federalism – the only form of government which in their opinion was appropriate to the disparate nature of Germany – and who accused Prussia of wishing to impose a form of centralized government on the German group of states. As an alternative to a Germany directed by Prussia in which its multiple nature would be crushed, it remained to Austria to propose a system which would strengthen the pact of the Confederation while continuing to respect the sovereign rights of the member states.

Conditions seemed favourable for such an endeavour. The supporters of a Greater German solution had formed an association: the *Deutscher Reformverein* (German reform society). Also, the reputation of Prussia had been affected by Bismarck's dictatorial measures, in which he ignored the opposition of the Diet in his implementation of the military reform which his sovereign had called for. During the spring and summer, Vienna prepared a plan for the reform of the Confederation's Constitution which was to be submitted to the German states for approval. Lastly, Franz Joseph gave his agreement to a project which involved the creation of an executive committee of five, with the Austrian emperor as president. In this he would be assisted by the kings of Prussia and Bavaria and by two other sovereigns elected by their peers. The Austrian leaders were careful to devise a system which would guarantee Austrian pre-eminence. It was hoped in Vienna that Bavaria and the other two states would side regularly with Austria. The Austrian plan also proposed the occasional meeting of an assembly of delegates to be elected by the different states of the Confederation.

This proposal was incontestably conservative in tone. Austria not only hoped to regain the advantage over Prussia, but also to build a defensive wall against the rise of liberalism. There was therefore less possibility than there had ever been that Franz Joseph would accept the election of a parliament based on democratic principles. Nor did he wish the expression 'popular representation' to be used in referring to the chamber of delegates. As well as acting just in a consultative capacity, it would meet only once every three years, and would be accompanied by an assembly of princes which would restrain its zeal if necessary.

Once this plan had been devised, Franz Joseph intended to submit it in mid-August to the approval of the German princes at a formal congress. Before sending out invitations, he wished to make sure that Prussia would attend. He therefore took advantage of Wilhelm I's stay at Bad Gastein to meet with him at the beginning of August and to inform him of his intentions. The king's reaction was reserved. He expressed his regret that he had not been involved in devising the plan, objected that notification of the congress was at too short notice and finally suggested that the questions should first be studied by established ministers. However, when the two sovereigns parted, nothing irreparable had taken place. Franz Joseph was even convinced that although it had initially raised objections, Prussia would eventully decide to participate in the congress, and so convinced was he of this that he gave instructions to send out the invitations. It was only at this stage that Prussia refused to take part. Although he had his reservations about the Austrian plan, Wilhelm was reluctant to remain aloof from a gathering which would bring together all the German princes. For him to give his refusal, it was necessary for Bismarck to use all his persuasive powers, suggesting to the king that he would be going to a second Canossa if he accepted Franz Joseph's invitation.

Matters had moved too far for Franz Joseph to consider giving up. In any case, Prussia's example was not followed by the other princes. Acceptances were soon flowing into Vienna. In such circumstances, Wilhelm I's absence had the advantage for Austria of demonstrating Prussia's isolation. A letter to Sophie sheds light on the attitude with which Franz Joseph approached the congress:

> It is the final attempt to unite Germany in order to place it in a position to achieve its goal of balance and peace in Europe. It is the final means of saving the German rulers from ruin in the face of the revolution. Unfortunately, through jealousy and blindness, Prussia refuses to associate itself with the attempt, which makes the matter far harder; but on the other hand acceptances have arrived from everywhere, even from those governments which until now have been entirely subservient to Prussia.[11]

Franz Joseph invited the German princes to meet from 16 August in Frankfurt. This choice was justified because Frankfurt was the seat of the German Confederation. But this choice was also the result of Franz Joseph's attempt to adhere to imperial tradition. The princes would find themselves in the city which had seen past Holy Roman emperors crowned. It was in any case in his role as the successor to these emperors that Franz Joseph undertook this journey. Passing through Munich and Stuttgart, his voyage took on the appearance of a triumphal progression as the Austrian emperor received ovations everywhere. This acclaim was the expression of the continued strength of the old feeling of loyalty to the empire among the southern German peoples. The future was to reveal this to be its swan-song, but for the time being, Franz Joseph was encouraged by it on the eve of a decisive meeting.

The congress opened on 17 August in the conference hall of the Thurn und Taxis palace with a speech by the Austrian emperor. Franz Joseph was hoping that matters would then progress quickly. He believed that a few days would be sufficient to obtain the agreement of the princes, but the congress quickly took a different turn from that which he had expected.

The princes were less amenable than Franz Joseph had imagined they would be. Some were ruffled by the casual manner in which they were informed at the last moment of the Austrian plan by the empire's diplomats. But Franz Joseph also found himself obliged to give way to the pressure of other princes who deplored Prussia's absence, and hoped that a new initiative could be taken to persuade it to go back on its decision. The king of Saxony was nominated by his peers to attempt to persuade Prussia to reconsider, but the Austrian proposal was still taken as the basis for discussions and this reduced his chances of success considerably. Nevertheless, Wilhelm was suffering because of his absence from Frankfurt. Some members of his family urged him to attend so as not to leave Austria a free field. Subjected to these various pressures, the king was on the verge of reconsidering his position, and Bismarck only managed to restrain him by throwing the full weight of his influence into persuading him otherwise.

The decisions taken by the congress, which resumed after the king of Saxony's return, confirmed Bismarck's predictions. Had Prussia been present at Frankfurt, it would have been pushed into the position of a minority and would have been obliged to conform. Because it was absent, it could upset Franz Joseph's plans. Many of the princes at Frankfurt had little wish to give a free hand to Austria, whether because they wanted to defend their individual liberties against the appetites of the great powers, or whether they wanted to please Prussia. The Austrian plan was certainly passed by a comfortable majority, but this approval was accompanied by a clause which restricted its implications considerably. It was agreed that those states which were absent should be allowed either to reject the proposal or to put forward counter-proposals before it was implemented. In effect, although Franz Joseph was not immediately aware of this, Bismarck was the true victor of the congress.

Unimpressed by the apparent unanimity surrounding the Austrian proposal, Bismarck clearly still had no intention of supporting it. Furthermore, moving into a counter-offensive, he was quick to present his alternative proposals which ran directly counter to it. He demanded equal status for Prussia with Austria and the election of a national parliament by universal suffrage, a demand which illustrated the limited nature of the congress of delegates proposed by Franz Joseph. The reaction of most the German states was muted, for many of them could smell the breath of war in Bismarck's proposals. Nevertheless these provided a good reason to resist Austria's persuasions and the Austrian proposal was stillborn.

The Affair of the Duchies

This failure strengthened the position of those who had remained sceptical over the plan for a congress of princes. Foremost among these was Rechberg, who could preen himself for having predicted that it was dangerous for Austria to base its German policy on an alliance with the lesser states. It confirmed that they could not be relied on as partners. It would therefore be wise to return to a policy of agreement with Prussia. Disheartened by the fate of his plan, Franz Joseph was open to persuasion.

The crisis of the two duchies of Schleswig-Holstein provided the Austrian diplomats with the opportunity to carry out this change of policy. After having been high on the political agenda in 1848, this question had been settled under the London Protocol, 1852, signed by the great European powers, who agreed to maintain the status quo. As a possession of the king of Denmark, Schleswig-Holstein had enjoyed personal links with Denmark since the fifteenth century. This situation particularly suited the maritime powers who had no wish to see Prussia taking over land which would give it access to both the Baltic and the North Sea.

The matter was complicated by the fact that most of the population of the duchies was German. Such a situation was anomalous in a period marked by the rise of nationalism, especially as Holstein's membership of the Confederation gave the German states an indirect interest in the duchies. The king of Denmark, Christian IX, was himself under pressure from the Danish nationalists, and made the decision to include Schleswig in his kingdom, and it was this act which lit the touchpaper in the last few months of 1863. Arguing that its authority extended to Holstein, the German Confederation reacted by sending an expeditionary force made up of Saxon and Hanoverian regiments. At the same time, it took up the cause of Friedrich von Augustenburg, the German claimant to the ducal throne, and installed him in Kiel which had been liberated.

Austria did not oppose this intervention, but had little enthusiasm for an initiative which would logically end in a consecration of nationalism in place of the conservative principle of respect for existing treaties. Prussia was no happier with the course of events. Coveting the duchies for itself, it had no sympathy for the prince of Augustenburg's cause. Bismarck's skill lay in initially concealing his true intentions, and in persuading Austria of their common interest in opposing the Diet of the Confederation which, in its support for Augustenburg, had chosen to uphold the liberal cause and wave the nationalist flag.

In the face of this combination of events, the two powers came to an agreement on 3 January 1864, to intervene together in the duchies in order to re-establish the institutional order which had been established under the London Protocol. The first result of this intervention was to end the Confederation's military campaign. The German states did not have the resources to stand up to the stronger powers. From this time on they were reduced to the role of spectators powerless to control the course of events.

This intervention could have caused an international crisis. The other signatories of the 1852 agreement did not look on a *fait accompli* with complacency. In addition to abandoning the status quo, it seemed to open the way to a change in the balance of power in this part of Europe. However, these countries showed themselves to be incapable of formulating any concerted response to this situation. The government most concerned with defending Denmark, the British cabinet, ended by shying away from confrontation, as it did not possess the military force necessary to enter a large-scale conflict on the Continent. France, for its part, had set itself a rule not to act independently of Britain. Lastly, Russia was preoccupied by the consequences of the Polish uprising, and the help which Prussia had provided in that instance meant that it would be embarrassing for Russia to show hostility over the Danish matter.

Obliged to fall back on its own resources unaided, Denmark could at best only put up a valiant defence. This victory certainly served as balm for Franz Joseph's heart, still wounded by the defeats of 1859. He had instructed Baron von Gablenz, the commander of the Austrian expeditionary force, to: 'revive the old Radetzky spirit so as to raise the army's morale which is still smarting from the 1859 defeat'.[12] He was not disappointed in his expectations. Everywhere it fought, the Austrian army showed itself to advantage. At the beginning of February, it won the first victories for the allied forces, and on several other occasions its intervention was decisive.

In the political sphere, the situation was not so bright. By dragging Austria into a shared military campaign, Bismarck had managed to shackle the monarchy, which had fallen into his trap. In following Prussia, the monarchy had broken away from the Confederation and cut itself off from the German states. At the end of the war it found itself facing Prussia alone. This was precisely the situation which Bismarck had set out to create, for the confrontation of the duchies already established in fact the equality which Austria had always refused its rival.

With the affair of the duchies, Bismarck found the means to bring the whole German issue into question. He would continue to hold on to Austria until relations between the two states had been firmly established on a new footing. It seems likely that at this time he did not see war as the only possible outcome of this conflict. It was possible that Austria's internal problems and the critical state of its finances might force the monarchy to resign itself to a recognition of the equal status of Prussia in the Confederation, rather than committing itself to the uncertainties of an armed conflict. He may have hoped that, in return for a few territorial concessions, it would agree to leave the duchies in Prussia's possession, providing Berlin with further arguments for taking control of northern Germany.

In Bismarck's mind, this distribution was only one step towards power. His ultimate objective was a Germany under Prussian control from which the Habsburg monarchy would have been excluded. He hoped that Austria might resign itself to this eventuality if Prussia were to guarantee it control of all its own territories, especially Venetia. Bismarck thus kept a wide field of possibilities open. For this reason, at the same time as he was negotiating with Austria, he was also working to isolate the monarchy in the field of diplomacy since, of the possibilities examined by Bismarck, war remained the most likely, even if its timing was as yet unclear.

It was already very improbable that Franz Joseph would agree to share authority with Prussia. It was in order to avoid such a situation five years earlier that he had hastened the conclusion of the peace treaty of Villafranca. It was therefore out of the question that he should agree to a proposal which would expel Austria from Germany. His acute sense of family tradition sufficed to discount such a possibility. For generations, the Habsburgs had been, and wished to be, the first of the German princes. It was ludicrous to expect Franz Joseph to allow this position to be taken away from him now without a fight.

Nevertheless he did remain loyal to the Prussian alliance which, for a long time, was to remain the cornerstone of his policies. In this, he had certainly not been struck with a sudden blindness to Prussian ambition, and he found Bismarck a difficult partner, although he did have a certain admiration for him. Like many Austrian conservatives, he was grateful to Bismarck for resisting liberal ideas within Prussia, and did not imagine that this champion of internal order would be prepared to make himself the tool of the revolution in his foreign policy. This was surely one of the keys to Franz Joseph's policies, for, by choosing the Prussian alliance, he believed himself to be returning to the tradition of the Holy Alliance. This conviction is clear in the letter which he sent to Wilhelm in October: 'It is, as you know, my unshakeable conviction that our alliance is the most secure bastion of the existing order against the serious political and social threats of our times.'[13]

Nonetheless, matters were not easy, for the fate of the duchies, which Denmark had returned to the victors, still had to be decided. Bismarck hoped for a simple annexation to Prussia, but Austria rejected this solution which, in failing to provide compensation for the monarchy, would strengthen Prussian influence in Germany. After long months of discussion, the two allies finally came to a temporary agreement which proposed the sharing of the administration of the duchies, Prussia receiving Schleswig and Austria Holstein. This agreement was confirmed by convention signed at Bad Gastein on 14 August 1865 by Bismarck for Prussia and Count Blome for Austria. Going against the advice of some of his ministers, Franz Joseph agreed to this plan only because it cemented the Austro-Prussian alliance. It nevertheless also had the effect of placing Austria a little more securely at the mercy of Bismarck's goodwill.

It was clear that Prussia held the winning hand. The Bad Gastein convention gave Austria responsibility for an area far from the empire but close to Prussia. This distance placed Austria in a vulnerable position. It exposed it in particular to Bismarck's provocations. He could now provoke incidents as he wished, which would furnish him with a *casus belli*. In the strength of this position, he did not hesitate to exploit the situation. The Bad Gastein convention thus had the result of turning the duchies into a powder keg which could be set off by Bismarck whenever he chose.

On the Eve of War

This threat did not prevent Franz Joseph from entering the year 1866 in a spirit of optimism. Following an interview with him in January Lord Bloomfield, British ambassador to Vienna, reported to his minister: 'His Imperial Majesty appeared to believe that there were no serious complications on the European horizon for the time being; he was confident that the year would unfold quietly and peacefully and that Austria would therefore be able to devote itself almost entirely to its internal affairs.'[14]

Events were soon to prove his optimism unfounded. Bismarck was not deflected from the objective he had set himself: the annexation of the two duchies. He promoted the development of an active propaganda campaign in favour of their incorporation into Prussian territory, behaviour which could only provoke irritation in his Austrian partner. A new stage was reached in the build-up of tension when he revealed the new Prussian plan for the redesigning of the institutions of the Confederation at the beginning of 1866. There was no longer any question of equal power for the two great German powers; this stage was over. Now Prussia was attempting to reorganize Germany in such a way that Austria would be excluded. In reply, Austria went over to the Prince von Augustenburg's cause. This about-turn provided Bismarck with additional ammunition. In particular, he could make use of it in his attempt to overcome the reluctance of his king, for, although the prospect of armed conflict was disliked by Wilhelm I, he would no doubt allow himself to be convinced if he could be persuaded of Austrian duplicity.

Bismarck was now determined to push matters to the point of war. To this end, his diplomatic preparations were stepped up. Bismarck first worked to ensure France's neutrality, although he was not prepared to go to the lengths of establishing a military alliance. In order to coax Napoleon III into his scheme, he dangled promises in front of him, while being careful not to commit himself by signing any undertakings. On the other hand it was essential for him to prevent the formation of a Franco-Austrian coalition. Bismarck was lucky that the choice of neutrality fitted in with Napoleon III's plans.

The French emperor chose to continue with the existing French policy towards Germany. His support for the principle of nationality made no difference to his policy: he had not suddenly turned into a champion of German unity. He was more inclined to support the continued division of Germany into Austrian and Prussian spheres of influence. By feeding the differences between the two powers, Germany would thus be weakened, leaving France in a strong position as possible arbitrator of German differences. In addition, Napoleon III was gambling on a long war, which would leave him a position to intervene at a suitable moment to dictate his terms to the opposing forces.

On the Russian front, Prussia hoped to benefit from the policies it had implemented since the time of the Crimean War. It had also recently built up further reasons for Russian gratitude by providing active support in the Polish uprising, whereas Austria had adopted an ambiguous attitude. Although Russia was unlikely to intervene through military means in the conflict which was developing, it would do nothing to impede Prussia's progress.

Britain's position was less clear. The Court of St James's certainly had little sympathy for Bismarck, whose frequently aggressive behaviour and authoritarian style was frowned upon. But the family connections with the Prussian royal family – Victoria's daughter had married the heir – prevented the British government from taking too hostile a view of Prussian policy. For the rest, the British also supported the concept of a 'little Germany' (*Kleindeutschland*). Lastly, Britain continued to have insufficient military means to intervene on the mainland of Europe.

But it was in Italy that the most positive aggressive intentions were to be found towards Austria. Hostility towards a common adversary must have suggested the advantages of an alliance between Italy and Prussia: the former would gain Venetia, the latter would find new support in its fight against Austria.

Bismarck indeed envisaged a war on two fronts which would keep a section of the Austrian army occupied in Italy and would thus lighten the task of the Prussian army. The Italian government would have preferred to settle the Venetian question through diplomatic means, but all its overtures had failed to produce a response. In the face of these repeated rebuffs, the Italian leaders decided to turn towards an alliance with Prussia. The two partners confirmed their commitment through a treaty signed on 8 April 1866. The contents of the agreement underlined Bismarck's aggressive intentions, for he had contrived that a clause should be included in the treaty which would limit it to a period of three months. In other words, he intended war to break out before the end of this period.

Austria could attempt to gain time by refusing to react to Bismarck's provocation.

This was the course which Franz Joseph first pursued. His memory of the disaster of 1859 made him wary of the trap held out by Bismarck. Furthermore, because it placed him in the position of the virtuous protagonist, he expected this tactic to strengthen Austria's diplomatic position. Lastly, Franz Joseph was still unconvinced of the inevitability of a break with Prussia. In following this moderate course, he could hope to thwart Bismarck's plans, for Vienna was not unaware that the king of Prussia balked at the prospect of war, and that a considerable portion of the Berlin court were encouraging him not to enter into a war with Austria.

Despite the precedent of 1859, Austria nevertheless had to bow to the demands of the security of the empire. Having taken this step the monarchy was locked into a fatal course. The Austrian military measures taken to safeguard against a surprise attack led to the initiation of counter-measures on the part of Prussia. This reaction allowed Bismarck to avoid the difficult position in which Vienna's patience had threatened to leave him, and gave him the means to convince his king that Prussia was the threatened party.

In the face of this acceleration of events, Franz Joseph was obliged to take decisions which had been unthinkable only a few weeks earlier. He could see no alternative but to give in to the bargain proposed by Napoleon III: to give up Venetia in return for French neutrality. Should he not agree to this arrangement, France would consider itself obliged to respond to the overtures of Prussia, which offered territories on the Rhine in return for its participation in the conflict. This was the implication of the 'very short, very simple proposal' which Napoleon III presented to Metternich on 8 June. Beneath the courteous proposal there lay an ultimatum, at least this was how it was read by Franz Joseph.

From 11 June, an extraordinary ministerial Council met. Here, neither Franz Joseph nor any of his ministers questioned the reality of the French threat nor of Prussian intentions. Franz Joseph felt himself to be forced to accept the unacceptable for: 'with a pistol held to our breast, it seems that we have no choice but to negotiate.'[15] On the following day, his foreign secretary, Count Mesdorff-Pouilly, and the French ambassador, the Duke of Gramont, signed the convention which made this official. The bargain struck between the two powers was not a fair one. Austria had protected itself from French military intervention, but it is not certain that Napoleon III had any serious intention of allying himself with Prussia. Certainly, the agreement allowed Franz Joseph to hope that should he win, he would be entitled to some territorial rights in Germany. He was probably thinking of Silesia, but this promise was matched by the reservation that any such gain 'should not upset the European balance', a clause which allowed Napoleon III an interest in German affairs. The loss of Venetia, on the other hand, was a bitter reality. Under the force of necessity, Franz Joseph resigned himself to a sacrifice which he had always refused to countenance until now. This concession was made under the worst of circumstances. Had it been made only a few months earlier, it could have guaranteed Austria Italian neutrality. Now it came too late for the monarchy to escape a war on two fronts if the conflict were to begin before the end of the three-month period designated in the treaty of 8 April.

In all, it is hard to imagine a more tragic and farcical situation. Whether it won or lost, Austria had lost Venetia, while Italy had committed itself to a conflict in return for the control of a province which, whatever the outcome, it was certain of gaining.

Franz Joseph hastened to sign the agreement with France, for events were fast reaching a point of no return in Germany. On 1 June, Austria made its break with Prussia official, by taking the question of the duchies to the Holstein Diet, through which it confirmed its support of Prince von Augustenburg's cause. These decisions indicated that Austria no longer considered itself bound by the agreement with Prussia, and could rejoin the alliance of lesser German states. For Bismarck this was a gift from the gods, providing him with an excuse for war, as Prussia was now in the position of the injured party. It was now of little importance that Prussia was condemned by the Confederation Diet, all that mattered to Bismarck was that he had achieved his main aim and he was already announcing the objectives of the war: to create a Germany directed by Prussia from which Austria would be excluded, and to elect a German parliament by universal suffrage.

Now that it was accepted that the Austro-Prussian differences would be settled by an armed conflict, preparation for war became a priority. Franz Joseph certainly had no intention of assuming command of his forces, having learned his lesson in 1859. But it would not have been true to his character had he rejected supreme command of military affairs. The important decisions would be referred back to him, leaving him in a position to choose the commanders-in-chief for both fronts of the war.

For the northern front he nominated General Benedek, and in Italy he chose Archduke Albert. After the event, these choices became the target of lively criticism. In sending Benedek, not Albert, to the northern front, it may be that Franz Joseph's main care was to safeguard the dynasty, but if this were true then he must have been anticipating a defeat. In fact, most military experts were predicting an Austrian victory and Franz Joseph shared their view. Following the logic of this thesis, he should have chosen Archduke Albert, not Benedek for the northern front. But this did not take into account the public favour in which the latter was held because of his achievements on the field at Solferino. His plebeian background also found favour in liberal circles. In such circumstances, the nomination of the Archduke Albert for the northern front would have been seen as the result of an intrigue on the part of the aristocratic *camarilla*.

However, this decision was not a good one. Benedek was certainly an excellent soldier who had demonstrated his fighting qualities in the various arenas in which he had seen combat, but he was certainly not a strategist capable of grasping the overall situation, and he was in no way prepared for the command of an army of over 200,000 men. It would have been wiser to have left him in Italy which he knew well and where he would have had command of smaller numbers, but instead, on the northern front, he was faced with the scientific strategy of von Moltke who made use of the advance of technology, and despite his courage he would soon reveal his limitations. He was himself aware of the problem, and he assumed his command in Bohemia wracked by doubts.

Franz Joseph could, however, be pleased that the king of Saxony had answered his call and was prepared to leave his own lands defenceless in order to add his troops to those under Benedek. Filled with gratitude, Franz Joseph assured his cousin Prince Albert of Saxony: 'For my part, it will be a matter of honour not to rest until Saxony emerges from this war which pits the forces of justice against trickery and piracy, both greater and stronger than before.'[16]

Sadowa

Events now followed an inexorable path: on 14 June Prussia announced that it no longer accepted the Constitution of the German Confederation; on the same day Prussian troops invaded Hanover and Hesse-Kassel; Holstein, which had been evacuated by the Austrians so as not to be cut off from their main forces, was occupied without opposition; and finally, on 18 June, Prussia and Italy jointly declared war on Austria.

Franz Joseph had decided not to intervene in the conduct of the war, but the successive missions of Lieutenant-Colonel Beck, one of his staff officers, to the side of the commander-in-chief demonstrate that Benedek's lack of action soon gave cause for concern. Indeed, it was essential in Franz Joseph's view that the army should move towards Bohemia, if only to join up with its Saxon allies. On two occasions, Beck's agruments had no effect on the chief of the armies. A third journey was required, in mid-June, before Benedek would give in. But the effect of this decision would remain limited if all he did was to move his troops. When on 26 June three Prussian armies marched into Bohemia from different points, he was only left with a few days to profit from his superior numbers before the enemy joined forces. But, clinging to a defensive strategy, he allowed his chance to pass. In any case, the news of the first clashes had dissuaded him from taking any risks. The ravages inflicted by the Prussian breech-loading rifles, and the weaknesses in the uppermost ranks of the Austrian command, boded ill for the outcome of the war. The confirmation of these first losses came on 29 June when the first corps of Clam-Gallas was shattered at Jičín.

In the face of these defeats, Benedek saw no other course open to him than to fall back on Olmütz where he could attempt to regroup his troops. It was a severely demoralized army which began its retreat, a fact emphasized by the disorder in which the withdrawal was accomplished. Sent once again to join Benedek on 1 July, Beck soon caught the military chiefs' mood of pessimism. In the face of this rapid deterioration in the situation, he convinced even Benedek to advise Franz Joseph at this early stage to put an end to the conflict in order to escape an even greater disaster. A telegram was sent to Franz Joseph to this effect: 'Implore Your Majesty to conclude peace settlement soonest; inevitable catastrophe for the army.'[17]

In Vienna, consternation reigned. Nothing was left of the joy caused by the news from the Italian front where Archduke Albert had defeated the Italians on 28 June at Custozza. Although it could do nothing to alter the fate of Venetia, at least this victory preserved Austrian honour. But this satisfaction was short-lived. With the first news from Bohemia, hope was replaced by doubt, all the more so because the court was dependent on the telegraph for its news, and this, of its nature, could only give a limited account of the situation. All in all, a degree of confusion developed in the communications between the battlefield and Vienna. News was already out of date by the time it came to Franz Joseph's ears. Furthermore, far from making matters clearer, Beck's presence complicated matters. Franz Joseph's decision to send him once again to Benedek's side betrayed his worry and uncertainty. He now found it hard to understand how the army could be facing defeat when it had not yet fought a proper battle. It is in this light that his reply to Benedek's telegram should be read: 'Impossible to make peace. I order you – if there is no alternative – to retreat in good order. Has there been a battle?'[18]

Franz Joseph thus appeared to consider Benedek's decision to retreat to be founded on good sense, but he categorically dismissed the possibility of ending the war. From Vienna, it appeared unthinkable for him to reach a settlement before all the armies had even been involved in a decisive battle. This accounted for the question with which the telegram ended, and which had been added by Count Crenneville, the emperor's adjutant general, but with the agreement of Franz Joseph. It can certainly be read as a sign of defiance, the more so because Crenneville's opinion of Benedek, as it is revealed in his diary, was unqualified. Reacting to Benedek's telegram he allowed his fury to escape: 'Odious telegram from Benedek who calls for peace at any price. Shameful! He neither knows how to win, nor how to lose with honour.'[19]

Crenneville's indignation may have influenced Franz Joseph, but it is also accepted that Benedek's hesitations had the effect of introducing doubts in Franz Joseph's mind over Benedek's ability to conduct the war. In addition to this, his sense of honour forbade Franz Joseph to consider himself beaten before he had even fought a real battle.

Did this reply lead Benedek to change his plans? He certainly saw it as a call to battle. It is also true that in the course of only two days the atmosphere changed. Dejection gave way to an optimism which, although it was certainly cautious, was real. The army had rested and regained its energy. Benedek could thus plan to halt his retreat and accept a fight. Battle was engaged on 3 July at Sadowa. Its course confirmed the lessons of the early encounters. Soldiers and officers did their duty with courage, but the finest virtues were not enough in the face of the fire-power of the Prussians. Furthermore, with its back to the Elbe, the army was in a terrible position to go into battle. To cap this misfortune, Benedek made a mistake in his calculations. Whereas he had expected to encounter only one army, the arrival of a second Prussian army split the Austrian forces. This soon left the general with no choice but to sound the retreat to avoid an even greater disaster.

In the Hofburg, the long wait ended only at seven in the evening when no doubt remained as to the outcome of the battle. Franz Joseph had no difficulty in assessing the magnitude of the disaster. There was now no more than a thin curtain of troops between Vienna and the Prussians, who might arrive at the gates of the empire's capital in a few days. In this situation, would it not be advisable to declare Vienna an open city? For the time being, Franz Joseph did not leave Vienna, but he decided that Elisabeth and the children should retreat to Buda.

Nevertheless, Franz Joseph did not give up the fight. He wanted to believe that the turn which the war had taken was not definitive. Indeed, he still had some trump cards left to play. He planned to bring the Italian army up to the northern front. These fresh troops could redress the numerical balance between the rival armies. Fresh from their victory at Custozza, these troops would raise the morale of an army eaten up with the disease of defeat. Finally, there were changes in the high command. Convinced of his own imcompetence, Benedek was replaced by Archduke Albert. Nor did the new commander-in-chief consider the game to be lost. It was essential that the army which had been defeated at Sadowa should regroup, while the divisions from Italy undertook the protection of Vienna and prevented the enemy from crossing the Danube. Once the fronts had thus been established, the conflict could shift to diplomatic ground.

Once again the key to the situation was to be found in Paris. Vienna did not expect Napoleon III to allow Prussia to take control of the whole of Germany, although the idea of a Germany divided between Prussia and Austria was now outmoded. If France did not hasten to throw the full weight of its influence into the conflict, it could find itself faced with a Germany united under Prussia. In these circumtances, Franz Joseph expected Napoleon III to make an armed intervention. To send or even to threaten to send a French army to the Rhine should be enough to force Bismarck to withdraw or face a war on two fronts. In an attempt to persuade Napoleon of the similarity of French and Austrian interests, Franz Joseph sent Baron Beust, who was still first minister of Saxony, and thus of the German state most committed to Austria's cause, to Paris.

Firm action was supported by many members of Napoleon III's court. The Empress Eugénie was known for her pro-Austrian sympathies. Drouyn de Lhuys, the foreign secretary, was worried at the dark future which the rise of Prussian power held for France. The French ambassador in Vienna, the duke of Gramont, was also in favour of military intervention. The hopes which Franz Joseph had pinned on the French emperor were nevertheless soon to collapse. Against the wishes of many of those closest to him, Napoleon III had no intention of any military intervention in the conflict. He informed Beust of this fact when he gave him an audience. For his part, the duke of Gramont was obliged to go against his deepest feelings, and inform the Austrians that there was no alternative but to attempt to make peace as soon as possible. The despatch from Drouyn de Lhuys was unequivocal:

> The emperor is convinced that to continue hostilities under the present circumstances would be disastrous for Austria. His Majesty is all the more reluctant to advise him to confront the enemy because he is not in a position to offer him the hope of armed assistance. He is effectively resolved, for the same reasons which have led him to adopt a policy of neutrality from the outset, not to tear the French nation from its work for peace only to impose on it the sacrifices and calamities of a war.[20]

The state of his army, part of which was still involved in distant Mexico, would not allow Napoleon III to enter a war with Prussia without risk. But it seems likely that the reason for his refusal was quite simply that he believed that he would be able to achieve his aims without having to resort to violence. The terms of the proposed peaceful arbitration presented by France to the two parties seems to corroborate this hypothesis. Thers was little question any more of Germany being divided into two spheres of influence, as it was clear that Austria would leave the German Confederation. But if Prussia were allowed to rally northern Germany around itself, and even to annex certain territories, France believed that it would not cross the Main. It would also be possible for the southern states to form a confederation which would form a counterpart to the organization of northern Germany.

Napoleon III therefore backed a tripartite system, for he could not believe that Austria would lose all interest in the fate of Germany, even if it was no longer a part of it on paper. On the contrary, the monarchy would not rest until it had wiped out the political consequences of Sadowa. Napoleon III was therefore betting on an aggravation of the divisions of Germany, which could only bring him joy, as it would enable him to retain mastery of the situation.

Now that the refusal of Napoleon III to give military support to Austria was known, it was left to Franz Joseph to make a settlement. There was no lack of supporters for the continuation of the war in his entourage, among them Archduke Albert. With the contribution of the Austrian army in Italy and of the final reserve forces, the number of men available to fight against the Prussians had risen to over 200,000. New lines of defence had been established. In addition, the Prussians were a long way from their home bases, which in the long run could cause them problems, and cholera had broken out among their ranks.

The arguments of the archduke were not enough to convince Franz Joseph. With the support of France, he would not have hesitated to continue the fight, but without this intervention the general outlook was altered. The chances of the advantage reverting to Austria became very slight. The prolonging of the conflict, on the other hand, might free hostile forces within the monarchy. Vienna was fully aware that Bismarck was financing the formation of a Hungarian legion which would be committed to inciting an uprising in Hungary behind the lines of the imperial army. In Bohemia, too, the Prussians were plotting to encourage the development of a separatist movement. These threats could become very serious if the war were to continue.

Although his reason convinced him, it was not without a great wrench that Franz Joseph decided on this course, for the price he would have to pay was the end of Austria's secular mission in Germany. He could only suffer in his heart that he should be the Habsburg who was obliged to close this illustrious chapter in the history of his dynasty. The terms of the armistice agreed at Nikolsburg on 26 July anticipated the peace treaty signed in Prague on 23 August. It was the official recognition of Austria's defeat, and of its withdrawal from Germany. Giving thought to the future, Bismarck was careful not to humiliate the monarchy, and imposed no loss of territory on it. Equally, a fine sense of the balance of power led him to decide not to push Prussian gains in Germany beyond those sanctioned by Napoleon III. The plan announced at the outset of the conflict was thus partly put on ice. Having increased its size through the territories which it had annexed (the duchies, Hanover, Hesse-Kassel, Nassau, and Frankfurt), Prussia contented itself with drawing together northern Germany under its aegis into a Confederation with itself at the heart, while the south was left to organize its own structure.

This comparative moderation no doubt provides the explanation for Franz Joseph's opinion, expressed as the armistice approached in a letter to Elisabeth, that the peace which was planned might be less unfavourable that he had expected. He even went so far as to pretend to be pleased with Austria's withdrawal from Germany: 'In any case we shall withdraw completely from Germany whether it is asked of us or not, and, following our experiences with our beloved allies in the German Confederation, I see it as a good thing for Austria.'[21] These remarks should not, however, be taken at face value. They were consigned to paper at a moment when Franz Joseph was at his most bitter towards the members of the Confederation who, with the exception of Saxony, had made Prussia's task easier through their apathy. But, whatever he wrote to Elisabeth, he was not reconciled to such an ending which closed the doors of Germany in Austria's face. At the end of October, the appointment of Baron Beust at the head of the foreign ministry soon confirmed this. As head of the Saxon diplomatic service since 1849, Beust had frequently opposed Prussian ambition and as a result, he had become one of Bismarck's pet hates. This was the man, then, whose name was a symbol of hostility to Prussia, to whom Franz Joseph confided the management of the Austrian diplomatic service. It is hard not to see in this choice an indication of his desire to eradicate the political consequences of Sadowa as soon as possible.

The weeks which followed the disaster of Sadowa and the Nikolsburg armistice were among the most painful in Franz Joseph's life. He was already suffering from having to face this ordeal alone for, with the threat of invasion, Elisabeth had taken the children to Buda. But when this threat seemed to have lifted, she refused to return to Vienna. She seized on any reason to delay her return: her state of health, the poisoned air of Vienna. But the truth of the matter was that she enjoyed being in Buda, if only for the contrast it made with Vienna, especially as the Magyars, who were aware of the advantage of having her support, surrounded her with care.

Franz Joseph was also worried about the extension of this stay for political reasons. It was not a very good thing for the empress to be won over by the charm of Hungary, and to espouse its point of view at a moment when decisive discussions about the fate of the monarchy were about to begin. To encourage her to return to Vienna, Franz Joseph sent her letters filled with touching humility: 'Come back to see me soon, if, of course, your strength and your health allow it, because, although you have been naughty and trying, I love you so much that I cannot be without you.'[22]

The tone of this provides a good illustration of the changes which the couple's relationship had undergone. Since the ultimatum sent by Elisabeth concerning Rudolf's education, she had developed a very acute awareness of the power which she had over him, and which she knew how to use. Learning his lesson from this refusal, Franz Joseph developed a sort of resignation which was to mark his relations with Elisabeth from now onwards: 'I shall patiently endure this loneliness to which I have long been accustomed. In this area I have already learned to endure much and in the end one grows used to it.'[23]

Nor was Franz Joseph unaware that as a result of the defeat, his popularity had fallen very low. A quatrain directly aimed at him appeared on the walls of the Hofburg:

> With volunteers with no buttons,
> Ministers with no heads,
> An emperor without a brain,
> How could we fail to lose?[24]

On his journey from Schönbrunn to Vienna he must have heard calls to abdicate from among the crowd. Even though he did not set out to seek popularity, these demonstrations added to his sadness.

A letter written to Sophie in the final days of August gives us a better idea of his feelings than his correspondence with Elisabeth. He remained convinced that, in this war, Austria had been fighting on the side of justice. If it had been defeated, it was because of an international plot between France, Prussia, and Italy who had united to bring about Austria's downfall. If the monarchy had sinned, then it was through its honesty in the face of adversaries with no scruples over their choice of means to an end: 'It is only that one can assess exactly the degree of infamy and of refined duplicity of which we have been the victims. Everything had been decided between Paris, Berlin and Florence and as for us, we were very upright, but also very stupid.'[25]

Nevertheless, in his view, this war was merely one act of a larger drama. Franz Joseph interpreted it as an episode in the conflict which had opposed the forces of legitimate rule and those of revolution in Europe since 1789. As the vocation of Austria was to be the bastion of the law, it became a natural target: 'This', Franz Joseph continued, 'is a fight to the death which is not yet over. The ultimate aim is the total destruction of Austria.'[26] It was for this reason that he still wished to believe that the last word had not been uttered and that, although this battle had been lost, there would be others. But hope only occupied a superficial level of Franz Joseph's feelings. During this period, pessimism reigned. For the first time, Franz Joseph recognized the possibility of the disappearance of the empire. His reaction in the face of this vision reveals his code of honour: 'When you have the whole world against you and you have no friends, there is no hope of winning, but you must still defend yourself for as long as possible, do your duty to the end, and finally, go down with honour.'[27] If time allowed it, Franz Joseph could regain his power, but the possibility of death would always be present on the horizon from now on.

The year 1866 marked a major turning-point in Franz Joseph's reign and, on a larger scale, for the Habsburg monarchy. In the course of a few weeks, Austria was excluded from its two traditional spheres of influence. Sadowa sounded the death knell for the Austrian mission in Germany. Although it would still encounter some resistance, the Hohenzollern state was now the only one to incite German nationalist feelings. In Italy, the process had already begun in 1859, but Franz Joseph had continued to hope that he could reverse the changes made at that time. Now that Venetia had been lost, there could no longer be any thought of this. Franz Joseph still had Italian subjects in Trieste, in the Tyrol, and in Dalmatia, but Austria had ceased to be an Italian power. Chased out of Germany, repulsed in Italy, there was little choice for Austria but to turn towards the Balkans where it might exert some influence to compensate for the losses in other areas. Although it did not enter this sphere until after 1871, this option was part of the scheme of possibilities for change from 1866 onwards.

Sadowa signalled the end of the Europe of the Vienna Congress shaped by Metternich. The principle of legitimate rule was fading in the face of new forces. The will to power was one of these. No doubt this phenomenon followed an established historical pattern. In the case of Prussia, the new element in its power lay in the fact that the emerging nation had managed to harness the forces of technical progress and the industrial revolution to provide the impetus for the destabilization of the existing order. But, above all, Sadowa represents the consecration of the eruption of nationalism as one of the forces which fashion the destinies of peoples. For all these reasons, Franz Joseph was justified in thinking, like Cardinal Antonelli, as he sighed over the news of Sadowa: *Casca il mondo.*

7

Times of Change (1867–1879)

After Sadowa, the winds of change blew across Franz Joseph's Austria. By removing Germany and Italy from its sphere of influence, the treaties of Prague and Vienna were the first confirmations of this transformation. In order to preserve its position as a great power, the monarchy would therefore embark on a series of changes to its policy in the Balkans, which, with the exception of the occasional crisis, had not figured large in the empire's concerns since the reign of Maria Theresa. The internal organization of the monarchy, too, would soon be turned upside down. With the 1867 *Ausgleich*, or Compromise, Schwarzenberg and Schmerling's unified state had incontestably come to an end, leaving in its place a double entity: the Austrian Empire had given way to the Austro-Hungarian monarchy.

In external affairs, Austria's Balkan policy placed it in opposition to Russia and led it to draw closer to the new Germany and, eventually, drawing a veil over past events, to form an alliance with the new nation. This alliance was to last for many years, and would form the unchangeable basis of the monarchy's foreign policy. In its internal affairs, Austria had reached the end of the period of fruitless experiments and fumblings. Despite the continued arrows of the critics, the dualist system resisted the test of time.

The sovereign who set out to implement these changes was a man who found himself increasingly alone. His mother, who had long been his true confidante, died in 1872. But, even in the sixties, her influence had been on the wane. Elisabeth, although she became caught up in the Hungarian cause, turned her back on political matters once the Compromise, which also represented a victory for her, had become a reality. Returning to her wandering life, she gradually drew further and further away from a husband who still loved her, but who had now learned to resign himself to long periods of separation. In short, through force of circumstance, loneliness became Franz Joseph's only true companion, if not his friend.

The Austro-Hungarian Compromise

The war had delayed the decisions which it was imperative to make over the structure of the empire. The unrest which had been revealed by the war, especially in

Hungary, had demonstrated that it was essential to find a solution. It was already the case that one of the factors involved in Franz Joseph's sacrifice of Austria's footholds in Germany had been the desire to save the empire from an internal crisis which might have unforeseeable consequences. Once peace had been restored, the settlement of this question became a priority.

Franz Joseph found himself at a crossroads: he could choose the federalist system or he could settle for a bipartite structure for the empire. The first option found a champion in the head of the government, Count Belcredi. Although he considered it desirable for an understanding with Hungary to be reached, he did not wish to infringe upon the interests of the other provinces of the monarchy. He feared that, if the Habsburg lands were reorganized according to a dualist system, the tensions between different nationalities would be increased. In his view, if the alternative course were taken, and responsibility were shared among several national groups along federalist lines, then there would be a good chance of establishing a new balance in the empire. Franz Joseph was not impervious to these arguments, but he had learned from his experiments at the outset of his reign that no constitutional reform could withstand the opposition of the Magyars. This realization was likely to lead him to favour an attempt at compromise with them, although such an agreement would preclude any other solution than dualism. Even if it were confined to the Austrian half of the monarchy, federalism was not acceptable to the Magyars, because there was a chance that it might spread, leading to the destabilization of Hungary.

Franz Joseph favoured an agreement with Hungary; before the war there had been many indications that he held this view. He was nevertheless still opposed to the creation of a system which would include a Hungarian executive and would put the seal on the fate of a single empire. Debate on this matter started up again even before the war had ended. This was connected to the pressure placed by Elisabeth on her husband. In Buda she allowed herself to be won over by the Hungarian cause and soon became a powerful ambassadress to Franz Joseph on their behalf. Count Andrassy even went so far as to hail her as the 'fortune' of his country.

This choice of action was only the extreme manifestation of the attachment which Elisabeth had developed towards Hungary. She had shown her affection for it previously, especially during her travels. Moreover, whereas she had made no effort to extend her knowledge of the Czech language beyond an elementary level, she worked hard to attain a perfect mastery of Hungarian, and succeeded to the point of making speeches, writing letters, and holding conversations with no difficulties in that language. Elisabeth also liked to surround herself with Hungarians. Many of her ladies-in-waiting, such as Countess Festetics and Ida Ferenczy, who read to her and was her confidante, were Hungarian.

Finally, there was her special relationship with Count Andrassy. From their first meetings, Elisabeth was fascinated by the charm of this Hungarian notable. But most of all, she saw in him the qualities which for her embodied Hungary: the spirit of independence and adherence to liberty. Was there any question of love? Whether she admitted it to herself or not, she looked at Andrassy like a woman in love. To this young woman whose need for love was not satisfied by her marriage, Andrassy must have appeared as the embodiment of her romantic dream, although she was well aware that their relationship must remain a platonic one. As for Andrassy, he was not in love. Although he felt a sincere and even fierce admiration for Elisabeth, he also knew how to maintain the degree of distance in their dealings which her rank demanded. Nevertheless he did not neglect to cultivate the friendship of the empress and to bind her closer to Hungary.

By unreservedly adopting the Hungarian cause, Elisabeth was overstepping her role as empress. Although it was acceptable for her to be concerned about Hungary's future, her mistake was to identify the interests of the monarchy with those of only one of its constituent parts. For some weeks, Elisabeth was transformed by passion. She maintained that the emperor should appoint Andrassy as foreign secretary. To achieve her ends, she bombarded Franz Joseph with letters and urged him to receive Andrassy without delay. Franz Joseph would not allow the choice of his foreign secretary to be dictated to him, but he did agree to give an audience to Andrassy and Deák. The threads of the discussion with Hungary were thus picked up again, but Franz Joseph was not won over to the Hungarian point of view.

His letters to Elisabeth show him to be caught between a degree of sympathy and unconcealed reservations. Although he wrote of Andrassy as a 'fine, honest, and very gifted man', he was nevertheless happy to be able to point out the lack of precision in his reform proposals.[1] Through his conversations with Deák, he developed 'a high esteem for his honesty, his sincerity, and his loyalty to the Monarchy'.[2] He was most impressed by Deák's declaration that Hungary would not add any further demands to those it had made before Sadowa. But these were still of a greater magnitude than he declared himself ready to accept. He criticized Andrassy for omitting to take the needs of other provinces into consideration. Although he acknowledged that Deák was more acutely aware of this, he blamed both men for putting forward excessive demands: 'They want everything, but they do not offer any substantial guarantees in return.'[3] In addition, he was not sure of the extent of their support within Hungary. Franz Joseph feared a re-enactment of the events involving the Old Conservatives which had taken place six years before. If he were to conclude an agreement with Deák and Andrassy, would he not be overwhelmed by the demands of supporters of the union of Austria and Hungary, or even of secession?

Although he satisfied Elisabeth by seeing Andrassy and Deák, Franz Joseph refrained from making any substantial concessions to her requests. The debate would continue for several months. Although he had not intended it, the decisive moment came when Franz Joseph nominated Baron Beust as foreign secretary. On his arrival in Austria, Beust had no particular opinion as to the form which the organization of power should take. On the other hand, he was convinced that the internal question should be settled as quickly as possible. For as long as this remained unsettled, the Austrian diplomatic service would continue to be powerless to act. If matters were looked on in this light, dualism seemed the only answer. It would be possible to reach an agreement quickly with Hungary on the basis of Deák's proposals. In the other camp, split between many national groups, the federalists could not agree, and this would render any settlement problematic, thereby reducing the political advantage that could be gained in any agreement with this faction. Lastly, the choice of federalism would set the Hungarians against Vienna, and their opposition would destroy the chances of any return to balance within the monarchy.

Beust had a maximalist view of dualism, since in his opinion, it was not simply a matter of dividing the monarchy, but involved placing each part under the control of one people: of the Germans in Austria and of the Magyars in Hungary. 'You will keep your hordes, we shall keep ours', he went so far as to say to the Hungarian representatives. The nature of this plan, which precluded any experiment in federalism in Cisleithania (the Austrian side of the river Leitha), made it likely to overcome the resistance of the Austrian liberals who, for the most part, had remained loyal to the Josephist concept of a unified state. Since beyond a certain point, the building of a single empire had turned out to be impossible, wisdom dictated an agreement with the ruling Hungarian classes on the basis of a division of power. A centrally controlled Austria would act in association with a united Hungary at the heart of a dualist monarchy.

These arguments finally persuaded Franz Joseph, for they touched on a sensitive area, the emperor being anxious to find a solution to the internal problems of the monarchy as soon as possible so that he could once again become active in foreign affairs. This urgency made him ready to acquiesce in Beust's opinion that only dualism could provide the monarchy with sufficient internal stability to give it the freedom of manoeuvre it required in external policy. His choice of Beust to continue the negotiations with Deák and Andrassy demonstrated that the balance had begun to swing towards dualism. This choice was confirmed definitively when the ministerial Council of 1 February 1867 decided in Beust's favour against Belcredi.

The latter could warn against the dangers of dualism, and put to the Council that there would be no true stability because such a decision would leave the Slav peoples ranged against the monarchy and would fatally weaken the empire, preventing it from developing any active policies in the Balkans, but to no avail. Beust had an advantage over his rival which was decisive, for he had reached an agreement with the Hungarian party. In order for it to be implemented it only remained to nominate a Hungarian prime minister who would submit it for the Diet's approval. Once this had been given, nothing more would lie in the way of the coronation of Franz Joseph and Elisabeth as king and queen of Hungary. With the prospect in view of an early peace with a subject people of the monarchy who had refused to forget the events of 1849, and whose resistance, however passive, had caused the government great problems, Belcredi's persuasions, however skilled, no longer had the power to restrain Franz Joseph.

The Compromise established the union of two sovereign states within one monarchy. The internal organization of each would be set out in a Constitution which fitted its individual needs. Accordingly, Franz Joseph would no longer reign in Hungary as Austrian emperor but only as king of Hungary. Hungary also exercised its own sovereign power in agreeing on an association with Austria and in recognizing their common interests. These could be divided into two groups. The first group, designated as 'pragmatic' in reference to the Pragmatic Sanction which had sealed the union of Hungary with the other provinces of the monarchy in the past, contained only three areas: foreign policy, defence, and the finances of the first two, which would be under the control of three ministers. These ministers would give an annual account of their management to the delegations, drawn from each of the two parliaments who would sit alternately in Vienna and Budapest. A second group of appointments would deal with those matters deemed to be of 'common interest', such as trade, currency, customs, transport, and indirect taxation which were theoretically the concern of each sovereign state, but which required a co-ordination of policy to create a cohesive whole. In order to meet common expenses a quota system was devised which established an economic imbalance between the two parts of the monarchy, Austria's contribution being fixed at 70 per cent, whereas Hungary would only be required to contribute the remaining 30 per cent of the total figure. Finally, following the example of international treaties – here again, Hungary's sovereignty should be remembered – provision was made for the economic clauses of the Compromise to be reviewed every ten years, which would also serve to adjust to the respective developments of the two signatories.

The price of this reconciliation with Hungary was high. In order to achieve it Franz Joseph had to agree to major sacrifices. From now on, the single empire of Joseph II and Schwarzenberg was gone forever, but, thanks to this agreement, Franz Joseph not only contrived to avoid the threat of secession, but to prevent Austria's relationship with Hungary from becoming merely a personal one. Above all, the Compromise left him with the upper hand in foreign policy and defence, the two elements which he had always considered to be fundamental, because, in the final analysis, it was these elements which determined the strength and position of the monarchy.

But the Compromise also led to a series of disruptions which caused as many problems as they solved. The first of these was the setting up of the three governments: on the one hand the joint ministry, and on the other the governments of Austria and Hungary. Although it was essential to the logic of the dual state in maintaining the areas of Austrian and Hungarian accord, the complexity of this machine threatened to reveal itself to be a weak link when put into practice. This problem was heightened because the Compromise created a shift in the monarchy's centre of gravity towards Hungary, although the numerical relationship favoured Austria (in the census of 1880, there were 15,642 Hungarians, as opposed to a population of 21,794,000 in Cisleithania).

In principle the dual state was made up of equal partners, but behind the fine words, the reality was quite different. There were many manifestations of this. Already the methods of implementation revealed inequality of representation, as the Compromise came into force before the *Reichsrat* of the Austrian provinces had even been elected. In other words, they were faced with a *fait accompli*, as their fate had already been decided by the Compromise which had been imposed on them by Hungary. Also, Hungary was in ancient country, and had the historical advantage of forming one political unit. The Magyars were dominant both in numbers and in influence, and their potential opponents were as yet merely disparate nationalities who were only just emerging from a long political hibernation and who, with the exception of the Croats, had no political tradition. Furthermore, an outrageously unequal electoral process would not be long in depriving these peoples of any means of organized opposition.

In contrast, the other half of the monarchy could call on no historical precedent. Even though it was habitually described as Austria, this was merely a term of convenience. Its anonymity was represented by the formula which would now designate it in official documents: 'the kingdoms and the provinces represented in the *Reichsrat*'. For lack of a better term, since the river Leitha formed the border between Hungary and the other lands of the monarchy, contemporary terminology made use of the term Cisleithania. But here again, this term had no foundation in historical tradition.

In its relationship with Hungary, its internal structure added to the fragility of Cisleithania. Whereas Hungary was strong in its political unity, Austria was divided into the seventeen provinces of the crown, made up of both administrative areas and regional groups, the props of local autonomy. Unless there were to be a return to absolutism, this politico-administrative organization set the limits of any plan for the reinforcement of central authority. Furthermore, the Germans did not have the same power over Cisleithania as the Magyars did over Hungary. One reason was that their numerical superiority was not so great. In 1880, they only represented 36.75 per cent of the Austrian population, whereas the percentage of Magyars in Hungary reached 41.2 per cent. But the biggest problem was that many of the peoples over whom they were meant to rule, whether Czech, Polish, or Italian, were the possessors of a level of political, cultural, and sometimes economic development which was far greater than that of the subject peoples of the Magyars. This narrower margin of difference suggested that the Germans would not have as much freedom of manoeuvre as the Magyars.

Finally, account should be taken of certain factors in the arrangements which threatened the stability of the whole organization. These factors were required by the Hungarians to emphasize the sovereignty of their country. For instance, the delegations from each country were expected to sit and to vote separately, communicating only in writing. There was an escape clause should there be prolonged disagreement, which permitted them to meet and to combine their votes, but they would nevertheless never have debated any issue together.

What was more serious was the requirement for a ten-yearly review. It was not unreasonable to allow for occasional changes so as to adapt to the development of the economic relationship between the two signatories, and it was thus natural that they should review their respective contributions to common expenditure at regular intervals. The danger lay elsewhere, in that the two partners placed different interpretations on the Compromise. Franz Joseph and the Austrian government continued to think in terms of the empire. They did not wish to perceive the Compromise as anything other than the extreme limit of the transfer of possible powers to Hungary. On the Magyar side, the prevailing view involved a completely different analysis of the situation. Hungary dismissed any reference to an empire to which Hungary would be subordinate, and declared the primacy of Hungarian sovereignty. From this time on, the Compromise was interpreted in Hungary as the furthermost limit to which Hungary was prepared to go in making concessions to the political whole.

For as long as the generation of founding fathers of the Compromise held the reins of power in Budapest, the status quo would probably not be threatened. But what would happen when new groups came to power? Less appreciative than their predecessors of the monarchy's sacrifices for the sake of accord, and more susceptible to the call of nationalism, it seemed likely that such successors would seek to profit from the ten-yearly review to place the delicate balance of the Compromise in jeopardy. Under the constant threat of this sword of Damocles, there was a risk that the Austro-Hungarian monarchy would effectively become a 'monarchy with notice to quit', as it was often described in the years that followed.

No doubt Franz Joseph did not clearly perceive all the logical consequences of the Compromise at the time he agreed to it. Most of these only emerged gradually in practice. He was quite clear, though, that he had chosen to share authority between Germans and Magyars and that he had recognized the two axes around which the reconstructed monarchy would revolve: 'I do not conceal from myself', he observed during the ministerial Council of 1 February 1867, 'that the Slav peoples of the monarchy may look on the new policies with distrust, but the government will never be able to satisfy every national group. This is why we must rely on those which are the strongest...that is, the Germans and the Hungarians.'[4]

However, it is unlikely that Franz Joseph perceived this relationship between nationalities as a brutal domination. His mind remained closed to the concept of nationalism. After the Compromise, as before, he saw himself as the sovereign of all the peoples of the empire. Nor did he consider that dualism made it impossible to form particular relationships with peoples other than the Magyars. In the following year, on a journey to Prague, he sought to renew his relationship with the Czech people. Nor did the dual monarchy prevent the Poles of Galicia from benefiting from a large degree of autonomy within the Cisleithan whole.

The Compromise did, however, lead to a cooling off in Franz Joseph's relations with his Slav subjects. The Slavs of Hungary had particular cause to consider themselves to have been abandoned. His constitutional obligations would from now on form a barrier between Franz Joseph and this group. The Hungarian minorities could no longer hope to find a protector in the Austrian emperor, as they had in 1848, against the abuses from which they suffered. As constitutional king of Hungary, Franz Joseph could communicate their requests to the Budapest government, but its members would simply file them, unless they wished to make use of them as a basis for the persecution of their originators. The Austrian Slavs also had cause for complaint. While Franz Joseph was seeking grounds for agreement with the Czechs, part of Bohemia was under a state of siege because of its opposition to the new order.

On a more general note, Franz Joseph's decision in favour of the dual monarchy showed that he had rejected the possibility of an Austro-Slav state which had been a possibility because of the numerical importance of the Slav people. In opting for an agreement with the Magyars, Franz Joseph had ignored the warning given by Palacký in 1865:

> On the day that a dual system is announced, we shall also see the birth of the Pan-Slavic movement in its least attractive form. Its godfathers will be the founders of the dual state themselves...We Slavs will receive the advent of dualism with a deep sadness, but with no fears. We existed before Austria, and we shall survive its downfall.[5]

The Coronation in Budapest

It was, however, not the moment for prognostications for the future. Franz Joseph was filled with satisfaction at what he had accomplished. From the day that a dual monarchy had been decided upon, it was also created in practice. Andrassy was placed at the head of the Hungarian government on 17 February. Soon after, Franz Joseph announced the restoration of the Constitution of April 1848, subject to the modifications made necessary by the Compromise. The path was now clear for the sovereigns to be crowned.

As the culmination of a process begun two years previously, this ceremony marked the reconciliation of the Habsburgs and Hungary. Of course there were still some extremists under Kossuth, who considered that all ties with Austria had been broken off in 1849. From his exile in London, Kossuth made a solemn protest at the abandoning of some rights of sovereignty which had been agreed by the negotiators of the Compromise. But most Hungarians were prepared to hope for a positive development of relations between Austria and Hungary, supported Andrassy and Deák, and greeted the coming coronation with joy.

Such an occasion called for extensive preparation. Most of the supplies necessary to support thousands of people, including a large part of the Viennese court, had to be brought from Vienna. Elisabeth was also pushed into action by the rituals which preceded the ceremonies, for this coronation represented, in some ways, the celebration of her triumph. However romantic a picture it may present, the portrayal of Franz Joseph giving way to his wife's blackmail or persuasions is probably a misrepresentation of the true course of events. Despite this, the path taken by Franz Joseph did correspond to Elisabeth's wishes and the Compromise was therefore a triumph for her which equalled her passion for Hungary. The Hungarians who, following Andrassy's lead, called her the fortune of their country were not wrong in doing so. Elisabeth, who balked at the formality of court life in Vienna, submitted with good grace to the necessities of the coronation rituals. Like each future queen before her, she had, in particular, to mend the royal robes. These were in sore need of such attention, for their great age made them effectively historical relics, and these symbols of royalty had also suffered from the recent treatment they had received. Just before leaving for exile, Kossuth had buried them on Hungarian soil to prevent Franz Joseph from taking them. It took four years of patient searching to find them again, and although they had been placed in a sealed box, they had clearly suffered from their lengthy stay in damp ground.

For the coronation ceremonies on 8 June 1867 Hungary put all its worldly splendours on display. Clothed in its most sumptuous attire, the Hungarian aristocracy ranged itself around its king and queen. Unaccustomed to this luxury which had an Eastern flavour, the Western observers marvelled at it, but also found it somewhat outdated. The festivities began at seven in the morning when the royal procession left the castle of Buda for Saint Matthias's Church, only a few hundred metres away. Clothed in the royal mantle, Franz Joseph was preceded by Count Andrassy who carried Saint Stephen's crown on a cushion. Then came Elisabeth, dressed in a gown by Worth, the great Paris designer. The brilliance of the ceremony was further heightened by the special Mass composed by Franz Liszt. The high moment of the ceremony came when, having been anointed by the Hungarian primate, the archbishop of Esztergom, Franz Joseph received the royal crown from Andrassy's hands. The taking of the oath was the other highlight of the day. It was described in *Le Temps*:

Once the Mass was over the new king of Hungary, wearing his crown, his mantle on his shoulder and his glaive at his side, crossed the bridge over the Danube, followed by a large and dazzling procession, in order to swear the constitutional oath in Pest; then, to the sound of trumpets, of artillery salutes, of *eljen** and nationalist *vivats*, he displayed himself to the people, standing on the traditional mound made up of clods of earth brought from all the Hungarian *komitats*; and there, brandishing his sword towards the four points of the compass, he expressed the renewal of the ancient pact between the Hungarian nation and the Austrian dynasty through this final symbolic act.[6]

A series of acts with both political and symbolic implications extended the coronation. Franz Joseph gave a gift of 100,000 golden ducats to the widows and orphans of those Hungarian soldiers who had fallen in the 1848–9 war. Immediately after the coronation, a general amnesty was declared, and was offered to all exiles provided that they swore the oath of fealty to the king, and of obedience to the laws of the kingdom. Still uncowed, Kossuth refused to make peace with the Habsburgs. On the other hand, General Klapka, who a few months earlier had raised a legion of Hungarians to fight with the Prussians against the imperial army, accepted these conditions.

Hungary reciprocated Franz Joseph's gift. To celebrate the reconciliation with the Habsburgs, the parliament made a gift of the castle of Gödöllö to the royal pair. This gift was also intended to induce them to remain in Hungary when official duties brought them to Budapest. The Hungarian government hoped that the sovereign would now live in Hungary for regular periods. In this matter, the choice of Gödöllö was a wise one. Situated only a few miles from Budapest, it was easy to get to. Furthermore, Andrassy was aware that Elisabeth had fallen in love with this castle, from which it was possible to go on lengthy rides across the Puszta. Now that her vow had been fulfilled, she would have an excellent excuse to flee the atmosphere of the Vienna court which she found so suffocating, to return to her beloved Hungary.

Doubtless Franz Joseph would often accompany her, for the settlement with Hungary had also had the effect of drawing husband and wife closer together. The couple were going through another happy period which brought an end to the troubled times which they had suffered in the course of the previous years. The announcement of a fourth prospective birth was the consecration of this renewed conjugal happiness. Elisabeth allowed it to be understood that she intended to involve Hungary closely with this birth. Not satisfied with giving birth in Budapest, she dreamed that the unborn child would be a son who would reign one day over an independent Hungary, thereby displaying little regard for the unity of the monarchy, or for the rights of Rudolf. This hope was not to last, though, for instead of a son, in April 1868 she brought a daughter, Maria Valeria, into the world. Although she could not aspire to the same destiny, Maria Valeria, born in Hungary, was to become Elisabeth's favourite child and the recipient of all her affection.

The Constitutional Laws of 1867

The Austrian lands were not only faced with a *fait accompli*. Dualism also determined the framework of their internal organization. The fundamental laws of

---

* Hungarian cries of acclaim

Hungary made explicit the requirement that this nation had made a commitment to a partner which itself should have a constitutional government. Beyond the ideological reasons for this, the Hungarians calculated that an absolutist Austria was more likely to succumb to the temptation to go against the Compromise and to revert to a military policy towards Hungary. The way in which the Compromise was set out also required that the Austrian lands should be structured in such a way that the main body of power was in the hands of the German middle classes.

The constitutional laws of December 1867 marked a new restriction of the powers of the monarch, if only because they were voted by the *Reichsrat* rather than granted by the emperor. Furthermore, they introduced the principle of ministerial responsibility to parliament, which Franz Joseph had opposed until now. The financial grants to the *Reichsrat* were also increased. These changes were not a serious challenge to the power of the sovereign, however. The Constitution approved by the *Reichsrat* followed the plan proposed by the government in its broad outlines. In accordance with the Compromise, the emperor would retain control of the foreign service and of defence, and would, in any case, have the power to call or dissolve the *Reichsrat*. He could also refuse to give his approval to any law which he did not agree with, and he could not only delay legislation, but use his right of veto to block it definitively. Although he would not abuse this right, Franz Joseph would not be prepared to allow it to lapse. As a final measure, article 14 of the Constitution gave the government the means to intervene if there were a parliamentary stalemate.

The organization of the *Reichsrat* acted as a further guarantee for Franz Joseph. The Lower House was matched by an Upper House known as the House of Lords, in which figures nominated by the emperor would sit beside the hereditary members, archdukes, and representatives of the ancient nobility and princes of the Church. As a result of its composition, this Upper House would serve to contain any excesses on the part of the Lower House. In all, despite the changes to Schmerling's system, Franz Joseph could consider his authority to be still intact.

On the political scale, Franz Joseph's Austria was of a moderate nature. It certainly remained a far cry from parliamentarianism on the British model, but it had equally declared its break with autocracy in the Russian style. The field of individual and collective freedoms had been extended, especially through the new right to form political groups and hold meetings. Furthermore, although the dominance of the German middle classes was assured – Schmerling's electoral model, which had not undergone any modification, made sure of this – in accordance with the liberal ideas of the Assembly, the nationalities of the empire were among those who benefited from the new era, through the recognition of their equal rights. This was brought in by article 19: 'All peoples of the state are equal, and each people has an inalienable right to preserve and cultivate its nationality and its language.'[7] The true effect of this article, which had been formulated along such liberal lines, would depend on the manner in which it was applied. But, such as it was, it was more detailed and went further than any text which had preceded it since the aborted Constitution of 1849. By defining language as one of the characteristics of national identity, it recognized the education system as one of the most important areas for the development and conservation of national identity. On a more general level, it set out the rules which would now control the relations between different nationalities.

Ultimately, the administrative structure brought into being in December 1867 was a double compromise. The first compromise was between Franz Joseph and liberalism. The emperor retained control of the government but the middle classes would participate more fully in the business of government and would enjoy greater civil liberties. The second compromise was struck among the liberals themselves. Being of a generation in which nationalist feeling had not reached its height, they were eager to reconcile a respect for their principles with the dominance of the German peoples in Austria.

This balance was also made possible by the preservation of a voting system which only allowed political rights to a minority, and at that time this formed only 6 per cent of the active male population. This group would certainly accept any compromise which favoured the financial and intellectual elites. Also, because of the narrow group from which it was drawn, the voting population could continue to resist the pressure of the lower social classes who were still excluded from official political life, to the exasperation of the nationalists.

The Liberal Era

In forming the first Austrian government of the new era, Franz Joseph turned to the liberals, who had gained a majority in the Lower House in the elections. There was no question that Beust should lead it. As foreign secretary, he would henceforth be part of a higher level of authority. As his first minister, Franz Joseph chose Prince Karl Auersperg. Auersperg was from an ancient aristocratic family and, having broken with the historical nobles when they formed an alliance with the Czechs against Schmerling's centralist policies, he had assumed the leadership of the Bohemian landowners who, in reaction, drew closer to the liberals. The formation of this government began the liberal era which, although briefly interrupted by Potocki and Hohenwart's terms of office, would last for nearly twelve years.

In forming a government which reflected the parliamentary majority, Franz Joseph was bowing to his position as constitutional monarch. He did not, however, feel at ease in his dealings with the liberals. His old prejudices were enough to prevent him from feeling any sympathy for their views. While his relationship with Schmerling had remained correct, it had always been characterized by a certain coldness. Nevertheless the liberalism of this generation of ministers remained moderate in character. For many of them, the execution of highly responsible duties in the service of the state before taking on ministerial posts had served to temper their liberal ideas.

This was not at all the case for the second generation of ministers. Their background placed them in a world which Franz Joseph had encountered only rarely. Already, their past histories diminished their standing in his eyes: for example, two of them, Giskra and Berger, had sat in the 1848 Frankfurt Parliament. Also, the liberalism of these new ministers was closer to the surface. Whereas their predecessors had automatically been concerned with the conservation of the powers of the monarch, the leanings of these ministers led them to display a greater susceptibility to ideological persuasions. Their training also frequently led them to give precedence to questions of law. It is significant that Edward Herbst, who would soon establish himself as the mentor of the liberal party, and Leopold von Hasner had both taught law at Prague University before joining the government.

In short, all the indications suggested that necessity alone had led to what can only be described as a marriage of convenience. In his conduct of this relationship, Franz Joseph demonstrated that over time he had developed an adaptability to events which had been lacking in his youth. It was nevertheless easy to guess that this would probably not be enough to avoid tensions. For the time being, the parliamentary situation left Franz Joseph with no choice but to adapt himself to this close relationship. But the nature of his true feelings suggested that he would be prepared to take advantage of any change in the political landscape to call a government more in keeping with his own convictions.

The time was not yet ready for such a step. The period was characterized by a speeding up of the process of domination on the part of the middle classes which in these years experienced its golden age. The members of the bourgeoisie could already congratulate themselves on having contributed to the consolidation of the constitutional regime, and their political powers were further extended to the economic field in a phase of vigorous expansion. The scale of this upsurge was all the more striking in that it followed a period during which the Austrian economy had experienced a marked cooling down. Had it followed the precedent set in 1859, the 1866 war might have made the situation even worse, but in fact the opposite happened: it liberated the monarchy from the heavy debts which had threatened its future. The German and Italian questions seemed to be settled for good, and the threat of a new war was very distant. Furthermore, there were drastic cuts in military spending which meant that the Austrian defence budget was below that of most of the leading European states, leaving the country free to work for peace.

This climate of confidence was strengthened by the belief that the monarchy, after a long period of hesitancy, had at last found a firm structure for its political administration. The liberal policies also contributed to a favourable framework for the development of the economy. Returning to Bruck's principles, they extended the field of application of liberal ideas to the monarchy's international trade, and many treaties based on the concept of free trade were agreed during these years.

Despite the predictions of pessimists that the Austrian economy would be weighed down by foreign competition, it transpired that in a period of growth the abandoning of protectionist measures served to enhance the general tendencies of the time. But there were also non-political reasons for this growth: a series of good harvests led to a heavy increase in the export of agricultural goods, which in turn entailed an increase in farming income and standard of living, benefiting the economy as a whole. These years also saw a spectacular return of railway construction: in only six years, 9,000 kilometres of track were brought into service. The size of this market gave a boost to Austrian heavy industry, although it was not extensive enough to supply all the railway's needs. General construction was also a prime source of economic growth, accompanied by an acceleration in the process of urbanization.

Following Vienna's example, the face of the main Austrian cities was gradually transformed. One after the other, they rid themselves of the city walls which inhibited their development. The physical expansion of the towns, like the increase in urban populations, created or increased a number of needs which formed one of the potential markets for Austrian industry. These included the demand for housing, although the building of workers' housing, which was less profitable than the construction of middle-class homes, remained insufficient for their needs, and rudimentary in its provisions for the inhabitants' comfort. They also included public schemes such as the building of arterial roads, the construction of water courses to supply drinking water to the cities, and of gas pipes.

Here again, the inspiration came from Vienna. A capital sometimes the object of envy, this city was nevertheless the only city in the monarchy to have reached the rank of metropolis, and as such it acted as a reference point, and set the style for other Austrian cities. More than any other work, the *Ringstrasse* symbolized the spirit of the period. Nearly 60 metres wide, it had the appearance of a boulevard bordered by an avenue of trees on each side. A first section which formed more than half of the intended total was opened on 1 May 1865 by Franz Joseph, who was driven along it in a carriage on returning from the traditional fair at the Prater. But the redesigning of this area had begun well before this date. In August 1862 an enormous park, the *Stadtpark*, whose frozen lake would be the joy of skaters during the winter months, was opened to the public. The *Ring*, too, soon began to be graced by official buildings: at the end of 1862, the Academy of Commerce (*Handelsakademie*) was opened; in May 1863 the first stone of the Imperial Opera House was laid, and this building, completed five years later, was to become one of the focus-points of Viennese life.

But most of all, the *Ring* began to be filled by sumptuous constructions, which were often described as palaces, in reference to the homes of the ancient nobility in the town centre. The aristocracy were not absent from these new residential districts, but the owners and inhabitants of these buildings were usually drawn from the upper middle classes, in particular from among bankers, businessmen, and chiefs of industry, many of whom were Jewish, to such a degree that the humorists of the time described the *Ring* as 'the street of Sion in the new Jerusalem'. Along these few kilometres of prestigious thoroughfare, a new financial and intellectual elite met. All the buildings were the expression of the success and power of this social class: the neo-Renaissance architecture, the decoration of the façades, the richness of the interiors in which furniture and pictures, carpets and hangings, vases and ornaments, potplants and statues mingled in exuberant excess.

Soon the *Ring* would also be ornamented by a series of public buildings which would each in its own way represent the rise of the middle classes and would confirm the influence of bourgeois values on society. For each of these buildings, a style was chosen which would serve to illustrate its position and its role in the liberal state. With its decorative façade inspired by the temples of antiquity, the Parliament building recalled ancient Greece, mother of constitutional government and freedom. The Town Hall would evoke the Flemish town halls, symbol of municipal freedom. For the University, there could be no better choice than the neo-Renaissance style which would connect it to the humanist tradition, and thus to science and progress, and finally, as liberalism sought to unite wealth and knowledge, the Stock Exchange, the other temple of the new era, would be built in the same style.

The Abolition of the Concordat

It was also on cultural grounds that the liberals engaged in their fight against the concordat of 1855. From the time of its signing, they had categorically condemned this treaty which did not content itself with freeing the Church from state control, but which also aspired to hand over to it large areas of social life, such as education. As they asserted that they had no quarrel with the Church, the liberals were all the more free to criticize this control for serving as a cover for obscurantism. They won the battle when, in December 1864, Pius IX declared war on the values of the modern world in his *Syllabus errorum*. The discrediting of this legacy of neo-absolutism thus figured among the priorities of the liberals.

A first attack was launched at the beginning of the sixties, and the defeats of 1859 provided additional ammunition for the liberals' reserve of arguments. Franz Joseph was not against some changes being made to the concordat. Despite the decisions he had made in the preceding decade, he had not broken off with the Josephist tradition and he would not be displeased to recover a number of the rights which the concordat had taken away from the state. Furthermore, the influence in court of the ecclesiastical party was on the wane, for Archduchess Sophie no longer occupied the central position that she had held a few years earlier.

But Franz Joseph wished such alterations to be the result of a direct agreement with the Vatican. In choosing this course, he was within his rights, because the concordat had the status of a diplomatic treaty, and any modification to it should therefore be negotiated by the two signatories. Above all, Franz Joseph wished to avoid a conflict with the Church, which would go against his own beliefs.

As a result of the Vatican's opposition to these changes, the first tentative discussions had come to an abrupt end. A new campaign began once the new *Reichsrat* had been called. This time, the political situation was more favourable. Franz Joseph was obliged to pay closer attention to the parliamentary majority, and the liberals held stronger views on the matter. Following the disaster of 1866, the liberals did not hesitate to complain about the power of the Church as they had in 1859. Beust joined his voice to theirs. Because it tarnished Austria's image in the eyes of the south German liberals, he considered that the concordat did not fit in with Vienna's German policy. Beust, like the liberals, was obliged to conclude that if Austria wanted to join the ranks of the states who were keeping abreast of progress it would be necessary to revoke the concordat, as one of the first acts of the new order. The president of the Lower House was echoing the views of most of his colleagues when he announced in his inaugural speech that one of the first tasks of the Assembly must be to 'accord equal rights to all beliefs and to free the state from the consequences of unfortunate treaties'.[8]

Franz Joseph would still have preferred a direct agreement with the Vatican which would have allowed him to put an end to this liberal offensive and to avoid a conflict with the Church. But new steps taken by him to achieve this end bore no fruit. Worse than this, a badly directed move on the part of the Austrian bishops led to a flare-up in the relationship between Church and State. After meeting in Vienna at the end of September 1867, to agree on a common stance, the bishops submitted an address to the emperor in which they urged him to preserve the concordat, and condemned the current attacks on the Church. This address caused a storm in the liberal ranks, but above all it hampered Franz Joseph's attempts to arrive at a compromise. The extreme position taken by the bishops seemed to him to be a criticism of his government. The curt tone of his reply is a measure of his annoyance. In it, he reproached the bishops for 'having chosen to make the government's task more difficult by submitting and publishing an address likely to stir up opinion, instead of supporting his attempts to find a solution to these important matters as he would have wished them to, in a spirit of conciliation and of understanding'.[9]

The balance of power, which at the time was strongly in favour of the liberals, no doubt obliged Franz Joseph to take a strong stance in his official reaction, but the severity he displayed was also the result of his Josephist upbringing which was coming to the surface. In his innermost self, despite the concordat, he had difficulty in allowing the Church any real independence. Like his predecessors, he expected the bishops to be the docile instruments of his will, awaiting its expression. Whatever inspired it, this reply indicated that even if Franz Joseph still did not wish for its suspension, he no longer considered it to be possible to maintain the concordat under its original terms. The confirmation of this soon came with article 15 of the December Constitution which, while allowing the Church self-rule, placed the act of confession under the general rules of the state. It was now only a question of time before the concordat was revised.

Three legal proposals soon attacked the major principles of the concordat. These were intended to reintroduce the civil marriage procedure, to withdraw the regulation of matrimonial matters from the jurisdiction of the Church, to free education from Church control, to allow everyone over fourteen the choice of whether to go to confession, and finally, to order that in mixed marriages, the sons would follow the father's religion and the daughters that of their mother. After being passed by the *Reichsrat*, these laws were promulgated in May 1868, and were generally referred to as the May legislation.

Franz Joseph did not refuse to give his signature to the proposals of the *Reichsrat*, but this was not to say that he truly agreed with the principles behind them. There are some indications that he did not fully approve them, for instance, on receiving a delegation of Catholic deputies from the Tyrol, who fought bitterly in the *Reichsrat* to defend the concordat, he congratulated Baron Giovanelli for his speech which, he assured him, had gone straight to his heart. However, he showed no opposition to the procedures which led to the adoption of these three legal proposals. Furthermore, when the Upper House had to make a decision on the marriage question, he ordered his great courtier, Prince Hohenlohe, to go to the upper Assembly to make his voice heard.

The key to this apparent contradiction is to be found in Franz Joseph's concern to respect scrupulously his obligations as constitutional monarch. It did not occur to him not to support the government he had appointed and which had, in his feudal view of the world, from that moment become 'his' government. But this loyalty placed him in a better position to act as a moderating influence. From the meeting of the ministerial Council which followed the promulgation of the May legislation, he set the limits for the new laws. There was no ambiguity in his speech concerning his decision:

> With the promulgation of these three laws, a new state of affairs has been created in the legislative field, which will only endure if it does not suffer infringements. I therefore expect that the methods of application and execution of the said decisions on an administrative level will dispel any disquiet they may have caused and that it will become increasingly clear that

their origin lies in the necessity for constitutional reform which has become imperative.[10]

It is impossible to misunderstand this declaration. Franz Joseph intended to restrict the interpretation of these laws. They had of course still served to deprive the concordat of part of its meaning, but in restricting the course of the liberal attack, Franz Joseph could feel that he had avoided the worst.

Ranged behind Cardinal Rauscher, most of the bishops interpreted events in this way, although they continued to condemn the May legislation. Furthermore, they had learned a lesson from the crisis in the relationship between the emperor and the Church of a few months earlier and, rather than risk losing Franz Joseph's support by mounting a systematic campaign of opposition to the new order, most of the bishops chose to make some attempt to adapt, so that the Church could save as much as possible from the situation. This stance was not, however, taken by all the Austrian Catholics. The concessions which Franz Joseph had permitted to be made might, in their opinion, lead to more. Also, even though the Church might believe that the worst had been avoided, it had nevertheless been deprived of the basis for its authority over some areas of social life.

The law of 14 May 1869 which called for a reorganization of the education system along the lines formulated a year previously, soon confirmed this fear, as the clergy only retained control of religious education. The legislation was intended, it was claimed in Catholic circles, to steal away the young from the influence of the Church, and to subjugate them to the authority of a 'state without God'. These intransigent Catholics therefore refused to recognize this new legislation and chose to resist it. They were strengthened in their resolve by the support of Pius IX who did not hesitate to describe the May laws as 'infamous laws' (*leges infandae*).

The most famous instance of resistance was that of the fiery bishop of Linz, Monsignor Franz Joseph Rudigier. Even before the promulgation of the May laws, he had made no secret of his intention to ignore them. Following their promulgation, he remained just as intractable. He committed a further offence by publishing a pastoral letter in which he defended the concordat, and made an outright condemnation of the Constitution and the new laws. This letter was immediately seized by the authorities, who thereby committed an offence against the freedom of expression which the concordat bestowed on the clergy. But the civil authorities went even further, charging the unfortunate bishop with breach of the peace.

Two opposing arguments were to be found in this situation. From the government's point of view, the Church and its dignitaries should respect civil law, and, if they should break the law, were liable to punishment by it. As far as the bishop of Linz was concerned, it was a contravention of the concordat for a member of the Church to be brought before a civil tribunal. He therefore did not reply to several court orders which were sent to him, so that, on 5 June 1869 he was dragged before the courts by force, and on 12 July following, he was condemned to fourteen days in prison.

Franz Joseph had until now refrained from intervening. Because Monsignor Rudigier had defied the authority of the state, he did not oppose the measures taken against him. However, he was not prepared to tolerate the scandal which the imprisonment of a bishop would involve in Catholic Austria. As a result, hardly had sentence been passed, than Monsignor Rudigier was granted an imperial pardon. This decision already suggests that it would be wrong to draw a parallel between Franz Joseph's Austria and the Germany of the *Kulturkampf*.

The debate over the concordat and the May legislation also resulted in the emergence of a Catholic conservative party which would quickly become a part of the Austrian political spectrum. Now that political influence was in part linked to the ability to command votes, it was natural that the largest bodies of opinion were attempting to organize themselves. Long accustomed to political battles, the liberals had a marked lead in this area. Outside Tyrol, the Catholics had not yet contrived to come together in an organized way. This was in part because the bishops were accustomed to applying to the emperor to defend the interests of the Church.

Events soon demonstrated that such an attitude was outmoded, for it could no longer be satisfactory, once Franz Joseph had justified his acceptance of the May legislation by referring to his constitutional obligations. This new turn of events meant that the Catholics would first have to rely on themselves and then on outside help from now on. This was the import of Monsignor Rudigier's words when he declared: 'When the emperor says: "I am a constitutional monarch," the Catholics should reply: "We are a constitutional people and, because of this fact, we must make use of constitutional rights." '[11]

Not all the bishops shared this viewpoint. Many of them, and first among them Cardinal Rauscher, looked with suspicion on a movement which threatened to pass out of their control. These reservations did not prevent this movement from making rapid progress. These years saw the creation of many Catholic associations, of varying size, admittedly, but some of which were large enough to demonstrate that a popular movement was developing around the Catholic cause. Taking advantage of the feeling provoked by Monsignor Rudigier, the Catholic Association of Upper Austria gained as many as 15,000 members.

The elections provided proof of the advance of this movement. The liberal candidates in 1870 faced an opposition which was far stronger than three years previously when they had won without any real competition. Although the towns remained bastions of liberalism, the conservative Catholics gained many rural areas in the Alps. These gains were not enough to affect the majority in the *Reichsrat*, but they introduced a new situation in the political game of which Franz Joseph could take advantage by drawing away from the liberals if the Catholics continued to grow in number.

This development of a Catholic political force was nevertheless not enough to save the concordat. Following the promulgation of the May legislation, Franz Joseph continued to display hostility to the annulment of the concordat. It took the proclamation of papal infallibility by the Vatican Council in July 1870 to make him change his position. Beust convinced him that this was a new departure, which, as a unilateral move on the part of the Vatican, removed any obligations on the part of the emperor towards Rome. Franz Joseph also took into account the position of the Austrian bishops in the debate over the declaration of papal infallibility. There were certainly some bishops who supported it, such as Monsignor Fessler, bishop of Sankt-Pölten, who had been chosen as secretary-general of the Council, and Monsignor Gasser, bishop of Brixen, who was also one of the authors of the text concerning the new dogma submitted to the Fathers of the Council.

However, most of the bishops followed the example of Cardinals Rauscher and Schwarzenberg who, along with the archbishop of Paris, Cardinal Darboy, led the opposition to papal infallibility. The force of this opposition impressed Franz Joseph who reacted to Pius IX's move in his role as guardian of the rights of the monarch, and led him to respond to it. He would later explain to his mother, who was upset by the dissolution of the concordat:

> When one takes stock of the bitterness and the sense of defeat with which our bishops returned from Rome, left without the slightest hope, without the slightest illusion, when one considers how the halo, which until now had surrounded Rome in their eyes, has completely disappeared, one would despair of the Church's future, if one were not firmly anchored in the belief and the hope that God will save his Church from further misfortune.[12]

Although he may have felt himself to have been obliged to go further than he had at first intended, Franz Joseph nevertheless did not wish his decision to be interpreted by the Church as a challenge. This concern was expressed in the manner in which the concordat was annulled, for it was done almost furtively, taking the form of a simple instruction sent by the emperor to the foreign secretary and then to the Austro-Hungarian chargé d'affaires in Rome, whose task it was to inform the Pope. The annulment of the concordat was as quiet an affair as its signing had been a solemn ceremony.

The Rise of the Federalist Opposition Parties

The Catholics were not the only opposition which the liberals in power had to contend with. They were also faced by the opposition of the federalist movements, among whom the Catholics held a strong position. Because it would involve the transfer of religious affairs to the hands of the provinces and kingdoms, a federalist system would allow the Catholics to escape the authority of the liberals in areas where they held a majority. But the federalist opposition parties also included most of the Slavs of Cisleithania, who criticized the dual monarchy, and protested against the centralist administration imposed by the constitutional laws of 1867. This opposition was, however, not united. The separate development of the Polish and Czech parties are an example of this.

On a theoretical level, the Polish conservatives who controlled the Galician Diet criticized dualism and inclined towards federalism. Their fear of Slav unity, too, would lead them to form an alliance with the Czechs. But other considerations made it attractive for them to follow a policy which would integrate them into the current system. The failure of the 1863 uprising in the Russian sector of what had been Poland taught them that the hopes of regaining independence for their country were very unlikely to be realized in the near future. The inclusion of Galicia in the Habsburg monarchy was thus a fact which they were obliged to accept. They were better able to do so, in that they had realized, by studying past Polish history, that independence was not the only means for a nation to continue to exist. Their concern to preserve the Polish identity within the group of lands under Austrian hegemony dictated their behaviour.

The Russian threat continued to haunt them, and played a major part in their decision to come to an agreement with Austria. The full weight of their history and culture led the Poles to perceive Russia in terms of modern barbarity while considering their own nation to be at the forefront of civilization. They also suspected the Russian Empire of nourishing Pan-Slavic projects. Because Poland was now split up, it was the duty of Austria to stand guard against Russia, as it had once guarded Europe against Islam.

There was one last reason for this moderation. The Polish aristocracy had not forgotten the great uprising of 1846. They were constantly aware that too outright an opposition to the monarchy might provoke the government to play its Ruthenian card. This threat had the effect of making the Poles act with prudence and of convincing them that their rule in Galicia continued subject to the approval of Vienna.

Despite their belief in the principles of federalism, the Polish conservatives did not push their opposition to the new order too far. Rather than bring about a serious crisis in their relationship with Vienna, they chose to support dualism and to limit their actions to the existing constitutional framework. In return for their conciliatory attitude, they hoped that Franz Joseph would not be ungrateful, and that Galicia would be given individual political status. As matters turned out, they could soon congratulate themselves on the results of this choice of tactics. It was no small achievement to have brought about, in 1869, the recognition of the Polish language as the internal language of the administration. Also, in 1869, the University of Cracow produced all lectures in Polish, and the University of Lemberg followed suit, at least in part, two years later. Effectively, these decisions led to the Polish ruling classes gaining control of Galicia.

In order for us to appreciate them properly, these gains must be compared with the fate of the Poles under their other rulers. While the process of the return to the Polish language gained ground in Galicia, the Vistula was subjected to an intensive process of Russification while a Germanicizing move would soon be launched by Bismarck in the Grand Duchy of Posen and in Silesia. Despite this, these measures did not satisfy the Poles who wished Galicia to have its own statutes. Aware that a concession in this area would make it hard for it to refuse the demands of the other minorities, such as the Czechs, the liberal government was not prepared to take the step of making Polish autonomy official. But, to make up for this, the Poles would have the right to a minister who would represent them in the government and who would include Polish affairs in his brief. In all, although it was not written into the fundamental laws of the monarchy, Poland enjoyed what was effectively an autonomy which, although it did not fulfil every Polish wish, left them in a far more favourable position than any other Slavs within the monarchy.

Unlike the Poles, the Czechs and their allies in the ancient nobility at first strongly opposed the new order. Having decided in April 1867 not to sit in the *Reichsrat*, the Bohemian opposition withdrew, the following year, from the Prague Diet. It had first reiterated the reasons for its opposition and the demands which it made in a solemn declaration on 22 August, 1868, written by Palacký and signed by eighty-eight Czech deputies. It refused to acknowledge a system, in the devising of which Bohemia had had no say and to which it had not given its agreement, which placed it under the authority of a state which had been created to order in 1867.

It is nonetheless striking to realize to what extent the Hungarian system inspired Czech behaviour and aims. When the Bohemian opposition boycotted the *Reichsrat*, it was not merely seeking to act out its principles. It hoped to obtain the same result as the Magyars had in making use of this weapon to bend the government to their will. As the Magyars considered that the Compromise of 1867 had been negotiated with their sovereign, without the interference of any foreign authority, the Czechs and the nobles considered that the Austrian cabinet had no authority to negotiate with Bohemia. An agreement could only be reached between the king and the nation, which would then be confirmed by the coronation of Franz Joseph in Prague and the taking of the royal oath. Although the state law forbade them to sit on the *Reichsrat*, the Czechs and their allies were prepared to agree that Bohemia had interests in common with the other provinces. For their debates, they envisaged another system based on compromise, in the form of meetings between a Bohemian delegation with the *Reichsrat*.

The number of analogies between the Czech demands and the Hungarian Compromise leave little doubt that Czech opposition to it lay in the fact that they had not benefited from a similar agreement. Their aim was thus to be recognized on an equal footing with Hungary, this equality being confirmed by historical rights, which in their view were just as incontestable as those of the Hungarians, as Rieger wrote: 'The rights of the imperial House over Bohemia are based on the same principles as those which it holds over Hungary. There is therefore no serious reason to refuse to Bohemia what has so generously been given to Hungary, that is the recognition of its historic rights and independent status.'[13]

Franz Joseph did not dismiss the possibility of an agreement with the Bohemian opposition and was well aware of the benefits which the monarchy could gain from such a compromise. Nor did he forget that an agreement with Bohemia would create the possibility for an alternative political force to the liberals. If the Czechs and their noble allies were to return to the *Reichsrat* this would provoke a swing in the parliamentary majority. This new majority could create a mainly conservative alliance within its ranks, combining the ancient Bohemian opposition with the Catholics from the Alps and with the Poles, who had no political sympathy with the liberals. Franz Joseph, nevertheless, had little room for manoeuvre to achieve this end. His obligations towards Hungary as much as those set out in the December Constitution created limits beyond which he did not feel he could go. It was thus impossible for any agreement reached with Bohemia to question the structure of the dual monarchy, and any such agreement would also have to fit in with the Austrian Constitution.

It was also clear that the liberals would not be prepared to help in the formulation of such a compromise, the more so because there were many Bohemian Germans among the liberal leaders. Several of the ministers of the period such as Prince Karl Auersperg, Karl Giskra, Leopold von Hasner, Edward Herbst, and Ignaz von Plener were of Bohemian or Moravian origin and the Bohemian Germans displayed a radical hostility to any idea of a compromise which, by linking political influence to demographic size threatened to leave them in a minority position in relation to the Czechs, in a kingdom where the Germans made up only a little more than a third of the population.

These pitfalls did not dissuade Franz Joseph from making overtures to the Bohemian opposition. Taking advantage of a journey to Prague in June 1868, he received Palacký and Rieger on behalf of the Czech national party, and Count Heinrich-Martinic as the representative of the conservative nobility. This meeting did not produce results. The conditions set by Franz Joseph were not considered acceptable by the opposition. The celebrations which, only two months earlier, had taken place in Prague on the occasion of the placing of the foundation stone of the National Threatre had demonstrated that there was a vast movement of popular support for the Bohemian opposition. The formal declaration of 22 August soon strengthened the national party's determination. For its part, the government returned the fire with the declaration of a state of siege in Prague and the surrounding area. This increase in hostilities demonstrated that Franz Joseph's move had failed, but his gesture still worried the liberals. Feeling himself betrayed because he was not informed of the emperor's intentions, Prince Auersperg went so far as to resign.

This failure did not discourage Franz Joseph. It simply taught him that the time was not ripe for his plans. A new opportunity nevertheless seemed to arise two years later. Differences of opinion had appeared at the heart of the government concerning the line to be taken against the federalist opposition. For their part, the opposition was not only growing but was becoming tougher. Following the Bohemian example, other groups joined in the boycott of the *Reichsrat*. The liberal majority was not threatened by this, but Franz Joseph considered the situation to be favourable for a new attempt at conciliation. This took the form, in April 1870, of the appointment of a government which was less strongly under the liberal influence.

The first minister, Count Alfred Potocki, reflected this change. This Galician magnate, the son of one of the most prestigious Polish families, showed every sign of loyalty to the crown. He was also a fervent Catholic who, so as not to betray his religious principles, would refuse to sign the document which denounced the concordat.

Potocki was ordered by Franz Joseph to prepare a compromise with the Bohemian opposition. To this end, he held a series of meetings in Prague in May 1870. Although he was liked by the Bohemian representatives, these talks ended in a further stalemate. The same thing happened in September following the dissolution of the Lower House of the *Reichsrat* at Potocki's instigation, in the hope that new elections would help to end the crisis. With the victory of the traditional nobility in the landowning *curiae*, the opposition soon gained a majority in the Prague Diet. Nevertheless, the impasse continued. On receiving a delegation from the Diet, Franz Joseph repeated his wish for compromise, but confirmed that he could not agree to reforms which ran counter to his constitutional obligations. He also insisted that the Czech deputies should bring an end to their parliamentary walk-out, for, he added, their return to the *Reichsrat* would make the formation of a new majority possible, a remark which suggests that in his view this was the main point of the exercise. In return, Franz Joseph promised to have himself crowned in Prague in the near future. These discussions still brought no response from the Bohemian opposition. Without a general agreement respecting Bohemian sovereignty, this ceremony would lose most of its meaning, and would become a fruitless diversion. The Bohemian leaders therefore saw no reason to change their position.

It seemed that nothing had shifted, and Franz Joseph must have tired of assimilating one refusal after another. He had not yet reached the limit of his patience, though. For two years, the various attempts at progress had been his doing and he still did not despair of persuading the other side to modify its demands. He was in any case already thinking of a new move. As Potocki's efforts had turned out to be fruitless, he was tempted to pass on the search for a basis for compromise to a different government. For this, he was considering new figures. His attention had recently been caught by a memorandum from the governor of Upper Austria, Count Karl von Hohenwart, who argued the case for an extensive programme of decentralization without bringing the December Constitution into question. Franz Joseph had also taken an interest in the federalist theories which Albert Schäffle, a Wurtemberg economist who had recently been appointed to the University of Vienna, had explained to him in the course of two audiences in October.

On being consulted, Hohenwart expressed himself willing to become head of a government whose principal task would be to find grounds for agreement with the Bohemian opposition. Nevertheless, the moment did not seem auspicious to him. He was of the opinion that it would probably be unwise to initiate such an extensive reform programme while the Franco-Prussian war was still going on. Franz Joseph was won over by this argument and it was decided that Potocki's cabinet should continue to deal with everyday matters until the appropriate moment was reached.

Towards a Reconciliation with France

The Franco-Prussian war of 1870 put a final end to the chapter of Habsburg history involving its participation in German affairs. The Treaty of Prague had already forced Austria out of Germany and in theory the monarchy was no longer concerned with German matters, but nevertheless Franz Joseph had not finally written off the tradition of Habsburg influence in Germany.

The Prussians' victory had brought them very close to achieving Bismarck's aims, but there were still a number of unknown variables from which Austria might benefit to the extent of regaining a foothold in Germany. The Treaty of Prague had left the possibility for the southern German states to form a confederation which would balance that in north Germany. In the longer term, Austria could hope to reopen the road to Germany by taking advantage of the bonds which it had reforged with these southern States. It is true that the line of the Main which was the traditional border between the two Germanies had already been partially breached. Immediately after the war, Bismarck had persuaded the southern States to bind themselves to Prussia through treaties which restricted their freedom of action. The ability of these governments to resist Prussia was thereby diminished, but public opinion remained largely hostile to a Prussian hegemony, and there was still widespread goodwill towards Austria.

The only hope for Franz Joseph's policy to become a reality lay in support for Austria by another great European power. He had learned his lesson after experiencing two wars in diplomatic isolation. There was no question of this power being Russia, as the Berlin–Saint Petersburg axis remained in place, and Russian resentment of Austria still existed. Britain held itself too aloof to make any active commitment on the mainland. There remained the possibility of an understanding with France. The French had made their position clear when Franz Joseph had asked for their help following the defeat at Sadowa and Napoleon III had expected to enjoy the fruits of his neutrality once peace had been declared. But the rewards which Bismarck had dangled in front of him without making any firm commitment soon vanished one after the other. This series of deceptions served to open Napoleon's eyes to Bismarck's methods. France should fear a growth in Prussian power just as much as Austria. Before the 1866 war, Napoleon III was prepared to allow Prussia to extend its borders as far as the Main. But his disappointments taught him that Prussian ambitions extended beyond this limit. As the next step, Prussia was aiming at no less an achievement than control of all Germany. France could not accept such a serious threat to its own security. Disabused of his illusions, Napoleon III now set himself the urgent task of halting the Prussian advance and of reducing Prussia to a level of power which would not present any challenge to French security. In this situation, he must be interested in a reconciliation with Austria which would open up the possibility of a defensive alliance against Prussia.

The Mexican Tragedy

It was for this reason that Napoleon III and the Empress Eugénie visited Franz Joseph and Elisabeth in Salzburg in August 1867. Officially, this journey had a different object, to provide the opportunity for the French imperial couple to present their condolences to their hosts following Maximilian's execution in Queretaro, an event which brought a tragic end to the Mexican expedition which had begun four years earlier.

Since he had nominated his brother as Governor-General of Lombardy-Venetia in 1857, relations between Franz Joseph and Maximilian had steadily grown worse. During the war, Ferdinand Maximilian had been given no role to play, and after it his only official position was that of inspector general of the Navy, a position which, although it was a high one, was nevertheless not a central one. This widening gap has been attributed by some to jealousy on Franz Joseph's part towards a brother who was said to be more gifted than he. It would, however, be closer to the truth to see this as a demonstration of a facet of Franz Joseph's character which would reveal itself on several future occasions: his fear that those members of the family who were closest to the crown would claim power. His behaviour cannot, however, be attributed to this motive alone. The instability of his brother's personality, his romantic impulses, and his taste for popularity led him to assume willingly a liberal stance, and this had not escaped Franz Joseph.

In his castle of Miramar, near to Trieste, Ferdinand Max was champing at the bit. Convinced that he could no longer hope to play a part in state affairs, he nursed his resentment and found refuge in his dreams. It was an embittered prince, tormented by doubts but still ambitious, who was approached in 1863 at Miramar by a delegation of Mexican officials who opposed President Juarez, and formally offered the Mexican imperial crown. This plan had already been a possibility, and under discussion at the Viennese court for two years. It was supported by Napoleon III who saw it as an opportunity to create a great Latin empire in South America under French influence. Of course the country was wracked by civil war. Supported by the great ecclesiastical landowners, the conservatives opposed President Juarez's republicans who depended on the liberals and the mass of the mixed-race population and the Indians for support. But with the intervention of the French expeditionary force which had been in the country since 1862, it was impossible to believe that the republicans would not eventually lose. Furthermore, now that Juarez and his followers had been chased out of Mexico, the Mexican conservatives' approach to Ferdinand Max could be the sign that the matter was nearly resolved.

The Mexican proposal immediately fascinated this thirty-year-old archduke in search of a future. He was also encouraged by his wife, Archduchess Charlotte, a Belgian princess who, like him, was eaten up by ambition, but who did not share his indecisiveness. There was no absence of warnings against accepting the crown, though, for despite appearances, the future was filled with uncertainties. Firstly, what was the real extent of Mexican support for the conservatives on whom the sovereign would depend? And was there not also the chance that the rebels represented a far more serious threat than the delegation suggested? In addition, the Monroe doctrine forbade the United States to accept any power on its borders which represented a foreign interest. It was true that the American civil war prevented them from interfering for now, but once it was over, the United States would not fail to display active resistance to this empire which had been imported from Europe.

In the Mexican venture, Franz Joseph may have welcomed an ideal way of ridding himself of a brother who had perhaps become an embarrassment. He would find himself glad at not having opposed the scheme when, following the defeat at Sadowa, he heard calls for his abdication in his brother's favour. But two years before this defeat, he had refrained from influencing Ferdinand Max's decision. Although he had not pushed him to enter an undertaking which he knew to be dangerous, he had made no attempt to dissuade him either. At the most, he had persuaded his brother to surround himself with guarantees. He had only intervened to the extent that he had imposed a family pact on him to renounce all his rights as archduke and to exclude him from the succession to the Austrian throne.

Different judgements have been passed on Franz Joseph's behaviour in this. Indeed, when the matter is examined in purely emotional terms, it is hard to portray this emperor who disinherited his brother in a kindly light. For his part, Ferdinand Max did not fail to interpret this final snub as a last demonstration of jealousy on Franz Joseph's part. The truth of the matter lies elsewhere. It should first be noticed that Franz Joseph was following his ministers' advice in taking this course, and that the decision was approved by the rest of the family. Once more, personal considerations were obliged to give way to state interests. In making Ferdinand Max sign this pact, Franz Joseph was not acting from any intent to humiliate him. He was instead concerned to keep Austria out of any undertaking in which its interests were not involved. At a time when it was fully occupied by German and Italian matters, the monarchy could not afford to extend its area of activity.

Thus, after a long period of resistance, Ferdinand Max resolved to accept the conditions imposed on him. The final meeting between the two brothers, on the morning of 9 April 1864, just before the signing of the Act of Renunciation, was a stormy one. In the course of these two hours together, with no witnesses, it appears that both brothers dropped their masks. Although Ferdinand Max gave way, he still considered his signature to have been forced. From the moment he set sail, he had no hesitation in going back on the agreement which had been forced out of him, not, however, that this change of heart had the slightest value in Franz Joseph's eyes.

It did not take long for the gloomiest predictions to be confirmed. Ferdinand Max, who was now known as Maximilian, emperor of Mexico, was to discover that his power rested on slender foundations. The groups who had come to find him had no real popular support in the country. Rejected by the great majority of Mexicans as a foreign power, the empire only managed to preserve the appearance of authority through the presence of the French troops. The situation became really critical when, once the North American civil war was over, the United States could provide efficient support for Juarez and stepped up their pressure on Napoleon III. Tired of throwing men and money into a venture which was turning out to be a fiasco, the French emperor finally took the decision to recall his Mexican troops in April 1866.

For Maximilian it was the hour of truth. When Marshal Bazaine, the commander of the French expeditionary force, offered to take him back to Europe, Maximilian did consider accepting the offer, but once again he displayed his indecision and allowed his conduct to be dictated by Charlotte who persuaded him to stay in Mexico, reminding him that for a sovereign, the mark of true greatness was to know how to face up to adversity:

> To abdicate is to condemn oneself and to give official recognition to one's failure: this course can only be excused in old men and idiots; it is not the act of a 34-year-old prince, full of life and with a great future. Sovereign power is the holiest gift bestowed on man; one does not abandon the throne as one does an assembly room surrounded by armed men.[14]

For her part, she was resolved to fight to the end, and paid a visit to Europe to seek aid. Her journey was nevertheless doomed to failure. The only interest of the people she wanted to help her was to bring the Mexican venture to a close. In undertaking this voyage just after the Austro-Prussian war, she was arriving at the worst possible moment. Napoleon III gave Charlotte an audience, but only in order to let her know that she should not cherish any illusions about obtaining aid from him. She had no greater success in Austria. Although he was concerned for his brother's fate, after Sadowa Franz Joseph had greater priorities than the sending of an armed force to help a non-European cause. Charlotte's tour ended in Rome where all Pius IX could give her were words of comfort. With this final blow her mental balance was overturned. Her reason could not withstand the misfortunes which afflicted her. Worn out with weariness, weighed down with disappointments, eaten up with anguish, she fell abruptly into a madness which would endure until her death in 1927.

In Mexico, the final act of the tragedy had begun. The noose was tightening around Maximilian's neck. Besieged in Queretaro, the final stronghold of the imperial forces, Maximilian eventually surrendered on 15 May 1867. The son of an Indian peasant, Juarez had none of the scruples of princes. Considering the empire to be a crime against the Mexican nation, he did not hesitate to condemn his prisoner to death. Maximilian faced the firing squad on 19 June in Queretaro with two loyal followers, under the circumstances represented in Manet's famous picture. Paradoxically, in the death throes of his empire Maximilian attained the greatness which had escaped him all his life for, although his continuation of the fight went against all reason, having refused to demean himself by abdicating he faced death with style.

The mortal remains of the poor hero were brought back to Europe a few months later on board the frigate *Novara* which had taken him out to Mexico three and a half years earlier in search of glory. Returned to the bosom of his family, Maximilian could take his rest among his ancestors in Vienna, in the Capuchin crypt, the final staging point of the earthly journey of the Habsburgs.

Franco-Austrian Reconciliation

When Franz Joseph and Napoleon III met in Salzburg neither was deceived by the other. Each knew the other's role in the tragedy which had just taken place. But it was no longer the moment for Franz Joseph to describe Napoleon as a scoundrel. Current needs dictated that he should put on a welcoming face for his guest. The two men shared an adversary in Bismarck and it was in their interest to co-ordinate their policies.

Franz Joseph was interested in a new relationship with Paris, but in order to fit in with his plans, any alliance must fulfil certain conditions. Franz Joseph was aware that, although many south Germans hated the concept of Prussian rule, their nationalist feeling was also aimed against France. There was therefore little room for manoeuvre. A war stemming from a French act of aggression would be the worst of catastrophes for it would provide Prussia with the chance to bind the whole of Germany to its side. Austria's chances of combining with the southern states to form a political bloc would then be over. On the other hand, a conflict in which France was not the aggressor would open up a range of possibilities for the monarchy. Austria would be able to involve itself without running the risk of being accused of betraying German interests. Beust even believed that, should war break out, it should be as a result of the Austro-Russian situation, into which Prussia and France would then be drawn in their turn.

This analysis underlined the importance which the Balkan question had gained since 1866 in the eyes of the Austro-Hungarian foreign service. Although Austria had not given up hopes of action in Germany, the consequences of Sadowa were beginning to be felt. This led Austria to turn towards south-eastern Europe as the only area in which it was free to exert its influence. Beust was therefore expecting any agreement between Paris and Vienna to provide a counter-balance to Russia, and to give Austria-Hungary the strength to enter the Balkans.

The Salzburg talks made a bridge between the two capitals possible. It was two months later, during Franz Joseph's visit to Paris for the Great Exhibition that their understanding took on a more precise form. During the ten days or so of his stay, Franz Joseph was surrounded with attentions from the French imperial couple. But, for his part, Franz Joseph was also able to win over the Parisian populace through a few simple gestures, for instance, by receiving a delegation of female market traders at the Elysée palace where he was staying. But he went further than this by returning their call soon afterwards. During a walk through the district of Les Halles, he was given an ovation by the crowd, and one of the stall-holders expressed the general feeling by avowing to a journalist that 'he was a very amiable emperor and he could be proud of the fact that the whole of Saint Eustache had a place for him in their hearts.'[15]

Franz Joseph was charmed by Paris on this his first and only visit. 'There is so much to see, and I do not cease to marvel and to admire', he wrote to Elisabeth who had the excellent excuse of early pregnancy for not accompanying him.[16] His stay was naturally filled with an official schedule of events: in addition to which he paid several visits to the Exhibition, attended various receptions at Saint-Cloud, at the Hôtel de Ville and Compiègne, reviewed the army in the Bois de Boulogne, and enjoyed several hunting expeditions. But Franz Joseph was just as happy to play the tourist. Notre Dame, the Sainte Chapelle, the Panthéon, the Invalides and Napoleon's tomb, the Tuileries, the Louvre, and the factory at the Gobelins were all visited in turn. At the Conciergerie he visited the cell in which his great grand-aunt, Marie Antoinette had been imprisoned. Accompanied by the French empress, he discovered the delights of Versailles. As a great admirer of Marie Antoinette, Eugénie showed him the collection of objects which she had assembled in the Petit-Trianon which bore witness to the life of the unfortunate queen. But Franz Joseph was also interested in the Paris of the present. Walking around the Parc Monceau, he admired the fine residential districts which had just been completed. His day would often end in a trip to the theatre. This visit was not without political activity, and although this took a back seat, it was also the occasion for meetings and announcements which confirmed the improvement in the relationship between the two empires. In the speech which he made at the Hôtel de Ville, Franz Joseph set the tone by emphasizing that old quarrels had been buried in the graves of his ancestors.

At first these talks took place between only the two empires, but soon Italy joined the discussions. Austria and France were not slow to realize that it would be necessary for Italy to be involved in their negotiations. For Austria, it was important to avoid any attack from behind in a situation where the monarchy was deploying its forces on other fronts. Italy, for its part, was interested in an agreement which would protect it from any attempt by Vienna to regain the Italian lands it had lost. Nevertheless these talks encountered a series of setbacks. The Italian government hoped to take advantage of the occasion to raise the question of Trentine, the Italian-speaking area of Tyrol, but Franz Joseph refused to entertain any question of the concession of lands.

But the greatest obstacle in the way of an agreement was the Roman question. In an exchange of letters with Napoleon III, Victor Emmanuel made a final commitment dependent on the application of the convention of 15 September 1864 which had agreed on the evacuation of the French troops who had been in Rome since 1849, in return for an assurance from the Italian government to respect the integrity of papal authority. The French troops had actually completed their withdrawal in December 1866, but a badly controlled attempt by Garibaldi to occupy Rome with his redshirts had led to their return in November of the following year. In addition Napoleon III in his obligation to take into account the opinion of the French Catholics, did not wish to risk a further disappointment. The discussions continued to come up against this obstacle, without contriving to find a way around it.

In the absence of the formulation of an agreement to confirm the understanding between the three parties, an exchange of letters between Franz Joseph and Napoleon III in September 1869 set out the reciprocal undertakings of Austria and France. Although this did not have the same value as a treaty, it at least had the advantage of binding the two parties together on a moral level. The task of the historian is complicated because there is no trace of Franz Joseph's letter in either the Paris or Vienna archives. It is nevertheless possible to reconstruct its contents on the basis of Napoleon III's reply:

> This sharing of interests and ideas can only promote peace in Europe. However, in the unlikely event that Your Majesty's empire should be threatened by an unforeseeable force, I would not hesitate for a moment in placing all the resources of France at its side. You may also be sure that I shall never undertake any discussion with a foreign power without first having reached an agreement with your empire.[17]

Beust would later insist that Austria-Hungary had only undertaken not to enter into any engagement with a third party without notifying France. However, in view of the decisions which were made in July 1870, and of the new attitude to foreign affairs in Austria following the Franco-Prussian war, Beust must have been obliged to play down the obligations which Austria-Hungary had earlier assumed towards France. It seems likely that in reality, in accordance with standard procedures in such cases, Napoleon III's reply had taken Franz Joseph's undertakings towards France, and repeated them towards Austria-Hungary.

The Opening of the Suez Canal

The following autumn was dominated by Franz Joseph's participation in the opening of the Suez canal. There were political motives for undertaking this journey. The building of the canal was the work of France, and Franz Joseph's presence beside Empress Eugénie of France was a demonstration of the accord between the two countries. It was also a reminder that Austria-Hungary was a Mediterranean power by virtue of its Adriatic coastline, and thus had interests in the Near East. This voyage was given additional lustre by Franz Joseph's visit, on the way to Egypt, to the sultan in Constantinople, followed by a trip to the Holy Land, the first by a German emperor since that of Frederic III in the fifteenth century.

Franz Joseph's letters to Elisabeth describe the different stages of this grand tour, from the end of October to the beginning of December 1869. From Constantinople onwards, the voyage took on an exotic and foreign character. On the banks of the Bosphorus, Franz Joseph could believe himself transported into the world of the *Arabian Nights*. His first impressions give an idea of his enthusiasm:

> I don't know how to describe what I am seeing and feeling. I have only one thought in my mind, the wish that you were here, only one hope, that you might be able to see all this: this setting, these waters, these palaces, the magnificent sunsets, the cypress trees, the host of boats, the colourful crush of people, the women, unhappily veiled, but with such eyes that you can only regret that they are, and this wonderful air.[18]

The sultan made sure that the stay in Palestine passed as comfortably as was possible. Nothing was left to change. A caravan of five hundred camels and dromedaries was put together for the Bedouin escort and the baggage train. In the evenings, the tents were pitched in the desert. Protected by a detachment of Ottoman horsemen, Franz Joseph slept on a silver bed which, at the sultan's orders, had been placed at his disposal for the entire journey.

When Jerusalem came into sight, his first act was to kneel down in the desert and kiss the ground. Many days were given over to visiting the holy places in Jerusalem and Bethlehem. In Jerusalem, Franz Joseph attended the Mass of the Holy Spirit and took communion there with many members of his retinue. As he was the protector of many different religions in the empire, he did not limit himself to encounters with Catholics, but also took care to meet the dignitaries of many of the different persuasions represented in the Holy City, whether Christian or otherwise.

Despite the care taken by the sultan, the journey was not without its dangers. It almost turned to tragedy in Jaffa, where the entrance to the harbour was barred by reefs, and the boats were obliged to anchor at sea. The only means of transport to and from the ships was by rowing boat, a simple exercise for the local boatmen, at least when the weather was good. On Franz Joseph's return to the *Grief* from Jaffa, the weather was terrible. Hoping to avoid delay, he decided to attempt the trip in spite of the conditions. The return journey was successful, but it was a miracle that his boat was not overturned or shattered on the reefs:

> The embarkation yesterday at eleven in the morning from Jaffa was very harrowing, due to the high tide and a very strong swell. I made the journey from Jaffa to the *Grief* in a small boat rowed by local people. Never in my life will I forget the way in which I was hoisted aboard in a sling, as horses are. I would not make the trip again for a million.[19]

The passengers of the other Austrian steamships, the *Elisabeth* and the *Gargnano* were obliged to wait for many hours before they could return on board. So as not to miss the meeting at Port Said, Franz Joseph gave the order to raise anchor without waiting for them. The other two ships would only set out the next day.

Once he had arrived in Port Said, the long procession of boats set out, on the morning of 17 November, along the Suez canal, writing a new page in the history books: at the head was the *Aigle*, Eugénie's vessel, followed by the *Grief*, the *Elisabeth*, and the *Gargnano*, and behind them the Prussian boat, an order which must have pleased Franz Joseph.

At Ismailia, half-way along the canal, a ball was given by the khedive in honour of his guests. During this ball, a crowd of many thousands thronged the palace, some of whom were clearly not to Franz Joseph's taste: 'Among the foreign figures of the first consequence from all over the world, there were many quite ordinary guests, and also many natives in costume. As the celebrations have drawn much riffraff to Egypt, Riciotti Garibaldi, the son of the famous Garibaldi was also present.'[20] Finally there came the arrival in Suez, the farewells to Eugénie, and the return by train to Cairo where Franz Joseph and his suite stayed for several days more before returning to Austria.

As the high point of his stay, Franz Joseph could not resist the pleasure of climbing Cheops, the highest pyramid in Ghiza. Taking seventeen minutes, the climb was not lacking in charm, according to the description given by Franz Joseph:

The ascent began at a fast pace. While a Bedouin seized me by the hand, another followed me in order to push me from behind when the blocks of stone were too high to be scaled, although this was only necessary five or six times. My mountain-climbing experience stood me in good stead. The Bedouins are very agile people, strong and confident. Mostly, they only wear a shirt, so when they are climbing, they leave a lot exposed. This must be the reason why English women so love to climb the pyramids.[21]

The Franco-Prussian War

On his return to Vienna, Franz Joseph also returned to the matter of relations between France and Austria. Since the exchange of letters between Franz Joseph and Napoleon III, the two empires had made no further progress towards an alliance. However, there had been contact made between the two armies, at the highest level. Napoleon III had expressed the desire for this when he confided in Prince Metternich: 'Should we ever have to take concerted military action, however far into the future it may be, it is very important that we should understand each other on military ground, in other words, we must form a joint strategy and should not, in the event, give way to foolish fumblings.'[22]

The inspector general of the Austro-Hungarian army, Archduke Albert, visited Paris in March and April 1870. This visit was returned by General Lebrun in Vienna in June. Although various strategic alternatives for German operations were examined, these discussions remained informal, so they did not end in the signing of a military agreement. Furthermore, on receiving General Lebrun, Franz Joseph was careful to remind him that he would only enter a war if forced to do so.

When, in the beginning of July 1870, the dispute between France and Prussia over the Spanish succession erupted, Franz Joseph's policy was determined: if the situation worsened, Austria-Hungary would only intervene on a military level in the unlikely event that France was attacked by Prussia. Not that Bismarck was against a war with France, indeed this was part of his calculations. Over the months, resistance to Prussian infiltration in southern Germany turned out to be stronger than he had predicted. He had hoped that the meeting of a customs union on the scale of the *Zollverein* would help him in his plans, by creating a common cause for all Germany. But to his great disappointment, the supporters of Prussia suffered serious election defeats in February and March 1868 in both Wurtemberg and Bavaria. Bismarck realized that these obstacles seemed likely to last for some time unless he could take advantage of an external crisis to shake up the southern German states. Although Bismarck had not brought it about, the Spanish question provided him with such an opportunity. The French reaction gave him the chance to turn the issue into one of national honour. Napoleon III pretended to believe that the candidacy of a Hohenzollern prince for the Spanish crown would expose France to a crisis on the scale of that faced in Charles V's time. Although this fear was a real one, Napoleon seized on this issue as a pretext to launch a counter-offensive against Prussia.

In fact, the behaviour of both sides was dictated by ulterior motives. Napoleon III demanded, following Prince Hohenzollern's withdrawal of his claim, an assurance from Wilhelm I that it would never be made again. This demand demonstrated that the French emperor's main objective was less to find an honourable way out for both parties than to humiliate Prussia. Bismarck, too, had ulterior motives when he composed the dispatch of Ems in such as way as to push Napoleon III to react in a way which made him the aggressor.

The line taken by the French worried Franz Joseph and Beust. The latter first warned the French leaders against a policy of direct confrontation with Prussia. When the conflict appeared about to explode, Austria-Hungary could no longer avoid taking an official stance in the matter, which would involve deciding whether to take part in the war or not. This was the object of the meeting of the crown Council on 18 July with Franz Joseph at its head. The personal inclinations of the members of this decisive meeting were not in doubt. All were in favour of France, whatever their opinion might be of Napoleon III's regime. Archduke Albert and the minister for war, General von Kuhn, went further, declaring themselves to be in favour of Austria joining the war on the French side. The monarchy, in their opinion, should seize on this final chance to restore its influence in Germany. The likelihood of a French victory reinforced this view.

These arguments did not, however, manage to sway the other members of the crown Council. Austria-Hungary, in Beust's opinion, was in no way obliged by its moral undertakings, set out in the exchange of letters in September 1869, to enter the conflict. Although it had been forced into the position by Bismarck, France was still the aggressor in the matter. Furthermore, this situation was precisely that most feared by the Austro-Hungarian diplomatic service. By portraying itself as the victim of French aggression, Prussia had rapidly succeeded in conjuring up a body of national feeling around itself, even from among the southern states. The defensive treaties concluded immediately after the Treaty of Prague were now called into play one after another.

If Austria-Hungary intervened in the war as Napoleon III's ally it would lose its bonds of friendship with the south German states. Nor could the Austrian government dismiss the possibility of a Russian attack. The army had still not recovered from the defeat of 1866, and was also suffering greatly from the effects of the budget cuts which had reduced the monarchy's military potential in comparison with the other European powers. In such a situation, it would be impossible for the monarchy to conduct a war on two fronts.

Andrassy had other reasons to oppose Austria-Hungary's participation in the war. As a Hungarian he had little concern for German affairs, but he was fully aware of the Russian threat. Nor did it escape him that the defeat of Prussia might involve a renewed questioning of the dual monarchy, and might affect the special position enjoyed by the Magyars within the monarchy. The revival of Austrian influence in Germany would inevitably involve a shift in the centre of gravity of the monarchy towards its German lands. Left in a position of greater freedom by such a victory, Franz Joseph might be tempted to go back on the concessions he had felt obliged to make to Hungary in 1867.

Caught in the midst of these various arguments, Franz Joseph took Beust's advice on 20 July and decided to play a waiting game. His evaluation of Austria-Hungary's strengths and weaknesses led him to adopt the course of armed neutrality. This would protect the monarchy from any surprise attack by Russia, a fear which continuously haunted the Austro-Hungarian ministers. But above all, such a decision allowed the monarchy to gain some time until the first armed engagements.

The possibility of joining the war soon receded as the French capitulation at Sedan and the collapse of the Second Empire brushed aside Franz Joseph's last doubts. In a way, Austria-Hungary did attempt to help France, by taking the step of creating a league of neutral states which would work for the return to peace. But, weakened by internal disputes, this league did not really hinder Bismarck, who was free to impose his own peace terms on the French. As a spectator, distressed by the Prussian successes, Franz Joseph looked on the future with trepidation: 'I see a very black future. It will be even more depressing than the present.'[23] At the end of the Franco-Prussian war, the situation was indeed harsh. The monarchy had been obliged to remain a powerless observer of the event which was the final blow to hopes of Habsburg influence in Germany: the proclamation on 18 January 1871 of the German Empire, in the Hall of Mirrors at Versailles. There was now nothing left of the hope which Franz Joseph had clung to after Sadowa that he would be able to reverse the march of history.

This break promised to have many consequences. It first threw the position of Austrian Germans into question. For the most part, they considered themselves bound to Austria by a dynastic patriotism. But how long would their loyalty to the Habsburgs resist the infection of the nationalist virus? Already, during the war, some Austrian Germans had loudly adopted the Prussian cause. While the government had difficulty in concealing their disappointment, Prussia's victories were hailed with joy in several towns of the monarchy. These outbursts annoyed Franz Joseph, who considered such behaviour to be unpatriotic, and he immediately ordered that they should not be tolerated by the forces of order. Vexation alone cannot explain such severity. It was also due to the belief that such demonstrations were founded on a system of thought which directly contradicted Austrian legitimacy. The fascination which the new Reich exercised on some Austrian Germans grew in proportion to their fear of becoming a minority in Austria. Before 1866, even, the Germans were only the largest national group, with nowhere near an absolute majority. But they were secure in the comfort of an organic link with the German Confederation, and felt the weight of all Germans behind them. Now they could rely only on themselves, and at a time when they faced the rise of nationalist movements among the other peoples of the monarchy. To escape this threat, some of them hoped that the unification process would extend to Austrian Germans, and this inclination was naturally strongest along the border with Germany, especially in Bohemia where they were under direct pressure from the Slavs.

It is unlikely that Bismarck envisaged such an eventuality, for he had already, in 1866, expressed his opposition to the annexation of Austrian territory. But this threat could not be ignored by the Austro-Hungarian government. Caution dictated that they should take care to refrain from a policy which was hostile to the new Germany. So already the creation of the new German Empire was affecting political decisions in Vienna. But its consequences were more far reaching. Franz Joseph was obliged to act upon the changes, and to adjust his foreign policy accordingly. Now that the German question was no longer open, the Danubian monarchy had no other choice than to turn its ambitions towards the south-east, and for this it was necessary to find an ally of sufficient strength to oppose the Russian threat. The defeat of France took it out of the reckoning for some time. Although Britain had its reasons to fear Russian expansionism it remained unlikely that it would intervene on the Continent. There remained the German Empire. For now, an Austro-German alliance seemed hard to imagine. The recent conflict had left scars which only time would heal. In addition, there was no reason for Bismarck to quarrel with Russia, whose friendship he had appreciated in the recent crises.

It was Beust who detected the new possibilities which might open up as a result of the completion of German unification, while matters were still undecided. From December 1870, he indicated the necessity for a reconciliation with Bismarck's Germany. After the Treaty of Frankfurt, which established a new power relationship in Europe, he went even further. In presenting his plans in May 1871 in a report to the emperor, he defined the main objective of his policy: 'the achievement of the dominance of central Europe in the balance of Europe's future through an agreement between Austria-Hungary and Prussian Germany embracing all current affairs with the declared aim of preserving world peace.'[24]

The Fundamental Articles

With the return of peace, Franz Joseph and Hohenwart's plans could be put into effect. On 7 February 1871, the *Weiner Zeitung* announced the appointment of Count Hohenwart at the head of a new government in Cisleithania. In the letter which set out his duties, Franz Joseph fixed the extent and limitations of Hohenwart's mission. Still refusing to be moved on this principle, he reminded him that the reforms must remain within the framework of the Constitution:

> Remaining within the terms of the Constitution which I have set out, I cannot doubt, despite the failure of previous attempts to unite all my faithful subjects in a common constitutional movement, that a minister who can stand above the different parties could succeed in bringing this mission to a successful conclusion, while taking care to respect the different interests concerned, to achieve the consolidation of the power and prosperity of the empire.[25]

It was clear that Franz Joseph was gambling on the success of Hohenwart's plan, for he ordered the government to 'seize the initiative by laying a series of papers before the *Reichsrat* and the Diets, with the intention of according greater judicial and administrative freedom to the provinces, in accordance with the essential unity of the empire, which supports each individual province.'[26] Franz Joseph still had no intention of allowing Bohemia the status of an independent state.

The situation only began to resolve itself in May, after the efforts of the government to increase the degree of autonomy enjoyed by the provinces had failed because of the opposition of the liberal majority in the Lower House of the *Reichsrat*. This failure illustrates the impossibility of the realization of the cabinet's programme without first reducing the parliamentary majority. This was why a new attempt at compromise with the Bohemian opposition was required. After two months of negotiation, the two sides managed to accommodate each other's viewpoint and to come to an agreement for a compromise. The government could congratulate itself that its obstinate refusal to revise the Constitution except by legal means had at last borne fruit. The Bohemian opposition decided not only to bring its parliamentary strike to an end, but also to agree that its compromise should be ratified by the *Reichsrat* after the Diets of the kingdom had voted on it. Another government success was to be found in the agreement concluded with the Czech national party and the historical aristocratic party, which did not shake the 1867 Compromise. Here again, Franz Joseph's determination had won through. The compromise which was drawn up would be inserted into the existing system of the dual monarchy.

Nevertheless, the fact remained that the government had finally recognized the statutory rights of the parties concerned. This was the import of the royal rescript read by Count Bohuslav Chotek, *Statthalter* of Bohemia, before the Prague Diet on 14 September:

> In consideration of the constitutional position of the crown of Bohemia, in measurement of the status and power which this crown has assured our ancestors and ourselves, and fully aware as we are of the unshakeable loyalty with which the Bohemian people has always supported our throne, we willingly recognize the rights of the Kingdom of Bohemia and we are prepared to reaffirm these through the vows taken at our coronation.[27]

Immediately after this announcement, the ratification of the compromise began. The fundamental articles formed its centrepiece. Inspired by a proposal elaborated by Count Clam-Martinic, they regulated the organization of power in Bohemia, and the kingdom's relations with the rest of the monarchy. Their first step was to recognize the Compromise of 1867. However, this only had the appearance of a concession, for the procedure served to establish the sovereignty of the kingdom. Bohemia submitted to the conditions of the Compromise, not as an agreement reached without Bohemian participation, but by conferring its approbation on the Compromise in the exercise of its own sovereignty.

Behind this procedure, the desire to see Bohemia treated on an equal footing with Hungary was clear. This was what the first articles emphasized. In them, the Kingdom of Bohemia recognized the common concerns which had been established between Hungary and the other provinces of the monarchy. Bohemia certainly recognized its obligations towards the non-Hungarian provinces, but article 9 specified that those Bohemian matters which were not common to all the provinces and kingdoms of the monarchy would become the responsibility of the Bohemian authorities. The sharing of responsibilities with the non-Hungarian provinces would then be merely the result of a delegation of sovereignty which did not threaten the constitutional body of Bohemia.

The restoration of statutory rights was demonstrated by the creation of a Bohemian executive which was responsible to the Diet. To lead it, the fundamental articles revived the post of chancellor which, until its disappearance under Maria Theresa, had been the embodiment of the Bohemian identity. Not all the ambiguities had disappeared, though. Although the fundamental articles contained the hope of parity with Hungary, they were nevertheless obliged to adapt themselves to the existing dualist framework. The despised word Cisleithania did not appear in them, but they were obliged to recognize a political body distinct from Hungary in the

Austro-Bohemian whole. The Austro-Bohemian countries, like Galicia, delegated a certain number of rights to a common political and legislative body. They also continued to sit in one Chamber of Delegates which matched that of Hungary. In addition, the chancellor was not only responsible for the direction of the Bohemian government, but also for the execution of the decisions made by the ministry common to the non-Hungarian provinces, and of the laws passed by this body. Bohemia was thus obliged, in these early stages, to confine its ambitions to the federalization of Austria. For the time, the system introduced by the fundamental articles was most noteworthy for its cumbersome nature, adding a third level of government to the body responsible for the monarchy as a whole, and the cabinet of the non-Hungarian provinces.

The fundamental articles were accompanied by a legal proposal which was intended to regulate the relations between Germans and Czechs. It was already innovative in its introduction of the principle of bilingualism in areas with mixed populations, while civil servants and judges would be obliged to speak both languages. But above all, it introduced a reorganization of the Diet, which would henceforth be divided into two national *curiae*. The main aim of this reform was to guarantee the cultural autonomy of each people. Once the funds for the joint institutions had been allocated, each *curia* had the right to an educational and cultural budget in proportion to the taxes paid by its people. A final provision was intended to reassure the Germans, and to protect them against the majority. This proposed that in any debate concerning the alteration of the law concerning languages, the proposal would be rejected if either side did not agree.

The compromise was nevertheless to collapse under the weight of opposition which it encountered, although the ratification procedure had begun under favourable conditions. On 10 August the government announced the dissolution of the Lower House of the *Reichsrat*, and of several Diets. In conjunction with a reduction in the minimum financial requirement for the vote, intended to strengthen the conservative vote and to increase the number of Slav voters, this decision was intended to provide the government with the majority it needed in the *Reichsrat*. Indeed, the elections were marked by a considerable reduction in the liberal vote, with the liberals losing control of many Diets, such as those of Upper Austria and of Moravia. The election of the Lower House of the *Reichsrat* confirmed the extent of this victory. The government could now rely on the two-thirds majority necessary to revise the Constitution.

The first problems appeared with the hostility voiced by the liberals. Denouncing the compromise as an act of aggression against the dominance of the Germans in Austria, this group decided to employ the tactic of a parliamentary walk-out which had been used so effectively by the opposition. Their hostility spread to the German middle classes through the great Viennese daily newspapers, one of the most influential of which was the *Neue Freie Presse*.

This hostility was particularly strong among the Bohemian Germans. As staunch supporters of a centralist system which, by connecting them closely with the German populations of the other provinces of the monarchy, served to cancel out their minority position in Bohemia, they rejected federalism for fear that it would break this tie. The guarantees written into the proposals concerning the protection of nationalities were not enough to calm these fears. On the contrary, the obligation imposed on civil servants and judges to master the two tongues of the kingdom released the anger of the Germans, for in reality this would inevitably work to the advantage of the Czechs. It was nevertheless very likely that Franz Joseph had allowed for the hostility of the liberals in his calculations and had accepted the risk involved. If such was the case, it should then be accepted that the reversal which led to the failure of the compromise was actually the result of the double involvement of Beust and Andrassy. Beust, who knew that this was a sensitive point, was eager to make clear to Franz Joseph that the enactment of the compromise could not fail to have an effect on the international standing of the monarchy. In a memorandum of 13 October, he set out to demonstrate to him that a policy which favoured the Czechs in Bohemia and which, moreover, reinforced the weight of the Slavs in Austria, would run counter to the policy which Austria-Hungary had followed in its relations with Berlin since the end of 1870. The recognition of a similar status for Galicia to that accorded to Bohemia would also lead to a deterioration of relations with Russia. The policies of Hohenwart's cabinet thus threatened to upset the efforts of the foreign service, by provoking a common Russo-German front against the monarchy.

Andrassy's intervention put the final seal on the fate of the compromise. The head of the Hungarian government soon became convinced that the new order of things required that an end should be put to any questioning of the dual system. Convinced of the threat which the compromise represented to Magyar rule in Hungary, he decided to add the weight of his influence to the debate.

The crown Council which Franz Joseph called on 20 October gave Beust and Andrassy the opportunity to deal the death blow. Their arguments succeeded in shaking the emperor who found himself in the same general situation as he had in February 1867 when he had been obliged to choose between Beust and Belcredi. His 1867 choice dictated that which he had to make now. Despite the rearguard action of Hohenwart, he gave his agreement to the draft rescript submitted to him by Beust and Andrassy as a reply to the address passed by the Bohemian Diet. Written in threatening terms, it effectively destroyed the compromise.

This was certainly how it was interpreted by the Bohemian opposition. The transformation of the compromise put an end to the current activity, and freed the historical nobility and the national party from any undertakings they had made. There was no longer any question, for instance, of a return to the *Reichsrat*. The Prague Diet confirmed this, on 4 November, by rejecting the imperial rescript and by formally reaffirming both its allegiance to the rights of the state and its refusal to participate in the *Reichsrat*. As for Hohenwart's government, quick to understand the betrayal to which it had been subjected, it immediately resigned.

This outcome constituted the failure of the first serious attempt to replace the liberal majority with a mainly conservative coalition. There is no doubt that Franz Joseph, who must have thought himself close to achieving this end, experienced a deep disappointment. This did not, however, absolve him from responsibility. His behaviour raises a number of questions. Franz Joseph refused to alter the Compromise of 1867 but it seems unlikely that he can have been unaware that in initiating a process which was intended to lead to a compromise with the Bohemian opposition, he was likely to undermine the foundations of the dual monarchy.

His actions thus suffered from an inner contradiction. Determined to prevent any threat to the Austro-Hungarian Compromise, he had none the less given his approval to a policy which was aimed at precisely this. He had apparently hoped to avoid this dilemma but when he was obliged to make a decision, he gave way to Andrassy's persuasions. This decision confirmed the imbalance which dualism had created within the monarchy to the Hungarians' advantage. It was now accepted that the members of the Hungarian government, who were in any case resolved to prevent any interference from the Cisleithan authorities in the internal affairs of the King-dom of Saint Stephen, considered it to be their right to interfere in the proceedings in the western part of the monarchy and would work to prevent any reform likely to have an effect on the internal balance of Hungary. Franz Joseph was brought to realize this, and this stillborn attempt at a constitutional revision was not renewed.

Also, it appears that, unlike Beust, Franz Joseph had not immediately taken stock of the international implications of the Bohemian compromise. Following the French defeat, it was becoming hard for Austria to allow itself to pursue any policy which might offend the new Germany, even in an internal matter. Thus the catastrophe of 1866 was slowly making its consequences felt and it would not be an exaggeration to consider the failure of the Bohemian compromise to be the precursor of the alliance of 1879.

From the point of view of home affairs, Franz Joseph's withdrawal had serious results. The failure of the compromise had a negative effect on the status of the crown in the eyes of the Czech people. Because Franz Joseph himself had given an undertaking in the first rescript to restore the historical rights of Bohemia and to be crowned in Prague, it was the sovereign himself who was compromised in this matter. This blow to the emperor's standing and authority would weigh strongly in future relations between Bohemia and the monarchy.

The Universal Exhibition and the 1873 Crash

The Hohenwart cabinet was soon to appear as no more than an interlude in the course of the liberal era. After Hohenwart's resignation, the liberals soon regained their power. Whatever it cost him, Franz Joseph was obliged to call them back to government. From November, Prince Adolf Auersperg was given the task of forming the new cabinet.

During this period, the Austro-Hungarian economy continued to expand. The volume of trade continued to increase. In the course of only one year, the export of sugar, which was a fast-growing area of the Bohemian and Moravian economies, increased by 130 per cent, although this was an extreme example. The corn trade, which was another key area of the economy, showed an increase of 20 per cent. Another sign of this growth was the 40 per cent increase in the importation of raw materials for industrial use between 1869 and 1873. The main beneficiary of this upturn was the railway construction industry which attracted vast capital sums. With the increase in concessions, the network soon resembled an enormous spider's web. The growth in the economy, which was generally believed to be without limits, guaranteed easy and considerable profits. The number of credit organizations and joint stock societies which were founded was an expression of this optimism and fervour for profit. During the seven years of the 'Austrian miracle', seventy banks were founded in Vienna, and sixty-five in the provinces. In 1872 alone, no fewer than 376 joint stock companies came into being.

In addition to this, the coming Universal Exhibition of 1873 promised to serve as a window display for the new Austria. After four exhibitions had been held, alternating between London and Paris, Franz Joseph mainly saw the holding of the fifth in Vienna as the sign that, despite the disaster of 1866, the monarchy was still a great power. But this exhibition was also the consecration of the triumph of a liberal and constitutional Austria, and this was why its organizers wished it to be as spectacular as possible. Set up on the Prater, the exhibition covered sixteen hectares, five times the size of the Paris exhibition of 1867. The central point was a vast rotunda which had a triumphal arch as its entrance, with the motto of the reign, *Viribus unitis*, inscribed on it, and surmounted by an enormous cupola with a diameter of 108 metres. Although it did not excite the Viennese who mocked it, calling it a giant cake, this curiosity set the tone for the exhibition and served as its symbol. The exhibition drew no fewer than 50,000 exhibitors from forty countries, of whom 15,000 came from Austria alone. Although the representation from Britain and the United States was modest, the organizers could nevertheless congratulate themselves on the major participation of several great industrial nations such as Germany, with 6,900 exhibitors, and France, and rejoice in the presence of many exhibitors from the Middle and Far East, such as Japan who, and this was a sign of the times, were participating for the first time in an international venture of this type.

After the official opening on 1 May, the weeks of the exhibition were very full for Franz Joseph. The crowned heads of state visited Vienna one after the other, according to a well-regulated sequence of arrivals, celebrations, and departures. The brilliance of society life could not conceal, however, that the final stocktake of the exhibition was not as stunning as had been expected. In place of the twenty million admissions which had been expected, only seven million were recorded. The rise in hotel prices partly explains this deficit. The cholera epidemic which hit Vienna from July onwards and which claimed nearly 3,000 victims also had a negative effect on the number of possible visitors. But the greatest irony lay in the fact that, only eight days after the opening of the exhibition proclaimed the superiority of the liberal system, the Vienna stock exchange collapse of 9 May shook that same system to its roots. The undermining of public opinion which the 'black Friday' crash brought about had a detrimental effect on the exhibition. Begun in a spirit of euphoria, it would end at the beginning of November with disenchantment, and even drama.

It was true that there were several pointers to a possible crisis in the months leading up to the crash, such as the cooling down of some areas of activity, but in the climate of exhilaration which prevailed at the time, these passed unnoticed. In addition, the financial possibilities opened up by the organization of the exhibition had delayed the crisis which was nevertheless inevitable. The runaway progress of the Austrian economy was not altogether built on healthy foundations. It was already dangerous that so much emphasis was placed on investments. What would happen if the discrepancy became too great between the production capacity of the companies and the demands of the internal market? But the obsession with quick profits also led to a number of speculative ventures which sometimes verged on fraud, although they were, for the most part, merely unwise. The atmosphere of confidence in unlimited possibilities for expansion might have seemed to justify the striking of deals which were partly dependent on future profits. On the other hand, the lightest puff of wind could soon turn into a tornado which would carry off this great house of cards.

Indeed, when the crisis came, it rapidly took on spectacular proportions. On 8 May, 110 societies found themselves in a state of insolvency; on the following day, the number rose to 230. In the course of the weeks which followed, failures and bankruptcies increased. In Austria alone, of the 147 banks which were open in May 1873, only 102 were left at the end of the year. Although every area of society was affected, the worst hit were the ranks of the lower middle class who, tempted by the lure of easy profits, had trusted their savings to supposedly safe investments. The effects of the crash were all the greater because the crisis continued. The Austrian crash was only a particularly dramatic example of a situation which was affecting the whole international economy.

Lasting as it did to the dawn of the eighties, the 'great depression' was in many respects the reversal of the achievements of the preceding period. Production and demand both dropped sharply. The main pillar of economic growth, railway construction, was hit very badly. The low water mark was reached in 1880 when only 75 kilometres of track were completed. This slump led to a reduction in the metal and mechanical industries. Construction was also badly hit, for example, work on the great buildings of state on the *Ring* was halted: the Parliament, the Town Hall, the Burgtheater, the University and the museums all fell behind schedule and would only be completed in the eighties.

To make matters worse, there was a series of poor harvests which reduced the purchasing power of the countryside. Famine returned to several areas. In conjunction with the effects of the cholera, famine claimed more than half a million victims in Hungary alone. The banks were also paying the price for their lack of caution. The seventy-two banks in Vienna in 1873 were reduced to eight in the course of the next ten years. At the same time, two-thirds of the provincial banks disappeared in the troubles. Ill-equipped to fight it, the artisan class and the small traders also figured among the victims of the economic crisis. Lastly, as is always the case in a recession, the working classes were severely affected, not only by a reduction in purchasing power, but also by the scourge of unemployment.

The crash and its consequences had an indelible effect on public opinion. Having set itself up as a universal solution, liberalism now found itself in the dock. The crisis threw it into question as a system of thought, as an economic construct, and as a social system. The optimism inspired by the successes of the preceding period did not last. It was replaced by a feeling which combined fatalism with an epicureanism, the roots of which went back to the baroque tradition, as epitomized by the words of one of the characters in *Fledermaus*, written in 1874: 'Happiness is forgetting what cannot be altered.'[28]

These events would result in the spread of a strong anti-capitalist feeling which did not disappear when the economy took a turn for the better, and became one of the basic currents of Austrian thought. Through this breach, many political and philosophical movements would pass (anti-semitism, Christian socialism, and socialism) which would each in its own way attack liberalism and precipitate its decline. Nevertheless, these political results of the crisis did not come about immediately. For the time being, the liberal government remained in power. If the elections to the

Lower House of the *Reichsrat* which took place in the autumn of 1873 had taken place under a system of universal suffrage, or under a system of extensive suffrage such as that in Britain, the liberals would undoubtedly have suffered a severe defeat. But the Austrian electoral system was so effective in choking off the movements of general opinion that although the liberals lost a number of seats to the federalists, these losses were no threat to their majority for as long as the Bohemian opposition continued to boycott the *Reichsrat*.

The crisis certainly didn't improve Franz Joseph's opinion of the liberals, especially as several of their leading members were left with egg on their faces by financial scandals. He expressed his views by refusing to allow any person who had been involved in these affairs, in any capacity, to remain in government. But in the political field, he still had no other choice than to join with the liberals.

The Confessional Laws of 1874

The economic crisis did not prevent the liberals from continuing to follow their programme of reforms. Auersperg's government confirmed this at the beginning of 1874 by registering four new draft papers concerning confessional practice with the *Reichsrat's* executive. In fact, these proposals were necessary to a redefinition of the relationship between Church and State and the place of the former in society, follow-ing the dismantling of the concordat. With a few differences, events took the same course as they had seven years earlier. Within his constitutional capacities, Franz Joseph held back the zeal of his ministers and acted to protect the Church. From the first ministerial Council of Auersperg's government, he made it very clear that the 'proposed legislation, following the repudiation of the concordat, should remain severely limited to what was absolutely necessary, and that nothing should be undertaken which might be understood as a concession to extremist groups in the *Reichsrat* or in the press'.[29]

Now that the concordat had been abolished, the liberals could have treated the Church according to their own principles and have taken up Cavour's aim of 'a free Church in a free State', but in so doing they would have stripped the state of its means of control over an institution which they still considered gripped by obscurant-ism, and which they also suspected of wishing to regain control over society. The solution which was reached was an attempt at a difficult compromise between the theory of the return of the Church to self-regulation and the Josephist tradition.

The first paper drawn up by Stremayr, minister for religious affairs, defined the Church as 'a favoured body of public rights'.[30] The law also recognized the right of the Church to the freedom to organize religion and make its own decisions on doctrine. Compared with the Josephist era, this was an undeniable advance. Another achievement of the fifties, the repeal of the *placet*, was not questioned. But it was also clear that the government had no intention of separating Church and State for, as the ruling stated, 'to return the Church to private regulation would not result in the reduction of the power of the Church, but would instead weaken the control of the Church by the State.'[31] It was clear that there was no question of giving the Church equal status with the state in temporal matters.

Having taken some areas of social life under its jurisdiction following the May legislation, the state now wished to ensure its control of the Church. To this end, it became a requirement for members of the clergy to be approved by the state, giving the government the right to be involved in their training. Going back on a major condition of the concordat, members of the clergy would be subject to civil law. It was also proposed that religious groups must have government approval before opening any convent on Austrian soil.

Faced with these proposals, the bishops were divided, as they had been in 1868. Cardinal Rauscher once again became the spokesman for a policy of compromise. Although he deplored the government decisions, he still considered them to be a lesser evil, given the threats which faced the Church, and compared with the fate reserved for the German Catholics at that time by the *Kulturkampf*. In addition, he had also had a hand in the comparatively moderate nature of the government demands. Although he did not negotiate with Stremayr, he directly involved himself through the activities of his bishop co-adjutor, Monsignor Kutschker, in persuading him to consider a compromise. Finally, and most important, he approached Franz Joseph himself, in the certainty that if it were to become necessary, the latter would restrain the government from taking more extreme action.

The other aspect of Rauscher's activity was his care to prevent all moves, whether from the bishops or from laymen, which might compromise his own intentions. He thus opposed the holding of a conference of Austrian bishops which might make a formal reaffirmation of the position of the Church before the government could even announce the measures which it proposed in place of the concordat. But once the contents of the government proposals became known, there was such indignation that he was soon obliged to give in to pressure, and resign himself to the convocation of an assembly of Austrian bishops.

When the conference opened on 12 March in Vienna, the tension had increased. Pius IX had just entered the debate, by publishing an encyclical on 7 March in which he called on the bishops to show resolve in opposing the moves of the liberal cabinet. This was accompanied by a letter from Pius IX to Franz Joseph in which he urged him to refuse to promulgate the confessional laws at the risk of incurring a religious sanction. Whereas this letter, with its veiled threat of excommunication, seemed to heighten the drama of the situation, Franz Joseph's reply served to defuse the crisis. On a serene note, he set out the justification for his policies since the agreement of the concordat, and assured the Pope that, far from nourishing hostile intentions towards the Church, he still saw himself as its protector. These explanations achieved their end for they did not fail to have an effect on the Vatican and finally convinced it that the Austrian government had no intention of taking matters to the extreme lengths which Bismarck had.

Reassured over Vienna's intentions, the Vatican would now preach moderation. From this time, the tension rapidly disappeared. Having considered, at one point, a boycott of the discussion of the proposals in the Upper House of the *Reichsrat*, the bishops changed their minds, thereby indicating that the Church would participate in the new legislation, despite its protestations. Franz Joseph, for his part, did not waver from the line of action which he had set out for himself, and respected the terms of his letter to Pius IX. Although he considered himself bound by his constitutional obligations, he succeeded in setting strict limits on the religious policies of the government and in protecting the Church from any rougher treatment. He was therefore not disguising the truth when he declared to the Bohemian bishops in 1876: 'Although until now, circumstances have prevented me from bringing about the protective measures for the Church which I would like in my heart to accomplish..., I am nevertheless aware that I have prevented many measures which might have caused greater wrongs to be done to the Church than the prejudices which it has actually had to endure.'[32]

Franz Joseph soon made good his declaration to defend the Church. After the Upper House had taken two years to confirm the vote of the Lower House, Franz Joseph exercised his right of veto in 1876 over the text which intended to subject the creation of religious establishments on Austrian soil to civil approval. With this refusal, the final word lay with Franz Joseph, who would henceforth be careful that the balance which had been reached between State and Church would not be threatened.

The Eastern Question

If the debate over the second attempt to change the confessional laws served to increase Franz Joseph's annoyance with the liberals, it at least took place in an area where he considered himself to be bound by his constitutional duties. This was not the case when the liberals questioned his policies concerning the uprising of the Bosnia-Herzegovinian Christians. The dispute here was on grounds which Franz Joseph considered to belong to the prerogative of the crown alone.

Since the monarchy had been forced out of Germany and Italy, Franz Joseph had made the decision to create an alternative area of influence in the Balkans. The political situation appeared to favour this, as the Ottoman Empire was falling apart with increasing speed. Its European possessions were particularly at risk as the Christian subjects of the sultan were becoming less and less tolerant of the Ottoman regime. It was certainly true that, since Metternich's era, the conservation of the integrity of the Ottoman Empire had been one of the tenets of Austrian foreign policy. Andrassy still followed this line, but he did not wish to exclude the possibility of a reduction in Ottoman power. Although he did not aspire to bring about a crisis which might hasten this process, neither was he prepared to cling to a vestige of the past.

Not all the leading figures of the monarchy were prepared to restrict themselves to this waiting game. In military circles, many eyes had long been turned towards Bosnia-Herzegovina, if only for strategic reasons. The Serbian and Croat officers, of whom there were many in the command structure, were also receptive to the cries of the Balkan Christians. These circles had good reason to believe that the emperor shared their opinion. Franz Joseph gave a clear indication of the importance which he attributed to these areas when he visited Dalmatia during the spring of 1875. His visit to this province (against Andrassy's advice) which was next to Bosnia-Herzegovina, on the even of an insurrection against the Turks, implied that the monarchy supported these subject peoples, but it also provided a clear indication of Austria-Hungary's intentions. In making this journey to the gates of the Ottoman Empire, he wished to make it plain that the Eastern question could not be resolved without the participation of Austria-Hungary. In particular, he did not conceal his rejection of any solution which, by entailing the creation of Slav states on its borders, would run counter to the fundamental interests of the monarchy.

The crisis soon became an international one, as the Turks were not able to suppress the insurrection which inflamed Bosnia-Herzegovina and which spread in April 1876 to the Bulgarian provinces. On 2 July 1876, Serbia and Montenegro declared war on the Sublime Porte. In April 1877, following the defeats suffered by the Serbs, it was Russia's turn to join the anti-Turkish alliance.

For the monarchy, the international nature of the conflict raised the question of its relations with Russia, for it was clear that Saint Petersburg had greater ambitions than to save Serbia. Austro-Russian relations had stabilized with the agreement concluded in June 1873 under Bismarck's aegis between Franz Joseph and Alexander II, for which Wilhelm I had declared his support in October. Bismarck, who was aiming to isolate France, found it essential to defuse Austro-Russian antagonism, and Austria-Hungary also benefited from this agreement because, although there were still three participants, this treaty could act as a foundation stone for a stronger relationship with Germany. In the meantime, it protected Austria-Hungary from an alliance between Germany and Russia which might channel its hostility towards the monarchy.

In the face of this sequence of events, Andrassy would no longer cling to his waiting policy. Although Austria-Hungary did not wish to join in the conflict, it was not prepared to leave the field open to Russia. As Saint Petersburg did not wish to open hostilities without having first ensured Vienna's neutrality, an agreement was drawn up which would set out the reciprocal undertakings and respective aims of the two empires. Because it respected the interests of the monarchy, Franz Joseph supported this solution. When Russia decided to enter the war against the Ottoman Empire, the terms were agreed in a secret convention between the monarchy and Russia on 15 January 1877, and completed in March of the same year. Franz Joseph had every reason to be satisfied because, without having even drawn sword, Austria-Hungary would receive Bosnia-Herzegovina in return for its sympathetic neutrality. In addition, the convention imposed strict limits on Russian expansion which, although it would gain southern Bessarabia, gave its undertaking not to create a greater Slav state out of the ruins of the Ottoman Empire.

Nevertheless, when the final Turkish defences in Europe crumbled in December 1877, events took an unexpected turn. In the euphoria of victory, the balance in Saint Petersburg swung towards the supporters of Pan-Slavism with General Ignatiev at their head. Russia imposed a peace treaty at San Stefano at the gates of Constantinople on 3 March which paid no heed to the terms of the convention signed with Austria-Hungary. Whereas the convention had excluded the possibility of the formation of a greater Slav state, the San Stefano treaty created precisely this, in the form of a greater Bulgaria which would extend to the Aegean Sea. Further-more, there was no longer any question of the annexation of Bosnia-Herzegovina by Austria-Hungary.

Ignatiev must have been very optimistic if he imagined that the other powers would accept such a change in the political map of south-eastern Europe. On the Austro-Hungarian side, neither Franz Joseph nor Andrassy considered accepting this move for a single moment. Vienna reacted by proposed a European congress to which the whole situation would be submitted. This idea was taken up by Bismarck who was concerned about the sudden deterioration in Austro-Russian relations, and who sent out invitations to a congress to be held in Berlin on 13 June.

Vienna could count on help from Disraeli's Britain, which had little desire to see Russia settled through its intermediary on the shores of the Aegean Sea. With the creation of this Anglo-Austrian front, a large-scale conflict would certainly follow if Russia clung to the gains of San Stefano. But Saint Petersburg was the battleground of a bitter fight between factions. The threat of a war against such a fearsome partnership, without German help, provided ammunition for the supporters of a more moderate policy who, with Prince Gorchakov the foreign minister, and Count Shouvalov, the Russian ambassador at the Court of Saint James's, remained loyal to a more traditional policy. As the voice of restraint finally won the day, the crisis was already effectively solved before the congress opened.

This meeting had been preceded by a number of bilateral agreements which anticipated the decisions it would make. Obliged to restrict its greed, Russia had to content itself with the annexation of southern Bessarabia and a few of the Asia possessions of the Ottoman Empire. The congress did create an independent Bulgaria which would be vulnerable to domination by Russia but it was smaller than the state envisaged by Russia at San Stefano and had no access to the Aegean. Austria-Hungary had a further reason to be satisfied, for the European meeting gave the monarchy the right to occupy and administer Bosnia-Herzegovina. Thus another clause of the San Stefano treaty was cancelled out, but the final agreement did not involve annexation.

Andrassy himself had wanted this limitation. Perhaps, in maintaining nominal Turkish sovereignty in these territories, he hoped to win Turkey's favour with an eye to possible future difficulties in the Balkans. But this choice was dictated above all by internal considerations. As a Hungarian he wished avoid any strengthening of Slav participation in the monarchy, which an annexation would inevitably entail. This was not the line he took with Franz Joseph, however. In order to convince him of the wisdom of this course of action, he emphasized that, while avoiding the problems of a real annexation, this occupation would in fact have the same effect. Andrassy hoped that the occupation of Bosnia-Herzegovina would be a simple formality. Had this taken place shortly after the beginning of the uprising in July 1875 the imperial and royal army would probably have been welcomed as a liberator. But by now, the Austro-Hungarians were widely resented, and not only by the Muslims, as a new occupying force. Before imposing their presence, they would have to fight a second uprising, deploy eleven army divisions and suffer heavy losses.

At the beginning of 1879, Franz Joseph could nevertheless congratulate himself on the successes of the monarchy: the obstacles placed in Russia's path and the occupation of Bosnia-Herzegovina. But most of all, he must have been glad that the succession of failures had come to an end. Nevertheless the conditions under which the occupation took effect cast a shadow over his relations with Andrassy. Franz Joseph was not impervious to the arguments of those critics who, having already reproached Andrassy for his opposition to the annexation of Bosnia-Herzegovina, now criticized him for not having foreseen the difficulties which the Austro-Hungarian expeditionary force was now encountering. Although he still officially held Franz Joseph's confidence, Andrassy's position was nonetheless weakened by this crisis.

The Break with the Liberals

It was the general outline of these policies which most liberals objected to. They were afraid that the Slav position within the monarchy would be strengthened by the decisions over Bosnia-Herzegovina, and that the dominance of the Austrian Germans would thereby be compromised. Baron Walterskirchen voiced these fears when he predicted a day when 'Germans will have become foreigners in the state which has lived by their sacrifices and devotion.'[33] The liberals were also shocked that the foreign policy of the monarchy should be conducted without parliamentary control. In answer to the official line that the foreign policy of the monarchy was the emperor's concern, and that of his foreign secretary, they argued that the Assemblies had the right to be kept informed of events, and to debate them.

The conflict was not long in emerging. No sooner had it become clear that the monarchy intended to become involved, together with Russia, in the Eastern crisis, than the liberals made their first move in October 1876, with a demand signed by 112 deputies. Prince Auersperg's reply led to a first flare-up. He informed the Assembly that Andrassy would not accept any interference in the conduct of foreign policy and 'would not allow himself to be swayed from his course, either by warmongering demonstrations, or by declarations intended to damage the authority and prestige of the monarchy'.[34]

The tension rose a notch when the liberals attempted to employ financial pressure to bring about the downfall of the government's policy. The opportunity for this was supplied by Andrassy's request to the delegations in March 1878 for a grant of 60 million florins, without revealing to what end he planned to use it; whether it was for a war against Russia or for the occupation of Bosnia-Herzegovina. In the Cisleithan delegation, most of the liberals voted to refuse this, and Andrassy needed the defection of some liberal nobles to win the day.

The opposition of the liberals did not diminish following the Berlin congress. Loyal to their principles, they blamed the government for having started the occupation of Bosnia-Herzegovina before the Treaty of Berlin had been approved by the Assemblies, and demanded that it should be ratified by parliament. The battle continued when the government submitted, not the final decision of the Berlin congress, but simply the incorporation of the port of Spizza into Dalmatia, to the *Reichsrat* for approval. The official reason for the debate seemed derisory. Furthermore, the liberals were aware that by the beginning of 1879 matters had gone too far for it to be reasonable to envisage a return to the previous state of play. However, a negative vote would act as the notification of the *Reichsrat*'s rejection of Franz Joseph's Balkan policies. This plan failed, but nearly two-thirds of the liberals combined their votes to confirm their opposition.

For the liberals, the worst was to come, because now that the international crisis had been resolved they would have to bear the consequences of their rashness. By aspiring to exercise a right of control over foreign policy, and by going so far as to criticize it, they were moving through a minefield. Whether they wanted it or not, their attacks inevitably took on the character of a challenge to Franz Joseph who, in spite of the changes to the Constitution which had taken place since 1860, had retained control of foreign policy. By disputing a foreign policy directly inspired by the emperor, the liberals were running a major risk. Indeed, Franz Joseph was not far from considering the opposition of most of the liberals to the occupation of Bosnia-Herzegovina as a form of treason. He was even less inclined to excuse them because they expressed their disapproval on a European level and almost weakened the international position of the monarchy. Because they challenged him in an area where he expected to exercise complete control, the liberals lost their right to act as trustworthy partners. As the parliamentary majority had broken down, Franz Joseph could not criticize his ministers for lack of loyalty, but the course of the debates and the way that the *Reichsrat* and the Austrian delegation voted showed that they no longer represented the majority of liberals. The government was like an officer who was no longer followed by his troops. Had the conservatives not come to its aid, it would have suffered the humiliation of being forced into a minority by its own supporters.

Since 1867, Franz Joseph had never held such a strong hand. He would still have to rely on a new majority, which meant that, once again, the Bohemian opposition would have to be persuaded to end its boycott of the *Reichsrat*. This was to be the task of Stremayr's cabinet which succeeded Prince Auersperg's government in mid-February 1879. The key figure in the new team was Count Edward Taaffe who became minister of the interior. In Franz Joseph's confidence, this great lord believed that the only function of the government was to be the faithful instrument of the emperor's policy. In his official capacity his main task would be to prepare for the legislative elections which would take place in the summer, and which, it was hoped in the Hofburg, would produce a new majority.

To this end, Taaffe entered into negotiation with the heads of the Bohemian opposition. His concern was to persuade them to rejoin the *Reichsrat* without a reconsideration of the 1867 Constitution. A few years earlier his talents as a negotiator would not have been enough but his opponents no longer took the same intransigent line as they had previously. The changes which had taken place in the Austrian political scene and the prospect of an end to the liberal era led them to take a different attitude to Taaffe's approach. But above all, they were obliged to admit the failure of their attempts to bring Franz Joseph round to their point of view.

From 1874 onwards, the Czech deputies had sat in the Moravian Diet. In Bohemia, they finally returned to the Diet in 1878. Certainly the question of their return to the *Reichsrat* remained unresolved, but this first step showed that the Bohemian opposition had begun to change its attitude. This was all the more so because cracks had appeared at the heart of the Czech movement. The Young Czechs were not afraid to criticize the tactics of the parliamentary walk-out and the alliance with the nobles. Matching their actions to their words, they returned to the Prague Diet in 1874. Behind their leader, Rieger, the Old Czechs, the moderate wing of the nationalist party, followed their example to prevent them from gaining popular support.

The discussions with Taaffe were made simpler by this development. Finally an agreement was reached under which the Czechs and their aristocratic allies would return to the *Reichsrat*, without Taaffe having to make any constitutional concessions. In return, he allowed for a number of measures which would strengthen the national rights of the Bohemian Czechs. Having achieved this, it remained to win the elections. Their results fulfilled Franz Joseph's hopes. The liberals lost the majority which they had held since 1867 in the Lower House. With 174 members, they were obliged to concede 36 seats. Opposite, the right-wing coalition totalled 168 deputies, of whom 54 represented the Czechs and the nobility, 57 the Poles, and 57 the conservatives in the alpine areas. Strengthened by several independent deputies, this coalition represented an alternative to the old liberal majority. In accordance with these results, Taaffe was called upon to form a new cabinet on 12 August.

After many difficulties, Franz Joseph's goal was at last in sight. From his point of view, the change in the government had been achieved through the most advantageous means. He had contrived to impose his conditions on the Bohemian opposition. Unlike in 1871, he did not have to pay for its return to the *Reichsrat* with a promise of constitutional change. The Taaffe government wished to be, according to its leader, 'the emperor's ministry' (*Kaiserministerium*), and Franz Joseph would therefore no longer be obliged to work with a team which did not represent his own personal inclinations. In short, after a decade of experimentation, he had at last managed, in Cisleithania at least, to bend the constitutional structure to regain his full authority over the machine of government.

The Austro-German Alliance

In the history of the reign, 1879 saw another great turning-point. On 7 October in Vienna, a treaty of alliance was signed with the German Empire. Beust had started Austria on the way, and after him, Andrassy gave priority to this course, for his aim was to bring about a treaty which would protect the monarchy from Russia. Franz Joseph was certainly not sympathetic to the German Empire, for he still smarted from the wound inflicted by the Germans in 1866. These memories did not, however, blind him, and his political choices were made according to a cold evaluation of the international situation. With the (temporary) decline of France as a world power, he, like his ministers, agreed on the necessity for a better relationship with the new Germany and considered that an alliance between the two empires to protect the monarchy's eastern borders was desirable.

It was still necessary to persuade Bismarck of the advantages of such an alliance. In 1875, shortly after the outbreak of the Balkan uprising, he was still unprepared to make a choice between Austria-Hungary and Russia: 'I don't want to become involved,' he confided in a friend, 'If I came down on one side, France would immediately support the other.'[35] But there was already a maggot in the fruit of the relationship between Russia and Germany. At the time of the crisis in 1875 which set Germany and France on opposing sides, Bismarck was disturbed by the position assumed by Russia in the person of Alexander II, who came to Berlin to preach moderation to him. But it was the Russian behaviour in the Balkans following the fall of the Turkish defences which gave him pause for thought. Although he described himself as an 'unbiased courtier', on inviting the two powers to meet in Berlin, this congress could only be intended to restrain Russian expansionism.

The Berlin congress was an important turning-point in the relationship between Germany and Russia. When presented with its decisions imposing a halt on Russian progress in the Balkans, the Tsar accused Bismarck of having been biased in his directorship of the negotiations. Hurt by this betrayal, he chose to make an issue of the matter by approaching Wilhelm I directly, warning him in August 1879 that 'the situation is too serious for me to be able to conceal my fear that the consequences for our two countries may be fatal.'[36] While it plunged Wilhelm into despair, Bismarck pretended to read this letter as a barely concealed threat: 'Such an attitude is usually the sign that there is about to be a split, when there are no treaties to stand in its way.'[37] Faced with this fresh situation, Germany had to reconsider the workings of its foreign policy and to turn to an entente with Austria-Hungary for its foundation in the future.

Without further ado, Bismarck proposed a treaty of alliance between the two empires on 27 August. Franz Joseph and his government received this proposal with favour as it coincided with their own desires. Once an accord had been reached on the general principle of an agreement, it remained to settle the detailed contents of the treaty. The Austro-Hungarian camp demanded that Russia should be named as the common enemy. On the other hand they refused to undertake any obligations concerning France, with whom they had no quarrel.

For several weeks, negotiations were held up by these crucial issues. Bismarck had to threaten to resign in order to overcome his sovereign's resistance, for Wilhelm considered himself to be bound to Russia by an agreement of honour, and did not wish for an alliance with Vienna. But in return for his acquiescence, the aged monarch demanded that Russia should not be mentioned in the treaty, which, in his view, would throw Russia and France into each other's arms. Presented with a proposal in which Russia was designated the only enemy, he protested: 'I cannot ratify this treaty: it would go against my beliefs, my character, and my honour.'[38] He would nevertheless have to sign, as Bismarck still held the threat of his resignation over his head. On 7 October, the treaty was concluded along the lines hoped for by Franz Joseph: if either of the two powers were attacked by Russia, they would join forces against the Russians; if there were an attack from a state other than Russia, each would extend the promise of friendly neutrality to the other.

This treaty constituted an undeniable success for the Austro-Hungarian diplomats. It had been their aim since 1871, but the initiative in the end came from Bismarck. It may have been the case that one of the reasons which led him to adopt this course was his awareness that, of the two possible partners for Germany, Austria-Hungary was the weaker. This seems possible, given that Bismarck had always suggested that in any partnership there is always a horse and a rider, and with time the relative strength of the partners would indeed become unequal. However, the fact remains that this treaty was drawn up along the lines formulated by Franz Joseph, and it was an event of primary importance. The alliance with Berlin would become the cornerstone of the monarchy's foreign policy. Overcoming the differences of the past, Franz Joseph followed this line unwaveringly, whatever the degree of annoyance which, on occasion, his ally was to cause him.

The signing of the treaty also marked the end of an era because it was almost immediately followed by Andrassy's departure. In fact, he had resigned over a month previously, but Franz Joseph had insisted that he remain in office until the treaty, in which he was closely involved, had been concluded. As often occurs in such a case, Andrassy gave reasons of health to explain his resignation. In fact, his main problem was the opposition which his policies had provoked in the army and in Cisleithan political circles, where all parties accused him of favouring the Hungarian interest. The election of a new majority, which included many Cisleithan Slavs, provided the moment to withdraw.

Mourning and Separations

Although Franz Joseph could consider the political situation in the final years of the decade to be a positive one, he did not benefit from a similar situation in his private affairs. A gap was beginning to open up around him. With the death of Archduchess Sophie at the age of sixty-seven in May 1872, one of the great figures of the first part of Franz Joseph's reign disappeared. This death meant the loss of one of Franz Joseph's closest relationships, although, over the years, his relationship with his mother had certainly changed. With the beginning of the constitutional era, Sophie had almost ceased to play any political role. Her final years brought her the sorrow of being a witness to the triumph of the forces which she had always resisted. The liberal takeover of Vienna and Budapest, the recognition of Hungarian sovereignty, and the dismantling of the concordat had all been harsh experiences for her. Partly as a result of advancing age, and partly because of the shock of Maximilian's death, she finally lost her fighting spirit.

Her disappointments had nevertheless not changed her relationship with Franz Joseph. Although she no longer gave him advice, he still took care to explain the reasons for his decisions to her. Sophie was also careful to retain a family atmosphere around herself. The family breakfasts certainly did not taken place as frequently as they had done in the past, but Franz Joseph would often seek out his mother for tea, or in the evening after the theatre. Brief though these moments were, they provided him with previous relaxation in the course of a day which was devoted to work or to other official duties. Sophie had thus succeeded in remaining a family axis.

Now that she was gone, it was certainly not her husband who would replace her in this capacity. For many years, Franz Karl had led a retired life which was now accompanied by declining health. He died in March 1879. But although he wept for his father, this death did not break the pattern of Franz Joseph's life. Franz Joseph also lost Gisela, who married Prince Leopold of Bavaria in 1873. But his main loss was the empress, who resumed her travels, and whose stays in Vienna became once again rare events. It took exceptional circumstances to hold her in the capital. When the exhibition was held there, she at first supported Franz Joseph who was weighed down by the constant stream of important visitors. But although her husband endured these duties with his habitual stoicism, it was not long before Elisabeth ceased to make any effort to conceal her boredom. After two long months, filled with visits, receptions, dinners, and balls, she decided that she had done enough. On the pretext that the state of her health demanded that she should leave Vienna, she abandoned Franz Joseph to the role which he performed so well.

Although he was not fooled by his wife's excuses, Franz Joseph would never have committed the indelicacy of requesting her return to Vienna had it not been necessary. This necessity arose in the person of the shah of Persia, Hasir al-Din, who, disappointed at not having met the empress whose beauty was so renowned, decided that he would await her return in Vienna. The court was not enchanted by the prospect of an extension of his stay. This Eastern potentate had habits which were disconcerting, if not offensive. He had, for instance, arrived in Vienna, accompanied not only by an impressive suite, but also by a number of animals, among which were forty or so sheep destined for the dinner table. In short, this prince lacked the civilized manners and sense of honour of the Viennese court, and he had become a burdensome guest. To find a way out of this diplomatic tangle, Elisabeth agreed to sacrifice her peace, and her return had the desired effect. Satisfied with having been given the opportunity to contemplate the beauty of the empress and to speak with her, the shah set out on his journey home soon afterwards.

After this Elisabeth appeared only rarely in Vienna. At first she spent a lot of time at Gödöllö, where she was sometimes joined by Franz Joseph, but he was usually unable to remain there for long. She planned her days to please only herself. Accompanied by the best Hungarian horsemen, she gave herself up completely to the joys of riding in the nearby Puszta. It was also at Gödöllö that her passion for hunting developed. But it was because of this that Gödöllö lost part of its charm. The ground there was wooded, and too flat to provide good hunting country, and Elisabeth now longed to go to England where she could find hunting which suited her. From 1874 onwards she made many journeys to England and Ireland, broken by a stay in Normandy. For appearance's sake, Elisabeth did ask Franz Joseph to join her. But he had neither the time, nor, it seems likely, the inclination. Although he was himself an excellent horseman, and did not scorn the pleasures of hunting, he did not like the lifestyle of Elisabeth's entourage. He preferred the simpler pleasures of hunting in the Ischl mountains. Elisabeth summed up their relationship in a few words: 'I know that you love me, even if you do not show it,' she wrote to her husband, 'and we are happy together because we do not interfere with each other's lives.'[39]

Franz Joseph kept Rudolf at his side, and the young man would sometimes help his father in his official role. When he was only just fifteen he accompanied his father during the ceremonies involved in the visits of foreign sovereigns to the exhibition. But in spite of appearances, Rudolf had few contacts with his father, and a gulf was already growing between the two men. This was partly the result of the education Rudolf had received from Joseph Latour, Elisabeth's personal choice of tutor. His liberal views led him to cast a critical eye on the state of the monarchy as the seventies drew to a close, and this was heightened because these years marked a decline in liberal influence. In the avowal which he wrote in 1878, as he was approaching twenty, and of which his father was clearly unaware, he denounced the current of reactionary feeling which he saw at work in Austria: 'there are reactionaries everywhere, but especially in Austria. This is the first step towards ruin. Reactionaries are Austria's most dangerous enemies.'[40]

The Silver Wedding

Franz Joseph nevertheless had the pleasure of seeing all his family around him for the celebrations in April 1879 of the imperial couple's silver wedding. The most important feature of these was the witness they bore to the intensity of the worship which was developing around Franz Joseph. The most spectacular event took place on 27 April bringing together all the guilds of the capital in a procession which lasted nearly three hours.

For the execution of this undertaking, which had been decided on by the city of Vienna, Hans Makart, the popular painter whose baroque luxury fitted in with the style of the *Ringstrasse*, was given a free hand. Often described as the 'Austrian Rubens', he decided to illustrate the guilds with forty or so *tableaux vivants* from the time of the German Renaissance. Several tens of thousands of people would thus progress along the *Ring* past Franz Joseph, Elisabeth, the whole imperial family, and several hundred thousand Viennese.

The procession opened with a herald, followed by twelve mounted trumpeters dressed in the livery of the city. There then followed, banners flying in the wind, the student societies, the shooting societies, the choral societies, and some eighty deputations from the guilds. Then came more than forty groups on carts, who enacted scenes depicting the activities of the different professions. With a series of hunting scenes, the organizers of the procession had devised a surprise for Franz Joseph which went straight to his heart: It was described by *Le Temps*:

> A many-chaptered marvel: fox-hunting, chamois-hunting, deer-hunting, boar-hunting, bear-hunting, and falconry. All these were represented in costumes from the time of Maximilian I, down to the smallest detail; the dogs, the game, the beards of the hunters, in the most accomplished manner. A splendid chariot followed, in which the king of the hunt sat enthroned among his companions, and horns sounding joyful fanfares.[41]

As the culmination of the procession, Makart led the final group, that of the artists, who, following the example of the master of ceremonies, modelled their costumes on the paintings of Rubens:

> Finally...the group of artists, which surpassed everything which had gone before in its splendour. Applause burst out more loudly than ever, for among the artists who preceded the *tableau* the crowd could see Hans Makart, the inventor and organizer of this fairy tale, perched on a white horse, dressed in black velvet, and surrounded by his staff-officers, painters, architects, and sculptors who had helped him to bring about this miracle.[42]

Looking back at the end of 1879, Franz Joseph might well have felt that the bad years of his reign were behind him, and that the monarchy had succeeded, after many setbacks, in arriving at a new state of equilibrium. After the series of defeats in Italy and Germany, the monarchy had now taken over Bosnia-Herzegovina. Its security was assured through the alliance with Germany, which also confirmed it as a world power. At home, Franz Joseph had been obliged to go against his personal principles and had come to terms with the liberal bourgeoisie, accepting the establishment of a constitutional regime. Threatened by a major crisis with the Magyars, he had resigned himself to the sacrifice of the single empire which he had hoped to build at the outset of his reign. But, within this system, he had contrived to retain control in the areas which he considered essential, and kept this sphere of influence beyond the control of the Assemblies, thus ensuring the unity of the monarchy, although it was now a dual one. And then, although he had had to await the decline of liberalism, he had finally contrived to turn the Constitution to his own ends in

Cisleithania. He now controlled a government which he would not be obliged to bow to, and which conceived its main function to be the implementation of the emperor's policies. Finally, thanks to the celebrations in April 1879, Franz Joseph had been able to register the extent of his popularity. This had been hard-won, for on several occasions, such as the time following the disasters of 1859 and 1866, it had been at a low ebb. But here too, time had done its work, and gradually the image of a sovereign entirely absorbed by his duties asserted itself.

These reasons for satisfaction were nevertheless tempered by the increasing solitude in which Franz Joseph shut himself. The good moments of family life in which he could find a counterpoint to the burden of his responsibilities disappeared from his everyday horizon. It was true that his character and his lifestyle did not lend themselves to such moments, but this was also a result of Elisabeth's behaviour, for she had ceased to make any effort to create an atmosphere of family warmth around herself. Completely free of the court, the empress only made occasional appearances in Vienna, and the relationship between husband and wife was mainly conducted by letter from this time on.

Franz Joseph also had only brief moments with his children. Following the departure of Gisela, Maria Valeria would often accompany her mother on her travels. Only Rudolf remained, but his military duties would soon take him far from Vienna, and in any case, father and son lived in completely different worlds and their paths began to diverge. Solitude had become the only true companion for an emperor, whose personal indentity, as he worked, gradually became indistinguishable from his official position.

8

Work and Daily Life

Although Franz Joseph was no monolith on which the passing years had no effect, there was nevertheless a strong element of continuity in his life, and this was the result of his working methods and the planning of his day. This is not to say that his life was one of monotony. On the occasion of visits from foreign sovereigns and princes, the normal timetable could not be adhered to in every detail, although care was taken not to upset it. This schedule was also interrupted by the times spent at Ischl which were generally holiday periods. Later on, too, with advancing age, modifications had to be made to Franz Joseph's schedule. However, despite these adaptations to circumstance or the march of time, the main characteristic of Franz Joseph's lifestyle was that of continuity. This allows us to sketch out a portrait of Franz Joseph's everyday life, his working methods, and his relationships with subordinates during the height of his reign in the early 1880s, which also provides a fair picture of the early years of his reign and which anticipates his later years.

The Residences

Following the 1867 Compromise, Vienna remained the emperor's primary city of residence (*Residenzstadt*), as it had been before. However much it might have wished to do so, the Hungarian capital could not compete for this role. Franz Joseph certainly stayed there when his constitutional duties required him to, and on such occasions he would stay in the royal palace of Buda. But on the whole, his stays would be flying visits, although they would sometimes end with a stay at Gödöllö, in spring to go riding and in autumn in order to hunt. Despite the creation of the dual monarchy, Vienna remained the monarchy's capital. This was partly because of tradition, but also because Vienna was the seat of the joint ministries and central administrative bodies, and it was there that the embassies of foreign powers were situated.

In Vienna, Franz Joseph would divide his time between two palaces, the grand old Hofburg palace at the heart of the capital, and the eighteenth-century Schönbrunn palace which at the time of its construction had been situated outside the city, but towards which the suburbs were now gradually creeping. Traditionally, Franz Joseph would spend his winter months at the Hofburg, this period corresponding with the high season at court, and would then go to Schönbrunn at Easter, where he would stay until the autumn. But even them he would go to the Hofburg almost every day for his work, holding audiences and carrying out various other duties there. He would travel there in an open carriage so that his subjects could see him and acknowledge him as he passed. During the final years of his life he would extend his stay in the Schönbrunn palace for as long as possible, and he would also reduce the number of journeys from there to the Hofburg. This change took place shortly before the outbreak of the First World War, which put an end to his comings and goings between the two palaces. From then onwards, Franz Joseph would practically never leave Schönbrunn until his death.

The rooms in which Franz Joseph spent most of his time, his study and his bedroom, were characterized by their simplicity. Had it not been for their setting, these rooms would have been in perfect accord with a middle-class home, and not even the richest of these, for the apartments and furnishings of the buildings on the *Ringstrasse* were in quite a different style. The furnishing of the bedroom in Schönbrunn was thus striking in its restraint: a few armchairs and a sofa covered in brown cloth. Franz Joseph slept on a simple iron bedstead which had a camelskin cover. Near the bed there stood his rudimentary toilet articles which included a washbasin, two pitchers and bowls and a bucket which he used as a chamber pot. Franz Joseph does not seem to have noticed these inconveniences. He never considered having a bathroom installed, and in this he provides us with a good example of his mistrust of things modern.

Unless matters kept him in Vienna or obliged him to cut his stays short, Franz Joseph would spend between one and two months of the year at Ischl (which became Bad Ischl in 1906) in the Upper Austrian Alps. This custom had started during his childhood, when Franz Joseph would stay at the Hotel Austria with his parents and his brothers. The family later stayed in one of the Ischl houses, the Eltz house, after it had been purchased by the Archduchess Sophie. This building became the *Kaiservilla* on Sophie's presentation of it to Franz Joseph and Elisabeth as an engagement gift. The rooms which Franz Joseph occupied displayed the same simplicity as those of the Vienna palaces. His last valet's memoirs record that the emperor's room was so narrow that there was only just enough room for a chest of drawers. It was a family tradition that Franz Joseph's birthday on 18 August should be celebrated at Ischl. This celebration took place within the small circle of those relations and administrators closest to the emperor. It could sometimes be a more formal occasion, as it was in 1910 on the occasion of the celebration of his eightieth birthday, when seventy-two members of the Austrian Royal House were gathered together. Although paperwork and audiences still took up a fair portion of Franz Joseph's time when he was staying at Ischl, life there had a more relaxed rhythm than in Vienna. There were many possibilities for excursions, and above all there was the chance to hunt, which Franz Joseph could enjoy here to the full.

The military manoeuvres which regularly took place in September set an obligatory time limit on the periods spent at Ischl. As supreme commander of the armies, Franz Joseph never failed to attend them. On these occasions, he would stay with a member of the local aristocracy who would place his house at the emperor's disposal. Joseph Roth's short story *The Emperor's Bust*, in which the author makes the emperor stay with Count Morstin, a Polish noble from Galicia, thus has its basis in reality.

Franz Joseph's Working Day

Wherever he was staying, most of Franz Joseph's time was taken up by his work. Although it is the image of the old sovereign bent over his desk which has endured, this habit began as soon as he came to the throne, and in a letter to Metternich, Schwarzenberg indicated that the young emperor worked at least ten hours a day. In order to do this, Franz Joseph had to rise early. In fact he would wake up at four in the morning, sometimes even at half past three. He would begin the day with a wash, invariably in cold water. Once he had completed his ablutions, he would don the infantry lieutenant's uniform which was his usual form of dress. This choice of clothing was intended to emphasize the special relationship between the emperor and his army. It also confirms the simple taste of the sovereign in everyday matters. His dress uniforms were reserved for state ceremonies when he had to appear in all the splendour of his imperial majesty. For his work, he preferred a simple lieutenant's uniform, shiny with use, to the fine dress of a *Feldmarschall*.

At five, Franz Joseph would settle down in his study. A pile of papers on current concerns would be waiting for him. He would begin the day's work by reading the letters from the foreign minister. There would also be a list of birthdays to acknowledge, and of congratulations and condolences to be sent. When draft telegrams were submitted for his approval, his delicate sense of tone would often lead him to correct them, or even to rewrite them completely. While he was working on these papers, a somewhat frugal breakfast would be served to him: a cup of coffee (replaced by tea in the second half of his reign), a buttered roll (the Viennese *Semmel*) and a slice of ham, except during Lent. Towards half past seven he would ring for his duty officer who would collect the briefcase containing the papers which he had dealt with.

Now the audiences would begin. The first encounter of the day would be the head of the military chancellery, followed by the head of the cabinet, and the ministers, among which encounters the meeting with the foreign minister would be the longest. There was no laxity of dress permitted to these top civilian dignitaries. They were obliged to appear in a suit and were expected to be perfectly punctual for the punctual for the audience, for which the time was fixed in advance.

Twice a week this programme was altered by the holding of general audiences, from ten o'clock onwards. Theoretically, any of the emperor's subjects was allowed to approach him, but in practice the head of the cabinet would sort through the requests. Until the 1890s, Franz Joseph would receive about a hundred people during the morning, but after this date this figure was reduced to about fifty so as to conserve his strength, but for the old man which he had become, this still remained an amazing performance. Although of necessity these audiences were short, they added to Franz Joseph's popularity. Whatever part of the empire he came from, each of his subjects knew that the emperor was accessible and could believe him to be prepared to listen to his problems.

When he did not join his family for lunch, Franz Joseph would eat in his office.

Once again the menu was a simple one: a bowl of soup, meat and vegetables, with beer to drink. Work would begin again immediately, and Franz Joseph would hear the daily report of the Vienna chief of police and would receive a press summary drawn from both domestic and foreign newspapers. This perusal, which would sometimes be accompanied by further audiences, would continue until dinner, which was served between five and six. Before leaving his office, Franz Joseph would always tidy it. He would clean it with a little brush and be careful to put aside the sheets of paper which he had not used.

In the time that his closest family members were still alive and were resident in Vienna, Franz Joseph would usually eat dinner with them. A dreary boredom reigned at these meals, as etiquette demanded that nobody could speak to the emperor unless he had first spoken to them. As Franz Joseph was naturally taciturn, there would be long periods of silence during these meals. But dinner would not last long, as Franz Joseph was in the habit of eating quickly. As for Elisabeth, when she was present, her preoccupation with preserving her slender figure led her barely to touch the dishes offered to her. As the meal was served according to the emperor's requirements, other members of the family would often go hungry. Following dinner, Franz Joseph liked to allow himself a brief moment of relaxation in smoking a Virginian cigarette. A great smoker during his youth, he cut down as he grew older, and fell back on cigars which had a milder tobacco. In the evening, he might sometimes go to the court theatre or to the opera. When old age forced him to rest more, he would go to bed earlier, between eight and half past eight. According to his letters, he would fall asleep quickly and would sleep well.

Although the rhythm was more relaxed at Ischl, Franz Joseph did not interrupt his work there. In the mornings, between eight and twelve, the emperor continued to work on his papers and to give audiences to ministers and political administrators when the necessity arose. Regardless of circumstances, he would receive the foreign minister at least once a week. The *Kaiservilla* was connected by telegraph to Vienna, so that Franz Joseph could be contacted quickly over urgent affairs. The installation of the telegraph was one of Franz Joseph's rare concessions to modern technology, and he made frequent use of this means of communication. He would use it to correspond with his employees at the Hofburg palace. On the other hand, he was to remain hostile to the telephone to the end. It seems possible that he sensed instinctively that such an invention would be as much a scourge as a boon. In giving instructions to his subordinates, he remained loyal to traditional methods. These instructions would be scribbled in pencil, and took the form of quick notes. He would already himself have cut larger sheets of paper into many pieces, another example of a personal characteristic which broke with the official pomp of the court.

The way in which he organized his time and working methods turned Franz Joseph into the first bureaucrat of his empire. It displays an exemplary sense of duty and already shows that the individual in Franz Joseph's character tended to retreat behind his official functions. It remains to assess the effectiveness of his methods. Many of Franz Joseph's contemporaries confirm his excellent knowledge of affairs at all stages of his reign. As a witness to the years of his youth, Duke Ernst von Saxe Coburg-Gotha declared himself to be impressed 'by the precision and knowledge of affairs which he displayed in mastering each problem'.[1] Albert Schäffle, who was one of his ministers in 1871, described him as having, among other qualities, 'an exceptional knowledge of matters and of men';[2] and a minister in one of his last administrations, Baron Spitzmüller, made the same comment.[3] It is true that Franz Joseph could rely on his own memory, which was well-ordered, in classifying documents and remembering names and faces.

However, it is questionable whether Franz Joseph's methods of working made it easy for him to take an overall view of the problems which faced the monarchy. The papers which were submitted to him did not undergo any strict sorting procedure, and this meant that Franz Joseph concerned himself equally with higher affairs of state which could affect the monarchy and with minor matters. In addition to the great waste of time which such a method involved, in depriving him of a sense of proportion, it threatened to prevent Franz Joseph from being able to look on matters from a sufficient height to be able to take in larger situations and dominate events.

Franz Joseph and his Advisers

Franz Joseph also filled the position of the empire's senior bureaucrat in his relations with his closest advisers, and most of all with his ministers. In truth, even within a constitutional system, he preserved a relationship with them which was feudal in character. In Franz Joseph's view, a minister carrying out his duties was on a mission in the service of his emperor. It would thus be unthinkable, in Franz Joseph's view for such a minister to shirk his duties. Any such refusal would be almost tantamount to desertion. Count Kielmansegg, who was hesitant about accepting the post of first minister in 1895 found himself saying: 'You have been an officer, and you know what it means when the emperor says "I order you." '[4]

This attitude on the part of the emperor gives on indication of the qualities which he valued most highly. Experience and a sense of duty acquired in the service of the state with an unswerving loyalty to the emperor were the qualities most likely to command his trust. For this reason, Franz Joseph naturally felt at ease with the senior officials who had long been in his own service and were only continuing this office in a different guise when they were called to join the government. Baron Beck, who was first minister in 1906, expressed a characteristic reaction: 'As a civil servant,' he explained later, 'I could not dream of refusing the task of creating and leading the government.'[5]

As an illustration of this special relationship, many former provincial governors (*Statthalter*) were among the figures chosen to lead the government. When they were selected by Franz Joseph, Belcredi, Hohenwart, Taaffe, Kielmansegg, and Badeni were all, or had recently been, governors. Besides the head of government, many ministries contained representatives from the top echelons of the administration, as well as political figures. This practice reached its most complete form with the *Beamtenministerien* (governments of administrators) which Franz Joseph would be obliged to form during the last period of his reign, as a result of the increase in confrontations between the parties and of the antagonism between nationalities which would between them lead to the paralysis of the parliamentary institutions.

It should finally be noted that Franz Joseph selected his first ministers from among the ranks of the upper classes, mostly from the aristocracy, but also, in later years, from the administrators who had served him. There were reasons for this preference. Franz Joseph had no wish to recognize specific powers for the nobility as a body, but the prestige of the great family names remained a marketable asset in a society which was still largely agricultural. This choice also illustrated the system of feudal values within which Franz Joseph lived. As has been mentioned, he perceived the nobles of his empire as vassals from whom he expected wholehearted devotion to the service of the crown.

It was therefore logical that Franz Joseph should keep a certain distance in his dealings with his ministers. It was not in his character to be too expansive, but this distance was primarily an indication of his concept of power which could be seen in the outward form of the relationships between Franz Joseph and his ministers. It would, for instance, be most unusual for him to shake hands with them. The same quality could be seen in his working relationships. When he met with his ministers, Franz Joseph made it a rule not to allow them to speak of matters outside their own field unless explicitly asked. It was therefore most unusual for him to consult them on matters which fell outside the area of their responsibilities. Later on, he would refrain from discussing questions concerning their previous sphere of office with ministers who had changed posts. This rule of conduct can be interpreted in the first case as a sign of tact towards other ministers and in the second as a concern not to embarrass a successor. But it also shows that, despite the constitutional changes which had taken place since the collapse of neo-absolutist rule, Franz Joseph still had difficulty in treating the government as a collective entity. As before, he continued to perceive the essential role of his ministers to be that of advisers to the crown and executives of the will of the crown.

His ministers were also aware that, even within their own domains, the emperor would not allow them to act independently. His reading of their reports was not a simple formality; Franz Joseph annotated these with indefatigable zeal, and anyone who ignored his comments would be extremely foolish. A minister could nevertheless be influential in his role as adviser to the emperor. If he avoided the transgression of the limits which had been set for him, he could rely on his sovereign's attention. The latter would only make decisions after having heard the arguments of the appropriate minister, as Schäffle recalls:

> It was always possible for me to ask him to give his attention to important matters...[Franz Joseph] examines each matter conscientiously and considers every detail but is never pedantic; he is always objective and sympathetic, he examines everything without prejudgements and never claims to know anything better than his minister before discussing it with him.[6]

His ministers also knew that they could rely on his complete support when they had to carry out a decision which he had approved.

There could, however, be rude awakenings. Franz Joseph did not appreciate any minister choosing his own moment to leave the government. Rechberg drew his monarch's anger down upon himself when in 1863 he asked to be relieved of his duties. Such a resignation was the equivalent of the desertion of his post. Franz Joseph therefore considered it to be perfectly in order that he should have refused him his request. The main reason for Franz Joseph's dislike of such behaviour was that it represented a reversal of roles, for in his view it was the emperor's right to decide on his ministers' terms of office. Once such a decision had been made, he would not be prepared to make any concessions, at least at the beginning of the reign.

The case of Baron von Bruck, whose harsh treatment at the hands of the emperor drove him to suicide, was certainly an exceptional one. Following the 1859 war he became the target of a smear campaign accusing him of corruption. He was informed of his dismissal through a note from the emperor at a time when the latter had just reiterated his confidence in him. Convinced that Franz Joseph had allowed himself to be persuaded by his accusers, and overwhelmed by such disgrace, he cut his throat in the hours which followed. Having learned the dangers of such summary measures from this tragedy, Franz Joseph would be careful in the future to use less brutal means of communication. A minister whom he wished to dismiss would receive a visit from a member of court, who was sent to inform him that His Majesty expected him to resign. A refinement of this method would occur when, in the course of a meeting with a minister, in particular with the first minister, who deserved a greater degree of consideration, Franz Joseph would allow it to be understood that the minister in question was approaching the end of his period of office. If he understood the message, he could be assured that his resignation would not be refused.

These procedures indicated the distance which separated Franz Joseph's Austria from contemporary parliamentary regimes. Save at the outset of the constitutional era, when Franz Joseph was dealing with a majority with whom he was not in agreement, the length of service of a minister depended more on the will of the emperor than on the parliamentary situation.

It is not hard to deduce from these practices that once the years of Franz Joseph's political apprenticeship had passed, no minister was likely to exert the degree of influence which Schwarzenberg had enjoyed. Should we then conclude from this, as Friedjung suggests, that Franz Joseph preferred to surround himself with mediocre figures? As a whole, his ministers displayed the same qualities as the Austrian administration in the execution of their task: loyalty, discipline, and efficiency. But with a few exceptions, they did not go beyond these in the execution of their new duties.

Although Franz Joseph did call some strong personalities to serve him, such as Bruck and Andrassy, his relations with these men were often difficult. He chose to make use of them because he knew of the services they could render to the monarchy, but there was no fellow-feeling in his dealings with them. Such behaviour should no doubt also be seen as a defensive reaction on the part of a monarch who was jealous of his prerogatives. Franz Joseph was always careful to maintain his distance, wary of allowing his colleagues to gain any influence which might lead to a loss of real power on his part. In support of such a theory, it should be noted that in the first part of the reign, Franz Joseph would often surround himself with advisers of widely differing and sometimes even conflicting opinions. The most spectacular example of this was the confrontation between Schmerling and Rechberg, both of whom were ministers in the same government. For more than three years, a first minister whose aim was to re-establish Austrian supremacy in Germany was in conflict with a foreign minister who was working to establish an agreement with Berlin.

This dualism might be, and probably was, to a certain extent, the manifestation of

Franz Joseph's lack of resolution in the face of contradictory possibilities for future policy. Such a practice of leaving the supporters of two opposing policies to fight out their differences threatened to give Austrian policy a bumpy ride which would eventually weaken it. Nevertheless, it is hard not to see this practice as a further demonstration of Franz Joseph's desire to remain master of events.

With consummate art, Franz Joseph accordingly set out to arrange his relations with his ministers in such a way as to prevent the possibility of any development which might result in transferring the powers of decision. In view of this, it is not surprising that he continued to be the true instigator of the monarchy's policies throughout his reign. On receiving a delegation of members of parliament at the height of the Bosnian crisis, he banished all doubt on this matter when he threw at them: 'You speak constantly of Andrassy's policy. Don't forget that it is my policy.'[7] It would therefore be unthinkable for a minister to behave towards him in the way that Bismarch behaved towards Wilhelm I when, after a real test of strength, he managed to force his sovereign to accept the alliance with Austria-Hungary. Had any of his ministers attempted to behave in such a manner towards Franz Joseph, he would have found himself immediately relieved of his duties.

But of all the ministers who worked with Franz Joseph, the one who was closest to him was doubtless his first Adjutant General. At the beginning of his reign, Count Grünne built up a considerable sphere of influence in this capacity. One of the powerful figures of neo-absolutism, he contrived to gain control of the army, playing a decisive role in the selection procedure. From this dominant position at the heart of the military institution, he had attempted to extend his field of influence to the political scene, with somewhat mixed results. The collapse of the neo-absolutist regime brought him down in its wake, for, although he did not disappear from the sovereign's retinue, he was relegated as Master of the Horse to a role which prevented him from participating in affairs of state. None of his successors, whether Count Crenneville, Count Bellegarde or Count Paar, achieved the same degree of influence, nor did they even think of aspiring to it.

Such a problem clearly did not exist for the four officers who, under the orders of the Adjutant General, were assigned as adjutants in the personal service of the emperor. Their tasks were clearly defined. Two of them were to hold themselves at the emperor's disposal at all times. The third was assigned to special duties, for instance, it fell to him to accompany Franz Joseph's guests during their stay in Vienna. The last adjutant would be on leave for a month. The day before these officers took up their duties, a carriage belonging to the court would come to collect them from their Vienna lodgings to take them to Schönbrunn where they would be quartered.

For the adjutant on duty, the day would begin at four in the morning, even if he was not called on until seven. Towards half past seven he would take the briefcase of files which Franz Joseph had been working on. For the rest of the day his main duty would be to admit the people who had been granted audiences. He was also involved in the preparations for the general audiences. It was his job to classify up to a hundred supplicants in order of precedence, often a delicate task. Of course there was no question of any familiarity with the emperor, and as he accompanied him he was obliged to remain silent, unless he was addressed by Franz Joseph.

For his part, Franz Joseph was not free with gestures which might introduce a note of familiarity into his relations with his adjutants. As proof of this, as with his other colleagues, he would very rarely shake hands with them. One of them, Baron Margutti, recalled that Franz Joseph had only shaken hands with him once in sixteen years, on the occasion of his promotion to Brigadier General.[8]

Franz Joseph's Tastes

Franz Joseph was thus almost completely absorbed by his duties as sovereign. Little time was left to him for cultural occupations. It is possible that Leo Thun was telling the truth when he gave his assurance that, other than reports and memoranda, Franz Joseph did not read a single book for pleasure following his accession to the throne. The question remains whether he would have wished to, for witnesses have not hesitated to describe him as a prosaic creature, completely impervious to aesthetic feeling. His visits to the Burgtheater and the Opera nevertheless seem to contradict this assertion, although it may be that he saw these visits as a duty, as they were theatres of the crown. Truth to tell, it is not hard to assemble a number of comments by Franz Joseph which demonstrate his boredom during some performances. A brief sample should suffice: as he wrote to his mother, 'Yesterday, Sissi and I saw *A Midsummer Night's Dream* by Shakespeare at the Burgtheater...It was rather boring, and very stupid.'[9] The evenings spent at the theatre or at the opera during his stay in Paris in October 1867 appear to have had a soporific effect on him, as his letters to Elisabeth show: 'At half past eight I was at the Théâtre Français where a long play was very well performed, but I slept a lot', or; 'I went to the Théâtre Lyrique where they were performing Gounaud's [*sic*] new opera *Romeo and Juliet*, and I slept very well once again.'[10]

Such comments were doubtless no longer surprising to Elisabeth. They also provide a key to the development of the relationship between husband and wife. To return to the example given above, Franz Joseph's letter to his mother gives no indication of Elisabeth's reaction to *A Midsummer Night's Dream*, but all the evidence of her character suggests that the poetic charm and the fantasy of this play would have enchanted her where her husband saw only insipid ineptitude. *A Midsummer Night's Dream* was one of the literary works which were most in tune with her imagination, to the point that she would soon identify herself with Titania and would often portray herself as the queen of the fairies in her poetry. In any case, Elisabeth was of all people the most convinced of Franz Joseph's imperviousness to artistic emotions. In going to the threatre, he was first acting out a social ritual. It would, however, be an exaggeration to suggest that he always succumbed to boredom. There was also the period from 1886 onwards during which he visited the Burgtheater for the pleasure of seeing Katharina Schratt perform. But usually, although serious or fantastic subjects left him cold, he enjoyed light comedy and vaudeville, confirming that he could have very bourgeois tastes.

Franz Joseph's encounters with music were passive. Unlike many of his ancestors, some of them recent – for instance Franz I who played chamber music – he did not play an instrument. Although he attended the Opera, he does not appear to have been concerned with the musical life of his time, despite the fact that Vienna continued to be one of the great musical centres of Europe.

On the other hand, Franz Joseph's interest in the plastic arts extended beyond the realm of duty. Even as a child he had enjoyed drawing and had shown some skill, and in 1848 he had brought back a book of sketches from his brief stay in the Italian army. In later life he had no time for such activities but he remained interested in art. His tastes were assuredly conventional. A soldier at heart, he inclined towards military subjects and as a huntsman he had a weakness for animal themes. In accordance with the tradition of princely houses, he also liked portraiture. One of the artists whom he valued particularly highly was Heinrich von Angeli, one of the official portrait painters of the court, whom he would often visit in his studio.

Hans Makart was also one of the painters afforded this honour. Indeed, it was largely to Franz Joseph that he owed his spectacular rise to fame. He established himself in Vienna following an imperial decree on 20 April 1869. His lodgings and studio were paid for and one of the principal rooms at the Hofburg was given over to an exhibition of his work. In addition to all this support, several of his paintings were bought from him by Franz Joseph. Later on, Makart was involved in the decoration of the Hermes villa and of the Kunsthistorisches Hof-Museum. In the work of this master, who style was reminiscent of both Rubens and Titian, Franz Joseph loved the historical subjects, the passion for luxury, the rich colours, and its baroque character in general.

In a way, Franz Joseph continued the tradition of princely patronage in this field, as is demonstrated by the number of paintings which he purchased for the imperial palaces and collections. In accord with the decisions announced on 20 December 1857, these collections were assembled in an imperial museum, the Kunsthistorisches Hof-Museum, which was opened by the emperor in October 1891. But he sometimes went beyond the duties of this role, for instance when he acted as arbitrator in the discussions concerning the interior decoration of official buildings. It was he who decided which paintings should be hung in the foyer of the Opera, and on the frescos for the Arsenal, the great military complex constructed during the neo-absolutist era on the outskirts of the city.

Franz Joseph's tastes did not alter with time. Anchored in his concept of beauty, he remained impervious to the tendencies of art nouveau which declared themselves at the end of the century with the *Wiener Sezession* and Gustav Klimt, and in this his reaction was in accordance with the majority of public opinion. Although he was not a follower of naturalism, he disliked any painter who took too many liberties with reality. An anecdote told by Horthy is significant in this respect. On visiting an exhibition, he fell into thought before a painting which depicted a hunting lodge. Clearly confused, he eventually asked the painter who was standing beside him:

'Is it a lake in front of the lodge?'
'No, your Majesty, it is a meadow.'
'But it's blue!'
'That's the way I see it.'
'In that case, you should not have become a painter.'[11]

It was with architecture, though, that Franz Joseph's preferences lay. He was closely involved in the programme for the construction of official buildings which were to mark points along the *Ring*. In many cases, it was he who influenced the final choices. The most well-known instance is that of the competition which was organized at the end of the 1860s for designs for the construction of the museums facing the Hofburg, in which he demanded that the architects should leave the prospect free between the Leopoldine wing of the palace and the court stables, the work of Fischer von Erlach. Franz Joseph's choice fell on the German architect Gottfried Semper and the Austrian Karl von Hasenauer. This proposal preserved the famous view, but also proposed the creation of a vast space which would bring together the Leopoldine wing, a new Hofburg, the museums, and the stables. Among its other merits, Franz Joseph appreciated this proposal's respect for the unity of the whole, for the new elements would be built in a neo-baroque style. On a more general level, this choice demonstrates Franz Joseph's taste for the baroque. Indeed, it had not escaped him that of all styles, the baroque corresponded most closely to the imperial majesty, and upheld it with the greatest splendour. It was closely associated with the rise of Austrian power under Leopold I and Maria Theresa and so it is natural that it should have been Franz Joseph's favourite architectural style.

The expression 'Franz Joseph style' sometimes used by historians seems broadly justified. It is not only accounted for by the length of his reign, it also represents the personal influence of the emperor on the architecture of the times. Franz Joseph obviously did not supervise the construction of all the official buildings across the empire. But the choices made in Vienna created a school. The solemnity of the neo-baroque style, and the rather austere elegance of the neo-renaissance style recommended these styles to the architects of imperial and royal buildings in other cities of the monarchy. Whether in Prague, in Brünn, in Cracow, in Lemberg, in Trieste, in Zagreb, in Presburg or even in Budapest, the influence of the Viennese style could be seen. Its spread gave urban landscapes a homogeneous character which transcended local and national variations, and was all the more marked because it was also used in cultural buildings and in middle-class domestic architecture. This unity of style reinforced the monarchy's common cultural heritage, and served as an integrating force against the forces of disorder at work elsewhere.

When he could escape the duties of his position, Franz Joseph was at his happiest when hunting. The stays at Ischl would be given over to this. For several weeks, Franz Joseph would devote himself to the sport. For the first and only time of the year, his time would be spent with different priorities from affairs of state. Even when the summer was over, he would not put away his rifles and cartridge belts. Although the demands of his work were heavy, he did not rule out a few moments respite in which to hunt. Hunting was part of the pattern of his days at Gödöllö. He also owned a hunting lodge at Mürzsteg in Styria, where he would sometimes entertain important guests who were visiting Vienna.

Franz Joseph the huntsman was quite a different character from the bureaucratic emperor or the soldier emperor. This difference can first be seen in his dress. At Ischl, Franz Joseph abandoned his uniform for his 'Styrian skins' as he liked to call his mountaineer's shoes, thick woollen socks, leather shorts, green jacket, and Tyrolean hat. The change was not merely a physical one. On these hunting expeditions, Franz Joseph was no longer the serious and rather stuffy monarch from Vienna, but became instead a jovial and good companion, capable of humour. It is likely that his taste for hunting was partly due to his skill at the sport, for his tally would eventually reach the impressive total of 55,000 trophies. But there was possibly a further reason. This sovereign who, with a sense of duty which has rarely been equalled, applied himself to the constraints of his office, may sometimes have felt the almost physical need to retreat and to re-establish a direct contact with nature. Such an explanation would suggest that there were two sides to Franz Joseph's character, the official figure, and another, far more secret character, which the former had not completely succeeded in crushing.

Beyond the occasional official guest, Franz Joseph chose his companions from a small circle. Duke Karl Theodor in Bavaria, his brother-in-law, known as Gackel in the family, and Ferdinand IV, the deposed grand duke of Tuscany, who was often called Nando, were often of the party. But the person who was indisputably the closest to him was his second cousin, Albert of Saxony. Albert was perhaps the only person who could call himself Franz Joseph's friend. Even more than by age (only two years separated them), they were drawn together by the similarity in their tastes. Both were at their happiest among soldiers and out hunting. As an exceptional privilege, they addressed each other by the familiar *du* rather than the formal *Sie*. When Albert, at the beginning of their friendship, wished to follow the general rule, Franz Joseph corrected him immediately: 'Concerning the letter you wrote to me, I was horrified that it began with "Your Majesty" and was filled with titles which I had hoped would be unnecessary between us: I beg you therefore to drop these formalities in the future and to address me in the simplest manner.'[12] The general tone of the correspondence with Albert of Saxony is relaxed, but Franz Joseph becomes positively jovial when he comes to his favourite subject, writing: 'Now that's enough of politics and let's talk woodcock.'[13]

Franz Joseph took on a character whose role he repeated day after day. His concept of power demanded this of him. For such a feat, no ordinary degree of self-discipline was required, but Franz Joseph forced himself to play this role with the heightened sense of duty which distinguishes him. This repetitive way of life must undoubtedly have confirmed the conservative streak in his innermost inclinations. As time and age demonstrated the rigidity of his character, running against the direction in which society was moving, the unchanging order of his days settled him into a 'grandiose *statisme*', to use the term which Franz Werfel applied to the old Austrian regime in the decades leading up to the First World War.

It is not hard to guess at the possible dangers of this, but in fact it contributed to the creation of a myth which began to develop around Franz Joseph even while he was still alive. Each of his subjects could, at any hour of the day, guess at what his sovereign was doing at that precise moment. This rigidity in the character he presented to the world helped him to appear to his people as the incarnation of a permanent principle, and helped to make them aware of the eternal nature of the Habsburg Empire through his person.

This meticulous sovereign who was so attentive to the observance of form, was also careful to arrange his relations with his subordinates in such a way as to preserve his power. The comparison which many have made with Queen Victoria ends there, for Franz Joseph was not a monarch along British lines contriving to combine the exercise of monarchical power with a constitutional structure. Although he had not been prepared for this confrontation, he soon took the measure of the constitutional regime. He accepted it as a necessity and adapted to it, but he also contrived to restrict it with such consummate skill that he precluded any possible threat to his own authority. It was still he who made the decisions, and provided the impetus for policy. Although he was affable towards them, his ministers knew the limits of their relations with their monarch and would not have dreamed of stepping outside them. Although he was not proud, his behaviour clearly indicated each person's place in the hierarchy and increased his imperial prestige. Franz Joseph was efficiently served with loyalty and devotion by everyone concerned in the administration of his policies, but the drawback of this distance was without a doubt that it condemned him to the ordeal of loneliness.

This solitude was the price Franz Joseph had to pay for a position whose demands created a personality which became second nature to him. From his childhood he had been brought up with a view to power. At an early age he moulded himself to the character for which he had been prepared with an ease which many of his contemporaries admired. The exercise of power further reduced what little spontaneity his education had left him with. But his upbringing could not entirely suppress his individuality. Although his official position monopolized the main part of his life, he did feel the need to preserve an area in which he was his own person, however narrow it might be. Despite the fact that this aspect of Franz Joseph's personality was usually hidden in the course of his daily activities, it cannot be ignored. His character was thus less one-sided than it might at first appear, although the official figure was almost always dominant.

9

Franz Joseph's Court

The dual nature of Franz Joseph's character was perhaps most in evidence at court. Like his ancestor Joseph II, Franz Joseph had no taste for luxury or formality in his personal life. The simplicity of his dress and of the rooms in which he chose to spend his time bears witness to this. But, when he assumed his official role, there was a complete change. Simplicity became majesty, and splendour and pomp were essential. The accounts and memoirs of those who came into contact with Franz Joseph are unanimous in hailing him as the archetype of the majestic monarch. At the end of his life, Admiral Horthy remembered: 'I never knew another monarch who was the personification of majesty in the way that he was.'[1] Count Ottokar Czernin, one of his ambassadors, confirms Horthy's view: 'The Emperor Franz Joseph was a great lord...Everyone left him aware of having been in the presence of an emperor.'[2] The impression which the emperor made on foreign visitors to Vienna was generally just as strong. On being received by Franz Joseph, Lord Rosebery declared to him that he was most accomplished gentleman that it had ever been his privilege to meet.[3]

The trappings of this majesty were in brilliant evidence at court where Franz Joseph was of course the central figure, as emperor, but also as head of the House of Habsburg, a role which he assumed from the moment he came to the throne. Under Franz Joseph, the court regained a long-lost lustre. During the time of the Vienna Congress (1815) it was lit with a thousand lights, but these were soon to go out. The spirit of the *Biedermeier* spread through the court as it had through the rest of society. Franz I had preferred the simplicity of family life, freed from the restrictions of court protocol, to the splendour of official ceremonies. Towards the end of his life he had also experienced the joys of developing his talents as a grandfather. Only wearing uniform when he was obliged to, he would like to walk among his subjects in the streets of Vienna and talk with them. Once Franz I had disappeared, there was little likelihood that the court would regain its brilliance under poor Ferdinand I.

With Franz Joseph's accession to the throne the outlook changed radically. The new emperor was young, dashing, and bursting with health. In Franz Joseph, the monarchy once again found a sovereign fit to fulfil his role, which, in any case, he had been prepared for by his education. These various factors were enough to bring the court out of the torpor into which it had sunk. But the changes did not end there, for the ceremonies and etiquette of the court were revived and strictly enforced. This rigorous regard for rules was a political decision. After the troubles of 1848 which had almost brought down the monarchy, and while liberal ideas had not been eradicated despite their defeat, it appeared essential to confirm the majesty of the emperor's person and his imperial role through a special display. This tightening of the application of the rules of ceremony and etiquette were therefore part of the move to restore the power of the monarch following the suppression of the revolution. The institutional system in Austria was certainly not inflexible, and at the end of the decade of neo-absolutist rule, the monarchy did introduce a constitutional regime, but even under this, there was still justification for a continued respect for court ritual. In the face of change, it reaffirmed the permanence of the principle of monarchy.

The Organization of the Court

From the most senior dignitaries to the most subordinate employees, the court made up a complex body of many thousands of people which required a very structured organization to be able to function. Indeed, there was a sort of internal government, formed by the four senior officials responsible for the different departments of the court administration.[4]

If only because he was the court finance minister, the Grand Master (*Obersthofmeister*) held the most powerful position in this group. Under his jurisdiction came court ceremonies, the organization of the emperor's travels, the chapel and court music, the gardens and hunting grounds of the various castles and lands of the crown. The doctors and pharmacists of the court were also under his authority. In addition, the *Obersthofmeister* was also responsible for the two royal theatres, the Burgtheater and the Opera, and this responsibility involved him in the cultural life of the capital. Finally, he was also closely involved in the devising of development projects for the land which had become available with the dismantling of the Viennese ramparts, and, more generally, with the transformation of the urban landscape. The incumbents of this post were all chosen from the greatest Austrian families. Prince Constantin Hohenlohe-Schillingsfürst, who held this appointment for nearly thirty years, from 1867 to 1896, left the mark of his personality on the post during the period in which the *Ring* took shape.

As part of his duties, the *Obersthofmeister* was directly concerned with this construction. It was therefore logical for him to sit on the commissions which took decisions concerning its essential planning. There were certain matters, though, which the prince followed with particular interest. The construction and the decoration of the Opera and the Burgtheater, the extension of the Hofburg and the opening of the court museums were under his control. It fell to him to examine the proposals, to present them to the emperor and to act as a link between Franz Joseph and the artists. His actions could be the deciding factor in their careers, as in the case of Makart. In drawing Franz Joseph's attention to this painter from Salzburg who had been living in Munich since 1860, Prince Hohenlohe-Schillingsfürst brought about Makart's return to Vienna in circumstances which freed him from all material worries and helped him to develop his talent.

Although his powers were broad, the Grand Master of the court did not have a monopoly over cultural affairs. Part of these were the concern of the Grand Chamberlain (*Oberstkämmerer*). The library and the court collections were given into his charge. It was his duty to protect them and to make regular additions to them by purchasing new works. The crown jewels were also his responsibility, but all these matters formed only a part of his duties. The main duty of the Grand Chamberlain was to control the army of footmen, valets, and chambermaids in the employ of the emperor. It was also his prerogative to bestow the *Hoffähigkeit*, the sanction which gave the right to appear at court. The holders of this position were also drawn from the great aristocratic families. Among them were Count Folliot de Crenneville, Count Abensperg und Traun, Count Gudenus, and Count Lanckorinski.

The Lord Marshal (*Obersthofmarschall*) and the Master of the Horse (*Obersthallmeister*) completed the group which ruled the court. The former was responsible for the court's internal regulation. In this capacity, he was called on to make decisions on everyday matters. He was also involved in more delicate questions concerning members of the House of Habsburg, for it was his role to ensure that members of the court obeyed the laws in the family statutes, which were under the control of the emperor. As for the Master of the Horse, he was in charge of the stables and the court carriages, which were a daily concern. The riding schools of the court were also under his control, and this included the famous Spanish riding School with its Lippizaner horses.

Apart from the members of these four departments, there were a series of household titles available, such as Private Adviser (*Geheimrat*), Chamberlain (*Kämmerer*), and Court Adviser (*Hofrat*), which could also provide the means of entry to court. In the eighteenth century and in the first decades of the nineteenth century, these functions were given only to members of the nobility. The rule of 1760 demanded eight noble quarterings on the father's side and four on the mother's side in order to aspire to these positions. In Franz Joseph's reign this quasi-monopoly was broken down. The dignity of *Geheimrat* or *Hofrat* could also be conferred on ministers and heads of departments, on university professors, and on industrialists in recognition of their merit, and for these middle-class notables these honorific titles set the seal of approval on their careers.

The companies of guards concerned with the security of the emperor and the Imperial House complete this picture of the court. The Noble Guard (*Adelige Leibgarde*) was created by Maria Theresa, who had made up this company from young nobles from the Austro-Bohemian area. Since 1806 its ranks had been open to commoners. This corps was made up of sixty experienced officers, and it was a tradition that its commander, the Captain of the Guard, and his second in command, the *Kapitänleutnant*, should be chosen from among the generals. The Captain of the Guard would often be an officer at the end of his career, such as Count Friedrich von Beck-Rzikowsky who, before being given this post in 1906, had been at the head of the army's General Staff headquarters for twenty-five years.

In Vienna, a Hungarian Guard (*ungarische Leibgarde*) was also in the sovereign's employ. Also created by Maria Theresa, this unit had evolved differently from the Noble Guard and was still confined to members of the nobility. Except for its officers, it was made up of young nobles who would serve in it for three or four years. They were not inconspicuous in their rich uniforms, especially in their dress uniforms: *kolpack*, panther skin across the breast, the red *attila*, silver facings, red trousers, and yellow boots.

With the exception of the Guards, this organization acted as the model for the courts which surrounded the other members of the Habsburg family, which were miniature reproductions of the imperial court, organized under the same rules. Of these households, that of the empress deserves particular mention. On her arrival in Vienna for her wedding, Elisabeth encountered a court which was already formed. Archduchess Sophie was responsible for the choice of the ladies-in-waiting who, under the *Obersthofmeisterin*, Countess Sophie Esterhazy, would make up the empress's suite. Naturally, she had been careful to choose princesses and countesses who owed their allegiance to her. In acting in this fashion, Sophie had no ill intentions. Well aware of the circumstances of Elisabeth's upbringing, she considered it necessary to provide her with an entourage which would help to train her for her duties as sovereign.

This system only lasted for a few years. As she acquired greater autonomy, Elisabeth set out to gain control of her own household. The first victim was Sophie Esterhazy, whom she had come to dislike. The countess was relieved of her post during the imperial couple's stay in Venice, at a time when Franz Joseph was filled with joy at the reunion with his wife after the long months of separation brought about by her stay on Corfu. The decisive step was taken two years later when she gained permission from Franz Joseph to select the members of her household herself. Elisabeth exercised this right to the full. Her choices reflected her tastes, which can be measured by the increasing number of Magyars in her retinue. The first was her new reader, Ida Ferenczy, a young Hungarian whose close relationship with Andrassy recommended her to Elisabeth's attention. She soon became the empress's confidante. Also, during the period in which the fate of Hungary was being decided, she acted as a link between the empress and Andrassy. Through his letters which were officially addressed to Ida, Andrassy could thus correspond with Elisabeth without arousing suspicion. The Hungarian clan took over another post when Countess Maria Festetics was made a lady-in-waiting.

Though both were devoted to Elizabeth, the two women were nevertheless very different. Ida was utterly absorbed in her service to the empress and had no other aims in life. During the bad days she was the friend in whom Elisabeth would confide her bitterness and her anguish when she sank into a depression. She was entirely at the disposal of the empress. A room was furnished for her next door to that of the empress so that she could attend her mistress when the latter was suffering from insomnia. Maria Festetics' loyalty was just as exemplary, but as the daughter of one of the great Hungarian families, she came from a different milieu, had a different circle of friends, and did not immerse herself so completely in her role. She would not allow herself to be blinded by Elisabeth's charm, and was capable of being critical of her.

Appointed Grand Master of the empress's court in 1868, Baron Nopcsa completed the Hungarian household which many considered a scandal. Even after the Compromise of 1867, Sophie's spirit still lived on in the Viennese court, and its members were quick to suspect the Magyars, especially when they formed an enclave, as they did in this case. Indeed, Hungarian was much spoken at the empress's court, and partly through inclination, and partly in a spirit of provocation, it was Elisabeth who set the example in this. When she was apart from them, she would write to Ida and Maria in their own language.

Franz Joseph as Head of the Imperial Family

The fact that Franz Joseph allowed Elisabeth to organize her own household was an indication of the love which he still felt for her, whatever the difficulties in their relationship. This was a favour which he allowed only to his wife. As head of the imperial family, he had an almost discretionary power over its members, and in this capacity, his authority extended to the composition of their households.

As soon as he became emperor, Franz Joseph's relationship with his family began to change. Baron Meyendorff remarked on it in 1850 in a report: 'He never allows himself a dangerous familiarity, either with his household or the archdukes.'[5] The procedures of etiquette built a barrier between Franz Joseph and the rest of his family which was demonstrated by the honorific terms which were used between them. These rules applied even to his brothers and his children. Although he would address them with the familiar *du*, they would use 'Your Majesty', at least in public.

The organization of the family was regulated by strict rules which were set out in the statute of 3 February 1839. This was also applied to the Tuscan and Modena branches of the family who had returned to the fold after being expelled from Italy in 1860, choosing Austria as their land of exile. The Tuscan Habsburgs had been prodigious in their offspring and their return strengthened the family ranks considerably. The 1839 statute set the annual incomes for each member of the family. It allowed 75,000 florins for the sons and brothers of the emperor. His daughters and sisters would receive only 42,000 florins. The other archdukes and archduchesses were subject to the same unequal treatment. Whereas the former would receive 45,000 florins, the latter would receive only 24,000 florins. These sums rightly appear to be considerable, but they were no greater than the income of some of the great aristocratic families such as the Liechtensteins or the Schwarzenbergs, and the archdukes and archduchesses were expected to pay their household expenses. These figures were sometimes increased, for instance, Ferdinand Max received 150,000 in 1856, and Ludwig Victor received 100,000 from his twentieth year. In the case of the archduchesses, account should also be taken of their dowries which were as much as 200,000 florins for the daughters or sisters of the sovereign, and 100,000 for the other female members of the family. Some of the archdukes also had comfortable personal fortunes, for instance Archduke Albert owned vast tracts of land in Teschen in Silesia, which he had received from his father the Archduke Karl, and which made him one of the richest landowners of the empire.

The empress was a special case. Elisabeth at first received an annual income of 100,000 florins, and in addition, Franz Joseph would subsidize some exceptional expenditure. But his financial situation did not initially allow him to increase these payments, for when he had abdicated, his uncle Ferdinand had kept his personal fortune, which was far greater than Franz Joseph's. This was a primary reason for Franz Joseph to be economical, but it was also the potential cause of a financial crisis, in conjunction with the international situation, the weight of military expenditure, and successive wars.

The death of Ferdinand in 1875 led to a new situation which completely freed Elisabeth from financial worries, which had been unbearable for an empress who was always ready to bemoan her fate, but rarely prepared to give up the benefits of her position. Without any direct descendants, Ferdinand left his estate to his successor. Franz Joseph made no changes in his personal way of life, but allowed his wife to be the main beneficiary of this godsend. Not satisfied with raising her income to 300,000, he also provided her with a capital sum of two million florins.

The dreamy Elisabeth displayed a sharp sense of realism in this area, making sure that at least part of these sums should be invested. She was shrewdly careful to spread her assets, buying shares in the railway companies, in the *Donauschiffahrtsgesellschaft* (the Danube Steamship Company), and opening a number of savings accounts under assumed names. She did not see fit to inform her husband of any of these activities. But in any case, there was now no wish of Elisabeth's which her husband was not prepared to grant. For her part, while giving him little in return, she knew how to choose the right tone and words to gain his agreement. She could now buy the most expensive hunters for her activities in England and Ireland; and although before 1867 he had refused to buy her Gödöllö, Franz Joseph acceded to Elisabeth's wish to build a house in Vienna, and later one in Corfu.

The 1839 statute placed the whole of the House of Habsburg under the emperor's authority. This guardianship was a real one, for, although his illness had prevented Ferdinand from doing so, Franz Joseph exercised his powers to the full. Accordingly, no member of the family was allowed to choose his or her place of residence, select his or her household, or travel abroad without the emperor's agreement. The latter could also banish an archduke or archduchess from court, or even from the empire if he considered his or her behaviour to have been morally reprehensible, or incompatible with the interests of the monarchy.

Franz Joseph did not joke where the honour of the family was concerned. His own brother, Archduke Ludwig Victor, who was not afraid to display his homosexual inclinations, learned this to his cost when Franz Joseph banished him to a castle near Salzburg. Archduke Stefan, whose behaviour in 1848 as Palatine of Hungary was judged to be criminal, was expelled from the monarchy once the revolution had been suppressed. Exiled to Nassau, he was only permitted to return to Austria in 1858 for Rudolf's christening. After this event, the empire's frontiers remained barred to him for ever.

These archdukes had not been deprived of their titles, though. The supreme sanction, expulsion from the imperial family and all the rights which went with membership, would be imposed on anyone who married without Franz Joseph's consent, or who chose to make a love match unworthy of their birth. Faced with this problem, Franz Joseph displayed greater severity than his grandfather had, when, in 1829, he had agreed to the marriage of the Archduke Johann with the daughter of a postmaster. Although his children were not allowed to be included in the succession, Johann had retained his title. This precedent did not make the law, however, and with only one exception, Franz Joseph always came down on the side of severity.

Several archdukes had to suffer Franz Joseph's anger. For instance, Archduke Leopold Ferdinand from the Tuscan branch of the family formed an attachment which his family wished to break off. When they decided to intervene at the beginning of 1902, Leopold Ferdinand had been living with a prostitute for many years.

To add to the scandal, succumbing to alcoholism, he suffered fits of delirium tremens for which he had to be treated in a clinic in the Rhineland. His parents, the grand duke and grand duchess of Tuscany, took advantage of the situation to persuade him to leave his mistress. In payment for this, she received the sum of 100,000 florins under a legal contract.

However, it soon became clear that this arrangement had not actually been implemented. Leopold Ferdinand soon wrote to the emperor to ask him to relieve him of his position as a prince of the imperial family. But Franz Joseph was not satisfied with this minor solution. The condemnation of his kinsman must be complete. Leopold Ferdinand would have to renounce all his titles, ranks, and orders. He would also lose his name and be banned from the lands of the monarchy. Under his new name of Leopold Wölflin he could now marry his mistress, and soon afterwards he obtained Swiss nationality. His bitterness was only partly assuaged by a gift of 200,000 florins, which was supplemented by an annual income of 30,000 florins from his parents. Leopold Wölflin would outlive the monarchy for long enough to enjoy some sort of revenge in publishing venomous memoirs of the Habsburgs and the imperial court.

Towards the end of the reign there was another case involving such a reduction in status. The victim was the Archduke Ferdinand Karl, one of the sons of Archduke Karl Ludwig. He not only chose to live with a woman of low birth, the daughter of a teacher of mathematics at the Technische Hochschule in Vienna, but he committed the unforgivable sin, in Franz Joseph's eyes, of marrying secretly, in August 1909. When Franz Joseph heard of the marriage, he exacted immediate punishment. Reduced to the status of a commoner, the former archduke took the name of Ferdinand Burg, in which choice a degree of mockery can be detected.

Life at Court

The court life from which these archdukes were banned was typified by exclusivity. In order to participate, it was necessary to prove membership of the ancient nobility, with at least eight noble quarterings on the father's side, which in principle excluded members of the second society. However, dispensations were possible, as has been described above, for senior officers, recently elevated nobles, and rich or learned figures from the middle classes who were given titles at court.

The annual court ball (*Hofball*) was open to the knights of the different Habsburg orders (the orders of Maria Theresa, of Leopold, of Stephen, of the Iron Crown) and to the officers of the Vienna garrison, not to mention the 'foreigners of distinction' who lived or were staying in Vienna, in such numbers that the guests would crowd into the Redoutensaal, the largest room in the Hofburg. For this event, the court appeared in all its splendour. Lit by ten thousand candles, the rooms were richly decorated: sumptuous tapestries decked the walls, complementing the traditional pot-plants and floral arrangements specially created for the event. The luxury of the ladies' toilettes and the brilliance of their jewels added to the splendour of the ball. For the men, official dress was obligatory, enlivened by the Austrian, Hungarian, and foreign decorations.

This high point of the Viennese Season, which took place in February, unfolded according to a carefully regulated procedure. In the dress uniform of a *Feldmarschall*, Franz Joseph would make his entrance, at half past eight, with the empress on his arm, or, in her absence, with the most senior archduchess according to rank, or with the most senior of the foreign sovereigns attending the ball. Then would come the archdukes and archduchesses with their retinues. With the members of the imperial family, Franz Joseph would take his place on a dais from which he would dominate the room. He would not, however, remain there for long. He would soon mingle with his guests and exchange a few words with several of them at random. While this was happening, the orchestra, under the direction of Johann Strauss or Carl Ziehrer, would continue to play and the dancers would continue to circle. Because there was so little space, there would not be many of them. Towards the middle of the ball, Franz Joseph, the imperial family, and a few distinguished guests would assemble in a neighbouring room where they would be served with a meal while the other guests would flock around an enormous buffet. The ball would then start up once again, but Franz Joseph would leave quite early. His departure would mark the end of the ball, which was announced to the guests by the last waltz.

The ball at court (*Ball bei Hof*) took place a few days later. Drawing together a smaller circle of guests (although there were still some 700 of them), this celebration was of a less solemn nature. Franz Joseph would wear the uniform of a mere colonel of one of his regiments. Following his example, the diplomats would attend this ball in their minor official dress. A supper would be served to all the guests. Comprising five dishes, the menu never changed: potted goose, fish with mayonnaise, paté, roast meat, and ice cream, with champagne to drink. Obedient to his habits, Franz Joseph would finish this meal in half an hour, to the great displeasure of his guests.

The gala dinners (*Galatafeln*) and the court dinners (*Hoftafeln*) also formed part of the duties which Franz Joseph set himself. The former were organized on the occasion of the visits of foreign sovereigns. The latter, which were more frequent, took place when Franz Joseph wished to honour large bodies or institutions, or figures at the forefront of their fields. Like all court ceremonies, these dinners, which rarely saw more than twenty or twenty-five guests at table with their emperor, would follow a strictly regulated ritual. No fewer than twelve dishes would be prepared by the royal kitchens. The dinner would often begin with oysters, served with chablis. With the exception of the soup, which was served with beer, each dish was accompanied by a different wine. The hors d'oeuvre would be accompanied by a Rhenish wine, the roast or game by sherry or madeira, and the dessert by a Tokay or a lachryma-christi. The meal was served by an army of footmen working in groups of four. The service assumed the appearance of a race against time, for these dinners would rarely last for more than an hour, to such a point that the guests, at best, would only just have time to taste the dishes which they were served. At a signal from the emperor, they would rise and go into the salon where they would be offered cigars with liqueurs and coffee. In these moments of relaxation, Franz Joseph would sit in a group, or would chat with individual guests.

Although they broke the routine of daily work, the visits of foreign sovereigns and princes did not bring any surprises, for they too followed an almost unvaried pattern. After having welcomed his guest at the station and having accompanied him or her to his or her Viennese residence, Franz Joseph would resume his day's work until the evening, when there would be a gala dinner at the Hofburg, usually followed by a performance at the Opera. On the following day, he would be received by his guest who would give a grand dinner in his honour.

These visits imposed strict rules of dress on Franz Joseph. Form demanded that he should wear the decorations of his guest's nation. Being a colonel of several foreign regiments, he also took it upon himself to wear a uniform from his guest's country. This would have been a simple matter, had each regiment not possessed an array of uniforms, as many as six in German regiments, of which the wearing was regulated by a very strict etiquette. But this was a skill which Franz Joseph had mastered to perfection. This variety of uniforms could necessitate many changes in the course of the day. The worst situation arose when the German sovereigns came to Vienna, in 1908, to congratulate him as a group on his jubilee. Following this ceremony, he received each guest individually and his sense of courtesy dictated that he should change his uniform after each audience. Franz Joseph even followed this procedure during his stays at Ischl. It was impossible to put him out of countenance, even by a unexpected visit, for instance on one occasion, on returning from a walk, he was informed that the British ambassador was awaiting an audience, and diplomatic proceedings had to wait while he removed his Tyrolean suit and donned a British uniform.[6]

Ambassadors were not the only ones to travel to Ischl. Many foreign sovereigns visited Franz Joseph there. Indeed, not a year passed when he did not receive one, if not several, European monarchs there. There were also visits from courtiers, and from ministers, and these visits led to the construction of new buildings, the Bauer and Elisabeth hotels, where these distinguished guests and their retinues were housed.

Among the court ceremonies, there were also many which had a religious character and which demonstrated the bond which existed between the Habsburgs and the Catholic Church. The laws of 1867 had certainly established freedom of worship in both Austria and Hungary, and Franz Joseph declared himself the protector of all the religions of the monarchy, but despite this recognition of religious pluralism, the monarchy remained a Catholic power. The tensions which had appeared between Church and State could not change this basic fact, and Franz Joseph would have been the last to question this family tradition.

Franz Joseph was possessed of a firm faith which had never undergone the test of doubt. He would never begin a day without kneeling and spending a few minutes in prayer. Once the powers of each had been clearly defined, Franz Joseph behaved as an exemplary son of the Church, respecting its commandments. It went without saying that he attended Mass every Sunday, and in Vienna this would take place in the royal chapel. He also went to confession and communion many times during the year, he did not eat meat on Friday, he scrupulously kept the Lenten laws, and from Maundy Thursday to Easter Sunday would eat as little as possible.

The Habsburgs' loyalty to the Catholic faith was also confirmed by a series of official acts. The ceremony of the washing of feet on Maundy Thursday was one of these venerable traditions. It emphasized the sacred aura which continued to surround the figure of the sovereign in the Austrian system of monarchy. Chosen from the city hospice of Vienna, twelve old men dressed in pilgrim garb would represent the apostles. The emperor would first serve each one with a meal on a wooden tray. Once the table had been cleared by the archdukes, officials would take off their shoes and their right socks. Franz Joseph would then kneel. Helped by two priests, he would carefully carry out his task, moving from one old man to the next. When he had finished, a page would give him a bowl and an equerry would fill it with water in which Franz Joseph would wash his hands. Then the Grand Master of the court would come forward with a towel on a silver tray for the emperor to dry himself. The final gesture would take place when Franz Joseph would hang a purse containing thirty silver florins round the neck of each old man.

Providing the occasion for a vast procession in the name of devotion to the Holy Sacrament, Corpus Christi was the time when the bond between the dynasty and the Catholic Church was most solemnly expressed. The court would appeared in all its magnificence and blend with the pomp of a Catholicism which was firmly rooted in the tradition of the Counter-Reformation and the baroque. Franz Joseph would first go to Saint Stephen's Cathedral, in a state coach drawn by six superb grays, where he would attend the High Mass celebrated by the cardinal archbishop of Vienna. An immense crowd would be assembled along the route of the procession which formed following the Mass. In ceremonial dress, the knights of the different orders of the monarchy would precede the cathedral chapter, and then, walking under a canopy, there would come the cardinal, holding the Holy Sacrament. In his *Feldmarschall*'s dress uniform, Franz Joseph would follow, bare-headed, and carrying a candle, followed by the archdukes and flanked by the Noble and Hungarian Guards. There would be a planned stop opposite the Capuchin church on the Neuer Markt, where a marquee had been erected for Franz Joseph and his suite, and they would pause there for a short while. After this halt, the procession would begin again and, having turned at the top of the Michaelerplatz, it would move along the Kohlmarkt, coming out onto the Graben and finally returning to the cathedral from whence Franz Joseph would return to the Hofburg.

Franz Joseph's Travels

In the course of the year, the stay at Ischl was not the only journey on Franz Joseph's schedule. From 1867, he was obliged, as constitutional king of Hungary, to go to Budapest every year. Furthermore, during September he would attend the manoeuvres of the imperial and royal army. But there were other journeys which, although they did not take place with the same regularity, were also necessary for Franz Joseph. There were the trips into the monarchy's provinces, his meetings with foreign sovereigns in other parts of the empire besides Vienna or Ischl, the official trips abroad, not to mention the journeys for exceptional reasons, such as the coronation in Buda in 1867, the opening of the Suez canal in 1869 or, in the 1890s, the holidays with Elisabeth in the south of France.

These journeys involved moving the court, for Franz Joseph would be accompanied by a suite which, although its composition certainly varied, would always be large. The coronation of 1867 was certainly an extreme case: the imperial couple's suite included no fewer than 837 members on that occasion. But for the journey in Lombardy-Venetia in 1856–7, which was expected to last four months, Franz Joseph and Elisabeth were still accompanied by 267 attendants, and when, in January 1866, he visited the Hungarian capital, this figure rose to 355.

The preparations for these journeys involved the different household departments, the more so because Franz Joseph would take mountains of linen, crockery, and bottles with him. For a visit to Trieste in 1850, he took 150 bottles of champagne, 150 bottles of Bordeaux, 100 bottles of Rhenish wine, and as many of Moselle. The household departments concerned with meals took up a good part of Franz Joseph's retinue: on the journey to Lombardy-Venetia, the court kitchens were represented by twenty members of staff, the cellars by twelve and the bakery by ten. The services of the master of the Horse were clearly required, especially at the beginning of the reign, when the rail network had only been partly developed. For the journey in Italy in 1856–7, Franz Joseph needed 37 carriages and 162 horses.

The receptions given for Franz Joseph in the cities of the monarchy were organized according to a practically unchanging scenario. On his arrival, he would be welcomed under a triumphal arch by the mayor and the municipal councillors. The keys of the city would often be presented to him at this ceremony. There would then be another stop at the centre of the town where the schoolchildren and local societies would cheer him. The populace would be gathered around the residence selected by the emperor for his stay, where the civil, military, and religious authorities would await him and where a small group would pay tribute to him. Before this, Franz Joseph would have passed between two ranks of young girls dressed in white who would have strewn flowers in his path. A full programme always awaited him. When he travelled alone, he would visit a representative range of the social and cultural institutions of the town. If he was with the empress, the visits would be divided between the couple. Elisabeth would visit the hospitals, the crèches, the girls' schools, and the institutes for the blind, deaf, and dumb, while the emperor would review the troops or give audiences. The couple would visit the monuments, museums, and churches together.

A visit by the emperor always provided the occasion for a wide range of festivities. If he was making a long stay, a ball would be held wherever the court was staying. A concert and a play would usually round off this programme. In addition, there would be a formal dinner every evening, to which the notables of the town and the district would be invited. At the very least, the town would be illuminated, and there would often be a torchlight procession in honour of the sovereigns. This would be accompanied by musical festivities (serenades and a concert by the local orchestra), Finally, there would often be a firework display as the high point of such days.

Court Society

In Vienna, the court did not shut itself up in the Hofburg or Schönbrunn palaces. Court life moved between a number of social centres, although these revolved around the central axis of the imperial court. Many archdukes no longer lived at the Hofburg, but would reside instead in palaces which they had inherited or bought. Archduke Albert lived in a palace which was close to the Hofburg but which was nevertheless separate from it; and Karl Ludwig acquired a palace in the Favoritengasse during the 1860s. These palaces each sheltered a miniature court life, which varied in brilliance according to the personalities involved. The great aristocratic families, especially those from the Austro-Bohemian region, occupied a prominent place in the ranks of this society. Many of them owned palaces in Vienna where they would stay every year from autumn to spring. Towards the middle of June these families would return to their estates, where they would spend the summer, unless they spent part of these months taking the waters at the fashionable thermal spas of Karlsbad, Marienbad, and Teplitz.

The nobles of the court were active participants in society life, in particular through their salons which were attended by a select group. Their success would largely be due to the personality of the hostess, as was clearly the case with Princess Pauline Metternich, one of the great figures of Viennese high society, and formerly one of the stars of Parisian social life when her husband was Austria's representative to Napoleon III. Her sparkling imagination, her ever lively humour, and her quick repartee gained her a celebrity which made her a queen of this milieu for many decades. This court society could also be found at the home of Princess Eleonore Schwarzenberg in the Mehlmarkt palace, and at the home of Princess Maria Hohenlohe-Schillingsfürst, wife of the Grand Master. It was also a tradition for these families to hold grand balls which were among the highlights of the Season.

The festivities organized by the great names of the nobility, often in aid of charitable works, animated society life. Of these, the theatrical performances deserve special mention. Princess Metternich once more displayed her talents here. Of all the performances which she directed, the one which left the strongest memories must surely have been that which was performed before Franz Joseph in 1886 at the Schwarzenberg palace in aid of the polyclinic of Vienna, with the title of *Twilight of the Gods (Götterdämmerung)*. This pleasant and light subject was appropriate to the tastes of the day. It describes how, pricked by the needle of curiousity, the gods and goddesses decided to come down from Olympus to enjoy the charms of the monarchy's capital. The *crème de la crème* of Viennese society was brought in to perform at Princess Metternich's side, the latter assuming the role of Juno. Their public proclaimed the amateur performance a triumph. Following the third and last performance, Princess Metternich was able to hand over 130,000 florins to the direction of the polyclinic, Professor Heinrich Schnitzler, father of the famous writer.

Horse trials and races also figured among the great society events. The biggest of these was the Derby which had been organized by the Austrian Jockey Club from the year it was founded in 1868. It was not uncommon for great aristocratic figures such as Count Nikolaus Esterhazy, and Count Karl Kinsky who attended the great British races, to compete in it. It was run at Freudenau on the first or second Sunday in June, and marked the official end of the Season. This event was patronized by Franz Joseph who attended it for as long as possible, until old age forced him to cut down his activities, and obliged him to send the archdukes to represent him.

This picture of court life is really that of the first part of the reign. From 1889 onwards there began a decline in life at court which had a number of causes: the brutal death of Rudolf, the absences of the empress, and later her death – in fact, all the natural consequences of old age. Prince von Reuss, who was the German ambassador to Vienna at this time wrote even in 1890: 'the concept of the imperial court is disappearing, and relations between the emperor and the members of the court are becoming increasingly distant.'[7]

The formal life of the court was now officially reduced little by little to those functions which Franz Joseph could not avoid. Society life was not unaffected by this change. Dinners, balls, and parties were less common. The development of more efficient means of transport also played a part in this change. The rise of the motor car accounts, for example, for the popularity of a resort such as Semmering, which was easy to reach from vienna, and which was visited regularly in the winter months, as well as in spring and summer. Some people would go even further afield, travelling in winter as far as Abbazia, the fashionable Austrian resort on the Adriatic, and to the Italian and French Rivieras.

Should we consider this court system to have served its purpose? The phenomenon of the court is clearly interlinked with the monarchy, but Franz Joseph did not limit himself to the system he had inherited, for under his rule, the system developed, and furthermore, the rules of etiquette and ceremonial were once more fully observed. This exaltation, sometimes verging on sanctification, of the imperial majesty had a basic purpose. In this multinational empire, the figure of the emperor was the major, and the strongest unifying factor. In this situation, the set of rules on which court ceremony was based was intended to create a charismatic aura around an emperor who needed to make his people submit to his authority. This need was even greater following the destabilizing effect of the 1848 revolution on the Habsburg monarchy.

The strengthening of the court system was thus inextricably linked with the restoration of the power of the monarch under neo-absolutist rule. But even when events had brought the monarchy back to a form of constitutional rule, the same need still existed. Austrian society had entered a period of change in which, if it were not strictly controlled, the worst might happen. When everything around him began to shift, the emperor remained the touchstone, the central axis of the system which united the different parts of the empire, and without which they might give way to centrifugal pressure, and separate. This suggests that all the pomp and ceremony of the court was less anachronistic than it might appear at first sight. Loudly proclaiming the permanence of the principle of kingship, the court, its ceremonies, and its splendours took on a highly political function. And indeed, without ever seeking it through behaviour or gestures, which would not have been in keeping with the dignity of his position, over the course of years, and through his trials, Franz Joseph eventually gained the popularity which had so long eluded him at the beginning of his reign. The almost universal respect in which he was held, and the cult which grew up around his person, cemented the monarchy.

Because they concerned him personally, did these feelings of respect also benefit the cause of the monarchy? The prestige which Franz Joseph conferred on the role of the monarch certainly did not disappear with his death. His successor could rely on this, provided that he compared favourably with Franz Joseph. If he did not have his predecessor's presence, he would need time to build up his own image. But what if there were no time?

10
The Height of the Reign

Although they ended in tragedy, the 1880s were the golden years of the reign. For Franz Joseph, who had now passed fifty, they were still years of maturity. Certainly, the signs of age were appearing on his face. Little by little, the picture which posterity has of him was developing: he went bald early, being left with just a crown of hair which had now gone grey; a thick moustache and side whiskers adorned his face; and the first wrinkles were appearing around his eyes. But Franz Joseph had the strength of an oak. The years did not seem to affect his health and he fought an exemplary battle against weariness. When he was on manoeuvres he could remain in the saddle for ten hours without showing the least trace of tiredness. His figure remained upright and the elasticity of his stride became proverbial.

Within the monarchy, the general feeling was one of relaxation. Franz Joseph knew that he could now count on a government which was not likely to take any rash initiatives. The problem of nationalism had clearly not disappeared, but among the Slavs of Cisleithania, the moderate element who were the loyal supporters of a collaboration with Vienna held the upper hand. In Hungary, the situation concerning national minorities might threaten ultimately to lead to an outburst, but for the time being, they did not have the legal means to challenge the supremacy of the Magyars who were in fact strengthening their hold. The economic situation during this decade was also positive. The monarchy had moved out of the depression into which it had been plunged following the *Krach* of May 1873. Economic growth started up again and flourished from 1879 onwards.

Franz Joseph could also congratulate himself that this decade saw the consolidation of the restoration of the monarchy's international influence. The alliance with Germany gave it the chance to put an end to the isolation which had been its downfall in previous conflicts. As a result of this alliance, Austria-Hungary was protected for the time being from possible Russian aggression. The inclusion of Italy also protected the monarchy from any attack from behind, on its southern flank. The monarchy could thus devote most of its attention to the Balkans, and occupy itself with counteracting Saint Petersburg's plans for this area, while increasing its own influence there.

It was probable that this calm was deceptive and was only a respite, that there were forces growing up which would soon shake or even overturn this balance which had been so hard-won, and that the monarchy's influence in the Balkans had no solid basis. However, Franz Joseph could at least observe that, after so many crises, a state of equilibrium had been achieved within the empire, and that the period of defeats in foreign affairs had come to an end.

Internal Appeasement

The general organization of the monarchy would henceforth be dictated by the dual state. Franz Joseph made no attempt to conceal its faults or its dangers. But the dual system had the incomparable advantage of settling the differences with Hungary and of guaranteeing a degree of stability on the home front which had not been achieved by a series of constitutional experiments.

Franz Joseph was therefore resolved to follow the Compromise of 1867 to the letter. Until now, the dual state had worked to his satisfaction. It was true that one by one the authors of the Compromise were leaving the political scene. Ferenc Deák died in 1876, and once he gave up the direction of the Austro-Hungarian diplomatic service, Andrassy ceased to have any close involvement with Hungarian politics. But some of those who had at first been opposed to the Compromise came round to supporting it. Kálmań Tisza, who headed the government from October 1875, was one of their number. Supported by a comfortable majority, in his policies he recognized that the position of the Magyars at the heart of Europe, where they were under pressure from the Slavs and exposed to the threat of Russian expansion, demanded that they should ally themselves with Austria.

Nevertheless, relations between Austria and Hungary continued to be founded on a difference of opinion, for Franz Joseph still thought of the monarchy as a single state whereas, even when they admitted the necessity of union with Austria, the Magyer rulers insisted on the primacy of Hungarian sovereignty. According to the logic of such an interpretation, the conditions of the Compromise would represent the upper limit of Hungarian concessions, and the aims of the Budapest government would be to reduce all connections with Vienna. Already the negotiations over the first ten-year renewal of the Compromise's economic stipulations had led to friction. Following bitter discussion, the Hungarian side managed to win a further victory in the decision to divide the national bank into two parts, one based in Vienna and the other in Budapest. The wisdom of the current leaders prevented any serious departures from the prescribed course of the Compromise, but such departures were a real possibility if their successors were to succumb to the lures of nationalism.

In Austria, with the return of the Czech deputies to the *Reichsrat*, the constitutional debate which had aroused such feeling for so long was now closed. The 1867 Constitution was in practice no longer challenged in the political arena. Furthermore, Franz Joseph had discovered a most satisfactory first minister in Edward Taaffe. This noble of Irish extraction, whose ancestors had once settled in the Habsburg lands to avoid serving a Protestant king was the prototype of the Austrian noble protected by his birth from nationalist feeling. When he took over as head of government, Taaffe had a long career as a senior civil servant behind him, in particular as *Statthalter* of Tyrol from 1871 to 1878. In addition to his recent participation in Stremayr's cabinet, he had served in one of the liberal governments towards the end of the sixties. He was not compromised by this fact, however, for his post had been due to his achievements in the service of the state rather than for his expressed political sympathies. In any case, finding himself in disagreement with the liberals' plans for centralization, he had finally handed in his resignation.

Never since the time of Schwarzenberg had Franz Joseph been in such accord with his first minister. He had no fears that Taaffe would attempt to follow his own ideas in directing the government. Their concepts of the distribution of power were in complete harmony on every count, considering that, in a monarchical system, it was the first duty of the government to turn the broad political directives of the sovereign into concrete policy. The idea of a conflict between the monarch and the head of government had no part in this view.

Nevertheless, Taaffe has not left a very positive impression on posterity. The liberal historians in particular, whose opinions prevailed for a long time, were noticeably set against him. He has been reproached for having lacked the inspiration of an overall vision, choosing his policies on a day-to-day basis. He has also been criticized for his part in heading the government which brought an end to the liberal era, and Taaffe certainly oversaw the return of the Czech opposition to the *Reichsrat*. Despite this, though, he personally would have preferred a government which included the more moderate liberals who had supported Franz Joseph's policy in the Balkans among its members, even if it did not include all of them. It was not his fault that this gesture was not received with favour. The liberals whose support he had hoped for backed down when faced with the possibility of a break in their own political group. They had also been influenced in this decision by the view that Taaffe's cabinet would only endure for a brief interim spell of office. This refusal of support pushed the new government's centre of gravity towards the Catholic right, and was thus deprived of its liberal wing. Some critics, of whom the foremost was Rudolf, used this fact as a basis for the accusation that Taaffe allowed himself to be manipulated by the obscurantists.

Within the immediate circle around the emperor, Rudolf was not the only one to criticize the first minister. The empress, who no longer concerned herself with political matters, but whose personal sympathies were in favour of the liberals, had similar feelings. This hostility was, however, not enough to shake Taaffe's position. Franz Joseph was grateful to him for having dealt with the constitutional question and for having given Austria the security of a long period of political stability. Remaining in his post for no fewer than fourteen years, Taaffe was the longest-serving minister under Franz Joseph, a record which none of his successors could surpass or even equal. For his part, Franz Joseph certainly made no criticism of Taaffe's policies for their lack of inspiration. Besides a profound mistrust of ideologies, he had learned from experience that a policy of gradual change was best suited to Austria's nature, for the empire was too fragile a body to be able to cope with radical treatments. Taaffe's merit lay precisely in his understanding of the fact that the varied nature of the constituent parts of Austria demanded gentle handling, or, in other words, that the truth was that Austria represented a permanent compromise.

The conditions under which the government was formed required Taaffe to make it a priority to settle some of the demands of the Czechs. After having suspended their programme for constitutional reform for the moment, they might be inclined to reconsider if they were not soon compensated for this concession. Taaffe's obligation was actually made simpler by the power relations within the Czech camp. In Bohemia they were under Rieger's leadership, and the moderates retained the upper hand, although the Young Czechs, who were more firmly based in the lower middle classes, were gradually gaining ground. The Czechs' support of the parliamentary majority was confirmed by their inclusion in the new government where a minister would represent them and defend their interests. For this post, Taaffe chose Alois Pražak, the spokesman for the Moravian wing of the national party, which traditionally contained its most moderate faction.

The Czechs enjoyed the first benefits of their support for the government in April 1880 with the promulgation of two language orders. Without throwing into question the use of German as the internal language of the administration, these declarations required that both the political and legal authorities should make use of the language of the peoples they were addressing in their dealings with the public. This reform was the beginning of a series of important changes in the relationship between the two peoples, for there were very few Germans who spoke Czech. Not only did they feel that there was no need, they also considered it to be an inferior language. The situation among the Czechs was very different. They learned at least the rudiments of German at school. Beyond this, knowledge of German was essential if they wished to rise in society and as a result, every Czech civil servant spoke German. This contrast seemed likely to give the Czechs the advantage within the Kingdom of Bohemia, and would also allow them to enter areas from which they had been effectively excluded until this time.

The right to share the respected University of Prague, the oldest university in central Europe, was the other major measure taken as a return for the Czech support of Count Taaffe's government. This was not to say that Czech culture had previously been banned, for the number of Czech teachers had been increasing since the beginning of the century. But now many areas of learning would be taught through the medium of Czech. These advances could in themselves provide sufficient reason for the foundation of a national Czech university, especially as the University of Prague officially retained its German character, despite the advances made in both the extent and quality of the use of Czech, and this situation was considered to be humiliating by an increasing number of Czechs. Just as they aimed to found a National Theatre, they believed that the creation of a Czech university would set the seal on the recognition of the individual nature of their culture and of its equal status with German culture.

Although some nobles, such as Count Leo Thun, warned against a split which ran counter to the concept of Bohemian patriotism which united the two peoples of the kingdom and instead confirmed the separation of their two cultures, these dissenters could not dissuade Taaffe from satisfying his Czech partners in 1882. Whether or not it was inevitable, this decision illustrated the growing pressure of nationalist feeling. Rather than embracing a course of action which, although it was not sufficiently speedy, would have left open the possibility for the co-existence of the two cultures, and even of a dialogue between them, the solution of a cultural split was favoured.

This series of measures was approved by the emperor. Franz Joseph did not wish to favour one people over another. Whatever his personal loyalties, he wished to act as a father to all his peoples. In this issue, he considered it right that the Czechs should benefit from a statute appropriate to the stage which their development had reached. Although, after the failure of the Bohemian compromise, he had hoped to avoid tackling this question from the constitutional angle, he was nevertheless prepared to extend the national rights of the Czechs.

It was, however, the fate of Austria to form a complex whole in which national interests could not be divided up into groups but instead were closely intertwined. Any advantage which was given to one nationality was likely to be interpreted by another national group as an infringement of its rights. This was precisely the reaction of the Bohemian Germans who felt that the legislation on language delivered them into the hands of the Czech majority. Between them, the liberals could rely on considerable electoral support and this policy alienated them from Taaffe's cabinet.

This decade did not bring such spectacular advantages to the Poles, who were the second partners in the coalition government. It did, however, consolidate the gains of the previous years. With control of the Diet of Lemberg and of the Polish parliamentary group in the Lower Chamber of the *Reichsrat*, the conservatives, who supported the 'Austrian way', were at this time the official voice of the Galician Poles. Their influence had grown over the years and they were no longer satisfied that their only representative in the government should be the minister for Galician affairs. They now took over other portfolios, such as that of the minister for finance, which was held by one of them, Julian Dunajewski, for almost the whole Taaffe era, and which subsequently became in some sense their private preserve. In this way, the decision to support Austria gradually bore fruit, and their loyalty tended to bring the Polish conservatives into government.

On entering the coalition government, the Catholic conservatives, the last group of supporters of the new order, could experience the satisfaction of driving the liberals out of power. They also hoped to achieve the cancellation of some of the measures which had deprived the Church of its influence in society, but it must be admitted that they had little success, for the legislation of the liberal era concerning the Catholic Church was left almost intact. Taaffe only made concessions in one matter: the duration of a child's schooling, which had been fixed at eight years by the liberals. This had been very badly received by the farmers who complained that this deprived them of their children's labour until the latter reached the age of fourteen. As the mouthpiece for the interests of the countryside, the Catholics espoused the farmers' cause. Finding himself obliged to make some concession to the Catholic part of his majority, Taaffe chose this area, in which nothing fundamental was affected. Without reconsidering the whole issue of the official length of schooling, he contented himself with the introduction of special exceptions for the children of farmers.

On the other hand, at the end of the period of Taaffe's government, the main demand of the Catholics, concerning the creation of a denominational school, had still not been met, while no attempt had been made to dismantle the reforms of 1868 and 1874. The modest nature of these results can no doubt be explained by the resistance towards such reforms at the heart of the coalition. Many of the Czech representatives felt no concern at all to defend Catholic interests, and they came close to the ideology of the liberals in this respect. But Taaffe's decisions chiefly represent the fact that Franz Joseph had chosen to settle for the position achieved during the 1860s and 1870s. The Josephist part of his nature was content with the balance they had achieved between Church and State. In the end, the only significant change – but it is an important one – was in the general spirit of the period, which saw the disappearance of anti-clerical feeling among the ruling classes.

Of the three members of the coalition, the Catholics gained the least from their support for the cabinet. This disappointment was not without consequences, but for the time being it posed no threat to the stability of power in Cisleithania. Taaffe demonstrated exemplary skill in the delicate art of holding together the different parts of a coalition government. Indeed, thanks to a slight adjustment to the electoral group, involving the extension of voting rights to some ranks of the lower middle classes who were often the losers under economic liberalism, he contrived to increase his majority in the 1885 elections. It was this stability which was the first benefit gained by Franz Joseph from Taaffe's government.

International Successes

The Austria-Hungary of the 1880s is disconcerting for anyone seeking coherence between internal and external policy. The same monarchy which had allied itself with the German Empire was initiating policies within its borders which threatened the primacy of Germans in Austria and, at least in the Cisleithan part of the monarchy, displayed an active sympathy towards the Slavs.

Whatever the annoyance which certain aspects of Austria-Hungary's internal policies caused in Berlin, the German alliance was firmly established. As he had done on the day of its signature. Franz Joseph expected the treaty to act as a guarantee against Russian invasion, for it was in the East that he thought the threat lay. His choice of Count Gustav Kálnoky, the dual monarchy's ambassador in Saint Petersburg, as Andrassy's real successor as foreign minister following the brief appointment of Baron Haymerle, further demonstrated this. Like Taaffe in Austria and Tisza in Hungary, Kálnoky would have the advantage of a long term of office. Appointed in November 1881, he remained in office until May 1895, a length of service which reflected the confidence which Franz Joseph had in him.

The priority assigned to relations with Germany continued with the inclusion of Italy in the alliance on 20 May 1882. The initiative for this came from Bismarck who hoped to include Rome in his network in order to complete France's isolation. He chose his moment well, following France's destruction of Italian ambitions in Tunisia in 1881. It was Franz Joseph's desire to continue the association with Germany which made agree to the Triple Alliance for, in high government circles in Austria, the dominant attitude towards Italy was one of defiance tinged with mistrust. But, although Austria-Hungary did not seek this alliance, it would also be possible to use it to advantage. The main gain for Austria from the Triple Alliance would be protection from attack from this quarter. Of course, Austria could not expect the campaigns of the Italian *irredentismo* to cease, but it was reasonable to hope that the obligations which the Italian government had agreed with Austria-Hungary would lead it to withdraw its support for these activities, concentrating instead on colonial expansion. Nevertheless, although Austro-Italian relations now entered a period of relaxation, they still suffered from tremors which, although not as serious as previous crises, proved this to be a weak link in the Austro-Hungarian diplomatic network.

Furthermore, although the Italian government no longer spoke for them, the treaty did not quiet the passions of the *irredentismo*. The threat of assassination hung over Franz Joseph's visit to Trieste in September 1882 on the occasion of the five hundredth anniversary of Habsburg control of the city. This threat was not just a figment of the police force's imagination: shortly before the sovereign's arrival, two conspirators were arrested, one of whom was a deserter from the imperial army, Guglielmo Oberdan, who had planned to assassinate Franz Joseph. Austria made the mistake of turning Oberdan into a martyr to the nationalist cause, for the nationalists did not hesitate to exploit his execution. There were soon many towns in Italy which contained a statue glorifying the hero who had died in the cause of the unification of Italy.

Finally, although on the expiry of the first treaty in February 1887, the two signatories were in agreement that their alliance should be renewed, there was a change in the renewed treaty's terms which threatened ultimately to disrupt Austro-Italian relations. Confronted with the threat of war with Russia, the Austro-Hungarian foreign service was obliged to agree to Italy's wish to have the right to be involved in Balkan affairs. Article 7 of the treaty of February 1887 included the provision that, in the event that the status quo in this region should prove impossible to maintain and that Austria-Hungary were obliged to proceed to a permanent, or even temporary, occupation of the territory, Italy would be entitled to compensation, effectively recognizing Italy's right to concern itself with Balkan matters. This was not an immediate problem, but this clause might cause future difficulties for the Austro-Hungarian government, and become a source of friction between the two allies.

For it was in the Balkans that Austria-Hungary's particular sphere of influence was developing. Kálnoky aimed to consolidate the monarchy's influence in this region, while being careful not to provoke Russia without cause. The decision to follow a peaceful course of action made him wary of any impulsive policy which might arouse a strong reaction from Saint Petersburg.

Kálnoky's prudent course was strongly criticized by those who wished to see the monarchy adopt a policy of aggression in the Balkans. Andrassy, who had not discounted a return to politics, was among these. He maintained that the monarchy had nothing to gain from a timorous policy which could only encourage Russia to be inflexible over Austrian goals. Instead, Austria should embark on a resolute course in the Balkans, helping the newly formed states to affirm their independence, without allowing itself to be paralysed by fear of a reaction from Russia, especially as the Tsar and his ministers would not risk the test of a conflict if they felt that Austro-Hungarian policy was being directed with a firm hand. Once again in disagreement with one of his father's ministers, Rudolf went even further in his hopes for a war which would allow the monarchy to rid the Balkans of Russia and to establish its own rule there.

These critics had no hope of success, for the simple reason that Kálnoky's policies were those which the emperor wanted. Having learned from two unfortunate experiments, Franz Joseph hoped to protect the monarchy from another war. It is likely that he did not rule out the possibility of a conflict. The army worked on this assumption and its annual manoeuvres were intended to prepare for such an eventuality. But the monarchy was not strong enough to support a war without serious risk to itself. It was therefore necessary for Franz Joseph's foreign policy to adapt to this situation. Franz Joseph was also aware that Bismarck would not support him if he were to embark on an active policy in the Balkans.

There was therefore no question of Franz Joseph contradicting his own policies when in June 1881 the Danubian monarchy signed a treaty with Germany and Russia which defined their relationship. The initiative for this treaty came from Bismarck. Haymerle, who was in charge of the Austro-Hungarian foreign service at this time, at first balked at it, but his fear of isolation eventually prevailed. The atmosphere was one of *détente*, and a protocol sketched out an arrangement with Russia. Vienna promised not to oppose the reunification of Bulgaria and Rumelia 'if it happened in the natural course of events'; and in return Austria-Hungary could annex Bosnia-Herzegovina when the moment seemed right.

During the years which followed, meetings between Franz Joseph and Alexander III, who succeed to his father's throne after the latter's assassination in March 1881, maintained contact at the highest level. First Franz Joseph visited the Tsar at Skierniewice in September 1884, only a few months after the renewal of the agreement between the three empires, and then Franz Joseph and Alexander III met at Kremsier in the following August. The political discussion which took place during these meetings certainly did not result in any changes. They would often highlight differences of opinion, but they managed to preserve appearances, already no small achievement, and above all, they ensured that the tensions between these two powers did not get out of control, which was a great achievement.

When the Bulgarian crisis broke in 1885, Franz Joseph displayed the same moderation, although it might have seemed a good opportunity for Vienna to replace Russia in its position of influence over the country. Although the Russians had brought him to Sofia, Prince Alexander of Battenberg soon displayed his independent will, to such an extend that the Saint Petersburg government withdrew its support when, on 20 September 1885, he made the unilateral decision to annex Rumelia. To have satisfied the supporters of an active policy in the Balkans, Austria-Hungary should have taken the side of Bulgaria in this split. Instead, Franz Joseph and Kálnoky continued to follow their policy of prudence. While announcing its support for Bulgarian independence, Vienna expressed the strongest reservations over an act which threatened to light the Balkan powder keg. In the event, this was precisely what happened. Considering himself justified in demanding compensation for the enlargement of Bulgaria's lands, King Milan took Serbia to war on 14 November. He was made to suffer for this move, for the defeat inflicted on him by the Bulgarians at Slivnica completely routed the Serbian army.

For Franz Joseph, the situation was serious. Before the conflict, he had attempted to dissuade Milan, who had been his ally since June 1881, from throwing himself into the venture. He was fairly annoyed that the king should have ignored his advice, but, however much Milan was at fault, he could not leave Serbia to be crushed. The Austro-Hungarian ambassador to Belgrade therefore received instructions to approach the victor and to enjoin him to halt his advance.

This intervention had the desired effect, but the end of the hostilities did not put an end to the crisis, which blew up again when the Russians decided to remove

Alexander from power, for although they were resigned to the *fait accompli* of the annexation of Rumelia, they could not forgive the king for rejecting their guardianship. To this end they devised a plan involving the group within the Bulgarian army which supported them. On 21 August 1886, a group of Bulgarian officers seized their sovereign and handed him over to the Russians. But the latter soon found themselves unable to convert their advantage. Most of the army refused to join the rebel forces, and the full weight of Bulgarian public opinion was unleashed against Russia in favour of the deposed prince. Under pressure from the international community, Russia decided to let Alexander go, and, although he abdicated soon afterwards, Saint Petersburg was no longer in a position to replace him with its own choice of king. When the *Sobranie*, the Bulgarian parliament, elected Prince Ferdinand of Saxe-Coburg, Russia might burst out in anger and protest, but short of provoking another war, there was no way for the Russians to prevent the new monarch from coming to the throne.

Confronted with this second stage of the crisis, Austria-Hungary's reaction remained moderate. The monarchy certainly supported Alexander, but Franz Joseph was not prepared to turn himself into a warmonger. Afterwards, although he eventually came round to supporting Ferdinand's candidacy, he would make no attempt to advance it in any way. This was strange behaviour given that, at the time of his election, Ferdinand was an officer in Franz Joseph's army. But beyond his personal feelings – he seems to have had little sympathy towards him – this course can be explained by Franz Joseph's continued desire to remain in the background. If he were to support Ferdinand openly, he would confirm Russian suspicions that it was a manoeuvre on the part of the Viennese foreign office. On the other hand, if he kept his distance, it would not prevent him from profiting from the situation. The establishment of Ferdinand on the Bulgarian throne was in all respects an indication of the decline of Russian influence, and the balance of power in the region was such that there was a strong likelihood that Austria-Hungary would be the first to benefit from the change in rulers.

Indeed, during this period, despite the reproaches of his critics who considered that Franz Joseph was lacking in audacity, Austria-Hungary increased its influence in the Balkans. Its first success was the signing of a treaty with Prince Milan Obrenovic of Serbia on 28 June 1881 which effectively established Serbia as an Austrian protectorate. In signing it, Milan was giving up the right to enter into any treaty with another state which might run counter to the 'spirit of the Austro-Serbian treaty'. For Franz Joseph this was a double advantage. A Serbia which was allied to Austria-Hungary could not hope to be the Piedmont of the southern Slavs. Such an alliance also reduced the possibility, at least for the time being, that Serbia might become a Russian outpost on the monarchy's southern border.

Austria-Hungary also made gains in Romania. Here, the monarchy took advantage of the bitterness felt by the Romanians as a result of the 1877–8 war. Although it had freed them from the last of their ties with the Ottoman Empire, the Russians had forced them to accept an exchange of land which they considered to be iniquitous. In return for giving up the riches of southern Bessarabia, the Romanians received only the north of Dobroudja in return, which was far less fertile. Their resentment grew with their fear of the Bulgarian state which had appeared on their borders, and which they expected to be manipulated by Russia as a pawn in its political manoeuvring.

The only source of help available to them was Austria-Hungary. The Transylvanian question was not enough to dissuade King Carol, for his concern over the security of the kingdom swept aside all objections and on 30 August 1883 he signed, in his return, a treaty of alliance with the dual monarchy.

The Russian infiltration of the Balkans had already been slowed by the congress of Berlin. Nine years later, it began a general withdrawal. Without having to enter into battle, Austria-Hungary managed to strengthen a sphere of influence which, in various forms, extended throughout the Balkan states. Serbia and Romania were bound to the monarchy by treaties of alliance, and although there was no question of alliance with Bulgaria, the failure of Russia in this area was enough to strengthen Austria-Hungary's position.

In the 1880s, the monarchy's influence in the Balkans was at its height, but this power rested on weak foundations. The inclusion of Serbia in the Austro-Hungarian area of influence depended entirely on a personal choice on the part of King Milan. Going against the feelings of most of his subjects, he hoped to regain, through Austria-Hungary, the public support which he had lost through his authoritarian rule and the scandals of his private life. When he finally abdicated in March 1889, the alliance became dependent on a boy of thirteen, assisted by a Council of Regency.

The Romanian alliance seems to have been founded on a more secure basis. Unlike Milan, Carol was not discredited, and Romanian hostility towards Russia held the alliance together. It was still essential that the Transylvanian question should not worsen, and upset the relations between the two states. Their agreement was unlikely to survive any worsening of the fate of the Romanian population of Transylvania.

There remained Bulgaria, where Austria-Hungary's position was not confirmed by any written treaty. Furthermore, despite its setbacks, there was still a current of opinion at work in Bulgaria which favoured Russia, and the situation might be reversed should there be changes, whether international or local.

The Rise of New Movements

Within the monarchy, too, there was cause for concern. The Taaffe era could easily become just an interlude, for there were movements growing up at the heart of its society which could threaten the fragile balance. The 1873 *Krach* had unleashed a strong anti-liberal movement which in 1879 had won its first victory although it had not attained its full dimensions. The exercise of political rights was still the privilege of a minority. Even after the 1882 reform, the electoral system continued to exclude most of the population from the right to vote, and these classes were becoming increasingly dissatisfied with their exclusion from political life. The liberals were not the only group to feel themselves threatened by these demands. The upper middle classes were eager to gain power, but were not prepared to share it with the lower classes. In the conservative camp, although there was general support for a reduction in the financial requirements to obtain the right to vote, this was seen as means of weakening the liberals, and there was no question of universal suffrage. In all, while bitterly disputing the right to rule amongst themselves, the sides shared an elitist and hierarchical vision of society and were in agreement over their opposition to a democratic political system.

During these years, this phenomenon was linked with another, that of the growth of nationalism, which soon showed a radical element. One of the major developments of the period was the rise of a German nationalist movement which had its origins in the 1866 break. Before Sadowa, although the Germans were certainly a minority within the monarchy, they had not been fully aware of this. Their influence in the administration and in society had been far stronger than their numbers warranted. Moreover, the Austro-Bohemian provinces had been part of the German Confederation, with the emperor as its president.

After Sadowa, this physical link was severed. The Austrian Germans found themselves faced with the brutal reality of their minority position in relation to the other nationalities of the empire. They were certainly far in advance of the other nationalities in terms of development, but this advantage could only decrease with time. The growth of nationalist feeling among the Austrian Germans should be seen as having initially been a defensive reaction.

This feeling increased when the liberals, who had been zealous defenders of the German interest, were ousted from power by the coalition which was dominated, at least numerically, by Slavs. This nationalism was fed by the successes of Bismarck's empire and it was easy to draw unfavourable comparisons between this and the mediocre outlook which Austria had to offer its German citizens. This period was also marked by an unprecedented spread of cultural movements which had originated in the *Reich*. Among these, the spread of Wagner's influence in Austria was a brilliant illustration of the close ties between politics and culture.

This exaltation of German nationalist feeling was strong enough among some groups to renounce any sort of Austrian patriotism, and their declared objective was the inclusion of the monarchy's Germanic lands in the *Reich*. However, even among these groups, this extremist solution was not universally adopted. Many Germans would be satisfied by a solution which would reduce the relationship with Hungary to a simple understanding, and would separate off Galicia from the body of the monarchy. This would ensure that there was a German majority in the Austrian part of the monarchy, and would provide the Germans with the political means to settle the Bohemian dispute with the Czechs to their advantage.

But, whether they took an extreme form or a moderate guise, these projects were incompatible with the needs of the Austrian authorities, or indeed with the very existence of the Habsburg monarchy. It is not surprising that Franz Joseph perceived these views as straightforward acts of betrayal. In truth, the threat was not an immediate one. Because of the voting structure of the monarchy, these theories had few supporters in the *Reichsrat*, and in any case they were only supported by a minority. Most of the rural population of the Alps, in particular, were indifferent to their blandishments. It was nevertheless a serious matter that such subversive ideas should be gaining ground in general opinion. But what was perhaps even more disturbing was that their influence went beyond their immediate circle of supporters, for those Germans who did not share them felt themselves obliged to take a stronger line so as not to be seen to leave the defence of German interest to the nationalists.

The Germans were not the only Cisleithan nationality to be infected by the nationalist virus. Among the Czechs the moderates were constantly losing ground to the Young Czechs who saw their relationship with the Germans to be one of confrontation. Choosing to see the German desires as an attack on the integrity of the

Kingdom of Bohemia, they were particularly opposed to any concession which might recognize special status for the areas which contained a German majority. The time was fast approaching when the extremists would have gained the upper hand on both sides and, once this occurred, invective, upsets, and violence would dominate the political debate in Bohemia.

These situations demonstrate that the theory which attempts to reduce the nationalist problem in Austria-Hungary to a paradigm involving the desire of one people, in this case the Germans, to assert its dominance over the other national groups, from Vienna, is not a satisfactory one. The facts of the matter were far more complex than this, for there were a number of nationalistic antagonisms and in many of these disputes, the Germans were not involved at all. These conflicts took place for the most part on a local level, in the commune, the borough or the province, and would only later find their echo in Vienna.

The arguments focused on certain issues and situations. The school classroom, in which a people could lay claim to its language and acquire its own cultural reference points, but which could equally be the place where it was deprived of them, was one of the principle areas of dispute. The existence of an official state language (which could only be German), which served for purposes of communication with the administrative and judicial authorities and the existence of a language internal to the provincial administration also aroused strong feelings when it was discussed. These feelings were not even appeased in death. Many communes did not hesitate to forbid families belonging to minorities to have their tombstones engraved in their own languages. Such a ban afflicted the Czechs of Dux in Bohemia, the Germans of Trente, and the Slovenes of Trieste.

In Hungary matters were far more simple, because here the state was directly identified with a national group. By providing the concept of a nation with political characteristics which were independent of ethnic and linguistic considerations, the Magyar political class supported the idea that the subjects of the Kingdom of Saint Stephen formed a single people. The logic of this theory led the Budapest government to refuse to accept any claims of national autonomy put forward by the minorities. Only Croatia was allowed a special status from 1868, which recognized its political existence and gave the Croats national rights, although the Hungarian authorities did try to deprive this compromise of most of its meaning. The fate of the other minorities was even less enviable and their nationalist aspirations were strongly opposed in the name of Hungarian unity.

The law surrounded the Magyar hegemony with guarantees. A carefully thought out electoral system meant that the representation of other nationalities in the Hungarian Diet was not related to their numbers. The few deputies who represented them could raise their voices in protest, but they had no hope of being heard. It is hardly necessary to mention that none of the minority populations had any connection with the government whatsoever. On the contrary, the Hungarian governments developed a policy of Magyarization towards the minorities of the kingdom, in particular through the education system.

This repressive system was fraught with dangers for the future. The Budapest authorities certainly had the means to overcome nationalist protests, whose size was limited by the poor organization of the political movements from which they came. But if the Hungarian ruling class were to persist in its refusal to pay attention to these grievances, it would be likely to create a favourable environment for the rise of separatist tendencies among these peoples. This was the more likely because some of these minorities might be tempted to listen to the voices of their fellow-nationals beyond the borders of the monarchy.

Franz Joseph remained silent in the face of the discrimination which his Slav and Romanian subjects suffered from at the hands of the Hungarian kingdom, despite the expectation among many of them that he would take them under his protection. But since he had negotiated the Compromise, he had decided not to intervene in matters which concerned the Hungarian Constitution. Obliged to choose between two evils, he considered it to be more dangerous for the monarchy to have to face Hungarian hostility.

The success of these political movements was linked with the urban development which was another feature of this period. In the larger towns, in particular, they encountered particularly favourable conditions for their development. Vienna had now grown into a metropolis, and was by far the largest city in central Europe, with 1,364,000 inhabitants in 1890 following the inclusion of the suburbs in the city limits. The growth of Budapest had become more rapid since the Compromise had confirmed its position as a capital city. At the beginning of the 1890s its population was nearly a million, and on a smaller scale, Prague, Brünne, Graz, Trieste, Lemberg, and Cracow had expanded to over 100,000 inhabitants.

The increase in urban populations was due only in small part to an increase in the existing inhabitants. It was mostly fed by the migratory movements which brought sectors of the rural population to the towns in search of a higher standard of living. Reality would often turn out to be quite different. Many of these new arrivals swelled the urban proletariat which supplied the workforce for the industries which were usually be situated on the outskirts of the towns. The workers faced living conditions which were almost always below the poverty line, involving an exhausting job with no security, seasonal lay-offs, poor salaries which were soon eaten up by rents and housekeeping, and the cramming of families into cramped and unhealthy accommodation. Here, as elsewhere, poverty was accompanied by various social ills. Cut off from their country roots, sharing the same way of life, pushed together into the same districts, the workers gradually developed a common class-consciousness which prepared them to join the ranks of socialism. There was another group of the urban population, formed in particular of craftsmen, for whom living conditions were hardly any better, but who refused to allow themselves to be swallowed up by the workers. This group shared the attitudes of the lower middle classes represented by small shopkeepers, office workers, and minor civil servants.

Among these groups there were very few who had the right to vote, which already explains their hostility towards the liberals. But this hostility also had economic grounds. In different ways, all these social groups had suffered from the liberals' economic policy. The factory workers were locked into a system which, until the beginning of the 1880s, provided no form of social protection. For their part, the craftsmen and shopkeepers suffered increasingly from the competition from large businesses, and were obliged to admit that their powers of resistance were diminishing.

This anti-liberal feeling was accompanied by the development of a strong movement of anti-semitism among the lower middle classes. The seeds of this fell on fertile ground. Originating in the general Christian hostility towards Jews in Europe, it had remained latent, and did not really become a political force until a reaction set in against the influence of the Jewish middle classes in Austrian society. The position held by Jews in the banking system was a major contributive factor in this. Many banks were owned by Jewish families: not only the Rothschilds, but also the Hirsch family, the Königswarters, the Springers, and the Todescos, whose financial power fed the campaigns against 'Jewish capitalism'. This hostility also fed on the influence which the Jews had gained in some professions. In 1861, 61 per cent of the Viennese medical profession was Jewish; in 1890, 50 per cent of journalist were Jewish; and in 1888, of 631 barristers in Vienna, 394 were Jews. As these professions were traditionally the bastions of liberal thought, it was tempting to combine the two facts, and to denounce liberalism as the product of the Jewish mind. Containing an economic element, directed by some towards a biological orientation, anti-semitism now became a political issue.

Faced with the increase in social problems, the government did not remain inactive. It is true that its answer, like Bismarck's, was a repressive one. But like Bismarck, Taaffe also conceded that the fight against socialism should be combined with a programme of social reform. The 1880s saw the passing of a series of legislative measures which, in this area, place Austria among the foremost European states, a long way in front of republican France. It was no small achievement to have reduced the working day to eleven hours, to have imposed strict controls on the employment of women and children, to have created a body of inspectors of working conditions, to have set up a scheme of accident and sickness insurance, and to have rationalized the relationship between larger industries and craftsmen. But although it established the foundations of the modern welfare state, this legislation did not provide a solution for the problems created by the narrow political base of the Austrian system. It is not therefore surprising that these measures were not sufficient to prevent the growth of movements which threw the system into question.

More than any other city, the Vienna of the 1880s was the centre for the development of new political movements. What was more, these groups which were to face each other in bitter confrontations in the future had originally sprung from the same mould, and before their ways parted had been united by the bonds of their common heritage. With its million inhabitants, Vienna had entered the era of the masses; the Pan-Germanism of Georg von Schönerer, the Christian Socialism of Karl Lueger, and Viktor Adler's Socialism all set out to rally the masses behind their banners.

Galvanized by these strong personalities, politics was no longer a matter for the elite. In adapting to the need to gain a broad base in public opinion, the conventions of the political battle had changed. This was the time when propaganda was first used as a weapon, and large public rallies were first organized. The tone of the speeches reflected this change. Written according to the laws of rhetoric, the speeches of the liberal orators had hoped to convince their audience through reason. In contrast, Schönerer and Lueger's harangues largely appealed to the irrational. In order to win crowds over to their side, these political figures cultivated the art of generating a climate of emotion, of speaking in the language of passion. This passion was not just verbal. When words failed them, some speakers, such as Schönerer, would not hesitate to resort to violence as a political means.

Schönerer and Lueger were both dissident liberals who had broken away from liberalism when they discovered its limitations, having accomplished most of the reforms set out in its manifesto. Before the former became recognized as the herald of Pan-Germanism, and before the latter moved towards Christian Socialism, Schönerer and Lueger gained a reputation for being democrats, the champions of the lower middle classes who were still deprived of the right to vote.

The break was made officially when this current of opinion which had its roots in liberalism, but which turned against it, provided itself with a doctrine in the form of the manifesto presented at Linz in 1882. This charter laid the foundations for a populism which combined a desire for democracy with violent anti-capitalist feeling and the intransigent defence of German interests. Its authors were agreed on a programme in which Austrian patriotism played very little part. Although this manifesto did not go so far as to propose the break-up of the Austro-Bohemian provinces and their inclusion in the Bismarckian *Reich*, which Schönerer strongly hoped for, it nevertheless proposed to tie them firmly to the German Empire by the inclusion of the 1879 alliance in the Cisleithan Constitution, and the establishment of a customs union between the two states. At home, the priority was to protect the Austrian Germans from the threat presented by other nationalities. The last bonds between Austria and Hungary would be severed, and they would only be united by a private agreement. In addition, in a Cisleithania which had lost Galicia, the Germans would form a majority and have the political means to impose their will on the Slavs.

Although his loyalty to the Habsburgs restrained Lueger from being associated with this manifesto, Schönerer here joined with other challengers of the existing political order, among them a young Jewish doctor, Viktor Adler, whose political theories attempted to reconcile the democratic tradition of 1848 with his support of socialism and a radical nationalism. Adler's case was not unique, and this combination of democratic aspirations and nationalism attracted many Austrian Jews at that time, such as Heinrich Friedjung the historian, and the journalist Theodor Herzl. There was thus a moment when Schönerer, one of the guiding figures of Hitler's thought, and Herzl, the future founder of Zionism, were part of the same movement. This combination is less paradoxical than it may seem at first. This is because the Jewish inhabitants of the western part of the monarchy were largely assimilated into society and considered themselves to be upholders of German culture. Some of them were so committed that they gave way to the temptation of nationalism. The split only came when Pan-Germanism developed an anti-semitic element and the nationalist associations began one by one to expel their Jewish members.

With this advance in anti-semitism, these movements began to develop individual characteristics and would soon find themselves violently opposed to each other. But the divisions between them remained fluid, and there were still links between the movements. Schönerer and Lueger joined together again in 1887 as part of the anti-liberal league of *Vereinigte Christen* (United Christians) before making the final break. All the same, even after this split, there continued to be a German nationalist branch of Christian Socialism for a long time.

The inheritor of a title through his father, a famous railway engineer, and the valued associate of Baron Rothschild, the knight Georg von Schönerer represented a new sort of politician. Unlike Lueger and Adler, he never gained the support of a powerful political force. The extremism of his proposals, the excess of his speeches, and the brutality of his methods precluded this. However, he was capable of arousing near-fanatical devotion among his supporters, many of whom were students. Although he did not invent the *Führerprinzip*, he was one of the first to apply it, suffering no disagreement, and demanding absolute obedience from his supporters.

Schönerer would not have been himself had he not surrounded himself with an atmosphere of violence. From his first term of election to the *Reichsrat* he introduced a new tone. As his theories became increasingly radical, he allowed his feelings full rein, making use of his skill of invective and his genius for insult without restraint. His supporters started scuffles and brawls at will, and he himself was personally involved in violence. But these excesses ruined his chances of a traditional political career. He increased the pace of events when on 8 March 1888, at the head of a squad of his followers, he invaded the premises of the *Neues Wiener Tagblatt*, one of the liberal Viennese newspapers, which had been so foolish as to announce the death of Wilhelm 1 prematurely.

As Moritz Szeps, the director of the newspaper, was Jewish, Schönerer did not fail to interpret this crime of lese-majesty as a confirmation of a Jewish plot against the German nation. This act as a self-appointed judge would cost him dear. For having ransacked the premises of the newspaper and molested the journalists, he was given a prison sentence and in addition he lost all his civil rights for a period of five years, a sentence which automatically lost him his title. Although Schönerer did not give up the political struggle, except for a brief period at the end of the following decade, he could not manage to regain the influence which he had held during the 1880s, especially in Vienna where his place had been taken by Lueger and the Christian Socialists.

Schönerer and Lueger long followed parallel careers. Like Schönerer, Lueger's political opinions were based on the democratic principles of 1848. They were also linked in their anti-semitism. But the similarities ended here. Whereas Schönerer was a member of the minor nobility, Lueger came from the Viennese lower middle classes. In addition, the former scholarship boy from the Theresianum was imbued with a deep Austrian patriotism. Finally, his anti-semitism was of a different type from that of Schönerer. When the Jewish question came to occupy a central position in his political thought, he already had more than ten years of political life behind him. There was certainly a large element of opportunism in his support of anti-semitism, and he only chose this line after having measured the strength of opinion among the working classes. Furthermore, his speeches were always made on a political and economic basis, and made no biological references to the Jews, another feature which distinguished him from Schönerer. At heart, Lueger's attitude towards the Jews was quite ambiguous. Although he did not omit to play this political card in the municipal elections, once he had become mayor of Vienna, he took no concrete measures against the Jews during the term of his administration.

A first step in the uniting of anti-semitic forces was taken in 1887, with the formation of the *Vereinigte Christen* which allied Lueger's democrats with the Christian Socialist Association, the *Roformverein*, which was the spearhead of anti-semitism among the Viennese craftsmen, and with Schönerer's German Nationalists. The reference to Christianity did not place this league under the flag of Catholicism for Schönerer denounced Catholicism as an anti-nationalist religion and would never have tolerated this. The term Christian should be understood in opposition to Jewish, without any real religious implications. In addition, after Schönerer had left the coalition, for personal as well as ideological reasons, there still remained an anti-clerical group within the league.

The departure of Schönerer nevertheless made the task of those who wished to introduce a Catholic element to the word 'Christian' an easier one. In this, the Catholics benefited from the work and ideas of those who, with Baron Vogelsang and Prince Aloys Liechtenstein, were concerned over the social problem, who set out to develop a number of solutions intended to wipe out poverty and who, on the international scale, joined in the meetings which were to produce the encyclical *Rerum Novarum*. The other determining factor in this was Lueger's return to his childhood faith, which had matured through his association with Vogelsang and acted as an impetus. Thus, at the end of the 1880s the gestation period of the political movement which was to organize the protests of the Viennese lower middle classes against liberalism was nearly complete. Assembled behind a charismatic leader, the Christian Socialist Party was ready to enter the political arena.

The end of the decade also saw the true birth of the Austrian Social Democrats. This group had already party come into being at the Neudörfl congress of 1874, but since that time it had sunk into apathy, undermined by constant disagreements between the supporters of Lasalle and the Marxists. Its weakness had also laid it open to the temptations of anarchism in the early 1880s. It was largely due to Viktor Adler that it emerged from this state of crisis. Following the episode of the Linz manifesto, he gave himself over completely to socialism and set out to cure it of the disease of dissension. This objective was achieved in January 1889 at Hainfeld where the congress of renewed unity was held. Once their differences had been overcome, the Social Democrats could hope to become one of the more important pieces on the political chessboard. It still remained to remove the restraint of the current electoral system, so the party was to concentrate in its fight on the issue of universal suffrage, which would also move it towards a position which supported social reform. In contriving to convince the members of the different nationalities who made up the party to remain united, Adler gave further proof of his diplomatic talents.

Indeed, of all the political parties, the Social Democrats were the only ones to transcend nationalist divisions, although of course this did not protect them from internal tensions, and in this respect they would prove to be a possible support for the monarchy. At the time, nobody in the government noticed this possibility, but in the face of the growth of nationalist feeling, Social Democracy might in the event turn out to be a valuable bastion against the different separatist elements.

As the end of the decade approached, the elements of a fundamental change in the political scene were thus in place. Although official political debate continued between the traditional parties, new trends of thought and new parties had been created or were emerging, which, because they aspired to be the mouthpiece of the people, would be impossible to accommodate in the political status quo. As the currents of internal, social, and national policies continued to be at odds with each other, and to grow in strength, it seemed likely that Franz Joseph was about to enter another stormy period.

The Travels of the Empress

Franz Joseph could now rely only on his own resources to find the inner strength necessary to face these difficulties. The family no longer provided the haven which he needed. In addition to the repeated absences of the empress, there were now also difficulties in his relations with Rudolf. Despite frequent visits to Vienna and to Ischl, Gisela spent most of her time in Bavaria, and however warm may have been the affection with which Maria Valeria surrounded her father, it was not enough to fill the emptiness.

The empress remained obstinately fixed in her lifestyle. Only her destinations changed. In 1882 Elisabeth ceased her journeys to England. However painful it might be for her to admit it, she came to this decision in the face of the onset of the infirmities of old age. Frustration may also have played a part in this decision. Since 1876, Elisabeth had had as her mentor one of the best horsemen in England, Captain Bay Middleton. Like most of the men who had the chance to grow close to her, he had not been long in falling under the spell of the empress. Strange though it might seem, this relationship between the empress and her British admirer was quite in keeping with her character. Perceiving love in the same light as the poets of courtly love, she conceived it as a feeling purged of all physical lust. She set the rules for her admirers, expecting them to sublimate their passion and to rise to her level of emotion. After this, her imagination would play with reality, and would transform it. Elisabeth found it completely natural to be idolized without giving anything in return. She also considered it to be almost an inconvenience if one of her admirers broke the spell of her fascination himself, and lowered himself to the level of mundane humanity, especially if he did so by entering into marriage. It so happened that Bay Middleton broke the rules set by this modern Astrée. He had just become engaged when he first met Elisabeth, and although he had long put off the event, he chose the love of a mere mortal in the end. But without Middleton, who had taught Elisabeth to put her whole soul into becoming one of the best horsewomen in Europe, hunting lost some of its appeal. As suddenly as she had become interested in these journeys, she closed the door on this period of her life.

This decision must have delighted Franz Joseph, who hoped that it might have the effect of bringing his wife back to Vienna. To achieve this end, he was prepared to pander to her whims and to agree to large financial concessions if necessary. Ill at ease in the great palaces of the Hofburg and Schönbrunn which she had almost come to hate, Elisabeth dreamed of a home on a human scale where she would no longer have to suffer the tyranny of the court ceremonial.

Franz Joseph estimated that such a gift could never cost him too dear if it would keep the empress in Vienna. As a site for the new residence, they chose the park at Lainz where Elisabeth could enjoy the pleasures of solitude in complete peace. This new residence would be in the form of a villa which she dedicated to Hermes, the god of travel, who was her favourite among the gods of Olympia. To keep her at his side, Franz Joseph was prepared to bring every persuasion to bear. The plans of the villa were designed by Hasenauer, the emperor's favourite architect; the decoration of the walls, in particular, was given over to the young talent of Gustav Klimt, who had been one of Makart's pupils, and who took some of Makart's sketches as his inspiration; nor did the emperor forget to provide a gymnasium in which the empress could exercise.

Nevertheless, all these attentions failed in their aim. Completed in 1887, the Villa Hermes soon began to feel like a museum, and Elisabeth only spent a few days a year there. Fleeing herself, as much as others, the empress continued her life of travel throughout Europe, although her preference took her to Greece. Having learnt Greek, she went in search of an aesthetic absolute which she had failed to find in the present, and which she hoped to discover among Greece's archaeological sites. A passionate reader of Homer, she wished to commune with her thoughts in the places where the spirits of the heroes of the *Iliad* and the *Odyssey* still floated. Visiting Ithaca in Ulysses' footsteps, she even wrote of her enthusiasm to Franz Joseph. She was wasting her time. In reply to this passionate epistle, he wrote a very flat letter for someone who was communing with gods and goddesses: 'I have difficulty in imagining what you can find to do in Ithaca for so many days. But the main thing is that you are well and happy, which seems to be the case.'[1] There were still further surprises in store for the poor emperor. He was soon to learn that, without a thought for the Villa Hermes, the empress was thinking of retiring to Corfu where she hoped to find peace surrounded by a natural splendour praised by the Greek poets.

The truth was that Franz Joseph was still as much in love with Elisabeth as when he first met her. This did not mean that there were no tensions in their relationship. Arguments would break out between husband and wife, and the structure of the court meant that these could not long remain secret. Everyone at court knew that the imperial couple had separate rooms. In addition, Elisabeth now displayed an almost pathological revulsion for physical love. Once the wonder of the early months had passed, the differences in character between Franz Joseph and Elisabeth had soon appeared. Following the crisis in the sixties, despite apparent reconciliations, the husband and wife were gradually growing further apart. Both now shut themselves off in a universe in which the other had no part. Although he was overwhelmed by affairs of state, Franz Joseph absorbed himself in repetitive tasks, and Elisabeth escaped more and more into an ethereal world inhabited by the poets and myths of the past.

Elisabeth still retained a friendly affection for Franz Joseph, but this affection could also be tinged with irony. An example of this was her habit of portraying Franz Joseph as one of the asses sighing for the hand of Titania. This charming animal was depicted next to the fairy in the picture which hung in the empress's bedroom in the Villa Hermes. This association also occurs in many of Elisabeth's poems. Although she would sometimes show a few of her works to Franz Joseph, we can be quite sure that she kept the following poem to herself, even though it shows undeniable sympathy for its subject:

> The little thoroughbred donkey
> So stubborn and so playful:
> He finally turned out to be a treasure,
> Despite all his harassment.
> He also has pride of place
> In my study![2]

Elisabeth's way of life increased Franz Joseph's loneliness and many members of the imperial suite judged her severely for it, among them Count Hübner: 'He often takes advantage of the final hours of the day to go to Laxenburg. He goes there alone, and he walks in the park alone as well. This prince who was made for family life is thus reduced to loneliness by the absence of the empress whom he continues to love with passion.'[3]

Elisabeth was certainly aware of the sadness of Franz Joseph's existence and she would sometimes even reproach herself for it. But as she had no intention of giving up her travels, she had to find another means of soothing her sense of guilt, and it was here that Katharina Schratt intervened.

Katharina Schratt

When she came into Franz Joseph's life, Katharina Schratt had just passed her thirtieth birthday and had recently joined the company at the Burgtheater. Despite her youth, she already had a long theatrical career behind her. As a child she had dreamed of becoming an actress, and as a young woman she had managed to persuade her father to agree to her choice of career. Under the direction of Heinrich Laube who, having raised the Burgtheater to the first rank of German theatres, had taken over the Stadttheater, she achieved resounding triumps from the age of twenty. Her marriage to a Hungarian gentleman, Nikolaus Kiss of Ittebe, caused her to leave the state for a time. Although this alliance theoretically raised her social status, it was a love match on her part. However, the idyll did not last for long. Without officially breaking off their marriage, the husband and wife soon decided to lead separate lives. Katharina retained custody of her young son Toni...and the debts left by her husband.

Through strength of will and through her talent, Katharina managed to return to the forefront of the Austrian stage. Realizing every actress's dream, she finally gained entry to the Burgtheater. Pretty, blonde and soft, Katharina was at the height of her beauty at this time. But her attraction did not only lie in her physical appearance. Her playful character and the vivacity of her mind added to her charm, which must have been great, for she had many admirers among the aristocracy as well as among the Viennese second society.

When, according to his custom, Franz Joseph gave an audience to the new member of the Burgtheater at the end of 1883, he may have remembered that she had been presented to him a few years earlier at the Stadttheater. This second encounter seems to have left him with a far stronger impression. The shyness and spontaneity displayed by this young woman during the audience diverted him greatly. Encountering Katharina again, some months later at the industrial ball, he spoke with her for so long that those present were struck by it. At this time the emperor went more frequently than usual to the Burgtheater and it so happened that he would attend on the very nights when Katharina Schratt was performing.

The matter would probably have ended there without the interference of the empress. It occurred to her that Franz Joseph might find in Katharina Schratt's presence the female companionship which he missed during her own absences. She was not put off by the fear that the ambiguity of such a relationship might give rise to malicious gossip. In any case, she knew the strength of her husband's feeling for her and she knew that, although he might have occasionally sought solace outside his marriage, his loyalty towards her precluded an affair. Finally, and most importantly, this arrangement would have the inestimable merit of relieving her of the weight of occasional remorse from which she suffered, and enabling her to continue with her own lifestyle.

It was still necessary to bring about the first step. Elisabeth had the idea of commissioning a portrait of Katharina Schratt from the court painter, Heinrich von Angeli, as a gift to her husband. She arranged that Katharina should be present when the imperial couple visited von Angeli's studio. This encounter on 21 May 1886 gave Franz Joseph the chance to have a few snatches of conversation with the young woman. These few stolen moments away from the monotony of his working days so charmed him that, on learning that Katharina would be spending some of the summer not far from Ischl, he promised to visit her.

Franz Joseph kept his word. Hardly had Katharina arrived than he notified her that he would visit her the following morning. This first visit would be followed by many others in the summer of 1886 and during later years, and Franz Joseph developed the habit of going up to Frauenstein, the house rented by the actress, and spending a part of each morning with her.

Speaking of Katharina Schratt, Hermann Bahr compared her to 'a Melusine with a ladle in her hand.'[4] This remark provides one of the keys to Franz Joseph's attraction towards her. Subjected to a life of strict etiquette, accustomed to the splendour of his palaces and the pomp of his official life, Franz Joseph nevertheless had a taste for family things. With Katharina Schratt he discovered a happiness which he had not encountered until this time. Sunk in a comfortable armchair, he loved to savour the coffee and delicious pastries she would serve him. While he smoked a cigarette, he would give himself up to the pleasure of the moment. With her witty conversation, Katharina had the gift of amusing him. In her company he discovered new worlds, entered the wings of the Burgtheater and the salons of lesser society. The emperor laughed as he had not done for a long time, and was filled with a gentle glow.

On his return to Vienna, he nevertheless denied himself the pleasure of reliving these delicious moments. His sense of honour preventing him from placing Katharina in a position which might compromise her, and he refused to visit her. On the other hand, it was within the bounds of respectability to walk with her in the grounds of the Schönbrunn palace. Beyond these brief encounters, he had to content himself with seeing her on stage, or at the dominical Mass which was celebrated at the Hofburg and which all the actors and actresses of the Burgtheater were allowed, by special privilege, to attend.

Although he could not meet her as often as he would have liked, at least he could write to her. It was the beginning of a long correspondence which very quickly, on his side, assumed the flavour of tender friendship. Franz Joseph and Katharina also developed the habit of exchanging gifts. It warmed his heart that she should give him little good luck charms such as four-leaf clovers which he would carefully preserve in his wallet, or useful items, for instance a calendar for his desk, or a cigar case which he could take hunting with him. For his part, without counting the cost, as was his habit, he would send her superb jewels.

Even from afar, Franz Joseph watched over Katharina. He made himself her 'finance minister', for, as much through carelessness as through her taste for luxury, she had a genius for piling up debts. Franz Joseph made it his duty to intervene regularly to pay off her creditors. For the sake of his friend he also broke the rule which he had made for himself never to become embroiled in the affairs of the Burgtheater. Katharina was annoyed that she was only allowed to act in the lighter plays in which she nevertheless excelled, and was vexed that the director of the theatre would not give her the great roles in the repertoire. An intervention on the emperor's part was enough to provide a solution to this serious problem. Franz Joseph also extended his protection to the young Toni: his mother wanted him to attend the Theresianum, the most sought-after educational establishment in the monarchy, and this wish was also soon to be realized.

Touched by so much generosity, and moved by Franz Joseph's loneliness, Katharina plucked up the courage to suggest that she should become his mistress. Unfortunately, the letter in which this proposition was made has been lost to posterity. It seems likely that Franz Joseph destroyed it before his death, but its contents can be deduced from his reply. The happiness which this letter caused him penetrates the humour which helped him to protect his feelings:

> To my great pleasure, I received your good letter today. The letter which was included with it, and which you describe as a 'letter of the feelings' made me very happy, and, if I were not confident that you are always honest with me, I would find it hard to believe, especially when I look in the mirror and see my old wrinkled face looking back at me.[5]

In this letter in which, albeit with modesty, he reveals the depths of his soul, Franz Joseph answered Katharina with a declaration of love: 'You no doubt already know that I adore you, or at least you must suspect it. This affection has done nothing but grow since the day on which I was fortunate enough to meet you.'[6] Although he allowed himself to make this declaration, he immediately imposed strict limits on his feelings. Despite his tenderness towards Katharina, the love which Franz Joseph continued to feel for Elisabeth prevented him from accepting her proposition, and in addition, the role played by the empress in the birth of their friendship was a further obstacle:

> Our relationship must remain in the future what it has been until now – that is if it should remain anything at all, and it must endure because it brings me so much happiness. You say that you will be able to control your feelings, and I shall try to do the same, which will not always be easy. But I shall do nothing wrong. I love my wife and I refuse to betray the confidence and friendship which she feels for me.[7]

Unable to become her lover, Franz Joseph placed himself in the role of 'paternal friend' towards Katharina. He soon developed the habit of calling her 'friend' (*Freundin*) and it was under this quasi-official title that she would soon appear in his correspondence with the empress.

The tone of his reply demonstrates that Franz Joseph was made of flesh and blood and was still capable of emotions and desires. There is no question that he must have had to wrestle with himself in order to control his feelings. But in the course of the preceding months, this friendship had become indispensable for him. Katharina's company allowed him to escape the loneliness which would otherwise have surrounded him, to give himself up to the illusion of having a private life for a few brief moments. In the gaiety of his friend he discovered a source of strength to combat the monotony of his daily existence. Katharina's spontaneity and sincerity which were displayed in both her actions and in her words made this friendship all the more precious, as Franz Joseph wrote to her: 'You cannot imagine how agreeable it is for a man in my position to have somebody as frank and true as you to speak to.'

But Katherina was not only his friend in his daily life (one cannot go so far as to say the happy times of his life). Franz Joseph also found her at his side in times of difficulty, especially when he had to face the tragedy of Mayerling.

Mayerling

The drama at Mayerling went back a long way. At an early stage in his life a gulf had developed between Rudolf and his family circle. Being deprived of the warmth of a family home when he was still young must have caused Rudolf distress. There was no question here over Franz Joseph's own feelings, for he adored the son whose birth had filled him with joy and pride. The problem lay more with the rules of the court which separated the imperial children from their parents at a very early age. Beyond his stays at Ischl, where he taught Rudolf to hunt, Franz Joseph, overwhelmed by the constraints of his position, had very little time to devote to his son. In the matter of his education, he could also only follow its progress from afar. As for Elisabeth, although she fought to be given the responsibility for her son's education, she soon lost interest in him, once she had won this battle.

The young archduke's formative years were even more significant, for he was exposed only to the influence of his teachers, without any real family interest to counterbalance this. Although these teachers were carefully chosen by Latour from among the best specialists in their own fields, it happened that almost all of them were members of the liberal camp. Their teachings won Rudolf over to ideas which were not well received at court, and were often frankly hated. Having assumed liberal values, he shared the liberals' worship of progress, believed in the value of science, and was a supporter of new technology.

From the end of the 1870s, the main patterns of Rudolf's thought were established. A good disciple of liberalism, he supported the idea of a constitutional monarchy, upheld by the bourgeoisie which would replace the aristocracy as the dominant class. While bestowing his full sympathies on the middle classes in recognition of their contribution to economic and cultural progress, Rudolf denounced the Austrian nobles for having failed in their duties. One of his favourite topics of conversation was the praise of culture as a middle-class value and its comparison with the aristocratic way of life which was given over to frivolous occupations and futile pleasures.

As far as religion was concerned, Rudolf was again the supported of liberal views. Here also, his position had been decided by the end of the 1870s. Although he conceded that religion had a social function, he criticized its involvement in politics, and denounced clericalism as one of the greatest enemies of the state and society. He wrote to Ludwig II of Bavaria:

> I respect religion for having taught the people in a truly useful manner, and for having instilled the first principles of moral feeling in the ordinary man, but I am suspicious of it when it is used by groups and parties as a weapon and a means to an end, when it induces blind faith and superstition among the people instead of a true culture.[8]

Unable to identify with Catholicism, and rejecting all forms of revealed religion, Rudolf was not, however, prepared to go as far as atheism. Instead, he believed in a moral deism, freed from the yoke of dogma, which was not far removed from the beliefs of the Freemasons, of whom there were many in his suite.

It is hardly surprising, given these facts, that Rudolf felt himself to be a stranger at court. Although his position forbade him to voice such views, he allowed enough of them to be understood for those in court circles to look on him with suspicion. Rudolf's political activities served to increase this atmosphere of distrust for, although he always showed the greatest respect for his father, he strongly condemned his ministers' policies, at least in Cisleithania. He was also concerned by the increase in Magyar nationalism, and only Tisza, who continued Andrassy's work in Hungary, could find favour in his eyes. Like the German liberals, he was a virulent critic of Taaffe's policies, the latter being his *bête noire*, and he could not find words harsh enough to condemn him.

Through the person of the first minister, his target was the ancient feudal and ultramontane camarilla which, according to him, had periodically imposed its demands on Austria since the Counter-Reformation. Hostile to federalism, which he considered to be reactionary, he found a further object for criticism in Taaffe's concessions to the Slavs which he believed to be a threat to the unity of the monarchy. In addition to these resentments, he was, as we have seen, a merciless critic of Kálnoky's policy. Hoping as he did that the monarchy would take a firm stand in the Balkans, rallying the small states of the area around itself, he was indignant that the fear of provoking the Russians should prevent such a move.

Rudolf's opposition to the policies of the ministers chosen by the emperor explains, at least in part, why he was not permitted to participate in any decision-making. In any case, there was no law which dictated that Franz Joseph should allow his eldest son any responsibility in government. Also, Franz Joseph's nature led him to be disinclined to share or even to delegate his authority. For the time being, he expected his son to devote himself to his military training and thus prepare himself for his future role as head of the imperial and royal army.

Whatever the reason, Rudolf was carefully kept away from political circles. His father's ministers, who were fully aware of his feelings towards them, even avoided giving him any information they might have. Partly because he considered the monarchy to be on a downward slope, and partly because he was eager to play a part in its government, Rudolf felt a painful resentment of this situation: 'the most minor court adviser has more to do with government than I do. I am condemned to inactivity.'[9]

Unhappy in the belief that he was considered to be of no importance, Rudolf decided to fall back on the press to get his message across. His friendship with Moritz Szeps, the director of the *Neues Wiener Tagblatt*, provided him with the means to achieve this. But in this he was increasing the gulf between himself and the court. In writing regular articles for this liberal mouthpiece, he was associating with a newspaper which was fighting against the policies of his father's ministers. Certainly his articles were unsigned, and Franz Joseph was probably unaware of the journalistic activities of his son, but although Rudolf attempted to conceal it, his friendship with Moritz Szeps did not escape Taaffe's vigilance. There is no need to emphasize that this must have confirmed the first minister's opinion of the heir.

Finding himself in a position where he had to keep secrets, Rudolf soon learned the art of concealment. His position demanded that in his public life he should keep an impassive face turned to the world. He may have occasionally enjoyed the process of fooling those around him, but it is unlikely that he can have found it easy to endure the equivocal position in which he was placed. If he were to suffer any doubts, or fall prey to a mental crisis, it was likely that the realization of the dead end into which such a double game threatened to lead him would increase his feeling of failure.

Rudolf did not find any greater security in his married life. Like most of the archdukes, he had enjoyed some amorous adventures before getting married and nobody would have thought of reproaching him for these. But the ease with which he achieved these conquests left him with a poor image of women, whom he tended to relegate to the status of objects of pleasure. His marriage to Princess Stephanie of Belgium did not bring him any stability. There was no place for feelings in this union which was contracted primarily for political reasons, which required that the wife of a future Austrian emperor should belong to a Catholic royal house.

In this matter, Rudolf acted as a dutiful son. Aware that this sacrifice was part of his fate, he agreed to marry the princess his father had chosen for him. But this marriage soon turned out to be a failure. From the wedding night itself, as a carriage bore the couple to Laxenburg after the ceremony, Stephanie had fears that this would be the case: 'We had nothing to say to each other, we were total strangers. It was in vain that I awaited a tender or kind word from him which might have distracted me from my thoughts. My weariness grew, and combined with feelings of fear and loneliness gave way to the heavy despair of exhaustion.'[10] The birth of a little girl, Elisabeth, in 1883, brought the hope that it might draw Rudolf and Stephanie together, and indeed, Rudolf loved his child, and showed himself to be a caring father. But the tastes, interests, and lifestyles of the couple were too disparate to achieve any lasting understanding. Following his marriage, Rudolf kept his bachelor quarters at the Hofburg, and continued to receive his mistresses there. In his marriage there was no trace of love. Less interested in conquest than in possession, Rudolf gave himself up to the demands of a strong sexual drive. He was perhaps also seeking a way of escaping the anguish which washed over him as his failures increased in other realms. But his pain was not just mental. At the beginning of 1887 he contracted a venereal disease which he believed to be incurable and with which he infected Stephanie. Her resultant barrenness was the final cause of their split, and they had only a formal relationship.

As the end of 1887 approached, events gathered speed. The plans which Rudolf had built up began to crumble one after the other. He had long dreamed of the creation of a liberal Europe in which his partners would be the heirs to the thrones of Germany and Britain, Frederic of Prussia and the Prince of Wales, both of whom were friendly with him. If it were extended to include republican France, this agreement would guarantee peace in Europe, and the new Germany might agree to give up Alsace-Lorraine for the common good. It did not matter that this idea of European harmony was viewed with scepticism. What was important was Rudolf's belief in it. Such a possibility was wiped out by the news at the end of 1887 that the heir to the German crown was afflicted by cancer of the throat, already in an advanced form. Wilhelm II could not be expected to follow his father's lead in his policies, for he was a champion of feudal values and adept in the use of force, expressing an iron mistrust of liberalism.

In the face of this blow struck by fate, Rudolf not only developed a fixation about Wilhelm II, whose destiny he constantly compared with his own, and whose successes contrasted with his own failures, but he also followed Maria Theresa and Kaunitz's line in opposing the alliance between the monarchy and the German *Reich*. Running against the current of events since 1879, he proposed the creation of an anti-German front, which would unite Austria-Hungary, Britain, France, and Russia.

The idea, which he had so recently espoused, of pursuing an active policy in the Balkans, was now out of the question. He even came round to the idea that the monarchy would benefit from abandoning Bosnia-Herzegovina. Russia was once more an acceptable ally and, aware that they were bound by superior interests, the two states would settle their differences by a direct agreement. This suggestion was as unrealistic as the previous one. As before, it would be impossible to achieve, as it was once again in opposition to his father's policies, and Franz Joseph had no intention of changing direction: 'I believe', he wrote to his friend Albert of Saxony, 'that the broadest agreement and the greatest solidarity with Germany in all political and military matters, is the linchpin of our policies.'[11] This disagreement would not have been very serious if Rudolf had confined himself to theoretical observations concerning the new elements of the international situation. But, with his usual impetuosity, he once again failed in his duty to remain aloof, and engaged in the active support of his beliefs. Although he was not in its front line, he encouraged the founding of the *Schwarz-Gelb* (Black and Yellow) review, which, from the autumn of 1888, in adopting a resolutely anti-German stance in the name of Austrian patriotism, supported the overthrow of existing alliances. Rudolf did not long succeed in concealing his part in this campaign. The revelation of this secret placed him in an extremely delicate position, for this was a highly sensitive issue which Franz Joseph had chosen to deal with himself, and which involved the relationship of the monarchy with foreign powers.

It is possible that it was this difference of opinion which led to the argument which took place between father and son on 26 January 1889, only four days before the fateful events at Mayerling, or it may have been another of Rudolf's activities which provoked Franz Joseph's anger, for in recent months, the deterioration of his relations with Stephanie had reached the point where he may have seen no other solution than that of divorce. To this end, it is possible that he may have taken it upon himself to write to Leo XIII, without consulting his father, to ask him for a dispensation which would allow their separation. The Pope's reply would probably have been sent to Franz Joseph, whose anger would have been as great as his surprise. As emperor and head of the House of Habsburg, he would have had many reasons for resenting his son's actions. As a Catholic sovereign, he could not accept a divorce on the part of the heir to the throne; as head of the House of Austria, he would have been just as shocked, as Rudolf's initiative would in effect have ignored his authority over the members of his family.

At the beginning of 1889, Rudolf was prematurely aged. He was filled with a sense of failure, which was all the more painful because he knew that his days were numbered. Worn down by illness, he suffered from problems with his eyes, and from coughing fits. To ease his pain, for several months he had been given morphine injections, and he sought oblivion in alcohol. But these were false comforters which in fact increased his susceptibility to the disease. The series of defeats which he had suffered had also been a severe test for his nerves. As the days went by, Rudolf displayed increasing instability, passing from moments of euphoria to deep depression. Convinced that he had no future, dominated by the advance of his illness, he reached such a state of physical and psychological breakdown that he could no longer see any way out other than suicide.

Although he had not definitely decided on this course, it is known that Rudolf was already considering such a possibility in the summer of 1888. This is demonstrated by his proposition to Mizzi Caspar, one of his mistresses, to join him in suicide. At first, the young woman did not really take this suggestion seriously, but she changed her attitude when Rudolf renewed his request. This behaviour, which he would repeat a few months later with Mary Vetsera, sheds light on the events at Mayerling. In particular, it puts an end to the idea that he was motivated by problems in love. Although Rudolf certainly felt a degree of tenderness towards Mizzi, there was no question of love in their relationship. The facts of the matter are far less romantic. Suspecting that he would not have the courage to end his life by himself, Rudolf needed to find a companion prepared to share his fate. The increasingly visible deterioration in Rudolf's health should have been obvious to Franz Joseph, even though their meetings were brief and infrequent, and should have made him question his condition. However, it seems that Franz Joseph did not note the change in his son's health. The same seems true of the empress, who, during these final weeks was living at Rudolf's side without any suspicion of the drama which was developing before her eyes.

Rudolf's destiny was decided in the dawn of 30 January 1889, in the hunting lodge at Mayerling, in the heart of the Viennese forest. Nevertheless, without the agreement of the young Baroness Mary Vetsera to join him in death, he would probably not have carried his plan through to the end. Forever associated with Rudolf, Mary Vetsera, who was only seventeen at the time of her death, passed through history like a meteorite.

The photographs we have of her depict a young woman only just out of childhood, but who is already secure in her powers of seduction. Although she may be lacking in the distinction of aristocratic grace, the shape of her lips, her slightly retroussé nose, her carnation skin heightened by the brilliance of her enormous blue eyes, her long black hair, and her already budding figure imbue her with a sensual charm which very soon attracted men towards her. The oriental elements of her beauty lay in her ancestry, for, through her mother, she was descended from the Baltazzi family which had recently come from Constantinople to settle in the lands of the monarchy. Since their arrival in Austria, the Baltazzis had devoted themselves to rising quickly in the social hierarchy, and were not satisfied with their conquest of the lower ranks of society. A number of alliances with aristocratic families had opened the doors to high society, but despite this rise, the Baltazzi's reputation suffered greatly from their vague origins and many considered them to be parvenus.

Before meeting Mary, Rudolf had already known her mother, Baroness Helen, who, ten or so years earlier, had literally thrown herself on his neck. It is possible that he remembered this when he received the letter in which Mary frankly declared her passion for him. We must assume that at first he was attracted by the possibility of an easy conquest. This relationship was different, though, from those which preceded it, although there was no question of love on Rudolf's part. How could this have been the case, when he spent the last evening before leaving for Mayerling with Mizzi Caspar? But although he must certainly have been moved by the passion which Mary offered him, an emotion to which his other mistresses had not accustomed him, her main attraction for him was her readiness to provide what Mizzi had refused, a love strong enough for her to give up her life for him.

It appears that the two lovers took the decision to die together on 13 January 1889. This pact was carried out seventeen days later in the Mayerling dawn. Mary first died by Rudolf's hand, who then, having closed off all possibility of retreat, shot himself in the head.

The news was brought to the Hofburg in mid-morning by Count Hoyos who had been invited to go hunting by Rudolf and was therefore at Mayerling. It was the task of the empress, who was the first to hear, to tell Franz Joseph the news. For the couple, the news of their son's death was a terrible shock, and bewilderment was added to pain. Elisabeth managed to draw on her reserves of strength to control her suffering when she told Franz Joseph of the misfortune which had struck them, but she knew instinctively that his strength would not last. Never had she so greatly appreciated the value of Katharina Schratt's friendship with the emperor. She could only beg her to give the emperor the support he needed in this time of suffering. It so happened that the actress was due to be received by Franz Joseph at the end of the morning. No sooner had she arrived that Elisabeth accompanied her into her husband's presence. Too sorely tried to play this role herself, she relied on Katharina to help him with the warmth of her presence, and to find the simple phrases which, although they could not ease his pain, would enable him to bear it. Franz Joseph would never forget this further proof of Katharina's affection for him which she gave him in some of the hardest hours of his life: 'Your true friendship and your tranquil sympathy which is such a comfort', he wrote to her on the day of the funeral, 'have been a great consolation to us both in these awful days.'[12]

Faced with this drama, Franz Joseph reacted both as a father and as a sovereign. Although he had not been aware of the depth of the divide which had grown up between them, he was sure of his deep love for his son. He had certainly never expected what he knew of Rudolf's opinions to assume such a tragic aspect. When some of his son's views were recounted to him, he would remark, 'Rudolf is gossiping again', more amused than worried. In his heart he believed that everything would resolve itself once Rudolf came to the throne. It was also to this end that he was working when he devoted himself to affairs of state. Loyal to his dynastic vision of power, he was working to leave Rudolf the monarchy as his heritage. His death not only wounded Franz Joseph in what he held most dear, but it also deprived his life of part of its meaning.

Even when he was shattered with grief, Franz Joseph could not long forget his duties as sovereign. He was soon going to have to create a version of events compatible with the honour of the dynasty. On the basis of the information brought by Count Hoyos, who, it seems, had not entered the room where the two corpses lay, it was first believed at the Hofburg that Rudolf had been poisoned by Mary Vetsera. But as there was no question of letting it be known that the heir to the throne had been found dead under adulterous circumstances, Mary's presence at Mayerling had to be kept secret. The first official version of events was therefore that the death was due to apoplexy. It was no longer possible to take this line once Franz Joseph had learned the truth from Dr Widerhofer, the court doctor, who had examined the two bodies at Mayerling. The discovery that Rudolf had committed suicide added to his suffering. However great a care he took in his official announcements or in his letters to Katharina to describe Rudolf as 'the best of sons and the most loyal of subjects',[13] in his heart he had judged him: suicide was a degrading death, unworthy of Rudolf, who was a soldier.

Franz Joseph was also to learn that his son had left him no farewell note, although he had written to his mother, to Stephanie, and to Maria Valeria. This silence should not just be seen in terms of his resentment of his father. Although he disagreed with many of his policies, Rudolf held his father in deep respect, but because of his subversive activities, he was also afraid of him, and feared nothing more than being obliged to explain or justify himself to him. In writing to him, he would have felt that he was being obliged to defend himself to him for a last time.

Because he died by his own hand, there was the chance that Rudolf's mortal remains could not be given over to Christian burial, and this would have been the supreme humiliation for the Austrian emperor. During this time Franz Joseph was filled with the worry that the religious authorities would be intransigent. He was saved by the autopsy report, in which the three doctors appointed to this duty revealed that the examination of the brain showed pathological indications which 'usually accompany mental disorders, and lead us to assume that the act was committed in a moment of psychological unbalance'.[14] It thus became possible to claim that the suicide had taken place while Rudolf was deranged, and, whether it was convinced or not, the Vatican allowed itself to be persuaded. It was not to be ignored that at the end of the nineteenth century there were few Catholic states left in Europe, and it was not therefore in the Vatican's interest to refuse Franz Joseph's request, thereby bringing about a serious dispute with the Habsburg monarchy.

At this time, a macabre operation took place near Mayerling. Although Rudolf asked to be buried with Mary, the ceremonial rules which surrounded the deaths as well as the lives of the members of the Habsburg family preluded the granting of this wish. Nor would it have been possible to comply with it without confirming the rumour that there had been a woman with Rudolf. Although they did not go so far as to make Mary's body disappear, the authorities decided to bury it secretly in the cemetery of the Abbey of the Holy Cross, near to Mayerling. Two of her uncles, Count Stockau and Alexander Baltazzi, were asked to accompany her remains to their final resting place. It is hard to imagine a more lugubrious scenario. Clothed in her dress and her coat, her head covered with her felt hat with black feathers, Mary was jammed between her uncles in the carriage which served as her hearse. Nature was in sympathy with this funeral journey. The wind was blowing in a tempest, and the rain beat down continuously on the roof and windows of the carriage. Inside, shaken by the jolting of the carriage, the corpse could not be kept upright. On more than one occasion, Mary fell onto one of her uncles. On their arrival at Heiligen-kreuz, a rough coffin constructed by the abbey's carpenter was awaiting her.

Following the administrative formalities which were carried out under the vigilant eyes of two senior officers from the Vienna police force, the religious ceremony was minimal. A few minutes were long enough to say a short prayer and to bless the body. The coffin was then given over to the gravedigger. Even then, due to the waterlogged state of the ground, it was necessary for the policemen and relatives to help him. All this had to be finished before any chance witnesses could discover that a burial had taken place in the abbey's cemetery.

The contrast between this burial and the pomp which surrounded Rudolf's funeral is striking. Knowing that she had not yet recovered, Franz Joseph hoped to spare Elisabeth this ordeal. During the funeral service she remained in a separate chapel. Once the service was over, the most heart-rending moment came when the coffin was taken down to the Capuchin crypt in the wake of monks who bore lighted torches. Although form dictated that Franz Joseph should leave his son at this point, Franz Joseph broke this rule by accompanying the procession. After a final blessing had been said by the cardinal of Vienna, he sank once again into prayer. Then, before withdrawing, he kissed the coffin farewell.

The final curtain had not yet fallen on the tragedy, for the emperor was still obliged to perform a number of official acts. In particular, he still had to thank the individuals and the organizations who had gathered together to share in the imperial family's mourning. It was not long, however, before Rudolf's name disappeared from official declarations and papers. References to him would be very rare from this time onwards until the end of the monarchy. Concerning the drama itself, the court and the authorities never went back on their version of events. Mary Vetsera's presence at Mayerling was never admitted. This did not prevent the circulation of rumours, sometimes of the most extravagant kind, from a very early date. They were fed by articles which would periodically revive the affair abroad. Although these publications were confiscated before they entered the monarchy, the echo at least of their contents reached Austria. But these rumours also fed on the efforts of the authorities to draw a veil of silence over events at Mayerling. Without a doubt, the legend which grew up and spread concerning this drama which tempts historians from time to time, and attracts sensation-seekers, owed much to these efforts to conceal the truth.

Although it was a spectacular event, Rudolf's brutal disappearance did not act as a break in the history of the reign. The internal policies of the monarchy did not change, nor were relations with Hungary modified, and Vienna's foreign policy did not suffer for it. There is little that is surprising in this, given that Rudolf was kept away from decision-making.

On the other hand, the death of his son marked a turning-point in Franz Joseph's personal life. The wound cut him to the quick, as his letters to Katharina reveal.

Writing from Budapest, to which he was obliged to travel only a few days after the funeral, he confided to her: 'The quantity of work and of worries caused by the present situation leave me no time to concern myself with my pain, and this is a good thing. But once I have gone to bed, it is hard for me to get to sleep, and I have the same problems when I wake up in the early morning.'[15] He found it impossible to prevent himself from thinking about the events which had led up to the tragedy, and from trying to explain it: 'Widerhofer spent more than an hour with me this afternoon. We spoke again of the sad events, and we tried to find a reason for them. All this is a waste of time, and, to tell the truth, has no purpose, but we can think of nothing else, and speaking of it brings some comfort.'[16] In the long term, Rudolf's death took away some of Franz Joseph's reason for living. Whatever his ties with the new heir, the latter was no long the flesh of his flesh. Although his sense of duty and his will gave Franz Joseph the strength to overcome this crisis, there is no doubt that it destroyed one of the most personal motivations of his life.

11

Rising Perils: Loneliness (1889–1908)

Although it could no longer have quite the same meaning for him after the events at Mayerling, Franz Joseph's sense of duty forced him to control his grief and to continue to bear the burden of the office to which he had been called by God. Even at the height of his suffering, it would never have occurred to him to abdicate, for such a decision would, in his view, have been tantamount to desertion. This meant that the new heir to the throne, Archduke Franz Ferdinand, Karl Ludwig's eldest son, was faced with the prospect of a long wait.

As an old campaigner who had not yet given up the fight, bowed down but not broken, Franz Joseph felt the need to continue in his task even more determinedly as the horizon darkened around him. Within the monarchy, Taaffe's system, which had provided Austria with a decade of relative stability, went into a process of decline, while Hungarian nationalism led to increasing difficulties in conforming to the rules of the Compromise. Internationally, new factors were changing the relationships between powers, and contained the seeds of crises in which the vital interests of the monarchy would be directly at stake.

The Seagull

The empress did not immediately resume her wandering life. Because she did not wish to leave her husband alone, she remained in Vienna. Nevertheless, it soon became apparent that it was Elisabeth who was least able to cope with the ordeal of their son's death. Whereas Franz Joseph channelled his suffering into his work, this outlet was not open to his wife. Without the help of occupations which could fill her thoughts, she found it impossible to come out of her grief. The shock was all the greater because of her fragile psychological equilibrium. A few years earlier, the tragic death of her cousin Ludwig II of Bavaria had had a serious effect on Elisabeth. From that time on, the thought had never left her that she too was afflicted by the curse of the Wittelsbachs. After Mayerling, this belief became an obsession. Because it had been officially recognized that Rudolf had committed suicide in a moment of mental derangement, she became convinced that it was through her that he had inherited his tendency to madness. Prince Reuss, the German ambassador in Vienna, was not exaggerating when he noted in a report: 'The empress has given herself up to perpetual contemplation of this event. She blames herself, and attributes the mental state of her unfortunate son to the blood of the Wittelsbachs.'[1]

Tortured by her belief in her own guilt, Elisabeth sank into a state of despair, and the thought of death never left her. This obsession was also a fascination. She had already displayed a curiosity concerning spiritualism, but following the blow of the Mayerling tragedy this ceased to be a simple amusement. She fell back on it in the hope that she could use it to enter into communication with Rudolf's spirit, and thus solve the mystery of his death. This ordeal also served to confirm the divergence of her religious beliefs from those of Catholicism. The God which she now called on was 'great Jehovah', who had decided men's destinies before they even appeared on earth.

From this time on, she gave up all interest in clothes, dressing only in black. The picture painted by Horowitz in 1890 shows her as a *mater dolorosa*, her long figure clothed in a black dress unrelieved by any ornament. Her face is as beautiful as ever, but her lips show barely the shadow of a smile, and she looks on the world through resigned eyes. Plaited into a crown, her hair is Elisabeth's only headdress, but its colour blends with the general tone of the portrait. The fan which she holds is also black, and this particular accessory would now practically never leave her hands. Along with her misanthropy, it helped Elisabeth to cut herself off from the world and, obsessed with old age, she would use it to conceal the wrinkles which began to appear on her beautiful face.

This succession of fits of depression interspersed with periods of elation made Elisabeth difficult to live with. She would regularly describe herself as a burden to her husband and those who loved her. She repeatedly claimed that death would be a happy release for her, and would also free her family. Unhappiness did not make communication between husband and wife any easier. Franz Joseph's prosaic attitudes continued to annoy Elisabeth, but their problem also lay in the difference between their sorrows. Elisabeth, in addition to the grief of losing a son, suffered from an existential despair which Franz Joseph's emotional stability and religious faith prevented him from experiencing.

The empress remained at Franz Joseph's side until the marriage of Maria Valeria. This separation was a fresh source of suffering for her. When Maria Valeria developed an affection for Archduke Franz Salvator, a cousin on the Tuscan side of the family, she did not oppose the match. But for a long time, at the mention of the possibility of this marriage she would melt into tears or sink into a state of depression. She even went so far as to speak of marriage to Maria Valeria with a bitterness which can hardly have been encouraging to the young girl, and which was in any case wounding for Franz Joseph: 'Marriage is an absurd institution. At the age of fifteen you are sold, you make a vow you do not understand, and you regret for thirty years or more that you cannot break it.'[2]

Delayed by the drama of Mayerling, the wedding took place on 30 July 1890 at Ischl. The emperor and empress had difficulty in hiding their sadness. Elisabeth suffered sorely from this separation and Franz Joseph knew that a new gap had been created in his intimate circle and also feared that after his daughter's departure, Elisabeth would not be long in resisting her urge to travel.

Indeed, once Maria Valeria had gone, Elisabeth resumed her itinerant way of life, only paying brief visits to the members of her family. She justified her refusal to stay longer with Maria Valeria, who hoped to keep her at her side, in the following terms: 'It is precisely because I am so happy here that I cannot stay. The swallows' nest is not approriate for the seagull.'[3]

These years of travel revealed a growing lack of stability in Elisabeth. She criss-crossed Europed tirelessly, without ever managing to stay in one place for any length of time. She herself explained her constant need for travel:

> If, having arrived somewhere, I knew that I would never have to leave it again, even a paradise would become hell for me. The thought of soon having to leave a place fills me with emotion and makes me love it. Thus on each occasion, I bury one dream which has evaporated only too quickly, in order to chase another.[4]

It was not without justification that Elisabeth compared herself to the Flying Dutchman. Fascinated by the sea, she discovered that its moods matched her own. She thus embarked on long cruises during which, far from society, she could live according to the rhythm of unspoilt Nature. But the strangeness of some of her behaviour disconcerted some of those close to her. Thus, memories of the tales of Antiquity were not enough to explain to her attendants why, in rough weather, she should have herself tied to the bridge of the sailing ship in order to enjoy the storm more. Were these just extravagances, or were they the sign of a deeper problem? Always quick to leap to Elisabeth's defence, Countess Festetics nevertheless found herself compelled to agree that there was 'a shadow floating across her soul'.[5]

For Franz Joseph, the opportunities to see Elisabeth became even rarer than before. She would often even refrain from returning for those celebrations which had once united the imperial family. The good wishes which her husband sent her from Munich where he was spending the Christmas of 1892 with Gisela, were in a very resigned tone: 'God bless you, protect you, and bring us the joy of meeting again. We can neither wish nor hope for more.'[6] When she returned to Vienna, the empress would shut herself away in her apartments, or would cloister herself in the Villa Hermes. Elisabeth had now almost completely opted out of her official duties. Even more than in the past, the responsibility thus fell on Franz Joseph's shoulders. Combined with the effects of old age, this failure on the part of the empress reduced the brilliance of court life.

As the empress's stays in Vienna became increasingly infrequent, Franz Joseph allowed himself a few extra vacations in order to be with her at some of her holiday resorts. He thus developed the habit of joining her for a few days on the French Côte D'Azur, at Cap Martin. He did not forget his duties while staying there. Each day a special courier would bring him papers from Vienna, and each morning, as in Vienna, he would carry out his duties as sovereign. These stays spent at Cap Martin also gave the imperial couple the chance to renew old acquaintances, for instance, Franz Joseph would visit Empress Eugénie who lived nearby. Time had long erased the antagonisms which had once set their Houses at odds, and Elisabeth and Franz Joseph shared with Eugénie the experience of losing a son under dramatic circumstances and this shared suffering brought them closer to each other.

The Gloriettegasse

In Vienna, Katharina Schratt's company provided Franz Joseph with a means of escape from total solitude. He could now enjoy once again, as at Ischl, the pleasure of breakfasts shared with his 'friend'. Katharina was now installed at Hietzing, at 9 Gloriettegasse, in a charming house in the baroque style, with yellow walls and green shutters, which she had acquired with the help of the emperor. It so happened that Gloriettegasse was close to the Schönbrunn and thus it was easy for Franz Joseph to visit when he was living there.

Katharina had contrived to create an atmosphere in this new home which suited her warm and gay personality. Franz Joseph liked to go there to savour a few mements of relaxation after having spent many hours of his morning on paperwork. While he enjoyed the breakfast prepared by Katharina's cook, his friend's volubility would distract him from the serious thoughts which occupied his mind elsewhere. Katharina would also sometimes receive her emperor in more intimate surroundings, having her breakfast served in her bedchamber. Franz Joseph was captivated by the charm of this exquisite hour: 'Do not get up too early tomorrow morning, I beg of you,' we read in their correspondence, 'Allow me to come and sit on your bed. You know that nothing gives me greater pleasure.'[7] But such wonderful moments did not occur every day, and this special favour did not become a habit. Following breakfast, Franz Joseph and Katharina only had to cross a road to find themselves in the grounds of the Schönbrunn. On returning from this walk, there would often be onlookers waiting for Franz Joseph to applaud him. Indeed, his visits to the Gloriettegasse had soon become known to the Viennese, and although not all those at court approved of his relationship with Katharina, the people showed a far greater tolerance.

During winter, the programme could not be the same, for Franz Joseph mostly lived in the Hofburg during this season. A discreet intervention on the part of the empress offered a solution to this problem. At the request of her mistress, Ida Ferenczy placed her apartment at the emperor's disposal. Although it was certainly not such a charming setting as Gloriettegasse, it nevertheless gave Franz Joseph the chance to see Katharina and to have breakfast with her.

Franz Joseph's attachment also took on very material forms. Only two months after Mayerling, he was careful to add a codicil to his will which guaranteed his friend's future. It allowed for the sum of 500,000 florins to be left to 'the court actress Katharina Kiss von Itebbe (née Schratt) to whom I am bound by the deepest and purest of friendships and who has always been loyally and faithfully at my side and at that of the empress during the hardest moments of our lives'.[8] Together with the other proofs of Franz Joseph's generosity, such as a palace on the *Ring* and a rich collection of jewels, this sum would assure Katharina one of the most substantial fortunes in the Austrian capital.

The Death of Elisabeth

Katharina's company did not relieve Franz Joseph from his worries over the health of the empress. More obsessed by death than ever before, she only rarely emerged from the state of melancholy which had become second nature to her. The drastic diet to which she subjected her system did nothing to soothe her nerves. Her slimming programmes also had the effect of weakening her constitution, as her obsession with her weight led her to real abuses. Although one of the court doctors had diagnosed that she was suffering from an oedema caused by starvation, Elisabeth made no changes in her eating habits. She was so weakened that in the last year of her life she had the greatest difficulties in walking. This was in sharp contrast with her previous lifestyle, which had continued until very recently, in which she had worn out the ladies-in-waiting who used to accompany her on her long walks. The signs of her deterioration, which was as much mental as physical, were so apparent at the beginning of 1897 that Franz Joseph felt himself obliged to warn Katharina Schratt who was about to join the imperial couple at Cap Martin.

If the appearance of the empress, which is sadly distressing, should shock you, do not show it, I beg you. Also, try to avoid the subject of her health, and, if you don't succeed, try to give her encouragement, and above all do not recommend any new treatments or remedies. You will find the empress completely exhausted, in great pain, and very demoralized. You may imagine how worried I am. This time, our holiday on the magnificent Côte d'Azur will be a sad one.[9]

When travelling abroad, the empress insisted that no special security measures should be taken. This was a further source of worry for Franz Joseph, for during these years there were a large number of anarchist attacks across Europe, aimed at princes or political figures. His warnings were of no use. Although the authorities of the countries which they visited were careful to set up security measures, these could only be light in view of the empress's request.

At the end of August 1898, Elisabeth arrived in Switzerland where she expected to spend a month at Territet. She expressed a wish for Franz Joseph to join her there, but the pressure of his duties following his return from holiday at Ischl, and in particular the army manoeuvres, prevented the emperor from considering such a possibility. On 9 September, the empress had planned to visit Baroness Julie von Rothschild at Prégny, not far from Geneva. She then expected to spend the night in Geneva, at the Beau Rivage hotel, before departing for Territet on the following day. As was usual in such circumstances, she was travelling incognito under the name of the 'Countess Hohenembs'. Everything would have gone off normally had not a Genevan newspaper seen fit to announce the Austrian empress's presence.

This indiscretion was the start of the trouble. The news caught the attention of Luigi Lucheni, a 26-year-old Italian mason, who nursed a hatred of those in power which was caused as much by his personal failures as by ideological conviction. He had at first selected as his target the Comte de Paris, pretender to the French throne, whose arrival in Geneva had been announced. But it so happened that the Comte de Paris changed his plans, and Lucheni may well have felt that fate was against him.

With the indiscretion of the Genevan newspaper, fate smiled on him. From the morning, Lucheni positioned himself near to the Beau Rivage. He was still watching when the empress left the hotel in the early afternoon to go down to the landing stage. It was then that he struck her in the breast with a file which he had sharpened himself. Losing her balance, Elisabeth slid to the ground where her thick hair cushioned her fall. She still had the strength to cover a hundred metres or so, but, on arriving at the boat, she collapsed and soon lost consciousness. Loosening her clothing, Countess Sztáray, her lady-in-waiting, discovered her injury. The empress was taken back to the hotel but it was already too late: all the doctors could do was confirm her death. The autopsy revealed that the blade had in any case penetrated 85 millimetres and had gone through her left ventricle, which would have been a mortal wound under any circumstances.

Hardly had the death been confirmed than Countess Sztáray sent a telegraph message to the Hofburg. Franz Joseph was working in his study, as he did every day, and was just dealing with the last of his papers before setting out to watch the army manoeuvres. As none of his daughters was with him, it was left to Count Paar to bring him the telegram, 'Her Majesty the empress has just died.'[10] Franz Joseph was at first frozen with shock, and then, sinking back into his armchair, he allowed the words to escape from his mouth: 'I shall then be spared nothing on this earth', words which were not an expression of revolt but of the suffering which he had carried in the innermost part of his being since Rudolf's death.[11] A few moments later, Count Paar heard him murmur to himself: 'Nobody knows how much we loved each other.'[12] This initial reaction, while his defences were lowered against the waves of his anguish, expresses the intimate truth about Franz Joseph, which was that there was another side to his character. The dignity of his position demanded that he should have control of his feelings and, in this circumstance, as in others, he knew how to do so. But when he saw Maria Valeria again, he could not suppress his tears. Katharina Schratt's presence brought him precious solace once again. At the beginning of this month of September, his 'friend' had taken a few days holiday to go mountain-climbing. As soon as she heard of the assassination of the empress, she hurried back to Vienna. Franz Joseph did not fail to express his thanks to her: 'It is so good of you to have come back. Who better could I have to speak of my lost one with than you?'[13]

In appearance, Franz Joseph's life very soon resumed its usual pattern. But, although his duties and the friendship of another human being might distract him, he carried a degree of suffering within himself which was all the heavier for being unexpressed. When she joined him for the first time since the funeral, Maria Valeria could only observe it: 'I know how deep and heavy his suffering is, but faced with so much pain, I am powerless.'[14]

The Cult of the Monarch

These new trials resulted in a strengthening of the respect which Franz Joseph's subjects felt towards their emperor. The latter had now assumed the appearance of the *alte Herr*, the 'old man', which remains most people's image of Franz Joseph. Although he still had his famous elastic step, the signs of old age were becoming increasingly obvious. Despite his continued vigour, he was beginning to stoop, and more and more, he took on the appearance of a gnarled old oak tree.

Franz Joseph's portrait was to be found all over the monarchy. There was no public place in which his picture did not hang, and many simple or bourgeois houses also contained his picture. It was to this image that the thoughts of the onlookers would turn in those scenes, familiar to garrison towns, in which military bands would march by playing the imperial hymn *Gott erhalte den Kaiser*.

As they had done twenty years before at the silver wedding, the celebrations which marked the fiftieth year of the reign, until the assassination of the empress in August put an end to them, bore witness to the popular feeling in support of the emperor. On 24 June, some 70,000 Viennese children paraded before him along the *Ring*. Some of these celebrations were picturesque in character, for instance, on the same day, 4,000 huntsmen in full dress gathered at Schönbrunn, and acclaimed Franz Joseph as the foremost among them. On 26 July, it was the turn of the cyclists to pay homage to him, in a ceremony which might be considered strange for an emperor who was generally hostile towards modern inventions.

Ten years later, the jubilee provided the occasion for further spectacular displays. Once again children were closely involved in these celebrations. A procession of 82,000 schoolchildren opened the jubilee ceremonies at Schönbrunn. On this occasion, there was also a revival of the fashion for *tableaux vivants*. It was decided to present Franz Joseph with a view of the history of his army since the birth of the House of Habsburg. This demonstration was also intended to express the unity of the peoples of the monarchy grouped around their emperor. Indeed, with the exception of the Czechs, no nationality was absent. For three hours, on the *Ring*, Franz Joseph saluted some 12,000 men, whose range of costumes and uniforms not only illustrated the course of the centuries, but also the diversity of the Habsburg lands.

This popularity also had a political significance and consequences. Naturally, a gathering of his peoples centred on the person of the sovereign, could be a point scored in favour of the monarchy. However, it could serve the opposite purpose, in demonstrating the fragility of the monarchy's unity. What other conclusion could be drawn at the sight of a political system whose only unifying factor, however strong, was the dynastic tie? Indeed, the celebration of these jubilees did nothing to calm the nationalist confrontations which were tearing the monarchy apart. In 1898, their exacerbation had the effect of paralysing the Austrian parliament, while in Bohemia there were frequent scuffles between Germans and Czechs, and in Galicia the tensions between Poles and Ruthenians were growing. The Magyars, for their part, aimed at a further reduction in their ties with the Austrian provinces in the name of the sovereignty of the Kingdom of Saint Stephen.

The political movements which had grown up in the course of the previous decade became more clearly defined and proclaimed the positions that they intended to take. Among most nationalities, the moderates gave way to the supporters of a more aggressive policy, and the nationalist disease continued to spread. At the same time, popular movements emerged at the centre of the political arena, and this contributed to a change in the political landscape.

The Fall of Taaffe

Count Taaffe's government was one of the first victims of this new spirit. The first minister hoped to settle the Bohemian question on the basis of a compromise between the Germans and the Czechs. Such an agreement would consolidate the position of the Old Czechs who were threatened by the rise of their Young Czech rivals. Once the Bohemian question had been settled, conditions would be ripe for some of the more moderate liberals to rejoin the coalition government.

Taaffe may have thought he was approaching his goal when the representatives of the two peoples, led by Rieger for the Czechs and Ernst von Plener for the Germans, contrived, with the support of the aristocracy, to reach an agreement at the beginning of 1890. This agreement proposed a division of the Diet into three *curiae*. The Germans and the Czechs would each be represented by one, and the third would be made up of the great landowners. In order to settle the education question, it was agreed that the Bohemian school council would be divided into a German and a Czech section. There was also a clause which allowed for the protection of ethnic minorities, under which the children of school age of any one nationality who numbered forty or more within a commune were entitled to be taught in their own language.

Nevertheless, from the moment it was concluded, this agreement was under serious threat. The Young Czechs had deliberately been kept out of these negotiations although their support among the public continued to grow. Taaffe would pay dearly for this mistake, for, had they been allowed to participate in this agreement, the Young Czechs might have taken a more moderate line, and might finally have come to support the proposed compromise. But because they were excluded, they attacked the agreement concluded by the Old Czechs and shortly afterwards they reaped the fruits of this larger gamble, triumphing in the *Reichsrat* elections, while their opponents were crushed. The first consequence of this turn of events was to bury the compromise before it could even begin to be effective. It was also a serious blow to the moderates of both parties. The Old Czechs, at least in Bohemia, almost ceased to exist as a political power, while among the Germans, it was the extremists who now had the upper hand.

In all, the result of Taaffe's move was the opposite of the one he had hoped for. Following the defeat of the Old Czechs, the Czech element of the government majority could no longer be relied on, and the cabinet's margin for manoeuvre was accordingly reduced. Faced with this new factor, Taaffe demonstrated that he was not the mediocre politician which liberal historians have suggested. On reflection, he decided that the adoption of universal suffrage would provide an answer to the rise in nationalist tensions illustrated by the crisis in Bohemia. It was not enough, though, for him to be convinced of this. Franz Joseph must also be persuaded, which would not be an easy task, for he might scent a spirit of militancy in this concession to democracy. But Taaffe knew how to develop the arguments necessary to bring him to support this reform. He sketched out his theory that the working classes had not been contaminated by the nationalist virus as much as the middle classes of the various communities which made up the Cisleithan whole. In acquiring a political voice, they would change the whole direction of the political debate, which would instead focus on social and economic issues, and would lead the various parties to organize themselves on this new basis, thereby relieving the pressure of the nationalist question.

The scheme devised by Taaffe did not, however, introduce full universal suffrage, and in fact retained the curial system. The new voters would be called on to vote in the rural and urban communes but the *curiae* of the major landowners and the chambers of commerce and industry would continue to exist. Even this was too much for the members of the coalition government. Being of the opinion that universal suffrage would bring about their downfall, they defended an elitist system which reserved power for a minority. In this they were very close to the liberals, most of whom did not support the principles of political democracy.

Disowned by the other partners in his government, Taaffe chose to resign. It was certainly hard for Franz Joseph to lose him. Their long association had given their relationship a personal note which broke with the usual sort of relationship between ministers and their monarch. Taaffe's departure also brought fourteen years of stable government to a close, and Franz Joseph may well have suspected that it would begin a period of political turmoil. But however great his annoyance, Franz Joseph behaved as a constitutional monarch should. He accordingly appointed a cabinet from those who had combined to oppose the electoral reform. The head of government, Alfred Windischgraetz, led a majority made up of the conservative and liberal right wings which until now had always been opposed to each other, but which were united in their opposition to universal suffrage. From its birth, this was a very tenuous coalition, as it was only united in its opposition. In particular, it was likely that it would be severely shaken once the question of nationalities became acute, setting Germans and Slavs against each other.

This was confirmed by the eruption of the Cilli affair. Cilli was a little town in southern Styria which had a German majority, but which was surrounded by countryside dominated by Slovenes. The situation here was a typical example of the bitter quarrel over education between the nationalities. At the school in Cilli, German had held a monopoly until the beginning of the 1890's. But the growth in the number of Slovenian pupils led them to demand the introduction of bilingual teaching. Feelings soon ran high and the Slovenes, who were members of the ruling majority, refused to accept defeat. On the German side, opposition to the move was all the stronger because this was an area on the border between the German and Slav communities. Prince Windischgraetz's cabinet did not survive this crisis, and foreseeing the consequences of this division in his government, he decided to resign in June 1895.

As a replacement, Franz Joseph called on the *Statthalter* of Lower Austria, Count Erich von Kielmansegg, who formed a cabinet in which there were many high-level administrators. This was only a transitional government, and in October of the same year, Kielmansegg gave way to Count Kasimir Badeni, a Polish noble, whose parliamentary majority was once again based on most of the Slav representatives and the Catholic conservatives of the Alpine provinces. But although Franz Joseph felt at ease with such a balance, in which the dominant figures were top administrators, this interval represented the first paralysis of the Austrian parliamentary system under growing nationalist pressure.

Lueger as Mayor of Vienna

The appearance of new political movements is illustrated by Lueger's conquest of the Vienna Town Hall at the head of the Christian Socialists. Since the fall of the neo-absolutist regime, the Vienna City Council had been controlled by the liberals, who had made it one of their strongholds. Until the mid-eighties, there was no opposition party of sufficient size to contest their position.

The political situation began to change when Lueger embarked on the task of drawing together the host of anti-liberal movements which had emerged and expanded over the preceding years. Strengthened by support from among the middle-class craftsmen and shopkeepers, the new party assembled behind its charismatic leader to mount its assault on the liberal citadel. According to the results of the elections of spring 1895, the two parties were almost equal in popularily, and the *Statthalter* of Lower Austria used this inconclusive result as an excuse to dissolve the City Council. But in September the Christian Socialists won a resounding victory against the liberal party by ninety-two seats to forty-six. On 29 October, Lueger was elected Mayor of Vienna.

All eyes now turned to the emperor, who had the power either to confirm Lueger's election, or to veto it. There can be no doubt that he had strong reservations concerning Lueger's character. He was harshly critical of his crude oratory, and disapproved of his anti-semitism. He probably also saw in Lueger and the Christian Socialists a face of democracy which he had never liked, whatever concessions he may have made to the spirit of the times. Nor was he unaware of Hungarian pressure on him to refuse to ratify Lueger's election, for the latter had never concealed his hostility towards the Magyars, whom he considered to be destroying the monarchy.

Franz Joseph decided not to ratify Lueger's election and the city council was dissolved once again. But this move failed in its aims. A plebiscite was held in Vienna in February 1896 which gave the Christian Socialists an increased majority. Franz Joseph could once again resort to a veto but after such electoral results, it was unclear what could be achieved by a new dissolution of the council. This crisis did not fail to have an effect on the erstwhile warm relationship between the Viennese and their emperor. Franz Joseph was no longer greeted with the same spontaneity when he travelled between the Schönbrunn and the Hofburg. Rather than allowing a situation which threatened the dynasty to deteriorate at a time when the monarchy had to face up to other problems, Franz Joseph decided on a compromise. He first gave Lueger an audience on 27 April. He then announced that 'for the time being' he would delay ratification of the election, and that the person involved had decided to support this decision. This established that his refusal was no longer an exclusive attack on Lueger.

Although he managed to salvage appearances by clinging to the advantage of having taken the initiative, in this compromise Franz Joseph had conceded an apparent victory to the Christian Socialists, for he was no longer opposed to their electoral victory. While waiting for Lueger to take his place at the head of the council, one of his colleagues, Joseph Strohbach, filled the post. Lueger's long journey towards the control of the city ended in the following year. On 8 April 1897, the city council once again voted for Lueger. This time, there was no hesitation in ratifying the appointment: Franz Joseph gave his agreement on 16 April. Once this hurdle had been passed, relations between the two men improved. Franz Joseph must have appreciated that Lueger behaved as a loyal subject. As first magistrate of Vienna, Lueger also demonstrated a sense of responsibility which was far greater than some of his speeches or behaviour might have led one to expect. Although he had made use of anti-semitic feeling as a lever, once he became mayor, he was careful to refrain from any infringement of the rights of his Jewish administrators. In addition, up until his death in 1910, he headed a vast modernization programme in the capital which at the turn of the century had already reached a population of 1,674,000.

As the instigator of socialism at municipal level, Lueger's main achievements were the development of the major infrastructures (the water and sewage system and the construction of gas and electricity plants) and the transport system (the tram and underground system), while planning for social improvements such as the financing of hospitals and a school system. It would fall to the Social Democrat council of 1918 to complete this work, especially by devising new solutions for the problem of housing which had been neglected by the Christian Socialist administration. Considered as a whole, Lueger's record is, however, a positive one. His work would serve as the foundations on which his successors would build their policies.

It was also in 1897 that the Social Democrats won their first electoral success. While it was still growing, this party adapted its internal structure to suit the national pluralism of Austria and, in effective, it became a party with a federal structure, comprising six principal nationalities (Germans, Czechs, Poles, Ruthenians, Italians, and Slovenes). Social Democracy could not, however, hope to play a major role in politics while the majority of the working classes were deprived of the right to vote. A new step towards universal suffrage was taken in 1896, for although Count Badeni had not suddenly been transformed into a champion of democracy, he felt that it was not possible to ignore the weight of opinion in favour of universal suffrage.

This accounted for the reform which was passed in 1896, which instituted an 'adjusted' universal suffrage. In addition to the four existing *curiae*, a fifth one would be created, in which all the newly created voters would vote. Accordingly, five and a half million voters would elect only 72 deputies. This voting system remained very unequal as at the same time 5,402 landowners would elect 85 deputies. But the elections of 1897 soon demonstrated that universal suffrage was nevertheless favourable to the people's parties. In the fifth *curiae* fifteen Social Democrats were elected, and it was from this sector that most of the twenty-eight Christian Socialist deputies came.

Tribulations

The preceding years had shown the potentially explosive power of nationalist feeling. The dam was breached in 1897. Austrian society and the new Chamber were shaken by real suffering following the publication on 5 April of two linguistic Orders which obliged the civil servants working throughout Bohemia to master, from July 1901 onwards, both the German and Czech languages. Count Badeni's decision in this matter was not motivated by aggression towards the Germans in Bohemia, and in theory such a proposal might appear reasonable. But beyond the limits of Galicia, where he had been governor before being called to Vienna, Badeni had no specific knowledge of the realities of Austria. In his analysis, he had clearly not taken sufficient account of the degree of mistrust and concealed feeling which poisoned relations between the two peoples concerned.

Confronted with these Orders, the German reaction was immediate. The Germans feared that the application of the linguistic Orders would deliver them into the hands of the Czechs and would destroy their hope of obtaining a statute of administrative autonomy in the areas where they had a majority. The massive influx of Czech administrators into these areas would make the realization of such a project impossible. On the other hand, this reform would satisfy the Czech belief in the unity of the Kingdom of Bohemia.

Badeni's Orders acted as a detonator. The disagreements which had been contained for many years were released. Bohemia became the theatre for a cycle of violence. But the unrest did not confine itself to Bohemia. Forming a kind of sacred union, the German parties took the fight against the 'villainous Orders' into the *Reichsrat*. Schönerer, who had resurfaced during the crisis, let loose his invective. At his side, the extremists set the tone for this movement of resistance. For fear of being accused of a lukewarm response, or even betrayal, the other parties, even the Christian Socialists and the Social Democrats, all assumed hardline positions. Only the Catholic conservatives remained aloof from the general feeling.

There would have been nothing abnormal in this confrontation between opposing points of view, if it had not been for the degeneration of the nature of these encounters, as the participants were carried away by strong feeling. The House of Deputies was borne off on a wave of madness. Every possible obstructive technique was employed. The speakers in the House would regularly be interrupted by verbal abuse or the banging of desks, and debates very soon escaped the control of the president. Partisans and adversaries did not stop at verbal insults, and the more excited members came to blows. To restore order, a law was passed ordering the suspension for a period of thirty days of any deputy who broke the rules of the Assembly. But this measure only increased the disruption. Far from dying down, there was renewed violence. The president's chair was assaulted by rowdies erupting with fury. The president found himself obliged to call for the physical enforcement of his decisions. Not contained within the *Reichsrat*, the disorder spread to the streets. The Pan-Germanists were not the only ones to demonstrate. Their ranks were reinforced by the Viennese, many of whom had voted for Lueger and who, although they were excellent Austrian patriots, were concerned about the fate of the Germans and wished to add their voices to those who sought to solicit Prussian favour. In the autumn of 1897, there was such a feverish atmosphere in Vienna that some observers feared the worst.

In light of this increase in unrest and the growing paralysis of the parliamentary institution, it was reasonable for Franz Joseph to feel that the time had come to bring an end to this experiment. Badeni had already offered to resign, but, typically, the emperor had at first retained his confidence in his first minister. Had he agreed to the resignation, he would have felt that he was giving in to the pressure on him to dismiss Badeni. However, he was finally obliged to adopt this course of action. On 27 November, Badeni's resignation, which was so eagerly awaited by the German Austrians, was accepted.

The resignation of a government was not enough, however, to bring an end to this crisis. Months of confrontation had left a profound mark on Austrian politics. Spread throughout Europe by the newspapers, and confirmed by ambassadors in their reports, the news of the scandalous scenes which had brought dishonour to the Austrian parliament had a serious effect on the international prestige of the monarchy. Many read in them the signs of a process of disintegration. Indeed, tensions did not slacken, although the battle lines were redrawn. The Czechs who had been delighted with the Orders considered themselves betrayed. Under the leadership of Baron Gautsch, the archetypical senior Austrian administrator, the new government did not cancel the Orders – they would be revoked only in 1899 – but he suspended their application, instituting more accommodating measures in their place which divided Bohemia into German, Czech or bilingual areas. It was now the turn of the Czechs to give free rein to their anger. In Prague, German students, proudly wearing the colours of their organization, were attacked in the city centre, and shops belonging to German traders were ransacked.

In answer to the Czech violence, the Pan-German extremists continued in their offensive against the Danubian monarchy. Denouncing the Catholic Church as a supporter of the Habsburg state, Schönerer launched the *Los von Rom* movement, which called on Austrian Germans to break with the Catholic Church and to convert to Lutheranism, which he portrayed as the supreme nationalist religion. Although this campaign did not bring about spectacular results, the number of converts, which reached around 40,000, was nevertheless considerable. But these attempts at conversion also had the converse effect of strengthening the loyalty of most Catholics towards Habsburg Austria.

Another consequence of the continuing crisis was an increase in the instability of the government. One after the another, governments would wear themselves out trying to devise a compromise which would settle the Bohemian question. In less than three years, following Badeni's resignation, there were four changes of government. For lack of a parliamentary majority, not a single law was passed by parliament in this period. Ministers were repeatedly reduced to falling back on article 14 of the Constitution which, in exceptional circumstances, authorized the government to operate without the approval of the Houses.

Another result of this paralysis of the parliamentary system was the weakening of Austria's position in its dealings with Hungary. The lack of a parliamentary majority constricted the Vienna government's power to act in its negotiations with its Budapest counterpart over the ten-yearly renewal of the Compromise. There was, however, provision to extend the existing agreement for a further year under such circumstances, so as to avoid the risk of an inevitable break if differences continued between the two parties when a ten-year period was up. This prevented the worst from happening, but it was a natural temptation for Hungary to take advantage of the weak state of the Austrian government and to increase its demands.

Franz Ferdinand's Marriage

In the midst of such worries, Franz Joseph was faced with the additional concern of Franz Ferdinand's intended marriage. The latter only officially became the heir to the throne in 1896 on the death of his father, but since Rudolf's death, nobody had seriously believed that Karl Ludwig could succeed Franz Joseph should he die suddenly. Already, before the matter of his marriage arose, Franz Ferdinand had had the chance to display his strength of character when, in 1895, he was diagnosed as having tuberculosis. General opinion considered that his days were numbered, and it did not escape him that many members of the court, in anticipation of his death, turned their attentions to his brother Otto, who would be the new heir in the event of his early demise. He had even considered the possibility that Franz Joseph, in establishing Otto in the Augarten palace, also supported this view. Faced with this test, he had refused to accept his fate, and had turned his will to the conquest of his illness, an effort which eventually met with success.

Franz Ferdinand displayed the same determination when he met with opposition from Franz Joseph over his intended marriage to Countess Sophie Chotek. Having experienced no qualms in refusing the marriage plans which Franz Joseph had devised on his behalf, he now aspired to choose his own wife! He had met Sophie Chotek when he was stationed in Prague and a deep feeling soon grew between them, which they nevertheless contrived to conceal from those around them for a long time. It was mere chance that the secret was revealed. Franz Ferdinand had long been in the habit of visiting one of his aunts, Archduchess Isabella, at Halbturn castle. Far from realizing that this assiduous attendance was due to Sophie Chotek's presence at Halbturn as a lady-in-waiting, the archduchess could only account for it by assuming that the heir to the throne must have an interest in one of her own daughters. The mystery was solved one day in the summer of 1898 when Franz Ferdinand left his fob-watch behind on the castle's tennis court. The archduchess could not resist the temptation of opening it in the hope of finding inside it a picture of one of her daughters who, she hoped, had conquered her illustrious visitor's heart. It was a painful surprise to discover the likeness of her lady-in-waiting. In her horror, she made the matter known to Franz Joseph.

At first believing it to be a passing affair, it was his turn to be surprised when Franz Ferdinand informed him of his wish to marry the countess. For Franz Joseph, such a marriage was unacceptable. Although the Choteks were a most worthy family of the Bohemian nobility whose respectability was not to be questioned, they were not among the noble houses with whom an archduke, especially the heir to the throne, could contract an alliance without losing prestige.

For nearly two years, uncle and nephew refused to budge. At the beginning of 1900, Franz Ferdinand wrote a letter to Franz Joseph to repeat to him that his happiness depended on marriage with Countess Chotek and that he could not work for the good of the monarchy if he was not happy in his private life:

> My wish to marry the countess does not spring from a whim, but is dictated by the deepest of attachments, which has survived the tests and sufferings of several years...This marriage with the countess is the way in which I can be turned into what I wish and ought to be for the whole length of my life: a man who is loyal to his duty and is happy. Without this marriage, I would lead a miserable life, as is already the case, which would prematurely age me...I cannot agree to any other marriage, and refuse to contract such an alliance, which would be repugnant to me. It is impossible for me to tie myself to another woman without love and to make her unhappy when my heart will always belong to the countess.[15]

These arguments do not appear to have moved Franz Joseph. However, his sister-in-law, Archduchess Maria Theresa, who, as the third wife of his dead brother

Karl Ludwig, was Franz Ferdinand's stepmother, seems to have been more persuasive. Maria Theresa was one of the few members of the court whose judgement was trusted by Franz Joseph, and she took Franz Ferdinand's part resolutely. However, her powers of persuasion are not enough to explain Franz Joseph's change of heart. We must assume that Franz Joseph did not wish to cause a crisis in the succession at the very moment when home affairs were becoming difficult. But although he eventually gave his consent to the wedding, he also set very harsh conditions concerning it. The marriage would be morganatic, in other words, Countess Chotek would not be made archduchess, and could not become empress of Austria, and any children which were born of the union would not have the right to succeed to the throne.

Despite its severity, Franz Ferdinand agreed to this arrangement, for he was fully aware that Franz Joseph would not make any further concessions. However, this compromise had the potential to cause problems, for, in particular, Hungarian law did not recognize morganatic marriages. Although it was a distant possibility, there was still a chance that, on the death of Franz Ferdinand, one of his sons might be recognized as sovereign in Hungary, although he could not reign in Austria.

For the affair to be brought to a close, Franz Ferdinand was obliged to swear an Act of Renunciation prepared by legal experts. Franz Joseph did not spare his nephew the full weight of Habsburg ceremonial in this. All the parties concerned, the dynasty, the monarchy, and the Church, were involved in the event. On 28 June 1900 all the archdukes, the foreign minister, the Austrian and Hungarian first ministers, the senior court officials, the cardinal of Vienna and the Hungarian Primate were gathered in the Geheime Ratsstube of the Hofburg. The atmosphere was icy, and all those present realized that this event would leave its mark. The dry and threatening tones in which Franz Joseph read the Act of Renunciation seemed to call down the wrath of the gods should Franz Ferdinand break his oath. Franz Ferdinand, for his part, hardly managed to conceal his anger. This ceremony was followed only four days later by the celebration of the wedding in the chapel of the castle of Reichstadt in Bohemia. Franz Joseph once again demonstrated his dissent by refusing to attend. His example was followed by the archdukes who were not prepared to brave his anger.

This marriage permanently changed the relationship between the emperor and his heir. In the course of this battle, two strong personalities had confronted each other, and each suffered from the concessions he had been obliged to make. Although he reluctantly gave his consent, Franz Joseph still perceived this alliance to be an attack on the order which regulated the organization and life of the imperial family. Furthermore, what was Franz Ferdinand's oath worth? Once he had succeeded to the throne, would he not soon tear up the Act of Renunciation?

Franz Ferdinand considered to conditions imposed on his marriage to be a humiliation. He had already endured the ceremony for the giving of the oath, which had been a real act of humiliation in his eyes. Now, at each official ceremony, the wound was reopened. Although as a wedding present, Franz Joseph had granted Sophie the title of princess of Hohenberg, this gesture did not alter the fact that she was not legally part of the imperial family. Thus, according to court protocol, the most minor of the archduchesses had precedence over the princess of Hohenberg.

Katharina's Departure

For Franz Joseph, 1900 was certainly not a happy year. In its course, the old emperor endured difficulties which affected even his private life, and which shook his relationship with Katharina Schratt. Following the death of the empress, Franz Joseph and Katharina had resumed their meetings, but a number of signs suggested a slow deterioration in their relationship. Franz Joseph's friendship with Katharina had never been fully approved at court, where there were many who disapproved of the position occupied by a commoner in the emperor's life. Maria Valeria, in particular, had always regarded this relationship with a critical eye.

While the empress had been alive she had protected Katharina from evil tongues, but once she was dead, these enmities gained new power. Maria Valeria who, in a way, had taken her mother's place, could be expected to use her influence with her father to attempt to extricate him from this friendship. Franz Joseph might even remarry. Certainly, Katharina's imagination led her to exaggerate these threats, and Franz Joseph was increasingly subjected to her moods. He himself was not always an easy companion and as the cares of old age came upon him his legendary courtesy would sometimes fail.

The uncertainties over her career also added to Katharina's worries. Paul Schlenther, the new director of the Burgtheater, was not a man to be impressed by the fame of an actress, nor to tolerate her fancies. Although he was very willing to recognize Katharina Schratt's talent, he expected to make his own decisions concerning the roles which he would give her. She, too, was suffering from the effects of age. Now that her looks had gone, there were problems in assigning her parts in which she had previously excelled. But she was not prepared to admit this to herself, and she was angry when she missed out on roles.

In these disputes, Katharina no longer received the support she expected from Franz Joseph. He did not once consider dismissing Schlenther as she had hoped. In addition, when her contract expired and Schlenther submitted a proposal to her which did not give her any special consideration, Franz Joseph advised her to swallow her resentment and to accept it. Another argument followed this which was worse than any before, judging by the letter which he wrote to her immediately after it, a letter which is poignant for the almost supplicatory tone in which it is written:

My dear and good friend,
In truth, I do not know whether I can still use these terms, and whether I should not be writing 'Dear Madam'. But I cannot give up the hope that yesterday's storm clouds will disperse, and that we may rediscover our old and happy friendship. You rejected my remonstrances and counsels with such obstinacy and passion, although they were sincere, and intended to further our common interest, that I allowed myself to be carried away by a strength of feeling which I now regret and for which I beg you with all my heart to forgive me. For my part, I would like to forget the insulting and painful (for me) manner in which you left me. But allow your good heart to be heard, examine the situation calmly, and you will realize that we cannot part. Ponder again on the long years of our serene friendship, of the joys and sufferings,

above all, alas, of the sufferings which we have shared together, and which you have helped me to bear. Think of the loved one we cannot forget, whom we both love, who watches over us like a guardian angel, and I hope that you will then be disposed towards a reconciliation...Every morning when I awake, my first thought has always been of you, the expectation of seeing you would give me the strength to face the day. I am sure that your kind heart will not wish all this to change and that I should end my old age deprived of your beloved company which brings me warmth and strength.[16]

This occasion was only a warning. The final dispute came when, ignoring Franz Joseph's advice, Katharina handed in her notice to the director of the Burgtheater. By all accounts, it seems that she was seeking a confrontation, counting on the intervention of the emperor, who would surely not allow things to progress too far. But Franz Joseph still made no move, and, adding to her worries, this disappointment made Katharina decide to leave him.

Franz Joseph's stay at Ischl in that year of 1900 ended in sadness. It was there that Katharina told him of her decision, after waiting for the end of the celebrations of his seventieth birthday. This news stupefied the emperor's suite. Maria Valeria's surprise was total when, his voice filled with tears, and his face contorted, her father informed her that he would see his friend for the last time on the following day.

Koerber's Government

As a result of this split, Franz Joseph faced the new century in increased solitude. His only consolation was that, after the unbridled passions of the previous years, he could enjoy a reduction in tension in the Austrian part of the monarchy. The period of government instability came to an end, and Koerber's cabinet was to remain in office until December 1904. Ernest von Koerber was another example of the senior Austrian civil servants so often appointed to political posts. Before his ministerial career, he had held major posts in railway administration and in the ministry of the interior.

Koerber did not succeed in resolving the Bohemian dispute any more than his predecessors had done. The new factor in the policies of his administration was his intention to reverse the order of priorities. Although he was clearly not in a position to ignore nationalist questions, his government could not afford to allow them to overwhelm it, for, should this occur, it might find itself locked into a logic which would favour interests and feelings in contradiction to the principles on which the Habsburg state was founded. In order to avoid this trap, Koerber hoped to set the assets of economic growth and an increase in prosperity against the destructive power of nationalism. By choosing a course which gave priority to material interests, he hoped to create an atmosphere which would defuse nationalist conflicts. To this end, he launched a vast programme, to the value of a million florins, of railway and canal construction.

Koerber's cabinet could also congratulate itself on its political successes. For the first time in many years, the *Reichsrat* voted in favour of the proposed 1901 budget. Elsewhere the negotiations concerning the renewal of the Hungarian Compromise had been completed. Although many people awaited the event with apprehension, the welcome given to Franz Joseph by the Bohemians in 1901 confirmed the atmosphere of *détente*. It also proved that Koerber's gamble was not an unrealistic one. Even in the areas containing the most violent clashes of opinion, no breaking point was reached. Loyalty to the dynasty was maintained and any secessionist movements had only a small following.

This face-lift did not, however, last for long. Although for a brief moment, they had been forced into the background, nationalist demands soon raised their voices once again. Degenerating once more into an arena for violent fisticuffs, the parliament was again paralysed by obstructive manoeuvres. Although it held out against these for longer than its predecessors had done, Koerber's government finally suffered the same fate and, exhausted by the incessant harangues of the deputies, the first minister finally resigned in December 1904.

We can draw only one conclusion from this experience. It had already been a great achievement for Koerber to last nearly five years in office, and he should therefore be given the credit for having brought Austria back to a stable position. But any assessment of his period of office should also take account of Koerber's objectives. Here, one is obliged to realize the distance between the declared ambitions of the government and the results it achieved. Whereas Koerber set himself the goal of reducing nationalist feeling, like his forerunners, he was finally to give way to the pressure they placed on him. This is not to say that his government should be dismissed as a failure. Koerber would have had to have been a magician to rid himself of the weight of problems accumulated over the decades. His policy certainly did not have all its intended results, but it had the merit of having shown one of the possible ways in which the monarchy could be saved. His assessment of the situation was in fact founded on the realization that national questions were not the only element in Austrian life. They could not eclipse the elements which were working towards the opposing goal of a unified Austria, not least the economic unity of the monarchy.

Universal Suffrage

Once the government had defined its objective as the inoculation of the masses against the disease of nationalism, it was logical to attempt the next step towards political democracy in Austria. It fell to Koerber's successor, Baron Gautsch, to formulate this project. Although this enterprise did not immediately meet with success, Gautsch could declare, as he was about to step down from office in the spring of 1906: 'People come and go, but ideas endure. My fall will not bury the campaign for electoral reform.'[17] Indeed, after him, Max Vladimir Beck took up the project once again and succeeded in bringing about this reform, by passing a motion which initiated direct universal suffrage and abolished the curial system for the Lower House of the *Reichsrat* (although this was still preserved by the Diets).

These decisions must certainly have taken account of the international situation. After the manifesto of 30 October 1905, in which Nicolas II promised universal suffrage to the Russian people, it must have been hard to imagine that Austria would not take a similar course. The response which was awakened by the Russian revolution in certain sectors of society did not pass unobserved by the Austrian government. Under such circumstances, electoral reform was also perceived as a means of relieving the growing tensions. Concern was far from meaning panic, however. Austria in 1905 was not suffering from the state of anarchy into which Russia had sunk at one point. In addition, the socialist threat remained theoretical at that time, for the Social Democrats could still ony boast twelve deputies in the *Reichsrat*. And, although it was certainly true that they had started to ask the government for direct universal suffrage, the street demonstrations which were organized were not of sufficient magnitude to persuade the government to commit itself to this course.

In truth, Franz Joseph's approval was essential to the making of this choice. At the time of his election, Gautsch had certainly had reservations concerning universal suffrage. It was only when he became convinced that this reform was also desired by Franz Joseph that he became its ardent champion. Equally, when Franz Joseph had called on Beck to form the new government, Beck had done so in the faith that he would be successful where his predecessor had just failed. Franz Joseph's views had not changed but he hoped that this reform, which would provide the working classes with an electoral voice in proportion to their numbers, would lead to a slowing down of the centrifugal movement which threatened the monarchy.

It was easy to foresee that the chief beneficiaries of universal suffrage would be the Christian Socialists and the Social Democrats. In the time since he had opposed Lueger's appointment as mayor of Vienna, Franz Joseph's prejudices against the Christian Socialists had disappeared. The performance of their municipal duties, and their solid record now surrounded them with an aura of respectability. The time was approaching when, reinforced by the Catholic deputies from the rural areas of the Alps, the Christian Socialists would become a major conservative force. In addition to this, and no less important, they professed a most proper patriotic support for the Habsburgs.

Concerning the Social Democrats the problems were certainly not the same. This was a party which aspired to the radical transformation of society and whose theories were hostile to the principles of the monarchy. It seemed reasonable, then, to fear that their entry into the *Reichsrat* in substantial numbers might pave the way for revolution. Franz Joseph, however, with the encouragement of Beck, saw matters in a different light. Far from reinforcing their extreme position, in his view, the increased participation of the Social Democrats in the parliamentary process was likely to lead them to take a more moderate stance.

What was more, the theories of the Social Democrats did not prevent them from adapting to the existence of the monarchy. While advocating a radical transformation of the structures of society, the Brünn Congress recognized the Habsburg state as a viable political and economic whole. Following this, Karl Renner, who supplied the party's doctrine on nationality, restricted his theories to this same framework. Set out in major works such as *The Fight of the Austrian Nations for a State*, in 1902, and *The Crisis of the Dual State*, in 1904, he developed his ideas around the concept of personal freedom. As a solution to the crisis, Renner proposed the establishment of a clear division between political and economic affairs on the one hand, and the question of nationality on the other. Although the way in which the former were handled presupposed a respect for the principle of territory, he rejected this in dealing with the latter. Maintaining that nationality was an individual attribute like religion, he concluded that the citizens of Austria should be called on to form national registers, irrespective of their territorial attachments. The people who made up a nation would form a moral body whose main aim would be to satisfy the need of its members and, to this end, would have its own legislation, budget, and administration. As a whole, this plan was intended to give the monarchy a lease of life. The details of the proposals did not concern Franz Joseph very much. For him, their importance lay in the objective support provided by the Social Democrats for the Habsburg state in the nationality question.

With the intention of removing the last obstacles from the path of universal suffrage, Franz Joseph chose Max Vladimir Beck as his first minister, who was yet another senior civil servant. Before this turning-point in his career, Beck had served the state for twenty years at the ministry of agriculture. Beck saw the emperor's request for his services as an order. Although for many years he had figured as one of the advisers to the heir to the throne, whose interests he had represented during the finalization of the Act of Renunciation, he was not allowed sufficient time to consult Franz Ferdinand, the latter being in Spain on official business.

Beck brought to the service of the reform programme his negotiating skills and his readiness to compromise. His task was not an easy one, for there was still considerable opposition to universal suffrage. In particular, Beck was faced with the delicate problem of the allocation of seats to the different nationalities. In this perilous exercise he would have to iron out the most striking injustices, while making sure that he did not infringe on the rights of those peoples who had benefited from the previous system. Among the latter were the Germans, who feared that they would become a minority, and the Poles, who were afraid that an increase in the number of Ruthenian representatives would endanger their control of Galicia.

Once the Chamber of Deputies had finally approved the reform, it was still necessary to obtain the agreement of the Upper House. This led to fresh confrontations. The nobles, who held the majority in this Assembly, and who would suffer greatly from universal suffrage, hoped to cause the project to fail, or at least to tone down its contents. Beck found himself fully occupied with the task of avoiding any changes which might distort the meaning of the reform. The battle was all the more harsh because the sector of the nobility which was hostile to reform had Franz Ferdinand's support.

For Beck, it was a painful experience to have oppose the prince with whom he had formerly been so closely allied that many observers had assumed that, when the time came, he would be his first minister. It was in vain that he attempted to dissuade him from openly supporting the nobles to oppose a now inevitable reform by suggesting that he might tarnish his public image, an argument which left Franz Ferdinand cold, for, unlike his uncle, he expected universal suffrage to work to the advantage of the enemies of the monarchy.

Behind this clash there lay a conflict between Franz Ferdinand and Franz Joseph himself. Indeed, right up to the final review, the latter maintained his official display of support for Beck. Nobody could be unaware of the importance which he placed on this reform. This commitment from the emperor weighed more heavily on Beck's shoulders than did Franz Ferdinand's opposition, and its full impact could be seen at the moment of the final vote in which the opposition could only summon up a handful of diehards.

Once this battle had been won, it still remained to be seen whether the reform would bring the results which Franz Joseph hoped for and it had to be admitted that it did not produce any miraculous effects. Universal suffrage failed to strike a fatal blow to nationalist feeling. But it would take time for all of its consequences to be realized. These questions aside, in the elections of 1907 universal suffrage favoured the two people's parties as had been predicted. With the support of the Alpine conservatives, the Christian Socialists became the largest parliamentary group, with ninety-seven members, while the Social Democrats gained eighty-seven seats.

Universal suffrage did not lead to the simplification of the political system which Franz Joseph had hoped for. Following these elections, there were no fewer than twenty-eight parties represented in the Chamber of Deputies. The Czechs were now split into six parties, and the Poles into five. The complexity of this situation was likely to make the running of Austria an even more difficult task. These results nevertheless contained the visible seeds of positive developments, for they effectively established the existence of alternative rallying points to that of nationalism. This was demonstrated by the case of the Social Democrats, whose parliamentary group contained deputies of several nationalities. The Christian Socialist parliamentary group, on the other hand, contained only German deputies. In addition to these new groupings, a further feature of these elections was the electoral breakthrough of the Czech Catholics, and on a more general scale there was a retreat of nationalist feeling in the empire's Czech possessions. The Young Czechs, who had dominated the political scene in these areas since the 1890s, were outnumbered by the agrarians who represented the interest of rural areas, and who, with the Catholics, raised a more moderate voice. All these developments show that Franz Joseph's gamble had not been an unrealistic one.

Tensions in Relations with Hungary

The debate over universal suffrage was not confined to Austria. It also gripped the heart of Hungarian political life, but in a different form. In Hungary, the threat of universal suffrage was manipulated against those factions which hoped to invalidate the Compromise by reducing relations between Austria and Hungary to a special agreement. Since 1867, Franz Joseph had followed a policy of scrupulous respect for the obligations which the Hungarian Constitution placed on him, and the way in which the dual state functional meant that he could no longer act as protector to the minorities who were under Magyar rule.

Proof of this had been given in 1892, when a delegation from the Transylvanian Romanians submitted a memorandum to the emperor which set out their grievances. Its authors had hoped that Franz Joseph would intervene with the Hungarian authorities on their behalf. But far from fulfilling this expectation, he had refused to act as an intermediary. All that he had been prepared to do was to pass the document on to the Hungarian government, who, considering the memo to be an act of high treason, had punished those Romanians responsible for it.

Faced with a similar dilemma shortly after, Franz Joseph had once again placed his duties as a constitutional monarch before his personal sympathies by promulgating a law, in December 1894, which made civil marriage obligatory in Hungary. The resentment brought about by this move did not die down immediately.

Franz Joseph was once again obliged to accept the resignation of Count Kálnoky. Following a tour of Hungary by the papal nuncio, who violently objected to the new legislation, the foreign minister came into conflict with the head of the Budapest government, Baron Banffy, over the response which should be made to this interference in the affairs of the kingdom. Rather than allowing this situation to develop into a crisis, Franz Joseph decided to sacrifice his minister, in whom he nevertheless continued to have confidence.

A remark made by Franz Joseph to Maria Valeria sheds some light on his actions: 'If I am to say "no", I must be in position to stick to it. But there are not the people in Hungary who would be necessary to support me in this. Those who might help are not in a political position to do so.'[18] The truth of the matter was that the Austrian government had little room for manoeuvre in Hungary and Franz Joseph had learned this the hard way. Certainly, the effects of this moderate stance could not be entirely positive, for in the long run such a stance was likely to alienate peoples who had previously been loyal to the monarchy. Franz Joseph nevertheless made the decision to adhere to it for as long as it continued to offer the advantages of the dual system, such as crown control of foreign affairs, and a united army. In this, he set a limit which the Hungarians would not be able to cross without provoking a serious crisis.

Franz Joseph was in fact aware that such a crisis was probably inevitable. The implications of the Hungarian interpretation of the Compromise, and the growing pressure of nationalism were such that, sooner or later, the Magyar demands would become too great in these areas. In their offensive, the Hungarians first turned their attention towards the army. Already, in the past, the discussions concerning military laws had led to impassioned debates. The members of the Budapest government who had originally negotiated the Compromise, and later their successors, had nevertheless contrived to restrain themselves. But, as the century came to an end, the balance of power was changing and the liberal party was being worn away by those in power.

In addition, there was an upsurge of nationalism which benefited the independence party, led by the great Kossuth's son. A champion of the solution of a special relationship, he was vociferous over the question of the army, considering the restraints which were imposed in this area by the Compromise to be incompatible with national sovereignty. The first area of attack was the monopoly of German as the language of military command in the imperial and royal army, which was the physical manifestation of military unity. But the independence party had other demands, in particular that the Hungarian regiments should not be stationed beyond Hungary's borders and that they should be obliged to swear to abide by the Hungarian Constitution. The implications of these demands were clear. They were intended to remove the Hungarian regiments from Vienna's control in order to create a national army which would receive its orders from Budapest. But this was something to which Franz Joseph was under no circumstances prepared to agree. Along with foreign affairs, the army was the last great institution to embody the tradition of the combined monarchy. Bound by their guiding principle of service to the dynasty into an indivisible unit, its officers had been sheltered from the pernicious influences of nationalism.

When this campaign, supported by the other opposition groups, grew to a point where it threatened to overwhelm the government, Franz Joseph considered it his duty to intervene. In September 1903 he seized the opportunity provided by the army manoeuvres which were being carried out at Chlopy in Galicia, to publish an order of the day in which he solemnly declared his will to protect the unity of the imperial and royal army. There was no ambiguity in his words:

> Its responsibility for all my subjects, and its unity are, and should continue to be, the main qualities of my army; a solid force which defends the Austro-Hungarian monarchy against all foes. Loyal to its oath, every part of my army must continue along its path, fulfilling its most sacred duty, imbued with a sense of unity and harmony which respects national characteristics and which bends the characteristics of each people to the service of the good of the whole.[19]

This declaration aroused contrasting reactions. In Cisleithania, Franz Joseph's firm stance won him the approval of many of his subjects, but on the other side of the Leitha, there was a radically different atmosphere. Here indignation reigned. Nevertheless, having set the limits of what he was prepared to tolerate, Franz Joseph did not refuse to accommodate the Hungarians with conciliatory gestures, which, although they provided no threat to the unity of the army, did serve to restore the *amour propre* of the Hungarians.

One illustration of this desire for conciliation is Franz Joseph's agreement to most of the points submitted to him by a committee of nine members of the liberal party, whose president was Count Istvan Tisza. Among the proposals was a call for the transfer of Hungarian officers to units stationed in Hungary and an increased use of Hungarian troops in these regiments. It was also decided that the regiments stationed in Hungary should make use of their Hungarian troops to establish good relations with the local authorities. It was also proposed that the Hungarian national flag should fly beside that of the empire over military establishments.

Tisza, the chief negotiator in this agreement, was then appointed head of the Hungarian cabinet by Franz Joseph. This fervent patriot was convinced that his country's prestige depended on maintaining its links with Austria. In his view, if Hungary were left to itself, it would soon be overwhelmed by the conflicts between nationalities, and would also be obliged to face the Russian threat alone. Nevertheless, the opposition did not change its position in the light of the agreement, and, considering the measures announced by Tisza to be insufficient, it continued in its demands.

Far from dying down, tensions in Hungary rose another notch. This time, it was the Budapest parliament that was the scene of the violence. The country was showing its sympathy for the opposition by refusing to pay its taxes, and there were desertions among army recruits. Tisza nevertheless chose this moment to call new elections, hoping that they would restore order, and counting on a reduction in public support for reform in reaction to the continued chaos. His calculations turned out to be wrong, though. Instead of supporting him against the extremists, the voters in the January 1905 election expressed their lack of confidence in Tisza. The liberal party lost its full majority, retaining only 159 of the 290 seats which it had previously held. Moreover, it was overtaken by the party for independence, which had now gained 166 elected members, and which was reinforced by 98 representatives of the smaller opposition parties.

In the face of this challenge, Franz Joseph took action, while making sure that a way had been left open for a compromise. His main aim was to pressurize the new majority into giving up the aspects of its manifesto which threatened the unity of the monarchy. His first move was to form a non-parliamentary government in June 1905 under the control of one of the few Hungarians in whom he had complete confidence, General Géza de Fejérváry, who at that time was the commander of the Royal Guard and Grand Master of the Order of Maria Theresa.

To help him to subject the Hungarian opposition party to his will, Franz Joseph had the advantage of a valuable weapon: the threat of universal suffrage, which had the potential to change entirely the structure of Hungarian politics. In this, he had the particular support of Franz Ferdinand who, because of his strong dislike of the Magyars whom he accused of working for the destruction of the monarchy, adopted the opposite position to that which he had held in the question of Austrian universal suffrage. His hope was that such a reform would end Magyar control in Hungary.

The firm attitude adopted by Franz Joseph was one which must have delighted his nephew. On 23 September he received the leaders of the opposition in Vienna. In five minutes all that there was to say had been said. In a tone which brooked no reply, Franz Joseph demanded that his visitors should cease to oppose the reforms which had been agreed two years earlier, that they should no longer demand that German should be abandoned as the language of government, bringing his remarks to a close with the threat of universal suffrage. The effects of this interview were not seen immediately, and the Hungarian political classes maintained their stand. Franz Joseph stepped up the pressure. In February 1906 events reached a new stage when he dissolved the Chamber of Deputies and had the Assembly forcibly evacuated by soldiers from a Romanian regiment. The opposition leaders expected this to rouse public opinion in favour of national representation, but it failed to do so. For the Hungarian opposition, this absence of reaction from the electorate brought about a realization of the true nature of the situation.

It did not matter that the results of the new elections reinforced the results of the previous year, giving the independence party a crushing majority, for this party still only represented the views of a minority, given that neither the urban nor the rural masses had any political rights. In addition, in the light of the reaction of the population to the current crisis, the Hungarian ruling classes feared that they would be submerged by weight of numbers if voting rights were extended. The threat was all the greater because the national minorities would also benefit from such a reform.

Confronted with this threat, the opposition leaders finally agreed to compromise. As Franz Joseph had never intended to push the tension to breaking point, an agreement was quickly reached, and it was decided that these parties would form a coalition government under Alexander Wekerle. For their part, the opposition leaders agreed that the consideration of the military question would not take place until there was universal suffrage. In short, the crisis was resolved by the re-establishment of the status quo.

Franz Joseph appeared to be the victor in this contest of strength, but he did not rejoice in his victory. It seems that he felt no sympathy towards the majority of the figures involved in the new government. A whole world of traditions and memories separated him, for instance, from Ferenc Kossuth. He could at least congratulate himself on having succeeded in imposing his conditions on the government, but he did not fool himself that this agreement protected Austria from the possibility of further crises in its relationship with Hungary: 'God will help us', he wrote to Katharina Schratt, 'but I can foresee more fights. I gave nothing away, but in the present circumstances, I find myself unable to look on the future with confidence.'[20] Certainly, there were no guarantees that the results of this crisis would be of long-term benefit to the monarchy. Perhaps, rather than a temporary success, this crisis should be looked upon as a missed opportunity. It had provided an opportunity to reconsider the question of the dual state, and to solve some of its problems through the means of universal suffrage. Universal suffrage would have given the non-Magyar nationalities of Hungary their rightful place in the government of their country, and would thus have opened the way to a restructuring of the monarchy. But in fact, Franz Joseph was perfectly satisfied with dualism, which had provided him with the priceless advantage of nearly forty years of stability. His first concern was therefore to retain the harmonious working of the Compromise. His severity and determination were now directed towards anyone who attempted to dismantle it, but he had absolutely no wish to enter into an institutional reform which would represent a leap in the dark. His intervention was therefore only to defend the status quo.

One particular feature of this line was that it led him to leave the Budapest leaders to develop their policy of Magyarization at the expense of the minorities, which policy was reinforced in 1907 by the educational laws introduced by Count Apponyi, the new minister for education. This legislation threatened to detach the minorities from the Habsburg Monarchy, by placing them under Magyar authority, and this meant that the monarchy was no longer fulfilling its role as protector of the minority populations of central Europe.

New International Factors

The threat created by this rejection of minority interests was all the more serious because these minorities might be tempted to turn elsewhere for support. The damaging effects of dualism were thus not confined to the Habsburg lands and, as they developed, had the potential to compromise the international position of the monarchy. It is true that after the events of the 1880s there was a period of relative stability in the Balkans until 1903. Like Franz Joseph, the foreign ministers Count Kálnoky, and later Count Agenor Goluchowski, a Polish noble, supported the status quo. Defending a conservative policy, they sought no confrontation with Russia, but instead supported a policy of co-operation with Saint Petersburg. This attitude was reciprocated by the Russian government which was also a conservative one at this time. In addition, during this period, its own expansion in central Asia and in the Far East so preoccupied Russia that it neglected its traditional areas of influence.

The nineties were nevertheless witness to an event which would transform the international political scene. Bismarck's great fear became a reality soon after his departure from the chancellorship in March 1890. Some twenty years after the Treaty of Frankfurt, France finally managed to emerge from its isolation, and in August 1892, concluded a treaty with Russia. The Franco-Russian alliance was the starting point for a readjustment of the relationships between the powers. Already shaken by the formation of the Paris–Saint Petersburg axis, Bismarck's system was showing an increasing number of cracks. The Franco-Italian agreements of 1900 and 1902 increased the fragility of the Triple Alliance to such an extent that the Austro-Hungarian leaders were justified in wondering whether Italy was still an ally or a potential enemy. Following the failure of its attempts to persuade Germany to put an end to its naval expansion, Britain decided to ally itself with France. Taking stock of their colonial aspirations, on 8 April 1904 the two countries signed an agreement which marked the birth of the Entente Cordiale.

Austro-Hungarian control of the Balkans did not escape the changes. The relationship with Serbia was the first link to give way. There, Austrian influence was mainly dependent on the personal decision of the sovereign. On 11 June 1903, King Alexander, his family, and his retainers were assassinated by a group of army officers who had not forgiven him the allegiance pledged on behalf of their country to Austria-Hungary. In a new episode of the war which had been going on between the rival families since the modern state of Serbia had been created, the Obrenovićs were replaced by the Karagjorgjevícs, whose family head assumed the throne as Peter I. This was not simply a palace revolution, though. The new rulers planned to end the policy of accord with Austria-Hungary, and to replace it with a Pan-Serbian programme. Because of their support for a reversal of alliances, they decided to turn towards Russia as the 'mother nation' of the Slavs for support and help.

Whatever his horror at the events in Belgrade, Franz Joseph rejected the idea of intervention. But surely this should have been the moment to nip the movement in the bud, for if it were allowed to develop, it could become a mortal threat to the monarchy. International opinion seemed to support this view. Germany would not oppose any action intended to restore order along the southern borders of the monarchy, while for its part, Russia was prevented from intervening by its concerns in the Far East, where it was about to engage in a conflict with Japan. Why then did Austria-Hungary remain passive? Many Austro-Hungarians did not realize the implications of events in Belgrade. In their opinion, Serbia remained as it had been before Alexander's assassination, a state incapable of any truly autonomous act. Franz Joseph did not, however, support this view. Undeceived by the monarchy's apparent power, he was well aware of its fragility. In his position at its head, he was sensitive to all the possible upheavals which might be unleashed by embarking on a military campaign, however simple it may have appeared. Also, he preferred to work for the preservation of peace rather than tempt fate.

This is how we should interpret his meeting with Nicolas II in October 1903. A hunting trip to Mürzsteg provided the opportunity for political discussions between the sovereigns and their foreign ministers. The worsening of the situation in Macedonia, where the Christian population was increasingly restless under Ottoman rule provided them with a good reason for this meeting. But, as war with Japan approached, Nicolas II's main concern was to make sure of Austria-Hungary's neutrality. The Tsar left the meeting satisfied. Russia had protected itself against a war on two fronts, and in return had agreed that Austria-Hungary should extend its sphere of influence to the western Balkans.

Although Franz Joseph dismissed the possibility of a military solution, relations with Serbia soon became soured. Indeed, from now on, the Serbian question would be a constant preoccupation in Vienna, especially as it had repercussions within the monarchy itself. The empire was now suffering from the disadvantages of its Hungarian policy concerning the minority populations. The Belgrade government's plan to unite all the monarchy's southern Slavs with Serbia would have encountered little support except among Serbians had the ground not already been prepared.

Actually, the pro-Yugoslav argument did not appeal much to the Slovenes, whose authority came directly from Vienna, and who were under a generally sympathetic administration. The grievances of the Croats had already gone further. Although many Croats had no thought of a future which would take them away from Habsburg rule, they hoped to replace the dual system by a triple one which would include the Croats and Slavs from the monarchy's southern provinces as its third political unit, thereby preventing them from succumbing to the lures of Serbia. There was, however, another current of opinion among the Croats which expressed dissatisfaction with the monarchy based on a strong disappointment that the monarchy had not rewarded Croat loyalty. Because they reflected this feeling, the Yugoslav ideas gained ground. In 1905 the Croat and Serbian Dalmatian deputies signed a joint declaration. Three years later, in the elections for the Agram (Zagreb) Diet, the victors were the supporters of the Serbo-Croat union. Although the restricted nature of the voting public limited the possible implications of this success, it nevertheless indicated a movement of thought among the Croat elite.

Having chosen not to use force on Serbia, Austria-Hungary put the economic thumbscrews on instead. It had been very tempting to fall back on this method of attack, as the monarchy was Serbia's main economic partner, receiving 80 per cent of its exports. Furthermore, this move was supported by the Hungarian landowners, for Serbia's main export was pork, and this led to competition in the marketplace which they were not at all happy with. This trade war did not, however, have the desired effect, for Austria-Hungary's place was quickly filled by Germany, Britain, and France. The latter, in particular, would supply Serbia with the military equipment which had come from Austria-Hungary until that time, and as a result of this Serbia became more firmly lodged in the camp of the Entente. But the main effect of this policy of economic sanctions was to strengthen Serbian feelings of resentment towards the monarchy.

The Annexation of Bosnia-Herzegovina

The increased tension in relations with Serbia led the Austro-Hungarian government to reinforce the ties which incorporated Bosnia-Herzegovina into the body of the monarchy. Of all Franz Joseph's possessions, Bosnia-Herzegovina was the only one whose statutory position was not clearly formulated. The question mark which had hung over the future of these lands since the Berlin congress had not troubled the monarchy for as long as Serbia remained a close ally. But, after 1903, the new Serbian ruling party were quick to exploit this uncertainty to achieve their own ends. Created in 1905 the *Slovensky Jug* society (Southern Slav society), with Belgrade as its base, developed an intensive pro-Serbian propaganda campaign in Bosnia-Herzegovina. By making the Austro-Hungarian presence in Bosnia-Herzegovina a permanent arrangement, the monarchy accordingly hoped to reinforce its defences against Serbian expansionist projects.

The international situation was favourable for this operation. Russia had still not rebuilt its military forces after the defeat it had suffered at the hands of the Japanese. Without Russian support, Vienna anticipated that Serbia would not dare to venture beyond a formal protest. It was no part of Franz Joseph's plan, or that of his new foreign minister, Baron Aehrenthal, to exploit this situation to bring about a direct confrontation with Russia. Indeed, before his appointment, Aehrenthal had been the Austrian representative in Saint Petersburg, where he had gained the reputation of being a strong supporter of close co-operation with Russia.

His nomination, which was also sought by Franz Ferdinand who, in the spirit of the defunct Holy Alliance, dreamed of a common front formed by the three great monarchies of central and northern Europe, was an indication of the importance which Franz Joseph attached to the continuation of good relations with Russia. Aehrenthal even considered, in return for Russian agreement in the matter of Bosnia-Herzegovina, an offer of Austrian support for a Russian application to the international community for freedom of passage through the straits of the Bosphorus, which would allow the Russian fleet access to the Mediterranean. But unlike the conservatism of his predecessors, Aehrenthal's was not static. He saw this annexation, not just as the end of a process begun in 1878, but also as a stage in a political progression of events which would resolve the problem of the southern Slavs. It was part of a plan by which he intended to bring all the monarchy's southern Slavs under a single authority. With the creation of this new centre of authority, bringing together a larger group than the peoples of tiny Serbia, the Slavs would no longer feel the need to look elsewhere for a national identity. Confined within its own borders and subjected to the combined pressure of the majority of southern Slavs, the Karagjorgjević state might soon even be reduced to the status of a satellite of the monarchy.

In order to achieve his ends, Aehrenthal nevertheless had to operate within a narrow field. There was no certainty that Russia would accept an annexation of Bosnia-Herzegovina which had been decided on unilaterally, especially as it might ultimately result in Serbian allegiance to the monarchy of the Danube. Russia was in an improved position to oppose such a move, as it had sunk its differences with Britain, and this had been confirmed by the agreement signed between the two countries on 30 August 1907. The Franco-Russian alliance was strengthened by the participants' individual agreements with Britain, and there was a possibility that the annexation might cause diplomatic complications as a result of the united front of these three powers. Vienna's advantage lay in Russia's state of military unpreparedness which would prevent the latter from considering any armed conflict. But this might not be enough to avoid an international confrontation.

The crisis blew up over a misunderstanding, whether unintended, or deliberately provoked. Alexander Isvolsky, the Russian foreign minister, stayed in Karlsbad in August 1908, and this provided the opportunity for a meeting with Aehrenthal at the castle of Buchlau, belonging to Count Berchtold, the Austrian representative at the court of Saint Petersburg. It has been established that Aehrenthal told his Russian counterpart of his intentions during this meeting, and promised diplomatic support for Russia concerning passage through the Bosphorus. Isvolsky does not appear to have raised any objections concerning the principle of the annexation of Bosnia-Herzegovina. The misunderstanding seems to have concerned the timetable for such an event. Later, Isvolsky was to maintain that no date had been discussed, whereas Aehrenthal insisted that he had spoken of such a possibility in the immediate future.

The accounts of the meeting differ on another essential point. The two men were agreed on the holding of an international conference which would bring together all the signatories of the Berlin Treaty. In Aehrenthal's view, this conference would merely serve to ratify the annexation of Bosnia-Herzegovina. Isvolsky did not see it in the same light. In his opinion, annexation should not take place until it had been authorized by the international community. The reasons for each minister's interpretation are easy to perceive. If a congress had to be held to make the annexation official, it would be likely to raise the whole question of the Balkans, and in such a case, Austria-Hungary would probably be obliged to make territorial concessions to Serbia in order to obtain agreement. It was precisely to avoid such a risk that Aehrenthal aimed to present Europe with a *fait accompli.*

When, on 5 October, Franz Joseph and Aehrenthal made their move, Isvolsky was surprised and protested. When Aehrenthal cited the Buchlau meetings, he replied that these had only been informal exchanges and that no agreement had been reached which had any diplomatic value. This argument was not without validity, but it was not enough to explain this hardening of the Russian attitude. Five weeks had passed since the Buchlau meeting. After leaving Aehrenthal, Isvolsky had travelled to several European capitals, and in particular to London.

We often date the deterioration in relations between Britain and Austria-Hungary from the annexation of Bosnia-Herzegovina. The result should not, however, be confused with the cause. London and Vienna had long been bound by a common hostility to Russian expansionism. This solidarity had been in evidence in particular in 1878 at the Berlin congress. It had been reconfirmed in March 1887 when Austria-Hungary joined Britain and Italy in a Mediterranean pact with Russia as its target. However, Britain did not wish to lose its right of influence over Balkan matters where its own interests were at stake, if only because of the proximity of the area to the Mediterranean. In addition, Aehrenthal's initiative, taken as it was, without consultation, could not fail to annoy Britain. But Britain's reaction should above all be perceived as the result of a change in London's foreign policy in the face of the growth of German power, and in particular, the programme of naval expansion decided on by Wilhelm II. It was its recognition of this threat which led the British government to decide on the necessity of a closer accord with France, and then with Russia, with a view to creating an anti-German front. It would also be with this in mind that Britain would now view its dealings with Austria-Hungary.

The latter was Germany's ally, and there was no sign that the monarchy was considering any revision of this alliance. Edward VII, who had succeeded his mother in 1901, certainly made considerable efforts to break it up. His frequent stays at Ischl provided him with the opportunity for this. He spent them trying to convince Franz Joseph to keep his distance from Germany. Having failed in this, he asked Franz Joseph to intervene on his behalf with Wilhelm II, in an attempt at least to slow down the expansion of the German navy, even if he would not call a halt to it. These efforts were in vain, for Franz Joseph remained deaf to the arguments and requests of his guest.

His sense of honour demanded that Franz Joseph should not encourage the British sovereign's advances. It prevented him from lending himself to any move which was directed against his ally. Franz Joseph may also have felt that he had no choice in this. In the midst of the changes in the international pattern, the alliance with German seemed to be the only solid element on which the monarchy could rely. But Britain also drew its own conclusions concerning this loyalty. Convinced that it would not succeed in breaking Austria-Hungary's ties with Germany, it no longer had any reason to accommodate the monarchy.

The ripples caused by the annexation of Bosnia-Herzegovina were large enough to provoke a major international crisis. Encouraged by Britain and supported by France, Isvolsky insisted that an international conference should be held. Serbia's response was unrestrained, especially as it was fully aware of the threat posed by the creation of a rallying-point for the majority of southern Slavs on its own doorstep. Determined to prevent the realization of the Austro-Hungarian plan, the Serbian government ordered military preparations to be made, counting on the support of Russia.

Having brought about this storm, Franz Joseph and Aehrenthal tried to calm matters down. They had no intention of going as far as armed conflict, although there was a body of military opinion which supported a preventative war against Serbia. Appointed head of the general staff in 1906, Conrad von Hötzendorf, one of Franz Ferdinand's protégés, was this group's spokesman. Wishing to modernize the Austro-Hungarian military machine, and possessed of a lively intelligence which inspired broad strategic visions, Conrad was also haunted by the fear that the monarchy would have to fight on several fronts in the case of a European conflict. In his view, the international situation provided a unique opportunity to eliminate Serbia as a political force without the risk of a broader conflagration, because there was no fear that Russia, still preoccupied by the disaster of its Far Eastern defeat, and by the revolution, would pick up the gauntlet. Conrad even hoped that the same fate would befall Italy, for he declared himself convinced that, given the right circumstances, it would turn against the monarchy.

These arguments did not convince Franz Joseph. Such a campaign would provide an easy victory for the imperial and royal army. But what would happen afterwards? If Russia was finally about to resign itself to the annexation of Bosnia-Herzegovina, it would be dangerous to push too far. Russia could never allow Austria-Hungary to crush Serbia. By setting off a chain reaction among the various alliances and ententes, a Russian intervention would be the signal for the broadening of the conflict.

Although it intensified on several occasions, this crisis was finally brought to a happy conclusion for the monarchy. In the final analysis, the course of events depended on Russia's decision. If it provided only moral support for Serbia, the latter would be obliged to withdraw; if, on the other hand, Russia encouraged the smaller state to put up an armed resistance, war would inevitably follow. Isvolsky had repeatedly informed the Serbian government of the limits of Russian support. Belgrade did not, however, wish to believe that Isvolsky's calls for caution could be Russia's final word. It was nevertheless obliged to change its mind in the middle of March 1909 when, under the weight of German pressure (Germany had decided to support its ally), a council of Russian commanders had no choice but to announce that they were opposed to war. From this moment, Serbia was left with no option but to give way.

This result was an undeniable success for the Austro-Hungarian diplomatic service. 'I believe that we can consider ourselves satisfied', Aehrenthal confided to Count Berchtold.[21] It was true that Bosnia-Herzegovina still retained a special status. Because of the problems which its inclusion in one or other of the two parts of the monarchy would entail, it was decided to make it into a province of the empire under the joint control of Austria and Hungary. But, as the final step in the process begun in 1878, the annexation consolidated Austro-Hungarian presence in Bosnia-Herzegovina and strengthened the monarchy's defences against a turbulent Serbia. Furthermore, this crisis demonstrated the solidarity of the alliance between the two central European powers. Franz Joseph could draw satisfaction from Germany's unwavering support in the preceding months. Lastly, the international community agreed to recognize the inevitability of the annexation of Bosnia-Herzegovina. The monarchy had thus demonstrated that, despite internal difficulties, it was still capable of an act of will which maintained its position as a great European power.

We should, however, question the reality of this apparent victory. As a result of this crisis, Austria-Hungary figured as the disruptive force at the heart of European agreement. This was the more so because elsewhere allegiances had become more clearly defined. Britain had clearly chosen its partners and there was no mystery over the inclinations of France. As for Serbia, it soon recovered from its resentment at Russia's desertion. There remained the Serbian hatred towards the Habsburg monarchy which it now considered to be its chief enemy.

An even more serious implication for the future was the deterioration of relations between Austria and Russia. Although its military situation prevented Russia from any armed intervention, Russia did not forgive the dual monarchy for the way in which it had been treated. Also, in order to preserve its credit with Serbia, Russia could not afford always to act as a restraint on the smaller state. In all, the future seemed filled with storm clouds. Berchtold was not painting a false picture in sending this pessimistic message to his minister: 'In this situation, there are enough incendiary elements involved to cause an explosion, if the conditions were more favourable, whose flowering might lead Russia to celebrate the restoration of its self-esteem.'[22]

12
Sarajevo

Repeatedly, in the course of the past three years, Franz Joseph had demonstrated both his ability to adapt to circumstances and his powers of initiative. He had imposed universal suffrage on his subjects, despite the resistance of most of the traditional elites; combining caution with firmness, he had controlled the crisis in Austro-Hungarian relations without any serious consequences for the unity of the army; and in Bosnia-Herzegovina he had transformed what had theoretically been a provisional occupation into a legal annexation. Nevertheless, it is questionable whether these were more than superficial successes. None of the fundamental problems faced by the monarchy had been resolved. Universal suffrage had not turned out to be a miracle cure for the disease which paralysed the Austrian political system; the detrimental effects of the dual state had not been wiped out; and lastly, in the Balkans, crises were becoming increasingly frequent, threatening the monarchy's position in the region, and deepening its obsession with the Serbian threat.

Pushed to the Limits of his Strength

Franz Joseph did not escape the effects of old age. In 1911, on visiting Maria Valeria's new home at Wallsee for Easter week, he was confined to his room as a result of a stubborn cough. The doctors even feared for the emperor's life and he was obliged to endure a long period of convalescence. In October, he was once again the victim of a chill which resulted from his carelessness at the wedding of Archduke Karl and Princess Zita of Bourbon-Parma, and which led to a relapse.

However, even at the height of his illness, Franz Joseph continued to work on his paperwork, which was prepared for him every day. Certainly, care was taken to conserve his strength, but Franz Joseph would not allow himself to be immured in the Schönbrunn or Hofburg palaces. Although he confided in Katharina Schratt that he was often weary, he still brought the same sense of duty to the fulfilment of his obligations as sovereign. He was all the more assiduous in this because he was aware of the extent to which his personal involvement and presence was important to the

cohesion of the monarchy. After the 1908 jubilee, there were other massive demonstrations of this, for instance at the congress of the Eucharist, held in Vienna in
1912.

But even outside these special occasions, on each of his excursions, Franz Joseph
could take stock of the extent of his personal popularity. Unless there was a very
good reason, he did not avoid the official ceremonies which he traditionally had to
attend. He also remained available to his subjects through the medium of the weekly
audiences for a long time, and continued to open exhibitions and conferences with
great stoicism. Not only did he travel around the capital, he was still prepared to
undergo the fatigues of long journeys. In 1909 he visited Tyrol for the centenary
celebrations of the uprising against the Franco-Bavarian occupation; just two years
after the annexation of Bosnia-Herzegovina, he did not fear to face the dangers and
exhaustion of journey to this distant province. Each year, too, at the beginning of
September, he would attend the army manoeuvres, and it was clear to everyone that
he was still an excellent horseman.

After the warning of 1911, his timetable was nevertheless revised to make his
duties lighter. He now only rarely visited the Hofburg, and spent most of his time at
Schönbrunn. His public appearances became rarer, but despite the fact that old age
now forced him to appear less often, over the years a myth had grown up around his
person which compensated for his absences. It no longer mattered that he hardly
ever left his Schönbrunn palace, for his subjects could see his likeness in the
innumerable portraits which hung in the most remote villages of the monarchy, from
Tyrol to the Carpathian mountains, from the depths of Galicia to the shores of the
Adriatic. Pictures, busts and statues of him were everywhere, sometimes in the most
crude forms, reflecting the cult which surrounded him. There was no business which
did not exploit this source of revenue. Thousands of tea and coffee services, glasses,
knives, and all sorts of everyday objects were decorated with his picture. Through
them, Franz Joseph embraced his subjects with a protective gaze, and indeed, he was
seen as a father figure by many of them.

There were few occasions for relaxation in the life of the old emperor. Although it
had gained ceremonial status, his stay in Ischl in July and August broke the monotony of his days. Although he still followed his habitual work-patterns while he was
there, and would sometimes receive foreign sovereigns and statesmen, his time was
nevertheless organized along different lines from when he was in Vienna. Despite the
weariness brought about by age, he was not prepared to give up the pleasures of
hunting in the Upper Austrian Alps and the chance to enjoy the countryside at first
hand. At Ischl, he also encountered close family members in a less formal environment than Vienna, for his daughters would regularly bring their children to stay.
The company of his grandchildren was one of his last pleasures. Also, when he got
the chance, he would enjoy spending a few days at Wallsee with Maria Valeria who
had provided him with no fewer than five granddaughters and four grandsons. His
relationship with his family reveals an unexpected side to Franz Joseph's character,
for in practising the art of being a grandfather he would not hesitate to sit on the
floor to play with his grandchildren, to marvel at the presents which they had
received for Christmas, and even to become involved in games of hide and seek in
order to please them: 'My only pleasure during your absence', he had written some
years previously to Katharina Schratt, 'has been in my seven grandchildren who,

with Valeria, have spent a number of weeks with me in the Schönbrunn palace. As one grows older, one returns to childhood. I am thus growing closer and closer to them.'[1]

But the most important factor in Franz Joseph's personal life was that his relationship with Katharina Schratt had survived the crisis which had troubled it. After her departure, many of those close to him, among them Princess Gisela, Prince Rudolf Liechtenstein, and Prince Eulenburg, German ambassador to Vienna, had been fervent in their efforts to persuade Katharina to put an end to a quarrel which left the emperor in despair. It was certainly true that on her return in June 1901 things did not revert to how they had been in the past. Katharina was still subject to changes of mood, and her absences were also more frequent than they had been, now that she was no longer attached to the Burgtheater. But when she was in Vienna, Franz Joseph and Katharina resumed their old habits, the only difference being that, careful to spare her too early an awakening, he would only appear at the Gloriettegasse after nine o'clock. The company of his friend also brought a ray of sunshine back into the emperor's life during his stays at Ischl.

Their friendship having attained a new level of serenity, Katharina surrounded Franz Joseph's old age with an affection which warmed his heart. Accustomed to a life of comfort, she set out to introduce a little of the comfort which she herself so enjoyed into the life of the emperor. She would give him a dressing gown, a bedside rug; or she would think to cheer up his study with flowers; when his doctors banned him from smoking Virginia cigars, she was careful that he should not be entirely deprived of this pleasure, presenting him with milder cigars to smoke. All those who were close to Franz Joseph at this time could confirm the importance of Katharina Schratt in his life at all levels. Ketterl, the emperor's last valet, remarked on his master's excitement when the actress was invited to lunch. In the few moments which preceded his friend's arrival, Franz Joseph could not resist rising repeatedly to tidy himself, or to brush his hair and beard.[2]

The Pressures of Nationalism

These moments of relaxation were all the more precious because, elsewhere, Franz Joseph's cares were increasing. The full consequences of universal suffrage had not yet appeared, but it was already clear that it would not be the panacea which had been hoped for by some leaders. Split into twenty-eight groups, the popular parties were incapable of forming a coherent majority. Nationalist feeling continued to dominate the parliamentary scene. The long-awaited general elections of 1911 did not bring about the improvement in conditions which had been hoped for. In these elections, the two parties which were most receptive towards a supranational view of the future of the monarchy even suffered losses.

Among the Christian Socialists there was no real successor to Lueger who had died the year before. Many of his lieutenants were beaten in the Vienna elections where a process was beginning which would ultimately lead, following the First World War, to a swing in the municipal vote in favour of the Social Democrats. For their part, for now, the Social Democrats were split by an internal crisis. Won over by nationalist fervour, the Czech socialists were no longer happy with the division of the party into national groups. Following the example of the trade unions, most of them broke away from the Viennese central administration.

The 1911 elections demonstrated the serious nature of the conflict. There were many clashes between Germans and Czechs in Bohemia, and following these, the deputies of the two nationalities sat in different groups, and would sometimes vote against each other. However, this crisis did not lead to a complete breakdown of the party. The wisdom of a number of the major figures in each camp still prevailed, preventing any official ratification of the split. But how long could they hold out for? Social Democracy was suffering in its turn from the general sickness which was eating away at Austrian society. Although the worst had been avoided for the time being, the party's capacity to resist the divisive force of nationalist feelings had clearly be diminished.

These internal developments within the Social Democrat Party provided the confirmation that the Bohemian question was still a major problem for Austrian politics. Most prime ministers attempted to formulate a compromise which would lift this weight from the political scene, but none of these attempts came to fruition. All were shattered against the barrier created by intransigence of the two sides. This was not to say that there were no moderate voices in either camp, but these were drowned out by those of the extremists. Successive governments were themselves out in their attempt to reconcile apparently contradictory demands: on the one hand the status of Bohemia as a unified province, which formed part of the Czech claim, and on the other hand, the German demand for self-rule in areas where Germans were in the majority.

These conflicts poisoned Austrian political life. They dragged on in the *Reichstrat*, where the German and Czech representatives pursued their quarrels. This tension in the German–Czech dispute was also integral to the composition of the Assembly elected in 1911. The Czech Social Democrats joined their voices to those of the nationalist parties; while in the other camp, it was significant that the Christian Socialists, who formed the Germanic group most sympathetic towards the multinational aspirations of the monarchy, made no gains among the Bohemian Germans, while the Pan-Germanists gained their best results from this group.

Reflecting these antagonisms, the parliamentary process continued to suffer from obstructive manoeuvres. Although steps were taken to impose a code of conduct on the members, this was not enough to restore calm. On March 1914, the last figure of the period to hold the position of first minister, Count Karl von Stürgkh, used this parliamentary paralysis as the grounds for dissolving the Lower Chamber of the *Reichsrat* and, following the example of many of his predecessors, he proceeded to direct the country under the special provisions of article 14. The lack of a clear majority also inhibited the government's powers of action. The 1907 electoral reform was the last major project which any government fought for. Mostly made up of administrators, the chief aim of subsequent governments was to avoid any further crises for the monarchy, rather than to introduce any initiative for reform in either the political system for Austrian society.

Hungary remained at the centre of Franz Joseph's concerns, but the worst of the crisis was already over. Franz Joseph would soon have the satisfaction of a Hungarian government which suited his own tastes. The May 1910 elections saw a complete reversal in the political situation, as Tisza's party gained an absolute majority, and Kossuth and his friends suffered a resounding defeat. Bolstered by this success, Tisza became the key figure in the new legislation. As president of the Chamber of Deputies, he managed to pass a law which called for an increase both in military spending and in the number of soldiers. In order to prevent any parliamentary initiatives for the introduction of electoral reform, he was not afraid to take a tough line against the opposition. Then, in June 1913, he regained his post of first minister. This strict Calvinist was a man of strong views, who combined a discreet patriotism with a belief in the union of Austria and Hungary which was all the stronger for being based on reason.

Tisza was admired by his sovereign, but not without reservations. Franz Joseph was well aware that Tisza's first concern was for the interest of Hungary, and that he had no respect for the imperial tradition. But Franz Joseph appreciated this Hungarian noble's loyalty, for he was not afraid to suffer unpopularity in order to remain true to his beliefs. His asperity and the strength of his principles made him a difficult man to deal with, but Franz Joseph was also aware that the monarchy could not afford to be without a man of his qualities.

But Tisza also showed intransigence towards the non-Magyar peoples of Hungary. They could hope for neither indulgence nor weakness from him. There was therefore no respite in the policy of Magyarization, to which there was a mixed reaction. The Slovak and German minorities suffered the most, while the southern Slavs and the Romanians were better able to resist the process. Taken in broad terms, this policy was successful. The ten-yearly censuses show that between 1880 and the eve of the First World War, the proportion of Magyars within the Hungarian population rose from 41.2 per cent to 48.1 per cent. But the policy also provoked strong reactions among the minorities, aggravated by the fact that it accelerated the process of growing national awareness and made it a political issue. The situation might have been more promising if the minorities had at least been given a voice in the official institutions of the kingdom. But in the Chamber which was elected in 1913, with the exception of the representatives from Croatia, which had enjoyed special status since the Compromise of 1868, there were only eighteen non-Magyar members.

In the course of these years, there was a hardening on all fronts. Resistance movements became organized, and unrest grew among the minorities subjected to Magyar rule. In Croatia, this opposition grew to the point of violence. There were assassination attempts directed at the head of administration appointed by the Hungarian government. As the government considered any questioning of the status quo to be an act of high treason, it reacted with the greatest harshness. Determined to crush this opposition, its reply was to increase the repression.

This intransigence could also be explained by the mounting international tension. This provided the excuse for the Hungarian leaders to justify their harshness by the connections which existed between many of the minority groups and foreign powers. They accordingly accused Romania of having a hand in fomenting the turmoil among the Romanians of Transylvania. There was no lack of proof, either, that Serbia was implicated in the troubles which shook Croatia.

The problem was nevertheless not insurmountable. Not all the minorities had been won over by separatist ideals. There were, for instance, many Croats who rejected Serbia's intervention, hoping for a solution to their problems within the framework of the monarchy. There were also many representatives of these minorities in Franz Ferdinand's suite. It was obvious that they would not be placing their confidence in the heir to the throne if they did not believe in the future of the monarchy. But although it was not irreversible, this sickness had nevertheless worsened. In the course of a few years, a series of powder kegs developed along Hungary's flanks which created a particularly dangerous situation, making the monarchy even more sensitive towards developments in the Balkans.

Balkan Storms

The series of defeats which the monarchy suffered in the Balkans increased this threat. This was the disadvantage of the annexation of Bosnia-Herzegovina, which in the course of time had turned out to be a hollow victory. Austria-Hungary found that it was constantly having to defend its actions before a combined front of states. Count Berchtold, who would succeed Aehrenthal, noted this problem in a report to Franz Joseph, shortly after he assumed his duties: 'We must not conceal from ourselves that the way in which we annexed Bosnia-Herzegovina has caused distrust of the monarchy to grow up among the governments of all the great powers, and has encouraged an unprecedented degree of agreement among them concerning their attitude towards our Eastern external policy.'[3] Combined with the defensive nature of its foreign policy, this discrediting of the monarchy benefited all those states which, while maintaining that their intentions were peaceful, planned to destroy the status quo in the Balkans.

This response began with the agreement concluded between Russia and Italy at Racconinghi on 24 October 1909. The two participating powers agreed that the status quo should be maintained in the Balkans, but their principal undertaking was to oppose any attempt by another power to change the situation. Only a year after the annexation of Bosnia-Herzegovina, it was clearly Austria to which they were referring. Russia was playing its usual role in attempting to cross its rival, while for Italy the signing of this agreement confirmed a movement which had begun in 1900. Italy's participation was also a reaction to the recent crisis, for it considered itself to have been deprived of the territorial compensation to which it was entitled under the treaty between itself and Austria-Hungary, in view of the latter's annexation of Bosnia-Herzegovina.

This agreement between Russia and Italy renewed the international debate over developments in Italy. Germany pretended that it was not bothered by Italy's flirtation with Russia. In Austria-Hungary, on the other hand, there was a conflict of opinion. Faithful to his new policy, and aware of the dangers which a break would entail, Aehrenthal wanted to avoid any move which might push Italy towards the Entente. On the other hand, Conrad von Hötzendorf was calling for strong measures to protect the monarchy from such a threat. The difference of opinion between the two men soon became worse. Conrad increased the number of his reports in which he hoped to warn the foreign minister of the increase in Italian military activity: at the same time he begged for reinforcements for the troops stationed on the monarchy's southern border. For his part, Aehrenthal considered these repeated interventions by the military Chief of Staff to be intolerable interference in matters which came under his own authority, while his underlying accusation was that they were a serious hinderance to Austro-Hungarian diplomatic activity.

At the pitch which it had reached, the conflict could only be settled by the intervention of the emperor. Beyond the individuals involved, this decision concerned two opposing policies, one which attempted to preserve the peace, and one which accepted the risk of war. It was hardly surprising that Franz Joseph opted in favour of Aehrenthal, after all, throughout his entire reign, his foreign ministers had never pursued any policy which had not previously been sanctioned by him. It was of this that he sharply reminded Conrad when he granted him an audience on 15 November 1911: 'These incessant attacks, especially these constantly repeated reproaches concerning policy towards Italy and the Balkans, are directed at me. I am the one who decided which path to take; this policy is mine.'[4] In this explanation which went straight to the heart of things, Franz Joseph provided the key to the ruling principle of his policy: 'My policy is one of peace. Everyone must adapt to this policy.'[5]

It should not be thought that Franz Joseph was nourishing any illusions concerning Italy. He was perfectly aware that his relationship with Rome had entered a difficult period. He knew that Italy had drawn closer to the member countries of the Entente, he was not blind to its interest in the Balkans and the lands still occupied by Austria-Hungary, and even recognized that a war with Italy was the most likely course of events. Given this situation, the monarchy would have been foolish to neglect its own security, and needed to ready its army for any eventual war. But it was still the duty of the Austrian foreign service to work to maintain peace. As a result, in the case of Italy, it was important that the ties which bound Italy to the central powers should not be broken, and this situation precluded any deliberately aggressive move. These conditions also prevailed in the Balkans, where the monarchy needed to play the role of moderator in order to avoid a situation in which a clash of interests and feelings might lead to a cataclysm into which it would be hard not to be dragged. Franz Joseph therefore made no plans to conquer new lands in this area.

This desire for peace can be attributed in the first instance to Franz Joseph's wish to end his reign without having to suffer another war. But, most of all, he had learned from past experience that the effects of war on any state are always destabilizing, but that in Austria-Hungary's case, there was an additional risk because of the fragility of the monarchy, which had been amply demonstrated by its internal conflicts. This led him to be wary of the temptation to use force. As a result of the intricate network of interests in Europe, and of its division into hostile political alliances, any war in which Austria-Hungary was involved would soon escalate. If such a war were to spread, there was no certainty that the monarchy would be able to survive the upheaval.

Franz Joseph's intervention in the quarrel between the two ministers led to Conrad's removal from power a few days after the audience described above. The problem which this dispute had raised nevertheless remained unresolved. This low-profile approach was not without its risks. It could be interpreted as a sign of weakness by the powers which were hostile to the monarchy, and might lead them to act in an aggressive manner, leading to the destabilizing of the Balkan political situation.

Franz Joseph's peace policy came under considerable strain. The war between Italy and Turkey which broke out in September 1911 was the first serious threat.

Although it took place far from the Balkans, and although Austria-Hungary was careful to prevent Italy from using the war as a means to gain a foothold in that area, Turkey's defeat was nevertheless not without consequences. There was a strong likelihood that some of the Balkan states would take advantage of the situation to raise the Macedonian question once again, and to attempt to drive Turkey out of Europe once and for all.

The war between Italy and Turkey did have the effect of hastening the development of a Balkan front directed against both Vienna and Istanbul. Serbia and Bulgaria set the example by signing a treaty on 13 March 1912, and Greece and Montenegro soon joined them. Austria-Hungary was one of the targets of this alliance. Under article 3 of their treaty, Bulgaria and Serbia undertook to oppose any attempt by a larger power to acquire any part of the Ottoman lands. As the treaty was signed under Russia's aegis, Austria-Hungary was the only great power in the area to which such a clause could apply. Russia's influence could be felt in this treaty. It had been preceded by a military convention which brought Bulgaria back into Saint Petersburg's sphere of influence. At the same time, Russia had built up a closer relationship between Belgrade and Sofia. This provides a measure of the change in the balance of power of this area compared with the 1880s, when Austro-Hungarian influence had been at its height.

Austria-Hungary was almost completely cut off from the Balkans; of the old alliances which it had built up, only that with Romania remained. Even this was not secure, for although King Carol in Bucharest still remained loyal, the Romanians did not support the alliance, becoming increasingly hostile towards the dual monarchy because of Hungarian policy in Transylvania.

At first, the monarchy had no control over the development of events. Count Berchtold, who succeeded Aehrenthal in February 1912, the latter suffering from cancer, would soon have to face up to the threat of war. The Turkish defeat was too good an occasion for the Balkan league to miss, to deliver the final blow to the Ottoman Empire.

When war broke out in October, Berchtold, under Franz Joseph's guidance, decided not to intervene. There was ample justification for this lack of action: before the monarchy threw itself into the dispute, it would be wise to await developments in the course of the war. This was especially true given that the alliance between the Balkan states was an entirely negative one, and it seemed likely that once the spoils came to be divided up among them, the victors would soon be tearing at each other's throats. In the light of this, having refrained from committing itself previously, the monarchy would be in an even stronger position to act as arbitrator.

The behaviour of the members of the Balkan league fulfilled Berchtold's expectations. Once the time came to draw up the new frontiers, the old Serbo-Bulgarian rivalry resurfaced. The clash between opposing interests became so acute that war broke out again in June 1913, but between different parties. Serbia, Greece, and Romania formed an alliance against Bulgaria, and the latter was soon attacked in turn by Turkey, hoping to regain part of the lands it had lost. However, Berchtold's reasoning contained a major flaw. By playing a waiting game, Austria-Hungary had been obliged to withdraw on the diplomatic front. For the monarchy, such a move had important implications for its policy, as it entailed a renunciation of any power to defend the status quo in the Balkans.

This did not mean that the monarchy was no longer capable of firm action. Although the preservation of the status quo was no longer the moving force in its policy, this did not mean that it would allow anything to happen. In particular, the Austro-Hungarian government had set itself the task of creating an Albanian principality which would block Serbian access to the Adriatic. Determined to deprive the Serbs of any coastline, the monarchy considered this to be an adequate reason for war. The Serbs would soon learn to their cost that these were not empty words. When, in October, Serbian troops entered Albania, Austria-Hungary ended its policy of restraint and called on Belgrade to withdraw immediately. As Russia considered that this matter was not worth a European war, Serbia was left with no choice but to comply with Vienna's demand. This success should not, however, conceal the fact that the monarchy's general score for these two years was negative. In concentrating on the Albanian question, Austria-Hungary had allowed Serbia to expand in other directions. After the Balkan wars, a greater Serbia was born, and one whose belief in its mission had been strengthened by its victories. There was no doubt that, as its prestige among the southern Slavs grew, there was a corresponding increase in the pressure which it was putting on the southern flank of the monarchy.

On a more general note, the monarchy's government must have been fully aware that its position in the Balkans had declined to a point which justified a reconsideration, at least in part, of the fundamental principles on which its Balkan policy was based. It had to deal with an increased belligerence on the part of Serbia, which would not forgive Austria-Hungary for upsetting its plans, and which, more than ever, considered the monarchy to be its sworn enemy. In the light of the events of 1913, the Austro-Hungarian leadership was also obliged to question the Romanian alliance. Although in 1912 Romania had renewed its treaty with the monarchy, it had still joined forces with Serbia during the second Balkan war. The monarchy might therefore be better advised to found its policy in the region on an agreement with Bulgaria.

The two states certainly had interests in common. In the second Balkan war, Bulgaria had been unable to resist the combined forces ranged against it. After its defeat, it had been obliged to abandon most of its gain from the previous war to its opponents, and it had also had to hand over the southern part of Dobroudja to Romania. Austria-Hungary and Bulgaria were thus the major losers in the Balkan wars, the former because of its loss of diplomatic influence, and the latter because it had failed to achieve its plans for expansion. Their failures and their hostility towards Serbia were natural grounds for an alliance between the two countries. Vienna was nevertheless careful not to push this too far, for fear of antagonizing Romania, which would be likely to make a firm commitment to the members of the Entente, if it were confronted with too close an alliance between Austria-Hungary and Bulgaria.

At the beginning of 1914, Austro-Hungarian foreign policy was steering a course between two contradictory lines, hoping to strengthen its ties with Sofia, but without breaking with Bucharest. While Austria-Hungary's behaviour was hesitant, the factors which would soon dictate the actions of the various actors on the Balkan stage were, by contrast, already firmly in place.

Unifying Features

These internal tensions and the deterioration of the monarchy's international position did not, however, succeed in destroying the Austro-Hungarian identity. Despite appearances, the fate of the Habsburg Empire had not yet been sealed. Parliamentary disorder, the atrophy of its institutions, and nationalist conflicts were certainly the symptoms of a major illness. But they should not conceal the continued existence of unifying features which countered the effect of the centrifugal forces.

It was no small matter that there were very few who actually called for the abolition of the Danubian monarchy. It was still considered by most governments as a European necessity, and more important, the majority of its subjects had no thought of an alternative framework to their lives. Although there was some middle-class support for independence, this had no influence in the countryside, and continued as a minor phenomenon. It was still considered to be the duty of the monarchy to act as a unifying force for the minorities of central Europe which were too weak to remain independent if left to their own devices.

This view was even shared by most of the opponents of dualism. Although they called for a basic reform of the existing order, they were still agreed that this should take place within the context of the Habsburg Empire. Some of those who would soon contribute to the destruction of the monarchy were at this stage unequivocal in their support for it. Who would have imagined that Tomaš Masaryk would be the future founder of Czechoslovakia, given the content of his final statement to the *Reichsrat*:

> It is because I do not wish to give myself over to dreams of the collapse of Austria; it is because I know that Austria, with all its good and bad qualities, is destined to survive, that I am taking the proposals for reform so seriously today. Our constitutional and administrative proposals are not intended to weaken the minorities, but to consolidate the edifice as a whole.[6]

The reforms which had taken place in the course of these years also tended to show that the problems of national rivalry were not insurmountable. For instance, in Moravia, the Czech and German populations came to an agreement in 1905 founded on a compromise over the principles of national autonomy and personal freedom. It projected the division of the Diet into two *curiae*, one Czech and one German. The voters would enter themselves on the electoral roles according to their nationality and would then vote for the members of one of the two *curiae*. The benefits of this system lay in its recognition that each nationality had the right to control its own affairs, especially in cultural matters, which were always the most sensitive area. It was perhaps to be regretted that it was necessary to seperate the nationalities in order to resolve their conflicts, but the agreement achieved its purpose. Intended to reduce the causes of friction between Czechs and Germans, the compromise satisfied both parties.

This compromise is also of interest because it was not the only one of its kind. It acted as a blueprint for the agreement reached between the Germans, Poles, Romanians, and Ruthenians of Bukovina in 1910. Its main concepts were also incorporated into the agreement between the Galician Poles and Ruthenians which was intended to end their differences. Unfortunately we cannot know whether it would have been successful, as it should have come into force in July 1914, and, overtaken by events, was never implemented. At least the positive results of the first two agreements provide encouragement for us to revise our image of an Austria condemned to collapse by its internal nationalist disagreements. They also show that these peoples both wished to and could find positive solutions to their problems and improve relations among themselves. Although these solutions may only have been local ones, it should be remembered that it is at this level, first and foremost, that relationships between national groups are defined. It is true that, of the lands of the crown, Moravia and Bukovina were not the most seriously affected by nationalist conflicts, but in Galicia, the hostilities between Poles and Ruthenians had been especially strong for a long time.

In fact, on the eve of the war, it seemed as though nationalist feelings were beginning to lose their intensity. A certain feeling of lassitude was beginning to appear in the face of the futility of these fights which often obscured other questions of equal importance, such as the issue of economic and social development. Although relations between the Czechs and Germans in Bohemia continued to cause serious problems, the general opinion was that, after so many attempts at reconciliation, the conflict between the two communities had become theoretical in nature, though this should not be taken as an indication that an agreement was imminent. A more relaxed climate was beginning to develop, although it was in its early stages and was naturally very fragile. Despite this, at the beginning of 1914, the worst was not inevitable.

Perhaps this relaxation of tensions can also be explained by the increase in economic growth and the corresponding improvement in the standard of living in Austria-Hungary which occurred in the final years of the nineteenth century. As is often the case, there is no evidence of a direct link between economic developments and changes in thought. But the time-lag between the two events is hardly surprising, given that it takes time for currents of thought to develop. It does, however, seem likely that the gradual maturing process was beginning to bear fruit on the eve of 1914.

On a world scale, Austria-Hungary always acted as a halfway house between the societies of eastern and western Europe. At the dawning of the twentieth century, only 32 per cent of its population had moved to urban areas, compared with 78 per cent in Britain, and, at the other extreme, 15 per cent in Russia. Certainly, the economic situation in Austria-Hungary still did not constitute a homogeneous whole. There continued to be large disparities between its active industrial areas and other areas verging on underdevelopment. The economic map of the monarchy had not changed very much. The only real change – although of considerable importance – was the development of Hungary as an industrial centre, especially in the area around Budapest, which demonstrates that the 1867 Compromise also had its economic consequences.

There was a wide range of expanding industrial concerns. On the one hand there were firms such as Skoda, whose reputations were international, and on the other, the smaller artisans, who remained an important part of Austrian industry. Although some of their traditional products were in demand not only at home but abroad as well, the trading sphere of many craftsmen did not extend beyond their small local markets. Nevertheless, the general movement in Austro-Hungarian industry was towards modernization. In this respect, it should be noted that the dual monarchy was not behindhand in exploiting all the most recent areas of development: expanding its electrical, mechanical, chemical, and pharmaceutical industries. Despite these disparities, the Austro-Hungarian economy was nevertheless a unified one. The monarchy provided agriculture and industry with a vast internal market of some 51 million consumers, whose needs increased with the rise in the standard of living. The traditional trading patterns continued: Hungary exported a part of its harvests to Austria, while the Austro-Hungarian whole produced mostly manufactured goods.

But the details of the economy were certainly more complex than this. Since the internal customs barriers had been abolished at the beginning of Franz Joseph's reign, products were free to circulate around the whole of the monarchy. The Hungarian political classes frequently demanded the reinstatement of these duties in order to protect national production. But these protests were mostly for the sake of appearances, as the benefits of free trade were greater than the drawbacks, and Hungary took full advantage of this vast commercial area of operations. Mutual benefit was also drawn from the special relationships between some provinces of the monarchy. The Viennese *Hinterland* extended as far as Bohemia, the monarchy's main industrial centre, which formed a single political body with the Austrian provinces. Vienna was also a major link in the movement of capital. The larger Viennese banks, the Creditanstalt, the Boden Creditanstalt, and the Länderbank, extended their influence over the whole of the monarchy, and were in part responsible for the financing of economic development.

In some respects, culture also acted as a unifying factor. In this matter, the arguments are complex. The basic question is whether national pluralism could be compatible with the affirmation of an Austrian cultural identity. Following the advances of the previous decades, the growth of autonomous national cultures, which were expressed across the artistic spectrum, was one of the major features of the period. Furthermore, in this phase of self-affirmation, these cultures placed great emphasis on the theme of nationalism. Literature, music, and painting each expressed nationalist sentiment in its own way. It is also clear that these various cultures did not grow up in a closed society, and they were often influenced by currents from outside the monarchy. For instance, before the flowering of their talent in their own countries, Benczur and Brozik were both influenced by the Barbizon school and were pupils of Courbet.

Was there any place then, in this situation, for an Austrian culture which transcended national differences? If, as Hugo von Hofmannsthal was to maintain, Austria should consider itself mainly to be a 'spiritual concept' (*geistiger Begriff*), linguistic pluralism was no longer an insurmountable problem. A whole range of proofs support this concept of a specific cultural domain at the heart of Europe, provided that we acknowledge that this culture did not grow up independently of the various national cultures, but that, instead, it absorbed their contributions, while feeding them.

This culture was primarily based on a common inheritance which had, as its main component, the baroque style, and its influence could already be seen in every urban landscape of the Danube. But, firmly ensconced as part of an agrarian and aristocratic society, it was not only an artistic concept but was also imbued with values which, in reaching out beyond the century in which it had flourished, had contributed, with other factors, to the development of the Austrian mentality. An aesthetic, and a way of thought and feeling, it was a permanent factor in the development of Danubian culture, and is essential to the understanding of that culture. Its earthy vigour can be found in the compositions of some of the musicians of the age, such as Anton Bruckner, the organist at Saint Florian's Abbey. Attracted by its sophistication, Hugo von Hofmannsthal took the baroque as one of his sources of inspiration, as can be seen in his *Rosenkavalier*; and its contemporary application could also be found in the art nouveau movement, in particular in the works of Gustav Klimt and Otto Wagner whose roots lay in the baroque tradition.

At its outset, this artistic movement was also supported by the government. Some Austrian statesmen hoped to recruit the services of art to exorcize the nationalist demons in the same way that they were counting on the benefits of economic development to help them achieve this aim. It would certainly be difficult in this case to speak of a Franz Joseph style, for the emperor was not involved in this initiative in the same way that he had been with the building of the *Ringstrasse*, and in the construction of the state buildings which are ranged along it. Furthermore, Franz Joseph was faithful to his tastes, and had no part in the daring experiments of art nouveau, but he at least allowed no feeling to colour his judgement of it.

This detachment was not shared by Franz Ferdinand, who was scandalized by the turpitudes of the works exhibited by the art nouveau painters, or in other words, the lasciviousness which they displayed. He was not the only one to object. Protests did not only come from the supporters of rationalism, but were also raised on moral grounds. These moral protesters were resisting a movement which, in their view, released the forces of uncertainty, and they soon persuaded the government to withdraw the support which it had previously lent to these artists. This ultimately had little effect for, even without official support, the style developed into a school and was emulated throughout the rest of the monarchy.

Once again the impetus had come from Vienna. This influence could also be seen in the urban landscapes of the monarchy. Even without the legacy of the baroque era, town centres still had a similarity of style which was not confined to official buildings, but could also be seen in the better residential areas. This was another sign of the existence of a common culture.

Franz Ferdinand

In all, the Monarchy was not without its strengths, but it still had to be able to withstand the challenges thrown at it. Given the size of the undertaking, there were some who suggested that Franz Joseph was too old to direct policies of sufficient scope to overcome these problems. Franz Ferdinand was certainly of this opinion. Although he refrained from expressing this belief in so crude a fashion, everybody was aware that he was suffering from the length of Franz Joseph's reign. His impatience can be explained by his fear that the monarchy was already living on borrowed time. There lay, here, a basic difference of opinion between uncle and nephew. Whereas Franz Joseph believed the monarchy to be too complex and too fragile to withstand strong measures. Franz Ferdinand believed that only drastic surgery could deal with its problems. The relationship between the two men had never been a warm one, and after the crisis of Franz Ferdinand's marriage plans, a rift developed between them. Neither would forgive the other's refusal to bend to his will. Furthermore, Franz Ferdinand considered the lowly status conferred on his wife to be a mortal insult.

This dispute also reflected a fundamental difference in the two men's temperaments. Franz Joseph was not unaware that Franz Ferdinand's strength of character only partly concealed a dangerous leaning towards violence. The archduke's behaviour when hunting illustrated this aspect of his character. Whereas Franz Joseph perceived hunting to be, first and foremost, a sport and a relaxation, on his hunting trips Franz Ferdinand displayed a sort of murderous frenzy. The impressive collection of trophies which adorned the walls of his residence of Konopiste in Bohemia, bears further witness to this disturbing aspect of his personality. This was matched by an distrust of others which was almost an illness, and which can be traced back to his youthful experience of the fickleness of the members of the court who, believing him to be on his deathbed, had turned their attentions to his younger brother. As though formally recognizing their lack of understanding for each other, uncle and nephew met only rarely. Franz Joseph, who found these encounters painful, hardly ever received Franz Ferdinand in private. As for Franz Ferdinand, the prospect of meeting Franz Joseph induced in him an unusual feverish state. However great his resolve to have a proper discussion with his uncle, the old emperor's majestic composure would always inhibit him.

It had never been Franz Joseph's custom to share power, and he was certainly not prepared to make an exception for Franz Ferdinand. For a long time, beyond his official military duties, the latter was only a figurehead. Despite the heir to the throne's impatience to become involved in government, Franz Joseph kept all political decisions for himself. As he had done in the past for Rudolf, he arranged for Franz Ferdinand to prepare himself for his task of government through a military training. This choice served to define the limits of the heir to the throne's responsibilities. It would be wrong, however, to attribute this choice of career just to Franz Joseph's desire to restrict Franz Ferdinand's power; it was also a reminder of the special relationship between the dynasty and the army.

But it was not only Franz Ferdinand's title which led to his rise in the military hierarchy, achieving the rank, in August 1913, of Inspector General of the armed forces. To the exercise of these responsibilities, he brought an enthusiasm and ability which were a far cry from the dilettante nonchalance displayed by many archdukes. He owed this enthusiasm to his soldier's heart, and this quality could not fail to please Franz Joseph. Convinced, like his uncle, of the army's role as the binding force of the monarchy, he differed with him in his consciousness of the importance of technology. He agreed with Conrad that it was a matter of urgency to modernize the Austro-Hungarian army. His influence in military matters provided him with the lever he needed in his attempt to be involved in political decision-making. Although the results of this were limited beyond his own field, in this specific area he built up sufficient authority for Franz Joseph to be obliged sometimes to accomodate his views.

Although Franz Joseph continued to hold the reins of power, as the years went by, Franz Ferdinand's shadow fell across the political arena. Despite the vigour displayed by the old emperor, there was a natural possibility that Franz Ferdinand might be called upon to succeed him at any moment, and political society was obliged to take account of this. Franz Ferdinand had long since built up a network of contacts in this area, but more importantly, he represented the hopes of many politicians and editors who criticized the activities of the Magyars in Hungary, and who protested that their influence was excessive within the monarchy. In accordance with his militant Catholicism, he kept in regular contact with the representatives of the Christian Socialist Party. Many members of the Bohemian aristocracy, with whom his marriage had cemented friendships, were also close to him. The network of Franz Ferdinand's contacts extended as far as Hungary, where it included the representatives of many nationalities suffering from the policies of the Hungarian government.

Highly placed within his inner circle were a Slovak, Milan Hodža, future first minister of the Czechoslovakian republic; a Croat, Josip Frank, the head of the party of the Right which had developed a policy hostile to both Magyars and Serbs; and a number of Romanians such as Vajda-Voevod, Juliu Maniu, and Aurel Popovici. The last of these, in particular, drew himself to Franz Ferdinand's attention. In 1906, in an essay entitled *The United States of Greater Austria*, he had sketched out the main features of a plan which anticipated the organization of the monarchy along federal lines, following the collapse of the dual state. He envisaged the creation of fifteen territorial units based on nationality which would enjoy a broad degree of autonomy on a basis similar to that of the Swiss cantons or the North American states, but which would be organically linked to the central power, whose authority would ultimately be consolidated by these units.

This group came to be known as the Belvedere party, taking its name from the archduke's Viennese residence. This group should certainly be seen as an informal one, and it would be excessive to consider the Belvedere circle to have been a real opposition party. It was certainly the case, though, that Franz Ferdinand served as a rallying point for a Greater Austrian movement, whose members believed in the future of a revived monarchy.

Although he was prepared to discuss current affairs, and to listen to opinions, Franz Ferdinand was careful not to tie himself down with undertakings. It would therefore be risky to speculate on the policies he might have adopted had fate not prevented him from coming to the throne. Such speculation should be all the more circumspect, given that his plans for reform changed over the years, even if the chief motivations of his thought remained unaltered. The first of these constants is clearly his aversion for the Magyars. The truth was that no Magyar could find favour in his eyes. He constantly criticized the Hungarians as 'traitors who fought with weapons against their sovereign and their dynasty, who destroyed their king and lord', and, in his opinion, they would be prepared to do so again.[7] If it was really the case, as he wrote to Wilhelm II, that 'the roots of all the problems which the monarchy has to face lie in Hungary', then it was logical to conclude that: 'If we want the Austrian monarchy to enjoy order and peace, if we want it to have the chance to follow, together with its allies, an active foreign policy which is favourable to all its peoples, there is only one means to achieve this, and this means is also an essential aim: to shatter Hungarian dominance.'[8] Such a declaration was effectively a condemnation of the Compromise.

For the Hungarians, this was the beginning of a difficult period. Although they had no precise knowledge of Franz Ferdinand's intentions, they knew enough of them to believe that once he was free to act he would clash with them. In such a situation, it was hardly surprising that they should reciprocate his hostility. Given the threat which his accession would have represented for them, the disappearance of the archduke was unlikely to provoke many regrets among the members of the Hungarian oligarchy. Many of them, heedless of any implications other than those which were immediate, would secretly hail it as an act of providence.

In contrast to this, the nationalities which suffered from Magyar domination were the objects of a very special solicitude on Franz Ferdinand's part. He remarked that to hand over a number of peoples, whose loyalty towards the ruling dynasty had never wavered, to the mercy of a national group which had often defied it, was not only a paradoxical act, but was a denial of justice. Such an act clearly risked the loss of their loyalty at a time when the international situation was becoming increasingly worrying.

Among these peoples, the Romanians in particular held Franz Ferdinand's attention. This interest was connected to the special position which he intended for Romania within the monarchy's diplomatic system. For this to be achieved, though, it would first be necessary to solve the problem of Transylvania. An alliance between Vienna and Bucharest would have no solid basis until the situation of the Romanians of this area had been improved. This is an instance of the close link established by Franz Ferdinand between the execution of internal reforms and the driving thought behind the monarchy's foreign policy.

This link can also be seen in the continued sympathy shown by him for the Croats. The military skills which they had long placed at the Habsburgs' service on the borders of the empire was the chief reason for their right to his concern. They also earned this by their hatred for the Magyars. Franz Ferdinand had not forgotten the role which had been played by Jellačić and his army in the fight against Kossuth's Hungary. But above all, he saw the liberation of the Croats from Magyar control, and their transformation into a new centre of influence, as probably the best way to combat Serbian aspirations.

Over the years, although Franz Ferdinand had a number of different visions of the new face which the monarchy would assume following his accession, all of these plans had the common desire to bring down the Magyars and to promote the Romanians and Croats on a political level. His first thoughts seem to have been of a confederation based on historical countries, with the exception of Hungary, which would be dismantled and divided into five bodies. After this, his attention was drawn by Popovici's ideas for a while, but towards 1908–9 he seemed to favour a tripartite system which would bring together all the southern Slavs of the monarchy. In 1911, new perspectives opened with the programme proposed by the head of his military chancellery, Commander Brosch von Aarenau. Brosch advised him to use the six-month delay before the new sovereign would have to swear to the Hungarian Constitution for the negotiation of a new Compromise. Should this fail, he would be free to take the decision to introduce universal suffrage and to create a cabinet which would be made up of representatives of all the kingdom's nationalities and, as a last resort, he could always use force, as Franz Joseph had done in 1849.

In all, Franz Joseph and Franz Ferdinand had very different policies towards

Hungary. Franz Joseph was capable of showing his strength and, if necessary, was prepared to stand firm in the face of a crisis, but only if the Magyars attempted to terminate the undertakings which they had made towards the crown. He refrained from taking advantage of the situation to impose a revision of the Compromise on the Hungarians, and in this he demonstrated that the main objective of his policies was to protect the status quo. Franz Ferdinand, on the other hand, chose an active policy which intended to go further than the Compromise, and this offensive strategy would make a confrontation with the Magyars almost inevitable.

Although they were less clear-cut, there were also disagreements between Franz Joseph and Franz Ferdinand concerning foreign policy. Contrary to a myth which has long been circulating, Franz Ferdinand was no hothead. In some matters he was even more cautious than Franz Joseph; for instance in 1908 he advised against the annexation of Bosnia-Herzegovina. Later, disapproving Conrad's warmongering stance, he declared himself to be opposed to the monarchy's intervention in the Balkan conflicts. Conrad, who was longing to take advantage of the situation to crush Serbia, had heard from Franz Ferdinand that he did not want to gain 'a single plum tree or a single sheep'[9] from the Balkans.

This can first be explained by Franz Ferdinand's belief that the monarchy should not allow itself to be drawn into an external conflict until it had sorted out its internal problems. This stance was further justified by other considerations. In his opposition to war with Serbia, Franz Ferdinand was not responding only to immediate circumstances. It was also his belief that it would be possible to reply to Serbia's challenge through other means than force. He believed that by introducing a reform which would make the Croats one of the pivots of the monarchy, he could also neutralize Belgrade's powers of attraction over the other southern Slavs. He must also have been aware that a conflict would probably destroy all chance of a reconciliation with Russia, and one of Franz Ferdinand's aims was to achieve precisely this, retying the knot which had been broken at the time of the Crimean War, and making it possible for the two powers to return to the understanding which had existed between them when they had faced the revolution together. Beyond this, he hoped for a broadening of the Austro-German alliance to include Russia, thereby establishing the solidarity of the three great monarchies of central and northern Europe.

It was therefore important that the monarchy should match its methods of foreign policy to this objective. In other words, while attempting to remove the threat of Serbia, this policy should not contain any aggressive initiatives which might provoke a violent reaction from Saint Petersburg. For Russia, as for Austria, Franz Ferdinand warned, such a confrontation would be the equivalent of suicide, for the bottom line was that such a war could end only in the destruction of both monarchies. The sole victor would be the revolution: 'Is it necessary', the archduke cried, 'for the Austrian emperor and the Tsar both to fling themselves from their thrones, leaving the way clear for the forces of the revolution?'[10]

Although they were in agreement over the basic need to maintain the peace, Franz Joseph and Franz Ferdinand did not agree on this last point either. The old emperor expressed his scepticism over the possibility of an alliance between Austria and Russia. Whatever importance he still attached to solidarity between monarchies, he was fully aware that the Holy Alliance was over. A call for a united front against the revolution was not enough to bring the policies of different states into line with each other. This would also require common material interests. In the case of Austria and Russia, in the relatively recent past, two attempts by Bismarck to bring them together had been shattered on the obstacle of their rivalry in the Balkans. Franz Joseph had no wish to conclude from these failures that conflict was inevitable, and that there was no other course left than to prepare for war. But, formally recording this possibility as a permanent truth, he felt that the foreign service should take account of this situation, and be careful to avoid any irrevocable step in relations between Austria and Russia, while remaining aware that any agreement between the two powers would be a fragile one, subjected as it was to constant opposing pressures.

The Assassination

The governments of Europe were therefore justified in their belief that the advent of Franz Ferdinand to the throne would presage major changes. However, there was no capital city in which this event was awaited with such anxiety as in Belgrade. Franz Ferdinand's plan to resolve the problem of the southern Slavs in the monarchy's favour made him a dangerous man for Serbia. In order to achieve its ends, the Serbian state was gambling on an increase in discontent in the states which it coveted. In order to speed up this process, Serbia itself was not afraid to send agents to stir up discontent and to spread pro-Serbian propaganda among these peoples.

The archduke's intention to review the relationship between Austria and Russia increased the peril, for Serbia would not be able to carry out its programme of territorial expansion without Russian help. All its dreams threatened to collapse if Franz Ferdinand managed to achieve a reconciliation between the two empires. Deprived of Russian support, Serbia would have no other hope for the future than to return to the orbit of the Habsburg monarchy. In short, it had to be admitted that if Franz Ferdinand were allowed to pursue his policy, it would run directly counter to Serbian ambitions.

In Belgrade there were those who were seriously considering taking the necessary steps to eliminate this obstacle. The initiative in this did not come from the government, but from the General Staff, within which some officers had formed a secret society, the Black Hand, which had almost come to be a state within a state. The head of the Black Hand, Colonel Dimitrijević, known as Apis, and his adjutant, Commander Tankosić, were not men to hesitate over the assissination of a prince, nor over its possible consequences. Apis had already been one of the instigators of the conspiracy which had led, in 1903, to the extermination of the Obrenović family. The members of the Black Hand now turned their attention to Austro-Hungarian dignitaries. There had already been a plan to shoot Franz Joseph on the occasion of his visit to Sarajevo in 1910. There had also been assassination attempts directed at the emperor's Croatian bans, and against the monarchy's representatives in Bosnia-Herzegovina.

Although they were in agreement that the southern Slavs should be united under Serbia's authority, the government in Belgrade was far from unanimous in approving the Black Hand's methods. But, born out of violence, the new regime could not afford to turn against those to whom it owed its power. King Peter and his ministers must certainly have privately condemned the aims and methods of the officers of the Black Hand, but they were too afraid of them to be prepared to embark on any course of action against these men who did not hesitate to use bombs, pistols, and daggers against their enemies.

It so happened that Franz Ferdinand had planned to attend the troop manoeuvres in Bosnia-Herzegovina during the last days of June 1914. At the beginning of June he seemed, however, to be hesitating to follow this plan. He was worried that he would not be able to endure the high temperatures which were customary in the area at this time of the year. Also, disquieting rumours which suggested that the archduke might be in danger of his life were beginning to circulate. On being consulted, Franz Joseph left his nephew free to make his own choice. Doubtless reluctant to be seen to withdraw in the face of the threat, in the end Franz Ferdinand made no change to his plans.

For their operation against the archduke, the Black Hand had drawn many young recruits from Bosnia who were prepared to lay down their lives in order to strike at the accursed race of the Habsburgs in the person of Franz Ferdinand. In their enthusiasm, they believed that the Serbian nation would greet them as heroes, and indeed, considerable national feeling had been aroused at the holding of these manoeuvres so close to Serbia's borders, which was seen as an act of provocation. It was again easy to arouse public opinion by pointing out that Franz Ferdinand's visit to Sarajevo, planned for 28 June, would coincide with a day of national mourning, on which the Serbs would commemorate one of the blackest moments of their history: the defeat suffered at Kossovo in 1389 against the Turks, which had deprived them of their state for several centuries.

After being trained in Belgrade, the young Black Hand recruits, among them Gavrilo Princip whose name was soon to appear in the history books, entered Bosnia, three weeks before the assassination, with the help of frontier guards who were connected with the society. All that it remained for them to do was to await the arrival of Franz Ferdinand, providing of course that their orders were not countermanded. There was a real possibility of this for Pašić, the Serbian first minister, eventually got wind of these preparations from agents who had infiltrated the Black Hand. It is in this matter that the problem of the complicity of the Serbian government presents itself.

It was certainly not Pašić's intention to have Franz Ferdinand assassinated. His minister, who were aware of the plan, also condemned it. Having said this, no effective measures were taken to prevent the assassination. The Serbian ambassador to Vienna limited himself to the expression of a fear to an Austrian minister that the archduke's life might be in danger during his visit to Sarajevo, but this remark was too vague for the Austrian to follow it up. Pašić's passivity can probably be explained by his unwillingness to enter into a contest of strength with the Black Hand. Or perhaps, like all the members of the Serbian administration, he was aware that sooner or later there would have to be a direct confrontation with Austria-Hungary, and it may be that this certainty helped him to resign himself to the situation.

Thus all the elements of the drama were already in place when Franz Ferdinand arrived in Sarajevo in the middle of the morning, accompanied by his wife. The inadequate security measures provided by the authorities, which can no doubt be explained by their concern not to antagonize the inhabitants of Sarajevo, made the conspirators' task all the easier. A first assassination attempt was made on the way to the Town Hall where the archduke was to be received by the notables of the city and the surrounding area. A bomb thrown by six conspirators who were spread out along the route of the procession injured two officers seated in the carriage directly behind that occupied by Franz Ferdinand and the duchess.

The matter might have ended there, but Franz Ferdinand expressed his desire, before leaving, to visit the two wounded men who had been taken to the garrison hospital, and this involved him retracing at least part of the same route. This would have been the moment to have the streets evacuated, but the only security measure taken was to avoid the centre of the city. Instead, the carriages would move along the Miljacke quay, thereby making a second assassination attempt more difficult.

It was here that fate intervened once again in the course of history. The first carriage followed the new route as it was meant to. But nobody remembered to notify the driver of the second carriage, in which Franz Ferdinand was sitting with General Potiorek, governor of Bosnia-Herzegovina. On arriving at the fork towards the centre of the town, he began to slow down in order to turn, and Potiorek, realizing the misunderstanding, ordered him to continue straight ahead. This lead to a manoeuvre which, for a brief moment, left the carriage almost stationary. This was enough to enable Princip to shoot at his target, hitting Franz Ferdinand many times. The Black Hand did not miss its mark, and added Sophie to its victims, for she, too, had been mortally wounded. Before losing consciousness, Franz Ferdinand still had the time to whisper in her ear: 'Sophie, my darling, don't die! Stay alive for the sake of the children.'[11] But when the carriage arrived at the governor's residence, the doctors were too late to do anything but record the death of the duchess. A few moments later, Franz Ferdinand also died. For the Austro-Hungarian monarchy, and for Europe, these two deaths were to be the first in an irreparable tragedy.

13
The End

It was not yet midday when the news of Franz Ferdinand's death was brought to Franz Joseph. His first reaction is revealing of his way of thought and his values: 'It is terrible,' he murmured to himself, 'the All-Powerful cannot be defied. A higher power has re-established the order which I had not managed to maintain.'[1] These remarks confirm that he had never been comfortable with a compromise to which he had been obliged to resign himself, but which he perceived to be a stain on the honour of his House. They also emphasize the priority which the dynasty had regained among his concerns. As the guardian of a higher order, Franz Joseph felt that he was guilty of having allowed its transgression. At the end of his life, he still viewed dynastic affairs in the light of the principle of the divine right of kings.

We should not expect Franz Joseph to have been as deeply affected by this event as he had been by Rudolf's suicide, and later by Elisabeth's assassination. On the day of the tragedy itself, Maria Valeria certainly found him upset by the news, but she guessed that he was not really suffering from it. When she saw him the next day, the previous day's emotion had disappeared. He was even pleased that he would be able to depend on the support of the new heir, Archduke Karl. His obvious affection for his great-nephew had always contrasted with the coldness which dominated his relationship with Franz Ferdinand. The tragedy was still too recent for him to be able to say more, but his calm manner was largely due to his confidence in his future successor.

The Ultimatum

Franz Joseph was fully aware that Franz Ferdinand's assassination had been a blow struck at the monarchy. Although until this time, he had always favoured a moderate course, on this occasion he found himself obliged to retaliate against Serbia on a serious scale as befitted the crime. Although he did not immediately have any proof of it, everyone guessed that the assassination had been planned in Belgrade. It remained for the nature, degree, and timing of his response to be decided. On this major issue, there were many conflicting viewpoints.

Conrad, who felt that his evaluation of the situation had been confirmed by events, and the minister of war, General von Krobatin, did not want to miss this opportunity to rid themselves of the threat of Serbian aggression. On the military side, the matter would be without risks providing, of course, that it remained a local affair. In order to avoid any international aspect to this conflict, it was essential to act as quickly as possible, especially as Europe was likely to abandon Serbia to its fate under the first shock of the attack, whereas once emotions had calmed, traditional divisions would come back into force.

The Hungarian first minister, on the other hand, warned against any precipitate action. Tisza had the opportunity to put forward his arguments during an audience with Franz Joseph on 1 July. He insisted that nothing irrevocable should be attempted until the Belgrade government's involvement in the affair had formally been established. It was also important for the monarchy to make sure of Berlin's support. His final argument was that it was important that the Balkan situation should be clarified before any move, or in other words, that favourable relations with Bulgaria should already have been consolidated to a point where they would compensate for Romania's weakness. All this caution can be explained by his fear of Russian involvement. It was also likely that, even if the conditions outlined by him were satisfied, Tisza would prefer to inflict a diplomatic punishment in Serbia rather than risk the hazards of war.

At the foreign ministry, general opinion was not far from considering Tisza to be overly cautious. This was a consequence of Berchtold's conclusions, set out in a memorandum written on the eve of the assassination, that it was now necessary for the monarchy to rethink its external policies along more severe lines. Analysing his own policies, he admitted that the monarchy had gained nothing by refraining from intervention in the Balkan wars. On the contrary, its enemies had exploited this to their own profit, while the international position of Austria-Hungary declined. For the monarchy, the problem was not merely a question of credibility. The almost total expulsion of the Ottoman Empire from Europe made Austria-Hungary the most likely next target for national grievances. The serious nature of the threat demanded that the monarchy's response to any future provocation should be a strong one. Emerging from its passive position, it would have to set itself to regain the initiative with, as its chief objective, the crushing of Serbia as the main centre of anti-Austrian intrigue. Berchtold was therefore immediately moved to defend the possibility of a military solution, even if it was obvious in his view that this should first be prepared on the diplomatic front.

Franz Joseph shared his foreign minister's opinion, and agreed that the public display of moderation on the part of the monarchy had had a negative effect, showing himself determined not to leave the crime of Sarajevo unpunished. This did not mean that he gave his backing to Conrad's plan. The time had not yet come when he would be prepared to make hasty decisions. But he was also restrained by the fact that he was not in a position to ignore Tisza's view. The distribution of power within the Habsburg monarchy precluded any decision which had not been approved by Hungary in so grave a matter.

Before taking any further steps, it would therefore be necessary to dispose of Tisza's objections. Although it was not likely that relations with Bulgaria and Romania could be clarified within a few days, or even weeks, it would nevertheless be possible to assemble the proofs of Serbia's involvement; and he also decided to investigate the intentions of the German government. This was the object of the mission of Count Hoyos, who was the closest of Berchtold's colleagues in the ministry, to Berlin. This step was all the more necessary because the German foreign service had not always understood Vienna's frozen stance towards Serbia and, during the Balkan wars in particular, had recently displayed a degree of distance in its dealings concerning the Austro-Hungarian position.

Count Hoyos brought a letter from Franz Joseph to Wilhelm II. His presentation rested on three points. Taking care to place the assassination in a general context in order to counteract any temptation to look on it as an isolated incident, Franz Joseph presented it as the result of a Pan-Slavist campaign which was directed from Saint Petersburg and Belgrade against both the monarchy and the Triple Alliance. His second point was his concern to demonstrate that the Belgrade government was directly implicated:

> The threads [of the conspiracy] can be traced back to Belgrade and, even if it is probably impossible to prove the complicity of the Serbian government, it cannot be doubted that its policy of bringing together all the southern Slavs under the Serbian flag must encourage such crimes, and that the perpetuation of such a state of affairs must represent a permanent threat to my House and my lands.[2]

The conclusion to be drawn from the first two points, argued Franz Joseph, was that it was clear that a decisive confrontation with Serbia could no longer be avoided. The seriousness of the danger, he assured Wilhelm, left the monarchy with no choice but to take the necessary measures to lance the abscess: 'After the terrible events which have just taken place at Sarajevo,' he concluded, 'you must be convinced that there can be no further thought of a diplomatic solution to our conflict with Serbia, and that the European monarchs' policy of peace will be under threat for as long as this centre of criminal unrest remains unpunished.'[3]

Franz Joseph's letter and Count Hoyos's mission achieved their aim. The Austro-Hungarian government need no longer fear that Germany might act to hold them back: recognizing that the fundamental interests of their ally were at stake, Wilhelm II and Bethmann-Hollweg left him free to determine Serbia's fate. They did not therefore raise any objections to the principle of a military operation. Furthermore, they did not conceal their preference for a radical solution and, given this, advised Franz Joseph to act quickly.

The assurances received by Count Hoyos, and echoed by the German ambassador in Vienna, could only serve to strengthen those who supported war in their discussions with Tisza. The position of the Hungarian first minister had become more flexible, for German support removed a number of his fears, but for all this, he did not join those who hoped for war. He remained convinced that the wisest course would be for the monarchy to be content with the inflicting of a resounding diplomatic defeat on Serbia rather than expose itself to the uncertainties of a war.

It was left to the ministerial Council, who met on 7 July after the return from Berlin, to make a decision. It comprised the Cisleithan and Hungarian first ministers, Count Stürgkh and Count Tisza, and the ministers in charge of 'pragmatic matters',

Count Berchtold, the minister of finance, the Pole, Bilinski, and the minister of war, General von Krobatin. With the exception of Tisza, all declared themselves to be in favour of quick military action, but Tisza's opposition still made it impossible to carry out the majority decision. A compromise was therefore reached, which discounted immediate military action, but which proposed the sending of an ultimatum to Belgrade. The Serbian government's reply would decide the nature and the extent of Austrian action. The debate was still not closed. The text which was to be submitted to the Serbian government would have to receive Tisza's approval. The need to accommodate him led to a fresh delay as time would have to be taken to devise an ultimatum and to discuss its terms. This was not all. Berchtold planned to create a file which would explain the Austro-Hungarian action, and would accompany the text of the ultimatum when it was sent to the other European governments. This additional delay was to plunge Europe into drama.

We can never be certain that if war had broken out during the first days of July, it would not have degenerated into a general conflict. It does, however, seem likely that the risk of a large-scale war would have been smaller. The effect of surprise would have acted in Austria-Hungary's favour. Faced with the *fait accompli* of an invasion of Serbia, would Russia have gone further than a simple protest, especially if the Austro-Hungarian army had won a quick victory? But after a certain amount of time had elapsed, each day that passed made this possibility less likely. Three weeks after the assassination, the situation had changed. The original cause of the crisis was gradually being lost sight of. As emotions died away, political logic took over once again, the powers collected themselves, and the blocs were re-formed. From now on, the monarchy's chances of avoiding European involvement in the crisis could only diminish.

It was necessary to wait until 19 July for the draft ultimatum to be discussed by the ministerial Council. This meeting recorded a shift in Tisza's position to that of the majority. Having reached the point of accepting now the risk of war with Serbia, he further became convinced of the necessity to impose severe conditions on Serbia. He did nevertheless make his agreement conditional on a solemn undertaking by the monarchy to renounce any territorial gains from its adversary. Concerned to avoid a broadening of the conflict, he believed that such a promise would serve as an argument against the provision of Russian military support to Serbia. It was agreed that this renunciation would be communicated to the powers when war was declared, should events reach such a pass.

The text of the ultimatum was then submitted to Franz Joseph, and was approved by him two days later. Berchtold, in his *Memoirs*, relates the impression which his sovereign made on him at this crucial moment:

> The emperor was fully conscious of the serious, I would even say tragic, nature of this historic moment... However difficult it may have been for him to take a decision which he must have known would have severe consequences, he took it with dignity and serenity, and gave, without hesitation, the order for it to be carried out.[4]

After Franz Joseph's agreement had been given, nothing could prevent the implementation of the measures which had been finalized by the ministers. The ultimatum would be sent to the Serbian government on 23 July at six in the evening. This government would have 48 hours in which to send a reply to the monarchy's ambassador in Belgrade.

The demands which the Belgrade government was called on to meet were intended to ensure the monarchy's security. But if they were accepted they would also have the effect of destroying Serbia as a political force. Serbia must for now make honourable amends, and must in future be prepared to take drastic measures to render impossible the continuation of any intrigue against Austria-Hungary, and what was more, all these measures were to be taken under the dual monarchy's vigilant eye. Indeed, the Serbian government would be obliged to condemn officially the propaganda campaigns directed against Austria-Hungary, and would have to recognize the involvement of Serbian officers and officials in these campaigns. It would also have to undertake to disband the societies implicated in these activities, to deal ruthlessly and with the greatest severity with those who might attempt such propaganda in the future, and to forbid any publication which might be intended to arouse hostility to the monarchy or to develop any Pan-Serbian projects.

Vienna also demanded a purging of the Serbian administration and army of any elements known to have taken part in these campaigns. As a defence against any sabotage attempts, Austro-Hungarian officials would be involved in the application of these measures. Lastly, legal proceedings would be begun against those implicated in the conspiracy. To avoid any attempt at a mock trial, it would also be arranged for Austro-Hungarians to take part in these proceedings.

The Move towards War

After Baron Giesl, the Austro-Hungarian ambassador, had handed the text of the ultimatum over to the Serbs, a two-day wait began for Franz Joseph. He called a meeting at Ischl for the afternoon of 25 July, which was to include Berchtold, Krobatin, and Bilinski, and which would discuss future steps once the Serbian reply was known. In the course of these two days, no news at all came out of Belgrade.

For Franz Joseph, 25 July began like a normal day. He entertained the duke of Cumberland and his family at his table, but in awaiting the news which might arrive at any moment, he had difficulty in concealing that his mind was elsewhere, according to Colonel Margutti's account.[5] Berchtold, who arrived at the *Kaiservilla* in the middle of the afternoon, found him 'preoccupied and nervous'.[6] This impression did not last for long, though: when he saw him at the beginning of the evening, Franz Joseph had taken a grip of himself, and no longer showed any external signs of worry, for in the intervening period he had received the Serbian government's reply, which had been made to Baron Giesl a mere ten minutes before the deadline. Belgrade accepted eight of the ten Austro-Hungarian demands, but not without accompanying this agreement with reservations which reduced its effect. But most of all, in refusing to accept the intervention of Austro-Hungarian officials on Serbian soil, the Belgrade government rejected the conditions which it considered to be a threat to its sovereignty. Judging this response to be insufficient, Baron Giesl immediately broke off diplomatic relations and left Belgrade without delay.

If Colonel Margutti is to be believed, Franz Joseph, on receiving this message, murmured to himself: 'the breaking off of diplomatic relations does not necessarily mean war.'[7] But when, shortly afterwards, he was joined by Berchtold and Krobatin, he showed no opposition to a process which, in all logic, must lead to precisely that. To his foreign minister, he gave the instruction to 'go all the way' if, after detailed examination, the Serbian reply was not judged to be satisfactory. He signed the mobilization order for eight army divisions there and then, in accordance with the plan which had already been devised for the eventuality of war with Serbia.

Unlike most senior officials in the foreign service, and the military chiefs, Franz Joseph had probably hoped for a positive response from Serbia, without really having any faith in it. After the assassination at Sarajevo, he had quickly become convinced that it would be dangerous to defer a test of strength. This was not simply a question of the honour of the dynasty, but of the very existence of the monarchy as a multinational entity. If Serbia were left to continue its undermining activities, it would soon become impossible to halt the progress of a separatist movement among the southern Slavs, and following their secession, the rot might then spread to the body of the monarchy. It was this fear which dictated Franz Joseph's confidence to Berchtold on 9 July, 'We cannot go back,'[8] and the words with which he dismissed his minister of war, having signed the mobilization order: 'Go! I cannot do otherwise.'[9]

It would be wrong to attribute these remarks merely to Franz Joseph's justifiable desire to be at peace with his own conscience. They should instead be seen as the sign of an internal struggle. Although he believed that he had no other choice but to cut out the cancer, he was also aware that the reasons which in the recent past had caused him to oppose a war still existed. The monarchy remained a fragile organism, and its ability to sustain a European war was questionable. Although his duty obliged Franz Joseph to commit himself fully, he could not rid himself of the forebodings which assailed him.

While more than three weeks had been allowed to elapse before reacting to the assassination, only three days now passed between the mobilization order and the declaration of war on Serbia. Tisza, whose reservations had contributed to the delay in the Austro-Hungarian reaction, had executed a complete about-face. In the belief that fresh delays would increase the risks of international involvement in the conflict, he now pressed Franz Joseph to act quickly: 'The slightest hesitation or lack of resolve', he wrote to him, 'would have a serious effect on any evaluation of the monarchy's energy and capacity to act, would influence our friends as well as our adversaries, not to mention those who remain undecided, and would have unfortunate consequences.'[10] Franz Joseph must certainly have agreed with this view, for on 26 July he approved the text of the manifesto 'To my People', in which he was to announce to his subjects the reasons which had forced him to declare war on Serbia, and would call on them to support him in this test. It was agreed that the manifesto would be made public on 29 July, which would be the day following the notification of Serbia that they were now at war.

On 28 July, the Austro-Hungarian government still wanted to believe that it could avoid an escalation of the conflict, but in fewer than 24 hours it would be obliged to reconsider its opinion in the light of events. For, on 29 July, Russia reacted to Vienna's decision by mobilizing thirteen army divisions against Austria-Hungary. This response confirmed the promise made by the Russian government to Serbia on 25 July that it would not abandon the smaller state if it became the object of aggression.

It must be acknowledged that the Austro-Hungarian diplomats had under-estimated Russia's possible reaction. Even if they were unaware of the exchanges between Saint Petersburg and Belgrade, they might have been warned by the rejec-tion of the ultimatum that Serbia had received solid assurances of support from Russia. There were certainly a whole series of rational arguments which could be made against Russia's joining the war. Its army had not yet managed to regain its former strength following its defeat by Japan. The events of 1905 had, in any case, set a precedent which gave Russia cause for concern. A new war might serve as a springboard for revolution, and threatened to imperil the very existence of the imperial regime. But there were also fears that Russia's reputation might be irreparably damaged if it were to allow Austria-Hungary to crush Serbia. As the empire had already failed to give its promised support to Belgrade in 1909 and 1913, it considered that it would be impossible for it to withhold its support again.

The systems of alliance were set in motion by this crisis, bringing with them the inevitable consequences. From the beginning, Germany had guaranteed its support for Austria-Hungary, while for its part, France would have the power to restrain Russia if it was prepared to announce that it would not become involved in a war in which its own interests were not at stake. But it had already intervened to this end in Saint Petersburg at the time of the Bosnian crisis, and it could not now afford to repeat this move without putting its alliance with Russia at risk.

The last-ditch attempts to draw Europe back from the edge of the abyss came to nothing. They had hardly got off the ground before they became the victims of the acceleration of events. Sir Edward Grey, the British foreign secretary, did indeed ask Austria-Hungary to content itself with occupying Belgrade as a security measure and to submit its differences with Serbia to the arbitration of the four great European powers. Vienna's reply, although polite, was nevertheless unchanged: hostilities would not cease until the monarchy had achieved the political objectives it had set itself. Austria-Hungary was rightly suspicious of the alleged disinterest of a tribunal of which three members, Russia, France, and Britain, were predisposed to be hostile towards the monarchy. In order to accommodate Germany, which had, briefly believed that the British plan offered a way out of the crisis, Berchtold was careful to present a measured reply: Austria-Hungary would not reject the process suggested by Sir Edward, but, at the same time, it refused to defer its military operations. In any case, with the Russian decision of 30 July to call a general mobilization, before the ministerial Council in Vienna had even agreed on the terms of its reply to the British proposal, this had automatically ceased to be an issue.

Following this Russian move, the scale of the conflict escalated. The race to prepare for war now dominated all other preoccupations. On 31 July, Germany's response took the form of an ultimatum addressed to both Russia and France, and of a proclamation of a 'state of possible war'. On that same day, Austria-Hungary in turn decided to make its mobilization a general one, in order to protect itself against Russian attack. Events moved forward inexorably. Having received no reply from Russia to its ultimatum, Germany declared war on that country. France had chosen merely to indicate in a laconic fashion that, should there be a Germano-Russian confrontation, it would act according to its own interests, which suggested that it would respect the terms of its alliance with Russia. As a result, Germany declared war on France on 3 August. For its part, Britain had never concealed the fact that it would act in the event of a German attack on France. The violation of Belgian neutrality, as part of Germany's execution of the Schlieffen plan, removed Britain's last doubts. The knot was tied when, following Germany's lead, Austria-Hungary declared war on Russia on 6 August. Franz Joseph accompanied this ultimate act with a symbolic gesture which was in keeping with his character: on the day that war was declared he removed from his breast the cross of Saint George, which had been a gift from Nicolas I in 1849 during the Hungarian campaign, and which he had worn on his uniform ever since, even when relations between the two empires were at their lowest ebb.

Franz Joseph had the satisfaction of seeing his subjects respond to his call. It had not been without some trepidation that the monarchy's administration had awaited the test of general mobilization. This now took place in a spirit of calm, and met with no resistance. Desertions were no more numerous than in other European countries. Even among the Czechs, who had displayed worrying signs of wavering in 1908, failure to respond was rare. Even better, the same signs of patriotism were in evidence among the monarchy's subjects as in the other warring states. It would be wrong to mistake the situation. The many internal problems which the monarchy faced had not magically disappeared. There was also a probability that if the war turned out to be a long one, this newly discovered unity would undergo a very bumpy ride. But for the time being, it was true that the forces of unity had won the day and that loyalty to the monarchy still had the power to bring together the different peoples of the empire.

The First Defeats

Franz Joseph could not find as much cause for satisfaction in the progress of military operations. On the Serbian front, the Austro-Hungarian forces were at a standstill. Three offensives were rebuffed by the stubborn resistance of the Serbs. Having been captured in December, Belgrade was soon lost again. At the beginning of 1915 the Austro-Hungarian troops had returned to their original positions. These failures can be partly explained by the fact that Conrad found it necessary to deprive his southern flank of several divisions which he needed to deploy on the eastern front against Russia.

In the confrontation with Russia, Conrad had not received the help which he had banked on from the German high command. Because the German plan required that they should first disable France before turning to the Russian front, German headquarters had concentrated most of its forces on the western front. To the east, plans had been made only for a defensive force to cover Prussia's eastern border under Hindenburg's command, and this army, despite avenging the disaster of the Teutonic Knights in a dazzling victory at Tannenberg, did not have the strength to support the three Austro-Hungarian armies which were subjected to the main force of the Russian attack.

The toll of the three weeks of fighting which had occurred in the Lemberg area from the end of August to mid-September was particularly grim. Most of Galicia had had to be evacuated. Through deaths, injuries, and men taken prisoner, the Austro-Hungarian army had lost a third of its force. Lastly, the backbone of the army, the corps of officers, had been decimated. The events which followed were equally disagreeable for the monarchy. A counter-offensive which this time included German reinforcements did not produce any results. Worse than this, at the end of November, as the Russian advance continued, Silesia and Hungary found themselves under threat. By mobilizing his reserves, Conrad did contrive to win the important victory of Limanowa–Lapanov between 3 and 14 December, which halted the Russian advance and saved the monarchy from further invasion. But he did not manage to swing the situation in the monarchy's favour, and after this burst of activity, the front settled down for the winter.

Franz Joseph clearly suffered from his army's defeats, but, accustomed to controlling his feelings, he greeted them with a stoicism which had been strengthened by the long series of misfortunes which had beset his life. Shut up in the Schönbrunn palace, which he now practically never left, he was kept informed by means of reports which were submitted to him daily, and he followed the progress of the military operations on maps. But he adhered firmly to the rules which he had set himself after the disillusionment of 1859. In contrast with his actions in 1866 he did not even attempt to influence events indirectly. Although he had reprimanded Conrad when the latter disagreed with the emperor's foreign policy, in the current situation he was careful to make no attempt to influence Conrad's strategic decisions and left him free to conduct the war for himself.

The Opening up of a Third Front: Italy's Defection

Franz Joseph nevertheless continued to leave his mark on Austro-Hungarian diplomacy. For the monarchy, the principal concern following its entry into the war was the attitude of those countries which had remained neutral, and foremost among these was Italy. In fact, nobody deluded themselves over the chances of Italy entering the war on the side of the central powers. In government circles, it would be considered a satisfactory outcome if Italy did not join the Entente. It was true that it had announced its intention to remain neutral on 31 July. But this announcement did not put an end to the question. It was to be feared that in making this move, Italy was merely establishing a temporary position, and it very soon became obvious that Italy was intending to make the most out of its neutrality.

In Vienna, everyone was fully aware of the seriousness of the threat which a third front would pose to the monarchy, especially as it was likely that Italy's example would soon be followed by Romania. In addition, the ministerial Council, meeting on 19 August to establish the monarchy's position, decided to initiate discussions with Rome over the terms of a possible agreement. This meeting was brought to a conclusion by Franz Joseph, who insisted on the importance of maintaining a measured tone in the negotiations.

At first, the positions of the two parties seemed hard to reconcile. Austria-Hungary would only consider the possibility of concessions in the Balkans or the Mediterranean. On the other hand, although they were not to be formulated for many months, it was understood that the Italian demands would involve territories under Austrian sovereignty: Trentino, and perhaps Trieste. In this matter, the Austro-Hungarian government dismissed the possibility of any incursion in the territorial integrity of the monarchy. Franz Joseph was categorical in this: 'I would rather lose everything and die with honour, than accept this odious brigandry', he declared to one of Wilhelm II's representatives.[11] Mainly dictated by moral reasons, this refusal represented the ethic, fed by feudal values, to which Franz Joseph would remain faithful to the end of his life. As it had done before the events of 1866, his code of honour forbade him to give up one of the empire's provinces without having drawn sword to defend it. There are also further political arguments justifying this intransigence, for if it were to give satisfaction to the Italian government, the monarchy would be creating a formidable precedent. Such a concession would place it in a delicate position in the future if it wished to reject similar demands from other states.

At the beginning of 1915, the Italian government considered that the time had come to increase its pressure on Austria-Hungary, which had been made vulnerable by its military failures. If the monarchy wished to avoid the creation of a third front, it was likely that it would have little choice from now on but to submit to the Italian conditions. On 11 January, the decisive step was taken. The Italian ambassador, the duke of Avarna, submitted a message from his minister, Sidney Sonnino, to Berchtold, requesting that discussions be opened 'on the possible concession of territory currently belonging to the Austro-Hungarian monarchy'.

Austria-Hungary's government had long been prepared for this move. On 9 January, Franz Joseph confirmed his refusal to Berchtold, and the latter passed this on to the Italian ambassador. But the monarchy found that this affair was not simply a matter of discussions with Italy. It was also to come under strong pressure from its German ally, worried by the threat of the creation of a new front. Germany showed itself generous with the possessions of others, for, although it had never been prepared to consider surrendering Alsace-Lorraine, the German government demanded that Austria-Hungary sacrifice Trentino if this measure would prevent Italy from going over to the enemy camp. Hoping to persuade Franz Joseph to reconsider his position, Wilhelm II went to the lengths of sending a personal envoy to Vienna. He might have spared his efforts, for the emperor remained firm in his refusal. In Vienna, this interference from Berlin in a matter which involved the sovereignty of the monarchy was considered to be unseemly. On the German side, though, there was already a certain degree of annoyance at some of the failures of the Austro-Hungarian armies, and there was little tolerance for Franz Joseph's obstinacy which, it was feared, threatened to compromise the central powers' chances of success.

Although the Italian demand came up against a blank wall, this rejection was not supported by all the members of the Austro-Hungarian government. The two first ministers were unreservedly in support of a firm course of action. Tisza was particularly vocal in this. He declared himself convinced that Rome would be quick to revise its demands if Germany were to change its attitude. He was well aware that a concession today over Trentino might lead to another tomorrow in Transylvania, at the expense of Hungary this time, if that were the price demanded by Romania for its continued neutrality. This intransigence did worry Berchtold, though. Fearing the consequences of a break with Italy, he advised that the possibility of an agreement should not be dismissed out of hand. After all, he argued, the essential interests of the monarchy were not in play in the matter of Trentino. Would it not now be wiser to accept its loss, so as to be left with a free hand in the Balkans? This difference of opinion was finally resolved by Berchtold's departure from government, for, finding himself opposed to the emperor and the two first ministers, he wisely chose to withdraw. On 13 January, he was replaced by Baron Stefan Burian, a Hungarian and a friend of Tisza, who, like him, supported a strong policy.

This substitution served only to delay the reckoning. Having unsuccessfully pursued a policy of intransigence, Burian was gradually obliged to retreat from his position, step by step. When the threat of Italy joining the war became clear, he, in turn, concluded that the best course would be to give up part, if not all, of Trentino. Tisza shifted position once again, while Franz Joseph finally resigned himself to the inevitable, but not without the rider, as in other cases, that he would not be prepared to make any further concessions.

This decision was finalized by the the crown Council on 8 March, but it was nevertheless not enough to satisfy the Italian government. In the course of its negotiations with the member states of the Entente, the Italian demands had increased. As well as the whole of Trentino, the monarchy would also have to give up the area of Bozen (Bolzano), Upper Isonzo, including the town of Görz (Gorizia), part of the Adriatic coast and a number of islands off the Dalmatian coast, would have to consent to the creation of Trieste as an independent state, and, lastly, would have to withdraw its interest in Albania. It seems unlikely that the Italian government really believed that Austria-Hungary would agree to this. Whatever it believed, when Burian submitted a series of counter-proposals which fell well short of its demands, but which did add to the original concessions of 8 March, it refused to consider them, declaring itself released from the terms of the treaty of alliance with the monarchy, and resuming its freedom of action.

This break can be explained for the most part by the treaty which Italy had just concluded in London on 26 April with the members of the Entente, who had not found it hard to offer it more than Austria-Hungary would ever be prepared to allow it. Thus, while the monarchy said that it would be prepared to recognize Italian ownership of Trentino, Italy's new partners promised it all of Tyrol as far as the Brenner Pass. In short, for Italy, the only advantage of an agreement with Vienna lay in the fact that it would save it from having to enter the war. But the wave of nationalism had now swept across Italy and, furthermore, Austria-Hungary, weakened by the defeats it had suffered in the past nine months, appeared to be an easy prey. When the escalation of hostilities reached its peak, on 23 May, with Italy's declaration of war, nobody could be surprised.

Faced with this new test, the peoples of the monarchy effectively displayed a solidarity which confirmed the validity of the upsurge of loyalty in August 1914. Despite an alliance which had lasted for over thirty years, they had always secretly considered the Italians to be their hereditary enemies. The Austro-Hungarian regiments engaged in this war, drawn from a variety of nationalities, would display an exemplary valour. The opening up of a third front also placed many areas containing national minorities on the front line. Under the threat of invasion, the Tyrolians had little difficulty in falling back on their tradition of self-defence. The southern Slavs, who had reason to fear the Italian plans for annexation, were also directly threatened.

The situation which the monarchy had to face nevertheless seemed likely to become serious. On the eve of the hostilities, Conrad could only provide a meagre line of defence. Even when reinforcements had been brought to the field of operations, the enemy troops outnumbered those of the monarchy by a considerable margin. However, the Italians failed to take advantage of this imbalance. Their advance was quickly halted, and for over a year, a. succession of offensives and counter-offensives to gain control of Upper Isonzo would make practically no change to the line of battle.

The Recovery of 1915

For Franz Joseph there were other reasons for satisfaction. On 2 May, a massive counter-offensive was launched in Galicia. This time the Germans agreed to engage their forces on his front on a large scale, bringing in their Eleventh Army, under the command of General von Mackensen. There was an immediate breakthrough. For many weeks, the Germans and Austro-Hungarians continued to advance. On 22 June, Lemberg was retaken; by mid-July the Russians had been expelled from almost all the areas of the monarchy which they had occupied at the outset of the war. The Serbian front also began to move forward again as autumn began. In six weeks, Serbia was put out of action. This success was again the result of a combined action between the Austro-Hungarian and German armies, and the Bulgarians.

The satisfaction of the monarchy's government was not, however, unreserved. Although, as a whole, the army had managed to survive the campaign, worrying symptoms appeared as 1915 progressed. At the beginning of April, the first Czech regiment surrendered to the Russians, practically without a fight. Could this failure be explained simply as the effect of nationalist and Pan-Slav propaganda? These certainly played a role. But other German and Hungarian regiments would also be affected, who had no obvious political motives. Few regiments, in the course of the whole war, would not experience moments of weakness. Whatever the reasons for this failing, the military authorities saw it as the sign of the growth of a spirit of defeatism in Czech public opinion, and considered it essential to place Bohemia under close surveillance.

Elsewhere, Autro-German relations suffered from the manner in which victory had been won. As much in Galicia as in Serbia, these successes were due to the intervention of Mackensen's German divisions. On the Austro-Hungarian side, the degree of the German contribution was not played down, but the part played by the monarchy's troops was treated by the Germans as negligible, and they suffered from this. Making no secret of the low opinion in which they held their allies, whose deficiencies they would describe freely, the German officers displayed a sense of superiority which wounded the pride of their Austro-Hungarian comrades. Mirroring this discord, at the top of the command structure, relations between Conrad and the new German generalissimo, General von Falkenhayn, were overtly poor. The two men did not only disagree on the conduct of the war. The autonomy of the Austro-Hungarian army also began to be called into question. On the eastern front, the Austro-Hungarian divisions had been integrated into Mackensen's Eleventh Army, and even more significantly, in October Mackensen received command of the armies fighting against Serbia.

This aside, the fundamental fact remained that, despite Italy's entry into the war, a spectacular recovery had been achieved. After the victories won during the autumn campaign, the monarchy's primary aim in the war, the occupation of Serbia, had been accomplished. To the east, not only were the Russians left with a very limited area of the monarchy's territory, but the war had now moved onto Russian soil. Despite German criticism, Austria-Hungary had demonstrated a remarkable capacity for recovery during the first two years of the conflict. The breaches which had appeared as a result of its considerable losses, both human and material, had been repaired. Since the outbreak of hostilities, five million men had been called up and armed. These results were a source of pleasure for the old emperor who, shut away in his Schönbrunn palace, had become a legend among his subjects, while millions of men were fighting in his name.

The Final Tests

However, 1916 did not begin well for the monarchy. As the Serbian front was no longer in existence, Conrad had planned an offensive which was intended to disable Italy in its turn. When he asked Falkenhayn to support his troops in this, on the eve of the attack on Verdun on the western front, the German general refused. This did not diminish Conrad's resolve, but he was now obliged to withdraw several divisions from the eastern front. He would not have been criticized by historians for this had he won a resounding victory, but because of poor weather conditions the launching of the offensive was delayed. Originally planned for March, it began only in mid-May. Because of this, he had lost the advantage of surprise. After a few initial successes, the forward thrust of the Austro-Hungarian troops foundered against the Italian defences. After more than a month of extremely bitter fighting, Conrad was obliged to call a halt to the offensive.

This decision was also brought about by the sudden turn which events had taken on the Russian front. Badly shaken by the attack on Verdun, the French had asked their ally to mount a diversion which would force the Germans to relax their hold. Launched on 4 June, General Brusilov's offensive succeeded beyond all expectations. Weakened by the loss of the divisions which had been moved to Trentino, the Austro-Hungarian forces gave ground at many points. What was more, the weakness shown in the previous year increased. Whole units were seized with panic, while Czech and Ruthenian regiments went over to the enemy.

These events certainly did nothing to improve the reputation of the Austro-Hungarian army in the eyes of the German troops. However, the Reich could not leave its main ally to be defeated. Germany was therefore obliged to throw several divisions into the fight in order to stop the Russian advance, and this move did have the desired effect. Brusilov's offensive began to run out of steam at the beginning of August, and one month later the Russian advance was finally halted. However, the toll taken by these four months of fighting was a heavy one. In the course of a few weeks, the Austro-Hungarian army lost 750,000 men, of whom 380,000 had been taken prisoner. The war had been brought back onto the monarchy's territory, where Russia had taken possession of Bukovina and the greater part of Galicia.

The flames now spread to the Carpathians. As was to be expected after the success of the Russian campaign, Romania decided, during the final days of August, to join the Entente. Once the Austro-Hungarian army appeared to be on the verge of collapse, Romania was not prepared to miss the opportunity to gain national unity. The Romanians found only a thin line of troops between themselves and Transylvania. General Arz von Straussenburg could only hope to slow the enemy advance, but he had considerable success in this, and managed to gain the time necessary to prepare for a counter-attack. Involving German, Austro-Hungarian, Bulgarian, and Turkish units, this attack, which was launched at the end of September, from Transylvania in the centre and from Dobroudja in the south, reversed the course of the campaign. Caught in a pincer movement, the Romanian army retreated before the blows of its enemy. Having first been forced out of Transylvania, it had to abandon Bucharest to the central allies.

Franz Joseph followed the progress of operations on the different fronts with mixed emotions. The anxiety of the first weeks now gave way to relief. After a moment in which it had been forced to bend, the army had not been broken. This satisfaction was nevertheless tempered by the realization that the weaknesses which had been observed in 1915 had not disappeared, and had in fact grown. These weaknesses were in some cases displayed by the troops, but in others they occurred within the command. For the first time, Conrad had to defend his actions, following the failure of his attack on the Italians and its consequences.

But even worse, on two occasions only German intervention had saved the Austro-Hungarian army from disaster. Nor had Conrad been able to prevent a restructuring of the division of responsibilities between the allies. Made strong by the increase in their contribution, the Germans first demanded and obtained control of the section of operations on the eastern front which had until then been under Austro-Hungarian command. Once this had been agreed between the two emperors, it was decided, at the end of July, that it would pass under Hindenburg's command, as the German commander-in-chief in the east. Out of consideration for the heir to the throne the group of armies under Archduke Karl's command remained outside his jurisdiction. But even here, care had been taken to provide him with a German Chief of Staff. But the Germans wanted more than this. The successive defeats brought about by bad co-ordination between the various fronts led them to the opinion that it would be necessary to create a supreme command for the allies, controlling all areas of operations. Despite Conrad's protests, the desire for efficiency led Franz Joseph to agree to such a measure. An agreement between the two emperors therefore proposed to place Wilhelm II at the head of all the armies of the central powers, a move which effectively placed this responsibility in the hands of the new German generalissimo, Marshal Hindenburg. The disparity between the Austro-Hungarian and German forces which had already appeared on the field had now been officially confirmed on paper, involving a reorganization of their relationship to take account of it.

Although the military situation had once again been rescued from failure, Franz Joseph was fully aware that the longer the conflict continued, the more likely it was that unrest and dissatisfaction would emerge within the monarchy. The splendid unity of the early months of the war was beginning to show cracks. The first problem was presented by the serious shortage of food faced by the civilian population, especially in the towns. The loss of Galicia alone, one of the main grain-suppliers of the monarchy, would have been enough to cause problems, but it was the additional ill fortune of the monarchy to suffer poor harvests during these years. Between 1914 and 1916 yields were reduced by a half. The effects of this dearth were not felt evenly across the whole monarchy. Hungary, which traditionally supplied Austria with cereals, was forced to keep its harvest for its own consumption, and although this move did not remove Hungary's problems, at least it protected it from the shortages which struck Cisleithania.

The continuation of the war also led to the reappearance of political tensions. The suspension of the activities of the political institutions had been accepted as a measure which was justified by the exceptional circumstances of the outbreak of war. Two years later, it did not meet with the same understanding. In political circles, impatience grew and there were many who hoped that the *Reichsrat* would quickly be recalled so as to provide the peoples of the monarchy with a forum for expression.

Bohemia was particularly affected. Having left the monarchy in the autumn of 1914, Masaryk had created a national Czecho-Slovak committee which campaigned for the unification of the two peoples within an independent state. With the support of some journalists and professors of the countries of the Entente, he worked to convince the governments of the Entente that the creation of a new order in central Europe would involve the destruction of Austria-Hungary and the granting of independence to those peoples still under the Habsburg yoke. This propaganda had not yet achieved its ends, for the European governments found it hard to imagine a Europe without the Habsburg monarchy, especially as they did not despair of breaking up its alliance with Germany. In Bohemia itself the response was still limited. The traditional political groups: conservative, agricultural, and Catholic, protested their loyalty to the monarchy. These declarations could not, however, conceal the existence of a general state of unease.

The Kramar affair confirmed this. Accused of intelligence activities on behalf of an enemy power, in this case Russia, this Young Czech leader was arrested and condemned to death. Were the charges brought by the army sufficient proof that his activities had been treasonable? For his part, Franz Joseph appears to have had his doubts. Whether or not the accusation was exaggerated, the most important feature of this affair is that it revealed a disturbing shift in opinion. Franz Joseph certainly saw it in this light. Unlike members of his immediate circle who wished the sentence to be carried out, he realized that Kramar's death might lead to an irreparable split between Czech public opinion and the central administration. This deterioration in the political climate was brutally illustrated on 21 October 1916, by the assassination of the first minister, Count Stürgkh, whose obstinate refusal to call the *Reichsrat* had brought him growing unpopularity. Indeed, it was because Friedrich Adler, son of the leader of the Social Democrats, had come to see him as the main obstacle to the resolution of the situation, that he decided to assassinate him.

Did Franz Joseph understand the implications of this warning? There was not sufficient time left to him to prove whether he did or not. He did confide at the height of Brusilov's offensive that he was resolved to begin an initiative for peace in 1917 if the war did not end in the intervening months. Would such a plan have been executed? Would it not have been prevented by his German ally? Or would his personal prestige have brought him success where his heir was to fail? Again, it is impossible to know. One thing was nevertheless certain: Franz Joseph had become aware that time was working against the monarchy.

The Death

In the course of these two years, there had not been any serious alarms over Franz Joseph's health. But those who were close to him realized that his strength was failing. This decline was not noticed by those occasional visitors who were struck by the vigour of his mind, and boasted of the sustained attention which he brought to his consideration of major matters. These two opinions were not contradictory. The strength of his constitution enabled Franz Joseph to continue to drive himself to exercise his role as sovereign. On the other hand, once he moved on to everyday matters, this effort ceased, and exhaustion increasingly took over.

Until the last days of October, however, Franz Joseph's state of health had not given serious cause for certain. But the signs of a relapse (fits of coughing, bouts of fever, loss of weight) suddenly appeared in the first days of November. The doctors diagnosed a return of the pulmonary congestion which had already caused serious alarm a few years earlier. The illness did not follow a steady course, and just before mid-November there even appeared to be an improvement. Franz Joseph had in any case done nothing to change the pattern of his day's work, although his great weariness was plain for all to see. Many of his visitors noted that he sometimes had difficulty in following their words. He would sometimes become sleepy, a previously unheard-of occurrence. It now cost him a great effort merely to move around, to sit down, or to rise from an armchair.

The improvement which was recorded shortly before mid-November did not last. Franz Joseph's health soon deteriorated to such a point that his death seemed imminent. During the evening of 20 November the doctors decided that the time had come to make the necessary arrangements for his approaching death. Franz Joseph nevertheless rose at half past three, as he had done since the beginning of the war, and started work as usual. After Franz Joseph had read through his papers, General Bolfras, his military head of household, made his report on the progress of military operations, as he did every morning. Up until this point, nothing out of the ordinary had occurred. But towards ten o'clock, the court chaplain appeared, from whose hands he received the sacrament. So as not to alarm him, the Grand Master at the court, Prince Montenuovo, had been careful to inform him that the prelate had been asked by the Pope to give him his blessing, for such a blessing should be preceded by communion.

By midday his temperature had risen to 39.5°C. Franz Joseph would not give up the rest of his work, although before completing his work for the day, he had been unable to prevent his head from sinking onto his arms on several occasions. Numb with exhaustion and fever, he finally dozed off. When Maria Valeria visited him shortly after his evening meal, he confessed to her that he was feeling very ill. Indeed, she must have been struck by the change which had occurred in the course of a few hours. Franz Joseph's face was burning with fever, he answered his daughter's questions in a suffocated voice, and was even beginning to have difficulty in finding his words. Shortly afterwards, when he wished to kneel down for his evening prayer, he did not have the strength to do so, and was obliged to remain sitting in his chair. After this, he needed the help of two servants to get himself to bed. Despite all this, he was still thinking about the work which he still had to do. When his valet came to receive his orders from him, he was still able to say to him, summing up a whole life in his final words: 'Tomorrow morning, at half past three'.

Franz Joseph now fell asleep. But everyone understood that the end was near. The time had come to complete the final part of the religious ceremony. Towards half past eight, the chaplain was called to the emperor's bedside to perform the rite of extreme unction. Franz Joseph expired gently and slowly, without any apparent suffering. Suddenly, he was seized by a fit of coughing, his body stiffened for a brief moment before falling back onto his bed. It was the end, and the death was recorded by the doctors. It then fell to Maria Valeria to perform the final gesture of filial piety, in closing her father's eyes.

The waiting crowd had been growing outside the emperor's apartments. In the funeral chamber, though, his friend of the past thirty years was missing. Shortly after nine, Prince Montenuovo had telephoned her to tell her the news, without providing any further details, but, with a consideration which showed the delicacy of his character, Karl, who was aware of the depth of affection which existed between his great-uncle and Katharina Schratt, soon requested that she come to the palace. When she arrived, the new sovereign himself accompanied her to where Franz Joseph's mortal remains were lying. There, with a last gesture of tenderness, Katharine placed two white roses, which had been grown in the Gloriettegasse greenhouse, between the hands of the deceased.

Tradition decreed that nine days had to pass before Franz Joseph could be laid in his final resting place. For his last journey, Franz Joseph was dressed in the state uniform of a *Feldmarschall* – a white tunic and red trousers, with gold trimmings. On the tunic the insignia of the Order of the Golden Fleece and the other crosses which he used to wear regularly were pinned. Thus, even in death, his special relationship with his army continued. For several days, his subjects could visit him as he lay on his camp bed. But with the transfer of his body to the Hofburg, he lay in state in the splendour expected of a state funeral. Franz Joseph's remains were displayed on a catafalque in the court chapel, surrounded by a mass of bouquets and wreaths. For a further three days, the Viennese people were able to file past to pay their last respects to their monarch.

On 30 November the pomp of the Habsburgs was paraded for the last time at the funeral service. Drawn by eight black horses, the hearse was preceded by carriages filled with wreaths, and by barouches in which the highest court dignitaries sat. There then followed the procession of carriages which contained the members of the imperial family and the foreign princes who were staying in Vienna. In their dress uniforms, the mounted guard escorted the deceased in this final progress through his capital, along the *Ringstrasse*, and then across the ancient city to Saint Stephen's Cathedral. After the funeral service, the funeral cortège covered the few hundred metres to the Capuchin crypt on foot.

The Grand Master of the court and the abbot then began the ritual dialogue which had to precede the entry of the Habsburg sovereigns into their final home, a dialogue in which temporal power bowed before the glory of God:

'Who are you? Who asks to enter here?'

'I am his Majesty the emperor of Austria, king of Hungary.

I am the Emperor Franz Joseph, Apostolic king of Hungary, king of Bohemia, king of Jerusalem, grand prince of Transylvania, grand duke of Tuscany and of Cracow, duke of Lorraine and of Salzburg ...'

'I do not know him. Who asks to enter here?'

Only when, on his knees, Prince Montenuovo began again: 'I am Franz Joseph, a poor sinner, and I beg God for mercy,' did the voice behind the door give permission to enter: 'Enter, then.'

When the heavy door opened, Franz Joseph had finally reached the end of his pilgrimage on earth. Handed into the care of the Capuchin brothers, he could now rest, in the midst of his ancestors, beside Elisabeth and Rudolf, to await the accomplishment of God's will.

Conclusion

The sixty-eight years of Franz Joseph's reign were marked by a series of impressive changes which affected the whole of political, economic, social, and cultural life. Although they appear to be separate phenomena, these changes were in fact closely linked. Over the years, undercurrents developed which bore Franz Joseph away from the world in which he had been brought up. After its swan-song during the first ten years of his reign, the age of absolutism was ended forever and the monarchy adopted the constitutional forms of a representative regime. Austria, even more than Hungary, had entered the era of the people, and this was reflected in the development of new ideas and in the appearance of modern political parties whose chief concern was with the masses. Even though in 1914 the dual monarchy was noticeably trailing behind the great economic powers of the period, profound changes had nevertheless taken place within its borders. Feudal society had not disappeared completely with the abolition of the feudal system, but the old aristocracy was increasingly losing its influence. Although the majority of the population still lived in the country and continued to work on the land, industrial centres had been created in many areas. This industrial growth was matched by a process of urbanization which brought about a transformation in the urban landscape. The prime example of this is Vienna, the chief city of the monarchy and the imperial residence, which in the course of sixty or so years, increased in size from 430,000 inhabitants to over two million.

These changes cannot be dissociated from the developments which had taken place in the field of science and technology, which had begun to loosen the constraints of distance and of time. Whereas at the outset of the reign, horseback and riverboat were by far the most common means of transport, there being only a few stretches of railway in existence, by 1914 Austria-Hungary had been covered by a network of 44,000 kilometres of track. By this time, the motor car was becoming important, and the turn of the aeroplane would soon come. In this same period, spectacular inventions revolutionized the communications system, with the appearance of the telephone, the phonograph, and the cinema. Last, and not least, all these material changes served to introduce ideas and values which must certainly have been unfamiliar to Franz Joseph.

Could the exceptional length of his reign be said to have had a destructive effect on the monarchy? It is certainly a possibility. If we follow this idea through to its logical conclusion, we may even question whether Franz Joseph himself was not partly responsible for the collapse of his empire, which occurred, after all, only two years after his death. It soon became apparent that his way of thought was far removed from the values and fundamental ideas of the age, and this distance increased with time. This would mean that the main criticism to be levelled at Franz Joseph is that he placed himself in the way of positive development, adopting policies which were unsuited to the challenges faced by the monarchy and which could even be described as resolutely opposed to progress. In particular, he has been criticized for having allowed the negative effects of dualism to develop through his refusal to review the 1867 Compromise with Hungary. Rather than averting the dangers which had grown up as a result of nationalist rivalries, his adherence to dualism instead increased them. The freedom of action granted to the Magyars in Hungary, who were beyond any real control from Vienna, would, according to this argument, have served to exacerbate these emotions to the point that they endangered the very existence of the Habsburg monarchy as a whole.

Seen in this light, Franz Joseph's empire would soon have turned into the Cacania described by Robert Musil. No longer able to maintain their central position, it could be argued that the authorities instead attempted to halt the march of time. According to this hypothesis, Franz Joseph followed the example of his grandfather, Franz I, fearing that to move any one of his pieces would result in the entire structure of the monarchy tumbling down. But, by refusing to accept change, the Austro–Hungarian monarchy would have become no more than a state 'which continued to exist only through force of habit.'[1]

However fruitful it may be, such an interpretation of events does not fully take into account what we know about Franz Joseph. Certainly, during his life as sovereign, political failures and military defeats were more common than victories. But it is nevertheless hard to restrict our view of him to the picture of an emperor afflicted by an inability to act. Although his dominant characteristics developed early, this does not oblige us to conclude that he was incapable of change. In many instances, he displayed an ability to adapt to new situations. He had long been accustomed to having to make quick decisions, and indeed some of these which had not been sufficiently thought out would sometimes miss their mark. In certain cases, these adaptations took the form of real about-turns, and this can best be illustrated by his policies concerning Hungary. At the beginning of the reign the Hungarians were perceived as rebels, then they were not only redeemed by the 1867 Compromise, but were also given a privileged position in the dual monarchy. The transition from neo-absolutism to a constitutional regime, initially under a single monarchy and then under the dual state, also demonstrates Franz Joseph's ability to accept change, all the more so because these choices ran counter to his deepest beliefs. Even at the end of his life, he continued to be active in promoting the plan for universal suffrage, in opposition to the views of the majority of the official classes.

It is true that these final decades of his reign taught Franz Joseph to exercise a greater degree of caution concerning sudden changes of policy. He increasingly adopted a policy of gradual change which could be seen at its zenith during Taaffe's administration. Once he had lost the vigour of youth, he introduced greater moderation in his behaviour. But, above all, once he was no longer restricted by a systematic approach, he developed a more pragmatic attitude. This was certainly in no way spectacular and may have been lacking in brilliance but, on the basis of his own experience, Franz Joseph concluded that it was the only policy which was appropriate to the heterogeneous structure of the monarchy.

There remains the problem of relations with Hungary after 1867. Here it is impossible to defend Franz Joseph against the accusation of non-activity. After concluding the agreement with Hungary, he insisted on adhering to it loyally, and was never prepared to agree to reconsider it. Although he was opposed to attempts by the Magyars to reduce the relationship between Austria and Hungary to a simple personal union, neither did he seize on any of the opportunities open to him to go back on the transfer of power which had been conceded in 1867. It is incontestable that these choices had a damaging effect on the minorities under Magyar rule. They also probably did long-term damage to the monarchy. But they did not result from an inability to accept change. They should instead be understood as a reaction to the disappointments of the first two decades of the reign. From the fumblings and failures of these years, Franz Joseph had learned that it would be impossible for the monarchy to achieve any enduring internal administrative structure without a settlement with Hungary. After 1867, he remained loyal to the terms of the Compromise, which recognized Hungary as one of the main rallying points of the monarchy. He was all the more respectful of these terms because dualism provided his empire with a stability which it had not enjoyed since 1848. This is not to say that he was blind to the imperfections of the dual system. But, knowing from experience how fragile the balance of power which it created actually was, he feared that in questioning it, he would set loose devils which he would be unable to control.

We should not lose sight of the fact that dualism did not resolve the problem of nationalism, and it should be borne in mind that, the nationalities which made up Cisleithania cannot be placed in the same category as the minority groups under the rule of Budapest. The Compromise certainly affected their relations with Vienna, but the policies of the Austrian government did not restrict their national development. They had come a long way since 1848. Among these peoples, elites had been formed or had been strengthened, and these played an increasing role in the different fields of Austrian activity. They spoke in assemblies from the commune to the *Reichsrat*, were given responsible positions in the local executives, had established a presence in the universities, and expressed themselves through the arts. The validity of this advance was not counteracted by the crises which shook the monarchy as a result of nationalist claims or worries. It would even be possible to assert without paradox that in many respects, it was precisely this development which led to such conflicts. In any case, we can no longer be satisfied with the simplified and polemic image of Austria as the 'prison of the peoples'.

Whatever the final assessment of his reign may be, Franz Joseph remains the most popular of all Austrian sovereigns, along with Maria Theresa. The legend which had already grown up around him during his lifetime has endured to the present day. A degree of nostalgia can certainly be seen in the continuation of this myth. This may possibly have been brought about by regrets for a lost youth on the part of some, for instance Joseph Roth, one of the major contributors to the myth in works such as

Radetzky's March and *The Capuchin Crypt*. Roth confided to a Vienna newspaper in 1935: 'All the Austrian emperors are my emperors. But Franz Joseph is my personal emperor, the emperor of my childhood. This is why, when I have the good fortune to return to Austria, I make a pilgrimage to the Capuchin crypt to salute my emperor.'[2] Another characteristic which is often associated with Franz Joseph's reign is that of stability. Despite the wars, the internal crises, the nationalist passions, and the disparity in living conditions, when we look on it through the legend, this period becomes 'the golden age of security', described by Stefan Zweig. Despite technical innovations, daily life still preserved the traditional rhythms which contrast with the rapid onslaught of progress in subsequent decades. But, primarily, this idealization should be understood as a reaction, whether conscious or not, to the many upheavals experienced by central Europe after 1918.

Above all, Franz Joseph was the majestic embodiment of a particular view of the monarchy. Had he not himself described himself as 'the last monarch of the old school'?[3] Although his pragmatism convinced him that it was necessary to make certain concessions to the spirit of the times, through all the length of his reign, he retained a deep scepticism towards constitutional forms of power. While displaying respect for his obligations in both Austria and Hungary, he had still retained a great degree of personal autonomy in the areas which he considered most important. In addition, as the inheritor of the most ancient European dynasty, and successor to the rulers of the Holy Roman Empire, Franz Joseph was surrounded by an aura of majesty which affected those who came into direct contact with him, as it did his most distant subjects.

There would be no exaggeration in saying that a real cult of the monarch grew up around Franz Joseph after he had reached maturity. The scrupulous con-scientiousness which he brought to his role as sovereign, even when his strength failed him, clearly had much to do with this. The long series of misfortunes which befell his family also contributed to it. But, above all, in the execution of his official duties, he was always clothed in a grandeur which set him apart from the rest of society, from the most humble to the most elevated of his subjects. Convinced that in keeping his distance, he increased the prestige of the monarch, his public behaviour was dictated by political considerations. The strict respect of court ceremony and the pomp of the Habsburgs were part of the same intention. Although the resulting constraints were often heavy, and he often had to pay a price in solitude, he achieved his objectives in this.

The paradox remains that this cult was based on a sovereign who had no excep-tional gifts. The main points in his favour were his sense of duty, his knowledge of affairs, and the experience he had acquired over the years. But Franz Joseph did not dominate his century in the same way as Napoleon or Bismarck. He possessed neither the genius of an empire builder, nor that of a strategist. Furthermore, beyond his official functions, his way of life and his tastes were simple, to the point of banality, and this contradiction was very evident. The relationship between Franz Joseph and his subjects was double in character. On the one hand, Franz Joseph clearly served as an example to them, but the terms of the relationship could often be reversed. As the monarchy's first bureaucrat, Franz Joseph reflected the charac-teristics and values of the servants of the state and this mirror image did not escape the writers of the time. When, in Roth's *Radetzky's March*, Franz Joseph and Baron von Trotta are brought face to face by the author, this is taken to such an extreme that the reader is obliged to question which is the double of the other.

Franz Joseph's fate was nevertheless of tragic proportions. His prestige held together the 50 million subjects who made up the eleven peoples under Habsburg rule, but these peoples were also filled with conflicting tensions, and influenced by centrifugal forces. Franz Joseph's empire provides the supreme example of a battle-ground between two conflicting ideologies and cultures: on the one hand, the multinational state, inheriting a long tradition which, through the Holy Roman Empire, could be traced back to ancient Rome, and on the other, the nation-state, inspired by the spirit of nationalism which was the moving force of the nineteenth century, and which completely transformed the map of Europe. In this con-frontation, the fate of the monarchy was sealed. As the years went by, and Franz Joseph suffered fresh ordeals, the struggle became more bitter and less certain. The acute sensitivity which Franz Joseph developed towards the vulnerability of his empire in the face of the nationalist advance largely provides an explanation of his policies. But in this fight we can also see the seeds of the upheavals which would radically transform the face of Europe, of the dramas whose consequences can still be felt. In this, should we not look on Franz Joseph's Austria as 'the experimental laboratory', to borrow Karl Kraus's image, for the decline of Europe?

Notes

NOTES TO CHAPTER 1

1 See Franz Herre, *Kaiser Franz Joseph von Österreich. Sein Leben-Seine Zeit*, Cologne, 1978, p. 29.

NOTES TO CHAPTER 2

1 See Jacques Droz, *L'Europe centrale. Evolution historique de l'idée de Mitteleuropa*, Paris, 1960, p. 43.
2 Charles Sealsfield, *Austria as it is: or Sketches of Continental Courts*, 1828.
3 Haus-, Hof- und Staatsarchiv (HHStA), Vienna, Familienurkunde Mr. 2347B, fols 1–2.

NOTES TO CHAPTER 3

1 See Droz, *L'Europe centrale. Evolution historique de l'idée de Mitteleuropa*, p. 67, letter from Františec Palacký to the Commission of Fifty.
2 Haus-, Hof- und Staatsarchiv (HHStA), bequest of the Archduchess Sophie, *Diary*, 13–15 March 1848.
3 Ibid., 19 March 1848.
4 Ibid., 25 March 1848.
5 Franz Schnürer (ed.), *Briefe Kaiser Franz Josephs I an seine Mutter 1838–1872*, Munich, 1930, p. 88, Bozen, 27 April 1848.
6 Ibid., p. 93, Verona, 6 May, 1848.
7 Ibid., p. 97, Verona, 11 May, 1848.
8 Ibid., pp. 102–3, Verona, 21 May 1848.
9 See Victor-L. Tapie, *Monarchie et Peuples du Danube*, Paris, 1969, p. 305.
10 See E. C. Corti, *Vom Kind zum Kaiser, Kindheit und erste Jugend Kaiser Franz Josephs I, und seiner Geschwister*, Graz, Salzburg, Vienna, 1950, p. 308.
11 See Heinrich Ritter von Srbik, *Deutsche Einheit*, Munich, 1935–42, vol. I, p. 389.

12   See Rudolf Kiszling, *Fürst Felix Schwarzenberg: der politische Lehrmeister Kaiser Franz Josephs*, Graz, Cologne, 1942, p. 52.
13   Archduchess Sophie, *Diary*, 2 December 1848.

NOTES TO CHAPTER 4

1   See Joseph Redlich, *Kaiser Franz Joseph von Österreich*, Berlin, 1928, p. 60.
2   Archduchess Sophie, *Diary*, 7 January 1849.
3   Archduchess Sophie, *Diary*, 6 May 1849.
4   Schnürer, *Briefe Kaiser Franz Josephs I*, p. 126, Schönbrunn, 28 August 1849.
5   See Paul Müller, *Feldmarschall Fürst Windischgraetz. Revolution und Gegenrevolution in Österreich*, Vienna, Leipzig, 1934, p. 199, letter from Windischgraetz to Prince Felix Schwarzenberg, 15 January 1849.
6   See Heinrich Friedjung, *Österreich von 1848–1860*, Stuttgart, Berlin, 1908–12, vol. I, p. 148.
7   See E. C. Corti, *Mensch und Herrscher. Wege und Schicksale Kaiser Franz Josephs I. zwischen Thronbesteigung und Berliner Kongress*, Graz, Vienna, 1952, p. 24, letter from Prince Windischgraetz to Franz Joseph, Olmütz, 17 April, 1849.
8   See R. Kiszling, *Fürst Felix Schwarzenberg: der politische Lehrmeister Kaiser Franz Josephs*, Graz, Cologne, 1952, pp. 169–70.
9   See Josef Karl Mayr (ed.), *Das Tagebuch des Polizeiministers Kempen von 1848 bis 1859*, Graz, Vienna, Leipzig, 1931, p. 204, 12 March 1851.
10   See Srbik, *Deutsche Einheit*, vol. II, pp. 80–91.
11   Count Friedrich Ferdinand von Beust, *Aus drei Vierteljahrhunderten. Erinnerungen und Aufzeichnungen*, Stuttgart, 1887, vol. I, p. 122.
12   See Srbik, *Deutsche Einheit*, vol. II, p. 89.
13   Schnürer, *Briefe Kaiser Franz Josephs I*, p. 166, Schönbrunn, 26 August, 1851.
14   See Corti, *Mensch und Herrscher*, p. 78.
15   On the matter of Metternich's position, see Heinrich Srbik's classic work, *Metternich. Der Staatsmann und der Mensch*, Munich, 1925, vol. II, pp. 442–50.

NOTES TO CHAPTER 5

1   Schnürer, *Briefe Kaiser Franz Josephs I*, p. 176, Vienna, 6 April, 1852.
2   Ibid., p. 179, Vienna, 14 April 1852.
3   Josef Karl Mayr, *Das Tagebuch des Polizeiministers Kempen von 1848 bis 1859*, p. 217, 2 June, 1851.
4   See Géza Kövess, *Feldzeugmeister Karl Ritter von Schoenhals, Ein Lebensbild*, unpublished dissertation, Vienna, 1932, p. 15.
5   See Corti, *Mensch und Herrscher*, p. 27.
6   See Erika Weinzierl, *Die österreichischen Konkordate von 1855 und 1933*, Vienna, 1960, p. 43.
7   Srbik, *Metternich*, II, pp. 454–9.
8   See Georg Franz, *Kulturkampf, Staat und katholische Kirche in Mitteleuropa von der Säkularisation bis zum Abschluss des preussischen Kulturkampfes*, Munich, 1954, p. 116.
9   See *Österreichische Rundschau*, 1905/IV, p. 588.
10   See Brigitte Hamann, *Elisabeth, Kaiserin ohne Willen*, Vienna, 1982, French translation *Elisabeth d'Autriche*, Paris, 1985, p. 32.
11   Archduchess Sophie, *Diary*, 18 August 1853.
12   B. Hamann, *Elisabeth d'Autriche*, p. 35.
13   Ibid.
14   Schnürer, *Briefe Kaiser Franz Josephs I*, p. 215, Munich, 17 October 1853.

15 Count A. von Hübner, *Neuf ans de souvenirs d'un ambassadeur d'Autriche à Paris sous le Second Empire*, Paris, 1904–8, vol. I, p. 229.
16 Archduchess Sophie, *Diary*, 24 April 1854.
17 Gérard de Nerval, *Voyage en Orient*, Oeuvres II, Paris, 1978, p. 36.
18 See Franz Rauchenberger, *Graf Buol-Schauenstein. Seine Politik im Krimkrieg*, unpublished dissertation, Graz, 1967, p. 66.
19 Schnürer, *Briefe Kaiser Franz Josephs I*, p. 232, Schönbrunn, 8 October 1854.
20 Ibid.
21 B. Hamann, *Elisabeth d'Autriche*, p. 82.
22 Schnürer, *Briefe Kaiser Franz Josephs I*, p. 270, telegram from Franz Joseph to Colonel Count Wurmbrand, Ofen, 29 May 1857.
23 Ibid., p. 280, Vienna, 3 November 1857.
24 *Wiener Zeitung*, 23 August 1858.
25 Count A. von Hübner *Neuf ans de souvenirs*, vol. II, p. 244.
26 On Napoleon III's policies, see Louis Girard, *Napoléon III*, Paris, 1986, pp. 278–92.
27 Schnürer, *Briefe Kaiser Franz Josephs I*, p. 292, Verona, 16 June 1859.
28 Ibid.
29 Georg Nostitz-Rieneck (ed.), *Briefe Kaiser Franz Josephs an Kaiserin Elisabeth*, 2 vols, Vienna, 1966, p. 14, Verona, 7 June 1859.
30 Ibid., p. 20, Verona, 15 June 1859.
31 Ibid.
32 Ibid., p. 35, Verona, 8 July, 1859.
33 Ibid., p. 28, Verona, 26 June 1859.
34 See Srbik, *Deutsche Einheit*, vol. II, p. 375.
35 Georg Nostitz-Rieneck, *Briefe Kaiser Franz Josephs*, p. 35, Verona, 8 July 1859.

NOTES TO CHAPTER 6

1   B. Hamann, *Elisabeth d'Autriche*, p. 155.
2   Ibid.
3   Ibid., p. 183.
4   See Walter Goldinger, 'Von Solferino bis zum Oktoberdiplom', *Mitteilungen des österreichischen Staatsarchivs*, vol. III, 1950, p. 121.
5   Schnürer, *Briefe Kaiser Franz Josephs I*, p. 302, Schönbrunn, 21 October 1860.
6   Ferenc Deák, *Pesti Naplo*, 16 April 1865.
7   Schnürer, *Briefe Kaiser Franz Josephs I*, p. 294, Laxenberg, 1 September 1859.
8   Ibid., Schönbrunn, 2 October 1860.
9   See Helmut Böhme, *Deutschlands Weg zur Grossmacht. Studien zum Verhältnis von Wirtschaft und Staat während der Reichsgründungszeit 1848–1881*, Cologne, Berlin, 1966, p. 55.
10 Albert Schäffle, 'Der preussisch-französische Handelsvertrag', *Deutsche Vierteljahresschrift*, vol. III, 1863, p. 290.
11 Schnürer, *Briefe Kaiser Franz Josephs I*, p. 320, Schönbrunn, 13 August 1863.
12 See F. Herre, *Kaiser Franz Joseph von Österreich. Sein Leben-Seine Zeit*, 1978, p. 196.
13 See Chester Wells Clark, *Franz Joseph and Bismarck. The Diplomacy of Austria before the War of 1866*, Cambridge, Mass., 1934, p. 149, note 139, letter from Franz Joseph to Wilhelm I, 22 October 1864.
14 Ibid., p. 333, dispatch from Lord Bloomfield to Lord Clarendon, 21 January 1866.
15 See Josef Redlich, *Das österreichische Staats und Reichsproblem*, Leipzig, 1920–6, vol. I, pp. 804–8.
16 O. Ernst (ed.), *Franz Joseph I in seinen Briefen*, Vienna, Leipzig, Munich, 1924, p. 164, letter from Franz Joseph to Albert of Saxony, Vienna, 20 June 1866.

17 See Edmund von Glaise-Horstenau, *Franz Josephs Weggefährte. Das Leben des Generalstabschefs Grafen Beck*, Zurich, Leipzig, Vienna, 1930, p. 114.

18 Ibid., p. 118.

19 Count Franz Folliot de Crenneville, *Tagebuch*, HHStA, bequest of Franz Folliot de Crenneville, box 13, 1 July 1866.

20 Austrian political correspondence, vol. 492 (July–August 1866), Foreign Ministry, telegraphic dispatch from Drouyn de Lhuys to the Duke of Gramont, 13 July 1866.

21 Georg Nostitz-Rieneck, *Briefe Kaiser Franz Josephs*, vol. I, p. 49, Vienna, 23 July 1866.

22 Ibid., p. 55, Schönbrunn, 4 August 1866.

23 Ibid., p. 58, Schönbrunn, 7 August 1866.

24 See A. Wandruszka, 'Die Habsburgermonarchie von der Revolution zur Gründerzeit', Exhibition catalogue for *Das Zeitalter Kaiser Franz Josephs. Von der Revolution zur Gründerzeit*, (Grafenegg Castle, May–October 1984), p. 9.

25 Schnürer, *Briefe Kaiser Franz Josephs I*, p. 358, Schönbrunn, 22 August 1866.

26 Ibid.

27 Ibid.

NOTES TO CHAPTER 7

1 Georg Nostitz-Rieneck, *Briefe Kaiser Franz Josephs*, p. 41, Vienna, 18 July 1866.

2 Ibid., pp. 44–5, Vienna, 20 July 1866.

3 Ibid., p. 48, Vienna, 22 July 1866.

4 E. C. Corti, *Mensch und Herrscher*, p. 387.

5 See J. Droz, *L'Europe centrale*, pp. 146–7.

6 *Le Temps*, 11 June 1867.

7 G. Stourzh, *Die Gleichberechtigung der Nationalitäten in der Verfassung und Verwaltung Österreichs 1848–1918*, Vienna, 1985, p. 56.

8 Erika Weinzierl, *Die österreichischen Konkordate*, p. 103.

9 *Wiener Zeitung*, 17 October 1867.

10 Kab. Archiv., Direktionsakten, 5/1868.

11 See Harry Slapnicka, *Bischof Rudigier. Eine Bildbiographie*, Linz, 1961, p. 52.

12 Schnürer, *Briefe Kaiser Franz Josephs I*, p. 377, Schönbrunn, 25 August 1870.

13 See Harald Bachmann, 'Riegers Memoire an Napoleon III aus dem Jahre 1869', *Festschrift zum 70. Geburtstag von Dr. Heribert Sturm*, Munich, Vienna, 1974, p. 184 (text in French).

14 HHStA, Braun bequest, note from Charlotte to Maximilian (beginning of July 1866).

15 *L'Univers Illustré*, 9 November 1867.

16 George Nostitz-Rieneck, *Briefe Kaiser Franz Josephs*, vol. I, p. 68, Paris, 24 October 1867.

17 *Les Origines diplomatiques de la guerre de 1870–1871*, collection of papers published by the French Foreign Office, vols. 11–29, Paris, 1920–31, vol. 25, p. 247.

18 Georg Nostitz-Rieneck, *Briefe Kaiser Franz Josephs*, vol. I, p. 84, Constantinople, 29 October 1869.

19 Ibid., p. 110, on board the *Greif*, 15 November 1869.

20 Ibid., p. 125, 20 November 1869.

21 Ibid., pp. 140–1, 27 November 1869.

22 See Hermann Oncken, *Die Rheinpolitik Kaiser Napoleons III*, 3 vols, Stuttgart, 1926, vol. III, p. 74.

23 Schnürer, *Briefe Kaiser Franz Josephs I*, p. 380–1, Schönbrunn, 23 October 1870.

24 See Heinrich Lutz, 'Die Stellung der Habsburger Monarchie in Europa', exhibition catalogue, *Das Zeitalter Kaiser Franz Josephs*, p. 319.

25 See Antonin Ottokar Zeithammer, *Zur Geschichte der böhmischen Ausgleichsversuche (1865–1871)*, 2 vols, Prague, 1912–13, vol. II, pp. 5–6; on the Bohemian Compromise, see also J. P.

Bled, *Les Fondements du conservatisme autrichien, 1859–1879*, Doctoral thesis, Sorbonne, submitted December 1982, vol. II, pp. 805–39.

26 Zeithammer, *Zur Geschichte der böhmischen Ausgleichsversuche (1865–1871)*, vol. II, pp. 5–6.

27 The text of the royal rescript is reproduced in G. Kolmer, *Parlament und Verfassung in Österreich*, 8 vols, Vienna, 1902–14, vol. II, pp. 172–3, and in Zeithammer, *Zur Geschichte der böhmischen Ausgleichsversuche (1865–1871)*, vol. II, p. 54.

28 See Roman Sandgruber, 'Der grosse Krach', exhibition catalogue for *Traum und Wirklichkeit. Wien 1870–1930*, (March–October 1985), p. 68.

29 F. Fellner, 'Kaiser Franz Joseph und das Parlament Materialien zur Geschichte der Innenpolitik in den Jahren 1867–1873', *Mitteilungen des österreichischen Staatsarchivs*, vol. IX, 1956, p. 316.

30 G. Franz, *Kulturkampf, Staat und katholische Kirche in Mitteleuropa von der Säkularisation bis zum Abschluss des preussischen Kulturkampfes*, pp. 147–8.

31 Ibid.

32 G. Kolmer, *Parlament und Verfassung in Österreich*, vol. II, p. 236.

33 *Stenographische Protokolle des Hauses der Abgeordneten des österreichischen Reichsrates*, vol. 8/414, 17.1.1879.

34 Theodor von Sosnosky, *Die Balkanpolitik Österreich-Ungarns seit 1866*, Stuttgart, Berlin, 1913, p. 175.

35 See Emil Ludwig, *Bismarck*, Paris, 1929, new edition 1984, p. 473.

36 Ibid., p. 483.

37 Ibid., p. 484.

38 See Pierre Renouvin, *Histoire des relations internationales*, vol. VI, 'Le XIXe siècle, II: de 1871 à 1914, l'apogée de l'Europe', Paris, 1955, p. 101.

39 E. C. Corti, *Elisabeth. Die seltsame Frau*, Graz, Salzburg, Vienna, 1954, p. 270.

40 See Baron Oskar von Mitis, *Das Leben des Kronprinzen Rudolf*, Leipzig, 1929, new edition, Vienna, Munich, 1971, p. 227.

41 *Le Temps*, 29 April 1879.

42 Ibid.

NOTES TO CHAPTER 8

1 Duke Ernst II von Sachsen-Coburg-Gotha, *Aus meinem Leben. Aus meiner Zeit*, Berlin, 1887, p. 51.

2 Albert Schäffle, *Aus meinem Leben*, 2 vols, Berlin, 1905, vol. II, p. 69.

3 Alexander von Spitzmüller, *Kaiser Franz Joseph als Staatsmann*, Vienna, 1935, p. 7.

4 Count Erich von Kielmansegg, *Kaiserhaus, Staatsmänner und Politiker*, Vienna, 1965, p. 44.

5 Baron Max Vladimir von Beck, 'Der Kaiser und die Wahlreform', in Eduard Ritter von Steinitz (ed.), *Erinnerungen an Franz Joseph I, Kaiser von Österreich-Apostolischer König von Ungarn*, Berlin, 1931, p. 202.

6 A. Schäffle, *Aus meinem Leben*, vol. I, p. 237.

7 See Count Friedrich von Beck-Rzikowsky, 'Das Dezennium vor dem des Bündnisses mit dem Deutschen Reich', in von Steinitz, *Erinnerungen an Franz Joseph I*, p. 85.

8 Baron Albert von Margutti, *Kaiser Franz Joseph*, Vienna, 1924, p. 51.

9 Schnürer, *Briefe Kaiser Franz Josephs I*, p. 233, Schönbrunn, 8 October 1854.

10 Georg Nostitz-Rieneck, *Briefe Kaiser Franz Josephs*, vol. I, p. 71, Paris, 26 October 1867 and p. 74, 30 October 1867.

11 Nikolaus von Horthy, *Ein Leben für Ungarn*, Bonn, 1953, pp. 58–9.

12 O. Ernst, *Franz Joseph I in seinen Briefen*, p. 158, letter from Franz Joseph to Albert of Saxony, Vienna, 11 April 1852.

13 Ibid., p. 250, letter from Franz Joseph to Albert of Saxony, Vienna, 4 April 1856.

NOTES TO CHAPTER 9

1 N. von Horthy, *Ein Leben für Ungarn*, p. 52.
2 See Michael McGarvie, *Francis Joseph I. A Study in Monarchy*, London 1976, p. 157.
3 Count Albert Mensdorff, 'Die Höfe von London und Wien', in von Steinitz, *Erinnerungen an Franz Joseph I*, p. 302.
4 On the organization of the court, see exhibition catalogue, *Uniform und Mode am Kaiserhof. Hofkleider und Ornate. Hofuniformen aus dem Monturdepot des Kunsthistorischen Museums Wien*, (Halbturn Castle, May–October 1983).
5 Otto Hoetzsch, (ed.), *Peter von Meyendorff. Ein russischer Diplomat an den Höfen von Berlin und Wien. Politischer und privater Briefwechsel 1826–1863*, 3 vols, Berlin, Leipzig, 1923, vol. II, dispatch from Baron Peter von Meyendorff to Count Nesselrode, Vienna, 24 February/8 March 1851.
6 Eugen Ketterl, *Der alte Kaiser. Wie nur Einer ihn sah*, Vienna, Munich, Zurich, Innsbruck, 1929, republished 1980, pp. 20–1.
7 See E. C. Corti and H. Sokol, *Der alte Kaiser. Franz Joseph I bis zu seinem Tode*, Graz, Vienna, Cologne, 1955, p. 152.

NOTES TO CHAPTER 10

1 Georg Nostitz-Rieneck, *Briefe Kaiser Franz Josephs*, vol. I, p. 190, Gödöllö, 1 November 1887.
2 B. Hamann, *Elisabeth d'Autriche*, p. 390.
3 University of Padua historical institute, diary of Count Alexander von Hübner, 24 July 1878.
4 See J. Haslip, *The Emperor and the Actress*, London, 1982, French translation *L'Empereur et la Comdienne*, Paris, 1985, p. 104.
5 Jean de Bourgoing (ed.), *Briefe Kaiser Franz Josephs an Katharina Schratt*, Vienna, 1949, republished 1964, p. 73, 14 February 1888.
6 Ibid.
7 Ibid.
8 Baron O. von Mitis, *Das Leben des Kronprinzen Rudolf*, p. 224; on Rudolf, see the biography by B. Hamann, *Rudolf, Kronprinz und Rebell*, Vienna, Munich, 1978.
9 Leopold von Chlumecky, *Erzherzog Franz Ferdinands Wirken und Wollen*, Berlin, 1929, p. 30.
10 Princess Stephanie of Belgium, *Ich sollte Kaiserin werden*, Leipzig, 1935, p. 82.
11 Corti and Sokol, *Der alte Kaiser. Franz Joseph I bis zu seinem Tode*, p. 92.
12 Bourgoing, *Briefe Kaiser Franz Josephs an Katharina Schratt*, p. 112, 5 February 1889.
13 Ibid., p. 113.
14 Corti and Sokol, *Der alte Kaiser*, p. 126.
15 Bourgoing, *Briefe Kaiser Franz Josephs an Katharina Schratt*, p. 121, 16 February 1889.
16 Ibid., p. 114, 5 March 1889.

NOTES TO CHAPTER 11

1 Foreign Policy Archives, Bonn, Osterreich 86, secret, 6 March 1889.
2 Diary of Archduchess Maria Valeria, 21 August 1888, see B. Hamann, *Elisabeth d'Autriche*, p. 567.
3 Corti and Sokol, *Der alte Kaiser*, p. 173.
4 Constantin Christomanos, *Tagebuchblätter*, Vienna, 1899, p. 133.
5 HHStA, Corti bequest, documents for the biography of the Empress Elisabeth.
6 Corti and Sokol, *Der alte Kaiser*, p. 173.

7　J. Haslip, *L'Empereur et la Comédienne*, pp. 213–14.
8　Ibid., p. 199.
9　Bourgoing, *Briefe Kaiser Franz Josephs an Katharina Schratt*, p. 284, letter of 3 March 1897.
10　Corti and Sokol, *Der alte Kaiser*, p. 234.
11　Ibid.
12　Ibid.
13　Bourgoing, *Briefe Kaiser Franz Josephs an Katharina Schratt*, p. 302, letter of 26 June 1898.
14　Corti and Sokol, *Der alte Kaiser*, p. 241.
15　Ibid., p. 254.
16　Bourgoing, *Briefe Kaiser Franz Josephs an Katharina Schratt*, pp. 323–4, letter of 7 March 1900.
17　See Hugo Hantsch, *Geschichte Österreichs*, 2 vols, Graz, Vienna, Cologne, 1950, 4th edition, 1968, vol. II, p. 461.
18　Corti and Sokol, *Der alte Kaiser*, p. 189.
19　V. L. Tapie, *Monarchie et Peuples du Danube*, pp. 375–6.
20　Bourgoing, *Briefe Kaiser Franz Josephs an Katharina Schratt*, p. 385, letter of 11 April 1906.
21　See H. Hantsch, *Leopold Graf Berchtold. Grandseigneur und Staatsmann*, 2 vols, Graz, Vienna, Cologne, 1963, vol. I, p. 176.
22　Ibid., p. 133.

NOTES TO CHAPTER 12

1　Bourgoing, *Briefe Kaiser Franz Josephs an Katharina Schratt*, p. 363, letter of 12 May 1902.
2　E. Ketterl, *Der alte Kaiser. Wie nur Einer ihn sah*, p. 71.
3　H. Hantsch, *Leopold Graf Berchtold. Grandseigneur und Staatsmann*, vol. I, p. 308.
4　Corti and Sokol, *Der alte Kaiser*, p. 363.
5　Ibid.
6　J. Droz, *L'Europe centrale. Evolution historique de l'idée de Mitteleuropa*, p. 198.
7　Kriegsarchiv (Vienna), Military Chancellery of Franz Ferdinand, box 39, letter from Franz Ferdinand to Baron Alois von Aerenthal, 20 July 1909.
8　See Robert A. Kann, *Erzherzog Franz Ferdinand Studien*, Vienna 1976, p. 62.
9　Conrad von Hötzendorf, *Aus meiner Dienstzeit 1908–1918*, 5 vols, Vienna 1921–5, vol. III, p. 127.
10　Baron Carl von Bardolff, *Soldat im alten Österreich. Erinnerungen aus meinem Leben*, Iena, 1938, p. 117.
11　See Friedrich Würthle, *Die Spur führt nach Belgrad. Die Hintergründe des Dramas von Sarajevo 1914*, Vienna, Munich, Zurich, 1975, p. 16.

NOTES TO CHAPTER 13

1　Corti and Sokol, *Der alte Kaiser*, p. 412.
2　H. Hantsch, *Leopold Graf Berchtold. Grandseigneur und Staatsmann*, vol. II, p. 568.
3　Ibid.
4　Ibid., p. 603.
5　Baron A. von Margutti, *Kaiser Franz Joseph*, p. 412.
6　H. Hantsch, *Leopold Graf Berchtold. Grandseigneur und Staatsmann*, vol. II, p. 612.
7　Baron A. von Margutti, *Kaiser Franz Joseph*, p. 415.
8　H. Hantsch, *Leopold Graf Berchtold. Grandseigneur und Staatsmann*, vol. II, p. 588.
9　Corti and Sokol, *Der alte Kaiser*, p. 421.

10 H. Hantsch, *Leopold Graf Berchtold. Grandseigneur und Staatsmann*, vol. II, p. 611.
11 Corti and Sokol, *Der alte Kaiser*, p. 437.

NOTES TO CONCLUSION

1 Robert Musil, *Der Mann ohne Eigenschaften*, 1930, French translation, *L'Homme sans qualités*, Paris, 1956, 5th edition 1982, vol. I, p. 40.
2 Joseph Roth, 'In der Kapuzinergruft', *Wiener Sonn-und Montagszeitung*, 27 May 1935.
3 J. Redich, *Kaiser Franz Joseph*, p. 13.

Chronology

1830   18 August   Birth of Franz Joseph.

1832   6 July   Birth of Ferdinand Maximilian.

1833   30 July   Birth of Karl Ludwig.

1835   2 March   Death of Emperor Franz I, his oldest son, Ferdinand I, succeeds him.

1842   15 May   Birth of Ludwig Victor.

1848   3 March   Kossuth's speech to the Hungarian Diet.
        13 March   Fall of Metternich.
        15 March   Ferdinand promises to grant a Constitution.
        17 March   Formation of Hungarian Government under Count Batthyány.
        8 April   Bohemian Charter.
        11 April   Promulgation of Hungarian Constitution.
        25 April   Baron Pillersdorf's draft Constitution published.
        26–8 April   Election of Frankfurt Parliament.
        29 April   Franz Joseph joins the army in Italy.
        6 May   Franz Joseph's first battle at Santa Lucia.
        19 May   Flight of the imperial family to Innsbruck.
        25 July   Radetzky beats the Piedmont army at Custozza.
        7 September   Abolition of the feudal system by the *Reichstag*.
        6 October   Street riots in Vienna.
        7 October   Imperial family leaves for Olmütz.
        31 October   Windischgraetz's army retakes Vienna.
        21 November   Formation of Prince Felix Schwarzenberg's government.
        2 December   Abdication of Ferdinand I and accession of Franz Joseph I.

1849   7 March   Dissolution of the *Reichstag* and promulgation of the Constitution granted by Franz Joseph.
        25 March   Radetzky beats the Piedmont army at Novara.
        28 March   Frankfurt Parliament offers the German crown to Friedrich Wilhelm IV.

3 April   Friedrich Wilhelm IV refuses the crown.

May   Beginning of Russian intervention in Hungary.

26 May   League of the three kingdoms (Prussia, Hanover, Saxony) begins the smaller German Union.

13 August   Hungary surrenders at Vilagos.

1850   March–April   Smaller German Union parliament passes a Constitution at Erfurt.

27–8 November   Retreat of Olmütz. Dissolution of smaller German Union.

1851   April   Dresden Conference.

31 December   Saint Sylvester patent abolishes the March Constitution.

1852   5 April   Death of Schwarzenberg.

1853   18 August   Engagement of Franz Joseph and Elisabeth.

1854   27 March   England and France declare war on Russia.

20 April   Austro-Prussian treaty of alliance.

24 April   Wedding of Franz Joseph and Elisabeth in Vienna.

2 December   Treaty of alliance between Austria, Britain, and France.

1855   5 March   Birth of the younger Sophie.

18 August   Signing of the concordat.

1856   30 May   Treaty of Paris.

15 July   Birth of Archduchess Gisela.

1857   29 May   Death of infant Sophie.

20 December   Order to demolish the Vienna city ramparts.

1858   5 January   Death of Radetzky.

21–2 July   Encounter of Napoleon and Cavour at Plombières.

21 August   Birth of Archduke Rudolf.

1859   19 April   Austrian ultimatum to Piedmont.

13 May   Count Rechberg becomes foreign minister.

4 June   Defeat at Magenta.

11 June   Death of Prince Metternich.

26 June   Defeat at Solferino.

11 July   Armistice of Villafranca.

15 July   Laxenberg manifesto.

1860   20 October   October Diploma.

November   Elisabeth leaves for Madeira.

18 December   Anton von Schmerling joins the government.

1861   28 February   February patent.

14 March   Creation of the Kingdom of Italy.

8 April   Hungarian Diet passes an address rejecting the February patent.

23 June   Elisabeth leaves for Corfu.

21 November   Dissolution of the Hungarian Diet.

| 1862 | 29 March   Franco–Prussian commercial treaty. |
| | 29 September   Bismarck becomes first minister in Prussia. |

1863   17 June   Departure of Czech deputies from the *Reichsrat*.
16 August – 1 September   Congress of the princes in Frankfurt.

1864   1 February   Austro-Prussian intervention in the duchies begins.
9 April   Franz Joseph and Ferdinand Maximilian bid each other farewell.
27 October   Resignation of Count Rechberg, who is succeeded by Count Alexander von Mensdorff-Pouilly.
30 October   Peace of Vienna.

1865   11 April   Publication of Deák's article in *Pesti Naplo*.
1 May   Opening of the *Ringstrasse*.
14 August   Bad Gastein convention.
20 September   Imperial manifesto suspends the February patent.
14 December   Convocation of the Hungarian Diet.

1866   8 April   Treaty of alliance between Prussia and Italy.
12 June   Franco-Austrian convention over Venice.
24 June   Victory of Custozza.
3 July   Disaster at Sadowa.
26 July   Peace talks at Nikolsburg.
23 August   Treaty of Prague.
30 October   Baron Beust becomes foreign minister.

1867   1 February   Franz Joseph decides in favour of dualism.
17 February   Count Gyula Andrassy is nominated Hungarian first minister.
29 May   Compromise approved by Hungarian Diet.
8 June   Franz Joseph crowned king of Hungary in Buda.
19 June   Execution of Maximilian in Queretaro.
18–20 August   Franz Joseph and Napoleon III meet in Salzburg.
End of October–beginning of November   Franz Joseph visits Paris.
21 December   Promulgation of Constitutional laws 'of the kingdoms and provinces represented by the *Reichsrat*'.
30 December   Prince Karl Auersperg becomes first minister.

1868   22 April   Birth of Archduchess Maria Valeria.
May   Promulgation of confessional laws known as 'May legislation'.
22 August   Declaration of eighty-eight Czech deputies of the Bohemian Diet.
September   Resignation of Prince Karl Auersperg who is replaced as head of government by Count Edward Taaffe.
12 September   Monsignor Rudigier's letter condemns the May legislation.

1869   14 May   Hasner law regulates new school system.
12 July   Rudigier condemned to fourteen days imprisonment.
End October – end November   Franz Joseph's journey to Near East for the opening of the Suez canal.
13 December   First major workers' demonstration in Vienna.

1870   1 February – 3 April   Leopold von Hasner's cabinet.
4 April   Count Alfred Potocki becomes first minister.

18 July   Crown Council decides that Austria-Hungary should remain neutral in Franco-Prussian war. Proclamation of doctrine of papal infallibility by the Vatican.
19 July   France declares war on Prussia.
30 July   Denunciation of concordat by Austrian government.

1871   18 January   Establishment of a German Empire declared at Versailles.
7 February   Hohenwart's cabinet is formed.
10 May   Frankfurt treaty.
14 September   Rescript in which Franz Joseph recognizes the state rights of Bohemia.
20–2 October   Crown Councils admit failure of Bohemian compromise.
27 October   Resignation of Hohenwart's cabinet.
8 November   Beust relieved of post of foreign minister.
13 November   Count Gyula Andrassy becomes foreign minister.
26 November   Prince Adolf Auersperg becomes first minister.

1872   28 May   Death of Archduchess Sophie.

1873   20 April   Marriage of Archduchess Gisela to Prince Leopold of Bavaria.
1 May   Opening of Universal Exhibition.
9 May   Viennese stock exchange crash.

1874   21 January   Deposition of new set of draft confessional laws.
7 March   Plus IX condemns proposed confessional laws.

1875   20 October   Koloman Tisza becomes first minister of Hungary.

1876   2 July   Serbia and Montenegro declare war on the Ottoman Empire.
8 July   Franz Joseph and Alexander II meet at Reichstadt.

1877   7 February   Death of Pius IX.
22 February   Election of Leo XIII.
18 March   Austro-Russian military convention.
12 April   Russia enters war against Ottoman Empire.

1878   3 March   Treaty of San Stefano.
8 March   Death of Archduke Franz Karl.
13 June – 13 July   Berlin Congress.
20 July – 20 October   Occupation of Bosnia-Herzegovina.

1879   15 February   Stremayr's cabinet is formed, with Count Edward Taaffe as minister of the interior.
27 April   Franz Joseph and Elisabeth's silver wedding – procession along the *Ringstrasse*.
24 June – 12 July   Election of the *Reichstrat* Chamber of Deputies, giving the majority to a coalition of conservative groups.
12 August   Taaffe forms his cabinet.
16 September   Return of the Bohemian opposition to the *Reichsrat*.
7 October   Treaty of alliance between Austria-Hungary and the German Empire is signed.
8 October   Count Andrassy resigns.

1881   14 March   Assassination of Tsar Alexander II.
6–10 May   Marriage of Archduke Rudolf and Princess Stephanie of Belgium.

18 June   Revival of league of the three emperors.
28 June   Secret Austro-Serbian treaty.
20 November   Count Gustav Kálnoky becomes foreign minister.

1882   20 May   Treaty with Italy, forming the Triple Alliance.
2 June   Linz programme.

1883   30 October   Secret treaty of alliance between Austria-Hungary and Romania.

1884   September   Alexander III, Franz Joseph, and Wilhelm I meet at Skierniewice.

1885   August   Meeting between Franz Joseph and Alexander II at Kremsier.

1886   20 May   Encounter between Franz Joseph and Katharina Schratt at von Angeli's studio.
23 May   Beginning of correspondence between Franz Joseph and Katharina Schratt.

1887   7 July   Ferdinand of Saxe-Coburg elected prince of Bulgaria.
25 November   Creation of the *Vereinigte Christen*.

1889   1 January   Austrian Social Democrat unification congress at Hainfeld.
30 January   Death of Archduke Rudolf at Mayerling.
March   Abdication of King Milan of Serbia in favour of his son Alexander.
13 March   Resignation of Tisza's cabinet in Hungary.

1890   31 July   Marriage of Archduchess Maria Valeria to Archduke Franz Salvator.

1891   27 August   Franco-Russian agreement begins alliance between the two countries.

1892   18 August   Signing of military convention between France and Russia.

1893   29 October   Count Taaffe resigns.
11 November   Prince Alfred Windischgraetz becomes first minister.

1895   15 May   Resignation of Count Kálnoky, who is succeeded by Count Agenor Goluchowski.
19 June   Resignation of Windischgraetz's cabinet.
2 October   Count Kasimir Badeni becomes first minister.
29 October   Karl Lueger elected mayor of Vienna.
5 November   Franz Joseph refuses to ratify Lueger's election.

1896   February-March   Christian Socialists gain two-thirds of the seats in the Vienna municipal elections.
8 April   Lueger is again elected mayor of Vienna.
27 April   Franz Joseph gives Lueger an audience, who provisionally renounces his post as mayor.
19 May   Death of Archduke Karl Ludwig. Archduke Franz Ferdinand becomes official heir to the throne.

1897   5 April   Promulgation of linguistic Orders by Court Badeni.
8 April   Lueger elected mayor of Vienna.
16 April   Franz Joseph ratifies Lueger's election.

November   Violent clashes in the *Reichsrat* Chamber of Deputies in reaction to the linguistic Orders.
27 November   Count Badeni relieved of office.

1898   7 March   Count Franz Thun becomes first minister.
10 September   Assassination of Empress Elisabeth by Luigi Lucheni.

1899   23 September   Thun's cabinet resigns.
17 October   Withdrawal of Badeni's linguistic Orders.

1900   18 January   Ernest von Koerber becomes first minister.
28 June   Act of Renunciation excluding Franz Ferdinand's heirs from the succession.
1 July   Marriage of Archduke Franz Ferdinand to Countess Sophie Chotek who is granted the title of Princess Hohenberg by Franz Joseph.

1902   1 November   Secret agreement between France and Italy.

1903   11 June   Assassination of King Alexander of Serbia and his family.
17 September   Chlopy order is given by Franz Joseph.
30 September – 3 October   Franz Joseph and Nicolas II meet at Mürzsteg.
3 November   Count Istvan Tisza becomes first minister in Hungary.

1904   8 April   Entente Cordiale is formed between France and Britain.
31 December   Resignation of Koerber's cabinet.

1905   1 January   Baron Paul von Gautsch becomes first minister.
January   Electoral defeat of Hungarian liberal party.
June   Resignation of Tisza's government which is replaced by a cabinet under General Geza von Fejérváry.

1906   8 April   Hungarian coalition government is formed under Alexander Wekerle.
30 April   Resignation of Gautsch's cabinet.
2 June   Baron Max Vladimir von Beck becomes first minister.
24 October   Baron Alois von Aehrenthal becomes foreign minister.
18 November   Baron Conrad von Hötzendorf is named head of the army's General Staff.

1907   20 January   Franz Joseph promulgates a law instituting universal suffrage in Cisleithania.
4–24 May   First elections under system of universal suffrage bring success to Christian Socialists and Social Democrats.

1908   5 October   Annexation of Bosnia-Herzegovina.
7 November   Resignation of Beck's cabinet.
25 November   Baron Richard von Bienerth becomes first minister.

1910   17 January   Wekerle's cabinet resigns in Hungary.
10 March   Karl Lueger dies.
May   Electoral victory of Istvan Tisza in Hungary.

1911   13–20 June   Elections for the Lower Chamber of the *Reichsrat*.
26 June   Bieneth's cabinet resigns.
21 October   Marriage of Archduke Karl to Princess Zita of Bourbon-Parma.

3 November   Count Karl von Stürgkh becomes first minister.
End of November   Dismissal of Conrad von Hötzendorf.

1912   17 February   Death of Count Aehrenthal who is succeeded by Court Leopold Berchtold.
13 March   Formation of Balkan league.
8 October   First Balkan war begins.
7 December   Conrad von Hötzendorf is recalled to his post as head of General Staff.

1913   10 June   Formation of Tisza's second cabinet.
25 June   Second Balkan war begins.
10 August   End of second Balkan war.

1914   March   *Reichsrat* is adjourned.
28 June   Assassination of Archduke Franz Ferdinand and the Duchess Hohenberg at Sarajevo.
23 July   Austria-Hungary sends Serbia an ultimatum.
28 July   Declaration of war by Austria-Hungary on Serbia.
30 July   Russian general mobilization.
31 July   Austro-Hungarian general mobilization. German ultimatum to Russia and France – Germany declares a 'state of possible war'.
1 August   Germany declares war on Russia.
3 August   Germany declares war on France.
4 August   Britain declares war on Germany.
6 August   Austria-Hungary declares war on Russia.
12 August   Britain and France declare war on Austria-Hungary.
12 August – end of August   Failure of first Austro-Hungarian offensive in Serbia.
23 August – 12 September   Series of battles which result in the occupation of most of Galicia by the Russians.
November-December   Failure of new offensive against Serbia.
3–12 December   Victory of Limanowa–Lapanov over Russia.

1915   13 January   Count Berchtold resigns and is succeeded by Baron Stephan Burian.
2 May   Beginning of Austro-German counter-offensive in Galicia.
4 May   Italy renounces the Triple Alliance.
23 May   Italy declares war on Austria-Hungary.
22 June   Lemberg retaken.
Mid-July   Russians driven out of almost all the monarchy's territory occupied by them at beginning of war.
6 October   Beginning of Austro-German offensive against Serbia.
24–5 November   Serbia defeated.

1916   15 May – 17 June   Failure of Austro-Hungarian offensive on Italian front.
4 June   Brusilov's offensive begins.
18 August   Romania joins the Entente.
21 October   Assassination of Count Stürgkh.
28 October   Ernest von Koerber becomes first minister.
21 November   Death of Franz Joseph at Schönbrunn.
30 November   Franz Joseph's funeral.

Bibliography

General history of the Habsburg monarchy

Hantsch, Hugo, *Geschichte Österreichs*, 2 vols, Graz, Vienna, Cologne, 1950, vol. I, 5th edition, 1969, vol. II, 4th edition, 1968.
Zöllner, Erich, *Geschichte Österreichs. Von den Anfängen bis zur Gegenwart*, Munich, 1961.
Tapie, Victor-L. *Monarchie et Peuples du Danube*, Paris, 1969.
Goerlich, Ernst Joseph and Felix Romanik, *Geschichte Österreichs*, Innsbruck, Munich, 1977.

Franz Joseph's reign

Friedjung, Heinrich, *Österreich von 1848–1860*, 2 vols, Stuttgart, Berlin, 1908–12.
Sieghart, Rudolf, *Die letzten Jahrzehnte einer Grossmacht. Menschen, Völker, Probleme des Habsburger Reiches*, Berlin, 1932.
Taylor, Alan J. P. *The Habsburg Monarchy 1809–1918. A History of the Austrian Empire and Austria-Hungary*, London, 1948, 2nd edition, 1964.
May, Arthur James, *The Habsburg Monarchy*, Harvard University Press, Cambridge (Mass), 1965.
Macartney, Carlile Aylmer, *The Habsburg Empire 1790–1918*, London, 1969.
Die Habsburgermonarchie, general collection editors Adam Wandruszka and Peter Urbanitsch. Of ten volumes, those already published are:
vol. I, *Die wirtschaftliche Entwicklung*, Vienna, 1973.
vol. II, *Verwaltung und Rechtswesen*, Vienna, 1975.
vol. III, *Die Völker des Reiches*, Vienna, 1980.
vol. IV, *Die Konfessionen*, Vienna, 1985.
Bled, Jean-Paul, *Les fondements du conservatisme autrichien 1859–1879*, thesis for *doctorat d'Etat*, submitted 1982, Sorbonne, 3 vols.
Exhibition catalogue, *Das Zeitalter Kaiser Franz Josephs. Von der Revolution zur Gründerzeit* (Grafenegg castle, May–October 1984).

Franz Joseph

The main reference work here is the three-part work by Count Egon Caesar Corti:
Vom Kind zum Kaiser. Kindheit und erste Jugend Kaiser Franz Josephs I und seiner Geschwister, Graz, Salzburg, Vienna, 1950.

Mensch und Herrscher. Wege und Schicksale Kaiser Franz Josephs I zwischen Thronbesteigung und Berliner Kongress, Graz, Vienna, 1952.

(with Hans Sokol) *Der alte Kaiser. Franz Joseph I bis zu seinem Tode*, Graz, Vienna, Cologne, 1955.

Friedjung, Heinrich, 'Kaiser Franz Josef I. Ein Charakterbild', *Historische Aufsätze*, Stuttgart, Berlin, 1919, pp. 493–541.

Margutti, Albert Baron von, *Kaiser Franz Joseph*, Vienna, Leipzig, 1924.

Redlich, Joseph, *Kaiser Franz Joseph von Österreich*, Berlin, 1928.

Ketterl, Eugen, *Der alte Kaiser. Wie nur Einer ihn sah*. Vienna, Munich, Zurich, Innsbruck, 1929, new edition 1980.

Steinitz, Eduard Ritter von (ed.), *Erinnerungen an Franz Joseph I, Kaiser von Österreich-Apostolischer König von Ungarn*, Berlin, 1931.

Heller, Edvard, *Kaiser Franz Joseph I. Ein Charakterbild*, Vienna, 1934.

Spitzmüller, Alexander Baron von, *Kaiser Franz Joseph als Staatsmann*, Vienna, 1935.

Saint-Aulaire, Comte de, *Francois-Joseph*, Paris, 1945.

Elmer, Hans, *Franz Joseph I von 1830–1859 im Urteil von Zeitgenossen und Nachwelt*, unpublished dissertation, Vienna, 1948.

Srbik, Heinrich Ritter von, 'Kaiser Franz Joseph I. Charakter und Regierungsgrundsätze', *Aus Österreichs Vergangenheit*, Salzburg, 1949, pp. 221–41.

McGarvie, Michael, *Francis Joseph I. A study in Monarchy*, London, 1960.

Herre Franz, *Kaiser Franz Joseph von Österreich. Sein Leben – Seine Zeit*, Cologne, 1978.

Haslip, Joan, *The Emperor and the Actress*, London, 1982.

Franz Joseph's correspondence

Ernst Otto (ed.), *Franz Joseph I in seinen Briefen*, Vienna, Leipzig, Munich, 1924.

Schnürer, Franz (ed.), *Briefe Kaiser Franz Josephs I an seine Mutter 1838–1872*, Munich, 1930.

Bourgoing, Jean de (ed.), *Briefe Kaiser Franz Josephs an Katharina Schratt*, Vienna, 1949, republished 1964.

Nostitz-Rieneck, Georg (ed.), *Briefe Kaiser Franz Josephs an Kaiserin Elisabeth*, 2 vols, Vienna, 1966.

The imperial family

Haslip, Joan, *The Lonely Empress*, London, 1965.

Corti, Egon Caesar Count, *Elisabeth. Die seltsame Frau*, Graz, Salzburg, Vienna, 1954.

Hamann, Brigitte, *Elisabeth, Kaiserin ohne Willen*, Vienna, 1982, French translation *Elisabeth d'Autriche*, Paris, 1985.

Haslip, Joan, *Imperial Adventurer. Emperor Maximilian of Mexico*, London, 1971.

Mitis, Oskar Baron von, *Das Leben des Kronprinzen Rudolf*, Leipzig, 1929, new edition, Vienna, Munich, 1971.

Hamann, Brigitte, *Rudolf. Kronprinz und Rebell*, Vienna, Munich, 1978.

Chlumecky, Leopold von, *Erzherzog Franz Ferdinands Wirken und Wollen*, Berlin, 1929.

Kann, Robert A., *Erzherzog Franz Ferdinand Studien*, Vienna, 1976.

The court

Fritsche, Viktor von, *Bilder aus dem österreichischen Hof- und Gesellschaftsleben*, Vienna, 1914.

Promintzer, Petra, *Die Reisen Kaiser Franz Josephs (1848–1867)*, unpublished dissertation, Vienna, 1967.

List, Joachim, *Beiträge zur Stellung und Aufgabe der Erzherzöge unter Kaiser Franz Joseph I*, unpublished dissertation, Vienna, 1962.

Exhibition catalogue *Uniform und Mode am Kaiserhof. Hofkleider und Ornate. Hofuniformen aus dem Monturdepot des Kunsthistorischen Museums Wien*, (Halbturn castle, May–October 1983).

Memoirs, diaries, firsthand accounts

Beust, Friedrich Ferdinand Count von, *Aus drei Vierteljahrhunderten. Erinnerungen und Aufzeichnungen*, 2 vols, Stuttgart, 1887.

Hübner, Alexander Count von, *Ein Jahr meines Lebens, 1848–1849*, Leipzig, 1891.

Hübner, Alexander Count von, *Neuf ans de souvenirs d'un ambassadeur d'Autriche à Paris sous le Second Empire*, 2 vols, Paris, 1904–8.

Stremayr, Carl von, *Erinnerungen aus dem Leben. Seinen Kindern erzählt*, Vienna, 1899.

Schäffle, Albert, *Aus meinem Leben*, 2 vols, Berlin, 1905.

Plener, Ernst von, *Erinnerungen*, 3 vols, Stuttgart, 1911–21.

Conrad von Hötzendorf, Count Franz, *Aus meiner Dienstzeit 1908–1918*, 5 vols, Vienna, 1921–5.

Baernreither, Josef M., *Fragmente eines politischen Tagebuches*, edited by Joseph Redlich, Vienna, 1928.

Mayr, Josef Karl (ed.), *Das Tagebuch des Polizeiministers Kempen von 1848 bis 1859*, Graz, Vienna, Leipzig, 1931.

Stephanie, Princess of Belgium, *Ich sollte Kaiserin werden*, Leipzig, 1935.

Funder, Friedrich, *Vom Gestern ins Heute. Aus dem Kaiserreich in die Republik*, Vienna, 1952.

Horthy, Nikolaus von, *Ein Leben für Ungarn*, Bonn, 1953.

Redlich, Joseph, *Schicksalsjahre Österreichs 1908–1919. Das politische Tagebuch*, edited by Fritz Fellner, 2 vols, Graz, Cologne, 1953–4.

Kielmansegg, Erich Count von, *Kaiserhaus, Staatsmänner und Politiker*, Vienna, 1965.

Szeps-Zuckerkandl, Berta, *Österreich intim*, Vienna, 1970.

Major figures (ministers, politicians, generals)

Wertheimer, Eduard von, *Graf Julius Andrassy. Sein Leben und seine Zeit*, 3 vols, Stuttgart, 1910–13.

Srbik, Heinrich Ritter von, *Metternich. Der Staatsmann und der Mensch*, 2 vols. Munich, 1925.

Engel-Janosi, Friedrich, *Graf Rechberg. Vier Kapitel zu seiner und Österreichs Geschichte*, Munich, Berlin, 1927.

Engel-Janosi, Friedrich, *Der Freiherr von Hübner 1811–1892. Eine Gestalt aus dem Österreich Kaiser Franz Josephs*, Innsbruck, 1933.

Müller, Paul, *Feldmarschall Fürst Windischgraetz. Revolution und Gegenrevolution in Österreich*, Vienna, Leipzig, 1934.

Szapary, Marianne, Countess, *Carl Graf Grünne, Generaladjudant des Kaisers Franz Joseph 1848–1859*, Vienna, 1935.

Loew, Hans, *Alexander Freiherr von Bach*, unpublished dissertation, Vienna, 1947.

Kiszling, Rudolf, *Fürst Felix Schwarzenberg: der politische Lehrmeister Kaiser Franz Josephs*, Graz, Cologne, 1952.

Allmayer-Beck, Johann Christoph, *Ministerpräsident Beck*, Munich, 1956.

Regele, Oskar, *Feldmarschall Radetzky. Leben und Leistung*, Vienna, 1957.

Regele, Oskar, *Feldzeugmeister Benedek. Der Weg nach Königgrätz*, Vienna, Munich, 1960.

Hantsch, Hugo, *Leopold Graf Berchtold. Grand Seigneur und Staatsmann*, 2 vols, Vienna, Graz, Cologne, 1963.

Thienen-Adlerflycht, Christoph, *Graf Leo Thun im Vormärz. Grundlagen des böhmischen Konservatismus im Kaisertum Österreich*, Vienna, Graz, Cologne, 1967.

Whiteside, Andrew G. *The Socialism of Fools. Georg Ritter von Schönerer and Austrian Pan-Germanism*, Berkeley, 1975.
Hawlik, Johannes, *Der Bürgerkaiser. Karl Lueger und seine Zeit*, Vienna, 1985.
Bertier de Sauvigny, Guillaume de, *Metternich*, Paris, 1985.

Constitutional history

Kolmer, Gustav, *Parlament und Verfassung in Österreich*, 8 vols, Vienna, 1902–14.
Belcredi, Ludwig Count (ed.), 'Fragmente aus dem Nachlass des ehemaligen Staatsministers Grafen Richard Belcredi', *Die Kultur*, vol. 7, 1906, p. 300.
Zeithammer, Antonin Ottokar, *Zur Geschichte der böhmischen Ausgleichsversuche (1865–1871)*, 2 vols, Prague, 1912–13.
Redlich, Joseph, *Das österreichische Staats und Reichsproblem*, 2 vols, Leipzig, 1920–6.
Goldinger Walter, 'Von Solferino bis zum Oktoberdiplom', *Mitteilungen des österreichischen Staatsarchivs*, vol. 3, 1950, pp. 106–26.
Fellner, Fritz, 'Kaiser Franz Joseph und das Parlament Materialien zur Geschichte der Innenpolitik in den Jahren 1867–1873', *Mitteilungen des österreichischen Staatsarchivs*, vol. 9, 1956, pp. 287–347.
Forschungsinstitut für den Donauraum (ed.), *Der österreichisch-ungarische Ausgleich von 1867. Vorgeschichte und Wirkungen*, Vienna, 1967.

Political life

Molisch, Paul, *Briefe der deutschen Politik in Österreich von 1848 bis 1918*, Vienna, Leipzig, 1934.
Fuchs, Albert, *Geistige Strömungen in Österreich*, Vienna, 1948.
Wandruszka, Adam, 'Osterreichs politische Struktur. Die Entstehung der Parteien und politischen Bewegungen', *Geschichte der Republik Österreich*, edited by Heinrich Benedikt, Vienna, 1954.
Eder, Karl, *Der Liberalismus in Altösterreich, Geisteshaltung, Politik und Kultur*, Vienna, Munich, 1955.
Allmayer-Beck, Johann Christoph, *Der Konservatismus in Österreich*, Munich, 1959.
Sutter, Berthold, *Die Badenischen Sprachverordnungen von 1897*, 2 vols, Graz, Cologne, 1960–5.
Jenks, William, *Austria under the Iron Ring 1879–1893*, Charlottesville, 1965.
Pulzer, Peter G. J., *Die Entstehung des politischen Antisemitismus, in Deutschland und Österreich*, Gütersloh, 1966.
Stölzl, Christoph, *Die Ära Bach in Böhmen*, Munich, Vienna, 1971.
Hellwing, Isak-Marie, *Der konfessionelle Antisemitismus im 19. Jahrhundert in Österreich*, Vienna, Friburg, Basle, 1972.
Knoll, Reinhold, *Zur Tradition der christlich-sozialen Partei. Ihre Früh und Entwicklungsgeschichte bis zu den Reichsratswahlen 1907*, Vienna, Graz, Cologne, 1973.
Boyer, John W., *Political Radicalism in Late Imperial Vienna. Origins of the Christian-Social Movement 1848–1897*, Chicago, 1981.

The nationality question

Kann, Robert A. *The Multinational Empire. Nationalism and National Reform in the Habsburg Monarchy 1848–1918*, 2 vols, New York, 1950.
Hantsch, Hugo, *Die Nationalitätengrage im alten Österreich*, Vienna, 1953.
Kramer, Hans, *Die Italiener unter der österreichisch-ungarischen Monarchie*, Vienna, Munich, 1954.
Plaschka, Richard-Georg, *Von Palacký bis Pekař. Geschichtswissenschaft und Nationalbewusstsein bei den Tschechen*, Graz, Cologne, 1955.

Droz, Jacques, *L'Europe centrale. Evolution historique de l'idée de Mitteleuropa*, Paris, 1960.

Wandycz, Piotre S., 'The Poles in the Habsburg Monarchy', *Austrian History Yearbook*, III/2, 1967, pp. 261–87.

Prinz, Friedrich, *Prag und Wien 1848. Problem der nationalen und sozialen Revolution im Spiegel der Wiener Ministerratsprotokolle*, Munich, 1968.

Forst-Battaglia, Jakub, *Die polnischen Konservativen Galiziens und die Slawen (1866–1879)*, unpublished dissertation, Vienna, 1979.

Goldinger, Walter, 'Das polnische Element in der Wiener Hochbureaukratie (1848–1918)', *Studia Austro-Polonica*, vol. I, 1978, pp. 106–26.

Urbanitsch, Peter, 'Die Deutschen in Österreich. Statistisch-deskriptiver Überblick', *Die Habsburgermonarchie*, III/1, pp. 33–153.

Sutter, Berthold, 'Die politische und rechtliche Stellung der Deutschen in Österreich 1848 bis 1918', *Die Habsburgermonarchie*, III/1, pp. 154–339.

Katus, Laszlo, 'Die Magyaren', *Die Habsburgermonarchie*, III/1, pp. 410–88.

Koralka, Jiri and R. J. Crampton, 'Die Tsechen', *Die Habsburgermonarchie*, III/1, pp. 489–521.

Batowski, Henryk, 'Die Polen', *Die Habsburgermonarchie*, III/1, pp. 522–44.

Bihl, Wolfdieter, 'Die Ruthenen', *Die Habsburgermonarchie*, III/1, pp. 555–84.

Bihl, Wolfdieter, 'Die Juden', *Die Habsburgermonarchie*, III/2, pp. 880–948.

Hitchins, Keith, 'Die Rumänen', *Die Habsburgermonarchie*, III/1, pp. 585–625.

Suppan, Arnold, 'Die Kroaten', *Die Habsburgermonarchie*, III/1, pp. 626–733.

Djordjevic, Dimitrije, 'Die Serben', *Die Habsburgermonarchie*, III/1, pp. 734–74.

Holotik, L'udovit, 'Die Slowaken', *Die Habsburgermonarchie*, III/2, pp. 775–800.

Pleterski, Janko, 'Die Slowenen', *Die Habsburgermonarchie*, III/2, pp. 801–38.

Corsini, Umberto, 'Die Italiener', *Die Habsburgermonarchie*, III/2.

Stourzh, Gerald, *Die Gleichberechtigung der Nationalitäten in der Verfassung und Verwaltung Österreichs 1848–1918*, Vienna, 1985.

Michel, Bernard, *La Mémoire de Prague. Conscience nationale et intelligentsia dans l'histoire tchéque et slovaque*, Paris, 1986.

Foreign policy

Friedjung, Heinrich, *Der Kampf um die Vorherreschaft in Deutschland 1859–1866*, 2 vols, Stuttgart, 1897–8.

Hoetzsch, Otto, (ed.), *Peter von Meyendorff. Ein russischer Diplomat an den Höfen von Berlin und Wien. Politischer und privater Briefwechsel 1826–1863*, 3 vols, Berlin, Leipzig, 1923.

Salomon, Henry, *L'Ambassade de Richard de Metternich à Paris*, Paris, 1930.

Clark, Chester Wells, *Franz Joseph and Bismarck. The Diplomacy of Austria before the War of 1866*, Cambridge, Harvard University Press, 1934.

Srbik, Heinrich Ritter von, *Deutsche Einheit. Idee und Wirklichkeit von Heiligen Reich bis Königgrätz*, 4 vols, Munich, 1935–42.

Ströher, Doris, *Die Okkupation Bosniens und der Herzegovina und die öffentliche Meinung Österreich-Ungarns*, unpublished dissertation, Vienna, 1949.

Fellner, Fritz, *Der Dreibund*, Munich, 1960.

Engel-Janosi, Friedrich, *Geschichte auf dem Ballhausplatz*, Graz, Vienna, Cologne, 1963.

Böhme, Helmut, *Deutschlands Weg zur Grossmacht. Studien zum Verhältnis von Wirtschaft und Staat während der Reichsgründungszeit 1848–1881*, Cologne, Berlin, 1966.

Wandruszka, Adam, *Schicksalsjahr 1866*, Graz, Vienna, Cologne, 1966.

Rauchenberger, Franz, *Graf Buol-Schauenstein. Seine Politik im Krimkrieg*, unpublished dissertation, Graz, 1967.

Jelavich, Barbara, *The Habsburg Empire in European Affairs 1814–1918*, Chicago, 1969.

Kann, Robert A, 'Kaiser Franz Joseph und der Ausbruch des Weltkrieges', Österreichische Akademie der Wissenschaften, Philosophisch-Historische Klasse, *Sitzungsberichte 274*, vol. 3, Vienna, 1971.

Tapie, Victor-L., 'Autour d'une tentative d'alliance entre la France et l'Autriche, 1867–1870', Österreichische Akademie der Wissenschaften, Philosophisch-Historische Klasse, *Sitzungsberichte 274*, vol. 5, Vienna, 1971.

Bridge, Francis Roy, *From Sadowa to Sarajevo. The foreign policy of Austria-Hungary, 1866–1914*, London, Boston, 1972.

Galantai, Jozsef, *Die Österreichisch-Ungarische Monarchie und der Weltkrieg*, Budapest, 1969.

Lutz, Heinrich, *Österreich-Ungarn und die Gründung des Deutschen Reiches, Europäische Entscheidungen 1867–1871*, Frankfurt, Berlin, Vienna, 1979.

The army and military policy

Glaise-Horstenau, Edmund von, *Franz Josephs Weggefährte. Das Leben des Generalstabschefs Grafen Beck*, Zurich, Leipzig, Vienna, 1930.

Allmayer-Beck, Johann Christoph and Erich Lessing, *Die K. (u.) K. Armee 1848–1914*, Munich, Vienna, 1974.

Schmidt-Brentano, Antonio, *Die Armee in Österreich. Militär, Staat und Gesellschaft 1848–1867*, Boppard am Rhein, 1975.

Rothenberg, Günther E., *The Army of Francis Joseph*, Purdue University Press, West Lafayette, 1976.

The Austrian economy

Benedikt, Heinirich, *Die wirtschaftliche Entwicklung in der Franz Joseph Zeit*, Vienna, Munich, 1957.

Matis, Herbert, *Österreichs Wirtschaft 1848–1913. Konjunkturelle Dynamik und gesellschäftlicher Wandel im Zeitalter Franz Josephs I*, Berlin, 1972.

Komlos, John (ed.), *Economic Development in the Habsburg Monarchy in the Nineteenth Century*, Boulder, 1983.

Religious policies

Franz, Georg, *Kulturkampf, Staat und katholische Kirche in Mitteleuropa von der Säkularisation bis zum Abschluss des preussischen Kulturkampfes*, Munich, 1954.

Weinzierl, Erika, *Die österreichischen Konkordate von 1855 und 1933*, Vienna, 1960.

Engel-Janosi, Friedrich, *Österreich und der Vatikan*, 2 vols, Graz, Vienna, Cologne, 1958–60.

Winter, Eduard, *Frühliberalismus in der Donaumonarchie. Religiöse, nationale und wissenschaftliche Strömungen von 1790–1868*, Berlin, 1968.

Lewis, Gavin, *Kirche und Partel im politischen Katholizismus*, Vienna, Salzburg, 1977.

Culture and society

Johnston, William M., *The Austrian Mind. An Intellectual and Social History 1848–1938*, Berkeley, 1972.

Springer, Elisabeth, *Geschichte und Kulturleben der Wiener Ringstrasse*, Wiesbaden, 1979.

Schorske, Carl E., *Fin de Siècle Vienna. Politics and Culture*, New York, 1980.

Exhibition catalogue, *Traum und Wirklichkeit Wien 1870–1930*, Vienna, (March–October 1985).

Meysels, Lucian O., *In meinem Salon ist Österreich. Berta Zuckerkandl und ihre Zelt*, Vienna, Munich, 1985.

Bruckmüller, Ernst, *Sozialgeschichte des Habsburgerreiches, 1526–1918*, Vienna, 1986.

Exhibition catalogue, *Vienna, 1880–1938. L'Apocalypse joyeuse*, Paris (February–May 1986).

Index

Jean-Paul Bled

Jean-Paul Bled is Professor at the Centre
for German Studies in the Robert
Schuman University in Strasbourg.